RELIGIOUS CHANGE IN EUROPE 1650–1914

John McManners

RELIGIOUS CHANGE IN EUROPE 1650–1914

Essays for John McManners

EDITED BY NIGEL ASTON

CLARENDON PRESS · OXFORD
1997

Oxford University Press, Great Clarendon Street, Oxford OX2 6DP

Oxford New York
Athens Auckland Bangkok Bombay
Calcutta Cape Town Dar es Salaam Delhi
Florence Hong Kong Istanbul Karachi
Kuala Lumpur Madras Madrid Melbourne
Mexico City Nairobi Paris Singapore
Taipei Tokyo Toronto
and associated companies in
Berlin Ibadan

Oxford is a trade mark of Oxford University Press

Published in the United States
by Oxford University Press Inc., New York

British Library Cataloguing in Publication Data
Data available

Library of Congress Cataloging in Publication Data
Religious change in Europe, 1650–1914 : essays for John McManners /
edited by Nigel Aston.
p. cm.
Includes bibliographical references and index.
1. Europe—Church history. 2. Europe—Religion. 3. McManners, John.
I. Aston, Nigel. II. McManners, John.
BR735.R4536 1996
274'.07—dc20 96-22714
ISBN 0-19-820596-1

1 3 5 7 9 10 8 6 4 2

Typeset by Best-set Typesetter Ltd., Hong Kong
Printed in Great Britain
on acid-free paper by
Bookcraft Ltd., Midsomer-Norton, Somerset

PREFACE

This book is a tribute to one of the most influential historians at work today, who has graced the profession for nearly fifty years. It is a symbol of our esteem as his friends and colleagues, with our hopes that he will have many more years yet of scholarship, good health, and happiness. I am deeply grateful to the publishers and to all the contributors for their encouragement and cooperation in the making of this book. I would also like to acknowledge with thanks the help and advice extended to me by John Bourne, Henry Chadwick, John Cowdrey, John Fenton, Eric Heaton, Roger Highfield, Sir Michael Howard, Arthur Middleton, Basil Mitchell, Harry Pitt, John Roberts, Philip Waller, Maurice Wiles, and Blair Worden. Bruce Mansfield and Richard Fargher read over and corrected the introductory chapter in the most painstaking manner. Any inaccuracies left in it are no fault of theirs. Caroline Aston's willing assistance was indispensable, while Tony Morris at OUP provided, as ever, essential advice and support. Finally, it is a great sadness for all of us that Peter Hinchliff, one of the contributors to this book and Jack's successor as Regius Professor of Ecclesiastical History, died before publication.

Nigel Aston

St Andrew's Day 1995

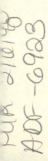

ACKNOWLEDGEMENTS

The editor is grateful for permission from Olive, Countess Fitzwilliam's Wentworth Settlement Trustees and the Director of Sheffield City Libraries to cite from the Wentworth Woodhouse Muniments. He would also like to gratefully acknowledge permission to cite material from the Fitzwilliam Manuscripts (Burke) in the Northamptonshire Record Office to The Fitzwilliam Milton Estates.

CONTENTS

NOTES ON CONTRIBUTORS

NIGEL ASTON is Lecturer in Modern History at the University of Luton, and the author of *The End of an Élite: The French Bishops and the Coming of the Revolution, 1786–1790* (Oxford, 1992).

GILES BARBER was Librarian of the Taylor Institution, Oxford, from 1970 to 1996, and University Lecturer in Continental Bibliography, 1969 to 1996. He has been a Fellow of Lincoln College since 1963.

DEREK BEALES is Professor of Modern History at the University of Cambridge and a Fellow of Sidney Sussex College. He is the author of Joseph II, i. *In the Shadow of Maria Theresa, 1741–1780* (Cambridge, 1987).

DOM AIDAN BELLENGER is a Benedictine monk and was Head Master of Downside School from 1991 to 1995. His writings include *The French Exiled Clergy in the British Isles after 1789* (Bath, 1986).

ROBIN BRIGGS is Senior Research Fellow of All Souls College, Oxford. His publications include *Witches and Neighbours* (London, 1996).

OWEN CHADWICK was formerly Regius Professor of Modern History at the University of Cambridge. He wrote the volume on *The Popes and European Revolution* in the Oxford History of the Christian Church (1981).

WILLIAM DOYLE is Professor of History at the University of Bristol. His publications include *The Oxford History of the French Revolution* and *Venality: The Sale of Offices in Eighteenth-Century France* (Oxford, 1989 and 1996, respectively).

GEOFFREY ELLIS is a Fellow of Hertford College and Lecturer in Modern History at Oxford. His *Napoleon* appeared in the Longmans Profiles in Power series in 1996.

RICHARD FARGHER is an Emeritus Fellow of St Edmund Hall, Oxford.

JACQUES GRES-GAYER is Professor of Church History at the Catholic University of America in Washington DC. His latest book is *Le Jansénisme en Sorbonne, 1643–1656* (Paris, 1996).

PETER HINCHLIFF was Regius Professor of Ecclesiastical History from 1992 until his death in November 1995. His biography of Archbishop Frederick Temple has been published posthumously by OUP.

COLIN KIDD is Lecturer in Scottish History at the University of Glasgow and author of *Subverting Scotland's Past: Scottish Whig Historians and the Creation of an Anglo-British Identity, 1689–c.1830* (Cambridge, 1993).

LAURENCE LE QUESNE taught history at Shrewsbury School and at the Universities of Sydney and Tasmania. He is the author of *Carlyle* in the OUP Past Masters series, and also of books on the Victorian diarist Francis Kilvert and on the bodyline bowling controversy in the 1930s.

SCOTT MANDELBROTE is a Fellow of All Souls College, Oxford, with research interests in the history of the uses of the Bible in late seventeenth- and early eighteenth-century England.

BRUCE MANSFIELD has been an Honorary Associate of the Department of History, University of Sydney, since 1992, and was formerly Professor of History and Deputy Vice-Chancellor of Macquarie University. He is the author of two volumes on interpretations of Erasmus, *c.*1550–1920.

AUBREY NEWMAN was originally appointed Assistant Lecturer in History, University of Leicester, in 1959, and is now Professor of History (Emeritus). He is Past-President of the Jewish Historical Society of England, 1977–9 and 1991–2. He has written on various aspects of modern Anglo-Jewish history, including the United Synagogue and the Board of Deputies of British Jews.

BRUNO NEVEU is Président of the École Pratique des Hautes Études, and the author of *Érudition et religion au XVIIᵉ et XVIIIᵉ siècles* (Paris, 1994). He was Director of the Maison Française in Oxford from 1981 to 1984 and, concurrently, a Member of Common Room at All Souls College.

EDWARD NORMAN is Canon Treasurer of York Minster, Hon. Professor of the University of York, and an Emeritus Fellow of Peterhouse, Cambridge. He was Chaplain of Christ Church College, Canterbury, from 1987 to 1995.

JOHN ROGISTER is Associate Director of Studies at the École Pratique des Hautes Études (IVᵉᵐᵉ Section), Sorbonne, Paris, and President of the International Commission for the History of Representative and Parliamentary Institutions. He is the author of *Louis XV and the* Parlement *of Paris, 1737–1755* (Cambridge, 1995).

GEOFFREY ROWELL is Bishop of Basingstoke and an Emeritus Fellow of Keble College, Oxford, where he was Fellow, Chaplain, and Tutor in Theology from 1972 to 1994, and a university lecturer. He has written extensively on nineteenth-century English Church history, in particular on the Oxford Movement. He is now Anglican Co-Chairman of the Anglican–Oriental Orthodox International Forum.

Introduction:

John McManners, Man and Historian

NIGEL ASTON

John McManners has an honoured and recognized place among this century's British historians of the Church. A man of great imaginative gifts, he has never confined himself to the minutiae of institutional developments or seen his work as in any sense a form of apologetics. Indeed, his scholarly breadth makes it difficult to describe him as a 'Church historian' in any other than the most formal sense, but the Church has always been an institution with enough human diversity and waywardness to serve as a starting-point for his studies, and he has paid it full tribute in his *Oxford History of Christianity*. That book, like his others, reaches out to an educated audience beyond his fellow historians, in a manner that marries expertise with accessibility; throughout his academic career he has appreciated that the most original material may be denied the impact it deserves unless the presentation is right. His first concern has been to respect and bring it to life for present-day readers through a clear, workmanlike prose that carries one along with it. His own personality runs through his writing, with its delight in diversity and benevolence towards men and women of every persuasion. John McManners is an optimist without illusions, whose general indulgence towards humanity is not untouched by irony. No one going to his writings will find in them any evidence of the author angling to attract personal notice through deliberate participation in historical controversy, academic politics, or the creation of a 'school'. He is simply not that sort of historian and it is a feature of his career that he has shouldered whatever working duties have come his way without fuss or drama.

His influence on colleagues, students, and the public (readers and worshippers) has been disproportionate to his natural modesty and now runs to two generations, extending far beyond Oxford. In a profession where individualism is threatened by the pressures of uniformity, he has always been his own man, happy in his individuality but the least egocentric of academics, competitive but also self-effacing. The northern saltiness, the priestly forbearance, and the intellectual acuteness are inseparable in his character, and go to make up what can perhaps best be described in an adjective from his native north-east England—

'canny'. But the twinkling eye and the sharp wit are not maliciously deployed, and in his writing and in his life generosity of spirit is always there at play. He knows human foibles and vanity as well as any scholar, but is patient of them. For him, 'tout comprendre, c'est tout pardonner', and this vision surely explains his illuminating insights into the lives of men and women in societies that are no more.

The making of his distinctive historical sensibility owes much to his family and the close-knit community life of County Durham. John McManners was born in a pitman's cottage on Christmas Day 1916 at Ferryhill (though he was christened John, family and friends have always known him as Jack, and Jack he will be throughout this introduction). His father, Joseph, was a miner and Socialist agitator, and his mother a schoolteacher, a woman of resolute character and a moderate High Church Anglican who passed on her faith to her children and, eventually, to her husband. Jack received a solid pre-war state education, first at a Church infants school, then at Dean Bank Council Boy's School, taking his place with other neighbourhood lads—many of them ragged and barefoot— who all too often incurred daily canings. At 11 he moved to the local grammar school at Spennymoor, the Alderman Wraith School, travelling the few miles from his home at Ferryhill by bus. It was during these early years that Jack's father, Joe, gave up his open hostility to Christianity after a confrontation while addressing a political gathering from his portable platform in Ferryhill market place one Saturday night with Canon Thomas Lomax, the remarkable vicar of the town. Joe never lost the fire in his belly, and still held political discussions at the coal face with his fellow miners at 'bait time'. Eventually, he left the pit after he was finally persuaded of the truth of the gospel by the example and persuasion of his wife and Canon Lomax, to whom he offered his services as a lay worker. Encouraged by Bishop Hensley Henson, Joe went off to Chichester Theological College at his own expense in 1928, and was ordained the next year—with a warning from the bishop not to 'misuse' his ministry by speaking on political platforms! Joe McManners served as curate in his own home village of Ferryhill (where he had lived without going to church) from 1929 to 1933, returning there as vicar in succession to Canon Lomax in 1940. The intervening years he spent as perpetual curate of nearby West Pelton. 'Father Mac' or 'Canon Joe' as he was variously known (Jack's medical brother was 'Dr Joe' to his family) never lost his character as a miner, and was more than once as a canon of Durham put in charge of the Miner's Gala. It was an occasion his son later compared to a French Revolutionary concourse: the shops were boarded up, the people had thronged the pubs, but his father strode through the streets and seemed to know everyone. 'By, Joe, you've a good job there lad,' they shouted, and he would cry back inviting them to the cathedral for the service. Long before the term 'social gospel' was invented, it was an integral part of Joe's ministry. His son has never lost touch with the folks of Ferryhill. While his parents were alive, the villagers would always ask after his parents first, a great indication of their worth.

If Jack McManners cannot be properly understood without appreciation of the place of his parents' work in the pit villages of inter-war County Durham, then no less significant in the formation of his character has been the University of Oxford, and St Edmund Hall in particular. He won an Exhibition to the Hall in 1936, and so began an association which, other than the war years, would run uninterrupted for the next twenty years. SEH was very much the personal fief of its principal, the redoubtable A. B. Emden, himself a historian, a vigorous campaigner on behalf of the Hall (new statutes of 1937 gave the Hall much greater independence than previously) and, in the words of one of his successors, John Kelly, a 'benevolent paternalist'. Jack McManners throve in the close, corporate but unconfined atmosphere of the pre-war Hall and read under the guidance of George Ramsay, Elizabethan economic historian and tutor in Modern History. He duly took first class honours in June 1939, less than three months before the outbreak of the Second World War.

Within a few weeks of the conflict starting, he had been interviewed and accepted for a commission. Though he knew his future would be in an infantry regiment, there was no immediate summons to a depot—the War Office had lost his papers for officer training—and so he went back to Oxford, where he began work on a thesis on the Scottish member of Charles II's cabal, John Maitland, duke of Lauderdale. But before he had advanced any distance with this project, he was ordered to report to Fenham Barracks, Newcastle, the home base of the Royal Northumberland Fusiliers, and had actually been appointed to the rank of lance corporal, before the papers offering him a commission finally turned up! At that point, he reported to the OCTU at Aldershot, and began specialist heavy machine-gun training.

In due course he was posted to the Eighth Army, and served as a platoon commander in the Western Desert, where he took part in the first siege of Tobruk, attached initially to an Australian Division and, when they were re-lieved, to the British one. Despite receiving a serious wound during the break-out from Tobruk to meet the relieving force, by the end of the Desert War in 1943 he had risen to be adjutant in the First Battalion of the Fusiliers. They were machine-gunners who in action operated as independent companies attached to infantry or tank units; these soldiers wore trousers rather than the ubiquitous khaki shorts, partly because red-hot cartridge cases from heavy Vickers machine-guns had a trick of getting into shorts! J. L. Hodson's *War in the Desert* quotes the young Jack McManners during a pause in the cricket match improvised between the Northumberlands and the Australians while they were stationed on the reserve line of defence at Tobruk: 'I was doing a thesis at Oxford on a seventeenth-century chap—doesn't seem so important now.' None the less, he found time to read. The Oxford edition of Donne's poetical works accompanied him everywhere until it was lost in the desert. Donne was supplemented when Jack was on leave by access to the library of the Union Club in Alexandria, where he read widely in works ranging from Gibbon to P. G. Wodehouse.

By 1941 Jack McManners was already thinking of taking Anglican holy orders after the cessation of hostilities, but other duties intervened once the German forces in North Africa had gone down to defeat in May 1943. He was transferred to command of 210 British Liaison Unit (the Greek Mission), with the rank of major, based at HQ in Cairo. The role of the unit was to ensure that a constitutional government was restored in Greece once the Germans had been defeated, and that could be done only by removing known Communists from what was left of the Greek army in exile (scattered in Egypt along the North African coast) and sending them to work camps in Eritrea. For his services he was in 1948 admitted as an Officer of the Order of King George I of the Hellenes.

As the war neared its end he finally decided to seek ordination, rather than go to Greece for a further two years for the resettlement with the rank of lieutenant-colonel. His recent familiarity with violent death, especially his first sight of a pile of dead bodies in Tobruk, was an important motivation, quite apart from his family background. During the war, he had written to the principal of St Chad's College, Durham, the Revd John Brewis, who between 1929 and 1937 had been vice-principal and tutor at St Edmund Hall, telling him that, if he returned safely, he intended to take holy orders. Brewis waited awhile and then, on hearing that Jack had come home to Ferryhill, wrote in 1945 to remind him of his pledge. In fact by then he had changed his mind, but was eventually per-suaded by Brewis to take up a government grant for two years' study of theology to test the original sense of vocation. Though it proved to be intact, it did not displace his original ambition to be a professional historian (dormant since 1939), and St Edmund Hall invited him to return to Oxford to become Chap-lain and Lecturer in History and Politics even before he had obtained his Diploma in Theology in June 1947.

Ordination to the diaconate followed quickly, but before proceeding to the Hall, he served almost a year in 1947–8 as one of six curates on the staff at Leeds Parish Church, all under the eye of Canon A. S. 'Rhino' Reeve, vicar of Leeds, former Cambridge rowing blue and future bishop of Lichfield. His curacy was an appointment arranged through the good offices of Brewis, and it helped that the distinguished Anglican scholar, Canon George Addleshaw, who served as Brewis's vice-principal at St Chad's between 1939 and 1946, had himself been named as lecturer at Leeds Parish Church in 1947. The short curacy turned out to be Jack McManners's only experience of pastoral life outside a university setting, but his experience did not deflect him from his other vocation as a historian or the post awaiting him in Oxford. But he enjoyed his year in Yorkshire, and found the classic Tractarian Anglicanism of 'LPC' much to his liking.

After ordination to priest's orders, he returned to St Edmund Hall in 1948 as Lecturer in History and as its chaplain, a post he held until 1956. The university was overflowing with undergraduates in those immediate post-war years, and the Hall experienced a huge influx, with no less than 262 students in residence in 1949. He worked hard to make the chapel a focal point of college life, especially important as so many men lived in lodgings. He also participated fully in most aspects of the Hall's life, taking a special interest in sport (he was already a formidable tennis player). But his duties did not stop with the chapel or the boathouse. With a small tutorial body, teaching responsibilities were heavy; a second fellow in modern history was badly needed. When elected as tutor and fellow at Michaelmas 1949, he was placed alongside his former tutor, George Ramsay, who did everything he could to make their new relationship work on a basis of equality. The undergraduates liked him, as their nickname of 'McHappy' made clear enough, for his serious interest in their work and well-being, expressed in an outgoing and unpompous manner.

In post-war Oxford one had to offer lectures to qualify for a CUF lectureship, indispensable for the finances of a fellow of a poor college. Accordingly, in 1949–50 Jack McManners taught on 'Church and Society in the Eighteenth Century' at a time when no one seemed to be offering anything on the *Ancien Régime* in France. He subsequently took over from Felix Markham (fellow of Hertford) responsibility for the Preliminary lectures on Tocqueville, a heavily subscribed first-year option, at the start of Hilary Term. Markham was glad to give up this duty, which he found a strain, not least the need to project his voice to 400 undergraduates at a time when the Schools lecture rooms were not equipped with microphones. Markham had no doubt that he had in Jack McManners the right man to take over his work—both for his formidable knowledge of Tocqueville and the appropriate manner of delivery. It was McManners the soldier as much as the scholar that Markham wanted, the note of authority that came from declamation rather than persuasion. Loud voice or not, McManners made the Tocqueville lectures his own every Michaelmas Term before his departure from Oxford in 1956 and after his return in 1973. The majority of first-year historians every year came into contact with him, and he with them. He took lecturing seriously enough to ensure that his observations were laced with a jocular streak that was never quite the same one year after another. So began the lecturing career that won the admiration of colleagues and students alike, not least for his sense of timing and his inspired deployment of the dramatic pause.

Teaching responsibilities reflected his new post-war research interests in eighteenth-century Europe and France in particular—in some respects an unusual choice for someone with his military connections and far from cosmopolitan background. He began to publish quite quickly. In 1953 he contributed the chapter on the nobility of France to a volume on the nobility of eighteenth-century Europe edited by Professor Albert Goodwin of the University of Manchester (he had moved there from Jesus College the same year), based on lectures given in Hilary Term 1951. The book brought him before the wider public for the first time, and Jack McManners retained a lasting sense of gratitude to Bert Goodwin for handing over to him the chapter on France, and taking for himself the less immediately appealing section on Prussia. It was also appreciated by his father. When he had finished his essay for the Goodwin collection he showed it to Canon Joe, who read it over silently. When he finished it, he put it down and said, 'Well, son, no wonder they had a revolution.' Jack McManners also collaborated in the early 1950s with his lifelong friend, John Bromley of Keble. Both men were to contribute to the *New Cambridge Modern History*, and meanwhile planned a joint textbook on the eighteenth century to follow Vivian Green's successful *Renaissance and Reformation*. For connoisseurs of the style and scholarship of the Oxford post-war generation, this would have been a remarkable book. Instead, it turned out to be a phantom volume, since Bromley never completed his division of the labour and the McManners chapters were not enough to make up a book in themselves.

Meanwhile his responsibilities at the Hall increased with his appointment to the important post of dean in 1951 (the same year that Emden retired from the principalship at the age of 63), with Graham Midgley as junior dean. Also in 1951 he married a geographer, Sarah Carruthers Errington, whose influence and support have been the lodestone of his life ever since. The young couple lived at the Hall, the first time since Principal Moore at the beginning of the century that a married fellow had done so. Jack and Sarah had an ever hospitable flat in the Besse Building, and there Hugh was born and became a great undergraduate favourite. He too quickly entered into the College Songbook:

> Joseph Hugh McManners is losing childish whims,
> He's reading Jean-Jacques Rousseau instead of Tiger Tims;
> He'll be giving Daddy's lectures on De Tocqueville for Prelims—
>   This time, next year.

In December 1956, after eight years' hard work at St Edmund Hall, Jack McManners opted for a radical change of scene, leaving not just Oxford but British academic life altogether. He travelled about as far from Oxford as it was possible to go, to the remotest backwater of the English-speaking academic world, the University of Tasmania at Hobart, where he looked forward to the challenge of building up the university and presiding over a department that needed some revamping as Professor C. S. King's tenureship (he had been in the department since 1919) ended—what his English successor called 'new creation in a new country'. The appointment made practical sense to a man with a growing family, but it also revealed something of Jack McManners's romantic streak and his sense of adventure. He once confessed to Graham Midgley that from boyhood Tasmania had been a place filled with a mysterious beauty and attraction, a sort of ideal dream of a distant land, and the picture may have been confirmed by the comments of a Tasmanian student encountered at the Hall. Possibly his first-hand experiences of Australians during the war also played their part. Such were the considerations as he hesitatingly dropped the letter in the post box in Queen's Lane, wondering if anything would come of the application. It did, and inaugurated a very skilful career course, one that confounded those dons who had wondered at his decision. The removal took him far away from the French archives, but appointment to a chair at least opened up the possibility of time for the sustained bouts of writing denied him by tutorial and chaplaincy duties at SEH. As far as the history department at Hobart was concerned, his arrival meant a jump of light years in terms of sophistication of scholarship, one of a bunch of young professors appointed at the same time, a ginger group in what was still a small community.

Hardly had he settled in than he was caught up in the notorious Orr case, arising from the university's dismissal, in confused circumstances, of its Professor of Philosophy, Sydney Sparkes Orr, for allegedly seducing a student. Australian academics waged a campaign on Orr's behalf, and compared him to Dreyfus. Jack McManners's position was straightforward: he deplored the University Council's refusal to accept Orr's resignation in preference for having him dismissed—because it thereby proclaimed 'an infallibility in its verdict which men do well not to assume unless they have to'. From these flawed tactics there arose a conflict between unions and university, and led to McManners's letter of July 1958 (intended for wide distribution) questioning the boycott which the academic unions decided to place on the University of Tasmania. He implored his colleagues in the Australian universities not to go hastily down that path because of the damage it could inflict on academic life. In the circumstances of the time Jack's letter was a work of both courage and percipience: full of personal reflections and experiences—especially his undisguised disappointment that his hopes of building up the department of history appeared to have foundered—but never straying very far from fundamental principles, and his conviction that the boycott was an extreme weapon, adopted 'with an assumption of infallibility' like the Council's. He urged the union leadership to come to Hobart to see for themselves the difficulties staff faced on every side, caught up 'in a struggle which is at once high-minded in principle and at the same time so grim and ruthless in form'. All they asked was a chance to sort out the affair for themselves.

The Orr affair did not prevent him from publishing material of wide interest based on his research on pre-Revolutionary France. In 1957 he saw to press a volume he edited jointly with J. M. Wallace-Hadrill: *France: Government and Society*, with his own chapter on 'The Revolution and its Antecedents (1774–1794)'. In Tasmania he was asked by Bert Goodwin to write the chapter on 'The Historiography of the French Revolution' for the late-eighteenth-century volume of the *New Cambridge Modern History*, a masterly overview that had its roots in his Tocqueville lecturing for Prelims. But the time in Tasmania also produced the book which made his reputation: *French Ecclesiastical Society under the Ancien Régime: A Study of Angers in the Eighteenth Century*, published by Manchester University Press in 1960. His distance from the town he was writing about—and his publishers—might have caused insuperable problems, but they were overcome by the amount of preparatory work already undertaken in France before the move to Hobart and also the editorial assistance from Oxford friends. The book was the culmination of a decade's research and study. Reading the picturesque biography of an Angevin priest, the *Souvenirs d'un nonagénaire* of F.-Y. Besnard,[1] had both confirmed his interest in the French eighteenth-century Church and introduced him to Angers. He followed it with a visit to the town, which soon became a regular long-vacation pilgrimage in the first half of the 1950s. The local Church seemed ripe for study. The archives were well calendered, and strong in notarial records and family papers. Even more helpful to his purpose was the availability of a vast publication by Canon Uzureau of original documents in *Anjou historique* and *Andegaviana* for many years from the beginning of the century until his death in 1947. He took immediate advantage of Uzureau's 'amazing production', supplemented it with work in other archives and libraries, and distilled it into his own direct, informal prose.

The outcome was an acclaimed case study of Church life in Angers before the Revolution, in which he brought to life both the structures of the *Ancien Régime* and the men who operated them. In so doing, he afforded insight and inspiration to eighteenth-century historians of France who had no particular interest in either Angers or the Gallican Church. His sympathetic presentation of his clerics never descended into apology, but throughout the book it is the human interest which catches his eye, the folk of all sorts and conditions absorbed in the sheer localness of Angevin affairs who are caught up in events beyond their knowledge or control. The affinities with other 'grass-roots' studies undertaken in the 1950s and 1960s by scholars like Richard Cobb, George Rudé, and their students are

---

[1] F.-Y. Besnard, *Souvenirs d'un nonagénaire*, ed. C. Port (2 vols.; Paris, 1880).

clear. *Angers* was universally well received, not least in France. One of the most prominent post-war Church historians in France, André Latreille, reviewed the work in the Australian *Journal of Religious History*, and his conclusion sums up the book's significance concisely:

Qu'un chercheur étranger ait pu à ce point entrer dans l'intelligence des réalités françaises et en donner un tableau aussi vivant et exact, je ne crains pas de dire qu'il y a là une étonnante réussite: McManners a fait preuve non seulement d'une culture historique peu commune, mais, ce qui est plus rare encore, d'un sens du concert humain et d'un talent littéraire hors de pair.[2]

The publication of *Angers* coincided with Jack McManners's moving from Hobart to another chair at Sydney. There is no question that the Orr affair had marred his experience of the University of Tasmania (his letter to Australian academics had not helped his cause with the vice-chancellor and the Governing Council), but he had no wish at this juncture to return to Britain. The Menzies government was then acting on the recommendations of the Murray committee for university expansion and upgrading, and there were many new opportunities arising in the Australian system. Indeed, he would not be drawn when informally asked by the vice-chancellor of Sydney in 1960 if he would apply for a newly created second chair of history should it be advertised. However vexed he was at the blighting effects of the Orr affair on his work in Hobart, he was grateful that the university had given a necessary £500 in public subsidy towards the publication costs of *Angers*, and that to leave abruptly would be to ignore the practical help and support most colleagues had offered. The Sydney chair was advertised, but no appointment was initially made, and when it was eventually readvertised, this time he successfully applied, despite parting recriminations from Professor Orr that he was deserting him in his hour of need.

His appointment at Sydney in late 1960 reinforced the central position of European history in a department that had grown fourfold to forty staff and 2,000 students in a decade. Library holdings were built up to permit the introduction of undergraduate dissertations on European topics and the range of courses on offer underwent steady and continuous expansion. His Honours seminar on 'Church, State and Society' was a pioneer in collaborative teaching, and he relished the collegiality it promoted—or 'staff development' as it would no doubt be called today! The freedom and openness of discussion in these seminars gave him no less satisfaction. In administration, his approach at Sydney (and, indeed, later in Leicester and Oxford) could be summed up neatly in the expression 'holy carelessness', a phrase probably originating with Canon Joe. It hints at the priorities of teaching and scholarship, and warns against over-anxiety,

---

[2] *Journal of Religious History*, 2 (1962), 156–9.

workaholism, bureaucratic obsessiveness. As professor, he was always willing to support colleagues with adventurous and imaginative proposals; he personally drew up plans for a course called 'Introduction to Historical Studies', built around the work of Macaulay, Carlyle, Tocqueville, Maitland, and Acton, and invited Laurence Le Quesne from Hobart to come to Sydney to teach it. It was an imaginative, cross-disciplinary scheme which aroused considerable opposition in the department before it finally appeared in 1965. But even those with whom he disagreed found it impossible to suggest that he was anything other than scrupulously fair: throughout his career, he had no interest in the petty jealousies and politics of personality that can plague academic life. There were no problems about the second professorship going to an Englishman. The history department at Sydney was genuinely international, with Jack McManners one of the eleven people born and educated overseas joining the permanent staff between 1958 and 1965 (out of a total of twenty-four appointments), a total partly explained by the then tiny higher education base in Australia.

The Sydney years were productive in terms of writing. He still had commitments to the next volume of the *New Cambridge Modern History* to be edited by John Bromley and covering the years 1688–1725. He was an obvious replacement for Norman Sykes, who had dropped out of the project at an early stage, and his essay on 'Religion and the Relations of Church and State' was the earliest submitted, though publication did not occur until 1970. It remains a useful introduction to the ecclesiastical life of the century. His main effort came in the book *Lectures on European History, 1789–1914: Men, Machines, and Freedom*, published in 1966, his last year at Sydney, a sequel to J. M. Thompson's *Lectures on European History*. The work reflected the Sydney pattern of courses, in which nineteenth-century European history had long been a great staple. It has remained the most intelligent short introduction to the period available to students.

His six years at Sydney were a very satisfying part of his life. He and Sarah were warm-hearted, hospitable, and much liked. The book on Angers had made his reputation, and the experience of sharing in the running of the history department with his colleague J. M. Ward reflected the broad human sympathies to be found in his writings, and his active membership of the Humanities Research Council made him known to a wide circle of Australian scholars. But there were two circumstances working against the likelihood of a long-term academic residence in Australia. First, his parents were ageing, and he wanted to be nearer to Ferryhill as Canon Joe's health deteriorated. Secondly, as a Europeanist, his distance from the primary sources could hardly have been greater. A year in 1965–6 as a senior visiting fellow at All Souls College, Oxford, went some way towards the replenishment of stores drawn from the great libraries and archives of the West, but it also had the effect of reinforcing his awareness about how much he needed to be near the sources if he was to produce a volume with as much original material in it as *Angers*.

Sydney was keen to retain him, as the vice-chancellor, Sir Stephen Roberts, made very clear when Jack McManners told him he wanted to return to Europe. Roberts, a specialist in French colonial policy but known worldwide for one of the first serious studies of the Nazi regime, *The House that Hitler Built* (1937), used the occasion of their last interview to articulate his triple categories for professors: those who cause no trouble, those who cause justified trouble, and those who cause unjustified trouble. McManners, he opined, was firmly in the fist bracket. But the desire to keep him was tempered by an appreciation of his family circumstances, so much so that the vice-chancellor invited him to resume his chair at whatever time his family responsibilities allowed. More immediately, Jack had a suitable post in view, the second chair (though his third) at the University of Leicester advertised while he was at All Souls, which he took up in 1967. Already ten years old as a fully independent university, Leicester was expanding quickly in the post-Robbins boom of the 1960s, and wanted a 'modern Europeanist' of McManners's calibre to work alongside Jack Simmons in Modern British studies. (Having two Jacks caused its own problems. With Simmons having first choice to it on the basis both of baptism and seniority, Jack happily reverted to 'John' to avoid the confusion it might have created.) The appointment was almost universally welcomed within the department, and he handled his placement near the top of the Leicester history hierarchy with characteristic sensitivity, respectful of a tightly knit department perhaps slightly unwilling to be stirred up from without. Simmons in fact fell ill soon after the new professor arrived, and Jack McManners acted as head of the department with confirmation of that status in 1969, the same year that he joined the University Senate. As at Sydney, he encouraged the gradual expansion of courses, beyond the core European and British options that had been available when he first joined: his own contribution was a 'Themes and Ideas' option for second- and third-year students. In particular, he formed an effective double act with Aubrey Newman: Newman taught seventeenth- and early eighteenth-century European courses, McManners the period down to 1914, with *Men, Machines, and Freedom* forming a convenient bedrock of his course.

He was popular with staff and students alike without going out of his way to cultivate opinion because he was so obviously his own man. Undergraduates had the sense of a teacher passing on truths in a deeper sense than the mere communication of factual information, while colleagues knew how much he battled to improve resources for them from his seat on Senate. The air of 'holy carelessness' was still there, the relish for the quirky side of academic life as he encountered it at Leicester, but so was the underlying seriousness of his commitment to the academic and administrative burdens entrusted to him. His inaugual lecture in 1967, *The Social Contract and Rousseau's Revolt against Society*, not only demonstrated his mastery of inaugurals (confirmed by his Oxford lecture of 1974), but revealed to a wide audience his profound understanding of Rousseau's political thought. Otherwise, there were two major publications while he was at Leicester. The first, in 1969, was *The French Revolution and the Church*, a much needed modern summary in English of the importance of religion and the Churches in the momentous events of the Revolution, in which the insights and judgements of other historians were supplemented by his own distinctive scholarship, particularly by his appreciation of the devastating effect of the Revolution on the lives of ordinary Catholics, and the way in which the well-chosen anecdote could bring the point home. It was followed in 1972 by *Church and State in France, 1870–1914*, a sister volume to the one on the French Revolution, with its origins in lecturing on the subject for many years. Solid, wide-ranging, and reliable, it served the needs of a generation of British undergraduates. Outside the university, he was appointed a Trustee of the National Portrait Gallery in 1970, a post held for eight years.

By the early 1970s his family was almost grown up. If Hugh's drumming in the garage was causing his father some irritation, he called on his son's advice when, unexpectedly, he was asked in 1972 by 10 Downing Street if he would take up the Regius Chair of Ecclesiastical History with a Canonry at Christ Church, Oxford. He took his time in confirming his acceptance. He was comfortable at Leicester in the word's non-complacent sense, but Sarah was keen to go back to Oxford, and the ease of access the new post would give to the Bodleian was tempting. Jack's rather stern diocesan, Bishop Ronald Williams of Leicester, had no doubts when he was told of the offer: 'Do it or the privilege will be eroded.' This was not quite how Jack saw it: while aware both of the continuities upheld since the chair's endowment in 1840 and that the Church of England was hardly rich in ordained historians during the 1970s, the idea that holy orders in themselves gave one any advantage in the academic world was one he deplored. But this was a man who had already held three chairs, and his publications spoke for themselves. There were some misgivings in the Oxford theology faculty that another non-theologian had been appointed. However, it strengthened his claims that the faculty was also keen to remove the restriction of the post to the early church period, since the Theology Schools syllabus had recently been modified so that all candidates worked in either the Reformation or the nineteenth century. This eased the way, while the history faculty was as near unanimous as a university body ever is. He also had the whole-hearted endorsement of Dean Henry Chadwick at Christ Church, and the statute which stated that the ecclesiastical history chair should be held by a scholar of the 'ancient' Church was duly amended. The concurrence of *both* faculties in wanting Jack McManners appointed clinched the matter in the mind of the patronage secretary at Downing Street and his name was duly submitted to the Queen. Interestingly, he knew the retiring professor, Stanley Greenslade (author of works on both fourth-century Christianity and Tudor biblical scholars, Tyndale and Coverdale), who had been his personal tutor at Durham (resident at the evangelical College of St John's) while he was training for ordination further down the Bailey at St Chad's.

Jack McManners thus took up two posts in Michaelmas Term 1972—the Professorship of Ecclesiastical History, and the Canonry of Christ Church, originally annexed to it under a statute of 1840. He enjoyed his membership of 'the House', and most of the college and cathedral duties associated with it. Here at last was the chance to live out a capitular life not wholly dissimilar from that depicted in the book on *Angers*, though it must be said that that the Christ Church Chapter, being academic and yoked to a much larger and more powerful governing body, was very untypical of its kind. As usual, he relished the more picturesque side of his responsibilities rather than either governing body or Chapter meetings, and none more so than when serving as canon in residence, keeping in his possession the key to the chest in which the college seal (which has to be used for any major financial transaction) is kept. The receptacle for the key is the little box which once housed Canon Claude Jenkins's teeth—his predecessor but one in the Regius Chair! He found the cathedral's then exclusive adherence to the Book of Common Prayer much to his taste, and was pleased at the regular opportunities to preach to the wider public as well as members of the university. Then there were his colleagues in the Chapter. The very variety of characters among his fellow canons, from John McQuarrie, the judicious theologian, to Carl Witton-Davies, classically Anglican and archidiaconal, obviously caught his eye as a historian who revels in the ways of clerics. He had cordial relationships with both the deans of Christ Church in his time: Henry Chadwick was a fellow historian whom McManners had known for many years, and Eric Heaton, whose combination of administrative and academic gifts made him one of the outstanding deans of his generation in the Church of England. Christ Church politics had a limited interest for him, and he took little part in the governing-body tensions between canons and students that occasionally flared up during the last half of Henry Chadwick's deanship. When Eric Heaton arrived from the Deanery of Durham in 1979 as his replacement, they tended to recede, but they had served to vivify for McManners the kind of squalls that occurred so often during the *Ancien Régime*.

Between 1972 and 1983 his principal professional concern lay with two faculties in the university: modern history and theology. He was a member of both boards during these years, and chairman of the Modern History Faculty Board from 1978 to 1981, a role he once memorably described as a cross between being manager of a football team and a godfather in the Mafia. For McManners the scholar, these may have been three years largely given over to administration, but Oxford history and historians were the beneficiaries of his immense experience, not to mention his tactfulness and fairness in dealing with problems when they arose. In faculty business he was a conciliator, but not at any cost, and presided with great skill and scrupulous fairness at the regular meetings. These qualities were particularly in evidence at the occasional meetings of representatives of the faculty with the Downing Street patronage secretary, and he saw to it as chairman that the faculty's views were properly conveyed in appointments involving the crown.

The good humour, even the fun of, History Faculty Board meetings were never lost on him, and there was always relief to hand when he participated in the less hectic gatherings of the Theology Board. In Oxford, as before at Sydney and Leicester (Hobart was probably the one exception), he took delight in the intricacies of academic politics; not as a power game, but he enjoyed it just *as* a game, and for the shafts of light it shed on human psychology. Other duties happily engaged him. There was the supervision of postgraduate students again and resuming the lecturing on Tocqueville to another generation of History Prelims candidates, for the last few years of the unreformed syllabus. In 1980–1 he was on leave in France as visiting professor in the IVème Section of the École pratique des Hautes Études, a place arranged for him by his old friend, Bruno Neveu, previously director of the Maison Française in Oxford. He lectured regularly at the Sorbonne (an unusual privilege for an Englishman) in his distinctive French accent with just the hint of Wearside still coming through, and found time to check a range of references at the Bibliothèque Nationale for forthcoming publications.

Despite the duties attendant on membership of two faculties, McManners crowned his return to Oxford in 1981 with the publication by Oxford University Press of *Death and the Enlightenment*, a book which earned him the Wolfson Prize for history-writing. It was a project that had been adumbrated in his Oxford inaugural lecture on 'Voltaire's Deathbed', and he had been sedulously gathering material for it since the late 1960s. Death was a subject first made fashionable by Phillipe Ariès with his *L'Homme devant la mort* (1977), and he openly admitted his debt to this pioneer in the field. His own book, while cognizant of French *Annaliste* scholarship, is an overview drawn from a multiplicity of angles, death as seen by the living, those who awaited a predictably grim senescence: relations, nurses, priests, executioners are all brought on to cast light on the experience of dying in eighteenth-century France. Changing contemporary views about the afterlife and the decreasing stress on the pains of hell are also laid out, changes fully in line with other shifts in spirituality. His text offers the reader many more facets of the Enlightenment than death. As the late Gary Bennett noted in the *Journal of Theological Studies*: 'Professor McManners is probably the only man who could have written a volume which has required not just the professional competence of a social and political historian, but the sympathy and skill of a theologian.'[3]

By the early 1980s Jack McManners was approaching the conventional retiring age for his chair. His achievements to date had been recognized by election as a Fellow of the British Academy in 1978, followed two years later by the conferment of a D.Litt. by Oxford University, and an honorary D.Litt. from Durham in 1983. Yet the prospect of 'retirement' in itself held little appeal. As Regius Professor, a royal appointee, McManners was technically entitled to hold his chair for life, though there was a voluntary agreement with the university that the holder would accept the customary upward limit of 67. He was, however, under no such constraint to give up his canonry of Christ Church at the same time. In point of fact, that decision had been made concurrently, since he knew he was moving to All Souls, but it was typical of the man that at the History Faculty dinner given to mark his retirement as Regius (and also to honour Richard Cobb), he determined to keep his colleagues guessing until the last moment. The chairs had been pushed back, the port was passing, the Regius Professor stood up to speak. From out of his pocket he pulled the Letters Patent of appointment promising to 'our trusty and well beloved John McManners' the full enjoyment of his cathedral stall for life. He looked across the room to see the reaction of the company, and it is clear that, at the time of speaking, more than one senior don genuinely believed he meant to do just that!

Aged 67, Jack McManners was appointed to the chaplaincy of All Souls College upon the proposal of the new warden, Sir Patrick Neill, a post he continues to fill at the time of writing, and complemented by the fellowship to which he was subsequently elected by the college as a whole in 1986. He has flourished within this small society, enjoyed its distinctive rituals, and once more been alert to any parallels with the *Ancien Régime*. In particular, there has been the chance to exercise influence on nominations to benefices historically in the gift of All Souls, a task he has discharged discreetly and with pastoral sensitivity. Links with parishes have been strengthened, with incumbents and church-wardens entertained on a regular basis. Here, as in most areas of college life, he was an invaluable lieutenant to Warden Neill, though, in line with the whole of his career, he was always ready to offer dispassionate advice and never identified

---

[3] *Journal of Theological Studies*, 34 (1983), 671.

himself with any one common-room faction. He has won widespread respect for his integrity, ingrained sense of equity, and good humour, and has amassed a range of friends across the college with fellows of every discipline and age. The chapel and its services—based exclusively, of course, on the Prayer Book—are dear to his heart, and he has taken delight in the restoration of the college's Mengs's 'Noli me tangere' painting and its return to the chapel.

In his own academic life, university lecturing stopped (invitations for special occasions were still accepted, witness the brilliant Emden Lecture in 1992 on eighteenth-century French church music), but reviewing and writing went on. In 1990 he published the best-selling *Oxford Illustrated History of Christianity*, a new sort of experience for him as general editor, marshalling the other contributors to the extent that he was ready to step in and write one of the assigned chapters himself when the person due to produce it resigned at a very late stage in production! The principal focus, however, has been on writing the two volumes on eighteenth-century France for the Oxford History of the Christian Church series. When published these will be the crowning glory of his lifetime's scholarship, based as they are on the materials he has accumulated in more than forty years of research.

When the books appear, they will be the product of a man whose background, breadth of interests, and range of human sympathies have made him such a distinctive and enriching presence in the profession. Historians write and lecture, but how many of them still preach? Jack McManners may well be one of the last professional historians to be found in the pulpit as well as at the lecture stand. Impishly, he has intimated that there is one major difference between preacher and lecturer—the former needs to believe in what he's saying—and this wry comment indirectly reveals just how important he thinks the preacher's task. One suspects a sneaking admiration for the comment of his old teacher at St Edmund Hall, John Brewis, who declared in his hearing that 'my object is to be a thundering success' as a preacher, and anyone who has heard McManners bring to imaginative life one of the Old Testament prophets or Pontius Pilate would know just how much overlap exists between historian and preacher, how much the one has helped to form the other. But few preachers thunder less than him!

His sermons are something to look forward to. While at All Souls he has preached regularly, and not just in college. Having given the University Sermon several times while a Canon of Christ Church, he has been subsequently requested at short notice to give it at St Mary's when the scheduled preacher has had to withdraw, and has deputized unfailingly. But dons and students have not been the exclusive auditors of a McManners sermon. Men and women whom he might never otherwise have reached have been part of the congregations in Sydney, Leicester, Oxford, and elsewhere, and have heard him bring scripture to life, yoking edification and entertainment harmoniously together in the service of truth. For the preacher, the obligation to disclose the message of salvation is paramount, while the lecturer has no such exalted task. Nevertheless, with a historian like Jack McManners, the sympathetic and accurate presentation of men and women in the past generates its own revelations into the endless predicaments of human beings and offers the reader insights, to share or to reject, which may not be unconnected with his own moral good.

Friends may think as much of McManners the lawn tennis player as of McManners the preacher. Ever a keen sportsman, he played soccer on the left wing in his younger days at St Chad's and St Edmund Hall (and was very vocal on the touchline), and has always relished an after-dinner game of snooker, but his first love is tennis. Wherever he has gone in the world his racket has gone— at once the supreme and indispensable recreation, and the perfect antidote to academic life. Dons from across the world have made up part of the 'McManners circuit', with some first playing him in Sydney later rejoining the show in the Parks at Oxford. He is unobtrusively but relentlessly competitive on the court, a skilled placer of the ball with a precise aim, whose talents have barely declined at all with age, as many of those habitually worsted by him would testify. In tennis as in history, he sets himself the ideal of leaving no angle unexplored. McManners takes tennis very seriously indeed, a commitment once memorably summed up by a regular partner at doubles, Robert Gasser, currently bursar at Brasenose College, that 'A day without tennis is a day wasted'. The game has brought him numerous happy friendships over time, and in its way contributed not a little to facilitating university business wherever he has happened to find himself. It would not be an exaggeration to suggest that the relaxed geniality these afternoon matches produce has in no small way helped to make innumerable academics happier in each other's company, and ensured that life off court and in the committee room has progressed rather more smoothly. The tennis anecdotes abound, but one from the 1970s neatly displays Jack McManners's humour. He had just been beaten for the first time by one of his regular opponents John Bourne (then of St John's) in their first game after Bourne's marriage. In shaking hands at the net, McManners simply said, 'John, marriage has really matured your game.'

Though his lecturing days are more or less over, the tennis continues alongside the writing, and Jack McManners at 80 remains a greatly liked and respected member of his profession. Historians, like modern politicians, in the 1990s tend increasingly to be rarely anything other than just that—historians (unless it be columnists in the public prints), and, perforce, administrators. It remains to be seen what the balance sheet will be for this concentration of energies or, as some might see it, unfortunate degree of removal from the wider sphere of human life and encounters with the range of men and women whose predecessors they are called on to write about. Jack McManners's career is a reminder of what the profession stands to gain from using the talents and insights of men and women who are more than mere historians, and particularly what it stands to lose from effectively severing the ancient links between the ordained ministry and the practice of history-writing. For him history has been the third of his careers, if the most important one, but he is also an Anglican priest. He has always been reluctant to talk about the beliefs which he has upheld throughout life, and the lack of any published version of his sermons makes any summary yet more elusive. Perhaps the most ample statement of McManners on Christianity can be gleaned from his essay on 'The Individual in the Church of England' in the 1981 report commissioned by the General Synod, *Believing in the Church* (typically, when he first received his invitation to serve on the Doctrine Commission, he assumed someone in Church House had mixed him up with John MacQuarrie), but there are other sources to scour. Tantalizingly, insights on his hopes and fears about such matters as the next world are to be found in his introduction to the *Oxford Illustrated History of Christianity*, which takes up some of the themes already laid bare at the beginning of *Death and the Enlightenment*. No one can doubt his acceptance of the faith as a historic corpus, but in every generation subject to all the vageries that people variously impose. Someone who has so sensitively examined the use and abuse of Christianity has a generous tolerance, ready to take delight in men and women of great faith—and none: 'We should not reproach those who are not Christians', he told a congregation in Christ Church cathedral in the late 1970s. 'To them we should say, "Do what you can; try to live for men as Jesus lived for men." The world of human relationships carries within itself, apart from the Gospel message, a clear demonstration of what is needed.'[4]

He has little time for churchmanship where ability is offset by dullness, seen well in his dismissal of the eighteenth-century Anglican Daniel Waterland (whose standing is high among most contemporary scholars) in a review of Robert Holtby's book as 'arid, dull, and humourless'.[5] He recognizes the mystery at the heart of responses to the Christian message, and, while valuing doctrine, would not overvalue it: 'Doctrines', he wrote in his General Synod essay, 'should look forward to the time nearer than we think for each of us, when they will have no further meaning.'[6] This generous Anglicanism would give individuals full opportunities for following their consciences, and he rejoices in what he (follow-

---

[4] 'The World, The Flesh and the Devil', sermon preached in Christ Church Cathedral, *Friends of Christ Church Cathedral Oxford Newsletter* (1977–8), 15–20, at 18.

[5] *Journal of Theological Studies*, 19 (1968), 683–5.

[6] 'The Individual in the Church of England', in *Believing in the Church: A Report by the Doctrine Commission of the Church of England* (London, 1981), 209–36, at 212.

ing St Paul in 1 Cor. 12: 4 ff.) has called the Holy Spirit's 'diversity of operations'. As he said in that Christ Church sermon quoted above, it 'is God's world, in which he wishes us to turn to him and to offer to him all our actions with all our accompanying doubts'.[7] He knows too that spiritual excellence is beyond most of us. To quote from his introduction to *The Oxford Illustrated History*: 'the way of St John of the Cross and of St Teresa is not for the generality of believers; it is, rather, meditation on the life, teaching, and death of Jesus and the hope that, in his resurrection, he will remember them.'[8]

Alongside this man of faith, the historian, sits the man-at-arms. For five years Jack McManners served as an army officer, and the importance of this time in his formation as a historian can hardly be overestimated. Edward Gibbon believed that his membership of the South Hampshire Militia during the Seven Years' War was of abundant value to his later career as a historian, and McManners, like his erstwhile All Souls colleague, Sir Michael Howard, and others of his wartime generation, has likewise had access to the range of insights into human behaviour denied to most scholars. Even at the mundane administrative level, he acquired skills as adjutant of his battalion that many such other comparatively junior officers failed to achieve: in afterlife this facility enabled him to clear his desk of administrative matters with astonishing rapidity and get down to writing history. Yet it was above all combat which gave him a sense of how far brute force can determine events, the importance of basic supplies in determining results, the power of personalities, the inability of militarization to suppress human individuality, and the supreme test of command: responsibility for others. If it is finally impossible to specify the impact of his military experience in his writings, one can safely say that, after the Second World War, the last thing history could be for McManners was a pattern of abstract influences. After demobilization, he took a continuing interest in things military. With his sons Hugh and Peter serving in the Falklands during the campaign of 1982, the experiences of the Second World War were made present again. His manifestly great pride in his sons was naturally combined with a fatherly anxiety which was the keener because of his own experiences of warfare and its unpredictable outcome. Such thoughts were all given voice in a memorable sermon that he preached in the chapel of St Edmund Hall while the Falklands fighting was going on.

The enriching effects of these different careers are less likely to be seen again in the profession, even among historians of religion, where individualism is still not hard to find. He may well turn out to be one of the last clergymen to hold the Oxford Regius Chair, since the General Synod, with the approval of Christ Church, has agreed that a lay canonry may in future be attached to it. That

---

[7] 'The World, The Flesh and the Devil', 19.
[8] *The Oxford Illustrated History of Christianity* (Oxford, 1990), 17.

change reflects the dearth of historian-priests in Anglican orders (a matter of primary and neglected concern to the Church of England rather than the academy), for, as Sir Michael Howard observed at a meeting of the General Board to discuss the priority to be given to filling the chair after his retirement, if the History Board thought it could produce another Jack McManners, they would put it top of their list. Yet it also reflects the way in which post-war professors of ecclesiastical history—Jenkins, Greenslade, McManners, Hinchliff—have not compromised their professional integrity as historians for any confessional considerations. Jack wrote for them all in the *Oxford Illustrated History* when he said that historians are obliged 'to treat seriously and with reverence all men and the social orders they build, to study everything, to explain without partisanship, insisting on the logical coherence of all things, without professing to know what the great design may be'.[9] None of them has allowed his Anglican identity to affect his scholarship and, thereby, all have participated in the wider transformation of attitudes among Church historians. Indeed, Jack McManners was firmly set against against the transferal of his chair to the Faculty of Theology for just such reasons. As Regius he disappointed two minorities: those who found his possession symbolically regrettable as a sign of the chair's position as an Anglican fiefdom, and those who wanted him to battle harder for the Church of England. He simply carried on writing good history in his habitual way where the characters of the men and women he treated were of intrinsic interest irrespective of their religious outlooks. Thus his contribution to the writing of Church history as it exists today, free from present-minded purpose, has been crucial. McManners may be a historian first, and a Church historian second, but he played his part as Regius in supporting the Ecclesiastical History Society, acting as president in 1977–8.

His character, too, is the product of a background that has few counterparts for variety among his contemporaries. That upbringing in the mining country of north-east England has subtly combined with the cultured Oxford don to make up a remarkable human being. Outward signs give one a handful of clues. His personal style has invariably been a mixture of the traditional and the formal with the informal and the sociable: ceremonial occasions are appreciated both because of the historical continuities they symbolize, and because of the opportunities for conviviality that they present. On every occasion, his sense of humour is rarely long in surfacing, never discomforting the vulnerable, but knowing, sometimes rollicking, and relishing initial puzzlement giving way to sharing the joke. Early on he was known and dreaded for his puns, the 'McHappy' of St Edmund Hall, as this Hall Smoker song makes plain:

[9] Ibid. 5.

McHappy makes puns at High Table,
He works them all out in his bath;
Then he steers round the whole conversation
And hopes that someone will laugh.

But latterly the wit has taken a different guise. Indeed, even his oldest and closest friends sometimes find it hard on occasion to see if tongue is in cheek. Thus when asked about Australia's greatest current need at a department-sponsored conference for secondary-school pupils at Sydney, his reply was: 'A stronger airforce and more Sunday schools'. The rejoinder nicely illustrates the extent to which earnestness and playfulness go together in unpredictable combinations.

Jack McManners has always possessed the gift of not making enemies, and he has virtually no competitor among Emeritus dons in receiving virtually universal plaudits for his range of human qualities: personal affection goes hand in hand with professional respect to form the happiest of combinations. There is a basic probity and directness that surely relates to his own illuminating admission that he has been at his happiest when possessed of a very simple purpose and was fulfilling it, for instance as a curate at Leeds, or as adjutant of the First Battalion of the Royal Northumberland Fusiliers. His balance, good sense, and inner repose owe as much to family as faith. First, to his parents, then to Sarah, whose love, support, and advice have been of incalculable value at every turn in their life together, finally to his sons, Hugh and Peter, and his daughters, Helen and Ann. Jack's resolve to do the job in hand to the best of his ability has marked out his life at every stage from Ferryhill to All Souls, and it is a pleasing coincidence, which neatly summarizes his work, that the word 'service' is crucial to tennis, the ministry, and the academic profession. His dedication to them all is justification enough for the life. Where should we look for him as a historian? One perhaps need go no further than Chapter three of *Angers*. It contains an affectionately droll portrait gallery of scholarly or would-be scholarly clerics, including the *curé* Robin, who justifies his addiction to historiography by invoking the long line of priest-historians throughout Europe. Modestly but proudly in this descent, John McManners places himself, along with the Angers clerics whom he so unforget-tably brought to life: 'Robin, Rangeard, Brossier and the rest of us, provincials as we are, [are] on the . . . fringes of a great tradition.'[10]

---

[10] *French Ecclesiastical Society under the Ancien Régime: A Study of Angers in the Eighteenth Century* (Manchester, 1960), 56.

1

The Science of Sin: Jacques de Sainte-Beuve and his Cas de conscience

ROBIN BRIGGS

If there was one area above all where the public doctrines of the Church intruded on private lives, it was through the disciplinary codes built on the concept of sin. This is an interesting phenomenon in itself, which also provides historians with much vital evidence about past lives and beliefs; one has only to think of the records of the Inquisition or of the English church courts. The perennial fascination of sin hardly requires much proof, in an age when much of the media appear to run on little else. The ambivalent position of those who make a vicarious living from both denouncing and publicizing 'wicked' conduct is also glaringly obvious. As generations of commentators have often ponderously shown, it is all about deviance, boundaries, inner drives, and repression. In our own postmodern age, however, moral codes have been extensively relativized, in response to a cognitively fragmented world. It was different once. Concepts of pollution and taboo functioned within a unified system, supposedly governed by immutable divine laws. Sin upset both the natural order and its ultimate ruler, carrying the twin threats of chaos and punishment. In this sense the world of our early modern ancestors was still much closer to that of primitive tribes than to our own. Clerics, rather than lawyers or policemen, drew the boundaries and tried to patrol them. For many centuries this last had been possible, to some limited extent, only through cooperation from the local community. The sixteenth and seventeenth centuries saw the emergence of the 'godly State', whose legislators and law enforcers shared, and sometimes threatened to take over, the clerical agenda. It is a moot point how far the effect was to sacralize the State, how far to secularize morality; in the very long run the latter trend would plainly win. In the short term, however, godly discipline was the theme of the age, for Catholics and Protestants alike.

Although this was in many ways no more than a reassertion of traditional Christian ethics, it also implied enormously higher demands on the general population. Broadly speaking, medieval Christianity had adopted a fairly realistic and workable series of compromises. Holiness was for the few, whether they were institutionalized in monasteries, wandering holy men like the friars, or self-selected members of the laity. Ordinary sinners hoped to benefit from these specialists in sanctity, through direct contact, general influence, and the range of ritual observances organized by the Church. The doctrine of purgatory was developed, with its corollary of innumerable foundations to say Masses for the Dead. The obligation of annual confession and communion, established in 1215, was for some centuries seen primarily as a means of fostering harmony within the community, through the reconciliation of enemies. Clerical intellectuals had worked out a much more demanding code of individual morality, but there were few effective means of transmitting this to local priests and parishioners. While disasters or great preachers might stir up ostentatious displays of self-abasement and repentance, these were isolated moments of heightened sensibility, always understood to be exceptional. Sin was effectively treated as a deficit towards God, something one bought back, by financial means if necessary. This was less a coherent theological position than the outcome of a long series of compromises between spiritual and worldly values.

Unease over such deviations from the principles of the early Church helped create the demands for religious reform which were central to the Reformation as a whole. Where moral theology was concerned, the Protestants won hands down, because they were pushing against an open door. The very existence of the schism became a reason for Catholics to seek explanations for God's displeasure. It was all too obvious, for many of them, that the immorality of clerics and laity alike was the fundamental cause of their predicament. The Catholic Reformation drew on the same sources as its counterpart, to produce remarkably similar results. As John Bossy has shown, the Seven Deadly Sins were progressively replaced by the Ten Commandments as the organizing system for morality.[1] While sins against the community and neighbours did not become irrelevant, they lost what had previously been their central place, as this was taken over by offences against God and true religion. The notion that a whole range of traditional activities involved at least tacit pacts with the devil was only one aspect of this evolution; as with just about everything else, the idea was not new, but the seriousness with which it was taken effectively transformed it from what had once been a marginal status. Meanwhile Catholic zealots came to share the view of their opponents about the drastic consequences of the fall. The great mass of mankind were destined for eternal torment, on the dual grounds of perpetual sinfulness and culpable ignorance.[2] This, too, was an ancient doctrine, which

---

[1] J. Bossy, 'Moral Arithmetic: Seven Sins into Ten Commandments', in E. Leites (ed.), *Conscience and Casuistry in Early Modern Europe* (Cambridge, 1988), 214–34.

[2] J. Delumeau, *Le Péché et la peur: La Culpabilisation en Occident (XIIIᵉ–XVIIIᵉ siècles)* (Paris, 1983), *passim* and 447–69, 'Un Dieu aux "yeux de Lynx"'.

created such psychological and pastoral difficulties that one may doubt if it was ever fully assimilated, even among those who preached it. Whatever reservations can be made about the internalization of these shifts, however, they clearly raised the stakes enormously where sin was concerned. Mitigation and compensation were no longer enough; even if the monster was known to be too powerful for mere humans to subdue, it was incumbent on the godly to fight it to their last gasp.

These were harsh and terrifying doctrines, which led into issues of great complexity and difficulty. With the advantage of hindsight, it seems plain that the relationships between sin, eternal punishment, salvation, and the divine purpose raised logical problems which neither human reason nor biblical and patristic authority could solve. Since such a conclusion was radically unacceptable to most early modern thinkers, the danger was that disputes around this nexus of questions would spiral out of control within the major denominations. The paradox for Catholicism was that the drive for religious renewal, itself stimulated by the first Protestant reformation, threatened to produce new schisms within the Church—yet the fear of schism was now so great, because of that devastating warning from experience, that dissentient groups in effect refused to leave. This was a situation in which the theoretical powers of the papacy were actually something of an embarrassment, for, while no shrewd pope would commit himself too far on this treacherous terrain, all parties in the various disputes were always trying to secure rulings in their own favour. Interpreting or misinterpreting the often ambiguous positions the Roman authorities were forced to adopt became something of an intellectual contest in its own right. For reasons which cannot be discussed here, it was in France that these conflicts proved most virulent. In 1713 the exasperated Louis XIV finally extracted the Bull *Unigenitus* from a reluctant pope, with predictably disastrous results which ironically vindicated earlier Roman caution. As so much of John McManners's work on the eighteenth-century French Church has shown, far from settling controversies, the Bull merely gave them new life and intensity, with far-reaching consequences for both Church and State.

The various disputants felt an urgent need to define their positions in relation to sin, not least because creative discussion of the subject allowed them to cover just about every area of human activity. In a sense it was the ideal busybody's charter, as Ben Jonson and other critics of the English Puritans saw. If all human life was to be measured against the divine purpose, then a meticulous grid of rules had to be established, starting with general principles, but ultimately getting down to specific examples. Much of this work had been accomplished during the later Middle Ages, in the numerous books of advice to confessors and similar manuals; one could represent the Catholic reformers as doing little more than exploit printing, better clerical training, and enhanced discipline to implement an existing programme. Despite these continuities, however, casuistry became a burning issue in the religious controversies of the age. The central Protestant attack was on grounds of principle, claiming to replace an allegedly mechanistic and deceitful system by one which offered both consolation and moral strength through faith alone. While the key distinction between mortal and venial sins was the target for much derision, perhaps the most passionate charge was that the casuists found multiple ways of permitting Catholics to tell lies. This was connected to the idea that people whose faith encouraged them to lie under oath could not be good citizens, especially in countries which tried to use oaths of allegiance and similar tests.[3] Casuistry thus became a dirty word, effectively a synonym for deviousness, particularly in the form of equivocation and mental reservations—what might be called the art of the misleading answer. The fundamental objection was that moral standards were absolute, so arguments based on expediency or logical hair-splitting merely compounded the original offence against God.

Debates over casuistry between French Catholics were inextricably bound up with the ambiguities surrounding the Order of Jesus. The alleged position of the Jesuits on the rawly sensitive question of tyrannicide, in the years when two French kings died at the hands of ultra-Catholic zealots, led many royalist Catholics to demand their expulsion. Although they survived this crisis, in the middle years of the seventeenth century a much broader attack emerged as the struggle over Jansenism took shape. Pascal's *Provincial Letters* gave brilliant expression to the image of the Jesuits as spiritual mountebanks, peddling a whole range of excuses for sinners, which involved grotesque perversions of divine law. This picture was at once monstrously unfair and very acute; Pascal's witty polemic had gone further than he intended, for its ultimate message was that no conceivable set of rules could meet all the contradictions thrown up by social life. Since no one could afford to admit this, the difficulties remained insuperable, and controversy was bound to continue.[4] It is all rather puzzling to modern eyes, since the French Jesuits at least held to what might now be considered impossibly stern principles. Father Bauny, whose *Somme des pechez* was singled out for ridicule, hardly sounds like an easy touch. In his preface he warned that, while penitents were supposed to accuse themselves, the confessor would probably have

---

[3] J. P. Sommerville, 'The "New Art of Lying": Equivocation, Mental Reservation, and Casuistry', in Leites (ed.), *Conscience and Casuistry*, 159–84; E. Rose, *Cases of Conscience: Alternatives Open to Recusants and Puritans under Elizabeth I and James I* (Cambridge, 1975). For an admirable recent survey, see Keith Thomas, 'Cases of Conscience in Seventeenth-Century England', in J. S. Morrill, P. A. Slack, and D. R. Woolf (eds.), *Public Duty and Private Conscience in Seventeenth-Century England: Essays Presented to G. E. Aylmer* (Oxford, 1993).

[4] For a fuller discussion of these points, see R. Briggs, *Communities of Belief: Cultural and Social Tensions in Early Modern France* (Oxford, 1989), esp. 285–92.

to help them out with a little interrogation about the sins they were likely to have committed. Of these,

Les plus communs parmi le vulgaire sont, les superstitions, les juremens, les maledictions, les haines, les querelles, mal parler d'autruy, le larcin, et l'usure; faire, dire, ou vouloir choses deshonnestes, et impudiques, n'entendre point la Messe les Dimanches et Festes, travailler ces jours-là, s'enyvrer, ne garder point les jeusnes qui sont commandez par l'Eglise: de toutes lesquelles actions il est besoin de s'accuser, et en cotter le nombre, quand l'on croit qu'elles sont mortelles; que si l'on n'en a pas la memoire, suffit de dire le temps auquel l'on pense avoir esté sujet à semblables imperfections, avec l'inclination à les commettre à peu près tant de fois en un jour, plus ou moins.[5]

In general it seems plain that Pascal and the rigorists won, on the formal level of moral teaching, with the Jesuits themselves forced to take a much harsher line towards sinners in their published works as the century progressed. It is equally clear that these doctrines cannot have been applied to any serious extent in practice, since the *dévots* themselves became increasingly despondent and defeatist about the society in which they lived. When writing on this topic before, I used works such as this one, alongside Augustinian or Jansenist compilations by such extreme rigorists as Habert and Treuvé, to build up a picture of the advice given to French confessors.[6] Although the detailed structure of these books varies, they form part of a long tradition, and their similarities generally far outweigh any real variations. The authors were, of course, free to determine how far they risked tackling the most controversial issues; some opted for generalized exhortation or mere dullness, rather than get into trouble. What I had always wanted to work into the discussion, yet never found room to give more than a passing mention, was an exceptional publication which breaks the normal mode, Jacques de Sainte-Beuve's *Resolutions de plusieurs cas de conscience touchant la morale et la discipline de l'Église*. Strictly speaking this is not a work intended for the public eye at all, and the first volume did not appear until the author had been dead for twelve years. Twenty-nine of the cases were published in 1666, apparently against Sainte-Beuve's wishes and without his knowledge, through the agency of the Jansenist bishop of Alet, Nicolas Pavillon. These reappear among the 207 cases which make up the volume of 1689; there are another 204 in the second volume of 1692, and 259 in the final one of 1704. In the handsome octavo of the early editions the cases extend to just over 2,000 pages; there is some attempt to group them by subject, but only in the final volume is this explicit.

[5] E. Bauny, *Somme des pechez qui se commettent en tous estats: De leurs conditions et qualitez: et en quelles occurrences ils sont mortels, ou veniels* (Paris, 1635), preface (unpaginated).
[6] R. Briggs, 'The Sins of the People: Auricular Confession and the Imposition of Social Norms', in *Communities of Belief*, 277–338.

Jacques de Sainte-Beuve (1613–77) was the son of a minor official (a *huissier*) in the *parlement* of Paris. He became a doctor of the Sorbonne in 1638, and *professeur royal de théologie* there in 1643. Already in 1641 he was among those invited by the Assembly of the Clergy, through the Paris Faculty of Theology, to correct the errors of the Jesuit casuists, and 'à faire concerter les conclusions les plus certaines de la théologie morale, afin que, parmi tant de diverses opinions qu'un chacun tâche de mettre en avant en cette matière, les fidèles sachent quelles sont les plus assurées . . .'[7] This charge could well be seen as setting the agenda for the rest of his life. Sainte-Beuve was in many ways a very typical product of his time and his milieu: a Gallican Augustinian, strongly drawn towards Jansenism, yet never a man who was comfortable in the *parti Janséniste*. He was deprived of his chair in 1656, when he refused to sign the condemnation of Antoine Arnauld. In 1661 he told Henri Arnauld that he would sign the formulary, out of respect for his superiors and for the sake of unity in the Church. He also stressed that one of the condemned propositions, that which declared God's commandments impossible to perform, was clearly heretical. Sainte-Beuve seems finally to have signed the condemnation of Arnauld around 1665–6. He refused to visit the dispersed nuns of Port-Royal when they asked for him, allegedly saying: 'Je n'irai point; si j'y allois, il y auroit aussitôt un livre imprimé contre moi . . . Le feu est aux quatre coins de l'Église, et au lieu de l'éteindre, on y jette toujours de l'huile: ils ne peuvent s'empêcher d'écrire.'[8] This was hardly a heroic attitude, although it does seem more reasonable than those taken by most of the combatants. Sainte-Beuve followed his own prescriptions by living in retreat in Paris, but was always ready to offer consultations, and his authority as a casuist became proverbial. In 1670 another assembly of the clergy voted him a pension, perhaps as one of the small acts of reconciliation associated with the 'Peace of the Church' of the previous year.[9] If so, it was peculiarly appropriate, for among so many virulent controversialists Sainte-Beuve stands out for his irenic temperament. So far as I know he never attacked the opinions of others (apart from Protestants), nor was he himself criticized.

One great interest of this enormous collection is that it was entirely generated

---

[7] Cited in the anonymous biography, *Jacques de Sainte-Beuve, Docteur de Sorbonne et Professeur Royal. Étude d'histoire privée contenant des détails inconnus sur le premier Jansénisme* (Paris, 1865), 73–5. This work was actually by a M. de Sainte-Beuve who was a magistrate in Normandy and prided himself on a (probably imaginary) family connection; for a ferocious critique, see C.-A. Sainte-Beuve (who disclaimed any relationship!), *Port-Royal* (Paris, 1840–59), iv, app. 'Sur M. de Sainte-Beuve'. This is on pp. 563–74 of the 9th edn.

[8] Sainte-Beuve, *Port-Royal*, iv. 172–3. The historian plainly regarded his namesake as a moral coward with a predilection for fence-sitting; he told a long story about his cover-up of the sexual and financial misdemeanours of a Parisian *curé* who was jobbed into a bishopric in order to reinforce the point (pp. 572–3 n. 1). While the story may be true, the authority for it is very weak.

[9] *Jacques de Sainte-Beuve*, 363.

by outside pressure. Sainte-Beuve wrote back to a great variety of individuals who sent in their individual problems for his advice, although unfortunately few of them can be identified by name. It is evident that a good proportion of the cases were real-life ones; others were no doubt more speculative, issues of principle raised in the course of seminary teaching or the *conférences ecclésiastiques*. On the whole what results is a selection which explores the frontiers between dogma and practicality, to reveal the doubts and preoccupations of the devout. Not all the cases are like this, however, and occasionally it is hard to see why advice was needed at all. One *curé* sent in a list of grave sinners in 1670, supposedly to discover whether he could absolve them, to draw a set of predictably crisp negations, such as 'ceux qui ont des inimitiés, et ne veulent pas se reconcilier avec leurs ennemis, ne sont pas aussi en état de recevoir l'absolution'.[10] Sainte-Beuve might justifiably have added that, if the *curé* did not know that, he had no business to be in possession of his benefice, still less administering the sacrament. Perhaps this priest and some other similarly ingenuous correspondents simply felt the need for outside help in their unequal battle with parishioners whose consciences were anything but scrupulous.

The wider *dévot* milieu seems to have worked through personal links in rather this way, with bishops and other leading figures in the provinces seeking approbation and support from sympathetic groups in Paris. Sainte-Beuve was consulted by the rigorist bishops of Alet and Pamiers, Nicolas Pavillon and François-Étienne Caulet, as they tried to impose an alien discipline on their recalcitrant Pyrenean dioceses. This led to an episode which, if we are to believe his brother, caused him some irritation. In 1666 Pavillon and others arranged the publication of twenty-nine responses, which were given the title *Resolutions de plusieurs cas importans pour la morale et pour la discipline ecclésiastique*, over the names of thirty doctors of the Paris Faculty of Theology. This was allegedly done without the knowledge or consent of the real author and his collaborator, Nicolas Porcher; Sainte-Beuve's brother asserted that he 'en fut surpris et en eut un veritable déplaisir', while the list of names made him fear he would be thought to have acted from 'un esprit de cabale dont il estoit très-éloigné'.[11] It is hard to believe that the doctor was really so innocent as this account implies, for the consultation formed part of a spectacular collision between Pavillon and his local enemies, which came to the attention of the king and his clerical advisers, with a special commission appointed to try the case. The near-contemporary Jansenist biography of Pavillon devotes a whole book to the story, making the claim that:

---

[10] *Resolutions de plusieurs cas* (hereafter *Cas*), ii. 105, *cas* XXVI.
[11] *Cas*, i, avertissement, sig. aii^v.

la résolution des Cas de Conscience, proposés en Sorbonne, signée par trente Docteurs, acheva de mettre le bon droit dans le plus grand jour. Rien de plus savant et de plus solide que cette réponse des Docteurs. Comme elle étoit parfaitement conforme aux maximes et à la conduite de M. d'Alet, elle porta le dernier coup à ses adversaires, qui en furent déconcertés.[12]

In other words, this was one of the many occasions when saintliness and absolute moral standards were mobilized very effectively to defend the Jansenist position. If Sainte-Beuve had not understood this, it was a startling and untypical display of naïvety. One may doubt whether his own scrupulous conscience would have allowed him to offer the type of disclaimer his brother was later prepared to make on his behalf.

The 'Cas d'Alet' were much reprinted in the ensuing years, and form cases CXII–CXL in the first volume of Sainte-Beuve's big collection; from his own references to them it would appear that he became reconciled to their notoriety.[13] Nevertheless he does seem to have suffered from what his namesake, the historian of Port-Royal, termed 'une sorte d'effroi de l'impression'.[14] Perhaps it was with this in mind that his brother began to publish the cases, by his own account, only when he heard of other projects to do so in a defective form, altered not merely by errors, but 'par la temerité de certaines gens, qui se piquant mal à propos d'une morale sévère, ont changé par des ratures ou par des additions, des réponses où ils s'imaginoient qu'il y avoit du relâchement'.[15] The implication is that the Jansenists were attempting a takeover of this prestigious yet marginal figure, whose apostasy had so disappointed them, and the publication was designed to prevent this. How seriously we should take such protestations it is difficult to judge, but the writings and the personal history do suggest a desire to compromise and to formulate a moderate Augustinianism, which was very typical of a wide group in the Gallican Church of the day.

Pavillon was certainly no moderate, for even those who shared his basic outlook often criticized him for a lack of realism in his approach. True to this reputation, the questions he put were of a strikingly subversive kind, for they largely concerned the economic tyranny of the rich over the poor. The fact that most of them were directly related to actual abuses which he attributed to his opponents gave them an additional edge. On the other hand, there is no sign that Sainte-Beuve flinched from the task, or that he found the issues uncongenial. The most prominent theme in both the 'Cas d'Alet' and his own great collection is the abuse of power. It not only appears in these explicit cases which consider

---

[12] [C. H. Le Febvre de Saint-Marc], *Vie de Monsieur Pavillon, evêque d'Alet* (3 vols.; Saint-Miel, 1738), ii, pt. 2, 64–142; quotation 136. A collection of documents on the dispute is printed in ibid. iii. 239–310. For Pavillon, see also E. Dejean, *Un prelat indépendant au 17ᵉ siècle, Nicolas Pavillon* (Paris, 1910), and P. Broutin, *La Réforme pastorale en France au 17ᵉ siècle* (Paris, 2 vols.; 1956), i. 199–214.

[13] *Cas*, i. 389–478.   [14] *Port-Royal*, iv. 570.   [15] *Cas*, i, avertissement, sig. aiiiʳ.

the social and economic problems of the time, but is also a frequent presence in the mass of rather technical cases about benefices and related clerical issues. One might further suggest that Sainte-Beuve found it easiest to discuss usury, on which his views were ultimately rather moderate, in terms of power relations. Like most of his contemporaries, he tried to approach this awkward problem by seeking various yardsticks by which one could determine fair shares in joint enterprises. Although the result is a type of hesitant liberalism which may seem odd, coming from a rigorist, Jansenist thought on usury was often more flexible than might have been expected.[16]

No merely normal amount of flexibility could have made the operations of state finance acceptable, so that clerical moralism was always going to be unwelcome to the government in this area. Pavillon's difficulties with the Aostenc brothers, major contractors for tax collection and winter quarter, were one example of this. For many years he denounced their manifold abuses and tried to have them condemned in the courts, only to find that they had too much influence in high places; he had to wait for the restoration of peace to succeed in dislodging them, now that the government could afford to dispense with agents of this type.[17] None of Sainte-Beuve's decisions seems to refer specifically to their case, but he cannot have endeared himself to a monarchy embroiled in a new series of expensive wars with his response to a consultation from February 1673. This concerned the practices of the Treasurer of the Estates of B. (presumably Brittany or Burgundy, since the 'grands emprunts' mentioned could hardly apply to Béarn or Bigorre), who had been obliged to advance the *don gratuit* for 1675 to the king two years early, and with royal permission was offering 10 per cent interest and reimbursement on demand to all lenders, with the eventual costs falling on the province.[18] Such terms do sound rather too good to be true, so it is interesting to see that one question is whether bankers could borrow elsewhere at *denier seize*, in order to lend to the Treasury at 10 per cent. Unsurprisingly, Sainte-Beuve condemned twelve separate possibilities as usurious, which seems reasonable enough, provided one takes the promises of repayment literally—it was, of course, precisely because no one trusted them that such high rates of interest had to be offered.

As might be expected, there is no suggestion that Sainte-Beuve thought the crown responsible for such abuses; he adopted the standard seventeenth-century posture of blaming subordinates and intermediaries who deviated from the good

[16] On this question generally, see R. Taveneaux, *Jansénisme et prêt à intérêt* (Paris, 1977); Sainte-Beuve's position is discussed on pp. 46–7.

[17] *Vie de Monsieur Pavillon*, ii, pt. 2, 109–25.

[18] *Cas*, ii. 419–22, CXXVI. For some of the dealings between the crown and the Breton Estates at this time, see J. B. Collins, *Classes, Estates, and Order in Early Modern Brittany* (Cambridge, 1994), esp. 219–22.

intentions of the prince. This issue came up in a rather different form where the *taille* and other taxes were concerned. Here again no criticism was directed to the crown, but the focus was on manifest and widespread abuse of power by the élites, to protect themselves and their dependents from the full weight of royal fiscality. One of the cases opens with 'Il y a presque par-tout une injustice horrible dans le partage des tailles, où les riches ne payent presque rien, et les pauvres presque tout.'[19] This was a fairly straightforward query about the position of *consuls* (elected local officials in southern France) who followed their predecessors by failing to tax the rich, because the latter were their creditors, or had other means of taking revenge on them. Sainte-Beuve insisted that they were still liable to make restitution if they failed to act properly, while suggesting that they should appeal to the royal intendant, who had the power to impose *taxes d'office* on the rich. In the third volume a far more elaborate discussion raises eighteen separate points, which might all be described as variations on the same theme. The very first question sounds like a response to the advice given earlier, with a denial that tax collectors can be compared with judges, who had chosen their positions, and could resign if they felt incapable of doing their duty properly. As the questioner put it:

Mais il n'en est pas de même des Collecteurs des tailles, qui, pour l'ordinaire y sont mis par force, à qui il en coûte beaucoup, et qui voudroient donner beaucoup pour ne le point être: et il semble bien dur de les obliger à la restitution, parcequ'ils ne sont pas entièrement ruinés comme ils auroient été s'ils avoient partagé les tailles équitablement. Car ce qu'on dit qu'ils doivent s'adresser aux Intendans des provinces est bien difficile en la pratique, et même inutile: car outre que ceux qui seront ainsi deferés à l'Intendant, étant puissans perdront ces pauvres gens, ils ont des amis auprès de l'Intendant, ou eux-mêmes sont amis, et ainsi on ne gagnera rien; ou bien ils plaidront, et feront de longues procedures qui ruineront ces pauvres gens, comme l'experience ordinaire le fait voir.[20]

Examples are then given, as when an attempt to assess the relative of a *Receveur des tailles* more harshly would cause the latter to throw the collector into gaol for the slightest delay in payment. The tone of the whole passage is strongly reminiscent of the bitter criticisms of the tax system as a series of protection rackets operated by the local nobility and officials, offered by the seigneurial judge Simon Estancheau in the Angoumois of the 1630s.[21] It is unfortunate than these consultations are not dated, since most historians have concluded that Colbert's regime did have considerable success in forcing the rich *roturiers* to pay a larger share of the taxes; it would be very interesting to know whether such complaints

[19] *Cas*, i. 496, CLV.
[20] Ibid. iii. 633–41, CCXIV; quotation 633–4.
[21] Y.-M. Bercé, *Histoire des croquants: Étude des soulèvements populaires au XVIIᵉ siècle dans le sud-ouest de la France* (2 vols.; Geneva, 1974), 377–9, 385–9, 746–9. See also my comments on Estancheau in *Communities of Belief*, 137–9.

predated these limited reforms, or showed their limitations.[22] Sainte-Beuve was predictably severe in his responses, insisting that the collectors must take responsibility in almost all situations, but softened this hard line a little at the end, conceding:

si un Collecteur est pauvre, il n'est pas dans le pouvoir de restituer. Quand il le pourroit, il faudroit que ce fut seulement dans l'ordre des restitutions; c'est à dire, après ceux qui ont profité du mal qu'il a fait, et après ceux qui l'auroient obligé à le faire. Dans ces circonstances, il seroit tenu de restituer à ceux qu'il auroit certainement oppressés; et il ne pourroit pas faire compensation à l'égard de ceux qu'il douteroit avoir traités injustement, mais dont il ne seroit pas assûré.[23]

Such a sweeping campaign to bring social justice into the tax system ought in principle to have pleased the government, but it would have brought the *curés* into head-on conflict with local vested interests. This was the crucial point at which the monarchy and its agents always finished by backing off, down to the final débâcle in the 1780s; the regime relied so heavily on these very people for its stability that it was ultimately not prepared to confront them. Although the need to preserve the tax base ensured some modest degree of royal protection for the local communities, this was always counterbalanced by an instinctive sympathy for privilege and social hierarchy. One of the clear examples of this was the abandonment of the *recherches de noblesse* instigated by Colbert in the 1660s; the central issue of these investigations shows up in a consultation from 1667, about the obligation to hand over to the local community legal documents undermining a gentleman's claim to tax exemption. The final remarks are revealing: 'On auroit inclination de favoriser le Gentilhomme, mais on ne veut point blesser sa conscience; et on estime qu'elle oblige à secourir les habitans, et à leur donner ce qu'ils demandent.'[24] Sainte-Beuve naturally insisted on this obligation; was the client anxious to cover himself for an apparent breach of noble honour and the duty of mutual support between gentlemen? It is also interesting to note that Estancheau had seen the *curés* as the best and most impartial persons to run local tax assessment, and had anticipated Vauban's idea that the tithe would be the best model for a fairer system. This approach sought to give the idea of the Church as the guarantor of morality and equity an unusually practical expression.

Whatever the date of the other tax cases, in 1671 Sainte-Beuve was still being consulted about similar abuses. It was alleged that a gentleman who had previously controlled the assessment directly was now acting through others, to avoid an open breach of royal orders. He was instructing the collectors to undercharge

---

[22] There is another case (*Cas*, ii. 516, CLVI) which is dated 1669; this also includes the advice to invoke the help of the royal intendant.
[23] *Cas*, iii. 640–1.   [24] Ibid. 590–1, CLXXXVIII.

his dependents, notably his tenants, while extracting higher rents from the latter as the price for his protection.[25] Of course these isolated reports do not establish general truths about the situation across the country, yet they are so much in line with other evidence that they seem to point to widespread problems. This was certainly the line taken by some of those who consulted the doctor; alongside the passage cited above, the most elaborate example begins:

L'abus aux partages des tailles est si ordinaire, et les restitutions ausquelles cet abus oblige sont si considérables, que pour ne rien faire mal à propos en cette affaire importante, on est obligé de faire plusieurs demandes pour s'en éclaircir. Il arrive en la plûpart des Paroisses, que les riches payent fort peu de chose, et les pauvres presque tout. C'est un grand mal, mais qui est presque sans remède: car ceux qui sont établis pour partager les tailles, sont comme obligés de laisser les choses comme ils les trouvent, n'osant pas charger les riches comme ils devroient, parcequ'ils leur doivent ou dépendent d'eux, ou parcequ'ils sont amis, parens, ou soûtenus des Receveurs qui perdroient ensuite ces pauvres Collecteurs.[26]

This radical pessimism in the face of worldliness and corruption is the authentic tone of voice of later seventeenth-century *dévots*, who were finding that reform of the Church was only a very small beginning towards a truly Christian society, of whose establishment they increasingly despaired. Attempts in this direction did of course raise further difficulties; how far should one go, for example, in enforcing restitution? Should Cardinal Tolet be taken literally when he stated that, if necessary, the offender should be reduced to begging for his bread? The questioner asked whether this was not:

contre l'usage des plus gens-de-bien, et même contre ce que l'on ordonna à feu Monsieur le Prince de C. [This was presumably Pavillon's star penitent the prince de Conti.]
    Un paysan qui a pris tantôt un boisseau de blé, tantôt un autre pendant plusieurs années, soit à son maître, soit à d'autres personnes riches, doit-il vendre tout ce qu'il a pour restituer, jusqu'à son lit, ayant particulièrement des enfans?

It is a relief to find an answer stressing that 'Il faut toujours que la restitution ou le dédommagement se fasse sans la perte de l'honneur, et sans qu'un homme se reduise lui et sa famille à la dernière extremité', so that the peasant in question could pay by instalments.[27]
    Numerous other cases could be cited to reinforce the general picture, but there is space to give only some of the headings; these are eloquent enough, as with a whole group from the third volume: 'Celui qui met sous le nom d'un autre une partie d'une terre, pour s'exemter d'en payer la taille, ne doit-il pas restituer à ceux qui ont été surchargés à cause qu'il a été déchargé?'; 'Si un seigneur qui a tiré de l'argent de ses vassaux pour des corvées qu'ils lui doivent, est obligé de leur

---

[25] Ibid. 643–4, CCXVI.   [26] Ibid. 633, CCXIV.   [27] Ibid. 648–9, CCXIX.

restituer'; 'Des Capitaines disent que leurs Compagnies sont complètes, les habitans qui devoient les loger traitent avec eux sur ce pied; la question est si ces Officiers ne sont pas obligés à restituer tout l'argent qu'ils ont reçû des habitants au-dessus du nombre des soldats qu'ils avoient, et si ils y sont obligés solidairement'; 'Si les cautions d'un Gentilhomme qui a pris et retient à ferme à vil prix et par force les dixmes de son village, ne sont pas obligés envers l'Église à la restitution du supplément du juste prix de cette ferme'.[28] To this selection of misdeeds by the rich one should add the various condemnations of animal share-cropping contracts, which were prominent among the 'Cas d'Alet', and are echoed elsewhere. In a typical instance 'contrats à gazaille' are declared illicit if the lessee is forced to bear half the costs when an animal dies. The same consultation includes an attack on village usury, but Sainte-Beuve wisely adds that the *curé* 'n'est pas en droit de se faire représenter les contrats que font ceux de la Paroisse qui passent pour usuriers, pour examiner leurs usures, devant se contenter de ce qu'ils lui declarent au tribunal de la Pénitence; et qu'en cas de refus par eux, il ne peut leur refuser l'absolution, ni la sepulture ecclésiastique en cas de mort'.[29] The notion of confessors inspecting written contracts for signs of usury would, one suspects, have provoked a violent reaction as a form of clerical tyranny. In another case with a strong resonance in our own times, Sainte-Beuve condemns lotteries, not least because they tempt the poor to invest more than they can afford, and thus lead to other moral offences. They are also tainted by 'l'esprit de cupidité et d'avarice', while, if theologians have been divided about their lawfulness since their appearance some eighty years earlier, there is unanimity that strict conditions of equity are required (which are far from being observed in France) if they are to be permitted at all. He further hopes they may be banned by the crown, like some other forms of gambling. This would have been a fine piece of hypocrisy, in the light of normal amusements at court.[30]

Exploitation in its various guises is a regular theme through the whole set of consultations; this might perhaps be taken as one expression of a society ruled by force and injustice. There is hardly any attention, however, to another notable feature of seventeenth-century life, the widespread resort to physical violence. Presumably this is primarily because no moral questions of great subtlety arose in this sphere. Sainte-Beuve did offer some cautionary advice to *curés* about taking any part in criminal prosecutions, and was severe about misconduct by judges.[31] He also dealt with one case where a female parishioner had bribed another poor woman to make false accusations about the revelation of secrets from the

---

[28] Ibid. 592–7, 617–22, 659–60, CLXXXIX, CXC, CCVII, CCXXXI.
[29] Ibid. ii. 457–61, CXXXVIII; quotation 460.   [30] Ibid. 618–25, CXCI.
[31] Ibid. i. 4, 371–80, II, CVI–CVIII; ii. 86–90, 197–202, XX–XXI, LXVII–LXVIII; iii. 174, 378, 381–2, L, CX, CXII.

confessional, and one where a parishioner (also a woman) had assaulted the priest at the altar on Palm Sunday.[32] It is of some interest to attempt a numerical breakdown of the cases, although this can be done only in a very approximate form, when many can be categorized under more than one heading, and some consultations covered a rag-bag of different topics. Rather more than half the total, about 350 out of 667, were devoted to the conduct of the clergy, ranging from technical questions about the legal rights of bishops and religious houses, through theological and disciplinary issues, to the proper conduct of confession itself. Around eighty cases dealt with aspects of marriage, shading into questions of sexuality. The final group in the major league contained at least 150 cases concerned with broadly economic issues, including usury, taxation, rents, leases of animals, and inheritance. The only other category to reach even double figures, with about a dozen mentions, was the observance of Sundays and feast days. These calculations agree remarkably well with earlier ones based on other works of casuistry, and with the wider picture of the Catholic reform painted by many recent historians. The clergy appear as deeply preoccupied with their own internal affairs, whose imperfections were so long blamed for the wider failure of true religion. Their jurisdiction over marriage naturally entangled them in a series of difficult questions; when, for example, was it legitimate to consider an absent spouse dead? Perhaps their most extensive and uncomfortable contact with that *esprit du siècle* most moralists denounced, however, could be assigned to the heading used for a group of such cases in the third volume, 'De l'injuste possession et acquisition des biens, et de la restitution'. This section included cases 186–213 inclusive, but nearly all the remainder to 259 really belonged to the same general category; they had been similarly prominent in the earlier volumes.

The prominence of marital questions did not necessarily imply any very deep analysis of the problems facing both Church and faithful in this area. Sainte-Beuve certainly envisaged sexuality in terms of pollution, yet in a strangely legalistic manner. In one curious instance a bishop reported a scandalous case of an affair between a married man and another man's wife which was openly tolerated by the wronged husband, to be told that only the husband could bring a charge of adultery, without which no ecclesiastical censures could be used.[33] The next case concerned a man who had sexual relations with two sisters, then married one of them, concealing his behaviour with the other. The answer was given in Latin, perhaps because it seemed rather lenient, for as long as the offence had been secret the bishop was allowed to give a dispensation.[34] A woman who

[32] Ibid. ii. 571–4, CLXXII; iii. 116–17, XXXI.   [33] Ibid. i. 235–6, LXIX.
[34] Ibid. 236, LXX.

had adulterous relations with her brother-in-law was still required to perform her conjugal duties—but if this had happened before the marriage, the latter would have been invalid.[35] Other questions concerned vows of chastity, and that old favourite of casuists, the wife who had a child by another man without her husband's knowledge. Here the wife was supposed to undertake the difficult task of keeping the matter secret while doing all she could to prevent any illegitimate children sharing the family inheritance—something the advice implicitly recognized might be impossible, since, if it could not be achieved, she was to have recourse to pious exercises and penitence.[36] Another traditional issue was how a young man should behave to a woman he had debauched. If she had not been deceived or coerced, then he had no obligation to marry her, but might be required to help her financially if she was poor and at risk of further degradation. Where there had been a promise of marriage, on the other hand, the man must honour it—unless the girl was of lower social status, when a dowry was sufficient compensation, for 'les filles ne peuvent pas dire qu'elles ayent été trompées: car elles n'ont pu raisonnablement se persuader qu'on les épouseroit'.[37]

These rather calculating responses often seem more concerned with the social order than with any paranoid concern with sexuality, of the kind sometimes linked to confessional techniques. Perhaps the nearest Sainte-Beuve comes to this tone is in a short but very explicit consultation (with no resort to concealment in Latin) on 'Attouchemens défendus entre mari et femme'. In this a wife is afraid she will be maltreated if she refuses her husband's demands for mutual genital caresses. A set of standard arguments is invoked, for, if such actions are a substitute for normal intercourse, then they breach the Pauline injunction that marital sexuality should be directed towards conceiving children. As the client puts it, behaviour which is 'si honteuse et si déreglée' does not even qualify for

le prétexte dont les gens mariés colorent leur incontinence dans l'usage du mariage, qui est le dessein d'éviter la fornication, &c. puisque de semblables actions ne font qu'allumer de plus en plus le feu de l'impureté, bien loin de l'éteindre ou de le diminuer, & d'elles-mêmes les disposent aux plus grands crimes. Si cela est permis, quelle différence y aura-t-il entre des Chrétiens et les Infidelles qui ne connoissent pas Dieu? Et où sera la pureté de cœur que l'Évangile nous préscrit pour voir Dieu, & cette sainteté dont parle saint Paul, sans laquelle personne ne le verra?

The reply stressed that such actions would be a venial sin even if they did not lead to pollution, but that in such a case the wife did not sin in obeying her husband. When they were a substitute for intercourse, however, they were a mortal sin, so she was obliged to leave him rather than comply, and otherwise could not be absolved.[38]

---

[35] Ibid. 236–7, LXXI.   [36] Ibid. 311, LXXXV.   [37] Ibid. 315–17, LXXXVIII.
[38] Ibid. ii. 349–50, CXV.

This was not the only potentially scabrous subject to appear in the collection, but the others were generally far more oblique. For example, was a priest who had sexual relations with his penitent liable to the penalties for 'spiritual incest'? Sainte-Beuve pointed out that the facts in the case were disputed anyway, while this description of the offence was more by analogy than by strict canon law.[39] A priest whose three children by his concubine were entirely dependent on him should not be obliged to become a Carthusian monk, since he had a Christian duty to care for them and educate them; he should live an austere life of fasting and prayer, unless the children died, when the Charterhouse would be appropriate for him.[40] A gentleman whose first marriage had never been consummated, and had then been annulled at the wife's request after a medical examination of his condition, had subsequently undergone surgery, married a second time, and fathered seven children. The second marriage was held to be valid on numerous grounds, despite protests from the first wife. Although this was getting close to the scandalous area of public trials of virility, the advice seems sober and sensible enough.[41] The most passionate opinions on marriage are in a very different context, that of unions between Catholics and Protestants. In four consultations, which extend over nearly fifty pages of dense argument, Sainte-Beuve repeatedly upholds the hardline opinion 'que ces sortes de mariages sont défendus par le droit naturel, divin & humain; & par conséquent, que les Superieurs ne doivent & ne peuvent permettre qu'on les contracte'.[42] To show the possible results, he cites the papal dispensation for the marriage of Charles I and Henrietta Maria, justified on the grounds that the lot of the English Catholics would be improved. Not only did the opposite prove to be true, the upshot was the death of the king, the exile of the queen, and the rebellion which for so long kept Charles II from the throne. What better evidence could there be that 'ces mariages déplaisent fort à Dieu'?[43] Not even the pope could validly dispense in such a case, he rather dangerously alleged.[44]

For whatever reason, Sainte-Beuve was hardly consulted at all on the subject of superstition and popular usages. He did denounce the general belief in the healing power of seventh sons; only the kings of France could cure scrofula by touching, he suggested, while their English counterparts merely pretended to similar divine gifts.[45] In 1671, at a crucial moment for official views on witchcraft, he gave a notably sceptical set of opinions on this vexed issue. The questions posed, with their reference to the king's intention to promulgate an

---

[39] Ibid. iii. 580–5, CLXXXIV.   [40] Ibid. ii. 603–4, CLXXXIV.
[41] Ibid. i. 522, CLXXI. For the wider issues, see P. Darmon, *Le Tribunal de l'impuissance: Virilité et défaillances conjugales dans l'Ancienne France* (Paris, 1979).
[42] *Cas*, i. 253–300, LXXVII–LXXX; quotation 258.   [43] Ibid. 299.   [44] Ibid. 293.
[45] Ibid. iii. 548–54, CLXX.

ordinance on the matter, sound as if they might well have come from some highly placed source. The consultation is dated 23 April 1671, and we know that just five days later Pierre Lalemant, prior of Sainte-Geneviève and chancellor of the University of Paris, sent a *mémoire* on the same subject to *premier président* Claude Pellot of the *parlement* of Rouen. Pellot, a close associate of Colbert, was trying to damp down on his court's enthusiasm for convicting witches, so consulted a leading Paris theologian. There are close similarities between the two opinions, although Lalemant's is much the longer and more complex of the two.[46] Sainte-Beuve stated firmly that, while the *parlement* of Paris might not condemn witches as such, there was no reason to doubt their existence or the scriptural texts on the subject. On the other hand, he followed the canon *Episcopi* in refusing to accept evidence from convicted witches about other people supposedly seen flying to the sabbat or participating in the doings there. Two irreproachable witnesses were needed, 'mais on ne conçoit pas qu'il puisse s'en trouver de tels pour déposer de ce transport & de ces abominations, comme de choses réelles & corporelles, & non pas seulement imaginaires: & elles peuvent être purement imaginaires, sans participation avec le démon, l'imagination étant blessée.' Another question was that of the diabolical mark, in the form of the imprint of a fingernail or an insensible place. Sainte-Beuve saw no reason why either should not have a purely natural explanation, and merely referred the question to 'des Médecins les plus capables'.[47] He clearly saw the dangers for clerics who became involved, for in another brief consultation on witchcraft he remarked: 'Pour ce qui regarde la dénonciation aux Juges séculiers, je ne voudrois pas que les Ecclésiastiques s'en mêlassent, vû qu'on n'a des preuves de ces choses que très-difficilement; & cela ne fait jamais un bon effet.'[48]

These sane, balanced views seem typical of a moral theologian whose realism and shrewdness rarely fail to impress a modern reader. Whether all his contemporaries would have seen his work in that light may be more doubtful. Sainte-Beuve's mastery of the scriptural and patristic sources was such that only the foolhardy would have challenged him, yet the lessons he drew from them were often as uncomfortable as those found by his great contemporary Blaise Pascal. Behind this great shield of learning the doctor of the Sorbonne was repeatedly subverting the basic assumptions of his age. In the unlikely event of his prescriptions being followed, they would have brought about sweeping changes in social and economic life, in the process undermining most of the tacit understandings on which Church and State really functioned. It was not simply a question of

---

[46] For the background, see R. Mandrou, *Magistrats et sorciers en France au 17ᵉ siècle: Une analyse de psychologie historique* (Paris, 1968), 449–58; Lalemant's *mémoire* is printed by Mandrou in *Possession et sorcellerie au XVIIᵉ siècle: Textes inédits* (Paris, 1979), 219–30.

[47] *Cas*, iii. 554–8, CLXXI. [48] Ibid. 560, CLXXIII.

public doctrines proving inapplicable to private lives, for in many ways it was the public and political implications of such thinking which made it impossible to realize. Like most of his kind, Sainte-Beuve was himself ultimately a conservative, who would never have taken his position through to its logical conclusions. Various compromises and equivocations which he adopted, some of them indicated above, make this plain enough. There could never be a true science of sin, because it was impossible to disentangle the subject matter from the whole of life. As seventeenth-century Augustinians believed, yet often found it hard to accept, that life was lived in the shadow of the fall and its consequences. Moralists could tell men and women how they ought to live; in their hearts they knew that only an elect few would be able to keep such standards. The true revolution was reserved for the moment of the Last Judgement, which so many early modern zealots hoped was almost upon them.

2

John Dury and the Practice of Irenicism

Scott Mandelbrote

It is true that the schisms which separate us from each other are not unrelieved tragedies—for they are the inevitable and inspirational outcome of the exercise of Christian liberty and the determination to preach the gospel in season and out of season. Even so, while we rejoice in the unique insights which our own branch of the Church has given us, we have a duty not to add to the tragic effects of disunity.[1]

In his contribution to the Report of the Doctrine Commission of the Church of England, John McManners sets out a contemporary interpretation of the relationship between the Church and the individual believer. Liberty of conscience, tempered by love for others and respect for the tradition and institutions of the Church, provides one of McManners's themes. He describes the conflict, and loss of Christian harmony, which have often resulted from too rigid a definition of the Church's doctrine, and advocates the alternative path of forbearance, concluding that, sometimes, 'it is God's will that we all agree to differ'. It is perhaps appropriate that so distinguished an ecclesiastical historian should have been chosen to write about the Church and the individual in this way. Doctrinal conflict has been an essential part of the history of the Christian Church, not least during the eighteenth century, of which John McManners is master. His judgement, that conviction should be softened by compassion for the views of others, is therefore grounded in a detailed knowledge of the destructive nature of dogmatism, both for the Church and for the individual. But despite his contemporary conclusions, McManners has never written at length about the history of the reconciliation of differences, either between individuals and the Church, or

I am grateful to Clare Griffiths and Charles Webster for their help with this paper, also to Nigel Aston for his tolerance. Passages from the Hartlib Papers in the Sheffield University Library are quoted from transcripts prepared by the Hartlib Papers Project, University of Sheffield, and are quoted by permission of the Project Directors and the University Librarian. I have occasionally modified the transcripts after reference to the original documents, but have followed their style. Elsewhere, I have followed normal conventions concerning spelling, punctuation, and so on.

[1] John McManners, 'The Individual in the Church of England', in *Believing in the Church: A Report by the Doctrine Commission of the Church of England* (London, 1981), 209–36, at 213.

between the various branches of the Christian Church itself. The subject of this essay, John Dury, has often been treated as an exemplary apostle for reconciliation. His travels across Europe in the seventeenth century, in pursuit of the reunion of the Churches, have been held up as a model of irenicism, even of ecumenism.[2] Here, I want to explore the context for Dury's irenicism, to discuss the convictions which underlay it, and to try to make sense of the apparent inconsistencies into which it led him. Dury's example helps to show that compassion and toleration in matters of religion are themselves historically constructed emotions. It is, in part, through reflection on the failure of the attempts of Dury, and others, to reunify the Churches that it becomes necessary to accept differences, and the benefits which diversity brings.

The world in which John Dury (1596–1680) lived, and which he laboured to transform, was shaped by two critical events that had occurred in 1618. The first of these was the outbreak of the Thirty Years War, which spread from Bohemia to engulf most of central Europe during the 1620s; the second was the meeting of the Synod of Dort, between November 1618 and May 1619. The course of the Thirty Years War, in particular the expulsion of the Elector Palatine from his lands and the conquest of Bohemia, seemed to make plain to many European Protestants the aggressive intentions of the Catholic powers, Spain and Austria. At the same time, the members of the Reformed Churches seemed themselves to lack clear leadership. The extent of the divisions among the Reformed Churches had been clearly visible at the Synod of Dort, which failed to resolve the quarrels which had broken out within the Dutch Church. The strict interpretation of Calvinist doctrine which the Synod endorsed seemed to undermine its long-term aim of bringing the Calvinist and Lutheran Churches of Europe together into one community. The Synod had also demonstrated the problems involved in trying to draw up a common statement of the beliefs of the various Calvinist Reformed Churches themselves. The political and religious events of 1618–19 exposed the idea of international cooperation, either between Calvinists, or between Calvinists and Lutherans, as a hollow dream. They showed that the Reformed Churches lacked political leadership of a kind which might transcend local or national concerns. They proved that, despite the urgency of the situation, gatherings of scholars and divines were incapable of formulating generous, or even pragmatic, doctrinal rules for one another.

Although his active career continued long after the Peace of Westphalia had brought the hostilities of the Thirty Years War to an end, Dury spent his life trying to heal the wounds of the years 1618–19. He travelled extensively across

---

[2] See e.g. J. Minton Batten, *John Dury: Advocate of Christian Reunion* (Chicago, 1944); John McManners, 'Enlightenment: Secular and Christian (1600–1800)', in McManners (ed.), *The Oxford History of Christianity* (Oxford, 1993), 277–309, at 283.

northern and central Europe, building a dialogue between the various branches of the Reformed and Lutheran Churches. Occasionally, he called for further synods or assemblies of clergy to try to settle doctrinal issues, serving himself in the Westminster Assembly on his return to England in 1645. But he preferred to work through individuals, placing particular faith in a succession of powerful secular leaders who seemed, at one time or another, to promise to draw the Protestant powers together into a grand alliance against Rome and her allies. Dury's pursuits were intellectual as well as irenic. Together with his friend and ally Samuel Hartlib, he worked to achieve a reform of learning which might help to teach people the essence of Christianity, and encourage them to think and act differently. He hoped to overcome the relentless, scholastic logic, which had driven the delegates at Dort to their conclusions, through a new, more practical divinity. He sought to tackle the causes of the conflict between the Churches, as well as to heal their open sores. In all of this, Dury was driven by the belief that God intended to unite the Protestant community, and that, once their pretensions were recognized by all, the power of the Roman Catholic Church, and of the papacy, would be broken. Dury appears to have believed that this transformation might happen as a result of the defeat of the intellectual power of scholasticism by the success of true, practical Christianity. Unlike many of his contemporaries and friends, Dury did not define the goal of a unified, Protestant alliance solely in military terms.

Dury's career as an irenicist began in 1628, when he was still serving as minister to the English Merchant Company at Elbing, on the shore of the Baltic Sea. In that year, Dury began to develop his plans to reunite the Protestant Churches, and petitioned the Swedish king, Gustavus Adolphus, to encourage this 'Universall, Spirituall, and truely Divine undertaking'.[3] Gustavus Adolphus seemed to be an ideal recipient for Dury's plans. He was already involved in the military defence of the Protestant cause, through his protection of the Lutheran city of Stralsund. He had shown himself to be a zealous and progressive monarch: he had sponsored reforms of the Swedish Church and constitution, and built up the army and navy. Importantly, in the eyes of someone like Dury, he had tried to reshape the Swedish school system, introducing new forms of education and new subjects of study.[4] By 1628 Dury had already begun to formulate some of his own ideas about the moral upbringing of children, and the proper role of education. Then, at Elbing, Dury had been encouraged to think about the

---

[3] G. H. Turnbull, *Hartlib, Dury and Comenius* (Liverpool, 1947), 129; Samuel Hartlib, *A Briefe Relation of that which hath been lately attempted to procure Ecclesiasticall Peace amongst Protestants* (London, 1641), 1; [John Dury], *The Copy of a Petition, as it was tendered by Mr. Dury, to Gustavus, the late King of Sweden* (London, 1641), 43.

[4] Michael Roberts, *Gustavus Adolphus: A History of Sweden 1611–1632* (2 vols.; London, 1953–8).

possibility of working for the reunion of the Protestant Churches by Jacob Godemann, one of Gustavus Adolphus' counsellors. Shortly after he had presented his petition to Gustavus Adolphus, Dury also encountered Sir Thomas Roe, who had been sent out from England to negotiate between the Swedes and the Poles. Roe was eager to involve Gustavus Adolphus in a broader, Protestant coalition to maintain the war in Europe. He was worried by the prospect of peace between Lutheran Denmark and the Catholic powers. Dury's project for the spiritual reunion of the Protestant Churches was, therefore, a useful diplomatic foil to Roe's own efforts among the Protestant communities of the Baltic.[5]

With Roe's encouragement, Dury came over to England in 1630. He was perhaps fortunate in having created for himself an opportunity for diplomatic employment, since, in 1628, the Polish Diet had dissolved the English Merchant Company at Elbing, and with it much of Dury's congregation. But he was able to persuade a number of prominent English divines, including Archbishop Abbott, of the sincerity of his purpose, and to win their support for a mission to the Protestant princes and communities of Germany. There, for a time, Gustavus Adolphus was carrying all before him, and he promised Dury that he would try to prepare the Lutherans for reunion, if Dury would make similar arrangements among the Calvinist Churches. The death of Gustavus Adolphus at the battle of Lützen in 1632 was, therefore, a set-back for Dury's work, although it also created the climate in which both Calvinist and Lutheran states in Germany were willing to come together in an Evangelical League, which Dury helped to sponsor.[6] Over the next ten years Dury moved between England, Germany, the Netherlands, and Sweden, negotiating for peace between the Churches, and for the cooperation of Protestant states in the war against the Emperor and his allies. Dury was very successful in obtaining audiences for himself with powerful figures, notably with the Swedish chancellor, Axel Oxenstierna, but his irenic efforts were constantly frustrated by clerical opposition, and by the differing objectives in politics, religion, and warfare of the various Protestant states.

Dury returned to England in 1641, in the expectation of serving as household chaplain to the Earl of Leicester, who had recently been appointed as lord-lieutenant in Ireland. Nevertheless, he continued his work for the reunion of the Churches. That work was always contingent upon Dury having the means to support himself, either through gifts and patronage, or through holding clerical appointments. As a result of the Irish rebellion of 1641, Dury never left to take up his new position, but, for him, the political turmoil in London during that year represented a moment of opportunity. His horizons were still shaped by

---

[5] Turnbull, *Hartlib, Dury and Comenius*, 128–32; Hartlib, *Briefe Relation*, 1–2; Michael Strachan, *Sir Thomas Roe 1581–1644: A Life* (Salisbury, 1989), 189–208.

[6] Hartlib, *Briefe Relation*, 2–6; Turnbull, *Hartlib, Dury and Comenius*, 129, 143–71.

events in central Europe, where he considered the dangers to the Protestant cause to be as great as ever. The meeting of the Long Parliament seemed to offer the possibility of a change in English policy, which might involve a more active role for England in the affairs of international Protestantism. With this in mind, Dury and Hartlib petitioned the parliament, and brought the leader of the dispossessed Bohemian Protestants, Jan Amos Komenský, over to England.[7] Comenius' stay in England proved brief however, and failed to win material support for his brethren. By May 1642 Dury himself had left England once again for the Hague. There, he served as chaplain to Charles I's daughter, Princess Mary, who had been betrothed to the prince of Orange in 1641. Dury eventually resigned this post, and, in 1644, went to work as chaplain to the Merchant Adventurers in Rotterdam, from whence he came over to England in 1645.

Dury's work throughout the period from 1628 to 1645 must be placed within the context of securing help for the recovery of the Elector Palatine's lost lands in Germany, and for the restoration of the Protestants in Bohemia. At this stage, he hoped that it might be possible to create a strengthened Protestant alliance which would inflict military defeat on the Habsburgs and their allies. By overcoming the religious differences which separated Protestants, it would be possible to encourage the pursuit of these goals.[8] There were many Protestants who shared Dury's concern for the situation in Germany, but there were also real issues which divided the Protestant world, and which made reunion impossible. It was not obviously in the interest of all Protestant states or rulers to support the Protestant cause in Germany. Partly for domestic reasons, the governments of James I and Charles I were reluctant to become involved in the war throughout the 1620s and 1630s. The Lutheran Elector of Saxony, and other Protestant German princes, benefited personally from the support which they gave to the Emperor against the Swedes. More importantly, there were significant doctrinal and institutional differences dividing the various Reformed Churches, which also separated them from the Lutherans. Thus, the decisions of the Synod of Dort on the questions of predestination, salvation, and reprobation made union with the Lutherans particularly difficult for the Dutch Church. The absence of episcopal government in the Reformed Churches, and its interruption during the Lutheran Reformation in Denmark, were obstacles to union with the Church of England. The differing interpretations of the status of the bread and the wine at the

---

[7] *John Dury His Petition to the Honourable House of Commons* (London, 1641); John Dury, *A Petition to the Honourable House of Commons* (London, 1642); Turnbull, *Hartlib, Dury and Comenius*, 330–3; Hugh Trevor-Roper, *Religion, the Reformation and Social Change* (London, 1967), 237–93.

[8] John Dury, *A Summary Discourse concerning the Work of Peace Ecclesiasticall* (Cambridge, 1641), 8–9, 27.

Eucharist provided a real theological distinction between the Lutheran Churches and all the Reformed Churches. Although Dury and others made out that the obstacles to union were slight, and that they were as much the consequence of the bickerings of clergymen as of genuine doctrinal differences, in practice the divisions were fundamental. They were not simply confined to adiaphora, but reflected the conclusions of the very debates which had brought the various Churches into existence, and which underwrote their separation from Rome.

These issues became clear during Dury's stay in Sweden between 1636 and 1638. Even though Dury had the support of Oxenstierna and his advisers, and of the archbishop of Uppsala, his schemes were successfully opposed by Johannes Rudbeckius, bishop of Västerås. Dury's Swedish opponents were able to point to the differences between their Church and the Calvinists on key points of doctrine, and to the political divisions which kept them apart from other Lutherans. Dury was himself worried that positions which had been taken up by the Church of England might alienate the Swedes. His supporters among the moderate, Calvinist bishops in England, like Archbishop Ussher or Bishops Bedell, Hall, or Davenant, were disturbed by the apparent idolatry of Lutheran theology, in particular the theology of the Eucharist. In the end, despite some brave sentiments, Dury's efforts in Sweden came to almost nothing. Although he shared common educational aims and interests with the Swedish bishops, and although he had had considerable political support, by 1639 Dury had retreated to Bremen, from whence he took up his hopeful correspondence, referring to the excellence and moderation of a fresh group of foreign divines.[9]

During the 1640s Dury became involved in the debates which were taking place in England about the nature of the Church. The Westminster Assembly, of which Dury was a member, discussed the fundamental doctrines, and forms of worship, required by a Reformed Church. Several members of Hartlib's circle considered the problem of toleration, with reference to those independent congregations which had already split from the Church of England. In the course of the exchange of letters within the Hartlib circle, Dury's own attitude to the boundaries of the Reformed Church became clearer. To some of Hartlib's correspondents, notably the merchant and economic reformer Henry Robinson,

---

[9] See Simon Lester Adams, 'The Protestant Cause: Religious Alliance with the West European Calvinist Communities as a Political Issue in England 1585–1630', unpublished D.Phil. thesis (Oxford, 1973); Anthony Milton, *Catholic and Reformed* (Cambridge, 1995), 377–447; W. J. Tighe, 'William Laud and the Reunion of the Churches: Some Evidence from 1637 and 1638', *Historical Journal*, 30 (1987), 717–27; Hartlib Papers, Sheffield University Library (hereafter HP), 4/4/18A–B (John Dury to Samuel Hartlib, 18 May 1661); Turnbull, *Hartlib, Dury and Comenius*, 183–8; Roberts, *Gustavus Adolphus*, i. 381–2; John Dury, 'A briefe Declaration of the severall formes of Government, received in the Reformed Churches beyond the Seas', in *Certain Briefe Treatises Written by Diverse Learned Men, concerning the Ancient and Modern Government of the Church* (Oxford, 1641), 123–7; Bodl., MS Rawlinson C 911, fos. 225–519 (copies of letters from Dury to various English correspondents, Aug. 1635 to June 1639).

it appeared that Dury valued liberty of conscience less than they did. Whereas Hartlib, and others, favoured the toleration of the Independents within a Church whose structure was based only on the essentials of the Christian religion, Dury appeared to accept the right of the magistrate or of the Church to define the rules of ecclesiastical government more closely. Robinson worried that 'you make Deutyes of practise no lesse fundamentall in the profession of Christianity then the knowledge of necessary truthes'.[10] Dury was afraid that the pursuit of toleration had become a mechanism for altering the fundamentals of the Church. Should this happen, he worried that latitude might be denied under any new settlement. In April 1646 he reminded Hartlib that liberty of conscience might not be increased by a weakening of Presbyterian control: 'doe yow not think that they [the Independents] will haue the same pretence of power ouer other Congregations as well as against the Presbyterians?'[11] Dury stressed the need to accept the decisions of legitimately constituted authorities (in this case, parliament), with regard to the structure of the Church. He drew up detailed advice to the magistrate on how to rule according to scripture. This advice contained an extensive list of doctrinal fundamentals, and exhorted the magistrate 'to declare for and to incourage all such Truths . . . and to discourage all such Errors, which the Scripture cleerly and plainly and most indisputably holds forth and disprooves'.[12] Dury was able to make this case within the bounds of his own conscience because he had always been sympathetic to classical Calvinism, and did not feel personally constrained by the Presbyterian settlement of the Church in England in the late 1640s. Furthermore, such a Calvinist form of Church government and discipline made the project of union between the English and the continental Reformed Churches easier. Thus Dury continued to be interested in the reunion of the Churches, and he was afraid of the destruction of the Church of England as a model for ecclesiastical settlement.

Dury's own religious and political beliefs came under close scrutiny in the years following 1649, as a result of his support for taking the Engagement. This oath of loyalty to the Republic proved controversial for a number of reasons. Its opponents argued that those who had taken the Covenant in the 1640s would perjure themselves by taking the Engagement. Nevertheless, several members of the Rump Parliament and of the Westminster Assembly, including Dury, took the new oath. Dury's action, and his advocacy of the Engagement in print, alienated some Presbyterians who had previously supported him. The most vociferous of these was William Prynne. In his *The Time-serving Proteus, and Ambidexter Divine* (1650), Prynne castigated Dury for what he saw as

---

[10] HP 10/10/1A–8B, at 7A.
[11] HP 3/3/10A–11B, at 10B; cf. the more open statements in Hartlib's hand at 17/18/1A–4B.
[12] HP 17/4/1A–8B, at 1A.

inconstancy in religion. According to Prynne, Dury had originally made his way in the world as a Presbyterian minister, but had then turned coat, and taken orders in the Church of England to engage the support of its bishops for his work. When political fortunes had changed, Prynne argued, Dury had trimmed to follow them. He had first taken the Covenant, and now the 'late change of affairs *metamorphosed* him into an *Independent*'.[13] In the 1640s Prynne had appeared to support Dury's irenic plans for the reunion of the Churches, and had attacked Archbishop Laud for his supposed lack of enthusiasm for Dury's work, in the account which he published of Laud's trial.[14] In Prynne's eyes, Dury had abandoned the cause of true religion and politics by writing in support of the Engagement. Dury had ceased to be a man of religion and honour, and had become a 'parasite', willing to do or say anything in order to gain preferment or to keep his place.[15]

Dury's advocacy of the Engagement must be placed in the context of his adherence to magisterial authority more generally. The *de facto* arguments which Dury advanced in favour of taking the Engagement were not substantialy different from those which he had always made in support of magisterial authority in the Church. Dury argued that it was not the place of the ministry to meddle in the affairs of the magistrate, stating that ministers 'are not properly *over men* as Magistrates are in humane affairs, to command and compell obedience to that which they inioyn'.[16] For Dury, the magistrate had a divinely given right to order the outward behaviour of his people. This authority resided in the magistrate as a result of his office, not of his person. If, as had recently happened in England, the authority of one magistrate (Charles I) had been replaced by that of another (the Republic), then that should be seen as reflecting God's will. Divine right, for Dury, was not hereditary. It could be won, or lost, by conquest, or as result of other signs of God's favour or displeasure, in the 'changes of Government, which Gods providence brings upon a Nation'.[17]

Following John Calvin, Dury argued that it was not reasonable for any private individual to refuse obedience to the magistrate in such circumstances. He characterized himself, and other private individuals, as 'strangers and pilgrims' in this world, arguing that 'a stranger, passenger and pilgrim, takes things as he finds them on his way, makes the best of them that he can, and meddles onely

---

[13] William Prynne, *The Time-serving Proteus, and Ambidexter Divine* ([London], 1650), title-page.

[14] William Prynne, *Canterburies Doome* (London, 1646), 541.

[15] Prynne, *Time-serving Proteus*, 4.

[16] John Dury, *A Case of Conscience . . . resolved more satisfactorily* (London, 1650), 52–4.

[17] John Dury, *Just Re-Proposals to Humble Proposals* (London, 1650), 2–3; Dury, *A Case of Conscience*, 74, 154, 162; cf. Dury, *A Case of Conscience resolved* (London, 1649), repr. in *The Harleian Miscellany*, ii (London, 1744), 523–32; Dury, *Considerations concerning the present Engagement* (London, 1650).

with his own matters'.[18] This argument was consistent with Dury's earlier rejection of independency in religion, even though it appeared, at least to Prynne, to make Dury a political ally of the Independents in 1650. Indeed, despite Prynne's allegations, Dury's writings display a considerable uniformity of attitude, both towards the power of the magistrate, and in terms of his own religious allegiance. In the petition which he sent to Gustavus Adolphus, Dury suggested that: 'You that are the Kings and Rulers of the world, you are gods among mortall men. God hath lent you his authority, his hand, and power, to put his work in execution . . . If you do not his work, and refuse to favour those that do it, you shall give account unto him.'[19]

At the time of the Synod of Dort, many divines had hoped that James I would take on the leadership of continental Protestantism. One of Dury's earliest patrons, Joseph Hall, bishop of Exeter, had stressed the links between the English and continental Churches during the 1620s, to remind Charles I of his responsibilities, and to warn against the more exclusive arguments of Richard Montagu, and other English Arminians.[20] It was important to Dury in the 1630s that his journeys in the course of irenicism should have the support of the king and of the Church of England. Similarly in the early 1640s, his petitions to parliament bear witness to his respect for the authority of king in parliament.[21] Throughout the turmoil of the 1640s, Dury continued to stress the need for the magistrate to correct evil, and to set England on the path to reformation once again.[22] In the 1650s Dury looked to 'the zeale which my Lord Protector hath to make a Mends unto Protestants in the behalfe of England'.[23] Although Dury left England in 1661, he was keen to stress that he did so because of his debts, not because of any lack of sympathy with the regime. He continued to recommend the schemes and needs of his friends to Charles II, and he remained confident about the nature of the king's personal religious belief, and his attitude towards the Protestant

---

[18] Quentin Skinner, 'Conquest and Consent: Thomas Hobbes and the Engagement Controversy', in Gerald Aylmer (ed.), *The Interregnum: The Quest for Settlement 1646–1660* (London, 1972), 79–98, esp. 81; John Calvin, *The Institutes of the Christian Religion*, ed. John T. McNeill, tr. Ford Lewis Battles (2 vols.; Philadelphia, 1960), ii. 1511–14; Dury, *Considerations concerning the present Engagement*, 10.

[19] Dury, *Copy of a Petition*, 41.

[20] Christopher Grayson, 'James I and the Religious Crisis in the United Provinces 1613–19', *Studies in Church History*, subsidia 2 (1979), 195–219; Peter Lake, 'The Moderate and Irenic Case for Religious War: Joseph Hall's *Via Media* in Context', in Susan D. Amussen and Mark A. Kishlansky (eds.), *Political Culture and Cultural Politics in Early Modern England* (Manchester, 1995), 55–83.

[21] e.g. *Dury His Petition*, sig. *2ᵛ.

[22] John Dury, *Englands Thankfulnesse* (1642); Dury, *Considerations tending to the happy accomplishment of Englands Reformation* (1647), both printed in Charles Webster (ed.), *Samuel Hartlib and the Advancement of Learning* (Cambridge, 1970), 90–7, 119–39, esp. at 93, 121–3.

[23] HP 4/3/63A–64B, at 63A (copy of a letter from Dury, 23 Nov. 1654); cf. Turnbull, *Hartlib, Dury and Comenius*, 274, 285.

Churches.[24] Dury was occasionally disillusioned by the failure of princes to carry out the providential tasks which he believed had been set for them. He was, however, confident that God punished princes who failed him, and sent other magistrates in their place to do his work. This was Dury's verdict on the fate of Charles I (although he later claimed to have tried to prevent that monarch's execution).[25] Only rarely did he feel that private individuals were justified in working without the full cooperation of princes, and he was generally confident, given his knowledge of the failures at Hampton Court, Dordrecht, and even at Westminster, that no conference or assembly 'will heal our breaches', unless carefully ordered from above.[26]

Despite the allegations of Prynne, Dury's religious allegiance also remained constant. He had begun his career as a Presbyterian minister in Elbing, and had indeed been ordained into the priesthood of the Church of England in 1634. By then, he had been taken up by a number of moderate Calvinist bishops and lay people within the English Church, who shared his interest in Protestant reunion. Like Dury, they were disillusioned by the failure of the Synod of Dort, although they were also sympathetic in principle to a Calvinist position in matters of doctrine and Church government. They blamed the intransigence of individuals, notably of the president of the Synod of Dort, Johannes Bogermann, for the decisions which had been taken in 1618 and 1619.[27] Dury himself was indifferent about episcopacy as a system of Church government, as he showed in 1642, and reiterated in 1650.[28] It was, however, important both to his allies in the Church of England, and, more seriously, to the king and to Archbishop Laud, whose favour Dury sought. It was not, therefore, surprising that Dury should have accepted episcopal reordination in 1634, particularly since this act carried with it the promise of patronage to church livings which might help to finance his travels. Dury's own liturgical and ceremonial preferences are made clear in a description of his ordering of the church in his charge as minister to the English

[24] See Turnbull, *Hartlib, Dury and Comenius*, 112–13, 292–3; *The Diary and Correspondence of Dr. John Worthington*, ed. James Crossley, i (Chetham Society, 13; 1847), 249; John Dury, *The Plain Way of Peace and Unity in Matters of Religion* (London, 1660), 9–14; Ernestine G. E. van der Wall, 'Prophecy and Profit: Nicolaes Van Rensselaer, Charles II and the Conversion of the Jews', in C. Augustijn, P. N. Holtrop, G. H. M. Posthumus Meyjes, and van der Wall (eds.), *Kerkhistorische Opstellen aangeboden aan Prof. dr. J. van den Berg* (Kampen, 1987), 75–87; cf. Henry More, *An Explanation of the Grand Mystery of Godliness* (London, 1660), p. xii.

[25] HP 4/3/63A; cf. Hartlib on the same subject, HP 17/18/1B; *A Declaration of John Durie* (London, 1660), 18, quoted in John M. Wallace, *Destiny His Choice* (Cambridge, 1968), 51.

[26] Bodl., MS Rawlinson C 911, fos. 476ᵛ–477; Dury, *The Plain Way of Peace*, 6. Dury attacked 'the vulgar notions of an Oecumenicall Counsel of Protestants & such like wayes which are imagined to bee intended by me', HP 4/3/121B.

[27] Bodl., MS Rawlinson C 911, fo. 225; John Platt, 'Eirenical Anglicans at the Synod of Dort', *Studies in Church History*, subsidia 2 (1979), 221–43.

[28] Turnbull, *Hartlib, Dury and Comenius*, 226; John Dury, *The Unchanged, Constant and Single-hearted Peace-maker* (London, 1650), 5.

Company at Rotterdam in 1644. He insisted on the role of preaching and reading in the service, removed the communion table which had been placed in the church like an altar, and celebrated communion in the manner of the Reformed Churches. He tolerated the kneeling of his congregation, but ensured that they were governed according to the principles of the Reformed, arranging for the election of elders and deacons.[29] Although Dury was following the instructions of parliament in pulling down the altar rail, his attitude to the congregation in Rotterdam suggests that his personal religious convictions, as well as his scrupulous sense of obedience to lawful authority, were involved in his reform of the Church. Dury himself regarded accusations of religious inconstancy as the occupational hazard of an irenicist. But his true beliefs were certain, and were known to his friends. He told Hartlib:

you know how that I haue beene heretofore blamed & suspected for walking more universally then others use to doe; sometymes I haue beene counted a Lutheran, sometymes an Arminian, sometymes a Canterburian Agent & such like; but what wrong hath beene done to me in all this yow also can sufficiently declare: the matter is the mistake of my waye, which is more uniuersall, & indifferent towards the good of all, (to gaine euery one to their duetie) then is usually aimed at by others; therefore such as mind only themselves, & think that nothing is right but what serveth precisely their turne, & which they can see a reason for, cannot but looke upon me with iealous eyes thinking that I am either a man of no Conscience, colluding with all sides for worldly endes, or else a deceitfull traytor of the good cause which I seeme to favour . . .[30]

These comments, which Dury made in 1644, anticipate the later criticism of his action at the time of the Engagement controversy. Then, the principal accusation levelled against Dury was that he was an Erastian. For Prynne, one aspect of Dury's Erastianism was his compromise with episcopacy; the second proof of it was his fellow-travelling with the Independents. In his replies to Prynne, Dury stressed that, just as he had not given himself up to prelacy in the past, he was not now about to abandon the principles embodied in the Covenant. However, he continued to believe that the words of the Covenant themselves were an indifferent matter, and that his allegiance to them was subordinate to his higher duty to God.[31] He defended his commitment to the Reformed Churches, but also to the authority of the magistrate over them. Dury did not advocate total freedom of conscience in areas of religion which went beyond the fundamentals on which all were agreed. He preferred the option of persuading the Independents to accept a Presbyterian settlement to that of granting them real toleration.

---

[29] Turnbull, *Hartlib, Dury and Comenius*, 243; HP 3/2/34A–35B.

[30] HP 3/2/2A–3B, at 2A (Dury, probably to Hartlib, 22 Feb./ 3 Mar. 1644).

[31] HP 9/11/31A–B, 33A–34B (Dury's answer to William Hamilton, with a covering letter by Hartlib, 25 Apr. 1657).

Yet his most passionate belief, reinforced by his experiences with the Churches abroad, was that it was not worth sacrificing the unity of the Church, or the harmony of the State, on behalf of the conscience of any one individual or group of individuals. In Dury's view, this was one of the most important justifications for the deposition of Charles I, from which the whole controversy had started.[32] For Dury, this did not constitute Erastianism, which he regarded as 'a scarre crowe'.[33] However, even sympathetic critics of Dury might conclude that 'nether is Mr. Durey directly an Erastiane, nether hath he much, that is considerable against it . . .'.[34]

The English Republic did not achieve the settlement of religion which Dury had hoped it would. However, he continued to be loyal to it, and to the regime of Cromwell which followed it. Throughout the period of the Interregnum, successive attempts were made to settle and unite the English Church. Like Dury, Cromwell was particularly concerned to bring about the union of the godly, and at the same time to allow for freedom of conscience within the limits set by the fundamental beliefs of Reformed Christianity. As Blair Worden has characterized them, Cromwell's beliefs both about the Church and about magisterial responsibility were at times very close to those of Dury. Cromwell was extremely sensitive to the providential aspects of his role as Lord Protector, believing that he was intended to do God's will, and that God would punish him for failure. He was concerned not to persecute Christians whose intentions were genuinely spiritual, but was afraid of the consequences for the union of the Church of permitting too much liberty in religion. He wished to preserve the community of the godly and to strive for national salvation.[35] For Dury, however, certain aspects of English policy during the 1650s were profoundly worrying. Between 1652 and 1654 England was at war with the Dutch, although by

[32] Prynne, *Time-serving Proteus*; Dury, *Unchanged, Constant and Single-hearted Peace-maker*, 11–12; J[ohn] D[ury], *Objections against the Taking of the Engagement Answered* (London, 1650), 17; Turnbull, *Hartlib, Dury and Comenius*, 226; cf. the judgement on Dury's actions in Anthony Milton, '"The Unchanged Peacemaker"? John Dury and the Politics of Irenicism in England, 1628–43', in Mark Greengrass, Michael Leslie, and Timothy Raylor (eds.), *Samuel Hartlib and Universal Reformation* (Cambridge, 1994), 95–117.

[33] HP 4/3/143A–B, at 143B ('Robertson' [John Dury] to Hartlib, 8 Jan. 1656).

[34] HP 9/11/30A–B, at 30A (Hamilton to Hartlib, 14/15 Oct. 1656).

[35] See Blair Worden, 'Toleration and the Cromwellian Protectorate', *Studies in Church History*, 21 (1984), 199–233; Worden, 'Providence and Politics in Cromwellian England', *Past and Present*, 109 (1985), 55–99; Worden, 'Oliver Cromwell and the Sin of Achan', in Derek Beales and Geoffrey Best (eds.), *History, Society and the Churches* (Cambridge, 1985), 125–45; cf. J. C. Davis, 'Cromwell's Religion', in John Morrill (ed.), *Oliver Cromwell and the English Revolution* (London, 1990), 181–208; Davis, 'Religion and the Struggle for Freedom in the English Revolution', *Historical Journal*, 35 (1992), 507–30; Davis, 'Against Formality: One Aspect of the English Revolution', *Transactions of the Royal Historical Society*, 6th ser., 3 (1993), 265–88.

the end of 1654 treaties had been concluded with both Holland and Sweden.[36] Dury himself visited Sweden in 1652, and went to The Hague in 1654, before travelling to Switzerland. Cromwell was interested in Dury's negotiations, which were given special urgency by the massacre of the Vaudois in the Piedmontese valleys.[37] But Dury was distressed by doubts which were being raised about the purity of his motives, and about the nature of English Christianity during the 1650s. Continental Protestants were disturbed by the apparent religious licence in England during the 1650s, and in particular by the spread to England of Socinian ideas, and of doubts about the Trinity. Although Dury had himself been involved in the condemnation of *The Racovian Catechism* in February 1652, arguments were now raised by various Reformed divines concerning the suitability of negotiating with him.[38] One of these divines was Samuel Des Marets, who, Dury wrote, 'falls extreame foule upon the Gouvernment of England for suffering Biddel his catechisme, & calls them all to bee favourers of such heresies'.[39] Dury's credibility as an irenicist within the Reformed Churches depended in part on the respect which those Churches had for the Church in England; by the 1650s that respect was wearing thin. In 1656 Dury even warned against the danger of making too many attempts at uniting foreign Protestants (especially in Germany), when they were unwilling to work for unity themselves.[40]

Dury's disillusionment was short-lived, however, and he considered making another journey to Germany in 1658. He continued to enjoy the friendship of other Protestant diplomats, scholars, and divines, who encouraged him in his work. After his return to England in 1657, Dury had written to Richard Baxter, to inform him of his progress and of his plans for union both at home and abroad. In 1658 the Worcestershire association of ministers, in which Baxter played a leading part, urged Dury on, and stressed the importance of scripture as the basis for determining the fundamentals of religion, which must be held in

[36] See Michael Roberts (ed.), *Swedish Diplomats at Cromwell's Court, 1655–1656* (Camden Fourth Series, 36; 1988); cf. HP 4/3/63A–64B; *The Correspondence of Henry Oldenburg*, i, eds. A. Rupert Hall and Marie Boas Hall, with the collaboration of Eberhard Reichmann (Madison, 1965), 21–30 (Oldenburg to Hans Jakob Ulrich, 4 Apr. 1654, and to the Senate of Bremen, 7 Apr. 1654).

[37] HP 4/3/102A–B (Dury to Hartlib, 18 June 1655); Zentralbibliothek, Zurich, MS E 15, fos. 562–82 (letters of Dury concerning the Piedmontese Waldenses), MS L 113; Turnbull, *Hartlib, Dury and Comenius*, 274. For English interest in the Piedmontese generally, see Euan Cameron, *The Reformation of the Heretics* (Oxford, 1984), 241–52.

[38] Peter Toon, *God's Statesman: The Life and Work of John Owen* (Exeter, 1971), 83–4; cf. Dury's report to Richard Baxter about Archbishop Ussher's reassurance that the biblical references to the Trinity are canonical, in *Calendar of the Correspondence of Richard Baxter*, ed. N. H. Keeble and Geoffrey F. Nuttall (2 vols.; Oxford, 1991), i. 93–4 (Dury to Baxter, 22 Feb. 1653).

[39] HP 4/3/62A–B (Dury, probably to Hartlib, 23 Nov. 1654); cf. Turnbull, *Hartlib, Dury and Comenius*, 275–6.

[40] Turnbull, *Hartlib, Dury and Comenius*, 280–1; cf. *Correspondence of Oldenburg*, i. 145–7 (Oldenburg to Dury, 14 Nov. 1657).

common by the Churches.[41] Baxter had been a correspondent of Dury for most of the 1650s, and shared his interest in establishing a national church, which would be governed to some extent along Presbyterian lines. The letters exchanged between Baxter and Dury give a sense of Dury's continuing optimism during the 1650s, and his belief that a lasting settlement in English religion was possible. In 1652 Dury was sure that Cromwell himself was searching for such a settlement, although he was also less naïvely enthusiastic about the prospects of success than was Baxter.[42] Both Dury and Baxter sought to maintain contact, not only with like-minded Presbyterians, but also with some Independents. They also sought out those leaders of the Church of England, like James Ussher, archbishop of Armagh, who were thought to be favourable to ecclesiastical compromise.[43] By April 1654, on the eve of his departure for The Hague, Dury was confident that Presbyterians and Independents would 'walk together in unity as brethren'. He did not 'think it needfull for me to stay any longer in these parts to attend to this designe seing the wheele is going, & I hope nothing will henceforth hinder it'.[44] As Dury discovered during his journeys on the continent between 1654 and 1657, his optimism had been premature. Nevertheless, his sentiments in 1654 support the conclusion that he regarded the achievement of religious peace in England as a necessary prelude to his irenic work abroad. It is also clear, however, that Dury still wanted English religion to be settled on the basis of uniformity of worship as well as of doctrine. Despite all the experience he had had, Dury continued to believe that such uniformity was compatible with the reunion of the Churches.[45]

In 1661 Dury went into exile, stressing that his reasons for doing so had nothing to do with the Restoration settlement of the Church in England, and hoping some day to return. He continued to travel in pursuit of the elusive goal of union amongst Protestants, visiting Switzerland and Germany, and settling finally in Cassel. His career ended unsuccessfully even there. By the time of his death he had lost the favour of the Elector of Brandenburg, who had supported his plans for reunion in the 1660s, and he had even been expelled from membership of the Reformed Church in Cassel itself.[46]

---

[41] *Calendar of the Correspondence of Richard Baxter*, i. 307–8, 321–2.

[42] Ibid. 85–6 (Dury to Baxter, 20 Oct. 1652).

[43] Ibid. 93–4, 127–8 (Dury to Baxter, 22 Feb. 1654), 133–5 (Dury to Baxter, 2 Apr. 1654); it is doubtful that Ussher was himself sympathetic to Presbyterian schemes for union, see William M. Abbott, 'James Ussher and "Ussherian Episcopacy", 1640–1656: The Primate and his *Reduction* Manuscript', *Albion*, 22 (1990), 237–59.

[44] *Calendar of the Correspondence of Richard Baxter*, i. 133–4.

[45] Ibid. 135.

[46] HP 4/4/27A–B (Dury to Hartlib, Amsterdam, 12 July 1661), in which Dury expresses his worries that the new regime in England might allow toleration to Catholics; Turnbull, *Hartlib, Dury and Comenius*, 292–300; Bibliothèque Publique et Universitaire, Geneva, Archives Tronchin, 46 and 50;

John Dury's career as an irenicist demonstrated enormous tenacity, not to say stubbornness. Dury was undoubtedly committed to the project of reuniting the Churches, but his view of the Church was too inflexible to make this possible. Nor did he have the power himself to make any real decisions about doctrine or discipline. His role was simply to persuade those who were in authority to take the right decisions. As I have suggested, Dury's reverence for authority, whilst gaining him support among kings, princes, and leaders of the Church, did not win him universal trust. It made it harder for him to win support from within the Churches themselves, even though he recognized that the work of reunion must reshape the hearts and minds of ordinary believers, as well as the ordinances which governed them. Before concluding, it is therefore worthwhile considering the motives which lay behind Dury's irenicism.

Dury's confidence in the power and authority of the magistrate was derived from his belief that God appointed rulers, and would have them govern according to his will. But Dury's providentialism underwrote the whole of his career, not merely his relationships with those in government. Dury believed that the events of the years through which he had lived had been predicted in the Bible, particularly in the Book of Revelation. He was confident that the terrors of the Thirty Years War were a prelude to the eventual overthrow of the power of the Roman Catholic Church.[47] Dury cast the events of his own time in biblical terms: the afflictions of the Protestant nations and Churches were like those of Israel, he himself was like Elijah, sent to exhort the rulers of Israel to true piety.[48] The Catholic powers who threatened the Protestants, Spain, and above all the Austrian Holy Roman Emperor, were likened to the biblical oppressors of Israel. The Emperor was 'this German Pharoah'.[49] The urgency which these beliefs gave to Dury's work helps to explain his strength of purpose. Yet, despite this, Dury did not agree with those Protestants who argued that the real purpose of reunion was simply to make war on Antichrist in the form of Catholic nations. He was enthusiastic about the prospects for evangelical union following the accession of the Swedish king, Charles X, who came to the throne at a time of frenzied

Richard H. Popkin, 'The End of the Career of a Great 17th Century Millenarian: John Dury', *Pietismus und Neuzeit*, 14 (1988), 203–20.

[47] See esp. [Abraham von Franckenburg], *Clavis Apocalyptica* (2nd edn., London, 1651), 160–1. This work has a dedication by Hartlib, and a lengthy preface by Dury (pp. 1–79). Cf. *Correspondence of Oldenburg*, i. 179–81 (Oldenburg to Hartlib, 12 Sept. 1658, on the apocalyptic context for Dury's current mission).

[48] HP 3/4/61A–68A, at 66A (letter from Dury, Amsterdam, 14/24 Jan. 1636).

[49] HP 4/3/17A–19A (Dury to Hartlib, Zurich, 22 July 1654); cf. John Philly, *An Arrainment of Christendom* (n.p., 1664, repr. Menston, 1971), a millenarian text attacking the Emperor Leopold I, written in Dury's system of phonetic spelling.

millenarian expectation, and who immediately made plans for war.[50] But even in the aftermath of the massacre in Piedmont, Dury was keen to stress that the achievement of the peace of the saints required more than acts of war:

Your freind giues it the name of a Warre Christiano-Political which hee would exhort the Protestant Princes unto, in opposing the Pope. whether the Dr. hath giuen it this terme I know not; it is likely hee may. Supposing then his scope to bee to stirre up all Protestant Princes iointly to oppose the Pope (for I take warring to bee nothing else but opposing that which is euill) & in a Christian & Politicall way; to strippe him of his usurped power & put an ende to his Tyrannie. I say supposing this to be his scope, would not your freind allow of it? if I take warre to bee only the Slaughtering of men; or think that the Dr. meanes nothing else by it, but outward brutish force to breake & teare all in pieces, I haue a very meane notion of the thing myself . . .[51]

For Dury, reunion was primarily a spiritual state, although it required political means to bring it about. Once achieved, reunion would also have political consequences, including the fall of the papacy and the conversion of the whole world to the true religion of the Reformed. Dury was conscious of the need to bring ordinary Christians into a state of readiness for union, and that Christians should spread their religion to embrace all the peoples of the earth. He believed that, until this was done, the true fruits of political union, which were everlasting peace, rather than further war, could not be attained. Throughout his career Dury strove to improve the education of Christians, and in particular their knowledge of the essential teachings of scripture. In 1642 he appealed to the parliament in England for the establishment of 'a professorship of Practicall Divinity in every University; and one in *London* . . . By which meanes, the second part of our Evangelicall profession will bee much advanced towards some perfection, chiefly in those that are desirous to leade a godly life.' In the same document he also asked that a lectureship, to teach the common people how to read and interpret the Bible, should be established in London, and hoped that it would soon be possible, through reforms in education, to '[find] out the true sense thereof'.[52] In his *Touchant l'intelligence de l'apocalypse*, which he published in 1674, Dury attempted to provide rational principles for the interpretation of the hardest of biblical texts, to enable people to understand the prophecies about the world in which they lived. His last work, *Le Véritable Chréstien* (Cassel,

[50] On the aftermath of the accession of Charles X, see Roberts (ed.), *Swedish Diplomats*, 142–3; Susanna Åkerman, *Queen Christina of Sweden and her Circle* (Leiden, 1991), 196–224.

[51] HP 4/3/121A–B, at 121A (letter from Dury, 25 Aug. 1655, discussing the writings of Dr George Horne).

[52] John Dury, *A Motion tending to the Publick Good of this Age* (London, 1642), printed in Webster (ed.), *Hartlib and the Advancement of Learning*, 97–110, esp. 102; see also Webster, *The Great Instauration* (London, 1975), 67, 213–34.

1676), sought to inculcate the inward principles of duty which must underpin true Christian practice.[53]

Whilst he was in England, Dury also worked to spread the essential message of Christianity to those who were ignorant of it, or rejected it. He sponsored the work of Samuel Chylinski, who sought help with the publication of a Lithuanian Bible.[54] Dury used the contacts which he made during his travels in Europe to aid in his plans for works of translation and Christian commentary; in particular he hoped to have published an edition of the Mishnah which would help to convert European Jews to Christianity. Through his acquaintance with the Amsterdam rabbi, Menasseh ben Israel, Dury became interested in the possibility that the apocalyptic moment of the rediscovery of the lost tribes of Israel had been reached. He hoped to be able to appeal to the Jews, and to bring all of them into the fold of Christianity. In the mid-1650s he worked for the readmission of the Jews into England, in order to be able to bring about their conversion. He realized, however, that practical arguments for their readmission, such as the help which the Jews might give England in its war with Spain, might prove more persuasive to the government.[55] He helped to raise money for the Ashkenazi community in Jerusalem, and, during the 1660s, remained receptive to the idea that a Jewish Messiah might be about to appear, and that, as a result, the Jews might be led to convert.[56] Dury's work for reunion was also supposed to expand the frontiers of the Christian Church, and to bring about the moment when God might depose Antichrist, and establish the dominion of his newly united saints over the earth.

[53] See Popkin, 'End of the Career'; cf. Dury's preface to [Franckenburg], *Clavis Apocalyptica*, and his comments on the interpretation of the Apocalypse, made in a letter to Baxter of 1673, *Calendar of the Correspondence of Richard Baxter*, ii. 141.

[54] *Diary of Worthington*, ed. Crossley, i. 249, 335.

[55] Ibid. 83, 250; HP 4/3/137A–139B ('Robertson' [Dury] to Hartlib, 1 Dec. 1655); John Dury, *A Case of Conscience, whether it be lawful to admit Jews into a Christian Commonwealth* (London, 1656), repr. in *The Harleian Miscellany*, vii (London, 1746); Thomas Thorowgood, *Jewes in America* (London, 1650), which contains a series of letters between Thorowgood and Dury; [John Dury], *An Information concerning the Present State of the Jewish Nation in Europe and Judea* (London, 1658); Menasseh ben Israel, *The Hope of Israel*, tr. Moses Wall, eds. Henry Méchoulan and Gérard Nahon (Oxford, 1987); Richard H. Popkin, 'The Rise and Fall of the Jewish Indian Theory', in Yosef Kaplan, Henry Méchoulan, and Popkin (eds.), *Menasseh ben Israel and his World* (Leiden, 1989), 63–82; J. van den Berg and Ernestine G. E. van der Wall (eds.), *Jewish–Christian Relations in the Seventeenth Century* (Dordrecht, 1988), esp. 145–9, 155–9; David S. Katz, *Philo-Semitism and the Readmission of the Jews to England 1603–1655* (Oxford, 1982), 127–231.

[56] David Katz, 'English Charity and Jewish Qualms: The Rescue of the Ashkenazi Community of Seventeenth-Century Jerusalem', in Ada Rapoport-Albert and Steven J. Zipperstein (eds.), *Jewish History: Essays in Honour of Chimen Abramsky* (London, 1988), 245–66; Richard H. Popkin, 'Rabbi Nathan Shapira's Visit to Amsterdam in 1657', *Dutch Jewish History*, 1 (1984), 185–205; Popkin, 'Two Unused Sources about Sabbatai Zevi and his Effect on European Communities', *Dutch Jewish History*, 2 (1989), 67–74.

Dury's irenicism was therefore a complete answer to the problems created for the Reformed Churches by the Synod of Dort and the Thirty Years War. It promised to reunite the Protestant nations politically, and to give them the strength to defend themselves against their adversaries. It offered mechanisms for the improvement of education and learning, so that a true understanding of the fundamentals of Christianity might be reached by all. As a result, it suggested that the power of the papacy might be destroyed, and a true, godly religion extended to all Christians, and, by them, to all the peoples of the world. In this way, God's final purposes for mankind might be fulfilled. For Dury, these ambitious aims were immediate prospects, if only Christian rulers could be persuaded to act as gods on earth, and work for the advancement of truth. Dury had set out these aims at the very start of his career in 1631, when he composed a document entitled 'The Purpose and Platforme of the Iourneyes that are vndertaken for the worke of Peace Ecclesiasticall'. In this paper Dury described his plans for working with the Protestant princes of Germany; for gathering up and making sense of the writings of Christian divines, and interpreting scripture; for making an embassy to the Jews; for increasing the understanding of nature; and for healing the divisions within the Churches.[57] At this early stage Dury intended only to make collections of information. As his career progressed, he turned to action. The eventual failure of his project should not obscure the extent of the ambitions which Dury nurtured, or the determination and consistency with which he pursued his ends.

Dury's apocalyptic setting for his work, his love of princes, his absolute conviction concerning the correctness of his own beliefs, and those of his Church, are all foreign to John McManners's account of the contemporary relationship of the Church and the individual. However, McManners's understanding is based on the knowledge that schemes like Dury's must fail, and that it is not enough to listen tolerantly to others, without also being prepared to accept that they may never change their minds.

[57] HP 18/17/1A–3B.

3

An Irish Opportunist in Paris: Dr Piers de Girardin

JACQUES M. GRES-GAYER

Insta opportune, importune

2 Tim. 4: 2

The publication in France of the bull *Unigenitus* (1713) triggered a vast debate, mostly in the form of anonymous tracts, *Relations*, and other *Tocsins* that were fabricated as the many weapons of an unending war associating religious, social, and political stances.[1] What did the adversaries find so exciting in a dispute about 101 propositions? Evidently, the themes not only stirred their imagination but also offered a rare opportunity both to speak up, to express themselves, on issues that mattered to them, and often to dream, to invent fresher and more gratifying interpretations of Christianity.

While worth investigating, this utopian facet of eighteenth-century Jansenism is difficult to document, as in most cases these 'prises de paroles'[2] were made under the protection of anonymity, or communicated piecemeal, often under a coded name, to a few chosen confidants. There must have been many individuals among those whose name is recorded in the *Constitution Unigenitus déférée à l'Église universelle*[3] for whom *Unigenitus* was the event of a lifetime, especially in the body where the conflict was for a while concentrated, the Faculty of Theology of Paris, commonly called the Sorbonne. What these 'Anticonstitutionnaires' really thought, what they specifically expected, will never be known. Most have sunk into oblivion, even their identity now difficult to ascertain. When it

---

[1] J. McManners, 'Jansenism and Politics in the Eighteenth Century', in D. Baker (ed.), *Church, Society, and Politics* (Oxford, 1975), 253–73; J. M. Gres-Gayer, 'The *Unigenitus* of Clement XI: A Fresh Look at the Issues', *Theological Studies*, 49 (1988), 259–82.

[2] To use the stimulating expression of M. de Certeau, *La Prise de parole: Pour une nouvelle culture* (Paris, 1968).

[3] [G. N. Nivelle], *La Constitution Unigenitus déférée à l'Église universelle, ou Recueil général des actes d'appel interjetés au Concile général de cette Constitution et des Lettres Pastoralis officii; avec les arrêts et autres actes du Parlement du royaume qui ont rapport à ces objets* (Cologne, 1757). Dominique Dinet and Marie-Claude Dinet-Lecomte, 'Les Appelants contre la bulle Unigenitus d'après Gabriel-Nicolas Nivelle', *Histoire, Économie et Société*, 9 (1990), 365–89.

happens that through an unusual twist of fate some have left behind enough documentation to provide for an investigation of their attitudes, the inquest brings back to life fascinating, although puzzling information. At least this is the case with Dr Patrick Piers de Girardin, one who seized this opportunity to dream a new world and also to advance his own interest.

Very little is known of the background of this cleric.[4] Queen Caroline, who came to know him, said that 'his true name was Price, but that he pretended to be of the Fitzgerald family in Ireland and hence took the name of Giraldon [*sic*]'.[5] The name Piers though seems authentic, as one cousin, also a doctor of theology of Paris, was R. Piers, sometime Bishop of Waterford.[6]

In 1691, at the age of 19, Piers came to France,[7] probably following the Treaty of Limerick,[8] and became a student at the University of Paris. He graduated in 1706, being awarded the seventy-fifth position in a class of ninety-nine at the Licence in theology, and he received the doctor's cap on 15 April 1707.[9] Of his many long years as a student we know nothing, for if he had any interest in Jansenism this was not the time to show it. Between the time of his *tentative*, the formal examination for the Bachelor of Divinity, to his reception in the *sacer ordo* of theologians, the Faculty of Paris had completely closed its ranks, requiring all new graduates to adhere to the formulary of Alexander VII on the Five Propositions. The Irish priest must have taken this talk, apparently without any personal problem.[10] When in 1714 the majority of the faculty received the Constitution *Unigenitus* that condemned excerpts from Quesnel's *Réflexions morales*, Piers's name does not appear in the ranks of either the defenders or the opponents of the papal document.[11]

[4] (1672–1762) *France littéraire*. 3, sup. 1764, 152. Sens, Collection Languet, VIII, 57.

[5] PRO, Egmont MSS, Diary of Queen Caroline, i. 396, cited in R. Clark, *Strangers and Sojourners at Port-Royal* (Cambridge, 1932), 259.

[6] Richard Piers, Doctor on 20 July 1688. *Series Episcoporum Ecclesiæ Catholicæ*, ed. P. B. Gams (Gratz, 1873), 228. See the letters of Piers de Girardin (hereafter PdeG) to William Wake (hereafter WW) (6 Dec. 1719), Christ Church, Oxford, Archiepiscopi Wake Epistolæ (hereafter AWE), xxix, fo. 63, published in J. M. Gres-Gayer, *Paris-Cantorbéry: Le Dossier d'un premier œcuménisme* (Paris, 1989) (hereafter *Paris-Cantorbéry*), and (11 Sept. 1723), AWE xxx, fo. 133, published in L. Adams (ed.), *William Wake's Gallican Correspondence and Related Documents, 1716–1731* (New York, 1988–92) (hereafter *Correspondence*), iv. 300.

[7] In 1723, he writes to Cardinal Fleury that he has been exiled for thiry-two years (PdeG to WW (27 Nov. 1723), AWE xxx, fo. 149, *Correspondence*, iv. 338–9).

[8] F. Eliot, 'L'Émigration irlandaise et les prêtres irlandais en France,' in L. Swords (ed.), *The Irish–French Connection, 1578–1978* (Paris, 1978), 88.

[9] Bibliothèque Nationale, Paris (hereafter BN), MS latin 15440, *Nomina et Ordo Licentiatorum in Sacra Facultate Theologiæ Parisiensi*, 371. *Nomina et Ordo Magistrorum Sacræ Facultatis Theologiæ Parisiensis* (Paris, 1723), 26. He took the doctoral oath on 2 May 1707: Archives nationales (hereafter AN) MM 255, *Registre des conclusion de la Sacrée Faculté théologie de Paris*, 210.

[10] PdeG to R. Hérault? (19 Aug. 1728), Bibliothèque de l'Arsenal, Paris, MS. 11004, fo. 374. *Correspondence*, vi. 412: 'Je déteste de tout mon cœur l'héréticité des Cinq Propositions et j'ai toujours distingué cette héréticité de mon appel de la Constitution.'

[11] J. M. Gres-Gayer, *Théologie et pouvoir en Sorbonne: La Faculté de théologie de Paris et la bulle Unigenitus* (Paris, 1991), 211–15.

Then everything changed. Louis XIV died (September 1715) and a complete turnaround was made by the duke of Orléans, who assumed the Regency, when he gave a place in his council to the principal opponent to the Constitution, Cardinal de Noailles, the archbishop of Paris. In less than a year, under the leadership of H. Ravechet, its imaginative *syndic*, the Faculty of Theology annulled its former reception of *Unigenitus*, initiated a Body of Doctrine countering the condemnations of the Bull, and, in a memorable meeting of *prima mensis*, in March 1717, solemnly appealed to the General Council. Piers de Girardin was one of the ninety-seven first *appellants*.[12]

The 'Hibernian doctor' did more than adhere to a movement of resistance that was the last and fullest expression of what is called *Richerism*, a form of Gallicanism that wanted to return to a more constitutional conception of the Church; he thought himself well qualified to influence it. He concocted the most ingenious schemes to propose to his colleagues of the Faculty of Paris. The marvel is that, not only was he able to interest some of them, but that he eventually succeeded in presenting his far-fetched plans to highly ranked persons in France and England. The circumstances seemed to favour him; the Anglo-French *rapprochement* negotiated by the Regent and his prime minister, Abbé Dubois, made it more possible, he thought, for a foreigner to intervene in French matters. In John Law and his *système* he saw a model and an incentive.[13] Piers came with a system of his own.

Piers's system,[14] it will soon appear, was quite extraordinary, since it envisioned no less than a complete reorganization of Christendom. This he saw possible through the establishment of an ecclesiastical axis Paris–Canterbury that would mirror and complete the diplomatic Anglo-French alliance. The way in which the Franco-Irish divine was able to initiate the project shows his industry. Having managed to meet William Beauvoir, the chaplain to Lord Stair, the British envoy in France,[15] Piers induced him to pass on to the archbishop of Canterbury, William Wake, a few notes related to French life. Mentioning the volatile religious situation in the country, he hinted that French Catholics were not averse to a union with the English Church. Piers must have known that he was approaching the right man. The primate already had the reputation of a great irenicist, although an early experience in Paris had made him rather sceptical about the French.[16] Conscious of his lack of appeal, Piers remained for a while

[12] Ibid. 58–9.

[13] 'M. Law, ce Joseph', PdeG to WW (20 Sept. 1719), AWE xxix, fo. 47, *Paris-Cantorbéry*, 409–11.

[14] PdeG to WW (27 March 1717), AWE xxv, fo. 124; xxix, fo. 168, *Paris-Cantorbéry*, 336–7.

[15] J. M. Gres-Gayer, 'Le Culte de l'ambassade de Grande-Bretagne à Paris au début de la Régence, 1715–1720', *Bulletin de la Société d'histoire du Protestantisme français*, 130 (1984), 30.

[16] N. Sykes, *William Wake, Archbishop of Canterbury, 1657–1737* (2 vols.; Cambridge, 1957), i. 16.

modestly behind L. Ellies Du Pin,[17] the famous church historian he had been able to recruit, being content to have Beauvoir pass on some of his remarks and interventions. Soon, however, a mere 'opinion' at a Sorbonne meeting, where more than 100 participants intervened, became an 'address' on the issue of reunion with the Anglicans and was communicated to the prelate, serving as a means of introduction. Thus, Wake accepted another Gallican correspondent. They were to keep in touch to the end of his life.

The letters saved by Wake are the major source of our knowledge of Piers de Girardin, appropriately enough, since it was this special relationship that gave consistency to the Hibernian's imaginative programme and obtained him accreditation with several great men and women. They represent mostly a *Gazette*, a collection of petty information and gossip such as people liked to exchange in those days. Piers wrote in French, occasionally interspersing English terms, probably to show that he had some knowledge of the language. His style is sufficiently pleasant and the details he reports are usually entertaining. But becomes more sombre, even poignant, when, moving from the citation of the latest *quatrain* against the Regent,[18] he turns to his system. Suddenly, he becomes the visionary who knows how to make others dream, the inspirer who gives form to their hopes, but also the doer, the go-between, never tired, never exhausted, never discouraged. For the venture he is sharing with his episcopal correspondent is not just his project but corresponds to the will of God. 'Que savons-nous, Monseigneur, si nous ne sommes pas du nombre des ces heureux mortels dont Dieu dont se servir pour commencer ce grand œuvre.'[19] His is a mission, an apostolate, modelled, nothing less, on the apostle who pressed Timothy to intervene 'opportune et inopportune': 'J'ai essuyé des chagrins, des traverses, des dangers par mer et par terre. Dieu m'a fait la grâce de les surmonter. J'ai parlé, j'ai écrit, j'ai pressé à temps et à contre-temps, le Seigneur en tirera son avantage quand il le jugera à propos.'[20] It is his dedication to peace[21] that empowers him, in a prophetic stance, to confront those in authority, ministers, princes, cardinals, even the pope,[22] with a 'liberty' that impresses them,[23] in order to convince them of the worthiness of his cause.

[17] J. M. Gres-Gayer, 'Un théologien gallican témoin de son temps, Louis Ellies Du Pin (1657–1719)', *Revue d'histoire de l'Église de France*, 72 (1986), 67–121.

[18] PdeG to WW (6 Aug. 1721), AWE xxix, fo. 305, *Correspondence*, iii. 188.

[19] PdeG to WW (23 Jan. 1723), AWE xxx, fo. 83, *Correspondence*, iv. 201.

[20] PdeG to WW (10 Mar. 1722), AWE xxx, fo. 6, *Correspondence*, iv. 21.

[21] PdeG to Fr. Le Quien o.p. (17 Apr. 1730), AN M 855, n° 10, 144¹.

[22] PdeG to WW (22 July 1724), AWE xxx, fo. 201, *Correspondence*, v. 61: 'L'abbé de G. écrira dans peu en droiture au pape [Benoît XIII]; il fera un petit précis de toutes les tentatives qu'on a faites depuis six ans pour la réunion de l'Église anglicane.'

[23] He meets Cardinal de Noailles: 'Je lui ai reproché vertement qu'il ne tendait pas les mains [à l'union avec les Anglicans] comme aurait dû faire un prélat de son pouvoir, de son zèle, de son savoir et de sa qualité. Il fût frappé de la liberté avec laquelle je lui parlais' (PdeG to WW (30 Dec. 1722), AWE xxx, fo.

Piers's great design was to heal the schism between the Churches of England and France, and through this 'reunion' to start a process of unification of Christianity. The first part of this project reflected a Gallican hope held by a number of theologians from Bossuet on. For its resolution there were major doctrinal issues to be discussed, but also practical ones. Piers was wise enough to leave these matters in the hands of more competent scholars, first L. Ellies Du Pin and later P. F. Le Courayer.[24] In his *Commonitorium*, an analysis of the Thirty-nine Articles, Du Pin offered a general assessment that resulted only in exasperating Wake. It was further weakened by the author's death and the intervention of the French state (1719), which seized all documents. The matter of apostolic succession in the Anglican hierarchy offered a more focused topic also of more immediate value. There Piers managed to collaborate with Wake in a pamphlet aimed at initiating a defence.[25] This association strengthened the relationship between the doctor and the primate, thus allowing more personal elements to appear in the correspondence that progressively reveal what this 'ecumenism' really meant for Piers.

From his general behaviour, it is clear that the Irish priest had assimilated the lessons learnt at the Faculty of Paris.[26] His perspectives, though, went much further than a mere defence of the classical Gallican ecclesiology.[27] For one thing, his interest in reunion did not have the patristic connotations of his friend Du Pin, who aimed at a healing of schism for the sake of Church unity; it represented more an alliance between sovereign powers, with the goal of redefining European politics and repairing in the Church the damages of 'two centuries of shameful blindness'.

En un mot on découvrirait bientôt l'aveuglement honteux dans lequel on a vécu de part et d'autres depuis près de deux siècles; on travaillerait efficacement à la Réformation de l'Église et on la purgerait de ces hommes audacieux qui (comme les mauvaises humeurs dans le corps humain) la dérangent et qui y font des révolutions qui tendent à la destruction totale.[28]

76, *Correspondence*, iv. 186). Later he writes to Noailles, 'une troisième lettre'. 'Je l'ai tellement talonné et pour ainsi dire harcelé qu'il lit actuellement la lettre latine touchant la succession de l'épiscopat en Angleterre depuis le commencement de la rupture. Je n'en demeurerai pas là. Je le presserai encore à temps et à contre-temps' (PdeG to WW (23 Jan. 1723), AWE xxx, fo. 83, *Correspondence*, iv. 201).

[24] E. Préclin, *L'Union des Églises gallicane et anglicane: Une tentative au temps de Louis XV. P. F. le Courayer (de 1681 à 1732) et Guillaume Wake* (Paris, 1928).

[25] *De Vera et non interrupta episcoporum ad nos usque Anglorum successione ad Amicum Epistola*. AWE xi, fo. 1; Préclin, *L'Union des Églises*, 19.

[26] In March 1720 he asks the faculty to provide a statute that henceforth at the licence examinations the bachelors would have to defend in their theses of *majeure ordinaire*, not only the Four Articles of 1682 but the decisions of the Councils of Constance and Basel: *Suite de la Relation des assemblées de Sorbonne*, vi. 271–2.

[27] J. M. Gres-Gayer, 'Le Gallicanisme de Louis Ellies Du Pin', *Lias*, 18 (1991), 37–82.

[28] PdeG to WW (30 Dec. 1722), AWE xxx, fo. 76, *Correspondence*, iv. 187.

In the international congress that was to meet at Cambrai in 1722–5 to negotiate the future of Europe, he saw the opportunity 'to mortify the Pope and demand the convocation of a general council'.[29] In the same manner, he advocated, that in the past Christian emperors could intervene to protect orthodoxy,[30] it was the duty of modern states to take such a step to protect the Christian religion from those who destroyed it from within.[31] If England and France would initiate the movement, the other participants would follow suit. Protected by the states from Roman interference, such a council would enjoy true freedom and deal with the reformation of the Church in a way that Trent had been incapable of accomplishing:

Quand ce concile serait assemblé, il y a apparence que les affaires ne s'y traiteraient point comme dans celui de Trente. Les ecclésiastiques, tant de l'Église romaine que de celles qui en sont séparées, sont aujourd'hui et plus savants et plus clairvoyants qu'ils ne l'étaient alors; les laïcs, surtout la noblesse, ne sont pas à beaucoup près ni si grossiers, ni si superstitieux. Toute l'Europe jouit d'une paix profonde, on est d'ailleurs revenu de cette terreur panique qu'imprimaient autrefois les foudres (*bruta fulmina*) du Vatican; un pape enfin, vieux, désinteressé et savant qui ne respire que de se distinguer de tous ses prédécesseurs. Toutes ces circonstances murement pesées, donnent toute une autre idée des affaires. Tout le monde est imbû de l'histoire de Fra Paolo qui rapporte si plaisamment qu'on envoyait le St Esprit dans une valise . . . Le concile, de plus, serait le point de vue de toute l'Europe; on ne sentirait que trop qu'il serait bien difficile d'en imposer aux Protestants et aux Jansénistes.[32]

It would accomplish such a reformation, 'in membris and capite',[33] that it would destroy once and for all most of the Protestant criticism of Catholicism. This council would be truly ecumenical,[34] as, since they were 'true bishops', the prelates of the Church of England would be invited to participate.[35] It could even

---

[29] PdeG to WW (14 Sept. 1970), AWE xxix, fo. 140, *Paris-Cantorbéry*, 500; PdeG to WW (23 Oct. 1720), AWE xxix, fo. 161, *Paris-Cantorbéry*, 502; PdeG. to WW (28 Dec 1720), AWE xxix, fo. 198, *Correspondence*, ii. 369.

[30] He gives the example of Sophronius 'qui fit revenir les quatre patriarchats d'Orient et celui d'Occident de l'erreur des Monothélites' (PdeG to WW (3 June 1722), AWE xxx, fo. 20, *Correspondence*, iv. 68).

[31] PdeG to WW (6 Apr. 1720), AWE xxix, fo. 91, *Paris-Cantorbéry*, 472.

[32] PdeG to WW (23 Sept. 1724), AWE xx, fos. 207–8, *Correspondence*, v. 81. See also a letter by J. H. Ott, Lambeth Palace Librarian, to WW (16 May 1726), AWE xi, fos. 248–9, *Correspondence*, v. 320; also Préclin, *L'Union des Églises*, 98.

[33] PdeG to WW (14 Sept. 1720), AWE xxix, fo. 140, *Paris-Cantorbéry*, 500.

[34] In opposition to an ecumenical interpretation of the Roman Synod of 1725: 'Le bruit court que Sa Sainteté emploiera son crédit auprès de tous les Princes catholiques pour qu'ils envoient des députés de leur clergé pour en examiner premièrement et ensuite pour en ratifier les décisions. Ainsi il y a apparence que ce concile sera dans la suite considéré comme œcuménique' (PdeG to WW (7 Jan. 1725), AWE xxx, fo. 226, *Correspondence*, v. 131.

[35] PdeG to WW (9 Apr. 1721), AWE xxix, fo. 253, *Correspondence*, iii. 77: 'Vrais évêques, les prélats de l'Église d'Angleterre ont le droit d'entrer au concile.'

change definitively the policy of the Church by taking in its hand the election of the next pontiff.[36]

This great design was a priority for Piers de Girardin;[37] he could not only hope for it but act 'opportune et inopportune'. This he did abundantly, taking some risk by travelling several times to England[38] in order to present his plan personally to those in a position of power[39] and to secure their assistance in convincing the Regent that it was in his best interest to support the Jansenists.[40] He also went to Brussels and envisaged a trip to the United Provinces.[41] The first step, he urged (in a sarcastic manner revealing himself to be a reader of the *Lettres persanes*), was to make Christian princes and their advisers realize that they were in an opportune situation to call a bluff and force the papacy to accept their views: 'Ces princes chrétiens seront-ils toujours tellement infâtués d'un fantôme de religion que de "donner de l'encens à une idole qui ne cherche qu'à la [l'Évangile] détruire", qui ne respire qu'une monarchie universelle sur les consciences'.[42] He had himself intended to show the way by writing to Clement XI adjuring him to renounce 'his pretended infallibility and his pretensions upon the temporal power of the kings', but was stopped by the pontiff's death.[43]

In addition to his fancy schemes and solemn admonitions, Piers was also progressing at a more modest level with the little group of ecclesiastics he had

---

[36] PdeG to WW (9 Apr. 1721), AWE xxx, fo. 253, *Correspondence*, iii. 76–7: 'Je crois que l'unique moyen, au moins le plus efficace, serait que deux ou trois princes protestassent contre l'élection d'un nouveau pape jusqu'à ce qu'un concile général fût assemblé et que là, ce corps *librement* et *canoniquement* uni, se choisit un chef, à qui l'on imposerait telle condition, qu'on trouverait à propos, le tout sous peine de nullité en cas de contravention et de *perdre même sa primauté*.'

[37] PdeG to WW (29 Mar. 1721), AWE xxix, fo. 245, *Correspondence*, iii. 59.

[38] He was arrested at Calais on his way to England: 'upon suspicion of his and his companion M. Carol being two coiners who were making their escape, which is supposed to be a trick played by some of his countrymen who know of his departure and did not fail to give notice of it to some Irish Priest in Calais, who are made use of to examine all persons who pass there from or to England. Upon the first notice Sir Robert [Schaub] had of it, he sent to the Cardinal Dubois who only laughed at the adventure and immediately sent an order for his being set a liberty' (William Ayerst, chaplain of the British embassy in Paris to WW (22 Oct. 1721), AWE xxix, fo. 340, *Correspondence*, iii. 314; F. Ravaisson, *Archives de la Bastille* (Paris, 1882), xiii. 321).

[39] He met Princess Caroline of Wales, Lord Carteret, Lord Stair (the former ambassador in Paris): PdeG to WW (25 Nov. 1721), AWE xxix, fo. 352, *Correspondence*, iii. 395. He asks Lord Sunderland to pension 'ceux de la Sorbonne qui menaient la bande' (PdeG to WW (28 Feb. 1722), AWE xxix, fo. 224, *Correspondence*, iv. 19[?]).

[40] W. Ayerst, embassy chaplain, to WW (25 Aug. 1720), AWE xxix, fos. 128–9, *Paris-Cantorbéry*, 496–7; PdeG to WW (15 Mar. 1722), AWE xxx, fo. 7, *Correspondence*, iv. 23: 'insinuer au Régent qu'il n'a pas de meilleurs amis que les Jansénistes.'

[41] PdeG to WW (30 Apr. 1722), AWE xxx, fo. 11, *Correspondence*, iv. 43; Préclin, *L'Union des églises*, 21.

[42] PdeG to WW (7 Nov. 1722), *Correspondence*, iv. 166. Cf. Montesquieu, *Lettres persanes*, Lettre XXIX.

[43] PdeG to WW (26 and 29 Mar. 1721), AWE xxix, fo. 243, 245, *Correspondence*, iii. 56–9.

enlisted, mostly members of the Faculty of Paris[44] and the successive chaplains of the British Embassy. The goal was to influence public opinion to a spirit of toleration and then force the leaders to act. He presumed that proving that the theological differences between the two Communions were not on essential matters (Du Pin's *Commonitorium*) and vindicating the validity of Anglican orders (Le Courayer's *Dissertations*) would overcome the main obstacles to a 'bonne intelligence entre les honnêtes gens, surtout les ecclésiastiques de bon aloi de part et d'autre. Ces ecclésiastiques ne cesseront d'en endoctriner le peuple à temps et à contre-temps, ce peuple, cette multitude endoctrinée entrainera à la fin, bon gré, mal gré, les princes chrétiens'.[45]

The defence of Anglican orders, therefore, was only the first step of a concerted effort to 'renew the minds on both sides';[46] they would then go on to 'show the nullity of the council of Trent, the sense of the real presence in a spiritual not a corporal manner'.[47] This was indeed a very liberal form of ecumenism, summarized by the abbé in a catchy formula: 'Je souhaite extrêmement que la religion réformée soit catholique et que la catholique soit réformée.'[48] Cardinal de Rohan, who was presented with such a version of the system, showed that he was not duped: 'Vous voudriez m'engager dans le tolérantisme avec vous. C'est le caractère que vous avez dans ce pays-ci.'[49]

Notwithstanding his personal style, it might be said that in his correspondence Piers often expressed what many Jansenists or Gallicans were not able to articulate or expose freely. He certainly shared with many a type of 'anti-Roman complex' that perceived the papacy as a factor of division and self-destruction in Catholicism,[50] fostered by the contempt shown to religious orders[51] and fuelled

---

[44] He names Drs Petitpied, Quinot, d'Arnaudin, Ph. Boidot: PdeG to WW (6 Sept. 1721), AWE xxix, fo. 321, *Correspondence*, iii. 218.

[45] PdeG to WW (24 Mar. 1723), AWE xxx, fo. 30, *Correspondence*, iv. 221.

[46] PdeG to WW (5 Feb. 1724), AWE xxx, fo. 172, *Correspondence*, iv. 392: 'Quand cet ouvrage prendra racine, je veux dire, quand tous nos savants seront entièrement revenus de leurs préjugés contre la validité des ordinations anglicanes, on s'attachera à éclairer un point de l'histoire ecclésiastique des six premiers siècles de l'Église, touchant un des points principaux de la croyance de l'Église anglicane. Cet eclaircissement ne servira pas peu à renouer les esprits de part et d'autre.'

[47] J. H. Ott to WW (16 May 1726), AWE xi, fo. 248, *Correspondence*, v. 320.

[48] PdeG to WW (28 Dec. 1720), AWE xxix, fo. 198, *Correspondence*, ii. 369.

[49] PdeG to WW (9 May 1722), AWE xxx, fo. 16, *Correspondence*, iv. 58.

[50] In Rome 'dans cette ancienne capitale du monde, le Pape y était adoré, la Vierge invoquée et Jésus-Christ ignoré' PdeG to WW (1 Nov. 1719), AWE xxix, fo. 54; *Paris-Cantorbéry*, 413. See also B. Neveu, 'Port-Royal à l'Age des Lumières: Les *Pensées* et les *Anecdotes* de l'abbé d'Etemare', in *Érudition et Religion aux XVIIe et XVIIIe siècles* (Paris, 1994), 285.

[51] PdeG to WW (5 July 1727), Bodl., MS Rawlinson, A.275, fos. 60–71, *Correspondence*, vi. 123: 'Les moines, en général, sont très méprisés en France, et tout le monde, grands et petits, ne vise qu'à s'en défaire. Cela n'arrivera pas de nos jours, mais cela arrivera tôt ou tard. Les moines eux-mêmes le sentent, leur déchés surtout depuis le milieu du siècle passé leur saute aux yeux. Les jésuites aussi vigilants que clairvoyants ne cessent de l'inculquer au corps des moines, afin de se les concilier et de se fortifier contre le corps du Clergé séculier qui ne travaille qu'à les rendre inutiles. Cette jalousie est si invétérée qu'elle ne finira qu'avec la ruine d'un des deux côtés.'

by the confrontation on the theme of *Unigenitus*.[52] He went much further, though, than most of his confrères[53] as he presented the Roman primacy only as a human institution that could be changed by a conciliar decision and should be if the need arose.[54] Determined to see a balancing of power, he did not hesitate to plan for the creation of another pole, a patriarchate, which might be in France[55] or—why not—in Canterbury.[56]

At that stage one might wonder if the abbé's vision was not just the lucubration of a 'heated character'.[57] Those who knew him well had warned Wake of his tendency 'to think askew',[58] 'd'être animé uniquement d'un esprit de parti et de vision qui donne témérairement dans les chimères'.[59] This must have been the perception of the important people he met during these years, mostly under the pretext of sponsoring his system of union, but also with the goal of obtaining a benefice.

Did Piers actually believe in his 'system', or was it an oblique way to advance his own interests? Probably both. He was very concerned about his need of a benefice and realized that being considered a friend of the archbishop of Canterbury at a time when foreign policy brought together France and Great Britain was an advantage. The way he pursued it is rather remarkable. Having set his eyes

[52] PdeG to WW (29 Nov. 1727), Bodl. MS Rawlinson, A.275, fos. 85–91, *Correspondence*, vi. 215: 'Le peu de cas que l'on fera de ces excommunications lancées de part et d'autre [concerning Bishop Soanen's deposition] causera un mépris dans l'esprit du peuple pour *l'autorité des clefs apostoliques*.'

[53] Following Gerson (*Questio in Vesperio, Opera*, ed. L. Ellies Du Pin (Anvers, 1706), i. 668), Gallican theologians taught that papal primacy could be transferred to another see. Y. Congar, 'Romanité et Catholicité', in *Eglise et papauté: Regards hisoriques* (Paris, 1994), 58.

[54] PdeG to WW (9 Apr. 1721), AWE xxix, fo. 253, *Correspondence*, iii. 77: 'Un concile général peut dépouiller non seulement le pape, mais même le siége de Rome de la primauté et l'attacher à Paris, Cantorbéry, Trèves etc. au cas qu'il ne se gouvernât pas selon les canons.'

[55] He meets Cardinal de Rohan and offers him 'de faire un patriarche en France et je lui fis sentir en même temps que je le désignais lui-même pour cette dignité' (PdeG to WW (13 May 1722), AWE xxx, fo. 16, *Correspondence*, iv. 59). A recurrent theme in Gallican history: *Correspondence*, iv. 58; see also *Paris-Cantorbéry*, 62–3.

[56] He wants the archbishop of Canterbury to have his nuncio in Paris: PdeG to WW (5 Feb. 1724), AWE xxx, fo. 172, *Correspondence*, iv. 392; (23 May 1724), AWE xxx, fo. 190, *Correspondence*, v. 30.

[57] Wednesday, 1 Feb. 1730: 'La conclusion précédente ayant été lue, M. Patrice Piers de Girardin, Hibernois, a lu à haute et intelligible voix, un acte d'opposition qu'il avait dressé . . . M. le Syndic a dit que M. Piers de Girardin s'était fait connaître depuis très longtemps et très souvent dans les assemblées de la Faculté pour un esprit très échauffé [*ferventioris ingenii*]; mais qu'il avait franchi toute borne par sa nouvelle opposition, qui était évidemment déplacée, nulle, pleine de faux et de calomnie' (*Acta et Decreta Sacræ Facultatis Theologiæ Parisiensis super constitutione S. D. N. Papæ Clementis XI quæ incipit Unigenitus Dei Filius, observanda et executioni demandanda* (Paris, 1730), 66–7, 69–70).

[58] J. Horner, embassy chaplain, to WW (29 Aug. 1722), AWE xxx, fo. 47, *Correspondence*, iv. 126: 'Il se peut que la fièvre ait contribué à l'abattement des esprits de M. l'abbé, mais je remarque qu'il pense assez souvent de travers et je n'en suis pas surpris. Les fâcheux contretemps et les fréquentes contradictions qu'on essuie dans le temps qu'on croit être bien fondé et avoir droit de prétendre un prompt avancement, excitent la passion et la mélancolie au point qu'on pense peu juste et qu'on parle de même.'

[59] J. Horner to WW (16 May 1722), AWE xxx, fos. 17–18, *Correspondence*, iv. 62.

on a vacant benefice, first the abbey of Saint-Crépin de Soissons,[60] giving an income of 5,000 *livres*,[61] then the more affluent abbey of Mont-Saint-Michel,[62] that produced 12,000 *livres*,[63] he devised a convoluted way for his name to reach the *feuille des bénéfices*. It was a chain of recommendations that originated with Wake, was endorsed by the princess of Wales, a close friend of the archbishop, who wrote to her kinswoman, Madame, the Regent's mother,[64] who in turn was expected to influence the duke Orléans himself.[65] But this combination did not produce any result. As Girardin knew only too well, his reputation was exceedingly suspect; this was the cross he had to bear.[66]

Piers resolved, therefore, to go to England for the second time[67] and press his patrons more directly: 'On ne peut rien obtenir chez les Grands qu'à force d'assiduité.'[68] All he was able to obtain was a letter of recommendation to Dubois from the princess of Wales.[69]

This led to a return to the diplomatic track through the British ambassador, Sir Robert Schaub. It seemed to be more effective, but, having convinced himself that the prime minister, Cardinal Dubois, 'personally liked him'[70] and actually protected him,[71] Girardin decided not to wait for the diplomat to act. He found a way to meet the prelate[72] and came out 'accablé de politesse'[73] and reasonably optimistic.[74] Still he was well aware that his future was not assured, as his trip to England had not improved his reputation: for now he was labelled not only a

---

[60] PdeG to WW (27 Mar. 1720), AWE xxix, fos. 88–9, also fo. 102 (25 May 1720), *Paris-Cantorbéry*, 486, *Correspondence*, ii. 149.

[61] [Dom Beaunier], *État des archevêchés, évêchés, abbayes et prieurés* (Paris, 1743), 579.

[62] PdeG to WW (11 Jan. 1721), AWE xxix, fo. 206, *Correspondence*, ii. 385.

[63] *État des archevêchés*, 725.

[64] PdeG to WW (20 Sept. 1719), AWE xxix, fo. 47, *Paris-Cantorbéry*, 409. He also suggests a more efficacious way, which would be to go through John Law: ibid.

[65] PdeG to WW (11 May 1720), AWE xxix, fo. 99, *Paris-Cantorbéry*, 483–4.

[66] PdeG to WW (18 Dec. 1721), AWE xxi, fo. 359, *Correspondence*, iv. 1: 'Nous ne nous sauverons jamais que par la croix, voici peut-être la mienne.'

[67] He was there in July 1719: PdeG to WW,' AWE xxix, fos. 41–2, *Paris-Cantorbéry*, 393–4.

[68] PdeG to WW (4 Apr. 1722 (NS)), AWE xxx, fo. 8, *Correspondence*, iv. 25.

[69] Letter prepared by Lord Carteret, secretary of state, to Cardinal Dubois: PdeG to WW (19 Jan. 1722), AWE xxix, fo. 205, *Correspondence*, iv. 10.

[70] Dubois 'l'aime personnellement et il dit qu'il l'a sauvé de l'exil dans le conseil de conscience' (J. Horner to WW (2 Jan. 1722), AWE xxix, fo. 1, *Correspondence*, iv. 7)

[71] J. Horner to WW (1 Nov. 1721), AWE xxix, fo. 345, *Correspondence*, iii. 327: 'M. le Cardinal Dubois a dit à M. Le Blanc: Je connais l'abbé de G. C'est un honnête homme, je répondrai même de lui.'

[72] He had already come to the attention of Dubois and had tried to meet in Feb. 1719: W. Beauvoir, embassy chaplain, to WW (8 Feb. 1719), AWE xxv, fo, 110, *Paris-Cantorbéry*, 311–12. He was formally introduced to him by Sir Robert Sutton, then ambassador, in Dec. 1720: PdeG to WW (21 Dec. 1720), AWE xxix, fo. 196, *Paris-Cantorbéry*, 509.

[73] PdeG to WW (11 July 1722), AWE xxx, fo. 27, *Correspondence*, iv. 87: 'Enfin la glace est rompue.' He alludes to his protection from the princess of Wales and Lord Carteret.

[74] But he did that without having the British envoy on his side, which infuriated the diplomat: J. Horner to WW (25 July 1722), AWE xxx, fo. 29, *Correspondence*, iv. 93.

Jansenist but also a Protestant[75] and a spy.[76] He was also perceived as 'an unprincipled man, a weather-flag'.[77] Nevertheless, Girardin thought that he could be assured of Dubois's protection, since the latter had taken his defence at the *Conseil de conscience* on the occasion of an intervention in the Faculty of Theology that had been denounced.[78] He accordingly praised him at a subsequent meeting at the Sorbonne[79] and made sure that the compliment would be communicated to the prime minister,[80] the more important since Dubois was then personally in charge of the *feuille des bénéfices*.[81] But Girardin's address did not please the cardinal, who, on the contrary, expressed his 'invincible antipathy'.[82]

Girardin then decided to return to the original scheme, with the modification that, through Wake and the princess of Wales, Madame would this time be asked to intervene with Cardinal de Noailles, archbishop of Paris.[83] Once again Piers decided to go his own way and attempted to meet Dubois personally.[84] To cover every possible track, he even found a way to be presented to the Spanish infanta, then betrothed to Louis XV, as the confessor of her court jester![85]

---

[75] PdeG to WW (3 Feb. 1720), AWE xxix, fo. 78, *Paris-Cantorbéry*, 438–9: 'La plupart de mes compatriotes me considèrent déjà comme un hérétique et même je suis connu sous le nom de *Protestant Doctor*.'

[76] The Jacobites claimed that he was a spy: PdeG to WW (16 Oct. 1723), AWE xxx, fo. 139, *Correspondence*, iii. 317.

[77] 'J. Horner to WW (16 May 1722), AWE xxx, fos. 17–18, *Correspondence*, iv. 62: 'La longue absence de l'abbé a trop fortifié les soupçons et les faux bruits que l'on a fait courir ici sur son changement de religion à Londres. . . . Notre abbé est ici marqué en encre rouge. Pour le noircir encore davantage, on nous soutient ici (et ce sont des personnes du premier rang) qu'il n'est pas un homme à principes, qu'il a toujours eu des hauts et des bas dans sa conduite et qu'il a changé comme a weatherflag. D'autres l'accusent d'avoir eu un zèle brûlant; c'est ce que m'ont dit les bénédictins. Et enfin, il y en a qui le taxent d'être animé uniquement d'un esprit de parti et de vision qui donne témérairement dans les chimères.'

[78] PdeG to WW (12 Aug. 1722), AWE xxx, fo. 41, *Correspondence*, iv. 114: 'Les Molinistes empoisonnèrent tout ce que j'ai dit au prima mensis. L'affaire fut porté au Conseil de conscience, le mercredi dernier 5ᵉ courant. Mais M. le cardinal Dubois soutint lui seul mon parti et ne balança pas de dire que j'avais raison d'opiner de la sorte.' (Also (22 Aug. 1722), AWE xxx, fo. 46.) PdeG to WW (24 Nov. 1722), AWE xxx, fo. 72, *Correspondence*, iv. 177: 'Son Eminence a empêché à elle seule que cet abbé [PdeG] ne soit exilé hors du royaume, il y a environ six semaines deux mois.'

[79] PdeG to WW (2 Sept. 1722), AWE xxx, fo. 49, *Correspondence*, iv. 131.

[80] J. Horner to WW (12 Sept. 1722), AWE xxx, fo. 53, *Correspondence*, iv. 137.

[81] J. Horner to WW (9 Sept. 1722), AWE xxx, fo. 52, *Correspondence*, iv. 136.

[82] J. Horner to WW (13 Oct. 1722), AWE xxx, fo. 61, *Correspondence*, iv. 154: 'Tous les bonnets rouges lui [PdeG] sont contraires, et ils prétendent que ce n'est pas à cause de ses principes mais parce qu'il n'en a point. Schaubb has attempted to 'faire valoir sa harangue, mais il n'a pas réussi: il paraît qu'on ait une antipathie invincible contre le pauvre abbé'.

[83] J. Horner to WW (13 Oct. 1722), AWE xxx, fo. 62, *Correspondence*, iv. 154. He adds later that Madame has given her word: J. Horner to WW (31 Oct. 1722), AWE xxx, fo. 67, *Correspondence*, iv. 165.

[84] PdeG 'ne tardera pas à faire une nouvelle tentative auprès du cardinal Dubois' (J. Horner to WW (30 Dec, 1722), AWE xxx, fo. 78, *Correspondence*, iv. 189).

[85] J. Horner to WW (9 Jan. 1723), AWE xxx, fo. 80, *Correspondence*, iv. 195: 'Il se fait présenter à l'infante reine par le Fol de la Reine, l'abbé se dit son confesseur.'

One of these stratagems must have been successful as, by the end of March 1732, Piers's name appeared on the proposed *feuille des bénéfices*, though Dubois still appeared to hesitate.[86] He seemed well inclined, but had to consider the bad name of the doctor.[87] Unexpectedly, Dubois died (10 August 1723), frustrating Piers's efforts.[88] All was not lost though, since the *feuille* had been given to a friend of a friend, M. du Parc, who confirmed that the doctor was still on the list, 'et même très avantageusement'.[89] Alas, when in October the nomination was published, Piers's name had been dropped. No Jansenist had been preferred.[90]

This was not enough to make Piers lose heart. He soon initiated a new strategy directed to the rising man, Bishop Fleury,[91] but, with the sudden death of the duke of Orléans,[92] M. du Parc lost the *feuille*. It was given to M. Melain, secretary of the duc de Bourbon, who fortunately happened to be another remote acquaintance.[93] Piers therefore increased pressure on his English connections,[94] making every effort to strengthen them. Always attentive to unusual events, he sent Wake a report of a miracle at the Faubourg Saint-Antoine asking him to communicate it to the princess of Wales, an oblique way to renew their acquaintance. Wake obliged,[95] but nothing happened. Feverish, anxious, and frustrated, Piers came close to losing heart and suspected the waning zeal of the British ambassador and his chaplain, his best supporters:[96] 'Ils promettent tout mais ne tiennent rien'.[97] To make things worse, Madame was now indisposed and could

---

[86] J. Horner to WW (31 Mar. 1723), AWE xxx, fo. 95, *Correspondence*, iv. 224.

[87] J. Horner to WW (26 May 1723), AWE xxx, fo. 108, *Correspondence*, iv. 245: 'Le cardinal paraît être assez bien disposé envers lui à présent, mais il ne peut s'empêcher de nous dire qu'il y a de grandes difficultés dans le chemin du pauvre abbé. On continue toujours à le décrier comme un homme sans foi, sans loi et sans principes. Et le cardinal de Rohan même, quoiqu'il lui en ait dit en dernier lieu, n'a pas cessé de le desservir auprès du premier ministre.'

[88] PdeG to WW (14 Aug. 1723), AWE xxx, fo. 129, *Correspondence*, iv. 291–2: 'On ne croit pas que l'on nomme demain aux bénéfices comme M. le cardinal se l'était proposé. . . . Me voilà encore frustré dans mes attentes. Il faut recommencer une nouvelle batterie pour me faire connaître du ministre présent . . . Un petit renouvellement de recommandation de la part de S.A.R. la Princesse de Galles mettrait les affaires en bon train.'

[89] J. Horner to WW (15 Sept. 1723), AWE xxx, fo. 134, *Correspondence*, iv. 302.

[90] J. Horner to WW (20 Oct. 1723), AWE xxx, fo. 140, *Correspondence*, iv. 319. But according to PdeG: 'on en a cependant donné à quelques Appelants' (PdeG to WW (30 Oct. 1723), AWE xxx, fo. 141, *Correspondence*, iv. 321).

[91] PdeG to WW (27 Nov. 1723), AWE xxx, fo. 149, *Correspondence*, iv. 338: 'Il a écrit une lettre très touchante et très respectueuse à M. de Fréjus.'

[92] PdeG to WW (4 Dec. 1723), AWE xxx, fo. 155, *Correspondence*, iv. 344.

[93] J. Horner to WW (10 Dec. 1723), AWE xxx, fo. 157, *Correspondence*, iv. 349.

[94] He asks Wake to introduce him to H. Walpole, the new envoy: PdeG to WW (30 May 1725), AWE xxx, fo. 233, *Correspondence*, v. 168.

[95] PdeG to WW (16 June 1725), AWE xxx, fos. 235–6, *Correspondence*, v. 178; PdeG to WW (22 Aug. 1725), AWE xxx, fo. 242, *Correspondence*, v. 216–17. Cf. B. R. Kreiser, *Miracles, Convulsions and Ecclesiastical Politics in Early Eighteenth Century Paris* (Princeton, 1978), 74.

[96] PdeG had offered 300 *livres* to Horner 's'il voulait contribuer à son avancement' (J. Horner to WW (17 Feb. 1723), AWE xxx, fo. 88, *Correspondence*, iv. 209).

[97] PdeG to WW (24 Nov. 1722), AWE xxx, fo. 72, *Correspondence*, iv. 177.

not be visited.[98] Nevertheless, Piers's vitality bounced back; he kept 'hoping against hope'[99] and continued to scheme. As soon as he heard of a proposal to marry Louis XV to an English princess, he asked Wake to suggest his name as her chaplain, since she would undoubtedly have to change her religion.[100] Faithful to his maxim, 'Il faut tout essayer. Qui quitte la partie, la perd,'[101] he embarked on another trip to England. But after five weeks, despite several meetings with the princess of Wales, he returned empty-handed.[102]

Despite his high hopes,[103] the accession to the throne of Queen Caroline's husband as George II in 1727 did not improve Piers's chances of obtaining the benefice he craved. By that time English protection was not as influential in France, where, under Cardinal Fleury's rule, opposition to the *Anticonstitutionnaires* had become harsher.[104] It did accomplish something though, as it shielded Girardin from being exiled or even *embastillé*[105] for his freedom of speech,[106] but he was finally expelled from the Faculty of Theology.[107]

Eventually, Piers flew again to England in 1732, 'being a busy Jansenist', to avoid the anger of Fleury, but at the desire of Queen Caroline he had permission to return unmolested. 'For which I have great obligation to the Cardinal,' said the queen, 'but it was on condition that, if he should play the fool again, I should never mediate more for him, for he would certainly send him to the Bastille.'[108]

---

[98] J. Horner to WW (14 Nov. 1722), AWE xxx, fo. 70, *Correspondence*, iv. 173: 'On ne peut donc lui demander des nouvelles au sujet de l'abbé G——n.'

[99] PdeG to WW (22 Aug. 1725), AWE xxx, fo. 242, *Correspondence*, v. 216: 'Espérer contre l'Espérance a toujour été le pivot de l'Église persécuté. Elle a toujours réussi. Elle réussira toujours et les portes de l'Enfer ne prévaudront jamais contre elle.'

[100] PdeG to WW (10 Mar. 1725), AWE xxx, fo. 180, *Correspondence*, v. 142–3.

[101] PdeG to WW (10 May 1726), AWE xxx, fo. 262, *Correspondence*, v. 311.

[102] PdeG to WW (12 May 1726), AWE xxx, fo. 263, *Correspondence*, v. 316.

[103] PdeG to WW (19 Feb. 1727), *Correspondence*, v. 72: 'Ceux qui sont au fait des intrigues de la Cour me disent qu'un recommandation réitérée de S. A. R. passera par dessus tout ce qu'on pourrait objecter au sujet de l'Appel, etc.' PdeG to WW (5 July 1727), *Correspondence*, vi. 122: 'Je vous suis redevable, Monseigneur, des nouvelles tentatives que vous avez bien voulu faire auprès de Sa Majesté la Reine d'Angleterre pour l'engager à faire sentir à la Cour de France que c'est *tout de bon* qu'elle s'intéresse pour moi.'

[104] In June 1726 Piers had been received by Fleury, 'qui l'a examiné de près et de loin' (PdeG to WW (8 June 1726), AWE xxx, fo. 265, *Correspondence*, v. 330).

[105] R. Herault to Cardinal Fleury (20 Feb. 1728), *Correspondence*, vi. 364–5: 'On a fait une visite des papiers de P. de G. On a trouvé une lettre du P. Le C[ourayer]. Il n'a pas cru devoir faire arrêter P. de G.' (He was under the protection of the archbishop of Canterbury and of the queen of England.)

[106] During a meeting of the Faculty of Theology of Paris (Dec. 1727): 'On a eu la charité d'en écrire au Cardinal Ministre. L'abbé lui a écrit aussi de son côté pour se disculper' (Bodl., MS Rawlinson, A.275, fos. 92–5, *Correspondence*, vi. 247.

[107] 1 Feb. 1730, *Acta et Decreta Sacræ Facultatis Theologiæ Parisiensis super consititutione S. D. N. Papæ Clementis XI quæ incipit Unigenitus Dei Filius, observanda et executioni demandanda* (Paris, 1730), 66–7, 69–70.

[108] PRO, Egmont MSS, Diary of Queen Caroline, i. 396, cited in Clark, *Strangers and Sojourners*, 260.

The quest for a benefice was certainly one of Piers's main concerns in life, but it was not his chief one.[109] He clearly realized that, were he to move to the other side of the Channel, his predicament would become easier, but he always rejected the suggestion.[110] He expressed his true mind in 1724, when, hearing that, upon Beauvoir's death, Wake might offer him the former chaplain's English benefice, he stated very clearly that he did not want to give up his system in order to be more comfortable.[111] If he wanted to stay in France, it was because, despite his difficulties, he believed not only in his great design, but also in the possibility to keep working at it.[112] In his eyes, it was not just a human conception but clearly the design of God, who often manifested his will and showed his protection: 'Quand je fais réflexion sur le progrès de cette entreprise, surtout depuis trois ans, sur le changement, sur la manière enfin dont le Seigneur s'est pris pour desiller les yeux de part et d'autre, je ne saurais m'empêcher de crier tout haut avec le prophète, *hæc mutatio dexteræ Excelsi* (Ps. 86: 11).'[113]

Piers's intuition was definitely eschatological;[114] in his eyes, the 'obscuring of truth',[115] blindness of the majority, similar to that of the Pharisees in Christ's time,[116] could not but eventually be reversed: 'Les hommes ont beau faire, Dieu est au dessus de tout. En vain voudra-t-on faire subsister l'Arche avec Dagon, Dagon tombera, l'Arche subsistera.'[117]

Here, of course, Girardin appears more than a mere opportunist scheming for

---

[109] When he heard that in order to receive a benefice he had to recant his appeal: 'à cette occasion il me chargea de dire au Chevalier Schaub que pour tous les bénéfices de la France il ne changerait jamais ses sentiments, dans la pensée que S. A. R. admirera sa fermeté et ne s'opposera point à son avancement' (J. Horner to WW (30 Sept. 1722), AWE xxx fo. 59, *Correspondence*, iv. 146).

[110] William Beauvoir to WW (15 May 1720), AWE xxix, fo. 96, *Paris-Cantorbéry*, 486–7.

[111] PdeG to WW (8 Mar. 1724), AWE xxx, fo. 177, *Correspondence*, iv. 406: 'P. de G. ne veut pas abandonner ce système pour se mettre à son aise.' He judged severely Le Courayer when the later decided to move to England: PdeG 'regrette cette décision. Cela signifie malheureusement que tout ce que celui-ci écrira par la suite ne sera plus considéré que comme hérétique' (PdeG to WW (11 Jan. 1728), *Correspondence*, vi. 278).

[112] This is the motivation he gave the princess of Wales, who asked him why he wanted to return to France: 'C'est là qu'il fallait et où il y avait à travailler' (PdeG to WW (12 May 1726), AWE xxx, fo. 263, *Correspondence*, v. 316).

[113] PdeG to WW (3 Feb. 1720), AWE xxix, fo. 78, *Paris-Cantorbéry*, 439. PdeG to WW (19 Feb. 1727), *Correspondence*, vi. 72: 'Au nom de Dieu, Monsigneur, connaissons-nous toujours de plus en plus de part et d'autre. Ne nous fatiguons jamais de notre commerce qui continue par un trait singulier de la Providence depuis une dizaine d'années. Qui est-ce qui pouvait dire à ce temps-lá que les choses viendraient au point où nous les voyons à présent?'

[114] PdeG to WW (23 June 1723), AWE xxx, fo. 117, *Correspondence*, iv. 266: 'Dieu qui aime souvent confondre les desseins des hommes . . . les renversera sans ressource et rehaussera l'éclat de son Église et de sa vérité.'

[115] PdeG to WW (23 Sept. 1724), AWE xxx, fo. 207, *Correspondence*, v. 81.

[116] PdeG to WW (6 Apr. 1720), AWE xxix, fos. 90–1, *Paris-Cantorbéry*, 472: 'Cet état d'aveuglement où nous sommes aujourd'hui.'

[117] 1 Sam. 5: 2–6. PdeG to WW (11 May 1720), AWE xxix, fo. 100, *Paris-Cantorbéry*, 485.

his own interests and definitively close to the movement that transformed its many frustrations with *Unigenitus* into a form of millerianism.[118] His interest in miraculous events has already been mentioned; it is not surprising that his name is reported at least once as a witness of the Convulsionaries at Saint-Médard.[119] Despite all his eccentricities, he was not alone in his desire to see an evolution of Catholicism and to accommodate it to his time.[120] É. Préclin, who first charted his career, noticed the existence within the French Church of 'a group of Free-Thinker Catholics', 'une société de pensées aux tendances philosophiques et libérales, une sorte de club de l'Entresol théologique'.[121] Girardin was certainly an active member of this society, more an inspirer than a theoretician.[122] Ph. Boidot, L. de Longuerue, P. F. Le Courayer were his associates.[123]

In the eyes of his superiors and also of many of his colleagues, Piers de Girardin was certainly an unconventional Irish clergyman, temperamental, even unstable, suspect for his association with Protestant England, suspicious in his irenicism, an opportunist, a plotter, and a devious one. Even his closest friends grew to distrust him[124] and consider him a traitor.[125] His attitude was certainly paradoxical: on the one hand, he stated his opinions and staunchly stood by them; on the other, he showed with authorities a flexibility that amounted to cowardice.[126] He did have a vivid imagination and repeatedly showed a

---

[118] C. Garret, *Respectable Folly: Millenarians and the French Revolution in France and England* (Baltimore, 1975), 21. C. L. Maire, *Les Convulsionnaires de Saint-Médard: Miracles, convulsions et prophéties à Paris au XVIIIe siècle* (Paris, 1985), 55–8.

[119] On 7 Aug. 1731, Girardin signed as a witness of a 'counter-miracle' on the grave of deacon Paris; Gabrielle Gautier, widow Lorme, found herself paralysed for pretending to be lame and incapacitated. Cf. *Journal de Barbier*, ii. 173–4; J. R. Armogathe 'A propos des miracles de Saint-Médard', *Revue de l'histoire des religions*, 180 (1971), 135–60.

[120] His correspondence with Wake manifests a certain scientific interest and a rationalistic attitude. Thus the plague that afflicted southern France, was not a punishment from God, but an 'ordinary disease' (PdeG to WW (27 Sept. 1721), AWE xxix, fo. 327, *Correspondence*, iii. 283–4).

[121] Préclin, *L'Union des églises*, 99.

[122] Though in a letter written to Wake, he alludes very discreetly to a work in progress: PdeG to WW (19 Feb. 1727), Bodl., MS Rawlinson A.275, fos. 40–3, *Correspondence*, vi. 72.

[123] Préclin, *L'Union des églises*, 98–9; *Les Jansénistes du XVIIIe siècle*, 167–73.

[124] M de Montenoi [pseudonym of l'abbé de la Vigne] to M. Langley [le P. le Courayer] (5 Feb. 1728), *Correspondence*, vi. 338: 'Je ne puis m'empêcher de vous dire à cette occasion, que M. de Bétizy [Girardin] me paraît homme trop peu attentif et trop babillard pour ne pas vous tenir avec lui simplement dans des généralités.'

[125] PdeG to R. Hérault? (19 Aug. 1728), MS Arsenal 11004, fo. 374, *Correspondence*, vi. 412: 'J'ai été trois fois faire ma cour, sans pouvoir vous aborder. Il court un certain bruit parmi les Jansénistes, que je vais nuitamment, comme un autre Nicodème, vous rendre compte, Monsieur, de tout ce qui se passe parmi eux . . . que c'est moi qui vous ai indiqué certaines personnes que vous avez mises à la Bastille.' Cf. Préclin, *L'Union des églises*, 149.

[126] PdeG to WW (10 Mar. 1722), AWE xxx, fo. 6, *Correspondence*, iv. 21: 'Si nous aimons la vérité, nous n'aimons pas moins la tranquilité publique. On m'attaque d'une manière sensible du côté de ma réputation, qui m'est aussi chère que la vie et que d'ailleurs je me trouve fort à l'étroit par rapport au nécessaire.'

lack of political *savoir faire*,[127] but on other occasions appeared shrewd and consistent.[128]

Yet his engagement into the project of union shows a true consistency and offers a principle of explanation that goes further than personal idiosyncracy. The contestation of *Unigenitus* gave him the opportunity of his life, not only to vent his frustration but to reconstruct the world, to envision a new type of Christianity, and also to aspire for a new society, free from despotism,[129] more peaceful, more fraternal. In all, it gave him a *raison d'être*, an identity. His name does not appear after the year 1732, unless he was the same person as the Patrick Pierre de Fitzgerald who, in 1734, was the chaplain of Notre-Dame des Rochers en la chapelle du Château de Bignan.[130] In which case, he finally received some earthly reward for all his toils.

[127] Thus his attitude of provocation at the Faculty of Theology, after it has been controlled by the Constitutionnaires, in proposing an 'allegorical case of conscience', when he knows very well that he runs the risk to be punished like the other opponents: *Nouvelles ecclésiastiques, Supplément pour 1730*, 25.

[128] One of the first *appellants* in 1717, he decided not to renew his appeal in 1721, because he planned to go to England during the Cambray Congress: PdeG to WW (12 mars 1721), AWE xxix, fo. 237, *Correspondence*, iii. 42.

[129] PdeG to WW (3 Oct. 1722), AWE xxx, fo. 60, *Correspondence*, iv. 148.

[130] Swords (ed.), *The Irish-French Connection*, 164.

4

'Il fallut même réveiller les Suisses': Aspects of Private Religious Practice in a Public Setting in Eighteenth-Century Versailles

GILES BARBER

The duc de Luynes, that informative memorialist on mid-eighteenth-century Versailles, records that Marie Leszczynska, 'Louis XV's sad queen' as Professor McManners once put it to the present writer, was an essentially, if not indeed excessively, religious person. She was naturally so; she had been brought up that way, and her marital experience left her few other options. She attended Mass even more assiduously than the royal routine required, being there at eight every morning—which, when the king was still abed, raised questions of protocol, since the drummers and guard who should accompany her could not perform their duties in the required manner. Sometimes she was even earlier, so that on one occasion, as Luynes reports, 'il fallut même réveiller les Suisses pour lui ouvrir la chapelle'.[1] Luynes's story brings into focus the strange juxtaposition of state panoply, the royal guard, and the need of one of the central figures of such official ceremony for the exercise of personal and private devotion. The aim of this article is to probe the relationship between personal piety and courtly display and to study, through the medium of surviving prayer books and their bindings, the expression and provision for these at Versailles during the early years of the Enlightenment, something touching, therefore, on a complex world, or series of worlds, and involving the interplay of religious history, personality groups, fashion, and publishing monopolies.

Writing in the memorial volume for Robert Shackleton, a close colleague and another great Enlightenment specialist, Professor McManners studied the

Apart from the persons who have kindly helped with this article mentioned in the notes, I would also like to thank the following for their assistance: Frère Michel Albaric, Professor W. H. Barber, M. Antoine Coron, Dr Mirjam Foot, M. André Jammes, Ms P. Marks, Professor Bruno Neveu, Mme Anne Sauvy-Wilkinson, and the staffs of the Special Collections Department and of Duke Humfrey's Library, the Bodleian Library.

[1] Charles-Phillipe d'Albert, duc de Luynes, *Mémoires du duc de Luynes sur la cour de Louis XV*, ed. L. E. Dussieux and E. Soulié (Paris, 1860–5) (hereafter Luynes), i. 412, ii. 97.

religious observances of Versailles under Louis XV.[2] In this rich and original article he dealt with what he termed this 'superficial theme', describing the 200 ecclesiastics on duty; the daily routine of devotions, formal and informal, of Masses and frequent prayers, inherited from Louis XIV; the precedence quarrels of bishops and *aumôniers*; the king as a parishioner; the sermons and, above all with Louis XV, the confessions of a king who believed in forgiveness and feared death. The scene is thus brilliantly set and, above all for that particular world, attention is properly focused on the central figure of the king. Politically this is, of course, true, but Versailles was a huge hive filled with many swarms, all, it is true clustered around the king, but separate universes each having their own galaxies, orbits, and life, and thus their own reflected problems of status, position, and precedence where favour and fashion played a major role.

By the time the young Polish princess was introduced in 1725 to a supercilious and snobbish French court which had just seen an Infanta set aside as a potential queen, the rituals and routine instituted under the old king as part of the new glittering world of Versailles were set and virtually immutable. The peripatetic lives of earlier kings had been abandoned, and a new political capital had been established in which new forms of worship evolved and aristocratic privileges were on a par with ecclesiastic requirements.

Of course the forms of worship practised in Western Europe had themselves already evolved slowly over the centuries, and the printed texts used in conjunction with them reflected both these changes and the ability of various sections of the congregation to use such works. The priestly celebration of divine service, carried out in a part of the church often physically separated from that for the laity, had encouraged the production of missals, breviaries, and psalters both for general use and for particular ceremonies from the later Middle Ages onwards. Ever since Carolingian times, when the preparation of collections such as the *Officia per ferias* had been placed under Alcuin's patronage, important or wealthy lay members of the faithful had also relied on their personal prayer books. The Book of Hours, bringing together prayers and extracts from the divine service, came into being, as Paul Saenger has shown, as a result of the advent of silent reading (itself a result of the systematic introduction of word separation in Europe in the early eleventh century).[3] Phonic literacy, as Saenger argues, allowed those who could recognize words to recite as it were by rote: comprehension literacy was another thing and could depend further on whether the reader

---

[2] J. McManners, 'The Religious Observances of Versailles under Louis XV', in G. Barber and C. P. Courtney (eds.), *Enlightenment Essays in Memory of Robert Shackleton* (Oxford, 1988), 175–88.

[3] P. Saenger, 'Books of Hours and the Reading Habits of the Later Middle Ages', in R. Chartier (ed.), *The Culture of Print* (Cambridge, 1989), 141–73.

knew Latin as well as French. From such abilities sprang the slow shift from the compulsory oral prayer of the Middle Ages to the silent, and thus more private, mode of prayer emerging in the fifteenth century. Thus, while the priest continued in Latin, some at least of the laity could occupy themselves with their own prayers based in the vernacular. Such moves are clearly of great significance for the history of private piety and for the evolution of Protestantism, but they are also behind that of a bilingual structure to the books for use in church. The custom of bringing Books of Hours and tracts on the Mass to church became common by the early fifteenth century and thus, as Saenger says, there was a great variety of separately programmed religious experiences cloaked beneath a single uniform Roman Mass.

To this had to be added the impact of printing and a growth in literacy, both presenting the traditional Catholic Church with problems which took time to solve. Following the Council of Trent, Pius V was therefore endeavouring not only to standardize the missal and the breviary, but also to impose on Catholic Europe a single uniform Latin text, together with a single set of prayers for the Mass. Ceremonies were not to be translated but could be explained orally, something basic to the oral preaching of the baroque Church. The evolution in French court circles in the seventeenth and early eighteenth centuries of bilingual church books was to underline the failure of this programme and the need felt by some at least of the faithful for a closer comprehension of, and participation in, the divine service. The Book of Hours had reflected medieval country life, and went into decline, as Albert Labarre has shown, from 1550, slowly to be replaced, from the mid-eighteenth century, by the modern *Paroissien*.[4] The most popular transitional manual, centred on Holy Week but containing the Mass, was to be a newly evolving work, the *Office de la Semaine sainte*.

Before proceeding further, a word should be said on the scale and nature of the production of such books. During the thirteenth century, in the then manuscript world, markets arose for both richly illuminated breviaries and Books of Hours for the powerful and wealthy, and simpler ones for other mortals. Many were for highly local use and related to the practices of a particular diocese, even if they were produced in the celebrated Parisian scriptoria of the fourteenth and fifteenth centuries. In the early years of printing, breviaries and missals were often all an itinerant printer might produce in a town before moving on, but here again the Parisian stationers, who had been providing manuscript prayer books and the like, soon turned to the new technology, and from around 1480 they began to dominate this field too. The first liturgical work printed at Paris was indeed a breviary for the diocese of Bourges. In the sixteenth century the new printing

---

[4] A. Labarre, *Histoire de l'édition française*, i (Paris, 1982), 212–14.

technology, combined with the ability to add illustrations in either woodcut or, later, engraved form, allowed the easy production of an item intended to serve both the literate layman able to understand the text and his less-skilled brother or sister for whom the illustrations would provide the necessary information and inspiration. A huge market opened up, and, in a field where numerous copies have doubtless disappeared, over 1,500 books of hours have been recorded, the vast majority being Paris printed. The scale of this market, supplied by a number of specialized dealers such as Antoine Vérard, Simon Vostre, and Thielman Kerver, is exemplified by the 1545 inventory of the stock of Guillaume Godard, who possessed 263,000 books, mostly liturgical, of which no less than 150,000 were Books of Hours.[5] Large-scale commercial considerations, therefore, begin to intrude themselves as well as both theological and literacy ones.

The turmoils of the sixteenth century altered this situation, creating a Protestant market, with its well-know *psautier*, which had Marot's translation on one side (including the numerous mid-seventeenth-century editions from Charenton), and diverting the Catholic production either to a more liturgical form closer to the missal or to an anthology of prayers. In 1568 the Council of Trent revised the breviary and prescribed the use of the reformed Roman text by all dioceses and religious orders not having had their own for at least 200 years. The monastic breviary and missal were again revised in 1612 and 1614, while the Roman ones were successively altered by Clement VIII and Urban VIII (1602, 1604 and 1631, 1634). Such innovations naturally led to enormous publishing operations. For the French world these were once again centred on Paris, where it is said that in the mid-seventeenth century fifteen presses and some fifty journeymen were constantly at work for the main publisher, the *Compagnie des usages*. This centralization had other aspects too. The introduction of the forty-hour vigil by Clement VIII in 1592 had introduced a highly sentimental type of popular piety, making much of the Virgin Mary. The early years of the century, and particularly the reign of Louis XIII, had thus seen a notable rise in the devotion to the Virgin and indeed in hagiography generally. The state propaganda machine could thus easily make good use of this powerful weapon, and attention has been drawn to the 1615 *Heures du roi*, intended in fact for a wide market, where the Virgin looks remarkably like Marie de Médicis and where the king and queen are represented and feature in important religious imagery.[6]

After the Fronde and under Louis XIV, a more united country with a large and stable court life was to be faced by other problems. Unlike Holland, where the demand for vernacular services was strong, in France the fact that the *bourgeoisie*

[5] Ibid.
[6] H.-J. Martin, *Livre pouvoirs et société à Paris au XVII*[e] *siècle* (Paris, 1982), 104–7, 163.

de robe had a reasonable command of Latin restrained this to some extent. Nevertheless, Protestant services in the vernacular led to a demand for versions of the Mass in French, a move seen by some as a step to the public saying of the Mass in that language and thus a desecration of a holy mystery. The members of Port-Royal initially adhered to the policy of explanations and devout prayers but progressively moved towards more historical discussions and even translations. A radical shift in approach was afoot and no less than four translations of the Ordinary of the Mass appeared between 1607 and 1651—that in the latter year, by Harlay, being much approved. The quarrel was to rumble on nevertheless. In 1660 the publication of a four-volume bilingual (Latin–French) missal by the Hebraist Joseph de Voisin (1610–85), *aumônier* to the prince de Conti, caused an immediate furore, being condemned by Pope Alexander VII and, recalcitrantly, by the Assembly of the French clergy, without, however, receiving any supporting official state condemnation in France. Its translator could even produce a full defence of it the following year and further, in 1662, his own translation of the *Office de la Semaine sainte*, to which the essentials of his translation of the Canon were prefixed.[7] By 1692 it is said that priests would translate at least the Gospel into French before explaining it.

The vernacular also impinged on another aspect of state policy, in that its use was directly relevant to Louis XIV's attitude to the conversion of French Protestants and the programme of support for the *nouveaux Catholiques*, whereby huge quantities of appropriate religious books were distributed to converts. This *voie de la douceur* avoided the Psalms but used pious works in French, and, although the papal nuncio specifically objected to the provision of any work containing the Canon of the Mass in French, Archbishop François de Harlay supported this. This book-centred campaign was on a vast scale, some million volumes being reputedly distributed in the years around 1685, many being published by precisely those Paris publishers also engaged in the *Office de la Semaine sainte*. Moreover some of the shorter texts, such as *L'Explication des parties de l'office et des cérémonies de la Messe*, were indeed initially produced in connection with it. The Revocation of the Edict of Nantes left the traditionalists with three options: ban all translations; tolerate an increasing flood of them; or attempt to compromise by allowing translations of certain special offices but continuing to ensure that the text of all daily Masses continued to be in Latin. For the faithful of the early eighteenth century, therefore, much continued as before, and the reading of devout works went on during services—something certain courtiers could profit from by substituting libertine texts. For others, however, bilingual texts were nevertheless to become increasingly available.

---

[7] H. Bremond, *Histoire littéraire du sentiment religieux en France*, ix (Paris, 1932), 178–92.

On an official level the 1685 revision of the Paris missal by Harlay was followed by another, in 1706, by Cardinal de Noailles, both of which moved closer to Roman practice in a number of details. However, the successor to Noailles, appointed by Fleury, was Charles Gaspard Guillaume de Vintimille (1655–1746), an ecclesiastic of Jansenist leaning, who, in turn, appointed Urbain Robinet as his vicar-general and charged him with a further revision. Robinet had already, in 1728, produced the *Breviarum ecclesiae Rotomagensis* for his then archbishop, Louis de La Vergne, a work incidentally printed by the local printers, the Jore family, who, some five years later, were to print Voltaire's *Lettres philosophiques.* This breviary was neither pro-Jansenist nor anti-Marian, but it did remove numerous saints and their lives while substituting many good hymns. The 1738 *Breviarium Parisiense* (4 volumes, 12°) pursued this line, cutting out feasts and putting its emphasis on Sundays, on Lent, and on the Psalms. There was an immediate outcry from the Jesuit side and the work was condemned. It had, however, been a prestige operation, being printed on special paper in two-column presentation with the rubrics in red, and with four engraved title-pages and vignettes by Boucher and Le Bas. It had cost the book trade a considerable sum and, while the original plates were destroyed, a second issue was prepared by introducing no less than fifty cancels to the original sheets. A new missal was published in 1738, equally under the authority of Charles de Vintimille, and, together with the 1742 French translation of the breviary, was to confirm this desire to return to the 'ancienne simplicité', which had already been expressed by the abbey of Cluny, by certain other dioceses such as Meaux, and in works such as J. Grancolas's *Commentaire historique sur le bréviaire romain* (1727), all of which urged a return to the worship of the central figure of Christ himself.[8]

Most of these changes, important in themselves, were, of course, essentially priestly ones, concerning the texts of the breviary and the liturgical books for divine service, the rituals for the administration of the sacraments, the missals for use in the Mass, and the ordinaries and other works describing various ceremonies. With the possible exception of the missal, these works were not for lay people. An increasingly literate market in this field was catered for by the successors of the older Book of Hours. The row over the translation published by Voisin showed, however, that there was a strong demand for such texts in French and a market for a general work of this kind. His edition of the missal was soon

---

[8] J.-B.-E. Pascal, *Origines et raison de la liturgie catholique* (Paris, Migne, 1844), 815–25, and *Dictionnaire d'archéologie chrétienne et de liturgie*, ed. F. Cabrol and H. Leclercq, ix (Paris, 1929), col. 1701. See also P. Guéranger, *Institutions liturgiques*, ii (Le Mans, 1841); M. Albaric *et al., Histoire du missel français* (Brussels, 1986), esp. 33–57; B. Chedozeau, 'Aux sources du missel en français à l'usage des laïcs: Port-Royal et la liturgie'; H. Tuechle *et al., Réforme et Contre-Réforme* (Paris, 1968); and E. Préclin and E. Jarry, *Les Luttes politiques et doctrinaires aux XVIIe et XVIIIe siècles* (Paris, 1955).

reprinted and led the way on a popular level for a whole host of similar works, often termed *Eucologue* or *Paroissien*, which were popular from the beginning of the eighteenth century, with the latter dominating the market after the Revolution.

The size of such markets has been stressed, and an associated point is that in fact very few specimens of any of these editions survive today. Most of these works belonged to private individuals (and often those who had few books), and since literary and religious fashions change these items were not kept. They were not seen as having any academic value and thus were not housed in libraries. Often, therefore, it is only an unusually fine binding which will have preserved them. Early manuscript devotional works have survived, together with a number of the blind panel-stamped bindings of the sixteenth century, but the great gold-tooled bindings of the latter period are essentially humanist works, Bibles, the Fathers, and similar folio volumes. The size of the market for Books of Hours was, however, such that panel stamps were used for some of these and in particular for those published by Simon Vostre in the first quarter of the century. Such items, although bearing some signs of mass production, were essentially single, personal, possessions. A style for a group of persons was nevertheless to come in. In 1578 Henri III created the Ordre du Saint-Esprit and its statutes were bound uniformly for members by Nicolas Eve, thus establishing a series or collective style. Similarly the members of the same king's Congregation des Penitents de l'Annonciation Notre-Dame, founded in 1583, had their books bound in a very similar funerary style, especially with regard to the spine. Further *Heures*, an *Office de la Vierge*, and a *Psautier* were all published in 1583 and 1586 by Jamet Mettayer for the use of the society. This example, together with the standing of the group concerned, established a certain fashion for uniformly bound series of religious books of this kind. It is indeed noticeable that from the 1570s many more religious service books generally, breviaries, missals, and Books of Hours, were bound in the best gold-tooled styles of the day, and this is probably in itself an indication, not only of the greater appreciation of smaller books, but also of the general growth of book-owning and collecting.

Against the above background, attention can now be given to a work, the popularity of which, from the mid-seventeenth to the later eighteenth centuries, has not yet been commented on: the *Office de la Semaine sainte*. Holy Week, or, as it is sometimes more extensively termed in French, 'la Quinzaine de Pasques', is naturally a vital moment in the Church's year, and occasional separate editions of the services for it, the *Officium hebdomadae sanctae*, are known from the early sixteenth century. However, the regular production of books giving the order of these services seems, at least in France, to date from the early seventeenth century. The story behind them, certainly for the early years, is not entirely clear. The young Michel de Marolles (1600–81) is said to have translated the text, as the *Office de la Semaine sainte*, around 1626 when tutor to the daughter of the strongly religious duc de Nevers. According to the testimony of Niceron (in 1735), the translation was printed the same year. No copy has been traced. Confusingly, however, the first work appearing to be such a translation would seem to be: *L'Office de la Semaine Saincte, selon le Bréuiaire et Messel Romain, reformé selon le décret du Concile de Trente, par le commandement de Pie V. Et reueu de l'authorité de Clément VIII*, published in Paris in 1619 by Clovis Eve, 'Relieur ordinaire du Roy', Rue St Jacques au Lion d'argent, the only recorded copy being in a *semé* binding with crowned L ciphers and fleurs-de-lys.[9] As yet unlocated, further details are not known.

From this date a number of editions with a French title-page begin to appear, starting with those of 1621 (Paris, Pierre Chevalier, 12°; 1627 Paris, Eustache Foucault, 8°; 1627 Paris, Gabriel I Clopejau, 18°). The latter edition, entitled *L'Office de la Semaine saincte, selon le Messel & le Bréuiaire romain. Imprimé par le commandement du Pape Pie cinquiesme. Et reueu par l'authorité de Clément VIII* is a small eighteenmo of 270 numbered folios, and appears to have survived probably only in one copy, that with the arms of Anne of Austria, now in Princeton University Library. Despite their title-page, however, the entire text of these editions is in Latin.[10]

The immediately subsequent bibliographical history is not yet clear either, being a mixture of editions reported by previous authorities and the location (and therefore more exact knowledge) of others. Certainly a very similar edition appeared in 1644, published at Paris by Antoine Ruette, who succeeded his father as *Relieur du Roi* in or around the same year. Copies are recorded in fine bindings, including one with, again, the arms of Anne of Austria. Ruette seems to have obtained a twenty-year *privilège* for the work around 1657 and to have republished it in 1661. The date of his death is not known, but there is evidence that suggests that his rights in the work passed to Charles Fosset, who continued to publish such editions until around 1700. The survival of copies of two editions, both with the arms of Anne of Austria, could be taken as an indication that the queen, from the years of her regency (1643–51) on, not only showed signs of the religious conversion, which followed her withdrawal from the centre of the political stage and especially marked her later years, but also gave patron-

---

[9] The binding and engraved title-page are both reproduced by L. Gruel, *Manuel historique et bibliographique de l'amateur de reliures* (Paris, 1887), 98.

[10] J.-C. Brunet, *Manuel du libraire et de l'amateur de livres*, suppl. 2 (Paris, 1880), col. 65, referring to the Yemeniz copy; *Bibliothèque Raphael Esmerian*, pt. 2 (Paris 1972), lot 40, and Sotheby's (Monaco) 16 June 1989, lot 94. I am also grateful to Margaret M. Sherry of Princeton University Libraries for information on the copy there.

age to this particular form of publication. The association of *libraires* who were also leading binders (as was possible up to 1686), Eve, Rocolet, and Ruette, is also interesting.

The history of de Marolles's translation is reviewed by the author himself in his preface to the reader in the 1662 duodecimo edition, where he writes:

Enfin, j'ay repassé les yeux & la main sur cette traduction de l'Office de la Semaine saincte que j'avois commencé dès l'année 1626. J'en ay mesmes corrigé les espreuves avec soin; & je croy que cette édition sera beaucoup meilleure & plus correcte que toutes celles qui l'ont précedée depuis trente ans, & mesmes depuis l'année 1634 que l'ayant rendue beaucoup meilleure qu'elle n'estoit la première fois, il plut à Monseigneur le Chancelier d'en accorder un privilège du Roy, lequel a este renouvelé depuis plusieurs fois, & particulièrement en 1650 & 1653 qu'il s'en fit pour une seule de ces années-là jusques à trois éditions: d'ou l'on peut juger du bonheur de ce petit ouvrage que l'on a vu sous diverses dedicaces, la première à Mademoiselle de Nevers, & les autres à Madame la Princesse Marie de Mantoue, à la Sérenissime Reyne de Pologne, & la dernière à Monsieur Mole Garde des sceaux de France. Une explication des cérémonies y fut adjoustée en 1651 par le R. Père Daniel de Cigongne religieux de l'ordre de S. François.[11]

Although this statement is not one of absolute clarity, it would seem that the translation was certainly in print by 1634, even if no copy appears to be easily traceable today. It was certainly available by 1645, an edition being published that year in Paris entitled *Office de la Semaine saincte, selon le missel et bréviaire romain, en Latin & en François*. As Marolles records, new editions appeared in 1650 and 1651, one of the latter being published by an interesting group of booksellers which included Clopejau's recently established sons as well as older members like D. Soubron, P. Rocolet, M. Hauteville, and J. Henault. They may have been the founders of the Compagnie des Libraires Associés au Livre de la Semaine Sainte, whose first edition under this rubric came out in 1655, with others continuing up to the 1680s.

Both forms of the book (French title-page but Latin text and openly bilingual version) show a slowly increasing frequency of edition, a matter possibly reflecting a concern to turn members of the élite (not least women) away from Protestantism. This goes on through every decade up to 1700, with a number of booksellers being involved: Charles Fosset, Denis Chenault (and later his widow), Frédéric Léonard, and those belonging to the Compagnie. Regardless of the title-page form of the work, the holding of the *privilège* of the two forms of the work appears to have been shared, since at one stage Pierre Le Petit, *Imprimeur ordinaire du Roi*, was involved. In 1673 Le Petit's entire stock was lost in the fire in the neighbouring Collège de Montaigu in the Rue des Sept Voyes

---

[11] I am grateful to Monsieur Jean-Marc Chatelain for information on the early editions of the *Office de la Semaine sainte* held by the Bibliothèque Nationale, Paris, and for drawing the preface of the 1662 edition (f. *2) to my attention.

and he consequently sought a long-term extension for all his *privilèges*, the text of this request (printed in his 1678 *Office de la Semaine sainte*) giving some insight into the sort of items held by such a bookseller. They included the *Œuvres et traductions par Arnauld d'Andilly*, the *Offices de l'Eglise, de la Messe, de la Semaine sainte*, the *Histoire du Vieux et du Nouveau testament*, the translations of the Psalms, Proverbs and so on, the 'Bibles imprimés par Vitre', and numerous other items, for all of which he was given rights for an unusual fifty years from the date of his first *privilège*. Le Petit's connection with Arnauld may suggest that his bilingual editions of the *Office* were of a Jansenist leaning.[12]

As the frequency of editions increases, so the number of copies surviving with the arms of members of the royal family increases as well. Apart from Anne d'Autriche, one finds Henriette d'Angleterre (d. 1670), the first wife of Philippe I, duc d'Orléans (1662), Marie-Thérèse d'Autriche (1671, 1674, 1680), the Princesse Palatine (Charlotte Elisabeth de Bavière, the second wife of Philippe I d'Orléans: 1674, 1688, 1698), Marie-Adélaïde de Savoie, duchesse de Burgundy (1691, 1701), James II (1691), Philippe II, duc d'Orléans (1703), Françoise Marie (Mlle de Blois), his wife (1708, 1711, 1718), and Mary of Modena, wife of James II (1708). It is, therefore, evident that from the 1670s, and even more the 1690s, members of the royal family tended to have well-bound copies of the *Office*, probably for their own personal use. The known copies with the arms of other members of the court support this. The arms of the king himself seem to occur only from the 1690s. A 1716 edition was dedicated to the wife of the Regent (who had assumed office the previous year), and in 1717 the uncommon first Collombat edition introduces the phrase 'à l'usage de la maison du Roy', a market statement of which the implications (discussed below) appear only some ten years later.

The Le Petit *privilège* for the Latin and French edition referred to earlier seems to have passed after his death in 1684 to Antoine Dezallier, who produced a number of editions in the first two decades of the eighteenth century, and after him to Grégoire Dupuis, the last of which came out, doubtless significantly, in 1724, just as the fifty-year *privilège* was running out. In the meantime the Latin-text-only versions had, from at least 1717, come from the firm of of Jacques Collombat. This important publisher, whose family originated from Grenoble, married into the powerful Parisian book-selling family of Hansy and was admitted *libraire* in 1695. He became associated with the household of Marie-Adélaïde de Savoie, duchesse de Bourgogne, becoming in 1705, through special interference, her *imprimeur* (and thus one of the only thirty-six allowed in Paris). By

---

[12] I am particularly grateful to Her Grace Mary, duchess of Roxburghe, who, among many other kindnesses, made her two copies of the *Office de la Semaine sainte* available to me at an early stage in the work for this article.

1714 he was printer in ordinary to the king and in 1718 installed a printing press in the Tuileries for the edification and amusement of the young king. His wealth came from these various appointments, from his considerable share in the market for religious books generally, and from his monopoly of the small-format court calendars, which were so well known that his name became synonymous with that of their format. The bilingual *privilège* seems, however, to have gone in 1728 to Pierre-Paule Garnier, widow of the bookseller Raymond Garnier (admitted 1702, d. 1715), and to her nephew, Jean Baptiste Garnier de la Heusse, who was admitted *libraire* by *arrêt du Conseil* in 1723 and in this connection granted the titles of *Imprimeur de la Reine et de l'Archevêque de Sens.*

Marie Leszczynska, the 22-year-old daughter of the dethroned king of Poland, arrived at Strasburg on 5 July 1725 and was engaged there, by proxy, to the 15-year-old Louis XV on 15 August, the marriage itself taking place at Fontainebleau on 5 September. Her sudden elevation had been promoted by Cardinal de Fleury, tutor and chief minister to the king. She had been selected basically on the grounds of the lack of qualifications in all other possible candidates and because of her reputed good health. Outstandingly, she was a devout Catholic, healthy, likely to bear children, and was not associated with any particular party at court. She was indeed almost totally foreign to court life and might therefore be reckoned to be grateful to, and dependant on, those ministers who had so signally promoted her and her family. From the start it was apparent that her very religious upbringing had had a deep effect on her character, and the suspicious Mathieu Marais comments in his *Mémoires* for July 1725 on her links with the Jesuits and on how she was sometimes referred to as 'Unigenita'. Marais also records that on arrival she had given the king 'des *Heures* qu'elle a faites et écrites de sa main pour présent de noces. On l'a envoyé relier à Metz et le maroquin a été achete à Paris. On est bien sûr que ce ne sont pas des *Heures* de Port Royal.'[13]

    Initially the royal marriage appeared to be a success and from the birth of twins in August 1727 (Louise-Elisabeth and Henriette), through that of Adélaïde eleven months later, the queen gave birth to no less than ten children (but importantly only one surviving boy) in as many years. By 1739, however, the king broke progressively away from the queen, who remained openly devoted to him but turned more and more to her religious nature and upbringing for consolation. Detailed information on her personal life is hard to come by, and both her first and second biographers, the lawyer Aublet de Maubuy (1773) and the Abbé Proyart (1784), can hardly be trusted as impartial and accurate

---

[13] M. Marais, *Mémoires* (Paris, 1864), iii. 205.

authorities. The memoirs of the duc de Luynes, despite the fact that he was a particularly close friend of the queen and a somewhat effusive admirer, do provide much first-hand, if pedantic, court information and allow one to catch contemporary glimpses of the queen's religious activities and routines.[14]

Thus in the early days of their marriage the king and queen jointly attended Mass daily at eight o'clock, although later this time seems to have varied and to have been either at ten or even eleven. Like many things in the royal routine, this was a ceremony and one for which the Swiss guard paraded. Normally the special motet started as the royal couple entered, but if the queen was attending alone she preferred to start with a period of silent prayer and would make a sign to her *aumônier* when the music might start.[15] Luynes was a stickler for protocol and there are therefore numerous discussions of the rights of the various members of the aristocracy and of the household to be seated in proximity to the royal persons. There is much too on the order of processions, where the approved order to follow the queen was: her *chevalier d'honneur*, the *premier écuyer*, the *écuyer de quartier*, the queen's confessor (usually a Polish priest), and finally the *officier des gardes*. There were also rules governing major ceremonies such as the *Fête Dieu*, which, like certain other major occasions, were attended at the parish church in Versailles itself. Here there had to be two carriages of *écuyers*, each drawn by a specified eight horses. This was an event requiring *le grand habit*, the train of which was held by a page, while the *grand parasol* was held by a *valet de pied*, Luynes noting carefully that, had the *petit parasol* been involved, it would have been held by the *premier écuyer*. The parasol was purple with gold fringes. Another row concerned the rights of the 'portemanteaux' to look after the queen's outer gown while she was in chapel, this being sparked off by the absence of the official in question on one occasion. The queen was regularly attended by her four ladies-in-waiting of the week, one group, consisting of Mesdames d'Ancenis, Fleury, Rupelmonde, and Talleyrand, being known as 'la semaine sainte', another (Mesdames de la Tournelle, Flavacourt, Antin, and Montauban) being termed 'la belle semaine'. In 1743 one of the latter complained that

[14] The following passages are based on numerous passages in Luynes: the main ones are from i. 345, 362, 412; ii. 97–101; iii. 110, 174; v. 2, 155, 458; vi. 472; vii. 21–3, 277; viii. 240; ix. 346; x. 99; xii. 349; xiv. 364; xv. 108. On the importance of precedence, see also A. Maral, *Autour de la chapelle royale de Versailles: Le Cadre archéologique et institutionel et les cérémonies religieuses sous Louis XIV* (École Nationale des Chartes, Positions des thèses, 1994), 129–33.

[15] The queen naturally had her own household and her own religious officers. Initially Cardinal Fleury was himself her *Grand aumônier*, the bishop de Saulx-Tavannes her *Premier aumônier*, and the abbé de Vienne *Aumônier ordinaire*, Tavannes being later promoted while the Abbé de Fleury succeeded him and St-Aulai:e became *Aumônier ordinaire*. At the end of her life her *Grand aumônier* was the archbishop of Rouen, Dominique de La Rochefoucauld de Saint Elpis, the *Premier aumônier* the bishop of Chartres, Pierre Augustin Bernard de Rosset de Rocozel de Fleury, while the Jesuit Père Radominowicz appears in the *Almanach royal* as her confessor from 1751. Her chaplain over a long earlier period was one Le Rouge. There were also four *Aumôniers de quartier* and four *Chapelains de quartier*.

their pews in chapel were too uncomfortable and within the week the bare boards and benches were covered in leather and purple velvet, while cushions and padded kneelers were provided. The queen's personal household linen ('linge et dentelles, tapisseries' and even 'les cassettes avec galons d'or') was renewed every three years, the old items going to her ladies-in-waiting, who were expected to hand these things on to the poor. Luynes suggested to the queen that there was some needless extravagance in this, but she refused to change the practice, both because it was an established one and because it gave pleasure to 'mes pauvres gens'! No reference is made to the books or other furnishings of the royal chapel.

Later in the day the king attended for a sermon at half past four, but the queen had often been at chapel for vespers starting at 3.30 p.m. Luynes specifies that the 'pain bénit' was 'brioche' and that, as he puts it, it was given 'même aux dames qui ont suivi la reine'. Financial generosity ('les quatre louis') was, however, restricted to 'la chapelle de la reine'—that is, to her appointed clergy and their assistants. On some occasions, probably at times of ill-health, the queen had a service said in her own room, but she never took communion there. Church services were public occasions and the rights of both clergy and court had to be observed. In chapel, Luynes records:

Lorsque la Reine communie, le grand ou le premier aumônier, ou en leur absence l'aumônier de quartier, dit la messe et communie la Reine; la seconde messe est dite par le chapelain de quartier; mais outre ce service il y en a un autre à faire auprès de la Reine. Il faut lui donner ses livres de prières, lui présenter l'Évangile à baiser, un moment avant l'oratoire lui apporter plusieurs hosties pour qu'elle choisisse celle qui doit être consacrée pour la communion etc; ce service ne peut être fait par celui qui dit la messe. Les chapelains prétendent qu'en l'absence de leurs supérieurs ils doivent les remplacer, et qu'il ne convenoit pas qu'on ait recours en pareil cas aux aumôniers du Roi.

Royal practice was closely watched and used to establish claims in precedence. 'Le vendredi saint [1741] à l'adoration de la croix, on remarqua une nouveauté. Mme la duchesse de Chartres avoit derrière elle son aumônier, qui lui porta son livre et son sac;[16] on n'avoit point encore vu de princesses du sang faire usage d'un

---

[16] The use of such bags in the provinces is described as follows: 'Si vous êtes à Foncine-le-haut, le jour des prières, vous ne laisserez point, sans y jeter un coup d'œil, passer les jeunes personnes qui portent ostensiblement à l'église de très belles heures reliées en maroquin verd et dorées sur tranches. Le sac fastueusement galonné des dévotes de la cour aurait, avec satisfaction, renfermé de pareilles heures, et l'on peut croir, sans téméraire soupçon, que la jouissance de ces aimables villageoises est autant dans la reliure opulente de leur livre, que dans les discours latins ou même français qu'elle couvre' (J. M. Lequino, *Voyage dans le Jura* (Paris, an IX), i. 144, quoted by A. Sauvy, in *Histoire de l'édition française* (Paris, 1984), ii. 438). On the same page there is also reference to a Breton priest who, in 1748, possessed a fine *Semaine Sainte* bound complete with silver clasps. The use of the book as a symbol and as an object for display is treated in J. Białostocki, *Livres de sagesse et livres de vanité* (Paris, 1993), and, with regard to lay Humanists at court, in F. Dupuigrenet Desroussilles, 'Le Livre à la cour: Livres des gentilshommes et des bouffons', in the important general volume, F. Dupuigrenet Desroussilles (ed.), *La Symbolique du livre dans l'art occidental du Haut Moyen Age à Rembrandt* (Paris, 1995), 86–7.

honneur qui n'est dû qu'au Roi', records and comments Luynes.[17] The Maundy Thursday service, one particularly dear to the queen since it introduced Christian humility into the otherwise vain life of the court, was usually held in the Salle des Gardes. After the sermon and benediction the queen washed, dried, and kissed the feet of twelve poor girls (the king doing the same for twelve old men) before serving them a thirteen-course meal and giving them each a purse full of money. The queen's ladies-in-waiting, six duchesses and six other ladies, handed the queen the necessary dishes. However, on a certain occasion one of the duchesses pushed in front of one of the other ladies in waiting so that a public brawl ensued. One side protested rank; the other pointed out that it was custom, when accompanying the queen in her coach, for the nearest person to get in after the queen, even if this meant that, despite the presence of a duchess, an untitled person could find herself sitting next to the queen. Fleury, forced into the role of Solomon, decided that the duchesses should have precedence—but only for the Eucharist and in processions.

The break-up of the royal marriage was reflected in these practices: the king's installation of a first major mistress, Mme de Mailly, has been variously dated between 1733 and 1737, but was publicly proclaimed, as it were, by his refusal to take communion at Easter 1738. The following year he acquired the property of Choisy—later to be a favourite residence with Mme de Pompadour. Easter saw the royal children actively participating in the services attended by the queen: Henriette being ill, Adélaïde carried the host; the very religious Dauphin, their cousin, the duc de Chartres, and others, all attended. The queen went frequently to church; the king hunted. Later the king was for a while to go so far as to forbid his children even to stand close to their mother on state occasions. His severe illness in 1745 and the dismissal of the then current mistresses brought a brief reconciliation, but it was only the advent of Mme de Pompadour, who deliberately made the king be civil with his wife, that improved matters, although even this could not make the queen accept the presence of the royal mistress as one of her company in church.

Progressively, the queen led her own quiet life more and more. She refused to attend military reviews; when obliged to go to the theatre, she took her handiwork along with her; she went more frequently to church. There arose the whole question of the Swiss guard turning out to accompany and attend her at early Mass: when she was *en haut* (there was a royal tribune centrally placed in the balcony and thus level with the first floor of the palace), only two or three stood at each arch but when she was *en bas* (at floor level) there were five. There was also the problem of whether the guard should turn out, and with them the

---

[17] Luynes, xi. 99.

drummers, when the queen went to early Mass, the king being still in bed close by. The matter was resolved in a typical and significant way by establishing a matter of principle in precedence: when she went alone early in the morning she did not go *en robe*; and was therefore going, not as queen, but *en particulier*, a phrase which reoccurs on a number of occasions. The guard need not therefore attend. The principle becomes established and later Luynes notes that, although the queen attended Mass on one day at 12.30, she had already been at 9.30, 'en particulier, suivie par une seule dame'. There were, however, matters of precedence for which she fought and which she obtained, as when, in 1749, it is recorded that: 'La Reine obtient du Roi de pouvoir se mettre sur le drap de pied [probably the black velvet cloth covering the royal prayer-stool, to approach which was a great ambition at court] sans être en grand habit.'

There were present, therefore, royalty, aristocracy, the clergy, the guard—and, on a number of occasions when the king or queen attended parish churches at Versailles or elsewhere—the common people. Mme Campan charmingly evokes their presence on an occasion when Cardinal de Luynes, another close friend of the queen, was in his diocese (Sens) at Fontainebleau. Rising at five in the morning, he would take the early service and preach his old homilies.

Toutes avaient été composées pour ramener les gens du grand monde aux modestes pratiques qui conviennent aux vrais chrétiens. Plusieures centaines de paysannes, assisses sur leurs sabots, environnées des paniers qui avaient servi à apporter leurs legumes ou leurs fruits au marché, écoutaient Son Éminence sans comprendre un mot de ce qu'il leur disait. Quelques personnes attachées à la cour, voulant assister à la messe avant de partir pour Paris, entendaient Son Éminence crier avec une émotion tout-a-fait pastorale: 'Mes chers frères, pourquoi le luxe vous accompagne-t-il jusqu'au pied du sanctuaire? Pourquoi ces coussins de velours et ces sacs couverts de galons et de franges précédent-ils votre entrée dans le temple du Seigneur? Quittez, quittez ces habitudes somptueuses que vous ne devez considérer que comme un gêne tenant à votre rang, et dont la présence de votre divin sauveur doit vous dégager.'

The cardinal's discourse soon became the talk of the town, and eventually those to whom the text more properly applied finally came to hear it—even if only out of curiosity.[18]

It could be argued that the queen would have been at one with either congregation. Her religious practice was essentially old-fashioned, simple, heart-felt, dutiful, and of notable generosity. Apart from a number of historical items, the surviving books which bear her arms are virtually all religious works: she upbraided her friend, the elder Helvétius, on the philosophical writings of his son; it is said that, reading the article on angels in the *Encyclopédie* (by the relatively safe Abbé E. F. Mallet, Professor of Theology at Paris), she condemned

[18] J. L. H. de Campan, *Mémoires sur la vie privée de Marie Antoinette* (Paris, 1823), iii. 75–6.

the entire work as damnable; and that, chancing at a bookstand on a copy of Voltaire's *La Religion naturelle*, she tore it into pieces, threatening that, if the bookseller continued to sell works of that kind she, the queen, would have the shop closed down. The Assumption was a notable event in her calendar, since she herself was, like the Virgin, called Mary. She also had a particular devotion to the Sacred Heart of Jesus and for the Carmelites. Her early biographer, Proyart, suggests that, in the manner of eighteenth-century royalty (Mme de Pompadour did the same), she had a small printing press in her appartment in Versailles and that she printed small, edifying, tracts and prayers there.[19] These were for distribution to her immediate entourage, although, sadly, none seems to have survived. Nor does this press feature in Lottin's 1789 list of private presses, but it may be linked to those used by Louis XV himself as a child or, more likely, to those of the Dauphine (1758) or the duc de Bourgogne (1760), both of which are credited with the production of short religious tracts.[20] If the queen was, in some ways, old-fashioned and bigoted, her generosity was, on the other hand, proverbial, and even a cause of embarrassment to her friends and staff. Although she herself had relatively little money (on two occasions the king had to pay her debts and in 1749 she was unable to give any family presents at Christmas), at least until her later years she spent a fair amount on minor evening gambling games and, as Luynes thought, had absolutely no sense of the value of money. She had, however, perhaps based on her own early experiences, a keen sense of need in others and the tales of her generosity towards the poor were legion.

Her closest friends, Luynes and Henault, paint frank, if courtierly, portraits of her, Luynes writing:

Il n'y a point d'humeur dans son caractère; elle a quelquefois des moments de vivacité, mais ils sont passagers; elle en est fâchée le moment d'après, et quand elle croit avoir fait peine à quelqu'un, elle est impatiente de le consoler par quelques marques de bonté. La Reine devroit savoir beaucoup, car elle a beaucoup lu, et même des livres difficiles à entendre, par exemple les ouvrages du P. Malebranche. Elle les lit avec plaisir; cependant quelques gens croient qu'elle peut bien ne pas les entendre. Ses principales lectures après celles de piété sont des livres d'histoire . . . il est aisé de voir qu'elle est instruite.

A reasonable conversationalist, the queen sang and painted tolerably well, as Henault remarks. Significantly for her later years, Luynes records:

Sa grande piété et sa vertu, qui viennent du tempérament et de l'éducation, l'ont mise à la portée de jouir d'une liberté que jamais reine n'avoit eue jusqu'à présent; elle a au moins deux heures de temps à être dans ses cabinets le matin, et trois ou quatre les après-dinée, les jours qu'elle ne va point l'après-dinée à l'église. Dans ses heures particulières, elle voit

---

[19] L. B. Proyart, *Vie de la reine de France Marie Lecksinska* (rev. edn., Paris, 1802), 250.

[20] [A. M. Lottin], *Catalogue chronologique des libraires et des libraires-imprimeurs de Paris* (Paris, 1789), 89–90.

qui elle veut, hommes et femmes, à son choix; mais quoi qu'elle ait le ton de galanterie, accompagné d'esprit et de prudence, et qu'elle entende parfaitement ce langage, elle a nulle idée du mal; elle n'en a que de l'horreur. Ce caractère naturel, soutenu par une piété vraie et éclairée, est le plus sûr de tout les préservatifs.[21]

Henault's portrait is equally positive:

Mais ce qui ne s'allie pas d'ordinaire, c'est que cette même princesse, si bonne, si simple, si douce, si affable, représente avec une dignité qui imprime le respect, et qui embarasseroit si elle ne daignoit pas vous rassurer: d'une chambre à l'autre elle redevient la Reine et conserve dans la Cour cette idée de grandeur, telle que l'on nous représente celle de Louis XIV. Ses lettres se ressentent de la noblesse de son âme et de la gaité de son caractere. Elle n'est mêlée en rien dans les affaires, et aussi jamais le Roi ne la refuse pour les choses qu'elle lui demande. Elle est sur la Religion d'une sévérité bien importante dans le siècle où nous sommes; elle pardonne tout, elle excuse tout, hors ce qui pourroit y donner quelque atteinte; et si on pouvoit la comparer, ce seroit à la reine Blanche.[22]

Thus Marie Leszczynska, in many ways remarkably adaptable to the considerable changes in role imposed on her, managed to create for herself something of a life of her own. She did not attempt to influence the king in their private concerns, conducted herself with dignity, and preached only by example. Her attitude towards the king is indeed described as one of great respect (something her father had always inculcated), bordering, even in the best days, almost on fear. She arrived at court as something of a poor relative and never succeeded in attaching the fickle king to her in any serious and lasting manner. She was subservient in politics, where her only real intervention appears to have been an attempt to persuade Choiseul not to ban the Jesuits—the creation of the *parti dévot* of the 1750s being more an alliance of closely interested court parties around the royal children rather than any association with the queen in a particularly active manner.

A matter of interest in the present context is, however, the way in which, in her early days, she accepted being seen as a new centre at court and allowed her household to be recognized as such. As soon as her arrival was announced, there had naturally been competition to be attached to posts associated with her. The earlier history of the *Office de la Semaine sainte* has indicated how this book became increasingly popular in royal circles during the latter years of Louis XIV, a fashion continued and enhanced under the Regency when the copies belonging to members of the court circle were given particularly attractive bindings. The

---

[21] Luynes, x. 168–9.

[22] C. J. F. Henault, *Mémoires, mis en ordre par le baron de Vigan* (Paris, 1855), 217–18. See also R.-L. de Voyer, marquis d'Argenson, *Journal et mémoires* (Paris, 1859–67), iv. 168–70. Henault's final comparison is presumably Blanche de Navarre (1331–98), who, engaged to the son of Philippe VI de Valois, married the father (1349), only to find herself a widow the following year. She retired to a devout life in Naples and steadfastly refused to become engaged in politics.

1717 edition, the first to be published by Collombat, appears to be the first claiming on its title-page to be 'imprimé par le commandement du Roy, pour le service de sa maison', although the earliest copies of any one edition to survive in several copies, all with either the royal arms or those of a leading member of the nobility, were from some ten years later.

Holy Week is, of course, the central season in the Christian year and was one in which both public and private commitment were on show. The *Encyclopédie*, written in the 1750s, says:

On l'appelle *grande semaine* à cause des grands mystères qu'on y célèbre.

Les Protestants en rapportent l'institution au tems des apôtres, aussi bien que les Catholiques chez qui elle est spécialement consacrée à honorer les mystères de la mort & passion de Jésus-Christ, & a les retracer à l'esprit & aux yeux des fidèles par les offices qu'on y chante & par les cérémonies dont on les accompagne.

Dans la primitive église, outre les jeunes rigoureux qu'on pratiquoit dans cette *semaine*, on s'y interdisoit les plaisirs les plus licites & les plus innocens; les fidèles ne s'y donnoient point le baiser de paix à l'église; tout travail étoit défendu; les tribunaux étoient fermés; on delivroit les prisonniers; enfin, on pratiquoit diverses mortifications, dont les princes mêmes & les empereurs n'étoient pas exempts.[23]

Following the royal marriage, the 1726 edition of the *Office de la Semaine sainte* promptly repeats, in the queen's name, the by-now standard phraseology and states: 'imprimé par ordre de la Reine, pour le service de sa maison'. In the following year, however, the first for which a large number of copies survive, the work is more graciously 'dedié à la Reine pour l'usage de Sa Maison'. It is now published by Pierre-Paul [*sic*] Garnier, the widow of Raymond Mazières, and her nephew, Jean Baptiste Garnier de la Heusse, who had, rather exceptionally, been admitted *libraire* by *Arrêt du Conseil du Roy* in February 1723. At some unspecified date around these years, the two seem to have acquired the title of Imprimeur de la Reine et de l'Archevêque de Sens, all evident signs of powerful protection.

It is doubtless also significant that the *privilège* states that the work was edited by Jean-Joseph Languet de Gergy (1677–1753), then bishop of Soissons but due to become archbishop of Sens in 1730. Languet de Gergy was the younger brother of the famous *curé* of Saint-Sulpice, Jean-Baptiste Languet de Gergy (1675–1750), whose highly irregular fund-raising activities (openly pocketing the table silver from his hosts as an enforced 'contribution' to the church-building programme) had incurred Buffon's irony. The bishop was a *protégé* of

---

[23] [D. Diderot, J. d'Alembert], *Encyclopédie* (Paris, [1766]), xiv. 936. It is interesting to note that the Larousse *Grand dictionnaire de XIXe siècle* paraphrases this text, adding after 'jeune' the phrase 'on s'y imposait la xérophagie, c'est-à-dire que l'on ne mangeait que des aliments secs', and ending 'les princes même et les empereurs en donnaient l'exemple', phrases which also occur in the introduction to the 1728 *Office*, but all of which may well be based on the usual source in St John Chrysostom.

Bossuet and a leader of the attack on the Jansenists, but also a paradoxical opponent of the miracles of the *diacre* Pâris, while, at the same time, forcefully and naïvely supporting those of Marie Alacoque. His popular *Traité de la confiance de la miséricorde de Dieu* appeared in 1725. The bishop's part in the 1727 *Office de la Semaine sainte* can, therefore, be seen as one of the moves by the anti-Jansenist party to ensure the adherence of the new queen to their side. Marie Leszczynska's early biographer, the Abbé Proyart, describes how the Jansenists had, early on, attempted to see that the library provided for the queen was largely of a Jansenist leaning, right down to the very Bible provided for her regular use. Proyart, whose testimony is evidently far from being unbiased, describes how she rapidly rejected all such works and indeed ordered them to be burnt.

Writing in 1794 and looking back on the queen's life, Proyart makes no specific mention of the *Office de la Semaine sainte* but, when describing the many ways in which she spent both time and money in support not only of her friends and staff at court but also of ordinary and needy persons, he records highly similar general activities, saying:

Un autre moyen de faire l'aumône spirituelle, qu'employoit souvent la Reine, c'étoit de répandre des Livres de Piété, qu'elle appeloit ses petits Missionaires. Elle faisoit faire à ses fraix des éditions des meilleurs Ouvrages en ce genre; elle en confioit la distribution à des Curés & à des Religieux, qui les donnoient, suivant son intention, aux Pauvres qui n'avoient pas le moyen de les achêter, & quelque-fois encore aux Riches qui n'en avoient pas la volonté.

This is further instanced by a late but well-substantiated inscription in a copy of the 1727 *Office de la quinzaine de Pasques*, an edition also dedicated to the queen, which records that 'à ses derniers moments cette reine fit distribuer à ses dames d'honneur, femmes de chambre et autres personnes pieuses qui se trouvaient alors auprès d'elle, ses livres de prières et autres objets de piété à son usage'.[24]

In the publisher's dedication much is made of the queen's 'bonté . . . grandeur . . . douceur', all of which are seen as being 'dans l'image de cette bonté divine', just as Marie is 'une Reine qui nous en montre un modèle si parfait dans sa conduite'. In the unsigned preface Languet de Gergy gives a brief history of *la grande semaine*, based largely on St John Chrysostom, and goes on with some interesting social comments to say that, while we may not today be able to observe the fasts and vigils as previous generations have done, we can at least endeavour to be as assiduous as possible in our participation at the central services. He also records that the edition has been carefully prepared: the translation of the *Office* is not new but based on the numerous previous ones; the

---

[24] Proyart, *Vie de la reine*, 32, and a manuscript inscription in Bibliothèque Municipale de Versailles, Res. C 345.

Ordinary of the Mass has been included; the Psalms are as approved by the bishops in the 1708 version; a preface has been added to each separate office and considerations on the Passion and Resurrection have been included between the offices in order to help fill out the long silences they contain. There is also advice on how to prepare for confession and to hear the Mass itself.

The bibliography of the *Office de la Semaine sainte*, in almost any edition, is far from being either straightforward or established and that of the 1728 editions is no exception. Copies exist with 624, 714, or 729 pages and variable contents. They were most probably issued in differing forms, possibly made up for particular clients, and at different times. Four facts are, however, of particular note in connection with the present study: (*a*) these editions are the most commonly surviving of any edition of the work; (*b*) the 1728 engraved title-page was not altered for at least one later edition, that of 1739 (marking a renewal of the original ten-year *privilège*), which can, however, be identified by the presence of the later extension of this *privilège*; (*c*) survival is doubtless assisted by the particularly large number of copies bearing fine bindings and armorial stamps; and (*d*) many of these, and outstandingly those with the arms of the queen herself, are impressed on the covers by means of a large gilt panel stamp to which the armorial stamp has been added in the otherwise blank central oval.

Copies of what is, in fact, basically the 1728 edition are easily found in libraries, in private collections, and in the book trade.[25] Bearing either the French royal arms or those of Marie Leszczynska, they turn up regularly and frequently at auction and in catalogues, optimistically (to put it no worse) described on occasion as the king's or queen's own personal copy. Among those bound in particularly fine bindings, similar to copies of immediately previous years, may indeed have been those few for royal use, but the more common ones with the panel stamps were clearly for general household distribution and indeed often bear the names of persons or convents to whom they had been given within a short time.[26] The 1728 edition is the first to be found with these panel stamps in a regular manner (only one or two 1727 copies also bear them), and this suggests that the edition was seen as one intended for a wide level of distribution (albeit

[25] Numerous bibliographical sources have been used to construct a provisional list of editions of the *Office de la Semaine sainte*; chief among these have been the on-line British, European, and US library databases now available. These were augmented by the catalogues of the Bodleian, the British Library, the National Union catalogue, and standard reference books, including especially those listing auction sale records in both the English- and French-speaking worlds. I hope to produce a checklist of all French editions 1600–1800 in due course.

[26] Evidence for an annual change is available for one case: a copy of the *Semaine sainte*, Veuve Mazières, 1726, is recorded with the arms of Louis XV and an inscription saying that the volume was used by the king and given by him to his tutor, the Abbé Perot, who, in turn presented it to the Bibliothèque du Chapitre de la Ville de Lyon in 1727. See E. Rahir, *Livres dans de riches reliures* (Paris, 1910), item 174. Other copies passed on include one of the 1728 edition which was in private hands in Versailles by 1756 and another copy of the same edition is recorded as being later in the convent of the Visitation at Rouen.

within a fairly limited circle) and that it was thus worthwhile having such stamps designed and cut specially for the book. Panel stamps (used blind, not gilt) had, of course, been used earlier and especially for Books of Hours in the sixteenth century, but they had fallen into abeyance well before 1600 so that their use here was a return to an old technique for the more rapid decoration of books where a number of copies were involved and where one wished to achieve a certain fashionable appearance without too much work or cost.

The panel stamps found on copies of the *Office de la Semaine sainte* are of two designs, both repeating the interlaced patterns, accompanied by small infilling tools, often in filigree, which were the structural basis of the so-called 'fanfare' style which was the height of fashion in the late sixteenth century and which continued, in one way and another, up to the end of the seventeenth. G. D. Hobson, the great historian of this style, viewed the panels on the *Office de la Semaine sainte* as the final degradation of a great Renaissance design, writing: 'Mais le décor à la fanfare va bientôt s'éteindre de façon misérable, avec de grossières reliures à plaque, sur des livres de messe et des almanachs.'[27] He does, however, illustrate the two designs, each of which leaves a space in the centre for an armorial stamp and another above and below this for further separate ornamentation. The tops and the bottoms of the panels are in fact mirror images of each other, and only a very careful inspection will allow for the identification of which way up the stamp may have been used—something which may naturally not be the same on the upper and lower cover of the same book. The panels themselves measure 19.5 by 12.5 cm (Fig. 4.1) and 18 by 11 cm (Figs. 4.2 and 4.3), the larger one requiring but a thin roll outside it (usually a fleur de lis and anthemion one) to cover the standard octavo volume, the smaller one leaving a larger space around it. The latter is in fact useful and may be indicative of the date of binding and therefore of publication, since the repeated use of the original engraved title-page can lead into error. Earlier bound copies of the 1728 edition usually have an outer roll with strongly undulating foliage surrounding six relatively crudely designed flowers before repeating itself (measuring 1.2 cm wide, and 9.9 cm before repetition of the design).[28] The panel does not fit the octavo page perfectly, and it may require the use of another thin decorative roll top and bottom. On later editions, such as those of the 1740s, these rolls are updated in fashion and, while still floral, are more sophisticated and naturalistic, the six flowers including a 'bearded' one which may be intended to be hops. Two rolls with the same design may be involved; a thinner one on the sides (measuring 1 cm across and repeating at 9.5 cm, and a fatter one, taking up more space top

[27] G. D. Hobson, *Les Reliures à la fanfare* (London, 1935), 66 and plate XXIII. Fig. 4.1 is on the right; Fig. 4.2, with the wider roll around, is on the left.
[28] See Figs. 4.1 and 4.2.

and bottom, measuring 1.5 cm across and 10.5 cm in length). The designs of all these rolls were common at the period and have therefore not yet been attributed to any particular binder of workshop.

The *Office de la Semaine sainte* panels have in fact a certain importance in the history of French book-binding in the eighteenth century, since they are the precursors of those used from the mid-1750s on copies of the *Almanach royal* and generally known as 'plaques Dubuisson', after the binder to whom their use at that time has been particularly attributed.[29] The *Office* panels occur from 1728 to the late 1740s, and the Dubuisson ones from just a few years later, the latter, however, being redesigned in the style of those times and indeed in a fairly wide variety of patterns, some of which were to be in use right up to the French Revolution. The technical function of the panels is evidently the same: the rapid production of a fashionable style suitable for a work appearing regularly in a steady market and thus justifying the expenses of manufacture. This industrial panel technique, using a press rather than hand tools, was to be typical of developments in book-binding in the eighteenth century, something in which the *Office* therefore led the way.

Two further points need to be made concerning these bindings: first, that while numerous copies are known with the arms either of France (usually attributed to the reigning monarch) or of Marie Leszczynska, single copies for single years are known with those of many other members of the court or associated groups (Louise Elisabeth d'Orléans, queen of Spain, Louis Dauphin, Louis d'Orléans, Mme de Pompadour, Mme de Lamballe, M. de Rohan, l'Archevêque de Tencin, Marie Thérèse Infante d'Espagne, Marie Joseph de Saxe, Mme Adélaïde). Some of these surviving examples suggest that certain people possessed or commissioned them fairly regularly over a number of years and indicate a relatively frequent rate of replacement (e.g. Louis d'Orléans 1728, 1730, 1735, 1745, 1752, 1753; Marie Thérèse 1743, 1745, 1746; Mme Adélaïde 1752, 1755, 1756, 1757, 1758). Secondly, the number of well-bound copies of the *Office de la Semaine sainte* recorded as surviving shows a very slowly rising profile from the mid-seventeenth century, followed by a sharp rise from the 1690s which reaches a peak between the 1720s and 1740s, to drop sharply in the next three decades with virtually no editions recorded at all from the 1780s onwards. Provincial editions appear most frequently in the 1740s and 1750s. The period of the work's high fashion thus seems established as the twenty years following the arrival of the queen in 1725. Marie died in 1768 and, while copies of the *Semaine* with the arms of Marie Antoinette just as she became Dauphine

---

[29] L.-M. Michon, *La Reliure française* (Paris, 1951), 90; E. Rahir, *Livres en de riches reliures* (Paris, 1910), no. 184 a-m.

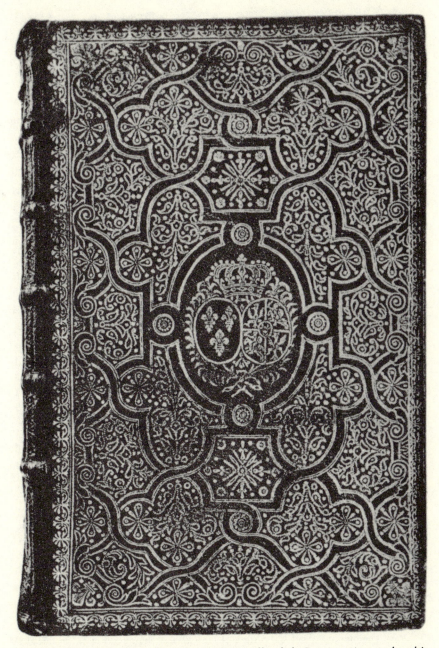

FIG. 4.1. The binding of a 1728 edition of the *Office de la Semaine sainte* produced in Paris by Veuve Mazières and Garnier. The central panel stamp (type A) shows the separate arms of Queen Marie Leszczynska.

Source: The print is taken from plate XXIII in G. D. Hobson, *Les reliures à la fanfare*, London, 1935.

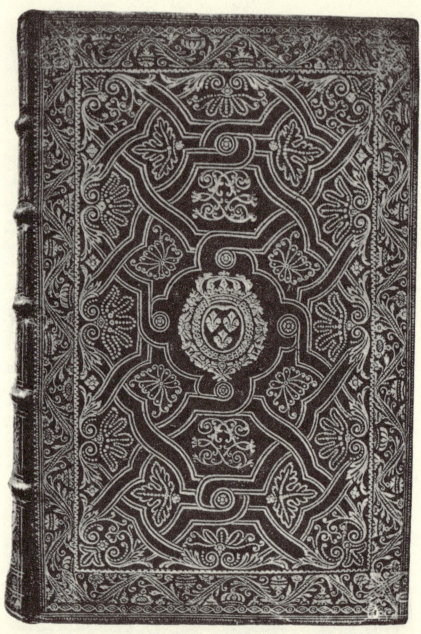

Fɪɢ. 4.2. The binding of a 1727 edition of the *Office de la Semaine sainte* produced in Paris by Veuve Mazières and Garnier. The rectangular inner panel stamp (type B) has, within it, the separate royal arms of France and the equally separate L cipher. Note the older zig-zag outer roll.

Source: The print is taken from plate XXIII in G. D. Hobson, *Les reliures à la fanfare*, London, 1935.

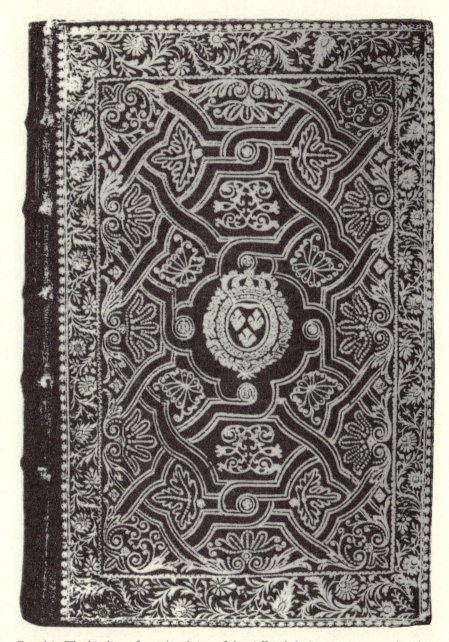

Fig. 4.3. The binding of a 1743 edition of the *Office de la Semaine sainte* produced in Paris by Collombat. The rectangular inner panel stamp is also type B but is upside down compared with Fig. 4.2. See the larger curls on the inner side of the ornament bottom left.

Source: The print is taken from lot 279 featured in the Sotheby's catalogue for the sale on 25 January 1949.

are known, there are few later. Of course the *Semaine sainte* was not the only personal liturgical work to be finely bound, but Michon's listing of recorded mosaic bindings in the first half of the eighteenth century puts it numerically on a level with the traditional Book of Hours, with all other 'offices' (for the dead, for the night, and so on) together coming to much the same figure. The *Semaine sainte* seems, therefore, to have had a particular popularity in this very competitive market at this period.

The emphasis placed by the Council of Trent on the Eucharist, and thus on the Easter period in particular, can be seen as one of the main features of baroque religiosity. However, in France at least the rise of absolute monarchy did much to counter, in a Gallican manner, the unified medieval Catholic world, to substitute moralism for mysticism, and progressively in its policies and laws to promote the State, and its priorities rather than those of the Church. The rise of religious erudition also entrained a continual revision and questioning of older accepted traditional forms.

The slow rise of the *Office de la Semaine sainte* in such popularity under Louis XIV seems likely to be associated both with the fact that it gave the major ceremonies 'en Latin et en François', and was thus the vehicle for the full comprehension of such services by a larger number of people, including the new circles growing up around the new court at Versailles. The religious tone imbued there under the older Louis XIV and Mme de Maintenon helped to establish the book as an increasingly common liturgical work by the early decades of the eighteenth century. The *Semaine sainte* seems to have been deliberately associated with the advent of a young and devout queen and positively promoted in connection with her household. The position and character of the queen herself are also relevant, since, while having to play a particular official role, she was deeply religious and of a highly sensitive and devout nature, seeking an inner balance in a very traditional—and possibly slightly naïve—way. She thus found herself forced into a double role whereby she was both 'la Reine' and a private person with her own religious needs, leading also what both friends and protocol viewed as her existence 'en particulier'. Without overstressing the connection, it is clear that the 1728 *Office de la Semaine sainte* was associated with her and with her household, its notable ensuing popularity ceasing immediately after her death. The outstanding success of the book should, however, be seen not just as the result of this connection with this particular queen and with the court, but quite as much as the outcome of a whole web of interconnecting elements—the rising popular desire for vernacular versions of liturgical texts allowing for a more general comprehension of services, the power struggles current in contemporary ecclesiastical controversy, personal connections and interests within the Parisian book trade, contemporary fashion in the decorative arts, and technical innovation within the bookbinding trade. Even in the Age of Enlightenment the publication of religious works was the major element in the Parisian book trade, and, while only a diminutive percentage of this production survives, it can, on occasion, show what contemporary religious needs, both state and private, were and how they were satisfied. The centralized monarchy established in France in the seventeenth century turned even private worship into a state ceremony and required the participation of all major royal figures. In the earlier eighteenth century the personal character of the queen—for whom the religious life was far from being empty or irrelevant—maintained something of a living flame in an otherwise indifferent world where the king's mistress sought, not salvation but the recognition and accolade of being one of the queen's *entourage* at Mass. The offshoots of ostentation may sometimes reveal the underlying human needs and mark, like other decorative trends, emotional changes. Absolutism bridged the period from late medieval religious Europe to the turbulance of the democratic, free-thinking, nineteenth century. The forms of worship accompanying it had necessarily to mirror and move with, albeit slowly and in their own various ways, these changes.

5

A Quest for Peace in the Church: The Abbé A. J. C. Clément's Journey to Rome of 1758

JOHN ROGISTER

In 1758 the Abbé Augustin-Jean-Charles Clément, treasurer and canon of the cathedral of Auxerre, set out on the first of two journeys to Rome with the aim of inducing the papacy to bring lasting peace to the Gallican Church, torn by the disputes over the Bull *Unigenitus*, by means of a restatement of the fundamental doctrines of the Catholic Church. Pope Benedict XIV died on the eve of the abbé's departure, but, although this event constituted a set-back, Clément nevertheless left for Rome in the hope that the circumstances surrounding the election of a new pope would advance the cause to which he was prepared to devote energy, time, and money. He felt that his presence there at the time of the conclave might serve a useful purpose and that, if the right pope were elected, he might be willing to make the desired pronouncement.

I should like to thank Dott.ssa Mireille Gille Pirchio for all her help and collaboration over the years and for her assistance during my visits to Pisa to collect material either on Abbé Clément or on Abate Antonio Niccolini, on whose study we are at present engaged. I should also like to express my gratitude to the librarians of the Scuola Normale Superiore in Pisa, where I was a visiting professor in 1988 at the invitation of Professor Furio Diaz, and of the University La Sapienza of Pisa. In Rome my thanks are due to Professor Maria Sofia Corciulo and Professor Marta Pieroni Francini for their help at the Accademia dei Lincei. Dott.ssa Enrica Schettini Piazza, curator of the Fondo Corsini, greatly facilitated my work at the Corsiniana; I express my gratitude to her and her colleagues for their assistance at a library which is still housed in Palazzo Corsini, where Clément visited it. In Paris my thanks are due to my friend and colleague, Professor Bruno Neveu; and to Père Irénée Noye, who kindly allowed me to work on the Fonds Clément at the Bibliothèque du Séminaire de Saint Sulpice in the rue du Regard. I should like to pay tribute to the memory of two men: the late André Gazier, curator of the Bibliothèque de la Société de Port-Royal, who gave me a free access to the Le Paige Collection thirty years ago and who later facilitated my work there by enabling me to microfilm and photocopy documents; and the late Michel Bruguière, my colleague at the École Pratique des Hautes Études (IVème Section), who gave me an experience in serendipidity; through his hospitality and that of his wife at Le Mage, I discovered Feillet. Michel Bruguière also drew my attention to the work of Abbé Godet and lent me his copy of it. I am grateful to the Research Fund Committee of the University of Durham for assistance with travel grants that enabled me to work in Paris, Rome, and Pisa. The research on which this article was based was also facilitated by a grant from the Scouloudi Foundation in association with the Institute of Historical Research in London. Finally, I should like to thank Miss Wendy Duery, who produced an impeccable typescript.

Clément's unofficial mission of 1758 did not have its desired effect, despite the discreet support which it received from certain official circles and from the influential contacts which he had made in Italy. His subsequent visits to Spain in 1768 and again to Rome in 1769–70 (in the wake of another papal election) were also less successful than he had hoped. After his return to France from the last of these journeys and around 1775, Clément began drafting a detailed account of his travels. He collated his manuscript in September 1785. The Revolution intervened, and in April 1793 he confided the manuscript to the Jansenist lawyer, Louis-Adrien Le Paige. He thought parts of it could usefully be published one day, but felt that, in the meantime, there could be no better place for it than in Le Paige's extensive library.

The treasurer had resigned his post at Auxerre in 1786. In 1789 one of his two surviving brothers, Jean-Chrysostome-Antoine, had joined the Emigration. On the death of another brother, Athanase-Alexandre, in August 1793 he retired to Livry (it was from Livry that he had arranged for his manuscript to be sent to Le Paige). The following year, Livry was occupied by one of the *armées révolutionnaires* and Clément was arrested. He still cut an impressive figure; according to a contemporary observer, he was 'non seulement chrétien et pieux, mais riche et noble'. He was conveyed to Paris and imprisoned in the former house of the English Benedictines, where he remained from 18 February until 9 October 1794. After his release he stayed on in Paris and contributed to the re-establishment of the Catholic Church. When public worship was permitted once again in May 1795, only the church of Saint-Médard was made available to Clément and his followers. In April 1797 he secured his election to the vacant bishopric of Versailles. He professed his loyalty to Pope Pius VI, who died, a prisoner of the French, in 1799. When Bonaparte came to power, steps were taken to restore formal links between Church and State, leading to the Concordat of 1802. In August 1801 the 'constitutional', or elected, French bishops like Clément, meeting in a council, resigned their sees in order to facilitate the introduction of the Concordat and the creation of a new hierarchy. By that stage Clément had recuperated his manuscript and felt the need to publish it, albeit with a few significant omissions and amendments. His account of travels made almost half a century earlier appeared in three volumes in 1802 under the title *Journal de correspondances et voyages d'Italie et d'Espagne, pour la paix de l'Église, en 1758, 1768 et 1769. Par M. Clément, alors trésorier de l'Église d'Auxerre, et depuis évêque de Versailles.* The publisher was the Parisian printer L. F. Longuet of 2, rue des Fossés Saint-Jacques.[1] Clément died suddenly on

---

[1] Bibliothèque Nationale, Paris (hereafter BN), Imprimés, G 21545; vol. I (340 pp), II (405 pp), III (187 pp). This set comes from Bishop Henri Grégoire's bequest.

13 March 1804 aged 87. Although Le Paige, by then totally blind, had died two years previously, Clément's original manuscript was once again in his collection at the time of his death.[2]

From the *Journal de correspondances* it is possible to glean much interesting information about the conditions and hazards of travel in the mid-eighteenth century—from the prerequisites of a journey, like the use of letters of recommendation, of bankers, and of letters of exchange, to the choice of itineraries, to the hospitality and the impressions created by the discovery of foreign countries, of ancient Rome, and of its inhabitants and their customs. On another level, the *Journal de correspondances* provides a fascinating insight into the workings of the Roman Church. Only the first of Clément's journeys forms the subject of this study. His account of it occupies the first volume of his book, but further details are provided by the original manuscript (now in the Bibliothèque de la Société de Port-Royal, Paris[3]), by Clément's papers (at the Bibliothèque de l'Arsenal and the Bibliothèque du Séminaire de Saint-Sulpice, Paris[4]), and by the Bottari papers (kept in the Corsiniana, at the Accademia dei Lincei, Rome[5]). The particular interest of the account and papers relating to the 1758 journey lies in what they reveal about the conclave of that year and the intrigues to which it gave rise, as well as their descriptions of the Roman milieux into which Clément was drawn.

The *Ancien Régime* thrived on networks and relationships: the overt ones of family, of province, of profession; the covert ones of shared experience in college, in the regiment, in the seminary or cathedral chapter. Hence, some knowledge of Clément's background may be helpful. His family came originally from Arles and owed its fortune to the practice of medicine. Antoine Clément was an apothecary in the town, but it was his son, Julien (1648–1728), who set the

---

[2] Bibliothèque de la Société de Port-Royal, Paris (hereafter BPR), Collection Le Paige (hereafter LP), vol. 550: 'Voiages [*sic*] en Italie et en Espagne pour procurer la paix de l'Église par le concert général d'une *Exposition de Doctrine*, par M. L'Abbé Clément, Trésorier de l'Eglise d'Auxerre'. An instruction in Clément's hand (p. 34) concerning a note that should be at the bottom of the page implies that this MS copy was the one used by the printer (cf. *Journal de correspondances* (hereafter *Journal*), i. 50). The MS does not include the preface that is found in the printed edition. After the passage ending with the words 'voyage d'Italie' (*Journal*, i. 26), the MS has the date (crossed out) and reference 'A Paris, ce 9 mai 1775'. At the end of the 'Préliminaires' and before the 'Avertissement', Clément has written and signed: 'Collationé [s] Clément, 7bre 1785'. There are two inscriptions relating to the provenance of the MS: the first states 'Oratorii Parisiensis Catalogo inscriptus | Ex dono Autoris'; the second states in a different hand: 'Oratoire St Honoré'. The letter from Clément to Le Paige of 27 Apr. 1793 is pasted into the inside front cover. According to Augustin Gazier, *Histoire générale du mouvement Janséniste, depuis ses origines jusqu'à nos jours* (Paris, 1922). ii. 109 n. 1, Clément had originally donated his MS to the Oratoire of the Rue St Honoré. When the religious orders were dissolved Clément retrieved his MS and gave it to Le Paige.

[3] BPR, LP 550: 'Voiages en Italie', *passim*.

[4] In particular see Bibliothèque de l'Arsenal, Paris (hereafter BA), MS 11,883 (Papiers Clément); Bibliothèque du Séminaire de Saint-Sulpice Paris (hereafter BSS), MS 1293 (Fonds Clément): 'Collection. Tome V. Pièces recueillies 1754–1785'.

[5] Accademia dei Lincei, Rome (hereafter AL), Corsiniana, MS 31, E. 8.

family on the road to success and ennoblement. He was 'accoucheur et premier valet de chambre de la Dauphine'.[6] He brought the children of the duchesse de Burgundy into the world, including probably the future Louis XV. He became 'médecin ordinaire du roi' and was ennobled in 1711. By his second wife, who was one of his cousins, he had a son, Alexandre-Julien (1684–1747), who was styled *seigneur* of Blavette, Berville (or Barville), Feillet, and Bussy, which were all places in the Perche, near Longny and Nogent. He was a godson of Louis XIV and he became a councillor at the second chamber of the *enquêtes* of the *parlement* of Paris in 1711. The old king signed his contract of marriage in 1714 to Catherine, daughter of Ambroise Gaudrin, *seigneur* de la Poterie, 'garde-joyaux' to the duc de Berry.[7] There were ten children of the marriage, including four sons: Ambroise-Julien (1715–78), known as Clément de Feillet; Athanase-Alexandre (1716–93), known as Clément de Blavette, or again as Clément de Boissy; Augustin-Jean-Charles (1717–1804), known sometimes as Clément du Tremblé (or Tremblay), the subject of this study; and Jean-Chrysostome-Antoine, known as Clément de Barville, whose dates are unknown, though he died in exile during the Revolution. As Ambroise-Julien, Athanase-Alexandre, and Augustin-Jean-Charles were all born in successive years, and as their mother produced twins on three occasions, Jean-Chysostome-Antoine may have been a twin of one of the others, or else he was born between 1718 and his mother's death on 19 October 1721 at the age of 23.[8]

In 1717 Alexandre-Julien bought the land and castle of Feillet (now in the *département* of the Orne) from a fellow *parlementaire*, Victor Le Mée. He restored and rebuilt parts of the château. His wife had died in Paris and was buried in their parish church there, Saint-Paul, on the right bank.[9] Her heart was brought to Feillet and buried in the crypt of the chapel in the château. When Alexandre-Julien died, also in Paris, he was buried on the left bank, in the cemetery of the church of Saint-André-des-Arts on 25 January 1747, and his heart was placed alongside that of his wife at Feillet the following April, in the

---

[6] On the Clément family, see the entry under that name in J. François Bluche, *L'Origine des magistrats du Parlement de Paris (1715–1771): Dictionnaire généalogique* in *Paris et Ile-de-France: Mémoires publiés par la Fédération des sociétés historiques et archéologiques de Paris et de l'Ile-de-France*, v–vi (Paris, 1953–4 [1956]), 135–6.

[7] Abbé Godet, *Mémoires sur les paroisses du Mage et de Feillet*, in *Documents sur la province du Perche*, 2nd ser., v (Mortagne, 1897–1903), 53, 150–1. I remain grateful to the late Michel Bruguière for bringing this work to my attention.

[8] Ibid. 53, 150–1 n. 1; see also [Saillant], *Mémoires secrets sur la vie de M. Clément, évêque de Versailles pour servir à l'histoire ecclésiastique du 18ème siècle* (Paris, 1812), 10: Saillant claims that Clément had three brothers; in fact he had four surviving brothers.

[9] Godet, *Mémoires*, 53. The church of St Paul, which was situated in the vicinity of the present 34, rue St Paul, was destroyed in 1796; see Yvan Christ, *Églises parisiennes actuelles et disparues* (Paris, 1947), 38 and pl. 78.

presence of his sons. A convex heart-shaped marble slab with a Latin inscription set in the wall of the chapel above the crypt still commemorates the event.[10]

The family was Jansenist. Alexandre-Julien's eldest son, Ambroise-Julien Clément de Feillet, was a councillor in the second chamber of the *enquêtes* like his father. He acquired the reputation of being a *zélé* in the course of the religious and procedural disputes of the 1750s.[11] Athanase-Alexandre Clément de Boissy (or de Blavette) was a humanist and scholar who became a member of another court, the *Chambre des Comptes* of Paris. During the period 1745–90, when he was a *maître des comptes*, he undertook the task of providing a guide to its records. From 1763 onwards, and with the assistance of his son and of four clerks, whom he paid out of his own pocket, he produced eighty volumes in folio and 50,000 extracts from the records. This collection was kept in boxes and used by the *Chambre des Comptes* on a daily basis.[12] Jean-Chysostome Clément de Barville, comte de Montgommery in Normandy, was a lawyer about whom little is known.

Augustin-Jean-Charles Clément du Tremblé was born at Créteil near Paris on 8 September 1717. He studied the humanities and law and chose to go into the Church. What is known about him comes not only from his *Journal de correspondances* and his papers, but also from the *Mémoires secrets sur la vie de M. Clément, évêque de Versailles, pour servir à l'histoire ecclésiastique de 18ème siècle* published in Paris in 1812. According to a note in the hand of Bishop Grégoire on the title-page of his copy (now in the Bibliothèque Nationale), the author of this work was Saillant, described as 'curé de Villiers-le-Bel, prêtre savant et très vertueux'.[13] There is a suggestion in the work that Saillant may have met Clément when they were both imprisoned in Paris in 1794.[14] According to Saillant, Clément received the tonsure with other clerks of the parish of Saint-Germain in Paris. He had not been required to sign the famous anti-Jansenist formulary required of all those going into holy orders, because Martin, the archbishop's secretary with responsibility for the clerks, did not exact the signature very strictly. Nevertheless, Archbishop de Vintimille was not prepared to allow Clément to proceed to the subdiaconate in 1740. This rejection earned the

---

[10] Godet, *Mémoires*, 151 n. 1, gives the text of the inscription. I should like to express my thanks to Comtesse Pierre de Laguiche, owner of the château de Feillet, who kindly showed me the inscription in 1983.

[11] On his activities in the *parlement* of Paris, see Dale Van Kley, *The Jansenists and the Expulsion of the Jesuits from France, 1759–1765* (New Haven, 1975), 44, 67, 115; and John Rogister, *Louis XV and the Parlement of Paris 1737–1755* (Cambridge, 1995), 20, 133–5, 195–6, 200.

[12] *Si la Révolution m'était comptée: Le Contrôle des finances publiques de la Monarchie à la République*, Association des Magistrats de la Cour des Comptes; catalogue de l'exposition, 17–29 novembre 1989 (Paris, 1989), 44.

[13] Saillant's work is bound with Grégoire's set of the *Journal de correspondances*. BN, Imprimés, G 21545. Villiers-le-Bel was a Jansenist parish north of Paris.

[14] [Saillant], *Mémoires secrets*, 45.

young man a letter of sympathy from the exiled Bishop Soanen of Senez, the standard-bearer of the Jansenist cause.[15] Rejected by Vintimille, Clément was taken under the wing of another Jansenist stalwart, Bishop de Caylus of Auxerre.[16] He was made a canon of Saint-Etienne of Auxerre on 17 December 1741 and finally ordained under that title as subdeacon on 21 September 1743. He became a deacon on 4 April 1744 and attained the priesthood in September of the same year.[17]

Ecclesiastical life at Auxerre in the late 1740s was tranquil and similar to that of Angers which John McManners has so evocatively described in his classic work.[18] Clément became the treasurer of the Chapter. In that capacity he showed zeal in his efforts to secure recognition for the relics of Saint-Germain, which had been removed by the Calvinists in 1569 and rediscovered in 1717. He maintained that the rediscovered relics were authentic in a controversy with Dom Vidal.[19] His circumstances changed, however, when Bishop de Caylus died on 2 April 1754. Although the treasurer administered the diocese while the see was vacant, he had little cause to be satisfied with the appointment of the successor to Caylus. Jacques-Marie de Caritat de Condorcet was made bishop on 16 December and soon revealed himself to be an active opponent of Jansenism.[20]

Bishop de Caylus had been in regular corrrespondence with Giovanni Gaetano Bottari, scholar, antiquary, keeper of the Vatican Library, and also a Jansenist.[21] Shortly before his death, the bishop had asked Clément to continue this correspondence for him, as well as another with Cardinal delle Lanze, scion of an illegitimate branch of the House of Savoy and grand almoner of Sardinia, resident in Turin.[22] In Clément's papers there are two interesting descriptions of Bottari dating from 1754. Perhaps the treasurer had felt the need to know more

[15] Ibid. 15. The letter from Soanen of 12 Feb. 1740 is printed in *La Vie et les lettres de Messire Jean Soanen, Evêque de Senez* (2 vols.; Cologne, 1750), ii. 74: letter no. 1567.

[16] Daniel-Charels-Gabriel de Tubières de Caylus (1669–1754); educated at the Jesuit college of Louis-le-Grand; doctor of the Sorbonne; bishop of Auxerre 1705–54; last *appelant* of the Bull *Unigenitus*; uncle of the artist and collector Anne-Claude-Philippe. comte de Caylus (1692–1765).

[17] [Saillant], *Mémoires secrets*, 16.

[18] John McManners, *French Ecclesiastical Society under the Ancien Régime: A Study of Angers in the Eighteenth Century* (Manchester, 1960); see, on Jansenism, pp. 9–11; on Auxerre, see P. Ordioni, *La Résistance gallicane et janséniste dans le diocèse d'Auxerre* (Paris, 1932), *passim*.

[19] [Saillant], *Mémoires secrets*, 17. On Saint-Germain, bishop of Auxerre, who visited Britain in AD 429 with the aim of combating Pelagianism, see E. A. Thompson, *Saint Germanus of Auxerre and the End of Roman Britain* (Woodbridge, 1985).

[20] *Journal*, i. 150. Bishop de Caylus died on 2 Apr. 1754. Jacques-Marie de Caritat de Condorcet (1703–83), bishop of Gap, 1741–54; bishop of Auxerre 1754–61; exiled Nov. 1756, translated to the see of Lisieux (where there were few Jansenists), 1761; uncle of the *philosophe*.

[21] *Journal*, i. 15. Giovanni Gaetano Bottari (1689–1775); apart from the entry on him in the *Dizionario biografico degli italiani*, see also R. Palozzi, 'Mons. Giovanni Bottari et il circolo dei giansenisti romani', in *Annali della R. Scuola Normale Superiore di Pisa*, 2nd series, x (1941–XX), 70–90, 199–220.

[22] Vittorio-Amadeo, cardinal delle Lanze (1712–84); son of Carlo-Agostino delle Lanze (c.1668–1749), a bastard of Carlo-Emanuele II, duke of Savoy.

about a correspondent with whom he was personally unacquainted. The first description, dated 12 May 1754, is in the hand of Abbé Cossoni, chaplain to Cardinal de Polignac (French ambassador in Rome 1724–32). Cossoni wrote:

M l'abbé Bottari est homme d'honneur et de mérite. Il a élevé M le prince Corsini, père des princes du même nom qui voyagent aujourd'huy en différentes cours de l'Europe. Cette maison a marqué de tout tems une grande et juste considération pour M Bottari, et Clément XII, oncle du prince, l'éleva au grade de prélat domestique. Il fut ensuite garde de la Bibliothèque du Vatican après la mort de M Maiella.

Ce poste convient parfaitment à M Bottari qui n'a de goût que pour l'érudition et la belle Littérature. Peu d'hommes en Italie sçavent l'italien aussi parfaitement que lui. Il a eu la plus grande part à la dernière édition du *Dizzionario della Crusca*. On a vu l'année passée dans les journaux une sçavante Notice des antiquitez que le pape d'aujourd'huy a ramassées dans le Capitoles [*sic*], dont M Bottari est autheur.

J'ai dit d'abord que c'est un homme d'honneur et cela est vrai dans toute l'étendue du mot. Il m'est bien connu, ainsi qu'à nos amis de là bas sous cette qualité.[23]

Cossoni's last observation related to the Jansenist milieu to which he and Bottari belonged. Bottari was the central figure in the Jansenist circle in Rome that was closely linked with the princely household of the Corsinis. Bottari lived in a house attached to Palazzo Corsini in the Lungara, and his circle was known as that of the Archetto. Like the Corsinis, Bottari and his friends, who included the patrician *abate marchese* Antonio Niccolini (whose brother had married a Corsini) and the theologian Foggini, were Florentines.[24] Another letter, dating from December 1754 and unfortunately incomplete, from another of Clément's correspondents, describes Bottari and his circle at that time:

Voici ce que je sais de M l'abbé Bottari. Il est sous le Cardinal Passionei un des gardes de la Bibliothèque de Vatican. L'autre garde est M Assamani, autre homme fort célèbre. Outre cela [il] est chapelain du pape et chanoine. Il jouit de 24,000 livres de revenu et il en a fait un très bon usage, car il distribue abondamment aux pauvres. Il a à sa table M Fogniani [*sic*] qui a donné les deux volumes de St Augustin, et il l'a fait nommer à la survivance de sa place de garde de la Bibliothèque. Outre le confessional, auquel il se prête, il s'occupe beaucoup au travail, et il a donné au public plusieurs ouvrages qui l'ont fait connaître. Ses liaisons sont principalement avec les cardinaux Passionei, Tamburini et Orsini [*sic*], et il a élevé celui-ci dont on dit beaucoup de bien; car ce cardinal est resté diacre, sans vouloir être prêtre, et cela par humilité.[25]

---

[23] BA, MS 11,883 (Papiers Clément), fos. 1–2: letter of 12 May 1754. Abbé Cossoni died at Utrecht c.1764.

[24] On the world of Italian Jansenism, see Palozzi, 'Mons. Giovanni Bottari'; N. Rodolico, *Stato e chiesa durante le reggenza lorenese* (Florence, 1910); Enrico Dammig, *Il movimento giansenista a Roma nella seconda meta del secolo xviii* (Vatican, 1945); Charles A. Bolton, *Church Reform in 18th Century Italy* (The Hague, 1969); and John Rogister, 'Jansénistes français et italiens au dix-huitième siècle', in *Bulletin de la société d'histoire moderne*, 16th ser., 23 (1984), 2–9.

[25] BSS, MS 1293 (Fonds Clément), no. 1: incomplete letter of 1 Dec. [1754] from an unidentified correspondent.

Two of the cardinals mentioned here, Passionei and Tamburini, had, together with Cardinal Neri Corsini, been singled out to Bishop de Caylus by Bottari as the only ones who read any good books or were enlightened. Only Tamburini, he added, perfectly understood Augustinianism and could sustain an argument about it. He dismissed the other cardinals as Molinists who were without any understanding of the Molinist, Thomist, or Augustinian systems.[26]

The correspondence between Clément and Bottari seems to have begun at the end of May 1754. Bottari wrote in Italian and, at the outset, Clément had some difficulty with that language. Later, one of the advantages which Clément hoped to derive from his journey to Italy was an improvement in his command of the language. His growing links with Bottari convinced him that he could go to Rome if the need arose and that he would find his stay there pleasant. Because of his problems with his new bishop, Clément could not foresee when that visit would take place.[27] During 1755 and 1756 his correspondence with Bottari turned chiefly on the development of the religious disputes within the French Church. In explaining the origins of Clément's visit to Rome in 1758, too much emphasis has usually been placed on the role of the prince de Conty's agent, the Jansenist lawyer, Louis-Adrien Le Paige, and insufficient attention given to the earlier links between Bottari and Clément in 1755–7.[28] The treasurer kept Bottari informed at the end of 1755 of the moves made by the official Clergy of France.[29] His correspondence also reveals that both men perceived a need to educate their fellow Catholics in sound religious doctrine in the midst of what Clément saw as a general decline in the quality of public education in France.[30] He informed Bottari, for instance, that a much-needed translation of the lesser works of St Augustine was under way.[31] The general theological climate in Italy was far more conducive to progress being made in this direction than it was in France: 'votre Italie', he told Bottari in July 1755, 'semble être aujourdhuy l'unique azile où la vérité se soit retirée, encore pour quelques jours de la vie du St Père.'[32]

On 24 November 1755 Clément sent Bottari a copy of the conflicting sets of

---

[26] BA, MS 11,883, fo. 3: Bottari to Caylus, Rome, 13 Apr. 1754: the letter arrived after the death of the bishop. On Cardinal Domenico Passionei (1682–1761), see Alberto Caracciolo, *Domenico Passionei tra Roma e la Repubblica delle lettere* (Rome, 1968); and Elio Sgreccia, 'Card. Domenico Passionei dall'incontro con i benedettini di S. Mauro a Parigi (1706) alla residenza nel romitorio di Camaldoli e Frascati (1761): Profili culturale e momenti polemici', in *Atti de I Convegno del Centro di Studi Avellaniti: Ascetica cristiana et ascetica giansenista e quietista nelle regioni d'influenza Avellanita* (Fonte Avellana, 1977), 27–109). Cardinal Fortunato Tamburini (b. *c.*1683) came from Modena and had been a Benedictine at Monte-Cassino; he was made a cardinal by Benedict XIV, 1743. On Cardinal Neri Corsiui, see n. 92 below.

[27] BA, MS 11,883. fo. 5: Bottari to Clément, Rome, 29 May 1754; *Journal*, i. 16.

[28] Dale Van Kley, *The Jansenists and the Expulsion of the Jesuits from France*, 73.

[29] AL, Corsiniana, MS 31, E. 8, fo. 375ʳ: Clément to Bottari, Auxerre, 28 Dec. 1755.

[30] Ibid., fo. 374ʳ: Clément to Bottari, 21 July 1755.

[31] Ibid., fo. 375ʳ: letter of 28 Dec. 1755.   [32] Ibid., letter of 21 July 1755.

articles which the contending parties in the Assembly of the Clergy wished to submit to the pope for his decision.[33] The king had not wanted the Assembly to send the articles as they stood. Hence, a collective letter to the pope on behalf of the bishops had been drafted in which he was asked for a decision on the articles. The text of this letter was handed to the king on 31 October; after having studied it, Louis XV was to forward it to the pope. The king sent it to the pope only on 19 December.[34] In the meantime, Clément had already sent the text of the articles to Bottari. Benedict XIV felt unable to decide the matter without reference to a consistory. The French ambassador in Rome, the Comte de Stainville, had been able to ensure that the composition of the consistory would be 'satisfactory'. The pope chose Cardinals Passionei, Landi, Tamburini, Galli, and Valenti.[35] Two of them, Passionei and Tamburini, had Jansenist tendencies, as it has already been noted. A printed copy of the bishops' collective letter to the pope had already been denounced at the *parlement* of Paris in December. The denunciation gave the *parlementaires* the opportunity to adopt nine points which helped to sustain the stand which the king wanted to adopt on the articles of the clergy. Clément implied to Bottari on 23 December that these measures had been taken in concert with Louis XV.[36]

The tripartite conflict between the court, the *parlement*, and the *Grand Conseil* in the last months of 1755 and early weeks of 1756 had led to a rift between Louis XV and his secret adviser, the prince de Conty. However, the rift was healed, and this event provided Clément with an opportunity to inform Bottari of his own indirect links with the prince. He wrote on 8 March 1756: 'j'apprens avec plaisir qu'il [Conty] a recommencé à travailler avec le Roy. C'est pourquoy on me prie de continuer de mettre votre prétieuse relation, Monseigneur, sur la réponse que les évêques attendent du Pape. On m'ajoute que les partisans du schisme ne cessent de quêter de tous côtés des signatures, qu'ils en acquièrent continuellement par le retard de la réponse . . . '.[37] Who were these intermediaries covered by the use of the word 'on'? They probably included the treasurer's brother, Clément de Feillet, and another *parlementaire*, President de Murard, who was attached to Conty's household, as well as Le Paige, who was himself the

[33] Ibid., fo. 376[r-v]: Clément to Bottari, Auxerre, 23 Dec. 1755 (with references to earlier letters of 17 and 24 Nov. and 2 Dec.).

[34] Maurice Boutry, *Choiseul à Rome 1754–1757: Lettres et mémoires inédits* (Paris, 1895), 58–9 n. 2 (letter to the pope), and 67 n. 1 (text of the king's letter to the pope of 19 Dec. 1755).

[35] Ibid. 65 n. 1: text of Benedict XIV's note to Stainville of Sunday [30 Nov. 1755].

[36] AL, Corsiniana, MS 31, E. 8, fos. 376[v]–377[r]; letter of 23 Dec. 1755: 'Enfin le Parlement veilloit de près et sous main concertoit avec soin ce qui convenoit le mieux au Roy à cet égard; les 9 articles que je joins icy et que le Roy a reçus le 18 de ce mois sont le résultat de ces sages démarches.' The correspondence between Clément and Bottari suffered delays, in part because Clément chose to send his letters by sea via Marseilles. In February 1756 he resolved to send them by the land route, with the added precaution of placing them inside a second envelope addressed to Bottari's superior at the Vatican Library, Cardinal Passionei: MS 31, E. 8, fo. 383[r]: Clément to Bottari, Auxerre, 10 Feb. 1756.

[37] AL, Corsiniana, MS 31, E. 8, fo. 387[r]: Clément to Bottari, Auxerre, 8 Mar. 1756.

bailli of the Temple and therefore linked to Conty as well in his capacity as grand prior of the French branch of the Order of Malta.[38]

For his part, Bottari kept Clément informed of developments in Rome, although it was Clément who told him the reasons for the pope's delay in responding to the king's request of 19 December. The treasurer's intermediaries had told him that the pope's reply would be conditioned by the views of the French court.

Le St Père travaille à l'importante réponse, au point de déranger ses audiances; il a peut-être déja fait un *poco di bozza*, mais sa réponse ne sera pas telle que vous la souhaîteriez: *non sara ottima*. La bulle fait un point de vue dont il ne peut se départir; mais elle n'aquérera [*sic*] aucun avantage. Nous savons d'autre part que la cour sollicite par Mr l'ambassadeur une très promte [*sic*] réponse, sans trop d'égard à nos maximes.[39]

The reason for the sudden impatience at Versailles was the rallying of support for *Unigenitus* among the ranks of the episcopate. On 24 March Bottari wrote to say that a draft of the pope's reply had been sent off four days earlier.[40] The information was correct.

In his draft reply the pope gave the king the choice between a new bull or an encyclical letter to the French bishops. The advantage to Louis XV of the second alternative was that such a letter did not have to be registered at the *parlement*.[41] Louis XV had arrived at this view after consulting, not only his ministers, but also the prelates and magistrates who made up the commission which he had set up in 1752 to advise him on the possibility of ending the disputes about *Unigenitus* by means of a new law.[42] Their views, favourable to the idea of an encyclical

---

[38] Louis-Adrien Le Paige (1712–1802), lawyer at the *parlement*; *bailli* of the Temple; *commissaire* of the *parlement* to examine the content of the first four volumes of the *Encyclopédie* in the light of the court's decision to proceed against that work and its authors, 1759. There is no full biography or study of this influential figure and prolific writer: see Augustin Gazier, *Histoire du mouvement Janséniste*, ii. 51, 111–12; Cécile Gazier, *Histoire de la Société et de la Bibliothèque de Port-Royal* (Paris, 1966), 24–7; John Rogister, 'Louis Adrien Lepaige and the attack on *De l'esprit* and the *Encyclopédie* in 1759', in *English Historical Review*, 92 (1977), 522–39. Le Paige was the author of the *Lettres historiques sur les fonctions essentielles du Parlement* (2 vols.; 'Amsterdam', 1753–4), and he provided material for the drafting of the 'Law of silence' of 1754.

[39] AL, Corsiniana, MS 31, E. 8, fo. 391ʳ: Clément to Bottari, Auxerre, 22 Mar. 1756.

[40] BA, MS 11,883, no. 62: Bottari to Clément, Rome, 24 Mar. 1756; see also Boutry, *Choiseul à Rome*, 113 n. 1 (for the text of Benedict XIV's letter to Louis XV of 20 Mar. 1756).

[41] Paul Nau, 'A l'origine des encycliques modernes: un épisode de la lutte des Évêques et des Parlements 1755–1756', in *Revue historique*, 4th ser., 33 (1953), 225–67, at 253.

[42] The members of the commission were: Cardinal F. J. de La Rochefoucauld (1701–57), archbishop of Bourges and former ambassador to Rome; Cardinal A. de Soubise (1717–56), bishop of Strasbourg; Cardinal N. C. de Saulx-Tavannes (1690–1759), archbishop of Rouen; J. F. J. de Rochchouart-Faudoas (1708–77), bishop-duke of Laon, ambassador to Rome, 1757; P. Gilbert de Voisins (1684–1769), D. C. Trudaine (1703–69), G. Castanier d'Auriac (1702–65), and J. L. Bidé de La Grandville (1688–1760), four *conseillers d'État*. On the work of this commission in 1752 when G. F. Joly de Fleury (1675–1756) was still a member of it, see Rogister, *Louis XV and the Parlement of Paris*, 122–4.

letter, were sent to Stainville on 14 May 1756.[43] Upon receipt of the memoranda from Versailles, the pope sent them to the cardinals whom he was consulting on the affair. Benedict XIV sent his observations to Louis XV on 18 July. There was a hardening of the position in Rome, because the pope now asked that the encyclical letter and accompanying brief addressed to the king should be buttressed by 'le secours de l'autorité royale'.[44] The effect of these observations was to induce further delays at the French court while the king again consulted his advisers. Nothing had been sent back to Rome by the time of the sudden death of Cardinal Valenti, the secretary of state, on 28 August. His successor, Cardinal Archinto, was expected by the French to be less cooperative, but their fears proved unfounded. At last, on 14 September, the king's reply was sent off. Louis XV asked for some modifications to be made to the draft of the encyclical. Before this request reached Rome, however, Christophe de Beaumont, archbishop of Paris and scourge of the Jansenists, stole a march on both the pope and the king by issuing a pastoral instruction on 19 September threatening with excommunication those who refused to accept *Unigenitus* and any magistrates who tried to compel priests to administer the sacrament to them.[45] Although Beaumont was in exile, his dramatic intervention was well timed and it served to complicate the action of both Louis XV and Benedict XIV. As Mme de Pompadour explained to Stainville on 17 October: 'L'Archevêque a été poussé à la démarche imprudente qu'il a faite par les évêques violents qui ont craint qu'il ne se soumit à la décision que le Pape va envoyer, et qui ont voulu tellement embrouiller les affaires, qu'il ne fût plus possible de se servir de l'autorité du Saint Siège. Ces motifs ne sont rien moins que célestes, mais au contraire de pure intrigue et par des vues très humaines.'[46] Clément was equally scathing in his indictment of the bishops who had inspired or supported Beaumont's move: 'Neuf évêques se sont déclarés unis à la même cause: Cambray, Bordeaux, Tours, Chartres, Mets [*sic*] et Verdun, Viviers, Sarlat et Lescar: presque tous la honte du clergé de nos jours, ou par une vie mondaine ou toute charnelle, ou par la plus crasse ignorance.'[47] These bishops had been exiled by the king.[48]

The encyclical letter, entitled *Ex omnibus*, was at last ready on 16 October. The following day, the parcel containing it, together with a papal brief and a personal letter, both addressed by the pope to the king, were dispatched from

[43] Nau, 'A l'origine des encycliques', 251–4.

[44] Boutry, *Choiseul à Rome*, 163–4 n. 1: text of Benedict XIV's letter to Louis XV, 18 July 1756.

[45] [Christophe de Beaumont], *Mandement et Instruction Pastorale de Monseigneur l'Archevêque de Paris, touchant l'autorité de l'Église, l'enseignement de la Foi, l'administration des Sacremens, la soumission due à la Constitution Unigenitus, portant défense de lire plusieurs Écrits* (A Paris, 1756), 273.

[46] Général de Piépape, 'Lettres de Mme de Pompadour au Comte de Stainville (Choiseul) Ambassadeur (1754–1757)', in *Revue d'histoire de Versailles et de Seine-et-Oise* (1917), 174.

[47] AL, Corsiniana, MS 31, E. 8, fo. 492ʳ: Clément to Bottari, Auxerre, 26 Oct. 1755.

[48] *Journal*, i. 21.

Rome. In the brief Benedict XIV asked the king to give the support of his full authority to the encyclical and to the protection of the jurisdiction of the Church.[49] Louis XV received the parcel on 27 October and immediately gave the required undertaking that the encyclical would be backed by the force of his authority.[50] There remained difficulties. *Ex omnibus* was addressed to the French bishops. In order to ensure secrecy, Louis XV had obtained the pope's agreement for the encyclical to be printed in Paris and transmitted directly to the bishops. From Auxerre, on 26 October, Clément had expressed his delight at the outcome in a letter to Bottari:

Vous ne sauriés [*sic*] croire, Monsieur, quelle sensible consolation nous donne l'assurance de votre part de l'existence du Bref en réponse du Pape à nos évêques dans le goust [*sic*] de la Déclaration de 1754, fruit d'une négociation personelle du Roy avec le St Père par son ambassadeur, car la politique de prince, extrémement rafinée [*sic*], l'a tenu depuis son arrivée icy [*sic*] si secret et si renfermé dans l'usage auquel il l'a apparement destiné.[51]

His enthusiasm was premature, as, at the time when he wrote his letter, the parcel from Rome had not yet reached the king. Clément was certain of its arrival only on 16 November, two days after Louis XV had dispatched the printed copies of the encyclical letter to each bishop under the seal of secrecy.[52] Although he was initially disappointed with the brief, Clément later came to recognize, in his *Journal de correspondances*, Benedict XIV's laudable aim of pacifying the disputes within the Gallican Church by minimizing the importance of the crime committed by those who opposed *Unigenitus*.[53] The respect which necessarily surrounded the Bull created a risk that resistance to it might result in a failure to submit to the authority of the Church. The pope wanted the bishops to look at cases individually and to take into account the inner motivation of such resistance, which might stem from a rightful or sincere fear of condemning holy doctrines.

To this analysis of *Ex omnibus* could be added other considerations. The pope

---

[49] Nau, 'A l'origine des encycliques', 255–6; Boutry, *Choiseul à Rome*, 185 n. 1.

[50] Boutry, *Choiseul à Rome*, 186 n. 1: extract from a letter from Rouillé (minister of foreign affairs) to Stainville, 1 Nov. 1756.

[51] AL, Corsiniana, MS 31, E. 8, fo. 401ʳ: Clément to Bottari, 26 Oct. 1755.

[52] Ibid., fo. 404ʳ: Clément to Bottari, Auxerre, 16 Nov. 1756; Nau, 'A l'origine des encycliques', 256–7.

[53] Clément was initially disappointed with the brief, and he told Bottari that Machault, the keeper of the seals, had been responsible for a decision which, in the treasurer's view, favoured the archbishop of Paris. Machault had thus vented his anger on the *parlementaires* for their recent remonstrances: 'On le sait de bonne part. Il [Machault] a fait illusion au Pape sur le succès d'un tel Bref par le canal de M. l'ambassadeur [Stainville]. Réuni icy aux autres ministres, il a surpris l'agrément du Roy pour l'envoyer aux Evêques, en lui faisant peur de l'Éclat des Excommunications que le Ministère a favorisé sous main' (AL, Corsiniana, MS 31, E. 8, fo. 407ʳ: Clément to Bottari, 23 Nov. 1756). In the present state of research it is not possible to confirm these allegations, which Clément did not repeat in his analysis of the brief in the *Journal* (cf. i. 20).

did not define *Unigenitus* as a 'rule of faith' or as 'a judgement of the Universal Church in matters of doctrine'. He maintained that, in effect, the sacrament could be denied only to those who publicly and 'notoriously' opposed the Bull, and not, therefore, to those who simply did not submit to it. Moreover, Benedict XIV qualified the right to deny the sacrament to the 'réfractaires publics et notoires' by setting sensible guidelines for the conduct of bishops in such cases.[54]

Louis XV honoured his undertaking to the pope by forcing through the *parlement* of Paris a *déclaration* that gave effect to the pontiff's decision. The first article of the new law enjoined the respect and submission that were due to the Bull *Unigenitus*, while declaring that the Bull could not be given the 'denomination, character, or effects of a rule of faith'. In the second article the king renewed the law of silence without, however, citing the *déclaration* of 2 September 1754 and also without prejudice to the right of the episcopate to teach matters of faith.[55] As Louis XV and Stainville had always found the pope willing to accept, as the basis of discussion, the principle that *Unigenitus* was not a 'rule of faith', that principle had been incorporated into the new law. Although the pope had shown his drafts to the king, the king had not shown his draft *déclaration* to the pope. Benedict XIV had reservations about a stipulation that was not included in *Ex omnibus*. Although he later endorsed the view that *Unigenitus* was not a 'rule of faith', he did so at a secret consistory.[56] Moreover, it was clear that, under the pretext of exercising the right to teach matters of faith, some bishops could continue to hound opponents of the Bull.

The *déclaration* of 10 December 1756 was deemed unacceptable by the *parlementaires*, partly on account of its second article and partly because it had been imposed at a *lit de justice*. A majority of the *parlementaires* had at once resigned. Damiens's attempt on the life of Louis XV further emphasized the failure of the measures taken to bring peace to the Gallican Church. The would-be assassin had clearly been influenced by the religious disputes, albeit in a vague, uninformed, way. Jansenists and supporters of the Jesuits accused each other of being his accomplices. With the entry of the Abbé Comte de Bernis into the royal council the day before the attempt on the king's life, and the dismissal of the rival ministers Machault and D'Argenson from their posts in February, there came the prospect of new initiatives by the government to resolve the disputes. Little was done, however, until after the resumption by the *parlement* of its duties in August and the subsequent replacement of First President de Maupeou by President Molé.

---

[54] The text of the encyclical letter *Ex omnibus* is reproduced in Boutry, *Choiseul à Rome*, 319–27; see also BN, Cabinet des MSS, Collection Joly de Fleury, vol. 570, fo. 390: memorandum on *Ex omnibus* by Jean-Omer Joly de Fleury, *premier avocat général* of the *parlement* of Paris.

[55] Ibid. (memorandum by J. O. Joly de Fleury).   [56] *Journal*, i. 21.

The king's speech to the reassembled *parlementaires* on 1 September 1757 reduced the *déclaration* of 10 December 1756 to the equivalent of a law of silence.[57] The *déclaration* was registered again with some complex modifications. The result was that it was deemed to have been abolished save in three important respects. The first article with its stipulation that *Unigenitus* could not have the denomination, character, or effects of a rule of faith remained in force. The second article imposing silence also remained in force, as well as the last part of the third article, which, in general terms, allowed magistrates to punish those who had rendered themselves guilty of unspecified offences in the course of the administration or the refusal of the sacrament.[58] In other respects the 1756 *déclaration* was held to be void. Nevertheless, uncertainty remained concerning the extent of the submission which the faithful were expected to display towards *Unigenitus* and the possibility for Jansenists of teaching the Augustinian corpus of theology.

With the Jesuits already in retreat over the condemnation of the second volume of Berruyer's *Histoire du peuple de Dieu* in 1756, and also in trouble with the king of Portugal, their Jansenist opponents seized their opportunity.[59] Their aim was chiefly to bring about peace within the Church through the clear restatement of its fundamental doctrines. It has been claimed that the move originated with Le Paige, responding to information received from Rome by his friend, Abbé Gourlin, a theological adviser to the pro-Jansenist Bishop FitzJames of Soissons.[60] Clément himself claimed that the move began with a letter of 29 November 1757 which he had received from another theologian, the Abbé Coudrette, who conveyed the same information, while at the same time asking Clément to tell Bottari that attempts by the pope to give new definitions to *Unigenitus* would only create problems, whereas an exposé of sound Church doctrine would achieve much good. Coudrette's informant in Italy was Monsignor Gasparo Cerati, commander of the Order of Santo Stefano and rector of the University of Pisa.[61] In Paris Coudrette, so he told Clément on 12 December, had seen Le Paige and Clément de Feillet; the first was going to act on the prince de Conty and the second on First President Molé. Coudrette also took Clément de Feillet to see Bishop FitzJames on 9 January 1758. It was in mid-February that

[57] BPR, LP 562, no. 176: note in the hand of L. A. Le Paige dated 25 Jan. 1767.

[58] Ibid. See also a note in French explaining the legal position in an unidentified hand addressed to Bottari on 12 Sept [1757]: AL, Corsiniana, MS 31, E. 8, fo. 483[r–v].

[59] Van Kley, *The Jansenists and the Expulsion of the Jesuits*, 74.

[60] Ibid. 73–5.

[61] *Journal*, i. 28–30; Gazier, *Histoire générale du mouvement Janséniste*, ii. 110–11. Abbé Christophe Coudrette (1701–74), known also as Le Prieur, an appellation which Clément gave him in his letters from Italy, had been a correspondent of Bishop de Caylus. On Gasparo Cerati (1690–1774), see Niccola Carranza, *Monsignor Gaspare Cerati provveditore dell'Università di Pisa nel Settecento delle riforme* (Pisa, 1974).

Le Paige and President de Murard thought of persuading Louis XV to reopen negotiations with Benedict XIV to obtain a new bull.[62] On 16 February Cerati wrote directly to Clément also suggesting that the French court should encourage the pope to reject publicly the definition of *Unigenitus* as a rule of faith, especially as the king had banned its use in what remained of the 1756 *déclaration*. Cerati urged Clément to come to Rome, a journey which would hold considerable advantages: 'Faites donc, Monsieur, tous les efforts pour exécuter ce proiet [*sic*] sans délai, parcequ'il vous seroit d'une grande instruction d'être présent à un conclave qui ne peut pas être éloigné et au commencement d'un nouveau pontificat.'[63] Cerati offered the hospitality of his house in Pisa (November to May) or in Florence (June to November). The initiative had come from Italy, and Clément was among the first, if not the first, to be approached.

A more significant point that needs to be made, however, is that the plan was adopted by others who could not be described as Jansenists: First President Molé, the Abbé Comte de Bernis, who had become minister of foreign affairs, and Louis XV himself, whose constant support for the project of approaching the pope anew was later stressed by Clément himself in his *Journal de correspondances*.[64] Le Paige prepared a lengthy memoir for the king, which was corrected by Molé and Murard on 13 April, and delivered to Bernis on 30 April. Le Paige's stated aim in the memoir was to obtain from the Pope a brief or a bull. Such a statement would declare 'd'une manière nette et précise et distincte, quels sont les articles de doctrine qu'on doit croire, ou au moins qu'on peut légitimement tenir, et quelles sont les erreurs qu'on doit rejetter, sur les matières doctrinales qui, par tant d'accusations vagues et indéterminées, sont devenues depuis un siècles [*sic*] l'occasion de tous les troubles; par cela seul, tout sera pleinement éclairci'.[65] Le Paige and the Abbé Gourlin busied themselves with making changes to the draft of a papal bull prepared by an earlier Jansenist theologian, Boursier, in 1724. On 12 May President du Murard took this corrected version to First President Molé, only to be told that a special courier had just brought the king the news that the pope had died on 3 May.[66]

The death of Benedict XIV spelled the end of the project, but Le Paige, Murard, and the First President met at the house of Clément de Feillet on 13 May and decided that the Abbé Clément should go to Rome for the sake of his health and also to form links in Rome which could be useful in the future and to send back 'portraits and characters' of the various cardinals, now that they were

---

[62] Van Kley, *The Jansenists and the Expulsion of the Jesuits*, 73.

[63] BA, MS 11,883, no. 131ʳ: Cerati to Clément, Pisa, 16 Feb. 1758.

[64] *Journal*, i, preface, p. viii, and p. 24.

[65] Ibid. i. 241. Clément gives the text of Le Paige's memorandum to the king of Apr. 1758 on pp. 233–45.

[66] Van Kley, *The Jansenists and the Expulsion of the Jesuits*, 74–5.

about to go into conclave. Those present at the meeting agreed that an alliance between the courts of Versailles, Vienna, Madrid, and Lisbon would facilitate the election of a 'good' pope.[67] Clément's departure for Italy only three days after this meeting is proof that he had been preparing himself for some time for the journey. It was one for which his established links with Bottari rendered him particularly suitable. Moreover, the support for his secret mission in the highest court circles makes it difficult to regard him as 'an unofficial ambassador charged with carrying out the equally official foreign policy of the *parti janséniste* of the *Parlement* of Paris'.[68] Through intermediaries like Conty, Molé, and Murard, Louis XV and Bernis encouraged his mission, even if they kept their distances and possibly employed other agents as well. The brother of one of Louis XV's known secret informants, the Abbé de Broglie, also went to Rome at the time of the conclave.[69]

Clément and his Jansenist friends were, however, kept in ignorance of one fundamental aspect of French policy following the death of Benedict XIV. Louis XV and Bernis intended to adopt a generally negative approach to the choice of a new pope. When the news of Benedict XIV's death had reached Versailles on 11 May, Bernis, upon informing the king at once, had also offered advice. He thought France needed to activate the friendly courts of Vienna, Madrid, Turin, and Naples, which had promised to act in concert with her to secure the election of a wise and virtuous pope. Secondly, according to Bernis, the king had to decide which of the two French cardinals who would attend the conclave, Gesvres or Luynes, should be entrusted with the 'secret' of his views. Thirdly, the king needed to put his full confidence in his new ambassador in Rome: Rochechouart, the bishop-duke of Laon, who, according to Bernis, 'jouit déjà à Rome d'une considération universelle'. As Gesvres and Luynes had no previous experience of conclaves, Bernis suggested that the ambassador should be authorized to place one of them in the hands of a good *conclaviste*. France also had to appoint a cardinal-protector of its interests; at the suggestion of Rochechouart, Bernis thought the king's choice should fall on Cardinal Colonna-Sciarra. Bernis concluded his report to the king with the fateful words: 'au reste pourveu [*sic*] qu'on ne place pas sur le trône pontifical un esprit turbulent il n'importe guère, depuis votre union avec la Cour de Vienne sur qui le choix tombera.'[70]

---

[67] Ibid. 75.

[68] Ibid.

[69] Abbé Charles de Broglie (1733–77) already had the promise of a cardinal's hat in 1757; agent general of the clergy, 1760–66; bishop-count of Noyon, 1766–77. He was the brother of Louis XV's secret agent, the comte de Broglie.

[70] *Bibliothèque d'un château de Bretagne, du château d'Ancy-le-Franc et à divers* (Paris, Nouveau Drouot, sale of 29 June 1981), lot 19, plate 19: Bernis to Louis XV, Versailles, 11 May 1758 (a letter of six pages with seventeen lines and the word 'approuvé' five times in the margin in the hand of Louis XV). Cardinal

There were reasons, which will be examined later, that may help to explain the clearly passive line which Louis XV and Bernis proposed to take over the forthcoming conclave. The Clément brothers and perhaps even First President Molé were probably not aware of this stance, although they felt that the bishop-duke of Laon did not share their views. For that reason they had tried to delay his departure for Rome in January.[71] They probably also did not know that his instructions consisted largely of convincing the Pope that the archbishop of Paris had only been exiled because, unlike the majority of the other bishops, he had failed to accept Benedict XIV's ruling concerning the denial of sacraments.[72]

Bottari had also urged Clément to come to Rome: the very thought of it rejuvenated him, so he wrote.[73] When the treasurer left Paris on Whit Monday, 15 May 1758, he was assured of being welcomed by friends. He also had letters of recommendation from the bishop of Soissons and from the duc de Mortemart, the kinsman of the ambassador. Gesvres and Luynes also left for Rome accompanied by their *conclavistes* (the Abbé de Lascaris, in the case of Gesvres, the cardinal who had been given the 'secret'), and a plethora of young, ambitious abbés in their train, including Abbé de Brienne, the future principal minister and cardinal. As he recalled in his *Journal de correspondances*, Clément left France at a time when those in positions of power were generally well disposed towards the pursuit of peace in the Church: not just Bernis and Molé, but also Bishop de Jarente of Orléans, who held the *feuille des bénéfices*, the councillors of state who had recently been appointed to the *Conseil des dépêches*, Gilbert de Voisins and Berryer, and several powerful ecclesiastics, like Montazet, the new archbishop of Lyons.[74]

Having left Paris in evening, Clément reached Auxerre the next morning on the first lap of his journey. Proceeding *en chaise de poste*, he went on to spend the following night at Châlons-sur-Saône and reached Lyons in the afternoon of 18 May: 'cent lieues de faites, sans fatigue, me firent espérer le même succés en ma santé pour le reste de mon voyage.'[75] At Lyons he saw the king of Sardinia's

---

Étienne-René Potier de Gesvres (1697–1774); bishop-count of Beauvais until 1772. Cardinal Paul d'Albert de Luynes (1703–88), archbishop of Sens, 1753–88; attended the conclaves of 1758, 1769, and 1775.

[71] *Journal*, i. 30.

[72] Archives du Ministère des Affaires Etrangères, Paris; Rome, Correspondance politique 824, fos. 131–2: 'Mémoire instructif sur l'exil de M. l'Archevêque de Paris'.

[73] *Journal*, i. 38; BA, MS 11,883, fo. 137ᵛ: Bottari to Clément, 22 Mar. 1758: 'il solo pensarvi mi fa ringiovanire'.

[74] Ibid. i. 40.

[75] Ibid. i. 44; BPR, LP 551, 'Clément. 13, Chisme [*sic*] 1758–59', unnumbered manuscript [hereafter u.m.] between tab nos. 9 and 10 of a thumb index: Clément to his brother, Lyon, 18 May 1758. This volume contains copies made by Le Paige of the correspondence between Clément and his brother (probably Clément de Feillet), and between Clément and President de Murard or Abbé Coudrette ('M Le Prieur'). These letters were the basis on which Clément compiled his *Journal de correspondances*.

agent, Bouvier, who had links with Cardinal delle Lanze. Through Bouvier, he was able to spend a night as the guest of the governor of Chambéry. The governor got him to take out *letters de cambiature* at each post so that his French currency would be less devalued when he came to pay for the hire of three horses and a *chaise de poste*. The governor also gave him a letter of recommendation for Martins, the court banker in Turin. Clément's crossing of the Mont-Cenis, carried on a wooden platform by hired bearers on 22 May, was relatively painless, except in financial terms. The advent of spring and the thaw had made his passage a less hazardous one than that of Louis XV's daughter, the duchess of Parma, a short while before: 'Md. de Parme y avoit passé quelques tems auparavant, pour se rendre à Versailles, porté [*sic*] par une trentaine d'hommes habillés, et comme enrégimentés exprès; elle y avoit perdu, par les neiges, quelques-unes de ses femmes.'[76]

Clément spent the day of 23 May in Turin. Visiting the royal palace, he admired, not so much its riches, but the presence of the works of Nicole and the *Catéchisme de Montpellier* in its secret oratory. He was well received by Raincei, the *premier commis* of the Ministry of Foreign Affairs, who was 'des nôtres' and a friend of Cardinal delle Lanze. He learnt from him that the election to the papacy of either Spinelli or Cavalchini would be vetoed. On the other hand, King Charles Emmanuel III wanted peace in the Church and had told his two cardinals to vote simply for the most worthy candidate.[77] However, as Clément learnt later, this stance was but an elaborate smokescreen. The next day he reached Milan: 'fort charmé de me revoir sur les vestiges anciens des Sts Ambroise, Augustin, et Charles Boromée.' He admired the paintings in the Duomo and the riches of the Ambrosiana. The wait was too long for him to see the body of St Charles Borromeo, 'qui se touche entier et bien conservé'; that of St Ambrose 'dans une urne ne se voit pas'. His journey took him on to Piacenza, a night near Parma, at Borgo San Danaino, Parma itself, Reggio, Modena, and Bologna. At Bologna he learnt that the route to Florence would be more difficult because of the mountains, so he chose the Adriatic route instead. It was from Pesaro by the sea that he wrote to his brother on 27 May, having, as he said, followed in the footsteps of the ancients: 'Bien des cardinaux d'icy sont sur la route: Malvezzi, Crescenzi, Pozobonelli, allant au conclave. Mais le fâcheux est que la poste de France ne passe point par ici, pour vous donner de mes nouvelles.'[78]

He wrote again upon reaching Narni in Sabina on 29 May, having passed through Fano and Fossombrone (the birthplace of Cardinal Passionei). He recalled his experience: 'On répètte toutes les horreurs des Alpes, pour regagner

[76] *Journal,* i. 51.
[77] BPR, LP 551, no. 9, um: Clément to [?Clément de Feillet], Pesaro, Saturday, 27 May [1758].
[78] Ibid.: 'De Narni en Sabine, Lundi soir' [29 May 1758].

Rome, en traversant l'Apennin. J'y ai passé tout habillé sur un lit une fort mince nuit de deux ou trois heures à Figillo.' A few hours rest at Spoleto and then a final crossing of the Apennines had brought him into Sabina and to Narni. 'M l'abbé de Lascaris a fait sans se blesser une chute qui l'a remis après moi; et j'en ai évitté mille. Je ne puis être occupé en y échapant que d'actions de grâces; le temps et tout m'a été favorable.'[79]

From a chance meeting with a Jesuit at Castelnivo, he learnt that the 55-year-old Ricci had been made general of the Order: 'exprès, me dit-il, pour les circonstances. On dit pourtant que c'est un bonhomme.' On 30 May he finally reached Rome after a journey that had lasted a fortnight. Bottari was still in the country, but his brother and the Abate Foggini were there to greet Clément on his arrival. Bottari himself returned the next day.[80] The Abbé de Lascaris undertook to present him to the French ambassador the next day with the aid of the learned bookseller Pagliarini. Bottari, Foggini, Pagliarini: it was the circle of the Archetto. Clément was first offered accommodation at the Hôtel de Portugal in Piazza di Spagna for forty *livres*: 'j'y serai tranquille, à grand compte, au bon air, et à portée de tout.'[81] However, he was expected to stay there for six months, and so he preferred instead to take cheaper lodgings which Pagliarini found for him in Piazza Farnese. He found these inconvenient, and he was to move again on 5 June to simpler accommodation in the house of the Abate Mazzi in the Strada Julia, near the Church of Sta Catarina della Rota.[82] He was just across the river from the Palazzo Corsini in the Lungara: 'je suis beaucoup mieux, plus à moi, décemment parceque, près du Palais Corsini, je suis fort loin du quartier recherché.'[83]

He quickly formed gloomy prognostications for the outcome of the conclave: 'on craint du choix futur, vû le crédit des Pères [Jesuites] ici, plus que l'on espère; mais on dit que si la France le veut autrement, elle peut tout.' A few brief words exchanged with Bottari, just before dinner and the departure of the post, enabled him to add a cryptic postscript about the *papabile* in his letter to his brother:

> *Excl.* Paolucci, Cavalchini, Imperiali violens
> *Desiderare multum* Tamburini, Mosca, Galli, Bardi;
> à l'impossible: Passionei, Corsini, Deslances [delle Lanze],
> *optimi.* Il est de la première importance de solliciter sur ce pied.[84]

[79] Ibid.   [80] Ibid.: 'Du 31 mai' [1758].
[81] Ibid.; *Journal,* i. 52. Abate Pier-Francesco Foggini (1715–83), a keeper of the Vatican Library; antiquary, scholar, and translator.
[82] Ibid.; *Journal,* i. 52. BPR, LP 551, no. 9, um: Clément to his brother, 'Rome Du 7 juin 1758' (copy in Le Paige's hand (hereafter LP copy)).
[83] BPR, LP 551: letter cited in n. 82. The Palazzo Corsini in Trastevere was sold to the Italian state by Prince Tommaso Corsini in 1883, when it became the seat of the Accademia dei Lincei. It houses the Corsiniana Library which the prince donated.
[84] Ibid.

Reactions from France were slow in coming, however, and Clément had still not received any news from his brother by 7 June, despite the three letters which he had written to him in the course of his journey.

On 31 May, accompanied by Bottari, the treasurer visited the Corsiniana, where he encountered Dangeuil,[85] a colleague of his brother, the *maître des comptes*; the economist and writer was on his way from St Petersburg to Naples. Bottari took him to meet a young secretary of the Congregation of Rites, Marefoschi, a gifted theologian later to become a cardinal. There he also found another theologian, the celebrated Père Mamachi, the Consulter of the Index.[86] On 1 June, the Octave of the Holy Sacrament, he watched the processions of the Chapter of St Mark of the Venetians and that of the Jesuits, which, he later recalled, 'formoit beaucoup de spectacle pour la richesse et la multitude de leurs chasubles'. The procession was followed by numerous cardinals and ambassadors.[87] Clément learnt that the Jesuits had fourteen houses and numbered about 600 in Rome: 'et y sont fort riches.'[88] That afternoon Bottari took him in his coach to see St John Lateran (where he probably saw the tomb of Clement XII in the Corsini chapel). He saw the Baptistery of St John (known as that of Constantine), the Scala Santa ('dont le prélat [Bottari] jugeoit sainement'[89]), the Church of San Clemente, the Colosseum.

He procured the appropriate black clothes and was able to present his respects to the French ambassador at the Palazzo Cesarini on 2 June. The bishop-duke invited him to stay for dinner: 'J'y dînai en grand comité; Mrs les abbés de Canillac, de Saint Simon, de Lascaris, le comte d'Osmont, l'Evêque de Carpi, un Grand-prieur de Malte Corsini,[90] et beaucoup de prélats italiens.'[91] Several Jesuits came to pay their respects to the ambassador. Clément was introduced to them but deflected awkward questions. The next day Bottari introduced him to another favoured nephew of Cardinal Neri Corsini,[92] the young Andrea

[85] Louis-Joseph Plumard de Dangeuil (b. 1722), *maître des comptes, maître d'hôtel de la Maison royale*, member of the Royal Academy of Sciences of Stockholm, 1758; writer (sometimes under the pseudonym of Sir John Nickolls). He was the author of *Remarques sur les avantages et désavantages de la France et de l'Angleterre* (Amsterdam [*sic*], 1754).

[86] BPR, LP 551: letter cited in n. 82; T. M. Mamachi (1713–92); Dominican theologian of Greek origin; at first supported Jansenist theology but later turned against it; author of *De costumi de primitivi christiani* (1753–7); not to be confused with the Jesuit priest of the same name.

[87] *Journal*, i. 53.

[88] BPR, LP 551: letter cited in n. 82.

[89] *Journal*, i. 53.

[90] Lorenzo Corsini (1730–1802), great-nephew of Cardinal Neri Corsini, was prior of Pisa of the Order of Malta at the age of 4 through the nepotism of Pope Clement XII. He later became an adviser of the Emperor Joseph II.

[91] BPR, LP 551: letter cited in n. 82.

[92] Cardinal Neri Corsini (1685–1770), nephew of Clement XII; started his career in the army and in diplomacy before entering the Church in 1730, when he was also made a cardinal; Protector of Ireland, 1737, and of Portugal, 1739. He was the patron of Bottari and shared many of his views. He founded the Archetto in 1749.

Corsini,[93] then at the start of his rapid career, and took him to visit St Peter's. On Sunday Clément attended Mass at San Luigi dei Francesi and vespers at the Dominicans of Santa Maria sopra Minerva. He saw the Piazza Navona. Having moved to the Strada Julia on Monday, he was formally presented to the Abbé de Canillac, who had twice served as *chargé d'affaires*, and, as *auditeur de Rote*, was the most senior French representative in Rome after the ambassador.[94] Bottari took him to dine with the Abbé Comte de Gross, an influential Piedmontese nobleman who had entered the Church and who shared their views. News of his brother came at last through Cardinal Corsini and from the conclave. Clément also learnt that he would be supplied with funds. He had also called for linguistic assistance: 'mon jeune homme qui vient par Marseille et Gênes, ne me poura arriver que vers le 25 de ce mois. Pour moi je suis obligé d'entendre et de balbutier l'italien toute la journée.' He wanted important letters sent to him care of Bottari, rather than at Strada Julia. He asked that they should always contain a reference to the effect that his own letters were being passed on to people in high places. His outward *persona* remained the same; he was, as he put it, 'un voyageur qui, pour sa santé visite les Églises, voit les monumens [*sic*] . . .'.[95] There was in any case some truth in that claim.

On 7 June Clément wrote a report, probably for President de Murard, stating that the rumour was that Cardinal Archinto would be elected and that, when they arrived for the conclave, the foreign cardinals would merely confirm that choice. There was, however, a powerful objection to Archinto's election: 'Le Népotisme est ici extrémement redouté, et le Milanais peu aimé au prix d'un Romain. Or il est milanais, et il a seulement 75 neveux auxquels il tient beaucoup, qu'il avanceroit, dont plusieurs sont jésuites et presque tous élevés chés eux.'[96] Cavalchini, Imperiali, and Paolucci were still being ruled out. Clément passed a hostile or negative judgement on Sacripanti, Oddi, Borghese, Galli, Pozobonelli, Mosca, and Durini, As for Passionei, the friend of the Jansenists, he had some good points: 'mais léger, point de tête, point de suite dans l'esprit; peu de résolution et peu en état de bien faire dans la première place.' The right man was Cardinal Tamburini. This prelate from Modena was modest, austere in his habits, sound and knowledgeable in matters of doctrine, and with no relatives. Clément outlined the strategy he thought the French should adopt. Tamburini should be allowed to emerge as a compromise candidate after they had run Cardinal Spinelli in the first instance.

[93] Abate Andrea Corsini (1735–95); cardinal, 1759; younger brother of Lorenzo Corsini (see n. 90); a member of the Archetto; succeeded his great-uncle Neri Corsini as one of the leaders of the anti-Jesuit party.

[94] Charles-François de Beaufort-Canillac-Montboissier (1693–1761); canon-count of Lyons, 1716; *conseiller d'État*, and a prelate of the Order of the St Esprit, 1753; *auditeur de Rote* for France, 1733. On his status, see Paul Lesourd, *L'Ambassade de France près le Saint-Siège (généralités)* (Paris, 1925), 206.

[95] BPR, LP 551: letter of 7 June cited in n. 82.   [96] Ibid.

Spinelli was the problem. He had been archbishop of Naples but had resigned his see in 1746 as a result of a dispute with the crown about the workings of the Inquisition.[97] Although formerly an adversary of the Jansenists, he had become an enemy of the Jesuits. He was a man of character and determination who had also supported France during the period of Stainville's embassy. He had been closely involved in the discussions that had produced the brief *Ex omnibus*.[98] Louix XV had expressed his appreciation of his services, and Spinelli had been informed that the king would always be disposed to show his gratitude. There were serious political and personal reasons, however, why Louis XV could not support his candidacy. Spinelli had been vetoed by the king of Naples. With the certain prospect of the death of Ferdinand VI of Spain, his half-brother King Charles of Naples would eventually return to Spain as his successor, taking with him his eldest sons but leaving the younger boy, Ferdinand, to reign in his place in Naples. Charles's younger brother, the infant-duke Philip of Parma and his ambitious wife, a daughter of Louis XV, had only an insecure hold over their duchy and were expecting to succeed to the Neapolitan inheritance themselves.[99] Charles was afraid that, if elected pope, the rancorous Spinelli might seek to favour the claims of the infant-duke. Naples was, after all, a papal fief, and the pope's suzerainty was recognized by the king's annual gift of a white palfrey and a sum of money. Louis XV found himself caught between his daughter and his daughter-in-law, the Dauphine, who was representing the interests of her sister, the queen of Naples, and of her children. Spinelli proved to be the victim of these dynastic considerations. Faced with a request to exclude him from the papacy, 'Sa Majesté [Louis XV] qui l'estime, et qui aime, comme il est naturel Madame de Parme, n'a pas voulu, et a dit que tout ce qu'elle pouroit faire, seroit de ne le pas recomander'.[100] This negative stance probably cost Spinelli the papacy. Clément hoped that his friends in France would succeed in obtaining the withdrawal of the Neapolitan veto. In that case, the Jesuits, whom he suspected of having engineered that veto, would settle for Tamburini and allow him to be elected: 'de peur de Spinelli, ils toléreroient Tamburini.'[101]

On 11 June news spread that the Jesuits had suffered a serious blow. The conclave heard that in April Benedict XIV, acting in concert with Archinto and Passionei, protector of Portugal, had issued a brief in which he appointed

[97] BPR, LP 551, no. 14, um: 'Traduction du Mémoire italien sur le Cardinal Spinelli'. Giuseppe Spinelli (d. 1763); cardinal, 1735; Archbishop of Naples, 1734.

[98] Boutry, *Choiseul à Rome*, 136, 224. Spinelli was at the head of Choiseul's list of preferred candidates for the papacy (pp. 225–8). Tamburini was also on the list (pp. 230–1).

[99] On the dynastic and diplomatic background, see Paolo Alatri, *L'Europa delle successioni (1731–1748)* (Palermo, 1989), 245.

[100] BPR, LP 551, no. 9, um: Clément to [Coudrette], 'de Rome, le 7 juin' [1758] (LP copy). Clément removed his reference to the Dauphine in the passage relating to these events in *Journal*, i. 75.

[101] Ibid.

Cardinal Saldanha to investigate the affairs of the Order in that kingdom. Saldanha had already begun his inquiry into its wealth and its conduct in the New World. The appointment of Cardinal Colonna-Sciarra as French protector was also made public at this time. Clément noted that the post carried large emoluments, and that Colonna-Sciarra came from a family which had become wealthy through a Barberini inheritance: 'C'est une famille haute, fastueuse, qui s'aigrit facilement, et qui était brouillée avec Valenti et ensuite avec Archinto.' He was thought to be fairly hostile to the Jesuits, having been educated by one of their enemies, Lazavini, professor at Padua. Colonna-Sciarra could carry the votes of five cardinals with him in the conclave.[102]

Clément discerned a feeling that the families of previous popes were no longer considered *papabile* so as to avoid the further accumulation of wealth. Foreigners were also excluded (though, on this occasion, it proved not to be the case), as were national protectors and a few others: 'ainsi cela va se réduire à un cercle plus étroit qu'à l'ordinaire.'[103] By 17 June most of the cardinals were in conclave. Fifty-five were eligible to attend, but only forty-three attended. News constantly leaked out of the conclave. Cardinal de Luynes had damaged Archinto's chances by publicly congratulating his nephew in advance on his probable election. Tamburini's chances remained high, especially as Colonna-Sciarra was prepared to support him. The courts of Turin and of Lisbon were also reported to be supporting his candidacy.[104] However, he still needed the help of the emperor and of Spain. Clément urged his friends in Paris to press for action: 'vous pouvés tout par le crédit que le roy a auprès de toutes les puissances catholiques; mais c'est le moment de ne pas épargner les courriers.'[105] The next day he sent news of the first ballot. Archinto had obtained twenty-three votes and was just short of the total which he needed; on the second ballot Cavalchini obtained twenty votes.[106] On 21 June Clément sent the 'portrait and character' of the various cardinals, and he continued to press his friends to act in favour of Spinelli.[107] He wanted Louis XV to inform the court of Naples that the delicate negotiations aimed at bringing peace to the Gallican Church in which Spinelli was involved made it necessary for the king, acting 'avec toute la fermeté qui convient à sa couronne', to ask for the choice to fall on the cardinal.[108] Besides, unlike France,

---

[102] BPR, LP 551, no. 9, um: Clément to [Coudrette?], 'Rome, du 14 juin' [1758], copy. Cardinal Prospero Colonna-Sciarra (1707–65) had been elevated to the purple in 1743.
[103] Ibid.
[104] Ibid.: '2ème Dépêche du même Jour. De Rome mercredi, 17 Juin' [1758].
[105] Ibid.
[106] Ibid.: 'Rome, 21 Juin'. Carlo-Alberto Cavalchini-Guidobono (1683–1774) had been made a cardinal in 1743.
[107] Ibid. List dated 'Rome 21 Juin' (LP copy). Clément printed an expanded version of his 'portraits' of the fifty-five cardinals in *Journal*, i. 57–73.
[108] Ibid.: letter quoted in n. 106.

Naples had no formal right to a veto. At the same time, Clément thought Colonna-Sciarra should be told to insist upon the election of Archinto, Spinelli, or Tamburini.[109]

While Clément was penning his letter, a *coup* had taken place at the conclave: the king of Sardinia had almost succeeded in securing the election of Cavalchini with thirty-three votes pledged. His see of Tortona was inside territory that had recently passed from the Habsburgs to the House of Savoy. Frederick II of Prussia was reputed to have commented that, in choosing Cavalchini, Charles Emmanuel III was in effect making himself 'king of Italy'. Cardinal de Rodt, who represented the interests of Maria Theresia, had not yet arrived at the conclave. The French cardinals had to take immediate action. Gesvres and Luynes brutally notified Delci, the dean of the Sacred College, of Louis XV's veto. They had it with them, although they had previously denied its existence.[110] Clément noted that the reputation of the French cardinals had not emerged unscathed from the affair. They had prevented Cavalchini's election, but at a price: 'On blâme beaucoup les Cardinaux français de s'être laissé amenés, faute d'ouverture avec les amis de la France à cette exclusive positive qui n'avoit pas d'exemple depuis très longtemps, et qu'il leur importoit davantage de ménager.'[111] Gesvres and Luynes blamed Rodt, whose absence had left them with no alternative if they wished to defend the interests of Louis XV's ally, the queen of Hungary, given that Albani, her cardinal-protector had not apparently received any instructions from her. The French had mishandled the affair, alienating the rest of the conclave, especially the Piedmontese. It was understandable that the cardinals who lived in Rome were eager to avoid being on the losing side in any papal election. Apart from the French cardinals, the only ones who had opposed Cavalchini were Colonna-Sciarra and Passionei, together with the Venetian Rezzonico, Sacripanti, G. F. Albani, Serbelloni, and the Milanese Stoppani. Delle Lanze and the other Piedmontese had supported him, and so had Neri Corsini and Tamburini. The French were shocked to find that both the cardinal duke of York and Cardinal Lante, two of their well-paid clients, had supported Cavalchini as well. Gesvres and Luynes did not help matters by coldly telling Spinelli, a potential ally, that they could not support him because of the Neapolitan veto.

Clément's reports were shown by President de Murard to First President

---

[109] Ibid.

[110] BPR, LP 551, no. 15, um: 'Relation traduite de l'Italien' (Du 24 Juin 1758)'; and no. 16, um: copy in Le Paige's hand of a report by Clément dated 'Rome, 28 juin'.

[111] BPR, LP 551, no. 16: report cited in note 110. Gesvres and Luynes had sought to avoid offending the Piedmontese and the Jesuits by simply declaring to Delci that the proposed election of Cavalchini was 'furtive, comme concertée de loin, irrégulière et simoniaque': LP 551 no. 16, um: report by Clément of 1 July 1758 (LP copy).

Molé, who gave an account of them to Bernis.[112] A letter from the already demoralized Bernis to Stainville at this time indicates that there was indecision at Versailles on the choice of a pope: 'M de Laon ne voudroit ni un moliniste outré ni un janséniste. Il vaut mieux aller au plus sûr. Je ne sais si l'on prendra un parti ici. Mais je sais bien que si l'on n'en prend pas, on perdra tout, et nous ne serons plus en mesure sur rien. Je suis aussi dégoûté de ma place que vous de la votre.'[113]

The reports from Rome became increasingly desperate and depressing. Without direction from the French court, Colonna-Sciarra was now favouring the candidacies of Crescenzi or Sacripanti. The latter was regarded by Clément as potentially sympathetic to the Jesuits on account of the support which he had given to the canonization of Bellarmin. According to Clément, he was the worst kind of prelate: 'c'est un homme de palais, intéressé, qui a beaucoup de pauvres parents et auxquels il est attaché; très ouvert par là aux sollicitations des RR.PP [Jésuites], d'autant qu'il est parfaitement ignorant des affaires de l'Église.'[114] The solemn entry of the French ambassador at the conclave on 2 July, followed by a dinner for 100 people, including Clément himself, offered the treasurer little consolation.[115]

On 5 July Clément's pessimism had turned to irritation. He had learnt that the Venetian, Cardinal Rezzonico, bishop of Padua, had been within one vote of being elected, thanks to the efforts of Passionei with the support of the French cardinals, and despite being a foreigner.

Quelle vraisemblance! Un Vénitien en ce moment!
Il a frères et neveux jésuites, et a un neveu plus que jésuite.
Il est lui-même plein de vénération pour la société, très ignorant et d'une dévotion affectée, tout occupé à courir d'Église en Église et aux saluts dans son évéché de Padoue, et n'a que 65 ans. Il est créature des Corsini et cardinal de Clément XII.[116]

It transpired that the French cardinals were able to draw on a million *livres* from the banker, Marchese Belloni, for their journey, and that they had taken 150,000 *livres* into the conclave. Clément thought money was being used to influence votes.[117] Gesvres and Luynes were now mending their fences and sensibly building up support. They could count on the votes of sixteen or seventeen cardinals.[118] On 6 July Rezzonico was elected pope and took the name Clement XIII.

In France Bernis was pleased with the choice; for him it also meant that his

---

[112] LP 551 no. 16, um: copies by Le Paige of an undated letter from Molé to Murard, and of one from Molé to Clément de Feillet of 3 July 1758.

[113] *Mémoires et lettres de François-Joachim de Pierre de Bernis (1715–1758)*, ed. Frédéric Masson (rev. edn., Paris, 1903), ii. 248: Bernis to Stainville, 7 July 1758.

[114] BPR, LP 551, no. 16, um: letter of 1 July 1758 (LP copy).

[115] Ibid.

[116] Ibid.: copy by Le Paige of a letter from Clément, 'Rome, 5 juillet' [First letter].

[117] Ibid.: third letter of 5 July 1758.   [118] Ibid.

own elevation to the purple, delayed by the death of Benedict XIV, could now go forward. As he told Stainville on 15 July: 'Autre bonne nouvelle: Rezzonico est pape, Archinto secrétaire d'État. Cela va bien. Je serai cardinal de votre façon bientôt. Le Roi a permis de solliciter cette grâce pour moi, et elle l'est et le sera par l'Espagne et la cour de Vienne.'[119]

The excitement was over. These events had come in high summer, and Clément was now able to enjoy its compensations. His health had improved. He devoted himself to the task of learning Italian with the aid of a tutor.[120] There were trips with 'toute la jeunesse française' out to the 'vines' of the Villa Pamphili, with everyone paying court to the young Abate Corsini, soon to be made a cardinal by the new pope in return for the support which Neri Corsini had given him in the conclave.[121] Clément went into the country to see the monuments or the 'vines' of the various cardinals. His diet was simple: 'Les fruits, abricots et figues sont en abondance. Les premiers ne se peuvent guères prendre que confits. Les deuxièmes sont excellentes et bien rafraîchissantes. C'est, avec le poisson qu'on a ici à choix, même les jours gras, ma principal [*sic*] nourriture.'[122] Like many travellers, before and since, he found the rate of exchange unfavourable: his 800 French *livres* were converted into 147 Roman *scudi* and 16 *baios* at a loss to him of the total sum of 64 *livres* and 4 *sols*.[123]

These distractions and concerns did not make him forget the main object of his mission. Rezzonico's election soon turned out to be less calamitous than it had seemed at first. Archinto, with whom *Ex omnibus* had been negotiated, was confirmed as secretary of state, and Spinelli was much in the new pope's confidence. On 10 August Clément took the drastic step of sending his servant back to France with an urgent message: the attempts to secure a new bull should be revived at once.[124] Advantage should be taken of the extraordinary General Assembly of the Clergy of France before it concluded its sessions in October. In face of what he saw as the continuous agitation of the Jesuits, he had come to the conclusion that they were responsible for the situation which he and his friends were seeking to remedy.[125] Could not Louis XV be urged to take a stand on the Order comparable to that of the king of Portugal and to communicate his views to the pope? After all, he had cause to complain of the Jesuits: 'Quelles plaintes n'a-t'il pas à porter de leurs factions continuelles, et par le Nonce, sur l'affaire de

---

[119] *Mémoires et lettres . . . de Bernis*, ed. Masson, ii. 250.

[120] BPR, LP 551 no. 16, um: copy by Le Paige of a letter from Clément, Rome, 5 July 1758 (second letter).

[121] Ibid.: letter cited in n. 116.

[122] Ibid.: letter cited in n. 120.

[123] Ibid.: fifth letter of 5 July 1758.

[124] Van Kley, *The Jansenists and the Expulsion of the Jesuits*, 77.

[125] BPR, LP 551, no. 25, um: 'De Rome [entre le 10 et le 12 août] intitulé *Réflexions sur l'exprès envoyé*', possibly addressed to Murard, first letter (LP copy).

Luçon, celle de la Sorbonne, et celle de M. l'Archevêque de Lion? C'est, dit-on, le moment de les congédier de la cour, et pour le parlement de poursuivre enfin leur négoce.'[126] This letter was written between 10 and 12 August 1758; it marks a new departure in Clément's thinking. His plan was now one of systematic subversion of the position of the Jesuit Order. The pope was to be induced to condemn the third part of the Jesuit Berruyer's *Histoire du peuple de Dieu*. Advantage should be taken of the favourable developments in Portugal and the foreseeable demise of the pro-Jesuit Ferdinand VI of Spain to weaken the position of the Order at the French court. The Order was strong in Rome only because of the protection which it enjoyed from various monarchs. Once that powerful protection was removed, there would be no reason why a pope should feel obliged to treat the Order with caution. Clément felt that the bishop-duke of Laon was too well disposed towards the Jesuits and should be replaced. Molé transmitted these views to Bernis and was assured that use had been made of them.[127]

By this time Clément's cover in Rome had been exposed. Gualterio, the nuncio in Paris, had branded him a Jansenist in his dispatches. He was in some danger of being regarded as an absentee in his diocese. Molé and Bernis had been obliged to take steps to protect him from this latter charge. For a while the ambassador froze him out; indeed, Clément wrote of 'le sec et la glace que je trouve chez son Excellence'.[128] He was no longer welcome at the table of Cardinal de Luynes. Cardinal de Gesvres continued to receive him.

Clément's desire to see a comprehensive restatement of the doctrine of the Church was further strengthened by the generally low opinion which he formed of the young French ecclesiastics who had gathered in Rome for the conclave, in the retinue of the ambassador, or of the two cardinals. A conversation with J. B. M. Champion de Cicé,[129] who was about to be consecrated in Rome as bishop of Troyes, was revealing in this respect:

Il s'est accoutumé en Sorbonne et auprès du Cardinal de La Rochefoucauld, à penser que tout ce qui se débat entre les Écoles, et ce qui se puise même dans St Augustin et St Thomas au delà des expressions du Concile de Trente, sont des choses de pure système, comme l'est la Concorde de Molina. Quand on sait ce dont il s'agit, et l'influence même de ces matières dans toute la morale, peut-on douter que ce ne soient des considérations humaines qui jetent dans des idées si évidemment détruites par une expérience constante de deux cents ans de disputes, qui mettent tout en confusion dans l'Église, et qui vont jusqu'à ébranler les États? Je n'ai eu garde d'en reparler avec lui.[130]

---

[126] Ibid.: 'autre lettre' [second letter].   [127] Ibid.: Molé to [Murard], 28 Aug. 1758 (LP copy).

[128] Ibid.: no. 26, um: Clément to his brother, 'Rome, 16 Août' (LP copy).

[129] Jean-Baptiste-Marie Champion de Cicé (1725–1806); doctor of the Sorbonne; bishop of Troyes, 1758–61, bishop of Auxerre, 1761–[92]. His younger brother, Joseph-Marie (1735–1810), became archbishop of Bordeaux, later of Aix, and keeper of the seals.

[130] BPR, LP 551, no. 26, um: Clément to [Coudrette/Murard], 'Rome, 19 Août [1758]' (LP copy).

Bottari and the other Italians were shocked at the ignorance of such ecclesiastics; they felt the French needed not so much pacific priests as knowledgeable ones ('éclairés'). Those who came to Rome gave the impression of being time-servers ('sujets dévoués'), secret adherents of Christophe de Beaumont, or else totally indifferent to the disputes of the Church. Clément told one of his Parisian correspondents that there was clearly a need to distribute ecclesiastical benefices and preferment differently: 'à décider tout le monde à la paix, à renouveller la lumière et le mérite dans le Clergé de France, et à dissiper toute faction secrète.' He hoped Montazet, the new archbishop of Lyons, might succeed in this aim. After being welcomed back to the ambassador's table on 27 August, possibly as a result of pressure from Versailles, Clément joined his suite to call on the cardinals, Cavalchini, Galli, Alexander, and G. F. Albani, but remaining always, as he wrote: 'fort sur la réserve et sans grande liaison avec toute une jeunesse montée par le jeu, la musique et les femmes si différemment de mes allures.'[131] The future of the Church of France was in the hands of these frivolous, carefree, young clerics, who included the Abbé de Brienne, who, on one occasion, delivered himself of the statement that the purpose of the Church was to save souls.

On 20 September Clément left for a month's holiday in Naples. During his absence, the repercussions of two notable events were felt: on 3 September there had been an unsuccessful attempt on the life of the king of Portugal, and on 30 September Cardinal Archinto died suddenly. These events were, of course, unconnected, but they had far-reaching consequences. In Portugal, Pombal claimed that the Jesuits were implicated in the attempt on the king's life and he set about destroying the Order, a process which Clément had already come to see as a prerequisite to the establishment of peace within the Church. The death of Archinto and his replacement by the pro-Jesuit Cardinal Torrigiani, on the other hand, put an end to any project of obtaining the desired papal restatement of fundamental doctrine. As Bottari observed, the new pontificate of Clement XIII no longer offered any hope for the peace of the Church.[132]

Clément returned to Rome on 17 October and began his journey home a few days later. This time he went back through Florence, where he met another

---

[131] Ibid.: no. 26, um: 'Du 30 Août 1758' (LP copy). For a list of the French ecclesiastics who came to Rome in 1758, see *Journal*, i. 55–6: they were de Lascaris (later bishop of Toulon), de Brienne (later archbishop of Toulouse and principal minister of Louis XVI), de Saint-Simon (later bishop of Agde), de Broglie (later bishop-count of Noyon), de Cicé (later bishop of Troyes and Auxerre), de Boisgelin (later bishop of Lavaur and archbishop of Aix), de Marbeuf (later bishop of Autun), de Cicé (later bishop of Rhodez, later archbishop of Bordeaux and keeper of the seals), de la Galaisière (later bishop of St Dié), de Salha (canon of the Sainte-Chapelle), de Malide (later bishop of Avranches, and later of Montpellier), d'Avrincourt, de Mazeas (ambassador's secretary), Ranchon (later canon of Chartres and biographer of princes), d'Osmont (later bishop of Comminges), de Murat and de Siougeat (both *aumôniers de la Cour* attached to Cardinal de Luynes), and Destables (a missionary, later a canon of Auxerre).

[132] *Journal*, i. 'Avertissement', p. xi: 'La mort violente et subite du Cardinal Archinto enleva cette espérance'; Van Kley, *The Jansenists and the Expulsion of the Jesuits*, 77.

distinguished member of the Archetto, the celebrated and learned Abate Marchese Antonio Niccolini.[133] In his flowery style Niccolini recalled his meeting with Clément and Champion de Cicé, now bishop of Troyes, in a letter to Bottari:

Avendo goduto in Firenze Le i buoni lumi e dell'aurea Compagina di Mgr di Cicé vescovo di Troia e di Mgr l'abbé Clément du Tremblé come da i medesimi forte . . . Io ho goduto moltissimo in vedere questi due degni soggetti contenti di Roma, avendari trovato quello, che non trovano in Francia, cioè che le opinioni sono opinioni e non Dogmi de Fede, come i Molinisti vorrebero che fossero. Nel vescove di Troyes ho avuto inoltre la consolazione di ritrovare una creatura del buon Cardinale de La Rochefoucauld, ed un amico delle aureo Presidente di Montesquieu, che alla sua morte procuro, che non mancatte delle assistenza necessaria tanto p. lo spirituale, che pel Temporale.[134]

Clément would probably have agreed that Rome was indeed a place where opinions were opinions and not rules of faith, but he would certainly have thought that, in Champion de Cicé's case, being a creature of Cardinal de La Rochefoucauld had been a mixed blessing.

The subsequent careers of Clément and Champion de Cicé form an interesting subject of comparison. Already a bishop at 33, Champion de Cicé was soon to move on to Auxerre in place of Condorcet in 1761. He implemented there an even-handed policy towards Jansenists and Jesuits. He was a gracious host to Edmund Burke when he visited Auxerre in 1773.[135] The bishop was elected to the Estates General in 1789 as a deputy of the clergy for the town. He opposed the Declaration of the Rights of Man, and he refused to adhere to the Civil Constitution of the Clergy. He was thereby deemed to have vacated his see, which was filled by his erstwhile companion in Rome in 1758, the former principal minister of Louis XVI, Loménie de Brienne. He emigrated in 1792 and went to live in Germany. He did not resign his see in 1801, as requested by the pope in order to facilitate the introduction of the Concordat, but he did not adhere to the protest of the bishops against the Concordat. He died at Halberstadt in 1806.

How different were Clément's career and opinions. He resigned the treasurership of Auxerre in 1786. He expressed approval of Pietro-Leopoldo's religious measures in Tuscany.[136] He supported the Civil Constitution of the Clergy and

[133] Antonio Niccolini (1700–69), patron of scholars, friend of Presidents de Montesquieu and de Brosses. Bottari described him to Clément in these terms: 'lo troverete un uomo sotto quanto possa esser mai in tutte Le scienze, e per molti anni ha girato per L'Europa. Egli è di buona dottrina e informatissimo delle questioni del tempo, e che conosce i Jesuiti meglio di noi' (BA, MS 11883, no. 144: letter of 29 Oct. 1758.

[134] AL, Corsiniana, MS 44, D. 47, fo. 295ᵛ: Niccolini to Bottari, 5 Nov. 1758.

[135] *The Correspondence of Edmund Burke*, ed. Lucy Sutherland (Oxford, 1958), ii. *July 1768–June 1774*, pp. 419 n. 2, 421–2. Burke and his son Richard were received in February 1773 at Auxerre by Champion de Cicé 'with cordial hospitality'; cf. his letter to Jane Burke of 4 Feb. 1773.

[136] BSS, MS 1292 (Fonds Clément), no. 230: Clément's observations on Pietro-Leopoldo's ordnance of May 1784 ordering ecclesiastics to sell their lands.

the consequent replacement of the old clergy by the new.[137] He wrote to Scipione de Ricci, the bishop of Pistoia and Prato, on 17 April 1791: 'Dans cette grande Révolution, pouvons-nous ne pas voir l'œuvre du Très Haut, le terme naturel du renversement que cet ancien clergé fait depuis quatre-vingts ans des dogmes les plus précieux, de la morale évangélique, de la sainte discipline, et de tout ce que la France avoit de vertus, de lumières et d'utiles établissements?'[138] He bought the abbey of Livry when it became a *bien national,* and he was elected bishop of Versailles. He facilitated the introduction of Bonaparte's Concordat by resigning his see. The contrast between him and Champion de Cicé could not be greater.

It would be misleading to conclude from Clément's account of his first journey to Italy that it simply depicts the activities, network, and ramifications of the so-called Jansenist party. The relative strength of that party depended largely upon the wider appeal of its aim to bring peace to the Gallican Church and to the subjects of the Most Christian King. In the particular political and ecclesiastical circumstances of 1757–8 that goal had at first seemed within reach: at court, in the *parlement* of Paris, within the Gallican Church, in Rome among some of the cardinals and among scholars and theologians of distinction, there was evidence of that desire and purpose. Events decided otherwise, and in that respect the death of Cardinal Archinto was probably more significant than the election of Clement XIII. Moreover, while Louis XV and Bernis definitely wanted peace within the Church, they also had other priorities. The dynastic complications created by Madame Infante's desire to place her husband on the Neapolitan throne inhibited French diplomacy in Rome over the crucial candidacy of Cardinal Spinelli. Besides, Louis XV and Bernis always had the tempting option of dealing with men rather than with issues. It was easier to appoint middle-of-the-road bishops like Champion de Cicé than to press for clear restatements of doctrine. The moment and the impetus were lost. The Jansenists for their part, encouraged by favourable circumstances in several countries, now turned their unstinting energies to the task of neutralizing the Jesuits. There too, in time, they were able to secure a measure of support and collaboration that extended beyond their ranks.

By the end of his long existence Clément had seen a new order and a new Church, and the events described in his *Journal de correspondances* belonged to the *tempi passati*. Pius VI had already consigned *Unigenitus* to the status of a purely historical document. When Clément wrote the *avertissement* to his work, he concluded it with a dismissive comment about a pontiff who, because he was 'étranger aux matières de doctrine, et sans lumière sur l'état de l'église, ne permet

---

[137] Gazier, *Histoire générale du mouvement Janséniste,* 142.

[138] Letter quoted in De Potter, *Vie et mémoires de Scipion de Ricci, Évêque de Pistoie et Prato, Réformateur du Catholicisme en Toscane, sous le Règne de Léopold* (Paris, 1826), ii. 404.

pas d'espérer qu'il soit jamais en état de remplir le plan qu'on se proposoit'.[139] Perhaps it was the forced removal of Pius VI from Rome by the French Revolutionary authorities, his dignified conduct, and his death while a prisoner at Valence in 1799 that led to this reference being deleted from the printed edition that appeared three years later.[140]

Of the *Journal de correspondances*, that monument to his activities, Clément had told Le Paige when confiding the manuscript to him in 1793: 'nous verrons, s'il plaît à Dieu, toutes ces précieuses vérités dans le Ciel, bien d'un autre œil.'[141] At his funeral at the cemetery of Sainte-Catherine in Paris, the pall was carried by four bishops. The oration was delivered by no less a person than Grégoire, who concluded it with the words: 'Consolons-nous! Notre existence ici bas n'est que le berceau de la vie. Le Dieu que nous servons ne sera pas toujours invisible; la splendeur du jour éternel paraîtra. Achevons notre voyage avec confiance, avec une inquiétude chrétienne, car nous ignorons qui de nous le premier arrivera au terme de sa course.'[142] Far from the 'vines' of the Villa Pamphili, Clément had started out on his last journey of hope.

---

[139] BPR, LP 550: MS of the *Journal de correspondances*, 2.

[140] Cf. *Journal*, i. 'Avertissement', p. xiii.

[141] BPR, LP 550: Clément to Le Paige, Livry, 23 Apr. 1793 (letter pasted into the inside front cover of the MS).

[142] [Saillant], *Mémoires secrets*, 128.

6

Secular Simony: The Clergy and the Sale of Offices in Eighteenth-Century France

WILLIAM DOYLE

Aversion to the sale of its own authority is one of the oldest established principles of the Christian Church. Ever since St Peter rebuked the sorcerer Simon Magus for attempting to buy spiritual powers from the apostles,[1] it has been axiomatic that priesthood and cure of souls may not be acquired for money. Yet, once benefices became entitlements to remuneration, the offence to which Simon gave his name became endemic in the Church. The frequency with which councils, popes, bishops, and divines condemned simony shows how persistent it was, and in the early modern Church it incurred the particular censure of the Council of Trent.[2]

An even older tradition, going back at least as far as Plato and Aristotle,[3] condemns the sale of public office. The powers of the magistrate rank second only in scope and importance to those of the priest, and their exercise requires qualities that no money can buy. Unlike the Christian condemnation of simony, the critique of venality derived not from authority but from principles of reason and justice. It was no less pointed for that. The sale, whether covert or overt, of public functions goes back as far as civil society itself—as once again the antiquity, number, and persistence of its critics show. Despite all their strictures, by the later Middle Ages the roots of civil venality were as deep as those of simony in the Church, and just as resistant to extirpation. In parts of early modern Europe, selling offices became the open and established practice of government at a time when it was easier to sell rich men honours than to tax them.[4] Nowhere

---

[1] Acts 8: 9–24.

[2] See R. A. Ryder, *Simony: An Historical Synopsis and Commentary* (Washington, DC, 1931).

[3] *Aristotle's Politics*, ed. H. W. C. Davis (Oxford, 1920), 94 (bk. ii, ch. 11); Plato, *The Republic*, ed. H. D. P. Lee (London, 1955), 322–3 (bk. viii, sect. 4).

[4] The standard general survey is K. W. Swart, *The Sale of Offices in the Seventeenth Century* (The Hague, 1949). More recent studies are I. Mieck (ed.), *Ämterhändel im Spätmittelalter und im 16 Jahrhundert* (Berlin, 1984), and A. M. Birke, I. Mieck, and K. Malettke (eds.), *Ämterkäuflichkeit: Aspekte sozialer Mobilität in Europäischen Vergleich (17 und 18 Jahrhundert)* (Berlin, 1980).

did it spread more widely than in France, where between the sixteenth and the eighteenth centuries all but a handful of public officials were recruited by purchase. It took a revolution to uproot this system. Even then vestiges of it survived, and survive still, though periodically denounced in arguments first heard several centuries before Christ.[5]

The practices of the Church were not unconnected with the development of French secular venality. The very definition of an office, when it solidified in an ordinance of 1467, had obvious parallels with an ecclesiastical benefice. It was defined as an appointment tenable for life. Its holder could be removed only by death, forfeiture, or resignation.[6] One reason why the sale of offices flourished in France was that from an early stage their holders enjoyed almost free disposal of their purchase to third parties. Not only did the king sell offices: he allowed buyers to sell them on, or to bequeath them to their own heirs. It was done through a *resignatio in favorem*, a conditional resignation, the condition being that a designated successor was provided. These instruments had first been developed for the transfer of ecclesiastical benefices in the gift of the pope, and they offered some of the most obvious opportunities for simony. Adapted for the transfer of French royal offices, the commercial purpose was undisguised. Only one constraint limited the free disposal of incumbents who resigned ecclesiastical benefices conditionally. If they died within twenty days of doing so, disposal reverted to the provisor.[7] In the 1530s a similar rule was introduced for French royal offices.[8] Offices conditionally resigned reverted to the crown if the officer resigning died within forty days. Insurance against this eventuality was the attraction of the *droit annuel* or *paulette* introduced in 1604, and destined to be the most effective and durable way of taxing venal office-holders.

The laws governing French venality were therefore deeply marked by the ways of the Church. This did not prevent the clergy, through their representatives in successive Estates-General, from taking a lead throughout the sixteenth century in denouncing the seemingly inexorable spread of the practice.[9] Among the most vocal of their spokesmen in the Estates-General of 1614, the last to convene before the Revolution, was Richelieu; and in the early years of his ministry a decade later this prince of the Church advised Louis XIII to undertake the entire abolition of the sale and heredity of offices.[10] By the time he died, however, the

[5] See W. Doyle, *Venality: The Sale of Offices in Eighteenth-Century France* (Oxford, 1996), esp. ch. 10.

[6] See R. Doucet, *Les Institutions de la France au XVIe siècle* (2 vols.; Paris, 1948), i. 406.

[7] M. Marion, *Dictionnaire des institutions de la France aux XVIIe et XVIIIe siècles* (Paris, 1923), 486. See also, on conditional resignations in the Church, C. Berthelot du Chesnay, 'Le Clergé diocésain français', *Revue d'histoire moderne et contemporaine*, x (1963), 241–69.

[8] The precise date has never been established. See R. Mousnier, *La Vénalité des offices sous Henri IV et Louis XIII* (2nd edn., Paris, 1970), 44–5.

[9] Ibid. 38, 42, 62, 332, 338, 609.   [10] Ibid. 645–6.

cardinal had concluded that any such attempt would be difficult, if not positively dangerous. He admitted that the general opinion of mankind, as well as reason and the best legal principles, were opposed to venality and heredity. But, 'en une ancienne Monarchie, dont les imperfections ont passé en habitude, et dont le désordre fait (non sans utilité) partie de l'ordre de l'État',[11] it was better to let well-established habits and institutions continue, until better men in a better age could undertake their reform with wisdom and safety. As a minister, Richelieu had come to know how the judicious exploitation of office-holders and their ambitions and appetites could help the state pursue its own. And, although these opinions did not become known until the publication of the cardinal's *Testament politique* in 1688, only Colbert among his ministerial successors thought that venality could be much curtailed. Richelieu's was to be the conventional wisdom of the eighteenth century, echoed and endorsed by Montesquieu: venality was ineradicable, and had some advantages. It was a necessary evil.

Confidence in the permanence of venality meant that venal offices retained their appeal throughout the eighteenth century. On the eve of the Revolution, many categories were more sought-after than ever, as rising prices testified.[12] A small but distinctive sector of the system was that of clerical counsellorships in the *parlements*. In medieval times clerics occupied a whole range of royal offices from which they would later be excluded,[13] but the *parlements* retained a handful of offices specifically reserved for clergy. When, under Francis I, the sale of offices in the *parlements* became avowed royal policy, no exception was made for *conseillers clercs*. Although holders of these offices were required to be in holy orders, they were still required to pay, and this purchase was not deemed simoniacal. The only concession to the cloth of clerical counsellors was that they were excused from sitting on cases whose outcome might involve the shedding of blood, and so avoided service in the *tournelles* or criminal chambers of these courts. Whereas a large provincial *parlement* like Bordeaux had only six clerical counsellors in the eighteenth century, in Paris there were twelve.[14] But not all these offices were occupied by clerics. Royal dispensations from major orders, or even any priestly qualifications at all, were easily obtained.[15] In 1725, four of the six clerical posts in the Bordeaux *parlement* were held by laymen.[16] There seems,

[11] *Maximes d'État, ou testament politique d'Armand du Plessis, Cardinal Duc de Richelieu* (2 vols.; Paris, 1764), i. 201.

[12] See Doyle, *Venality*, ch. 7, *passim*.   [13] Mousnier, *La Vénalité*, 31.

[14] W. Doyle, *The Parlement of Bordeaux and the End of the Old Regime 1774–1790* (London, 1974), 43; F. Bluche, *Les Magistrats du parlement de Paris au XVIIIᵉ siècle (1715–1771)* (Paris, 1960), 49. Bluche attributes all to the *grand' chambre*, but elsewhere he makes clear that (as in other *parlements*) no chamber had a fixed complement of clerics. But clerics served long, so most were likely to be in the *grand' chambre*.

[15] Bluche, *Magistrats*, 55, 64–5.   [16] Doyle, *Parlement of Bordeaux*, 43.

in fact, to have been limited competition among properly qualified candidates. A new clerical counsellorship created in the *parlement* of Besançon in 1704 failed to find a buyer, and four years later was laïcized;[17] and prices for these charges throughout the kingdom tended to be markedly lower than for lay counsellorships.[18]

It is not difficult to understand why. Even if a cleric could afford an office, he lacked the layman's incentive of children to pass it on to. The higher age of entry of most clerical counsellors[19] also suggests that a legal career might be a last resort, when other hopes of preferment had faded. The typical clerical counsellor was a younger son from a family already represented in the same court. These offices enabled well-born priests of modest means to establish themselves with dignity in positions that reflected well on their families. Remuneration for service in a *parlement* was unspectacular,[20] but an assiduous counsellor would find it a useful supplement to other resources. Besides, being a member of the *parlement* could bring additional advancement in the Church. In Paris, at least, where the king needed political support inside the court, assiduity could be rewarded with benefices in the royal gift. Most clerical counsellors in the capital had prebends or stalls in well-endowed chapters, and a score of them were commendatory abbots, often of several houses.[21] Two even went on to be appointed bishops.[22] For those achieving ecclesiastical preferment in this way, purchase of an office was a sort of simony at one remove, but without the stigma.

To become a bishop, however (unless one of those deemed a peer, with rights of session), was to move outside the *parlement*, which few established clerical counsellors ever did. They were indeed among the longest serving of magistrates.[23] When they moved on, it was more by chance than from expectation. Thus it was an old friendship with the family of Mme de Pompadour which brought the Abbé de Salaberry promotion, at 61, to one of the ecclesiastical seats on the Council of State in 1758. When he died three years later, he was succeeded there by the Abbé Bertin, of the *parlement* of Bordeaux, brother as it happened to the comptroller-general of the finances.[24] The most famous (or notorious) success story was that of the Abbé Terray, who in 1769 became

[17] M. Gresset, *Gens de justice à Besançon, 1674–1789* (2 vols.; Paris, 1978), i. 41.

[18] Doyle, *Parlement of Bordeaux*, 28–9; Bluche, *Magistrats*, 165.

[19] Ibid. 58.

[20] Ibid. 170–2; B. Stone, *The French Parlements and the Crisis of the Old Regime* (Chapel Hill, NC, 1986), 55–6.

[21] Ibid. 219–21.

[22] Ibid. 63.

[23] Bluche, *Magistrats*, 63.

[24] M. Antoine, *Le Conseil du roi sous le règne de Louis XV* (Paris, 1970), 187–8. See too the same author's *Le Gouvernement et l'administration sous Louis XV: Dictionnaire biographique* (Paris, 1978), 33–4, 227. Unusually, Abbé Bertin was an elder brother.

comptroller-general himself. His promotion, after thirty-three years in the *parlement*, caused universal surprise, but perhaps should not have. He owed it to Chancellor Maupeou, with whom he had worked closely in the *parlement* throughout the mid-1760s. Maupeou had then been prime president, and Terray, *rapporteur de la cour*.

Here was one position, not an office, to which a clerical counsellor in Paris might legitimately aspire, since it traditionally went to one of them. Salaberry had been Terray's predecessor, and only once subsequently, between 1781 and 1785, was the *rapporteur* a lay counsellor, much to the outrage of all the clerics.[25] The responsibilities of the *rapporteur* were heavy. In cooperation with the procurator-general, he was required to present and explain legislation sent by the king for registration in the *parlement*. Considerable abilities and tactical sense were required, and, as the government's financial difficulties deepened over the century, the demands of the post grew ever more daunting. When in 1785 it was recaptured for the clerics by the Abbé Tandeau, it was reputedly with the inducement of an abbacy worth 25,001 *livres* a year.[26] These duties provided a very effective training for the formulation, understanding, and conduct of high policy, as Terray went on to demonstrate; but no doubt his ruthless and extortionate record in power helped to ensure that no subsequent clerical counsellor was offered the chance to emulate him.

The original rationale of having clerical counsellors in the *parlements* was to safeguard the legal interests of the Church. Worldly men of business like Salaberry, Terray, or Tandeau in the eighteenth century devoted little enough of their time or energies to that. It largely became the monopoly of those who took a distinctive view of the Church's interests, seeing them as under fundamental threat from everything to do with *Unigenitus*. Although most of the identifiable Jansenists within the *parlement* of Paris were laymen,[27] there was a core of clerical counsellors down the generations, from the Abbé Pucelle, who led the early opposition to the Bull under the Regency, or his ally the Abbé de Guillebauld, to men like the Abbés Chauvelin or Nigon de Berty, who came to prominence when the quarrels were rekindled in mid-century by the refusal of sacraments.[28] Placed as they were in the premier court of the kingdom, these men were

---

[25] [L. Petit de Bachaumont], *Mémoires secrets pour servir à l'histoire de la république des lettres en France depuis 1762 jusqu'à nos jours* (36 vols.; London, 1784–9), xvii, 25 juillet 1781. See also B. Stone, *The Parlement of Paris, 1774–1789* (Chapel Hill, NC 1981), 25.

[26] M. de Lescure (ed.), *Correspondance secrète inédite sur Louis XVI, Marie Antoinette, la Cour et le Ville* (2 vols.; Paris, 1866), ii. 6, 18 Jan. 1786.

[27] On the problems of identifying them, see D. Van Kley, *The Jansenists and the Expulsion of the Jesuits from France 1757–1765* (New Haven, 1975), ch. 2.

[28] On Chauvelin, see ibid. 50–1; on Nigon de Berty, see B. Lacombe, *La Résistance Janséniste et parlementaire au temps de Louis XV: L'Abbé Nigon de Berty (1702–1774)* (Paris, 1948).

sometimes able to play a crucial role in politics, as when Chauvelin launched the *parlement*'s great attack on the Jesuits in 1761.[29] And, whether or not he was acting on that famous occasion as the agent, or puppet, of deeper forces, his status as a cleric lent authority to his denunciation.

It is true that at the time, and since, doubts were raised about how sincere a Jansenist Chauvelin was, if indeed he was one at all.[30] Jansenism always flourished behind a fog of denials and dubious attributions. Sincere 'friends of the truth' in the *parlement*, however, had the very basis of their power questioned by one of the leading Jansenist writers on politics when his most important posthumous work appeared in 1739. The Abbé Jacques-Joseph Duguet, some-time priest of the Oratory, had written his *Institution d'un prince* in 1699,[31] perhaps in response to the literary sensation caused by the appearance of Richelieu's *Testament politique*. Certainly it was a comprehensive polemic against the practices and instruments of French absolutism, including the surrender of authority by kings to ministers. But Duguet never allowed its publication during his lifetime. Too much of it was scarcely veiled criticism of Louis XIV; and by the time the author died, in 1736, another cardinal was exercising the royal author-ity. Duguet, like most Jansenists, vaunted the role of the *parlement* in public affairs, and defended the right of remonstrance. He praised the virtues of mag-istrates bred from generations on the bench. But he denounced the sale of judicial offices as a 'désordre contraire à la Justice' leading to excessive costs. Princes had a duty to bring an end to both.[32]

Duguet's denunciation of venality was sustained and impassioned. The sale of judicial offices meant that only the rich and presumptuous ever became magis-trates, whereas the best princes had always preferred to appoint men who shunned authority. Since the highest duty of the prince was to choose the men who would sit in judgement over his subjects, it was a prerogative which should never be alienated—least of all for reasons of transient financial need, which left a permanent burden of debt for the state. In a series of rhetorical questions which recalled a sermon, Duguet reviewed the evils of selling the right to judge. Since when had riches been a proof of integrity, knowledge, or a zeal for justice? Was all wealth virtuously acquired? What would become of impecunious men of

[29] See Van Kley, *The Jansenists*, 109–12, and J. Swann, *Politics and the Parlement of Paris under Louis XV, 1754–1774* (Cambridge, 1995), 206–13.

[30] See Van Kley, *The Jansenists*, 50–1.

[31] *Institution d'un prince, ou traité des qualitez des vertus et des devoirs d'un souverain, soit par rapport au gouvernement temporel de ses états, ou comme chef d'une société chrétienne qui est nécessairement liée avec la religion. En quatre parties* (London, 1739). See A. Sedgwick, *Jansenism in Seventeenth Century France: Voices from the Wilderness* (Charlottesville, Va., 1977), 182–7.

[32] *Institution d'un prince*, ch. 6.

virtue and talent, and what sort of example was it that their qualities should be left to languish 'dans la poussière et l'oubli'? 'Où sera l'émulation des belles choses, si les Richesses seules sont la porte de tous les Emplois?'[33] And would not those who had bought the power of justice also sell it? Venality forced men of good birth and background from the bench, replacing them with 'des hommes nouveaux, obscurs, sans nom, sans alliance, sans élévation, sans courage' for whom the public would have no respect. When magistracy was venal, greed became the measure of all things; and even in respectable families necessary investment in offices immobilized capital and warped inheritances. Above all, however, a venal magistracy meant that the dispensation of justice was the only profession needing neither ability, aptitude, nor knowledge, when none demanded these qualities more. Who would employ a doctor, or even a humble artisan, or servant, solely on the basis of his or her wealth? Money was the enemy of all virtue and public good.

Nor did Duguet accept (responding most obviously in this to the recently revealed arguments of Richelieu) that 'si c'est un mal . . . il est désormais sans remède; et il ne faut pas perdre le tems à le déplorer sans aucun fruit'. On the contrary, 'il est impossible qu'un Prince, touché de ce désordre et de ses funestes suites, n'y cherche pas des remèdes, sans se laisser vaincre par les difficultez, qui paroissent insurmontables'.[34] He accepted the injustice of outright abolition or confiscation of offices that had become property. Their holders would need to be reimbursed. Nor would it be just to buy them out at the original, often remote, selling price. A fixed 'milieu' should be established, and declared permanent and invariable, and at this price the prince would pay off office-holders 'par degrez'. Those reimbursed would be replaced by nominees where necessary; but, since the over-proliferation of judges through venality was, in Duguet's opinion, one of the main causes of the high costs of justice, not all of those bought out would have successors.

A quarter of a century after Duguet wrote, but the same length of time before his treatise was finally published, another clerical writer also addressed the problem of judicial costs. Anxious to rehabilitate himself after public criticism of the scarcely cold Louis XIV had brought his expulsion from the French Academy in 1718, in 1725 the Abbé de Saint-Pierre published a *Mémoire pour diminuer le nombre des procès*. In his view, a wide range of factors had made the French litigious and kept the costs of justice high, but venality was undoubtedly one among them. Jurisdictions had proliferated in order that offices might be sold within them, and all investors in office expected a return. And nobody could disagree that to award judicial office to the highest bidder irrespective of capacity

---

[33] Ibid. 164.   [34] Ibid. 163, 167.

was a 'grand inconvénient'.[35] Yet Saint-Pierre, too, had obviously read Richelieu; and he repeated the argument, which the cardinal claimed first to have heard from Sully, that venality had saved France from a judiciary recruited from among the clients and retainers of powerful magnates.[36] Other things being equal, it was better, argued Saint-Pierre (this time echoing Aristotle[37]) that rich men rather than poor should be judges, since their wealth placed them beyond corruption. Most important was that appointment should depend not on wealth alone. Prices should be held at modest levels, so that there was no shortage of candidates among whom members of a venal company should then choose by election. 'Ainsi je suis pour la vénalité, pourvu qu'elle soit contenuë dans de justes bornes, mais que le prix soit modique, afin qu'il y ait en même-tems dans les prétendans, richesse, émulation, concurrence, et choix des Magistrats entre concurrens.'[38]

Saint-Pierre, a worldly cleric, proto-*philosophe*, and polymath, had little in common with the austere Duguet. He was equally remote from perhaps the best-known churchman to write on public affairs in the eighteenth century, Fénelon. Though no Jansenist, like Duguet the archbishop of Cambrai was moved to write by what he saw as the unbridled excesses of a monarch obsessed by wars and glory. And, as with Duguet, his more extreme pronouncements did not become public until after his death. Appearing fleetingly as an appendix to a rapidly suppressed edition of *Télémaque* in 1734, his *Lettre à Louis XIV* of *c*.1702, and *Examen de conscience sur les devoirs de la royauté*, prepared for the duke of Burgundy in 1711, became generally available only in 1747.[39] In both, Fénelon concentrated his attack on the over-proliferation of venality rather than the thing itself. By over-creation of offices to sell, Louis XIV had burdened posterity with perpetual debts, only repayable at ruinous cost to the taxpayer. He had pushed up the costs of justice through the greed of office-buyers to recoup their outlay at the people's expense. He had, indeed, destabilized the entire good order of the state by making most functions venal monopolies. Justice was now more venal, reform increasingly impossible. Ten years of funding wars by such expedients had done damage that might take centuries to repair.[40] Nowhere did Fénelon suggest the entire abandonment of venality, although he advised the duke of Burgundy to abolish it in the army, and suppress hundreds of special jurisdictions whose members were recruited by purchase. He advocated the gradual elimination of the *paulette*, and the expulsion from the royal council of masters of requests 'introduits sans mérite pour de l'argent'.[41] Here Fénelon's contempt

---

[35] *Mémoire pour diminuer le nombre des procès* (Paris, 1725), 225–6.
[36] Ibid. 226; *Maximes d'État*, p. 200.   [37] *Politics*, ii, ch. xi.   [38] *Mémoire*, 229–30.
[39] See A. Chérel, *Fénelon au XVIIIᵉ siècle en France (1715–1820)* (Paris, 1917), 339–43.
[40] 'Lettre à Louis XIV', in C. Urbain (ed.), *Fénelon: Écrits et lettres politiques* (Paris, 1920), 48–9.
[41] 'Plans de gouvernement concertés avec le duc de Chevreuse pour être proposés au duc de Bourgogne', in ibid., 117, 120, 122.

for the very principle of venality came through clearly enough. But, like Richelieu, he appears to have believed that there was little prospect of eliminating it entirely, even under the model king he hoped Burgundy would be.

In this, his writings when they appeared underscored the conventional wisdom of the eighteenth century. Over the last century of its existence the sale and heredity of public offices in France found no more defenders than it ever had.[42] But the issue provoked no public debate, because the impossibility of eliminating it entirely was taken for granted. The most anybody dared suggest was ways to trim it, while disagreements largely centred on whether this public malady had any redeeming features. Clerical writers were as divided on these questions as any, but Duguet was alone in believing the evil eradicable. He appears to have persuaded nobody else; but his attack was resounding enough to have alarmed a man with more to lose from the abolition of venality than anybody else. Louis-Auguste Bertin was treasurer-general of the *Parties Casuelles*, the bureau from which most of the venal system was administered. He was, perhaps unsurprisingly, the only person in this whole century to mount an unequivocal public defence of the sale of offices.[43] And in a private manuscript dictionary of offices he picked out Duguet by name as a misguided critic to be refuted.[44]

Interestingly, none of the clerical writers who discussed venality drew the parallel with simony. It was left to Voltaire to make that connection, characteristically to disparage both. Venality was worse than simony, he observed in a late edition of the *Précis du siècle de Louis XV*, because selling judicial authority placed the lives and livelihoods of citizens in potentially incompetent hands. Buying ecclesiastical benefices had no such concrete and practical consequences.[45]

Few clerics would have agreed that simony was so harmless, even if it had not implied agreeing with an opinion of Voltaire. But it was not merely a handful of clerical writers who condemned or criticized the sale of public offices. When they were given the opportunity to pronounce publicly on the state of the kingdom, the eighteenth-century French clergy as a whole yielded nothing to their sixteenth- and seventeenth-century predecessors in their denunciation of venality and its consequences. As in earlier centuries, their opportunity came with the

[42] See W. Doyle, '4 August 1789: The Intellectual Background to the Abolition of Venality of Offices', in *Officers, Nobles and Revolutionaries* (London, 1995), 141–53; and 'Voltaire and Venality: The Ambiguities of an Abuse', in T. D. Hemming, E. Freeman, and D. Meakin (eds.), *The Secular City: Studies in the Enlightenment* (Exeter, 1994), 102–11.

[43] 'Réflexions sur la vénalité des charges en France', in *Histoire de l'Académie Royale des Inscriptions et Belles Lettres avec les Mémoires de Littérature tirés des registres de cette Académie depuis l'année MCCCXLIX jusques et compris l'année MDCCLI*, xxiii. 278–83.

[44] BN MSS Fr. n. a. 2495, fo. 129. Bertin was not related to the comptroller-general and his clerical brother of the same surname mentioned above.

[45] Doyle, 'Voltaire and Venality', 107.

convocation of the estates-general and the drawing-up of *cahiers* to guide the deliberations of chosen deputies. All bishops and parish priests, and elected representatives from the capitular and regular clergy, participated in the electoral assemblies which produced these *cahiers*, of which 158 survive.[46] A survey of 150, therefore, gives a uniquely full picture of clerical opinion on the eve of the Revolution.

When Richelieu had been young the introduction of overt venality by Francis I was still just within living memory; and it remained possible to hope that its advance might yet be curbed. What is remarkable in the clerical *cahiers* of 1789 is that, even after two further centuries during which the sale of offices had continued to root itself in almost every corner of public life, it remained in clerical eyes an unacceptable abuse. Not a single clerical *cahier* defended it, although seven (or 4.66 per cent of the total) recognized that it might not be possible to buy out venal public offices entirely. This was a lower proportion than either the third estate (6.34 per cent) or the nobility (9.8 per cent), suggesting a less compromising, or perhaps more utopian, attitude to reform among the clergy. It is true that only ten (6.66 per cent) clerical *cahiers* condemned venality in general, as opposed to eighteen noble (11.76 per cent) and twenty-six (13.75 per cent) third estate. General condemnations, however, did not bulk large in any of the *cahiers*. It was normally condemned in specific contexts, where its disadvantages were demonstrated in practice. Thus thirty clerical *cahiers* denounced judicial venality. The terms used by the clergy of Loudun were typical,[47] with that blend of moral earnestness and practical naïvety so characteristic of the spirit of 1789:

Par un abus déplorable, les richesses, presque partout, tenant lieu des lumières et quelquefois de probité, nous voyons avec douleur que les charges de magistrature pour la plupart sont acquises par des hommes qui n'ont d'autre mérite qu'assez d'argent pour acheter le droit de juger leurs concitoyens; c'est dans notre gouvernement un vice radical qui cause bien des malheurs, mais on y pourroit rémédier . . . surtout en abolissant, s'il est possible, la vénalité des offices . . . alors, ne choisissant qu'entre hommes éclairés, d'un âge mûr, et d'une probité reconnue, la balance de la justice ne pencheroit plus sans discernement, ni au gré des passions, parce qu'elle seroit confiée à des mains sûres.

Eleven clerical *cahiers* also condemned venal ennoblement, but this was a far less immediate preoccupation for clerics than for nobles deploring adulteration (seventy-nine *cahiers*, almost 52 per cent) or lay commoners resenting the role of naked wealth in social promotion (forty-six *cahiers*, 24 per cent). The clergy noticed the effects of venality most when it impinged on the lives of their

[46] See B. F. Hyslop, *A Guide to the General Cahiers of 1789* (New York, 1968), 144. Most of the texts are to be found in the first six volumes of J. Madival and E. Laurent (eds.), *Archives parlementaires de 1787 à 1860* (hereafter *AP*) (90 vols.; Paris, 1879–).

[47] Ibid. iii. 590–1.

parishioners. Eight per cent of their *cahiers*, for instance, complained of the depredations of the water and forest tribunals, whose magistrates recouped their outlay in fees levied on country people. 'C'est un abus', declared the clergy of Mantes, 'que les maîtrises des eaux et forêts se donnent le droit d'exiger tantôt 30, tantôt 36, tantôt 40 sous, et même d'avantage, pour la permission donné à un particulier, d'abattre un arbre qui souvent n'a pas cette valeur.'[48] More clerical *cahiers* evoked this source of grievance than third-estate ones, though not those of the woodland-owning nobility. And if the tax-exempt clergy were much less concerned than the other two orders about the activities of the exceptional courts which enforced the state's fiscal demands, they fully shared their anger at the most deeply felt grievance related to venality to emerge from the *cahiers*, the recently enhanced monopoly of the auctioneer-valuers (*huissiers-priseurs*).[49] These functions had been a venal monopoly in principle since the time of Louis XIV, but in 1780 Necker had authorized a tightening of the monopoly prior to remarketing the offices at a higher price. The result was to flood the kingdom in the years down to 1789 with predatory swarms of officials demanding fees on every form of non-commercial property transfer. Nearly a third of all *cahiers* (32 per cent) complained about them, including a fifth of all clerical ones.

On réclamerait aussi [declared the clergy of Beauvais] la suppression de l'office des huissiers-priseurs nouvellement créés par le Roi. Ces officiers oppriment singulièrement la veuve et l'orphelin, et généralement les gens de la campagne, en assujetissant leurs successions à des frais énormes qu'elles ne sont pas en état de supporter, et dans le cas ou cette suppression n'aurait pas lieu, nous réclamons au moins la concurrence . . . telle qu'elle a toujours été demandée par les seigneurs et officiers des hautes justices.[50]

Despite differences of emphasis and concern, in general the clergy of 1789 showed themselves exercised about the same elements in venality as the other two orders. The *cahiers* reveal little specific to clerical opinion. Apart from the question of venal ennoblement, the greatest contrast in emphasis was over compensation to office-holders when venality should be abolished or pruned. The problem of reimbursement had always seemed decisive proof that venality could never be eliminated. Nowhere in the *cahiers* was it ever suggested that it should be abolished or curtailed without compensation. But, whereas 31 per cent of third-estate and 23 per cent of noble *cahiers* insisted that whatever happened the losers must be paid for their losses, only 15 clerical *cahiers*, or 10 per cent, showed any interest in this problem. One at least[51] suggested a solution already helping since 1776 to phase out purchase among army officers—a 25 per cent diminution of price at each successive mutation, eliminating any capital value entirely over four exchanges, but imposing real losses on each successive seller.

---

[48] Ibid. 659.   [49] See Doyle, *Officers, Nobles and Revolutionaries*, 149–51.   [50] *AP* i. 291.
[51] *AP* v. 649, clergy of Saint-Quentin.

Were the clergy less concerned than the laity about compensating those who profited from an abuse that must be ended? Or did they fear that to insist on compensation would lead legislators to seek means of funding reimbursement at the Church's expense? Voltaire had already hinted that it would be better to sell all church plate than to sell justice.[52] And here and there among the *cahiers* of the two lay orders there were suggestions that ecclesiastical wealth could be used to fund the diminution of venality.[53] If this was the clergy's fear, it was eventually to be realized.

On the night of 4 August 1789, along with many of the basic social institutions of the *Ancien Régime*, venality and heredity of judicial and municipal offices were abolished by the National Assembly.[54] Before the Assembly finally dispersed, that abolition had been extended to all forms of venality. And within days of the first abolition, on 11 August, the principle had been accepted that the Nation would compensate holders of formerly venal offices for their losses. Isolated voices warning of the financial burdens that this would entail were quite drowned out. Nevertheless the problem they raised was real enough. Brought into being by a monarchy no longer able to meet its debts unaided, the representative body that became the National Assembly committed itself from the outset to honouring the state's commitments. Within months, however, it had come to recognize that there was no prospect of doing so without the extraordinary expedient of nationalizing the lands of the Church to provide a new fund of confidence. The Church was to bear the cost of satisfying the Nation's creditors.

In a sense the capital tied up in venal offices was part of the state's funded debt. To abolish them meant repaying it, and the knowledge that this commitment had been made can only have spurred the deputies into their fateful decision to confiscate ecclesiastical wealth. In the event it proved even more costly than most deputies had foreseen, since reimbursing office-holders involved refunding what they had paid to their predecessors rather than simply the capital which the crown had received when offices were first marketed. Eventually the Assembly felt unable to make complete restitution, despite earlier promises. But even then the cost was so high that a massive expansion in the planned quantity of *assignats* issued on the security of former church lands had to be authorized—the first step towards the catastrophic monetary inflation that marked the revolutionary years. Dispossessed clerics could take solace that God had thus punished the Revolution for its plunder of the Church; but there was little consolation in the knowledge that so much of their former property was dispersed to liquidate a practice which they had always denounced. Ironically, the only clerics to reap any

---

[52] Doyle, 'Voltaire and Venality', 110.   [53] e.g. AP iii. 403, Nobility of Gien.
[54] On this process and its vicissitudes, see Doyle, *Venality*, ch. 9.

benefit were that handful who had accepted venality—the clerical counsellors in the *parlements*, reimbursed in full[55] for the loss of the only positions available for purchase by priests.

[55] Most office-holders were reimbursed on the basis of values declared for tax in 1771. The *parlements*, however, had been exempted from this requirement, and offices within them were liquidated on the basis of the last contract of sale.

7

'Superstitious enemies of the flesh'? The Variety of Benedictine Responses to the Enlightenment

DOM AIDAN BELLENGER

Monks and the Enlightenment, at first sight, make strange bedfellows. And, yet, linguistically at least, they share some common features. Ideas of light and enlightenment are central to the spirituality of the Christian monk, and St Benedict, the sixth-century patriarch of Western monasticism, as recorded by his biographer St Gregory the Great, had a vision in which the whole world was gathered up before his eyes in what appeared to be a single ray of light.[1] It is not the intention here to trace the continuity of the theme of enlightenment throughout the history of monasticism but to look at the attitudes of Benedictine monks across Europe in the intellectual environment of the eighteenth-century Enlightenment. The thinkers of the European Enlightenment were born into a Christian world and, however jaundiced the views of many of them became of the 'ascetic, superstitious enemies of the flesh',[2] it is remarkable how some kind of dialogue was maintained between many Church members, including monks, and those who, to use one of Peter Gay's definitions of Enlightenment, looked towards 'the organized habit of criticism'.[3] Both those who remained attached to the Church and those who chose to reject it shared a love of classical antiquity and a lack of appreciation for the Middle Ages. When we look at Benedictine monasticism today, we tend to look through a neo-Gothic filter of revived medievalism. If we look at eighteenth-century Benedictine monasticism, we are looking at a Counter-Reformation phenomenon.[4] Even the learned Benedictines of Saint-Maur, instinctive historians steeped in medieval manuscripts, lived in courtly classical monasteries and 'were unable to read the language of cathedral

---

[1] In Chapter 35 of the Second Book of the Dialogues. See Adalbert de Vogüé and Paul Austin, *Grégoire le Grand Dialogues II, Sources Chétiennes*, 260 (Paris, 1979), 239. A footnote compares Benedict's vision with similar experiences in classical antiquity recorded by Cicero and Seneca.
[2] Peter Gay, *The Enlightenment: An Interpretation: The Rise of Modern Paganism* (New York, 1966), 33.
[3] Ibid. 130.
[4] See e.g. Yves Chaussy, *Les Bénédictines et la Réforme Catholique en France au XVIIe siècle* (Paris, 1975).

sculpture'.[5] Although Counter-Reformation in their education and their intellectual formation, the Benedictines maintained at least some of their most characteristic charism—their autonomy. The tendency of post-Tridentine monks to move away from abbatial rule towards congregational government (groups of monasteries under a president or superior general) encouraged by the commendatory system did not prevent strong regional variations and loyalties. In what follows I will look at three parts of the European Benedictine world: the German-, French-, and English-speaking monasteries.[6]

The complexity of the pre-German unification political geography of central Europe and the effectiveness of the closure of many monasteries make it difficult at times to appreciate the vast scale of the monastic presence, particularly in Bavaria and Austria. In the German-speaking countries there were 154 abbeys, twenty-five of which were either imperial foundations or prince abbacies. In the second half of the eighteenth century, the German bishops, who wanted to impose their authority on the independent monasteries, fixed the age of profession at 23.[7] The German monasteries were distinguished, unlike their French and English contemporaries, by some great monastic leaders, including Dom Martin Gerbert, prince abbot of Saint-Blasien (1764–93), who combined administrative competence with genuine intellectual and religious reform.[8] They were also characterized by a strongly localized and anti-congregational feel rather than a national spirit. In the course of two years, 1802 and 1803, under the anti-monastic influence of Josephism, 159 monasteries were dissolved in Bavaria and the Upper Palatinate.[9] The outstanding scholarly achievement of these monks is documented, as a recent writer on the dispersion of Bavarian monastic books has pointed out, not only in their published academic works and in their teaching activities in schools, monastic academies, and universities, but also in numerous letters exchanged among themselves and, in the years immediately preceding the secularization, between them and the bureaucrats.[10]

This meeting of minds supports the suggestion of Professor W. R. Ward, reviewing a recent book on the 'Katholische Aufklärüng' in Germany, that the

---

[5] Gay, *The Enlightenment*, 353. The Maurists did, however, attempt to use a Gothic medium in some of their buildings. See Joan Evans, *Monastic Architecture in France from the Renaissance to the Revolution* (Cambridge, 1964), 18.

[6] For the history of the Benedictines in Italy, the publications of the Centro Storico Benedittino Italiano include Francesco Trolese (ed.), *Il monachesimo italiano dalle riforme illuministiche all'unita nazionale (1768–1870)* (Cesena, 1992), which, despite its title, makes few references to the Enlightenment. For the general Italian background, see F. Venturi, *Italy and the Enlightenment* (London, 1972). For Spain, see D. Goodman, 'Science and the Clergy in the Spanish Enlightenment', *History of Science*, 21 (1983), 111–40.

[7] Patrice Cousin, *Précis d'histoire monastique* (Paris, 1956), 455–6.

[8] See Henrich Heidegger and Hogo Ott (eds.), *St Blasien* (Munich, 1983), 111–94.

[9] Bettina Wagner, 'Bodleian Incunables from Bavarian Monasteries', *Bodleian Library Record*, 15 (1995), 92. See also Joseph Hemmerle, *Die Benediktinklöster in Bayern* (Augsburg, 1970).

[10] Wagner, 'Bodleian Incunables', 91.

Enlightenment in Catholic Germany did not sustain the animosity against the Church which may have been more noticeable in France.[11] There is always a temptation in Enlightenment studies to pay too much attention to France. As Professor Beales has argued, the Austrian Enlightenment had a strongly Christian character, and Joseph II himself, the hammer of the monks, was a Christian reformer not a destroyer.[12] In a religiously divided society like Germany, the Catholic teaching of *Lumen Naturale* could offer greater hospitality to the Enlightenment than Lutheran doctrines of total depravity. Throughout the eighteenth century, when many Benedictine houses were being lavishly refurbished in baroque style, some also reached a new maturity in learning. Benedictines ran the university of Salzburg, an independent Catholic prince archbishopric and a self-conscious centre of higher culture, in its best years,[13] and others established *Ritterakademien*, to provide a proper education in modern subjects. Joseph II notwithstanding, in many ways eighteenth-century Austrian Benedictinism experienced an Enlightenment golden age: 'Österreich' truly was 'Klösterreich'.

This is perhaps no more physically apparent than at Kremsmunster, south-west of Linz. Its extraordinary set of buildings includes a series of late-seventeenth-century Palladian-collonaded fishponds, which were used as a display area for the heads of the stags hunted by the abbots. Hunting seems an even more incongruous pastime for a monk than pursuing the Enlightenment. The most striking if not the most beautiful part of the ensemble is the observatory, the *Sternwarte*, architecturally reminiscent of an Eastern European tower block, some seventy metres high. It is sometimes known as the 'Mathematical Tower'. It was constructed between 1746 and 1759 as a home for the scientific and artistic collections of the monastery. It is an encyclopaedia in stone with an implicit hierarchy of the sciences in the ascending order of its seven floors, with geology at the base and astronomy at the pinnacle via palaeontology, mineralogy, physics, zoology, and anthropology. Astronomy's pre-eminence was reinforced by the presence of a statue of a great astronomer ranging from Ptolemy to Kepler on each landing.[14]

---

[11] W. R. Ward, *Journal of Ecclesiastical History*, 46 (1995), 160–1, reviewing H. Klueting *et al.* (eds.), *Aufklärung in Katholische Deutschland* (Hamburg, 1993). Particularly helpful for this chapter was Georg Heilingsetzer, 'Die Benediktiner in 18. Jahrhundert Wissenschaft und Gelehrsankeit im suddeutsch-österreichischen Raum', in Klueting *et al.* (eds.), 208–24, which provides an extensive bibliography in its notes.

[12] D. Beales, 'Christians and "philosophes": The Case of the Austrian Enlightenment', in D. Beales and G. Best (eds.), *History, Society and the Churches: Essays in Honour of Owen Chadwick* (Cambridge, 1985), 189.

[13] See Magnus Sattler, *Collectanea Blätter zur Geschichte der ehemaligen Benediktiner-Universitat Salzburg* (Kempton, 1889), which lists the Benedictine professors and provides a comprehensive bibliography for their works.

[14] For Kremsmunster, see *Cremifanum 777–1977: Festschift zur 1200-Jahr-Feier des Stiftes*

Astronomy was perhaps the key area of dialogue between Enlightenment and religion, even if quite different inferences could be drawn from its observations. Astronomy could be seen as 'the model of a successful science' with its observational and theoretical dimensions, a symbol of the triumphs of the scientific method.[15] Newton's solution to the problem of the motion of the planets was seen as an unparalleled scientific achievement by the apostles of Newtonianism, who included not a few monks. Newton's natural philosophy, it could be argued, had cast light on the hitherto unknown intricacies of God's glorious design. John McManners has suggested that by 1778, the year of the deaths of Voltaire and Rousseau, all the stock arguments against Christianity had been formulated with the exception of the 'science-versus-religion' antithesis, 'a gambit as yet undetected behind the "Wisdom of God manifest in the Works of Creation" theme that had inspired John Ray, Robert Boyle, and Isaac Newton'.[16] Edmond Halley's prediction of the return of the comet (subsequently named after him) in 1759 reinforced the feeling that Newtonian science had achieved prophetic power over celestial events. It was significantly in 1759 that the Kremsmunster observatory was opened, with its first resident astronomer, Dom Placidus Fixlmillner, brother of the then abbot. It became known for certain discoveries about the movement of the stars and planets, but was famous (as it is today) for its long unbroken and precise meteorological measurements.[17] Monastic astronomy tended to observe revolutions rather than make them. The baroque monasteries of central Europe thus provided foyers of culture where the sciences were practised and the arts celebrated as part of an integrated view of life and faith.[18]

In terms of their physical appearance there is something much more severe about the remaining monastic buildings of seventeenth- and eighteenth-century France than there is about their German counterparts.[19] The French Benedictines had some 400 houses in the eighteenth century, the largest number in any country. Along with the Jesuits and the Oratorians, they were celebrated for their schools as well as for their learning. Many of their recruits were drawn from the aristocracy. The first part of the eighteenth century was distinguished by conflicts

Kremsmunster (Linz, 1977). See Germain Bazin, *Les Palais de la foi* (Fribourg, 1981), for Kremsmunster in its baroque context.

[15] See Jan Glinski, 'Astronomy', in John W. Yolton *et al.* (eds.), *The Blackwell Companion to the Englightenment* (Oxford, 1991), 44.

[16] John McManners, 'Enlightenment: Secular and Christian (1600–1800)', in *The Oxford Illustrated History of Christianity* (Oxford, 1990), 281–2.

[17] See Konradin d'Occhieppo, 'Placidus Fixlmillner, Kremsmunsters bedentedster Astronom', *Cremifarnum 777–1977*, 75–9.

[18] Bazin, *Les Palais de la foi*, 80.

[19] For the French buildings, see M. Bugner, *Cadre architectural et vie monastique des bénédictins de la congrégation de Saint-Maur* (Noget-le-Roi, 1984), and Evans, *Monastic Architecture*, 6–53.

about Jansenism, the second part by a state onslaught which predated the Revolution. The 'Commission des Réguliers', set up in 1766, decreed in 1768 that religious profession could not be made until the age of 21. This had an immediate effect on recruitment. Among the French Cluniacs numbers fell from 671 in 1768 to 600 in 1785.[20] Many of the houses, over 190 in total, were of the Maurist congregation (French Benedictinism was never monolithic), and this was the congregation above all where the figure of the monk-scholar predominates. It was at the forefront of historical, or at least of antiquarian and diplomatic study from the seventeenth century onwards, and Dom David Knowles counts the labours of its members, communally as well as individually (Mabillon's name still compels respect, as do others), for such works as the *Gallia Christiana* among his great historical enterprises.[21] Indeed, as far as the study of history was concerned, the French monasteries were far ahead of their German-speaking brethren, with whom they nevertheless corresponded. In the Habsburg Empire, Melk was to achieve an enviable reputation as a centre of historical learning. Bernard Pez was perhaps its greatest historian, the editor of the six-volume *Thesaurus anecdotomen novessimus* (1721–9). He wanted to start a collection of the writings of all monks, but the project came to nothing. Abbot Berthold Dietmayr wanted to concentrate all Melk's resources on buildings. Grandeur not learning was his guiding light.[22] French monasticism was most subject to the critics of the Enlightenment and suffered remorselessly from the wit of Voltaire and others, as John McManners has demonstrated.[23] In 1754 Voltaire spent almost a month with Abbot Augustin Calmet (1672–1757) at the abbey of Senones, a Vannist house. The formidably learned Calmet had the urge to be encyclopaedic before Diderot, but fawned on Voltaire. At the age of 83 the monk climbed up a high and unsteady ladder to pull out old books for the *philosophe*. Voltaire responded by describing his host as a 'naïve compiler of so many fantasies and imbecilities, whose simplicity has made him invaluable to whoever wishes to laugh at ancient follies'.[24] Dom Calmet was the quintessential French Benedictine of his time. He combined curiosity with credulity, social grace with eccentricity, a quest for new learning with a mind still dominated by the mentality of an enclosed cloister. Yet the reformers of French monasticism, in the romantic afterglow of the Revolution, tried to distance themselves in all but its learned tradition from the Maurists. They were suspected of a light-hearted indifference and even of harbouring too many Freemasons among their

---

[20] Cousin, *Précis d'histoire monastique*, 450–4.
[21] David Knowles, *Great Historical Enterprises* (London, 1963), 35–61.
[22] See B. Ellegast *et al.*, *Stift Melk: Geschichte und Gegenwart* (Melk, 1981).
[23] John McManners, 'Voltaire and the Monks', in W. J. Sheils (ed.), *Monks, Hermits, and the Ascetic Tradition* (Studies in Church History, 22; Oxford, 1985), 319–42.
[24] Ibid. 324.

number. Indeed, a recent prosophographer of the Maurists, Dom Charvin, has tried to identify those who actually belonged to Freemasonic lodges.[25] This association was seen as going too far in the direction of the spirit of the age.

Dom Yves Chaussy, whose *aperçu historique* of the Maurists appeared in 1989, provides an excellent introduction to the institutional and congregational history of the Benedictines of Saint-Maur but devotes surprisingly little space to the relationship between the French monastic order and the Enlightenment.[26] I suspect that he, like many French Catholic ecclesiastical historians, is more interested in the apogee of the congregation in the second half of the seventeenth century than with what he would consider its decline. There is, too, the whole vexed question of Jansenism and it relationship—or otherwise—to the Christian Enlightenment and the way in which the fall of the Jesuits may have increased Benedictine influence, albeit for a few years. In the last thirty years before the French Revolution, the Maurists' well-tempered, ordered life continued to survive and continued to produce scholars and writers.

The majority of their publications were in the historical or scriptural fields. But there were others. Dom Léger-Marie Deschamps, author of *Letters sur l'esprit du siècle* (1761) and *La Voix de la raison contre la raison du temps* (1770), has been seen as an antecedent to Hegelienism. He corresponded widely with the *philosophes,* arguing that the existing 'état des lois' had to be contrasted with the 'état des mœurs', where social rule is irrelevant and where equality rules. Dom Nicholas Grenier gave (in 1767) his *avis* to naturalists as well as to antiquarians. Dom Joseph Pernetty, as well as producing a mathematical *cours,* Newtonian in tone, collaborated with Dom François de Brézillac in writings on mythology and fine art, accompanied the naturalist Bougainville, and looked to the new world both literally and metaphorically. Pernetty was completely at home in an Enlightenment environment and, like many of his confrères, saw all learning as part of God's great canvas of universal knowledge. In 1790 he reconsidered his Enlightenment past and produced a work *La Vertu, le pouvoir, la clémence et la gloire de Marie, mère de dieu* which suggested a substantial shift away from the Enlightenment. Some did not leave it so late. Dom Pierre Deforis, who was to die in 1794 on the scaffold, took up arms with Rousseau over *Émile* in 1762, and in 1768 produced an apologia for the religious life. In 1777 Dom Jacques Wilson, a monk of Jumièges, translated into French Dom Charles Walmesley's profoundly anti-Enlightenment *General History of the Church.*[27]

---

[25] G. Charvin, 'Les Religieux de la Congrégation de Saint-Maur pendant la Révolution', *Revue Mabillon*, lv–lvii (1965–8).

[26] Yves Chaussy, *Les Bénédictins de Saint-Maur Aperçu Historique* (Paris, 1989).

[27] Bibliographical details are taken from C. de Lama, *Bibliothèque des écrivains de la Congrégation de Saint-Maur* (Munich, 1882). Jean Godefroy, in *Bibliothèque des Bénédictins de la Congrégation de Saint-Vanne et Saint Hydulphe* (Ligugé, 1925), shows the continuing scholarly endeavours of non-Maurist

The person of Charles Walmesley, of whom more later, leads us to the English Benedictines, whose life and history up to the French Revolution were intimately connected with the French Church and its monastic order. In 1992 Dom Geoffrey Scott's work about English monks in the Age of Enlightenment appeared with the intriguing title *Gothic Rage Undone*, which refers to a verse written in 1749 by Dom Augustine Walker rejecting the contempory identification of monasticism with superstition and seeing it instead as the antidote to barbarism:

> A Gothic deluge learning overrun.
> But monks undo what Gothic rage had done.[28]

The English Benedictine congregation, a missionary-based body with seventeenth-century constitutions, revised under French government reforms, was, in many ways, the poor relation of the great continental monastic families (with the exception of its baroque abbey at Lambspring near Hildesheim), but its very smallness allows a clearer overview than might be possible in a more complex and elaborate organization. In its origins, and until the late nineteenth century, when it became more self-consciously conventual, the English Benedictine congregation was dedicated to working on the English mission. The Benedictines in the French priories at Douai, Dieulouard, and Paris, on the other hand, were nourished by the intellectual vitality of the country. Douai had a well-established and thriving university,[29] but it was Paris which by the late eighteenth century was the place where the latest theological ideas were taught by such as Luke Joseph Hooke, the anglophone theologian (born in Dublin in 1714) who was at various times Professor of Theology, Professor of Hebrew and Chaldean, and head of the Mazarine Library. Thomas O'Connor, in a recent book, has suggested that Hooke was at the very centre of the French Catholic Enlightenment in his fresh approach to theological studies. Hooke was having to cope creatively with the whole range of new forces thrown up by Enlightenment France: the demand for religious toleration, the severity of deist criticism, the discovery of other world religions, the widening interference of secular authority in the ecclesiastical sphere. His response was to modernize without

---

French Benedictines in the eighteenth century. Apart from Dom Calmet, writers included Dom Jean-Baptiste Aubry, who explored contemporary metaphysics, Dom Pierre Massuet, an expert on matters medical, and Dom Donat-François Porro, a mathematician. Dom Jean François, who died in 1791, one of the most learned of Vannist monks, produced a four-volume *Biliothèque générale des écrivains de l'ordre de Saint Benoît* (Bouillon, 1777–78). In his preface (p. vi) he reflects how Totila, king of the Goths, was transformed by meeting St Benedict: 'On dit que le goth parut beaucoup moins barbare après cette entreuve.'

[28] Geoffrey Scott, *Gothic Rage Undone* (Bath, 1992), 155.
[29] See Gilbert Dehon 'L'Université de Douai au XVIIème et au XVIIIème siècle', unpublished doctoral thesis (Lille, n.d.). An observatory for astronomical observations was opened at Douai in 1761 (p. 255).

compromising. As a modernizer, Hooke saw religion as the necessary foundation of all knowledge and all political life. The sacred and the secular are not distinct but part of one world, the product of the one divine wisdom, the one great *religio*.[30] Hooke's majesterial *Religionis naturalis et revelatae principia*, originally published in 1752–4, appeared in a second edition in 1774 prepared by one of his students, the English Benedictine, Dom Bede Brewer.[31]

The learned English Benedictine was not typically a theologian, but a historian combining, or at least being influenced by, the two traditions of the Maurist *érudits* and the non-juring antiquarians, influences discussed at length by Scott.[32] The scholarly monk, even on the mission, was a familiar type, an early eighteenth-century example was Dom Gilbert Knowles, whose *Materia medica botanica* appeared in 1723 and provided a description of 400 herbs strung together with Latin hexameters. This was the first non-religious work produced by an English monk.[33] Under continental and particularly French influence, more obviously enlightened ideas swept through the young men in the congregation in the mid-century. In 1749 an English Benedictine academy, the Society of St Edmund, dedicated itself to scientific study, hoping to combat disbelief through the proper study of 'Sacred and profane history' and 'Mathematics and . . . all Natural History'. Its guiding light was Walmesley.[34] It can be compared with the much greater-scale Bavarian academy, which in 1759 accepted into its membership Dom Ildephonsus Kennedy, a Scots monk and a graduate of Erfurt, who was to play a leading part in its enquiries for forty years.[35]

As the eighteenth century moved into its later phase there was a growing divergence between religion and the Enlightenment. Some among the reduced number of Benedictines continued to flirt with its less controversial areas through the arts and a common aesthetic. Others, even those who had sought to modernize theology, moved towards a more pessimistic view. In the latter camp was Charles Walmesley, the eighteenth-century monk who perhaps is the best Benedictine exemplar of both the acceptance and the repudiation of the Enlightenment.[36] Charles Walmesley, born near Wigan on 13 January 1722, was educated

[30] Thomas O'Connor, *An Irish Theologian in Enlightenment France: Luke Joseph Hooke 1714–16* (Dublin, 1995).

[31] Ibid. 102.   [32] Scott, *Gothic Rage*, 145–89.   [33] Ibid. 150.

[34] Ibid. 155. Five volumes of the Society's transactions are preserved in the archives at Douai Abbey, Woolhampton (Memoirs of the Society, 1749–56).

[35] See Eric G. Forbes, 'Ildephonse Kennedy, OSB (1722–1804) and the Bavarian Academy of Sciences', *Innes Review*, 32 (1981), 93–9. The context is set by Mark Goldie in three articles, 'The Scottish Catholic Enlightenment', *Journal of British Studies*, 30 (1991), 20–62; 'Common Sense Philosophy and Catholic Theology in the Scottish Enlightenment', *Studies on Voltaire and the Eighteenth Century*, 302 (1992), 281–320, and 'Bishop Hay, Bishop Geddes and the Scottish Catholic Enlightenment', *Innes Review*, 44 (1994), 82–6.

[36] For Walmesley, see Geoffrey Scott, *Gothic Rage, passim*, and ' "The Times are Fast Approaching": Bishop Charles Walmesley O.S.B. (1722–1797) as Prophet', *Journal of Ecclesiastical History*, 36 (1985), 590–604. The present author contributed a short biography of Walmesley to the *Dictionaire de spiritualité*, 16 (1994), 1303–6.

at St Gregory's, Douai, and made his profession as a monk of St Edmund's, the English Benedictine priory in the rue Saint-Jacques in Paris, on 29 September 1739. He had a distinguished academic career which combined a doctorate in Theology at the Sorbonne with mathematical and astronomical interests, which duly led to his election to the Royal Society of London in 1750. As a young monk he made a scientific expedition to Mount Etna in Sicily. He advised the British government on the change from the Julian to the Gregorian calendar. He continued to pursue his interests when offices of administration began to be given to him. He served as prior of his Paris community from 1749 to 1753 and went to Rome as procurator of the English Benedictines in 1754. He was consecrated bishop of Rama in 1756 and appointed coadjutor to the vicar apostolic of the Western District succeeding to the charge in 1779. He lived at Bath from then until his death on 25 November 1797. In 1780 his residence and chapel were destroyed and his papers burnt in a local outburst of the 'No Popery' or Gordon riots. It is said that this episode put an end to his scientific career. Previously, he could be so distracted at Mass that he found himself making diagrams on the linen of the altar with his paten. The end of his mathematical endeavours are said to have caused much concern to the *philosophe* D'Alembert.[37] Walmesley advised his successor Dom Gregory Sharrock that the reading needed for the mission was not the same as that needed in France.[38] As senior vicar apostolic he defended episcopal rights against those, especially among the 'Old Catholic' gentry families, who favoured a more lay-dominated church. On 15 August 1790 he consecrated John Carroll as the first bishop of the new North American hierarchy, the public act with which he is most associated.

Walmesley became a noted writer.[39] His early publications were purely scientific and mathematical and reflected his enthusiasm for Newtonian science, a love of many Enlightened Benedictines of the time. In 1749, for example, he published an investigation of the motion of the lunar apsides, a study he continued with further works until 1761. His conclusions were confirmed by the distinguished mathematician Matthew Stewart (1717–85). The insights provided by these studies were employed by Walmesley in his most important work, published in London in 1771 under the *alias* of Signor Pastorini and entitled *The General History of the Christian Church from her Birth to Final Triumphant State in Heaven, Chiefly Deduced from the Apocalypse of St John the Apostle.* This work,

[37] Downside Abbey Archives, MS 846, Athanasius Allanson, 'Biography of the English Benedictines', ii (Bishop Walmesley), 5.

[38] Clifton Diocesan Archives, Correspondence 1772–88, Document 12, Walmesley to Sharrock, 2 Jan. 1780.

[39] For a bibliography, see J. Gillow, *Bibliographical Dictionary of the English Catholics*, v (London, 1885), 569–70.

principally a commentary on the Book of Revelation and an analysis of Christian history, reflects Walmesley's wide reading and acute intellect. It owed much to the claustrophobic atmosphere of eighteenth-century English Catholicism, and something to English Protestant writing, but its thought was widely European in its influences. Like Newton, he turned his glass from the heavenly bodies to the visions of the apocalypse.[40] French commentators on the Book of Revelation, including Bossuet and the Benedictine Calmet, were crucial influences. Walmesley shared the Counter-Reformation interpretation of history, which presented Protestantism as a secession from the true Church. His view of the future had no time for any abrupt Protestant millenarianism but, in the short term, looked forward to a period of gloom and despondency. Walmesley was original in his approach to the place of his own age in the history of the Church. He saw himself, with characteristic mathematical precision, as living in the second half of the fifth of the seven ages (1675–1835), coinciding roughly with what we might call the 'Age of Enlightenment' in which the Reformation was continued by 'Methodists and Huthinsonians' and other sects who would produce 'a defection from religion' and lead to latitudinarianism, deism, free thought, and atheism. This text was enlivened by the experiences and examples of his scientific research. Thus, he believed that St John was speaking of the 'firing of Carbines' when he spoke of Antichrist's cavalry wearing breast plates of fire and of hyacinth and brimstone (Rev. 19: 9–17). *The General History* was his principal work, although its themes were later explored in *Ezechiel's Vision Explained* (London 1778). Walmesley's work on the books of Revelation and Ezechiel were pioneer studies in the growing disillusionment of the European Catholic intelligentsia with the Enlightenment. They became popular within reading circles and were translated into many languages. Walmesley's central idea that contemporary suffering and natural disasters were largely the result of a turning-away from God and a general infidelity became increasingly persuasive as an age of reason gave way in the Benedictine world to an age of anxiety.

Walmesley's passage from the Enlightenment to dark depression reflected an intellectual's personal progress. Most of his English Benedictine *confrères* were content with less profound thoughts. Not all monks of the Enlightenment period were enlightened, nor were they all *savants*, despite their broad classical education. The Revd William Cole, an Anglican antiquary, expected to find all Benedictines as learned as the Maurists, or at least as intelligent and personable as the monk missioners he had encountered in England. He found the prior of St Gregory's Douai a sad disappointment, who, though 'the brother of a baronet and quite civil, was of a rough and clownish carriage and of no striking address

---

[40] Downside Abbey Archives, Allanson, 'Biography', ii. 4.

or behaviour'. He was similarly disappointed at St Edmund's Paris. There was civility, as J. C. H. Aveling put it, but no meeting of minds.[41]

The English Benedictines of the eighteenth century tended to be stolidly pragmatic and few would fall into the categories discussed by Joseph Chinnici in his book on *The English Catholic Enlightenment* published in 1980. He uses a definition of Bernard Plongeron, which sees the practitioners of the Catholic Enlightenment as those who sought 'to promote a mystique of salvation in conformity with the development of secular knowledge and the perfectibility of the person in his social environment, his customs and language'.[42] Chinnici sees those in the English Cisalpine group as attempting to synthesize their Catholic faith and the thought of the Enlightenment in five areas: Church–State relations, theology, ecclesiology, history, and religious practice. They advocated political secularization, religious liberty, and a contractual theory of both civil and ecclesiastical government; they applied a critical methodology to various intellectual and theological disciplines and exhibited 'a culturally open approach to dogma and piety'.[43] A reasonable working hypothesis, but few (if any) individual Benedictine would fall into this definition. In the increasingly utilitarian world of the Enlightenment, monasticism was failing to show its social or economic usefulness. For all its learning and broadly based culture, the monastic ideal seemed socially irrelevant and economically unsound.[44] And yet for the greater part of the eighteenth century monks and the Enlightenment coexisted.

This chapter suggests rather that within this Enlightenment *milieu* the monks played a not inconsiderable part. The greater emphasis on critical logic in the university courses at Paris and elsewhere and the broadening curriculum in monastic education formed a generation.[45] The shift in the contents of monastic libraries from Counter-Reformation polemic to a more humane aspiration for universal knowledge is apparent in the baroque buildings of Benedictine Europe and their burgeoning libraries.[46] The monastic Enlightenment had the confidence that universal knowledge was still attainable as a complete system in which both theology and the natural sciences had full rights of citizenship in a serene harmony. Thus the Spanish Benito Feijoó, an insatiable encyclopaedist, who taught philosophy and theology at the University of Oviedo, was a model

[41] Quoted by J. C. H. Aveling, 'The Eighteenth Century English Benedictines', in Eamon Duffy (ed.), *Challoner and his Church* (London, 1981), 164.

[42] Joseph P. Chinnici, *The English Catholic Enlightenment: John Lingard and the Civalpine Movement* (Shepardstown, 1980), p. x.

[43] Ibid., pp. x–xi.

[44] McManners, 'Voltaire and the Monks', 339–42. See also John McManners, *The French Revolution and the Church* (London, 1969), 9–11.

[45] See e.g. J. C. H. Aveling, 'The Education of Eighteenth-Century English Monks', *Downside Review* 76 (1961), 135–52.

[46] See e.g. Elmar Mittler and Wolfgang Müller, *Die Bibliothek des Klosters St Peter* (Bühl, 1972).

Enlightenment monk who took every opportunity to displace superstition with fact. He visited the chapel of St Louis at Cangas de Tineo to see the miracle of the tiny white flowers which covered so much of the interior of the buildings and its contents and concluded on close examination that they were insects: 'The people saw these eggs elsewhere—but in the hermitage they were sure that they were flowers.'[47] A niggle, however, always remained in the monastic mind. Plongeron's view that there was a European Catholic élite bound together to make the Christian faith intelligible to an Enlightenment person is appealing.[48] In 1754, when the entrance gate of the great abbey of Saint-Vaast at Arras was rebuilt, it was adorned with equally balanced statues of religion and learning.[49] The Christian Enlightenment tried to put over the message that its faith was a coherent whole and not, as Voltaire said of Shakespeare, a dunghill strewn with diamonds.[50] And yet, in reducing the *mystique* and emphasizing the logic, there was a danger of blandness and elegant torpidity. In essence, Christianity and the Enlightenment have different agendas in their search for the truth.

In the Austrian monastery at Altenburg, through the painting of Paul Troger, light is presented in all its aspects and is placed, with a flourish and precision typical of its age, in the appropriate places.[51] The light of faith illuminates the staircase and the imperial apartments, the light of glory the church vault, the light of wisdom the library, and natural light the great *salon*, the Marmorsaal. But at the heart of the scheme, under the library, is the funeral vault, depicting the vanity of human learning. In this image we see the essential ambiguity of a Christocentric enlightenment.

[47] Owen Chadwick, *The Popes and European Revolution* (Oxford, 1981), 5.
[48] Chinicci, *The English Catholic Enlightenment*, 4.
[49] Joan Evans, *Monastic Iconography in France* (Cambridge, 1970), 17.
[50] Gay, *The Enlightenment*, 5.
[51] Bazin, *Les palais de la foi*, 123. For a full description of the Altenburg buildings, see Hanna Egger *et al.*, *Stift Altenburg* (St Pölten, 1981).

8

Joseph II and the Monasteries of Austria and Hungary

Derek Beales

Everyone who visits rural Austria for the first time is struck by the number and size of the working monasteries that dominate its landscape. Among them are the vast Augustinian house of St Florian near Linz, Cistercian Wilhering with its exuberant rococo decoration, and the monumental Benedictine abbey of Melk towering above the Danube valley. In the cities of Salzburg and Vienna, too, ancient Benedictine abbeys, St Peter's and the Schottenstift, remain a formidable presence. Most of these institutions appear to date from the late seventeenth and early eighteenth centuries, when they were lavishly refurbished or rebuilt. But one by one they are celebrating their eight-hundredth, nine-hundredth, thousandth, even twelve-hundredth anniversaries. By contrast, almost everywhere in Western Europe monasteries were eradicated either by the Reformation, by the French Revolution, or under the aegis of Napoleon. Further east, in the Czech Republic, for example, many lasted into the twentieth century but succumbed to communist regimes after the Second World War. The almost unique continuity of monastic life in many of the great Austrian foundations was breached only for a few years, during the Nazi regime. If the visitor knows that the emperor Joseph II, as ruler of the Austrian Monarchy in the 1780s, is notorious for having carried through a drastic programme of church reform which included the suppression of numerous monasteries, he will wonder how on earth these vast establishments came to survive.

Figures about Joseph's suppressions remained inconsistent and unreliable until Professor Peter Dickson published in 1987 his *Finance and Government under Maria Theresia 1740–1780*, followed by his article in the *Historical Journal* of 1993, 'Joseph II's Re-Shaping of the Austrian Church'. These two magisterial works have cleared up most of the uncertainties in the statistics. In the entire Austrian Monarchy, including the geographically separated provinces of Belgium and Lombardy, there were just over 2,000 religious houses when Joseph II succeeded his mother in 1780. In the lands that were in a stricter sense Austrian provinces, that is, Upper and Lower Austria, Inner Austria, Tyrol and Vorarlberg, and Further Austria, monasteries held an especially important position. This area contained more than 500 houses, with altogether about 10,000 monks and over 1,000 nuns. As against these more than 11,000 regular clergy, there were only about 6,500 secular, that is non-monastic, clergy. Monasteries owned nearly half of all Church land, and therefore something like 20 per cent of all land. In most of these Austrian provinces, unlike other parts of the Monarchy except the Netherlands, the local representative assemblies or Estates were headed by a First Estate consisting entirely or largely of abbots of monasteries of ancient foundation. Bishops, of whom there were in any case very few, were not always included. The president of the First Estate of Lower Austria was the abbot of Melk, who, after the *Landmarschall,* the government's representative, was usually the most important member of the permanent subcommittee (*Landes-Ausschuss*) which conducted the business of the Estates between Diets. There is some force in the ancient catchphrase 'Österreich, Klösterreich', which might be translated 'Austria, the monasteries' state'. During the 1780s, however, Joseph II directed a barrage of ordinances at the monasteries, and by 1790, when he died and a halt was called, there remained in these Austrian provinces fewer than 250 houses and 5,000 regular clergy.

This policy evoked both enthusiasm and indignation in its day, and is still highly controversial in Austria itself. But its results seem rather limited if they are set against the total suppressions carried out in France by 1792, and in Germany and nearly all of Italy by 1812. On the other hand, it was easily the most radical monastic policy enacted by any eighteenth-century Catholic government before the Revolution. Dickson is not primarily concerned with the content of Joseph's ecclesiastical legislation nor with the philosophy behind it. He rightly points out that they have been much better studied than the matters he has examined— namely, Joseph's investigation and reorganization of the Church in the central lands. As he says, the emperor's principal aims are well known: to subject the Church to state control in all save purely spiritual matters; to introduce legal toleration for the main Protestant Churches and for Jews; to strengthen the episcopate; and to reshape 'the church away from its traditional emphasis on monasticism towards a more numerous, better educated, secular clergy'.[1]

---

[1] This essay follows from the discussion of monasteries and their reform in P. G. M. Dickson, *Finance and Government under Maria Theresia* (2 vols.; Oxford, 1987), esp. i, chs. 4, 11, and pp. 103, 446, and 'Joseph II's Reshaping of the Austrian Church, *Historical Journal,* 36 (1993), 89–114. Professor Dickson not only gave me copies of these works but has been unfailingly generous with help and advice over many years. He made most useful comments on an earlier draft of this essay. On the Estates, see also H. Stradal, 'Die Prälatenkurie der österreichischen Landstände', *Anciens pays et assemblées d'états,* 53 (1970), 117–80. The Austrian provinces of the eighteenth century include all of modern Austria except Salzburg and its region, which then made up an independent prince-archbishopric, and Burgenland, then a part of Hungary. On the other hand, part of the Tyrol and all of Further Austria are no longer Austrian territory. There is no general survey of the history or place of monasteries in the Austrian Monarchy.

While it is true that Joseph's policy has often been described, certain of its aspects have still not been adequately covered. In this chapter I shall consider some of them, using new or little-known material from the Vatican, Austrian, and Hungarian archives. I shall concentrate on the following issues: the relationship between Maria Theresa's monastic policy and her son's; the involvement of monasteries in parochial work; hitherto unsuspected opposition to Joseph's policy at the highest level of the bureaucracy; and the impact of his legislation in Hungary, which was significantly different from its effect in Austria itself. The subject is so complex and the documentation so vast that I cannot pretend to deal exhaustively with any of these topics. What I hope to do is to open up some neglected themes and to show how much remains to be found out.

It was probably in 1750 that Maria Theresa dictated the first version of her political testament. This was just after she had forced through a reform of the constitution of her central lands, curbing the power of the Estates—and therefore of the great abbeys of Austria—in order to increase her revenue and army.[2] In this document she declared that the clergy of the German lands were in a good and flourishing condition and needed no more of the lavish assistance that they had been receiving from the State, or from her predecessors. In fact, she went on, 'they do not—alas!—apply what they have as they should, and moreover, they constitute a heavy burden on the public. For no monastic House observes the limitations of its statutes, and many idlers are admitted; all this will call for a great remedy, which I propose to effect in good time and after due consideration.' But, she continued,

I except from such measures the Kingdom of Hungary, where much still remains to be done for religion, in which task I shall require the clergy there to cooperate, but not work with them alone, but concert chiefly with laymen on the principles to be followed, the chief aim of which must be to introduce seminaries, colleges, academies, hospitals for the sick and injured, conservatories (as in Italy) for unmarried women, for the better instruction of the young etc., taking careful pains to support and develop what is useful to the public, and not what profits the private advantage of the clergy, monks and nuns in any Province.[3]

This is an astonishing pronouncement coming from a young and devout monarch, still with a Jesuit confessor, and heiress to Charles VI, who had yearned to complete a palace-monastery for himself by remodelling the ancient Augustinian house of Klosterneuburg.[4] It is deservedly a famous passage, and it has been

---

[2] J. Kallbrunner (ed.), *Kaiserin Maria Theresias politisches Testament* (Vienna, 1952), has the best text of the testament. A. Ritter von Arneth, 'Zwei Denkschriften der Kaiserin Maria Theresias', *Archiv für österreichische Geschichte* (hereafter *AÖG*), xlvii (1871), 267–354, is more accessible. On the dates of the two versions see Dickson, *Finance and Government*, ii. 3 n. On the constitutional reform, see F. Walter, *Die theresianische Staatsreform von 1749* (Vienna, 1958).

[3] Kallbrunner, *Kaiserin Maria Theresias politisches Testament*, 38.

[4] D. Beales, *Joseph II*, i. *In the Shadow of Maria Theresa, 1741–1780* (Cambridge, 1987), 23.

asserted that from this utterance stems the whole gamut of Church legislation associated with her and with Joseph II, that what is known as Josephism or Josephinism actually derives from Maria Theresa's 'great remedy'.[5]

There are many difficulties about placing so much weight on this statement. The greatest is that, under examination, the programme, like the syntax, appears both incoherent and elusive. On the one hand, she says it is desirable that the Catholic religion should flourish and that the condition of the clergy should be good; on the other hand, *what is useful to the public* is a touchstone. She declares that monasteries should observe the limitations of their statutes and not admit idlers, but she does not condemn them in principle. She envisages different remedies for the central lands and for Hungary. It is with specific reference to Hungary that she makes one of her most radical statements: that she will require the clergy to cooperate with laymen in reform. But it sounds as though she thinks the Church in Hungary, unlike that in the central lands, needs *more* priests and *more* endowments. One cannot tell from her words what her concept of 'utility to the public' amounts to, or what her attitude is to monasteries of contemplative Orders. The meaning of 'useful' can be almost infinitely variable. Even in Joseph II's reign, in 1781, one of his most trusted ministers, Count Hatzfeld, president of the *Staatsrat*, argued that contemplative orders ought to be regarded as contributing to *das allgemeine Beste*—the general advantage—through their prayers and worship.[6] It is virtually certain that Maria Theresa would have agreed with him.

If one takes down the nine volumes of Maria Theresa's published edicts, it is disconcerting to find that the third item, of early 1741, is a prohibition on erecting maypoles because it employs labour and wastes wood.[7] That might be an edict of Joseph's, though environmentalism seems here to take precedence over objections to superstition. Contrariwise, a month before he died, Joseph was taking great pains to ensure that the Catholic Church founded by Joseph I in St Petersburg should be well supplied with silver, missals, and vestments from dissolved monasteries, 'since [he said] it is highly desirable, indeed necessary, that I should give an example in supporting and glorifying my true religion, especially in foreign countries'.[8] He and his mother, for all their violent disputes, were not *diametrically* opposed to each other. Both wished in some sense to promote Roman Catholicism in their dominions. But many historians of the last fifty

[5] See F. Maaß, *Der Josephinismus: Quellen zu seiner Geschichte in Österreich, 1760–1850* (Fontes rerum austriacarum (hereafter FRA); 5 vols.; Vienna, 1951–61), i. 5–9, and *Der Frühjosephinismus* (Vienna, 1969); E. Wangermann, *The Austrian Achievement, 1700–1800* (London, 1973), 74–88.

[6] C. Freiherr von Hock, *Der österreichische Straatsrath* (Vienna, 1879), 397–8.

[7] *Sammlung aller k.k. Verordnungen und Gesetze vom Jahre 1740, bis 1780 . . .* (9 vols.; Vienna, 1787), i. 6.

[8] Hock, *Staatsrath*, 413.

years, by urging that Joseph's measures derived directly from Maria Theresa's, have underrated the differences between them.

Despite what she said in the first version of her testament—no similar passage occurs in the second of 1756—Maria Theresa did nothing concrete about general monastic reform until after 1765, when Joseph II succeeded his father and became Holy Roman Emperor and co-regent of the Austrian Monarchy. As emperor he had some rather ill-defined powers over the Church in the *Reich*. As co-regent he had no power in his own right, but much opportunity to put his views and influence policy. In a memorandum of 1765 'on the defects of the present system and the most effectual means of remedying them'—a document which is perhaps even more famous and notable than Maria Theresa's political testament—he set out his plans for the reform of the Monarchy. He devoted a section to the monasteries. He declares that they are too thriving for the good of the State. They ensnare people into taking vows who are too young to know what they are doing, thus depriving the State of the services of men of genius. He would raise the age of profession to 25—that was a very big rise: following the dictates of the Council of Trent, profession for men was legal at 16. He would appoint a commission to investigate all monasteries, to reform them, and to use them 'for pious purposes which would be at the same time useful to the state, such as the education of children who, while becoming Christians, would become good subjects'. Perhaps one in twenty monasteries should be reformed, in order to distribute ecclesiastics more evenly over the country.

This pronouncement shows that Joseph had no thought of abolishing all monasteries, at least in 1765. To reform one in twenty was a very modest proposal. On the other hand, he spoke very ill of Catholic education, much of which was in monastic hands, and urged that it should be drastically reformed.[9]

At Maria Theresa's request, Prince Kaunitz, her chief minister, wrote a lengthy response, dated 18 February 1766, to the vast range of proposals in this memorandum.[10] What he had to say on monasteries is unexpected—indeed, given his reputation as an Enlightened reformer of the Church, positively embarrassing. Maaß, in his five indispensable volumes of documents on Josephism, whose thesis is that Kaunitz was the mastermind behind the movement, does not bring himself even to mention it;[11] and Dickson gives it only a reluctant footnote as

---

[9] A. Ritter von Arneth (ed.), *Maria Theresia und Joseph II. Ihre Correspondenz* (3 vols.; Vienna, 1867–8), iii. 348–51.

[10] Kaunitz's response to Joseph's memorandum was published in A. Beer, 'Denkschriften des Fürsten Wenzel Kaunitz-Rittberg', *AÖG* xlviii (1872). See esp. pp. 107–9.

[11] Maaß, *Josephinismus*. Maaß does make one back-handed reference to the document in his article 'Vorbereitung und Anfänge des Josephinismus im amtlichen Schriftwechsel des Staatskanzlers ... mit ... Firmian, 1763 bis 1770', *Mitteilungen des österreichischen Staatsarchivs* (hereafter *MÖSA*), i (1948), 301.

evidence of Kaunitz's inconsistency.[12] The chancellor refutes the emperor's state-ments point by point. He questions whether there are too many monks in the German hereditary lands. There are only 23,000, he says—in fact this may be too high a figure.[13] He scoffs at the idea that they include thwarted geniuses. Most monks are virtually unemployable outside their houses, and there are too few benefices to go round in any case. The convents are performing a service by maintaining such people. Then he defends the usefulness of monasteries. Unless religious worship is to be curtailed, the monks' contribution to it is indispensa-ble: 'It is true that there could be fewer monks if there were more secular priests. But it is not less true that the cost of priests is much higher than that of monks, for it is clear that three monks can live in a community on what it would be necessary to pay one priest living on his own.' Among the assumptions behind this defence are, first, that the provision of parish priests is of prime concern to the State; secondly, that such provision is or ought to be the most important function of the Church, overriding all others; and, thirdly, that monasteries have a vital role in this provision. Parish priests were considered to be central not only to strictly religious activity, as the Council of Trent had laid down, but also to the life of society as a whole, and to the State. Religious teaching, whether in church or in school, was seen as a first essential of education, and was expected to inculcate obedience and service to the State. How useful the parish clergy could be to the State was shown when Joseph compelled them to assist his reforms by ordering them to read certain of his edicts from the pulpit. The number of persons who thereby gained knowledge of his ordinances must have exceeded by hundreds of times the ordinary print-run of publications in this period.[14]

In countries other than the *Reich* and the Austrian Monarchy, monks were normally thought of as distinct from parish clergy. This separation was nowhere complete. Throughout the Catholic world, for example, the Premonstratensian Order exploited a unique papal privilege allowing it to supply parish clergy from its own ranks—600 of them, for example, in France before the Revolution.[15] The rule of the Augustinian canons permitted them to work outside their monaster-ies. But in the German and Austrian lands other orders did so too, in large numbers and as a normal practice—Franciscans, Benedictines, and Cistercians, for example. This point is seldom emphasized, and has sometimes not been grasped, by historians of the subject.[16] But, unless it is appreciated, neither

[12] Dickson, 'Joseph II's Reshaping', 97 n.   [13] Ibid. 94 ff.

[14] Ibid. 97 n. My calculation is as follows: in the Austrian duchies there were about 2,500 parishes. If we suppose that only 100 persons on average attended the main service at which these edicts were read out, 250,000 heard them in Austria alone.

[15] J. de Viguerie (ed.), *La Vocation religieuse et sacerdotale en France, XVII–XIX siècles* (Angers, 1979), 52.

[16] P. von Mitrofanov (*Josef II* (2 vols.; Vienna, 1910)) appears to miss this point, and even Dickson (see n. 1 above) barely refers to it. It emerges clearly from such works as G. Winner, *Die Klosteraufhebungen*

Kaunitz's attitude to the monasteries in his memorandum, nor Joseph II's policy towards them, can be understood.

The Austrian duchies are the most striking case. In 1780 at least 20 per cent of all the land of Lower Austria was owned by monasteries, and more than 70 per cent of all clergy were monastic.[17] The Benedictine abbey of Melk, with an income of over 50,000 florins a year, supplied around twenty-five priests from its own numbers for the cure of souls in fourteen parishes.[18] In 1743 the Augustinian house of St Florian in Upper Austria, which was nearly as rich, had thirty-one of its canons, that is two-thirds of them, working out of the monastery in twenty-three parishes.[19] All large monasteries were also seminaries, and these clergy received their basic training in theology and philosophy in their houses. They did not necessarily go on to university—not even to the University of Salzburg, which was itself run by the Benedictines of St Peter's.[20]

Kaunitz, despite what he had said in replying to Joseph's memorandum in 1766, began promoting monastic reform in the duchy of Milan, of which he was effectively the ruling minister, in 1767. He told Count Firmian, the governor there, that it would have to proceed step by step, because, first, it was necessary not to offend the religious sentiments of the sovereign, and, secondly, 'the number of monastic professions in Italy, though prodigious, is to some degree the result of the constitution of the country and of families.'[21] While Maria Theresa had to be humoured, pressure in the opposite direction from the new co-regent must have been a factor in Kaunitz's espousing monastic reform. An inquiry was set up, and in 1769 the process began of abolishing small convents. The same justification was put forward as Pope Innocent X had given in the mid-seventeenth century, that a house with fewer than twelve religious was not viable. A deal was then done by Maria Theresa's government with Pope Clement XIV under which small monasteries, rather than being straightforwardly dissolved, were united with others. The resulting rather limited profits were applied to parishes, hospitals, and orphanages. By the death of Maria Theresa, sixty-five out of 291 male monasteries had been suppressed in Lombardy, and the number of

---

in Niederösterreich und Wien (Vienna, 1967); *Welt des Barock* (2 vols.; Linz, 1986); *Josefinische Pfarrgründungen in Wien* (Historisches Museum der Stadt Wien, 1985); L. Raber, *Die österreichischen Franziskaner im Josefinismus* (Maria Enzersdorf, ?1983).

[17] Dickson, *Finance and Government*, i. 103, and 'Joseph II's Reshaping', 95–8.

[18] B. Ellegast, 'Vernunft und Glaube', in *900 Jahre Benediktiner in Melk* (Melk, 1989), 364, and data in the permanent exhibition on view at Melk.

[19] F. Reisinger, 'Ein Herz und eine Seele in Gott', *Welt des Barock*, ii. 326.

[20] For the University of Salzburg, see, most recently, H. Klueting (ed.), *Katholische Aufklärung—Aufklärung im katholischen Deutschland* (Hamburg, 1993), esp. the essays of G. Heilingsetzer and L. Hammermayer.

[21] C. Capra in D. Sella and C. Capra, *Il ducato di Milano dal 1535 al 1796* (*Storia d'Italia*, ed. G. Galasso, vol. xi), 398 (19 Nov. 1768). Kaunitz is presumably referring to the practice, widespread and generally accepted among the Italian landed classes, of placing surplus sons and (especially) daughters in monasteries.

monks had fallen from 5,500 to 4,330. Only six out of 176 nunneries had gone, because the bishops fought for their retention. Monasteries had been suppressed mainly on the ground that they were small, but with some regard to their 'uselessness' and to the possible utility of their buildings. These Italian measures are often treated as a trial run for the whole Monarchy, and this is true in the limited sense that any dissolutions constituted a precedent for other dissolutions. It is also true that much the same criteria were adopted in dissolving a rather similar proportion of the monasteries of Galicia soon after Austria acquired that province by the first partition of Poland in 1772. There 214 houses were reduced to 187, and 3,212 regulars to 2,895 by 1777.[22] But the situation in Lombardy was quite different from that in the German lands. Hardly any Italian monasteries were involved in parish provision, and they had no role in any form of Estates.

In 1770 Kaunitz emerged as a monastic reformer for the whole Monarchy. In this case he himself stated that he was partly influenced by the wishes of Joseph II. Kaunitz is now to be found vigorously arguing that the number of monks and nuns was 'far too high' and should be reduced by the State raising the age of profession to 24. This should be done without papal authority or concurrence. It was clear, he said, that Protestant countries benefited from having fewer monks, and fewer celibates generally. Monasteries, because their property was inalienable, distorted the market in land. Monks are not necessary to Christianity—they are not to be found in the Church before the fourth century. Then he produced another telling calculation: 'A parish priest in the countryside with three chaplains or "cooperators" can provide worship and cure of souls for 4,000 persons.' If that is so, the same four clergymen can do as much in a town. Yet the density of clergy in Vienna is far higher than that. The position will be better in every way if there are fewer monks and priests but all have a genuine vocation.[23] He has certainly changed his tune since 1766, but he still assumes that many parish priests will be regulars. However, he insists that they must be educated not as they have been hitherto, but on the same basis as in the universities, according to a curriculum approved by the government. He does not yet propose that the training of priests be taken out of the hands of their monasteries altogether.

Maria Theresa agreed to raise the age of profession to 24—not to 25, as appears in my *Joseph II*—and to imposing all kinds of often petty restrictions on monasteries, as to number of monks, reception of novices, education of priests, relations with superiors and foreign houses, and so forth.[24] But she never ap-

---

[22] For the whole paragraph, see ibid. 398–400, 497. For Galicia, H. Glassl, *Das österreichische Einrichtungswerk in Galizien (1772–1790)* (Wiesbaden, 1975), 135–40.

[23] Maaß, *Josephinismus*, ii. 139–41.

[24] See Beales, *Joseph II*, 450–2 and the sources there cited. I owe thanks to Prof. E. Wangermann for pointing out to me my mistake about the age of profession.

pointed a commission of inquiry into them and she dissolved none in the German lands or in Hungary—with the enormous exception of the Jesuits.

In 1773 the Society of Jesus was completely suppressed in Maria Theresa's territories. This was a draconian measure, and of huge importance. I cannot deal with it fully here, but it can hardly be ignored. What follows is a brief survey, based on work which I hope will soon be published elsewhere. Paradoxically, the story of the suppression of the Jesuits in the Austrian Monarchy reinforces the argument that Maria Theresa's policy—and even Joseph's—were not doctrinairely anti-monastic.[25]

At least until the late 1750s, the Jesuits were from many points of view the most powerful of all monastic orders in the Monarchy. Their houses were not so wealthy as the greater monasteries of the old Orders. They had no seats in the Estates. But, as the vanguard of the Counter-Reformation, they had acquired a near-monopoly of university education and the major role in secondary education. They played the chief part in the censorship of books and they supplied confessors to all members of the royal family.

In the 1750s Maria Theresa began to assail the monopolies and privileges of the Society. In 1759 they were deprived of their controlling position in the universities and the censorship, and in the following year the first non-Jesuit royal confessor was appointed. Whatever the long-term implications of these measures for the power of the Church, in the short run they were a victory both for the secular clergy as against the regulars, and for the old religious orders as against the Jesuits. Theology could now, for example, be taught in universities by Benedictines, Augustinians, and Dominicans, whose approach and tradition were different from the Jesuits'. When Maria Theresa chose a non-Jesuit confessor for herself in 1767, he was Ignaz Müller, provost of the Augustinian monastery of St Dorothea in Vienna. She came to believe that the moral teaching of the Jesuits was dangerous. In a certain sense she can even be classed as a Jansenist. She objected to certain aspects of baroque piety, she attached great importance to private devotions, and some of the religious books she recommended to her children were undoubtedly Jansenist.[26]

Meanwhile, much more drastic measures were being taken against the Jesuits in other Catholic countries. In 1765 they were expelled from France, as they had previously been from other Catholic countries. In the circumstances it is

---

[25] On Joseph II and the Jesuits, see ibid. 460–4, and my forthcoming paper in a collection on their suppression edited by Dr R. Oresko, based on the proceedings of a conference which he organized some years ago at the Institute of Historical Research in London.

[26] Beales, *Joseph II*, 54, 60, 65–6, 81, 441–4. The classic treatment is G. Klingenstein, *Staatsverwaltung und kirchliche Autorität im 18. Jahrhundert* (Vienna, 1970). Cf. P. Hersche, 'War Maria Theresia eine Jansenistin?', *Österreich in Geschichte und Literatur*, 15 (1971), 14–25 and his important book, *Der Spätjansenismus in Österreich* (Vienna, 1977).

extraordinary that Joseph did not so much as mention the issue in his great memorandum of that year, in which he discussed so many other matters; and nor did Kaunitz in his reply. Nor were the Jesuits considered in relation to the Italian monastic suppressions.[27]

In 1769–71 a great debate took place at the highest level about how a State educational system might be established in the Monarchy. The role of the Jesuits in education was so important that this was almost a debate about the Society. There were those who, like Count Pergen in a notorious paper of 1769, argued that all regular clergy should simply be debarred from any role in education because their influence was inevitably pernicious. But Maria Theresa, Joseph, and Kaunitz, in a rare display of unanimity, all agreed that this was not a practical possibility. They concurred that there were nowhere near enough secular clergy, and especially secular clergy of calibre, to satisfy existing educational demands, let alone to man an expanded system. They went on to agree that, since it was necessary to go on using monks as teachers, it was essential to re-educate them so that they would not inculcate 'superstition' but would instead teach 'sound religion'. Contrary to what is commonly believed, Joseph and Kaunitz as well as—perhaps more than—Maria Theresa were admirers of the Jesuits, or at least of some of them and of some of what they did, especially in education and scholarship, and refused to assist actively the movement for their suppression. The rulers of Austria acquiesced in it eventually in order to please their Bourbon allies, who were determined to force the pope to suppress the Society completely. Joseph could, of course, see how the dissolution could be turned to advantage provided that the Jesuits' property could be taken over by the State. A cartoon depicted him washing his hands and saying 'I am innocent of the blood of this just Society.' But he believed that most of the criticisms made of their activities in other countries did not apply in the Monarchy.

The suppression meant the dissolution of 192 houses in Austria and Hungary. Afterwards, the rulers of Austria demanded permission from the pope to continue employing ex-Jesuits in education, where their services were held to be indispensable. Those who did not find new posts were given a pension. Other Catholic states were much less generous. In 1775 the Empress gave remarkable testimony of her respect for Jesuit scholarship: she rejected the idea of forming a Vienna Academy on the ground that she would become a laughing-stock, since nearly all those who could possibly be appointed to it were ex-Jesuits whom, in obedience to the pope, she had just turned out of their houses.[28]

---

[27] See the works cited in nn. 9, 10, and 21.

[28] For this and the previous paragraph, see Beales, *Joseph II*, 455–64; Dickson, *Finance and Government*, i. 65–8. More recently, on education J. V. H. Melton, *Absolutism and the Eighteenth-Century Origins of Compulsory Schooling in Prussia and Austria* (Cambridge, 1988), esp. 204–9. On Pergen, see P. P.

So it was the pope and the other Catholic powers who imposed on Maria Theresa and Joseph the suppression of the Jesuits. The only initiative she herself took in suppressing monasteries was the limited programme carried through in Lombardy and Galicia. On this basis it is hard to regard her actual legislation as amounting either to the 'great remedy' which she spoke of in 1750 but never defined, or to the blueprint for Joseph's programme.

Within a few months of the death of Maria Theresa, Joseph set about serious reform of the monasteries in the Monarchy. It is worth stressing that he rarely offered as a justification the existence of abuses such as laxity, frivolity, and cruelty in particular houses. He operated instead on general principles. He first abolished all the connections that existed between houses in his territories and superiors or monasteries in other states. Then, late in 1781, he decreed the suppression in the central lands of all purely contemplative monasteries, which, being 'utterly and completely useless to their neighbours', 'could not be pleasing to God'. These were the houses of Orders like the Carthusians, whose rule and vows prohibited them from doing what Joseph saw as useful work.

He next turned to other Orders, intending that no monastery of any kind would be allowed to survive unless it performed a useful function. That meant, in Joseph's own first draft for the Council of State (*Staatsrat*), only educating youth or looking after sick persons. To these qualifying functions were added, after discussion, 'preaching, hearing confessions and attending deathbeds', and, later still, cure of souls.[29] In the summer of 1782 an Ecclesiastical Commission was established to implement this policy in the central lands and in Hungary. The emperor appointed as its chairman Freiherr von Kressel, declaring that under his direction he was confident the commission would produce 'in this business so near to my heart . . . the best results for religion and the state'.[30] Thirty-two years after Maria Theresa had spoken in her political testament of applying a 'great remedy' to the Church, Joseph at last ordered a full survey of monasteries as part of an elaborate and detailed survey of all Church land. Pending its report, Joseph forbade monasteries to take any new novices. On 24 October 1783 a decree was issued that envisaged the establishment of new parishes wherever too many people were included within an existing parish or were too far away from an existing church. It was now within this context of

---

Bernard, *From the Enlightenment to the Police State: The Public Life of Johann Anton Pergen* (Urbana, Ill., 1991), esp. ch. 3. Franz A. J. Szabo, *Kaunitz and Enlightened Absolutism 1753–1780* (Cambridge, 1994), esp. 241–7, supports this view of Kaunitz's attitude to the Jesuits. For the cartoon about Joseph, see Winner, *Klosteraufhebungen*, 29.

[29] For this and the previous paragraph, see Hock, *Staatsrath*, 295–6.

[30] Joseph to Kressel, 22 July 1782, in H. Schlitter (ed.), *Pius VI. und Josef II.* (FRA XLVII/2; Vienna, 1894), 147–8. Schlitter prints the draft instruction for the Ecclesiastical Commission on pp. 41–6.

improving the provision for the cure of souls that the fate of all monasteries was to be decided:

Among monasteries, those will be retained which are necessary either to staff their own parishes or to assist the cure of souls, and for these houses an appropriate number of clergy will be laid down, enough to meet all contingencies. The other monasteries that are entirely unnecessary for the cure of souls will wither away [*gehen nach und nach ein*] . . .

Monks were encouraged to leave their Order and become parish clergy or be pensioned. If they stayed in their Order, they might still become parish priests but otherwise would find themselves in the course of time moved, and brought together with members of other suppressed monasteries of their Order into one house until they died out. It must be emphasized that, unlike the initial dissolution of contemplative Orders, these measures were not, at least in principle, directed at entire Orders. Every single monastery was to be considered on its merits—a recipe for delay, uncertainty, ill feeling, and inconsistency.[31]

The financial mechanics of the process were that the property of the suppressed houses, or the proceeds of its sale, was transferred to a religious fund, established early in 1782. Maria Theresa had set up a fund of the same name, but that was entirely devoted to converting Protestants to Catholicism.[32] The first charge on the new fund was the payment of pensions to the ejected monks and nuns who could not find employment. The emperor was especially hostile to nuns as almost wholly useless: they could not be priests, confessors, or preachers, and few of them undertook charitable work. Most nunneries were therefore suppressed but, since former nuns were unlikely to find jobs, to pension them proved particularly costly. The second charge on the religious fund was the creation and endowment of the new parishes, parish clergy, and parish churches.

How these measures worked in practice has not been fully studied, but Dr Ludwig Raber has written an excellent account of their impact on the Franciscan houses of Austria, with special reference to Lower Austria, in which he has published many of the original documents.[33] The Franciscan Order, of course, is a mendicant Order, which raises an important question not yet addressed, the emperor's attitude to begging. He would have liked to stop it altogether. He disapproved of it on principle, as obstructing market forces, discouraging people from working hard, and denying personal responsibility. He believed that the regularized mendicancy of the Orders imposed a special and unjustifiable burden

---

[31] *Sammlung der kaiserlichen-königlichen Landesfürstlichen Gesetze und Verordnungen in Publico-Ecclesiasticis vom Jahre 1782 bis 1783* (Vienna, 1784), 109–13.

[32] Hock, *Staatsrath*, 415.

[33] For this and the next paragraph, see Raber, *Die österreichischen Franziskaner, passim.* The quotations come from pp. 139 and 236. See esp. p. 219. Dickson ('Joseph II's Reshaping') draws attention to the importance of the distinction between mendicant and other Orders.

on the poor. Further, he and his sympathizers thought that mendicant monks used improper spiritual inducements to extract alms, and that during their begging tours they preached superstition and bigotry. However, he was forced to admit that the monasteries of these Orders could not survive financially without some revenue additional to that supplied by their endowments. He was therefore compelled in the short run to make numerous exceptions to the prohibition on begging, and in the longer run to provide alternative revenue for the monks, confusingly known as pensions, further reducing the financial returns from his ecclesiastical measures.

There were sixteen Franciscan monasteries in Austria at the beginning of Joseph's reign. They were the largest single Order in the area. On the basis of the returns they made to the inquiry on ecclesiastical revenues and provision, the Commission decided that thirteen of the sixteen should be suppressed, leaving only the three located in Vienna and its suburbs. These three were to supply parish priests from their own number, to house secular priests to whom some of the Franciscan monks would act as assistants in parish work, and to maintain a kind of reserve of clergy to stand in when incumbents were ill or absent or died. Perhaps the most striking detail to emerge from Raber's account is that the thirteen monasteries were not all suppressed at once. The bureaucracy pointed out that, under the terms of the emperor's edicts, this was impossible. In Raber's words,

The priority was to make room in the monasteries by transferring the younger Fathers, and later the lay brothers, to the cure of souls or to other available posts. Thus a logical sequence was arrived at: monasteries were suppressed in order to procure personnel for the cure of souls, and monks were sent to parish work in order that monasteries could be dissolved.

The most that could be hoped for was to suppress one house a year, and that target was not always achieved. By the time Joseph died in February 1790, four of the thirteen houses had still not been dissolved, one saved by the intercession of the bishop of St Pölten, the others waiting their turn to be suppressed. The death of Joseph and the accession of Leopold II procured them a stay of execution. If this pattern was applicable to all Orders, it becomes easier to understand how Joseph's policy turned out to be less drastic in result than in intention. Some of the statistical uncertainties may spring from confusion between those houses that were actually suppressed and other houses that had been condemned but were not actually suppressed in time. This issue needs further research.

However, the policy of converting monks into parish clergy certainly achieved notable success with the Franciscans of Austria. Raber reports:

Between 1783 and 1790 were transferred to the cure of souls:

in the diocese of Linz	15 Fathers
in the diocese of St Pölten	55 Fathers
in the archdiocese of Vienna	107 Fathers
as army chaplains	4 Fathers
TOTAL	181 Fathers

In Lower Austria there had been 325 Fathers in 1783. Clearly that figure is not calculated for the same area as those in the table, but it would appear that a very considerable proportion of all Franciscan priests—perhaps a half—became parish clergy.

Taking again the example of the Austrian duchies, according to Dickson's tables, 1,178 additional secular clergy, over and above the 6,500 recorded in 1780, were in post or in training in 1790 as a result of Joseph's suppressions. In the whole Monarchy, almost 5,000 secular clergy were added to the previous total.[34]

Suppression of monasteries and the creation of new parishes formed part of a much broader programme of Church reform. In 1783 all religious brotherhoods were dissolved—thousands of them, involving tens of thousands of lay persons. All seminaries run by bishops and monasteries were shut down, and it was decreed that all those training for the priesthood must go into the small number of new general seminaries established to teach the sort of theology and canon law that the regime approved. Not only begging, but also the giving of unsystematic charity, was condemned. All charity, or poor relief, was in future to be distributed by a single 'institution for the love of one's neighbour', relying on the confiscated funds of the brotherhoods and on contributions from the private sector.[35]

So far as the monasteries were concerned, it is important to understand that Joseph was not content with suppressing half of them outright. He did not leave the other half untouched. It was not only the dissolved monasteries whose funds were tapped. If a house had surplus revenue, the religious fund might take it without the house being dissolved. When an abbot died, Joseph generally forbade the monks to elect a successor. Instead, they were allowed to choose a prior to be the spiritual head of the institution on a three-year tenure, while an outsider, perhaps a layman, was appointed to administer the temporalities to the benefit of the religious fund. This arrangement incidentally deprived the abbey of representation in the Estates. A house might be peremptorily ordered to create

---

[34] Ibid. 105, 110.
[35] A convenient account of the whole policy is E. Bradler-Rottmann, *Die Reformen Kaiser Josephs II* (Göppingen, 1973), ch. VI. On brotherhoods, see P. Ardaillou, 'Les Confréries viennoises aux 17e et 18e siècles', *Revue d'histoire ecclésiastique*, 87 (1992), 745–58.

a new parish out of its existing benefices and to build a parish church out of its own revenues—as the Vienna Schottenstift was compelled to do with the church of St Laurenz in the eighth district of Vienna. According to a modern abbot, his predecessor in Joseph's reign, Benno Pointner,

> made a courageous stand against the Josephist pamphlets and also fought for the rights of the parishes, to which he sent at least half his priests for the cure of souls . . . There was no avoiding the incorporation of more parishes into the foundation, so that the number of Schotten parishes reached 18—a much too high number considering the heavy obligations associated with the foundation in Vienna. But perhaps that excessive burden was necessary in order to stave off the danger of the monastery's suppression by Joseph's administration or of the appointment of a so-called 'commendatory abbot' who would not have to belong to the Order.

Melk too now sent the majority of its monks into parishes. The Premonstratensian monastery of Geras raised the number of parishes it owned and serviced from ten to seventeen. Between 1782 and 1791 it spent 14,000 florins on four new priest houses, eight schools, and a new church.[36] This must have been the pattern in all the surviving houses, except for the few which had been allowed to exist because of their contribution to education and the care of the sick rather than because they provided parishes and clergy. Overall figures appear not to be available, but the increased provision of parish clergy by the remaining monasteries from the ranks of their own monks must have added substantially to the total number of those charged with the cure of souls, over and above those supplied by the religious fund. Doubtless these people would have been classed as regulars in the statistics.

With their young monks away at the general seminaries and their able-bodied priests working in parishes, monasteries found it difficult, if not impossible, to maintain a proper community life. Choral services were drastically cut down, on the ground that, now that monks were required to be useful, all this singing, especially in the middle of the night, would be injurious to their health and therefore to the spiritual well-being of their flocks. Half the monasteries survived, it is true, but only as half-monasteries. In cases where it seemed to the government more convenient or economical, they were allowed to live on, but as depleted, cowed communities to be bullied, mulcted, scattered, and stripped of their traditions, of their independence and of their role in the Estates.[37]

---

[36] J. Kellner (ed.), *Pfarre Sankt Lorenz am Schottenfeld 1786–1796* (St Pölten, 1986). H. Peichl, 'Die Schottenabtei in der Neuzeit', in F. Krones (ed.), *800 Jahre Schottenabtei* (Vienna, 1960), 56–7. For Melk, see Ellegast, 'Vernunft und Glaube', 362–4; for Geras, J. Ambrósy and A. J. Pfiffig, *Stift Geras und seine Kunstschätze* (St Pölten, 1989), 34. I owe my knowledge of Kellner's book to Professor Donal Kerr.

[37] See the accounts of Winner, *Klosteraufhebungen*, and R. Hittmair, *Der josefinische Klostersturm im Land ob der Enns* (Freiburg im Breisgan, 1907).

In attempting to answer the question why Joseph allowed so many monasteries to survive, another part of the explanation must lie in the relations between the emperor and his civil servants. New light is thrown on this aspect of the problem, as on the whole story of Joseph's reign, by material in the dispatches sent to Rome by the papal nuncios, Giuseppe Garampi down to 1785 and Giovanni Battista Caprara thereafter.[38] For ordinary purposes the dispatches of nuncios are not as valuable for this as for earlier periods, when the pope was a militant player in international politics. But on religious questions, which in Joseph's reign bulked so large, the reports of Garampi and Caprara are far superior to those of other envoys. While 2,500 parish priests in Austria could be compelled to read the emperor's edicts from the pulpit, at least as many clergy may well have been happy to provide unsolicited information to the pope's representatives. Although some of their dispatches have been published, many of them have been neglected by historians,[39] and they turn out to be wonderfully full.

Among their most interesting features are the strikingly different impressions that the two nuncios give of Joseph II's relationship with his officials. Garampi, who had been in Vienna during the last five years of Maria Theresa's reign, was emphatic that tremendous changes were occurring. Even before a single monastery had been suppressed, he talked of 'a crisis similar to that which the Church suffered in the sixteenth century'.

All the regulars [he wrote] are so shaken that they not only carry out punctiliously the orders they receive but they actually go beyond the royal instructions . . . I'm reminded at this juncture of the fatalism of the Turks who, unnerved by the fear that their monarchy is in decay, calmly await its end, making no effort to prevent it, and excusing their supine inaction as what they call resignation to the divine will and to the inevitability of Fate.

He had no doubt at all that the emperor himself was the prime mover and that he was having to dragoon his officials into implementing his policy. Garampi informed Rome in July 1781, and again in November, that he could not square it with his conscience to administer the Easter sacrament to Joseph, the nuncio's traditional privilege, because the emperor's measures revealed him to be a

---

[38] Archivio segreto vaticano: Nunziatura di Vienna (hereafter ASVNV), 179–84, 197A, 199–200. I am grateful to Mgr Charles Burns for much generous help during my work in the Vatican Archives.

[39] H. Schlitter (*Die Reise des Papstes Pius VI. nach Wien* and *Pius VI. und Josef II.* (FRA XLVII; Vienna, 1892, 1894)) uses these files and gives extensive extracts from them, but it seems clear that many of the most confidential documents were not available to him. G. Soranzo, *Peregrinus apostolicus* (Milan, 1937), is rather fuller on the papal side. E. Kovács, *Der Pabst in Teutschland* (Munich, 1983), relies on these two works. T. Vanyó, *A bécsi pápai követség levéltárának iratai Magyarországról, 1611–1786* (Budapest, 1986), is largely confined to references to specifically Hungarian affairs. I am grateful to Professor István Tóth for the reference to Vanyó's book. Since I wrote this essay Father Umberto Dell'Orto, with whom I had valuable conversations in Rome, has generously sent me a copy of his very important study, *La Nunziatura a Vienna di Giuseppe Garampi, 1776–1785* (Collectanea Archivi Vaticani; Vatican City, 1995).

Jansenist heretic. This suggestion clearly alarmed the pope and must have helped to induce him to make his famous journey to Vienna, where he arrived in time to administer communion personally to the emperor on Easter Day.[40]

One of the commonplaces of historians, without a single exception, is that the president of the ecclesiastical commission, Baron Kressel, said to have been a Freemason, was a zealous promoter of Church reform.[41] As we have seen, Joseph thought so too. But on 5 May 1783 Garampi, in one of his huge, especially confidential dispatches sent by safe courier, reported a secret conversation with Kressel. The baron

in no way concealed the torment he suffered [in carrying through these reforms]; but he added that . . . despite his feelings he remains in his post, no longer with the hope of doing good, but merely of diminishing evil. He foresees that, if he gives it up, there are now too many capital enemies of the Church and blind flatterers of the sovereign who would weakly follow instantly every hasty idea or command he gives.

Kressel, while bitterly regretting the harm done to the Church, thinks he has succeeded in minimizing its effects. 'He assured me that, once the emperor has adopted a principle, it is a waste of time to try to oppose it. The only thing to do is to bring up one by one the difficulties that make it awkward to carry out.' By this means, he said, he had succeeded in preventing Joseph carrying out his plan to put all clergy on fixed salaries, and had persuaded him that the best course was to leave them with their possessions and in control of them. He believes that anyone else would have acquiesced in Joseph's scheme of destroying all ecclesiastical foundations. Some of his colleagues, he said, 'professed a hatred of everything that is piety, church, order, hierarchy and monks'. He reckoned that 'the multiplication of parishes was a bottomless pit for which the funds would never suffice'.[42]

The nuncio can hardly have invented this conversation, surprising though it is, and Kressel would hardly have spoken in this foolhardy way if he had not felt passionately about these issues. Had Joseph known of Kressel's private views and of his contacts with the nuncio, far from expressing such confidence in him, he would surely have sacked him. But the obstruction Kressel describes himself as practising is uncannily like the sort of behaviour Joseph complained of among bureaucrats in his famous pastoral letter of December 1783.[43] The bitter disputes among his servants, and their secret undermining of his plans, go far to account for the dilution of his policies as they were translated into decrees.

---

[40] ASVNV 180, Garampi's dispatches of 20 July and 18 Nov. 1781.

[41] e.g. E. Wangermann, *From Joseph II to the Jacobin Trials* (2nd edn., Oxford, 1969), 6; L. Bodi, *Tauwetter in Wien* (Frankfurt, 1977), 228.

[42] ASVNV 182, Garampi's dispatch of 5 May 1783, section on 'Kroesel'.

[43] *Joseph des Zweyten Erinnerung an seine Staatsbeamten, am Schlusse des 1783ten Jahres* (Vienna, [1783]).

On the other hand, as the nuncios realized with horror, there were also genuine radicals near the centre of power. Joseph von Sonnenfels, famous as Professor of Political Economy, dramatic critic, official censor, and Freemason, wrote confidently and rejoicingly, when the Jesuits were dissolved, that all other Orders would shortly follow.[44] Ignaz von Born, a noted metallurgist and an even more prominent Freemason than Sonnenfels, published in 1783 *Monachologia*, a satirical classification of monks on the Linnaean system, anticipating the extinction of all their species.[45] The progressive canonist, Johann Valentin Eybel, wrote not only *Was ist der Pabst?* (*What is the Pope?*), *Sieben Kapitel von Klosterleuten* (*Seven Chapters of Monks and Nuns*), and sundry other pamphlets highly critical of the traditional Church, but was also employed by Joseph II as ecclesiastical commissioner in Upper Austria, where he derived particular pleasure from ordering great abbots about and taking part in the formalities attending the suppression of monastic houses.[46]

Caprara was as certain as Garampi had been that it was Joseph who genuinely took the decisions. But he saw the emperor, for all that he abominated his measures, as the only bulwark against still worse changes. Joseph alone, he thought, stood in the way of the total abolition of clerical celibacy, which Eybel and others advocated. If Caprara both exaggerated the influence of the extremists and sometimes proved too optimistic about Joseph's attitudes, he was certainly right that the emperor's radicalism had its limits, and that a married clergy was beyond them.[47] Joseph undoubtedly saved some monasteries from suppression. Eybel kept on recommending that the great house of St Florian should be dissolved to endow the new bishopric of Linz. In the end the bishop was assigned some of the monastery's revenues and the provost's house in Linz for his palace. But Joseph ordered Eybel never again to raise the question of suppressing the foundation. It was too useful as a provider of parish priests.[48] In Bohemia, the emperor was asked to suppress the rich Premonstratensian house at Strahov on the castle hill in Prague. It had just built itself a second 'philosophical' library to match its 'theological' library of the seventeenth century. In so doing it used bookcases and accommodated books from dissolved monasteries, and placed a bust of Joseph in the pediment of the new building. He declared the monastery

---

[44] *Sonnenfels gesammelte Schriften* (10 vols.; Vienna, 1783–7), viii. 329–30 (from *Deutsches Museum*, Apr. 1782).

[45] The first edition was in Latin: *Joannis Physiophili Specimen Monachologiae methodo Linnaeana* (Augsburg, 1783).

[46] See Bodi, *Tauwetter in Wien*, 53, 125. Hittmair, *Der josefinische Klostersturm*, is very informative about Eybel's activities in Upper Austria, and M. Brandl, *Der Kanonist Joseph Valentin Eybel (1741–1805): Sein Beitrag zur Aufklärung in Österreich* (Steyr, 1976), about his writings.

[47] e.g. Caprara's dispatch of 3 Aug. 1786 (ASVNV 199). Cf. Dickson, 'Joseph II's Reshaping', 97 n.

[48] Hittmair, *Der josefinische Klostersturm*, 253–4.

too useful to destroy.[49] On the other hand, as late as 1789 the emperor agreed to suppress the major Cistercian monastery of Lilienfeld on the special ground that its spendthrift abbot had run it into debt. Since the religious fund was over-stretched, Joseph's officials were always looking for excuses for dissolving juicy foundations.[50]

The emperor had travelled a long way since he had proposed to his mother in 1765 that one in twenty monasteries should be abolished. Evidence known to me does not settle the question whether by the end of his life he would have had any religious qualms about suppressing all monasteries. But he certainly still held the view that there were practical advantages in preserving some of them.

In her testament of 1750 Maria Theresa had promised to give special treatment to Hungary, 'where much remains to be done for religion'. It is likely that she had in mind, first, that there remained many Protestants in Hungary—perhaps a quarter of the population—and that the campaign waged by the Catholic Church, with the support of the Habsburg dynasty, to convert them to Rome had so far achieved only partial success. Secondly, she must have known that the overall provision of Catholic parishes was thin. To try to remedy this lack, her father Charles VI had established in 1733 a fund to create new parishes. But after her death, while the population of Hungary was twice as large as that of the Austrian lands, there were one-and-a-half times as many Austrian as Hungarian clergy, and the total revenues of the Hungarian Church fell much below those of the Austrian. The provision was also very uneven. In the western and north-western counties the Church was strong and comparatively rich; in the rest of the country much less so. In two of the ten districts into which Joseph divided Hungary, his inspectors in 1786-7 credited the Church with a million florins of income, and four districts had over 1,000 clergy. In four there were under 500 clergy and Church income was under 300,000 florins. This variation arose partly because some of the strongholds of Protestantism lay in the east. But it had much more to do with the historical experience of the different regions of the country. The extreme west had experienced only rare Turkish incursions and was closely tied to Austria. An intervening area had been won back from the Turks imme-diately after the siege of Vienna of 1683. But the more easterly regions had come under the effective control of the Habsburgs only after the great Rákóczi revolt had been defeated in 1711. Here the Catholic Church was truly a missionary church. The central and western lands of the Monarchy had seen a massive rebuilding and refurbishing of churches and monasteries in the late seventeenth

[49] Hock, *Staatsrath*, 407; F. and R. Malecek, *Strahov Praha* (Prague, ?1993). I owe the latter reference to Dr L. C. Van Dijck.
[50] For supplying me with material about the case of Lilienfeld, I am very grateful to Miss E. Fattinger.

and early eighteenth centuries—by Italian standards a much delayed flowering of the Counter-Reformation. The Hungarian Counter-Reformation came even later, and Hungarian churches were mostly rebuilt from ruins or from scratch in the eighteenth century, and in a distinctly less opulent manner than to the west. Whereas the Austrian Church seems virtually to have stopped building and to have lost its missionary *élan* around 1750, the Hungarian Church was advancing and expanding right up to Joseph's accession.[51]

In Marczali's words.

In the counties formerly occupied by the Turks, where there was scarcely any other foe to contend with except the havoc and destruction that had been wrought, and where the life not merely of the Catholic Church but of Western Christianity had become entirely extinct, the chief rôle among the champions of the Church was still played by the Franciscans . . . their numbers continually grew in dimensions.[52]

In Hungary there were four times as many mendicants, mainly Franciscans, as endowed monks, whereas in Austria the mendicants outnumbered the non-mendicants by less than two to one. The ancient Orders that dominated Austria had only a few houses in Hungary, and their role in the Church was relatively insignificant. One of them, Pannonhalma, celebrates its nine-hundredth anniversary in 1996, but in fact they had ceased to exist during the Turkish occupation and had to be refounded after the Turks had been driven out. The relative poverty and weakness of Hungarian monasteries overall is shown by Table 8.1, based on Dickson's figures.[53]

So Maria Theresa was absolutely right that the religious situation in Hungary was markedly different from that in the central and western lands of the Monarchy. However, despite what she said in her testament of 1750, her legislation did not take much account of the difference. The most distinctive of her Hungarian Church measures, apart from those especially concerning the Greek Orthodox minority, was the establishment of three new bishoprics in 1777, though even that was paralleled in Bohemia.[54]

[51] My main published sources on the Hungarian Church are Dickson, *Finance and Government*, i, esp. ch. 4, and 'Joseph II's Reshaping'; H. Marczali, *Hungary in the Eighteenth Century* (Cambridge, 1910), esp. ch. IV; B. K. Király, 'The Hungarian Church', in the maddeningly footnote-less collection, W. J. Callahan and D. Higgs, *Church and Society in Catholic Europe in the Eighteenth Century* (Cambridge, 1979); and L. Csóka, *Geschichte des benediktinischen Mönchtums in Ungarn* (Studia Hungarica, Munich, 1980), esp. 312–64. For sources in the Hungarian National Archives, see n. 55 below—my comments on uneven provision derive from file C.107 of the Ecclesiastical Commission, reinforced by the graphic evidence in the remarkable articles of G. Tüskés and E. Knapp, esp. 'Österreichisch-ungarische interethnische Verbindungen im Spiegel des barockzeitlichen Wallfahrtwesens', *Bayerisches Jahrbuch für Volkskunde* (1990), 1–42, and 'Bruderschaften in Ungarn im 17. und 18. Jahrhundert', ibid. (1992), 1–23. Many Hungarian scholars have helped me to understand better the differences between the Hungarian and Austrian churches. I should particularly like to thank here Professor D. Kosáry and Professor L. Péter.

[52] Marczali, *Hungary in the Eighteenth Century*, 271.

[53] From *Finance and Government*, i. 35, 39, and 'Joseph II's Reshaping', 98.

[54] J. Tomko, *Die Errichtung der Diözesen Zips, Neusohl und Rosenau (1776) und das königliche Patronatsrecht in Ungarn* (Vienna, 1968). I owe this reference to Professor R. J. W. Evans.

TABLE 8.1. *Monastic Wealth in Lower Austria and Hungary*

Area	Population (approx.)	Mendicants	Endowed monks	Monastic revenue (approx.) (florins)
Lower Austria	1 m.	1,805	1,047	1.4 m.
Hungary	8 m.	3,736	988	1.2 m.

Joseph's approach was in some respects the opposite of his mother's. His travels had given him unique first-hand knowledge of the varied character of his dominions. But this only strengthened his determination to unite his disparate territories and to make them as uniform as possible. In his orders to the Hungarian authorities he regularly spoke of the need for *Gleichförmigkeit* in the Monarchy's legislation. His instructions about monastic reform were virtually identical for Hungary and the central lands, and Kressel's Ecclesiastical Commission, despite considerable Hungarian opposition, was placed in charge of both areas.[55] But the situation in Hungary was so unlike the position in Austria that identical policies, administered by the same men, produced significantly different results.

One perhaps unimportant difference was that the main group of suppressions, which in Austria began in 1783, did not start in Hungary until 1786–7, which was when the inquiry into the Church's revenues reported. Once the process had started, however, it seems to have proceeded rapidly. As always, it is difficult to establish precise figures for monastic suppressions. A major part of the problem is that the emperor's officials used varying definitions of Hungary, and it is not easy for historians to sort them out and decide between them. The most thorough study, a recently published article by Péter Bán, relying on a series of tables prepared for the Hungarian Diet of 1790–1, concludes that, in Hungary widely defined, there were 255 monasteries in 1782, not including those of the Piarists, the Brothers of Mercy and the Basilians. Out of the 255, 136 were dissolved and 119 survived.[56] To make the comparison with Lower Austria again, Dickson's

[55] These remarks are based partly on research in the Hungarian National Archives on the collections of Joseph's Normalia (A 58) and the papers of the Ecclesiastical Commission (C 70–107). Professor Éva Balázs made my work possible, and I was greatly assisted by Dr Éva Hoós and Dr Márta Velladics, who unselfishly abstracted material for me and directed me to appropriate files. I owe special thanks too to the staff of the National Archives, who gave me help far beyond the call of duty.

[56] P. Bán, 'Új adatok a szerzetesrendek II. József korabeli megszüntetéséről', *Baranya*, 3 (1990–1), 61–71. The three Orders mentioned are excluded because the source lacks figures for their houses. Dr Velladics very kindly supplied me with a xerox of Bán's important article. Dickson's figure of 117 Hungarian monasteries dissolved (*Finance and Government*, i. 76) refers to a smaller definition of Hungary, but still including Croatia. His figure of 154 as the total number before dissolution (ibid. 446 and 'Joseph II's Reshaping', 114 n.) is not comparable, since it excludes e.g. Croatia. M. von Schwartner, *Statistik des Königreiches Ungern* (2 vols.; Budapest, 1809), i. 171, gives a figure of 147 Hungarian monasteries spared by Joseph II, including Piarist houses.

calculations show that in 1790 the revenue of that province's monasteries was still almost a million florins, having been reduced by only a third since 1780. In Hungary total monastic revenue was in 1790 less than 600,000 florins, under half the total in 1780. However, both in Lower Austria and in Hungary the number of regulars in 1790 was about half the number in 1780.[57]

In total contrast to what happened in the German lands (and in Belgium), in Hungary only two of the eight Benedictine houses, and those not the richest, were spared, and all eight Premonstratensian houses were suppressed. Despite the prejudice of the Emperor and his supporters against mendicant Orders, eighty-one out of 116 Franciscan houses and eleven out of nineteen Capuchin houses survived.[58] This difference between Hungary and other parts of the Monarchy has scarcely been noticed, let alone studied. Much more research is needed before a full analysis can be provided. But here is a tentative explanation. The abbots of the great Hungarian monasteries had places in the Diet, but they were few and unimportant compared with their Austrian counterparts. In Hungary the bishops, and especially the archbishop of Esztergom, dominated the First Estate.[59] However, this difference was of limited importance, because Joseph had no intention of calling a Diet, whereas the Austrian Estates continued, if grudgingly, to work with his government. He deliberately flouted Hungarian susceptibilities, imposing his preferred policies regardless of opposition. It must be significant that, unlike in Austria, the monasteries he suppressed in Hungary were the rich ones. The Benedictine and Premonstratensian houses might be few, but they were on average *forty* times wealthier than Franciscan houses.[60] In the case of Pannonhalma at least, there was an inconclusive negotiation between the monastery and the government as to whether the monks would run a school in order to make their institution qualify as useful. It appears that even the Premonstratensians supplied few parish priests, but they surely could have supplied more.[61] Presumably, given the especially poor provision of clergy and the relatively low income of the Church in Hungary, the government simply could not finance the creation and maintenance of a satisfactory number of new parish clergy without taking over the revenues of the particularly wealthy monasteries. It was the Franciscans who had been conspicuous in parochial work before 1780, and it is to be presumed that they played an even greater role in it after Joseph II's reforms. Overall, the suppressions seem to have made it possible to supply

---

[57] Dickson, 'Joseph II's Reshaping', 98, 108.   [58] Bán, 'Új adatok', 61–2, 65–6.

[59] The nature of ecclesiastical representation in the Diet is remarkably difficult to discover. I here rely, uncomfortably, on Király, 'The Hungarian Church', 111.

[60] Bán, 'Új adatok', 68.

[61] Cf. Csóka, *Geschichte des benediktinischen Mönchtums in Ungarn*, 348–52, 262. The tables in C.107 (see n. 55 above) give tiny figures for monks acting as parish clergy in Hungary before 1786 (cf. Dickson, 'Joseph II's Reshaping', 101 n. 30, for figures for other provinces).

2,212 additional secular clergy for Hungary, a percentage increase much greater than elsewhere in the Monarchy.[62]

The policy of Joseph II towards the monasteries owed little to his mother's example. She took only limited measures against them, and much of what she did do—most importantly, the raising of the age of profession—was influenced by his views. There is no reason to think that she was hostile to contemplative monasteries as such, or to nunneries—two of Joseph's main targets. But his overriding concern was to improve parochial provision, either by dissolving monasteries and using the resulting funds to create new parishes and parish clergy, or by forcing surviving monasteries to make such provision themselves.

Both Garampi and Caprara may have been right in their differing estimates of the emperor's role in the 1780s. At the beginning of his sole reign he was goading a reluctant bureaucracy to drastic reform. By the end, many of the officials in charge of ecclesiastical matters were extremists whom he was reining in. The treatment meted out to the surviving monasteries showed little respect for their rules and traditions, and seemed to threaten the whole basis of monasticism. But, in the central lands at least, many of the major communities managed to maintain themselves after a fashion. When Joseph died in February 1790, it was still easy to muster the prescribed eight mitred abbots to accompany his corpse to the crypt of the Capuchins.[63]

By then the French Revolution had withdrawn State recognition from monastic vows and seized most Church lands. In the Monarchy, however, Joseph's successor Leopold inaugurated at almost the same time the opposite process of restoring the monasteries' position, abolishing the general seminaries, and permitting the revival of theological training in the cloister, re-establishing Lilienfeld and allowing abbots to be elected. He seemed to agree in principle to the restoration of some Hungarian monasteries, but no action was taken.[64] In 1801 Francis I was finally persuaded to assist the revival of the old Orders in Hungary, and in 1827 he permitted new foundations of contemplative Orders in his empire.[65] Though he maintained Joseph's ecclesiastical position in most respects, here he diverged from it. Those monasteries that had been spared in Austria now enjoyed again the favour of the government, some of them were given an important role in higher education, and they could return to a monastic regimen closer to that of the period before 1770.

---

[62] Dickson, 'Joseph II's Reshaping', 105.   [63] ASVNV 200, Caprara's dispatch of 22 Feb. 1790.
[64] Winner, *Klosteraufhebungen*; Maaß, *Josefinismus*, iv. esp. 3–13.
[65] Ibid. iv. 51; J. L. E. Graf von Barth-Barthenstein, *Das Ganze der österreichischen politischen Administration* (4 vols.; Vienna, 1838–43), ii. 133. This, of course, helps to account for the fact, noted by Dickson ('Joseph II's Reshaping', 114), that there were more Hungarian monasteries in 1847 than in 1780.

A book published in 1951 to celebrate the mere five-hundredth anniversary of the Franciscan Order in Austria contains this passage:

Certainly parishes were imposed on us by necessity, for both under Joseph II and also under the Nazi persecution the acceptance of a parish was the last expedient to preserve the monastery from suppression . . . [But] what originally happened under duress is also in the line of modern development, and it is possible to see here the hand of Providence.[66]

Austrian monasteries play a larger role in parochial work than those of any other European country. This peculiarity, and the fact that Austria is the one state in Europe where a large number of ancient and splendid Catholic houses can boast an almost continuous existence from the Middle Ages into the late twentieth century, are largely explained by the complex story of Joseph II's dealings with the monasteries.

[66] *500 Jahre Franziskaner der österreichischen Ordens-Provinz* (Vienna, 1951), 189. Cf. J. Hollnsteiner, 'Die Orden und Kongregationen in Österreich', in A. Hudal (ed.), *Der Katholizismus in Österreich* (Innsbruck, 1931), 110–19.

9

A 'lay divine': Burke, Christianity, and the Preservation of the British State, 1790–1797

Nigel Aston

The place of religion in the life of Edmund Burke remains a phenomenon as elusive as it is compelling, central to his vision in the 1790s. There are some areas of consensus. Most scholars, for instance, are in no doubt about the importance of religion for Burke in validating the existence of the State through an established Church, and in 'consecrating' its laws and institutions.[1] This chapter would not contest these conclusions. Instead, its concern is the much more problematic issue of Burke's specifically Christian identity, particularly in his later years. His religious position is undeniably complicated and the element of the *politique* in his views steadily diminishes. He ends as catholic and eirenic, but not Roman Catholic, within an irreducible Anglican framework that defied both ready labelling or reduction to expediency, and satisfied his unshakable sense of the divine reality.[2] Christianity was for Burke the justification for the monarchical status quo in Britain (and indeed of all decently ordered European states): it was the experience of true religion by the individual—for 'man is by his constitution a religious animal'[3]—as mediated by (pre-eminently) the Anglican

I am grateful to Dom Aidan Bellenger, Ian R. Christie, Grayson Ditchfield, Ian Harris, Leslie Mitchell, and Brian Young for their comments on an earlier version of this chapter.

[1] 'We know, and what is better we feel inwardly, that religion is the basis of civil society, and the source of all good and of all comfort' (*Reflections on the Revolution in France*, 141, in *The Writings and Speeches of Edmund Burke*, viii. *The French Revolution 1790–1794*, ed. L. G. Mitchell (Oxford, 1989)). Alfred Cobban pointed out that for Burke 'the state itself has a religious sanction, the church is a national church not by accident but by its essential nature' (*Edmund Burke and the Revolt against the Eighteenth Century* (2nd edn., London, 1960), 93). See also Frederick Dreyer, 'Burke's Religion', *Studies in Burke and his Time*, 17 (1976), 199–212, at 209; Peter J. Stanlis, *Edmund Burke and the Natural Law* (Ann Arbor, 1958), 74; John Dinwiddy, 'Interpretations of Anti-Jacobinism', in Mark Philp (ed.), *The French Revolution and British Popular Politics* (Cambridge, 1991), 38–49, at 44.

[2] 'Whoever goes to the task of Investigation must go with his heart inclined to faith—he must forget geers and gibing and quizing at this very important moment. He must dwell on his first Sentiment; that there is a God' (*Extracts from Mr Burke's Table-Talk, at Crewe Hall. Written down by Mrs Crewe* (Miscellanies of the Philobiblon Society, 7; London, 1862–3), 57). See also 'Burke's Answer to a Sceptic; Written down by, possibly, William Burke, 'For Mrs. Burke"', Wentworth Woodhouse Muniments, Bk. 26d, Sheffield City Archives. The document dates from the mid-1790s.

[3] *Reflections*, ed. Mitchell, 142.

Church, that would ensure the providential securing of the British state against the fearsome pressures for change from its enemies.[4] This presentation of Christianity in all its forms—'our boast and comfort, and one great source of civilization amongst us'[5]—to form, with aristocracy, a bulwark against barbarism, soon became personally associated with Burke by the British public, so much so that it has masked recognition that an overriding emphasis on the Christian character of the polity has nothing like the same prominence in his earlier speeches and writings and constitutes a major reordering of his thinking.[6] Like many Whigs, he developed a new appreciation of religion and its institutions as both making for public stability and satisfying the human heart. As Ian Harris recently observed, 'Burke conceived the Revolution in terms of his theology and the views of society he had constructed around it.'[7] But this conclusion poses questions so often overlaid in Burke studies—is Christianity any more for him than the most effective means to defend establishments against assault? What is the faith's intrinsic value for the individual as well as for the commonwealth? It there more to Anglicanism than its uses as a political theology?

Burke is too often presented as the spokesman for impersonal religious truths of use to the British state in its hour of need in the 1790s—truths that are deeply felt and ingeniously articulated, but in themselves offer little insight into his theological understanding, the nature of his private piety, or the character and form of his churchmanship. These are vital aspects of Burke's religious life that historians continue to neglect, and are in need of recovery. This study looks at his Anglicanism in relation to his support of Roman Catholicism in its Irish and French guises to see how it confirmed his own confessional loyalty and made religion central to his political vision in the 1790s, so much so that even his arch-enemy, Joseph Priestley, considered Burke entitled to the status of 'lay divine'.[8]

Yet when the *Reflections on the Revolution in France* were first published in November 1790, Burke's reputation as an Anglican layman was not his defining characteristic as a public figure. Indeed, he had been unable to shake off the allegations that he was a secret Roman Catholic, claims which had attended him from his appointment as secretary to the marquess of Rockingham in 1765.[9] In

---

[4] And provide the key to its past. See W. J. McCormack, *Ascendancy and Tradition in Anglo-Irish Literary History from 1789 to 1939* (Oxford, 1985), 64: 'Burke's view of history was not so much Irish or English but Anglican.'

[5] *Reflections*, ed. Mitchell, 142.

[6] As a writer in the *Critical Review* commented: 'revolutions, or the calamities of kings have not formerly been odious to Mr Burke.'

[7] Ian Harris, 'Paine and Burke: God, Nature and Politics', in Michael Bentley (ed.), *Public and Private Doctrine. Essays in British History Presented to Maurice Cowling* (Cambridge, 1993), 34–62, at 58.

[8] Joseph Priestley, *Letters to the Right Honourable Edmund Burke, Occasioned by his Reflections on the Revolution in France* (London, 1791), 91; Stanlis, *Burke and the Natural Law*, 147–8.

[9] Lord Charlemont observed that Burke's mind had 'an almost constitutional bent towards the Popish party' (HMC Twelfth Report, Appendix, Part X, *The Manuscripts and Correspondence of James, First Earl*

contemporary caricatures Burke was invariably depicted as a Jesuit decked out with papistical paraphernalia—cassocks, birettas, rosaries—a caricature that culminated in William Holland's famous 'Knight of the Woeful Countenance'.[10] His own Irishness and family background (his mother was a Catholic, and he remained in close and friendly contact with her relatives all his life) lent some superficial credence to these vague and amusing allegations, and they surfaced from time to time for consumption by a public where anti-Catholicism retained a dynamic it was losing in élite society.

Burke publicly proclaimed his confessional allegiance more than once. Perhaps the most emphatic was heard on 20 June 1780, when Burke told the Commons in debate that 'he had been educated as a Protestant of the Church of England'.[11] Indeed, he declared he had read all the theological publications on all sides written during the seventeenth and eighteenth centuries and had concluded that, as such studies merely tended to confuse, he had no difficulty about remaining in the Church of England. Such a statement, while unambiguous in its own way, does not suggest a man compellingly persuaded of the *via media*'s claims to a truthfulness or to spiritual benefits unknown to either Rome or Geneva. Instead, his membership was elicited by the Church's national character and established status, and its symbolic importance in contributing to social harmony. Despite his massive and eclectic reading in theology,[12] Burke was not in the early 1780s a professed and exclusive lover of the Anglican spiritual tradition, nor particularly appreciative of the Caroline divines that meant so much to the resurgent High Church party of George III's reign and their sense of the established Church's inalienably divine character.[13]

---

of Charlemont (2 vols.; London, 1891), i. 149). See also Thomas W. Copeland, *Edmund Burke, Six Essays* (London, 1950), 39–40; Carl B. Cone, *Burke and the Nature of Politics: The Age of the American Revolution* (Kentucky, 1957), 71–2; Thomas H. D. Mahoney, *Burke and Ireland* (Cambridge, Mass., 1960), 29, 95. His supposed education at Saint-Omer resulted in the recurrent nicknames of 'Neddy St Omers', and 'Jesuit Ned'. This story appeared the more plausible after praise of the Gallican Church was such a feature of the *Reflections*. See *Writings and Speeches of Burke*, viii. 24–5, citing [D. I. Eaton], *A Defence of the Political and Parliamentary Conduct of the Rt. Honourable Edmund Burke* (London, n.d.), 6.

[10] Dorothy M. George, *English Political Caricature to 1792: A Study of Opinion and Propaganda* (Oxford, 1959), 167, 170, 189, 192, 203, 209–10; *English Political Caricature, 1792–1832; A Study of Opinion and Propaganda* (Oxford, 1959), 4, 106.

[11] Quoted in James Prior, *Memoirs of the Life and Character of the Right Hon. Edmund Burke* (London, 1824), 11. The strength of the affirmation may well have a temporary significance: it would be a very expedient comment for Burke to make in the aftermath of the Gordon Riots. I owe this suggestion to Ian Harris.

[12] For early views on Christian doctrine, see *Correspondence of Edmund Burke*, ed. Thomas W. Copeland [*et al.*] (10 vols.; Cambridge, 1958–78), i. 32–3, 35–6. See also *Burke's Table-Talk*, 55; Stanlis, *Burke and the Natural Law*, 180–1.

[13] F. C. Mather, *Bishop Samuel Horsley (1733–1806) and the Caroline Tradition in the later Georgian Church* (Oxford, 1992), and Peter B. Nockles, *The Oxford Movement: Anglican High Churchmanship in Context, 1760–1857* (Cambridge, 1994). Their work makes Dreyer's conclusion that this was 'an age when latitudinarianism was the conventional and orthodox fashion for men of his [Burke's] station and circumstances' ('Burke's Religion', 212) seem more unpersuasive than ever.

Burke's own pre-1790 Anglicanism had a moderate Erastian character typical of the Rockingham Whigs and their Pelhamite predecessors. To call him a latitudinarian would be inexact at a time when influential younger Anglicans to whom that label might have been applicable earlier in the century[14] (especially those Cambridge clerics connected with Bishop Edmund Law of Carlisle, the master of Peterhouse, and the university chancellor, the duke of Grafton[15]) were tempted to deviate from credal orthodoxy—and succumbed. Grafton himself developed a loose alliance with the opposition after he left North's government in 1775, but, unlike the duke, the great majority of Rockingham's allies in both houses were uncomplicated churchmen with like-minded clergy friends.[16] There is no evidence that at any point during the 1770s or 1780s was Burke tempted to adopt any non-Athanasian version of Christianity. Like most Rockinghamites (including the marquess himself), his Anglican attachment was assumed to be both genuine and unconstrained, with faith and membership of the political order coexisting happily.[17]

His well-known speeches on the Feathers' Tavern Petition of 1772 and on the dissenting ministers' petition the following year showed Burke's commitment to the established Church in line with his understanding of the Revolution settlement of 1689 and the Lockian theory of the Church as a voluntary society.[18] Fundamental was his willingness to uphold the Toleration Act,[19] and, where it could be safely achieved, extend it for the benefit of Protestant dissenters: 'Zealous as I am for the principle of an establishment', Burke noted in 1773, 'so

[14] Cf. Dreyer, 'Burke's Religion', 201: 'His tradition of churchmanship was broad and low. Like the latitudinarians he was tolerant and open-minded in matters of dogmatic orthodoxy; he regarded matters of liturgical practice as questions of convenience and expediency. . . . He looked upon all churches as merely human associations, administering a purely human jurisdiction.' The use of these Victorian church-party labels is misleading, and Burke's respect for natural theology was hardly unusual among eighteenth-century Anglicans, and was not exclusively associated with Dreyer's 'latitudinarians'. See S. J. C. Taylor's reservations about use of that term in 'Church and State in England in the Mid-Eighteenth Century: The Newcastle Years, 1742–1762', Ph.D. thesis (Cambridge, 1987), app.

[15] John Gascoigne, 'Anglican Latitudinarianism and Political Radicalism in the Late Eighteenth Century', *History*, 71 (1986), 22–38, at 25–6; J. C. D. Clark, *English Society 1660–1832* (Cambridge, 1985), 311–15.

[16] Apart from his well-known tie with the Revd Christopher Wyvill, Rockingham himself was close to John Fountayne, dean of York, and the poet and precentor at the minster, the poet William Mason; the fringe Rockinghamite, the second earl of Hardwicke, had a large circle of clerical friends, See S. M. Farrell, 'Divisions, Debates and 'Dis-Ease': The Rockingham Whig Party and the House of Lords, 1760–1785', Ph.D. thesis (Cambridge, 1993), 390.

[17] App. B in Norman Sykes's *Church and State in the XVIIIth Century* (Cambridge, 1934) remains illuminating. It prints the prayers produced for the duke of Newcastle in his last years by Bishop John Hume.

[18] Robert Hole, *Pulpit, Politics and Public Order, 1760–1832* (Cambridge, 1989), 56–8, is generally excellent on Burke's position in the crisis of 1772–3, but one should be wary of endorsing without qualification his claim that 'Burke had no conception of a 'true church' which must be defended from imposter sects by establishment'.

[19] Frank O'Gorman, *Edmund Burke: His Political Philosophy* (London, 1973), 63–6, who observes at p. 64: 'Burke's ideas on toleration, in his earlier career, at least, lack both depth and coherence.'

just an abhorrence do I conceive against whatever may shake it, I know nothing but the supposed necessity of persecution that can make an establishment disgusting. I would have toleration a part of establishment, as a principle favourable to Christianity, and as a part of Christianity.' The Church of England should look outwards with charity towards those who could not in conscience join her, tempting them back by her dignified restraint: 'I would have her cherish all those who are within, and pity all those who are without; I would have her a common blessing to the world, an example, if not an instructor, to those who have not the happiness to belong to her.'[20] Throughout the 1770s Burke was principally concerned to uphold Christian orthodoxy, which he considered more seriously threatened by Anglican sponsors of subscriptional and liturgical changes than by the vast majority of dissenters. The latters' refusal to join the Church of England may have limited their political entitlement, but it should not affect their right to worship freely—as long as they were Trinitarian.[21]

Burke's considered justification of toleration for Protestant dissenters held less intrinsic appeal for clerics and politicians who identified with a loosely Tory tradition of Anglican theologico-politics. Comments such as those to be found in his speech of 1773 on behalf of dissenting ministers seeking relief from subscription to the Thirty-nine Articles were too detached from the established Church's fundamental well-being to endear Burke to such churchmen: 'Long may we enjoy our church under a learned and edifying episcopacy. But episcopacy may fail, and religion exist.' Such an observation offended a wider range of Anglican opinion than Burke in the early 1770s may have imagined, especially those who regarded bishops as a distinguishing mark of their Church, for which a martyred monarch had laid down his life just over a century earlier. References to 'The cause of the Church of England is included in that of religion, not that of religion in the Church of England'[22] offered no more reassurance to the country gentlemen behind the treasury bench in the House of Commons. Moreover, though averse to clergy not approving 'that state of religious things which are the sole end' of their ordination,[23] he did not rule out completely changes in the Church's outward form of worship, as Oxford Anglicans like North and, even more emphatically, the University's MP, Sir Roger Newdigate, had been ready to do in 1772.[24]

[20] *The Works of the Right Honourable Edmund Burke* (2 vols.; London, 1834), ii. 470, 73.

[21] F. P. Lock, *Burke's Reflections on the Revolution in France* (London, 1985), 42. Burke's attitude to dissenters in the 1770s is persuasively set out by Dreyer, 'Burke's Religion', 203.

[22] 'Speech on a Bill for the Relief of Protestant Dissenters', in *Works*, ii. 474.

[23] See the interesting draft on the liturgy in Northamptonshire Record Office (hereafter NRO), Fitzwilliam MSS. A. xxvii. 49.

[24] M. J. Piper, ' "The Philosopher in Action": A Study of the Relationship between Burke's Religious Thought and his Political Activity', MA thesis (Manchester, 1969), 38–41.

Burke then stood at a remove from clerical circles, and certainly from those around Lord North, patron of Oxford High Churchmen both as chancellor of the university from 1772 and as prime minister. A range of policies divided Burke as a loyal Rockinghamite from such natural supporters of the government of 1770–82: the place of party in the constitution, the alleged revival of royal power, above all the American War. His parliamentary attack on the convocation of Oxford University for its vote in June 1775 in support of government policy towards the rebellious colonies won Burke much opprobrium in conservative academic circles, where 'the specious sophistry of this frothy orator' and 'the shameful arrogance of those right honourable traitors' associated with him were roundly condemned.[25] Perhaps unsurprisingly with such attacks on the politics of the clergy, Burke's friends and acquaintances within the Anglican hierarchy in the 1770s were few,[26] especially as he had no sympathy for those heterodox (or crypto-heterodox) Anglicans prepared to contemplate leaving their mother church over failure to reform the Articles and liturgy. Though they tended to be critics of North's policies on America, Burke maintained his distance from them.

The upheavals of 1782–4 began the process of bringing Burke into closer contact with Anglican opinion. If the dismissal of the Fox–North coalition had kept the power of the crown as an issue, the thirteen colonies had received their independence, and North had become a fellow member of the opposition. Indeed, the presence of the Northites helped to give the Portland Whigs whatever distinctive Anglican colouring they possessed,[27] for Fox's downright hostility to the privileges of the Church of England was as vital a factor as any in opening up the distance between Burke and the party leadership after the marquess's death in 1782.[28] Burke himself scarcely added to his acquaintance on the bench of bishops during the parliament of 1784–90.[29] Such additional Anglican colouring as did attach to him came primarily from his developing friendship with the Laurence brothers and Walker King, though as followers rather than colleagues.

[25] *The Honor of the University of Oxford defended, against the Illiberal Aspersions of E—d B—e, Esq: with Pertinent Observations on the Present Rebellion in America. Translated from the original Latin of E.B.—* (London, 1776), 1, 17. Note also Burke's refusal, along with the rest of the opposition, to observe the Fast-day proclaimed for 30 Oct. 1776. To Richard Champion, 9 Dec. 1776, *Correspondence*, iii. 302.

[26] They included James Birt, canon of Hereford; Thomas King, rector of Woodstock; Thomas Bernard, dean of Londonderry and future bishop, and William Markham, archbishop of York. I am writing fully elsewhere on the subject of Burke's Anglican friends both in Ireland and England.

[27] Ian R. Christie, 'The Anatomy of the Opposition in the Parliament of 1784', *Parliamentary History*, 9 (1990), 50–77, deals authoritatively with North's friends.

[28] Frank O'Gorman, *The Whig Party and the French Revolution* (London, 1967), on Burke in 1789— 'the very nadir' of his political fortunes (pp. 39–42); B. W. Hill, 'Fox and Burke: The Whig Party and the Question of Principles, 1784–1789', *English Historical Review* (hereafter EHR), 89 (1974), 1–24.

[29] See Laurence French to Burke, 20 Oct. 1790: 'I do not overvalue your interest with the Bench of Bishops; yet I think it a little higher than you allow it to be, though not so high, as ought to be the interest of a man of exemplary life, various information, pre-eminent talents, and a true friend of Religion' (*The Epistolary Correspondence of The Right Hon. Edmund Burke and Dr. French Laurence* (London, 1827), 13).

All had worked with Burke on the *Annual Register* at some point.[30] French Laurence, a civilian lawyer in Foxite circles, had by the late 1780s written in opposition newspapers and become close to Burke, thanks to his assistance in Hastings's impeachment, and was regularly with him at home in Beaconsfield. French was a biblical student, while his brother, Richard, took Anglican orders and rose to become archbishop of Cashel.[31] Another young friend advanced to the episcopate after Burke's death was Walker King, who, with his two brothers, was well known to the whole Burke family as early as 1773.[32]

The fact remained that before 1790 Burke was simply not the sort of lay politician Anglican apologists would tend to cite in their support: his attitude to dissenters had too much of a Whiggish cordiality for that. Nevertheless, even before publication of the *Reflections*, there were signs of a guardedness towards dissent that had not been present earlier, and a corresponding appreciation of the established Church as a foundation of good order and sound belief.[33] The part dissenters had played in securing the victory of Pitt's government at the general election of 1784 did not endear their cause to Burke,[34] but it was the open heterodoxy of spokesmen for 'rational dissent' like Price and Priestley that kindled his suspicions of the threat to the established order in the late 1780s:[35] in 1772 the dissenters had solicited protection, but fifteen years later some of them like Joseph Priestley had made clear that they were looking to subvert the established Church.[36] Significantly, Burke refused to lend his active assistance to Henry Beaufoy's campaign for repeal of the Test and Corporation Acts.[37]

---

[30] *Notes & Queries*, 1st ser., 12 (1855), 171.

[31] After Burke's death French Laurence published *Critical Remarks on Detached Passages of the New Testament, particularly the Revelation of St John*. See *Poetical Remains of French Laurence, D.C.L., M.P. and Richard Laurence, D.C.L.* (Dublin, 1872), 4, 6, 11, and obituary in the *Gentleman's Magazine* (1809), i. 282. His younger brother, Richard, was appointed to the vicarage of Coleshill, Berks., in 1787 by Jacob, second Earl of Radnor (*Poetical Remains*, 111).

[32] Walker King. Matric. Brasenose Coll., Oxf., 1768, aet. 16; moved to Corpus Christi, BA, 1771; MA, 1775; BD and DD, 1788; Preacher, Gray's Inn; Canon of Wells, 1796; preb. of Canterbury, 1803; Bp. of Rochester, 1809–27.

[33] In 1785 the Scottish minister, Thomas Somerville, thought he found in Burke 'an illiberal and excessive Partiality to the Episcopalian government and forms of worship' (*My Own Life and Times 1741–1814* (Edinburgh, 1861), 222).

[34] To Richard Bright, 8, 9 May 1789, *Correspondence*, v. 471.

[35] Cone (*The Age of the French Revolution*, 292) notes that in Sept. 1789 Burke was urging Fox to court the dissenters. Yet a few months later some dissenters were deploring his hostility to their interests and attacked his violent censures 'which have neither dignity nor moderation' ([J. Smith], *Some Remarks on the Resolutions of the Clergy of the Archdeaconry of Chester* (Liverpool, 1790), 42). Piper, '"The Philosopher in Action"', 56 ff., charts these changes well.

[36] Robert Bisset, LL.D., *The Life of Edmund Burke* (London, 1789), 162; Piper, '"The Philosopher in Action"', 26. See also Nigel Aston, 'Horne and Heterodoxy: The Defence of Anglican Beliefs in the late Enlightenment', *EHR* 108 (1993), 895–920.

[37] G. M. Ditchfield, 'The Parliamentary Struggle over the Repeal of the Test and Corporation Acts, 1787–90', *EHR* 79 (1974), 551–77, esp. 567–8; U. R. Q. Henriques, *Religious Toleration in England, 1787–1833* (London, 1961), 105, 109–10; Hole, *Pulpits, Politics and Public Order*, 123–4.

Though he had not abandoned his belief in a renegotiated *modus vivendi* for Church and nonconformists that could dispense with a sacramental test (seen in his encouragement for the repeal of the same in Scotland in the later 1770s), Burke by early 1790 was insistent that dissenters must speak less stridently: 'they must cease to *alarm* the Church establishment; which many people believe (and I among them) to be connected, in its safety or danger, with many *other* establishments which form parts of our constitution. They will consider the Church, as a *jealous friend* to be *reconciled,* and not as an *adversary* that must be vanquished.'[38]

The debate in the Commons on 2 March 1790 on the motion for the repeal of the Test and Corporation Acts made public Burke's intensified concern for the fate of Christian orthodoxy and the established Churches which upheld it. The appearance of Richard Price's notorious sermon *A Discourse on the Love of our Country* had confirmed Burke's suspicions about the menace of 'rational dissent', and the minority inspired by the French example to foment revolutionary upheaval at home. Burke drew the attention of the House to the catechisms recently produced for the young by leading nonconformist preachers such as Robert Robinson and Samuel Palmer, works 'grossly libelling the national establishment in every part and passage', and the product of ministers too inclined to flirt with Socinianism.[39] Burke was so worried that he concluded 'our establishment appeared to be in much more serious danger than the Church of France was in a year or two ago'. Accordingly, nothing should be done precipitately.[40]

His obvious alarm revealed the extent to which Burke's thought had changed under the impact of the Revolution, above all by giving it an ecclesiological dimension that has never been adequately appreciated.[41] In highlighting the domestic and foreign threats to the settled character of the British state, Burke's appreciation of theology had suddenly become—and would remain—more appreciable than ever before in his political career.[42] It is too easily forgotten that the predominant religious element contained in the *Reflections* in November

---

[38] To John Nobel, 14 Mar. 1790, *Correspondence,* vi. 104, where Burke still claimed to be their 'well-wisher'; Priestley, *Letters,* iv. 52–3; O'Gorman, *Edmund Burke,* 138–9; *Whig Party,* 49. See also J. G. A. Pocock, 'Edmund Burke and the Redefinition of Enthusiasm: The Context as Counter-Revolution', in François Furet and Mona Ozouf, *The French Revolution and the Creation of Modern Political Culture,* iii. *The Transformation of Political Culture 1789–1848* (Oxford, 1989), 19–44, at 24–5.

[39] *The Speeches of the Right Honourable Edmund Burke* (4 vols., London, 1816), iii. 477, 81. Discussed in Piper, '"The Philosopher in Action"', 71–2. Here, as elsewhere, there are good grounds for treating with great caution John Dinwiddy's argument that 'there is little to suggest that he [Burke] was interested, for their own sake, in the *doctrinal* differences, which separated the Church of England from Dissent' (Dinwiddy, 'Interpretations of Anti-Jacobinism', 44).

[40] *Speeches,* iii. 478, 80.

[41] Cf. Clark, *English Society,* 250.

[42] J. C. D. Clark, *The Language of Liberty 1688–1832: Political Discourse and Social Dynamics in the Anglo-American World* (Cambridge, 1994), 278.

1790 took the public by surprise. These clerical preoccupations were not ones particularly associated with Burke in the past; that said, they were indicative of that wider sense of security in the Church of England shared by many conservative Whigs as 'a great national benefit, a great publick blessing'.[43] Foxite colleagues among the Portland Whigs, however much they had come to see 'the Philosopher of Beaconsfield'[44] as eccentric and unpredictable, were taken aback by what one radical commentator, Charles Pigott, referred to in 1791 as 'the New Political Tenets of the Right Honourable Edmund Burke'. Fox himself scorned the *Reflections* as a book 'in very bad taste' and as 'favouring Tory principles'.[45] Journalists were fascinated. What would become of what *The Times* called that 'tria juncta in Uno (Mr Fox, Mr Burke, and Mr Sheridan) who had hitherto been so united in politics that nothing could shake or disunite them'?[46]

As is well known, Burke was by no means the first commentator on events in France to notice their wider menace. High Church clerics like William Jones of Nayland were in no doubt that the Revolution was 'the most terrible threat, not merely to a particular political regime, but to Christian civilisation',[47] and so prepared the public for Burke's uncompromising condemnation. The *Reflections* gave 'eloquent but unoriginal expression' to a well-rehearsed tradition of Anglican theology, but the extent of Burke's identification with it had previously been in doubt.[48] His expressions of horror at the abolition of tithe in France, the nationalization of Church lands, and the imposition of the Civil Constitution of the Clergy pre-empted the possibility that any agitation by radical dissenters such as Priestley and Price (sponsored by extreme Anglican latitudinarians such as Burke's *bête noir*, the marquess of Lansdowne) for a similar spoliation in England

[43] 'Speech on the Petition of the Unitarians (1792)', *Works*, ii. 478.

[44] Expression used in *Philo-Theodosius: or, A New Edition of Theodosius with a new Character of Mr Burke* (London, 1790), 11.

[45] British Library (hereafter BL) Add. MSS 47590, fo. 24, Commonplace Book of Samuel Rogers; West Suffolk County Record Office, Grafton MSS, fo. 741, Bishop of Peterborough to Duke of Grafton, 7 Dec. 1790, quoted in L. G. Mitchell, *Charles James Fox* (Oxford, 1992), 113; *Charles James Fox and the Disintegration of the Whig Party 1782–1794* (Oxford, 1971), 158–9, 163–87. Priestley accused him of supporting passive obedience and non-resistance, principles 'peculiar to the Tories and the friends of arbitrary power' (*Letters*, p. viii). Another commentator deplored Burke's repudiation of the 'standard of opposition' through a new-found attachment to kings and the Popish Church in France (*Philo-Theodosius*, 6).

[46] *The Times*, 30 Nov. 1790. For the range of press views, see Frank O'Gorman, *The Whig Party and the French Revolution* (London, 1967), 57 n., 69 n. He quotes the *Morning Chronicle*, 21 Feb. 1791: 'the orb which once shone in full splendour, is now hastening to its wane. You have passed the meredian of life, and in a few years you will be among the silent dead.'

[47] Clark, *English Society*, 227, citing William Jones, *Popular Commotions Considered as Signs of the Approaching End of the World: A Sermon Preached in the Metropolitan Church of Canterbury, on Sunday, September 20, 1789* (London, 1789); Robert Hole, 'English Sermons and Tracts as Media of Debate on the French Revolution 1789–99', in Philp (ed.), *The French Revolution and British Popular Politics*, 18–37, at 21–2; Mather, *Horsley*, 76.

[48] Clark, *English Society*, 249.

would have any prospect of success. But was this dramatic restatement of the rights and privileges of the established order marked by an enhanced appreciation of the religious truths distinctively conveyed by the Church of England or of its primitive episcopalian character? Justification of the Church hierarchy in the *Reflections* at least showed a willingness to uphold the teaching ministry of the lower clergy, and to defend the bishops' political role.[49] Otherwise, Burke's restatement of his attachment to the national Church in January 1791 showed a continuing restraint: 'My particular religious sentiments are not of much importance to anyone but myself. I am attached to Christianity at large; much from conviction; more from affection. I would risque a great deal to prevent its being extinguished anywhere or in any of its shapes.'[50] To another correspondent in 1791 who had enquired about his religious beliefs, Burke felt the desirability of emphasizing that he saw no cause to abandon the Church of England: 'When I do, I shall act upon my conviction, or my mistake. I think that church harmonizes with our civil constitution . . . I am attached to Christianity at large; much from conviction: More from affection.'[51] Conor Cruise O'Brien has called this sort of reference 'cool and politic, provisional and contingent', and argued that Burke did 'not feel himself to be quite in the right platoon'.[52] Caution is surely required here. Mere absence of fulsomeness is not in itself evidence that Burke did not feel the Church of England was a spiritual home in which he could be personally comfortable.

Instead, the leaders of Anglican opinion preferred to overlook these generous hesitations, and announce Burke's uncompromising identity with the established Church anyway, on the reasonable assumption that this point had not been his primary concern in the *Reflections*.[53] His defence of the Church of England there and on other occasions (such as leading opposition to the Petition of the Unitarians for toleration in 1792) was far too compelling to be ignored by the episcopate, however distant and uncertain its previous relations with him, and gave him an enhanced authority inside his own communion.[54] Burke had re-

---

[49] Dreyer ('Burke's Religion', 205) plausibly finds Paleyian justification of the hierarchy, but exaggerates in writing that comments on episcopacy in the *Reflections* show that 'his case was argued entirely in utilitarian terms'.

[50] 26 Jan. 1791, to unknown, *Correspondence*, vi. 215.

[51] 26 Jan. 1791, *Correspendence*, vi. 214–16.

[52] *Burke: Reflections on the Revolution in France*, ed. Conor Cruise O'Brien (Harmondsworth, 1969), 29.

[53] See Roger Wells, 'English Society and Revolutionary Politics in the 1790s: The Case for Insurrection', in Philp (ed.), *The French Revolution and British Popular Politics*, 188–226, at 196–7. I am writing elsewhere about the nature of the Anglican response to Burke in the 1790s.

[54] It was perhaps more from hope than expectation of Burke's influence in the area of ecclesiastical patronage that he was approached by French Laurence in October 1790 with a view to enlisting his aid in obtaining the vacant chancellorships of the dioceses of either Bristol or Ely (Bodl., MS. Eng. lett. d. 5, (fo. 56)).

ceived generous acknowledgement of his part in enhancing the intellectual distinction of Anglican political theology from Bishop George Horne of Norwich only a few months before his death in January 1792[55] and he was greatly esteemed by another High Church champion, Bishop Samuel Horsley of St Davids, who had an unusual Whig–dissenting background. Lesser clergy could refer to the *Reflections* confident that Burke's name had a currency without parallel among their parishioners as a defender of the established order and the reinvigorator of Anglican loyalism. Burke had a better appreciation of the High Church position in the 1790s than ever before, and was unswerving in his admiration of prelates like Horne and Horsley, but nevertheless continued to occupy ground at some remove from their own. If 'latitudinarian' offers little insight into his religious mentality in the last few years of his life, then 'High Churchman' is only marginally less appropriate. He could not accede without qualification to the normal commonplaces of the ascendant orthodox 'party'[56] on the apostolic integrity of the Church of England, the authentic primitiveness of its government and liturgy, or its distinctive independent existence from the State. Neither is there evidence that Burke held the Anglican doctors from Lancelot Andrewes to the Nonjurors in unique esteem; in as much as he admitted any single Anglican authority, he looked rather to Joseph Butler,[57] and beyond him to Richard Hooker, whose following among the 'orthodox party' at the end of the eighteenth century was at best limited.

But if Burke identified incompletely with Anglican divines who gloried in their Nonjuring and Caroline heritage,[58] their esteem for him in 1791–4 was increasing. Nothing marked it more than his gradual rehabilitation in Oxford circles. The *Gentleman's Magazine* of February 1791 contained a complimentary address from the resident graduates in the university that was conveyed to Burke by William Windham. But his gesture was a consolation prize for the denial to Burke of an honorary degree. An attempt to persuade convocation in December 1790 to award him a DCL by diploma was thwarted, and he received only 'the unauthorised compliments of a baffled minority'.[59] It unquestionably piqued

---

[55] George Horne, *A Charge Intended to have been Delivered to the Clergy of Norwich at the Primary Visitation of George, Lord Bishop of that Diocese* (Norwich, 1791), 33.

[56] P. B. Nockles, 'Church Parties in the Pre-Tractarian Church of England 1750–1833: The "Orthodox"—Some Problems of Definition and Identity', in John Walsh, Colin Haydon, and Stephen Taylor (eds.), *The Church of England c.1689–c.1833: From Toleration to Tractarianism* (Cambridge, 1993), 334–59.

[57] B. A. W. Young, '"Orthodoxy Assail'd": An Historical Examination of Some Metaphysical and Theological Debates in England from Locke to Burke', D.Phil. thesis (Oxford, 1990), 331.

[58] See Burke's disclaimers to aspirations 'to the Glory of being a distinguished Zealot for any National Church' (to Dr John Erskine, 12 June 1779, *Correspondence*, iv. 83–8, at 85).

[59] *Gentleman's Magazine*, 61 (1791), 99–100, 210; Countess of Minto (ed.), *Life and Letters of Sir Gilbert Elliot, First Earl of Minto from 1751 to 1806* (3 vols., London, 1874), ii. 153.

Burke and his friends that forgiveness for his Whig past was so slow in forth-coming. Nevertheless, the thaw continued, part of the recognition accorded by the university to the cautious, conservative position adopted by the Portland Whigs towards the Revolution, and their resulting cooperation with Pitt's government. With the full backing of the ministry,[60] the duke of Portland (himself a Christ Church graduate) was nominated to succeed Lord Guilford (the former premier, Lord North) as chancellor in 1792. Burke came in person to Oxford that summer for Portland's installation as chancellor,[61] and the next summer learnt that the duke had recommended him for an honorary doctorate. Burke was unimpressed. To Portland's irritation, he considered it lesser recognition than the one originally proposed, and allowed it to go instead to his son Richard.[62]

The embarrassment over the Oxford degrees neatly symbolized Burke's uneasy relations with the Anglican hierarchy. His celebrity and status among churchmen generally did little to increase his contacts with the higher clergy, let alone establish new intimacy with any of them, with the notable exception of Bishop John Douglas of Carlisle (translated to Salisbury in 1791).[63] And that contact was offset by the final break-up of his friendship with the archbishop of York, William Markham, during the last phase of the Hastings impeachment.[64] The fact remained that, from 1792 to his death in 1797, Burke's course in religion still lay at one remove from the majority of the Church of England. His identification with the established Church remained incomplete. The main apology for it had come in the *Reflections*; thereafter, as events moved on, Burke's attention turned elsewhere in the confident knowledge that the Church of England would not want for eloquent spokesmen against detractors. He used his influence in government circles on behalf of Anglican friends, notably the Laurence brothers,[65] but otherwise kept his distance, while never losing his conviction that the established Church and the British constitution would stand or fall together and required constant watchfulness against 'the new fanatical religion, now in the heat of its first ferment, of the Rights of Man, which rejects all ecclesiastical, and in truth all civil order'.[66]

[60] *Correspondence*, vii. 168; W. R. Ward, *Victorian Oxford* (London, 1965), 3; O'Gorman, *Whig Party*, 103–4.

[61] *Correspondence*, vii. 224, 227–8.

[62] Bisset, *Life*, 547–8; Sir Gilbert to Lady Elliot, 3 July 1793, in Minto (ed.), *Life and Letters*, ii. 153–4.

[63] *Correspondence*, vi. 157 n., 282–3, 305, 308–9, 368; vii. 98.

[64] Burke complained (incorrectly) that the 'Corps of Bishops' had contributed to the failure of the impeachment (*Correspondence*, vii. 372).

[65] Portland nominated French Laurence to the Regius Chair in Civil Law on Burke's recommendation in 1796 (Burke, *Correspondence*, ix. 147).

[66] Letter to Richard Burke, post 19 Feb. 1792, in R. B. McDowell (ed.), *The Writings and Speeches of Edmund Burke*, ix. *The Revolutionary War 1794–1797, and Ireland* (Oxford, 1991), 647.

Yet, if Burke had actively ceased to support Protestant dissenters, in the 1790s he favoured Irish Roman Catholics far more ardently. A degree of caution is required here, since Conor Cruise O'Brien's recent biography *The Great Melody* has distorted the rationale underscoring Burke's campaigning by depicting him as, in Jim Smyth's telling words, a 'sort of sublimated Irish Catholic' himself.[67] That was far from the case: Burke was and remained a Protestant, keen to maintain the established Church of Ireland.[68] Nevertheless, it was Burke's determination to do all in his power to improve the civil status of the Irish majority[69] that tempered the admiration for his anti-Revolutionary writings found among fellow Anglicans, and induced caution within the episcopate against too close an association with this maverick defender of the faith.[70] Many English prelates, like the majority of Pitt's cabinet, were not averse to further relaxation of the disabilities imposed on Irish Catholics since the Revolution settlement, but it was Burke's zealotry in this cause that embarrassed them, threatened to compromise his character as a churchman, called into question his political judgement, and suggested (quite rightly) his limited and not uncritical attachment to Anglican supremacy.

Burke's espousal of the Irish Catholic cause was equally impelled by his genuine belief in their loyalty and his fear that to ignore their grievances would drive them into Jacobinism[71] and imperil the security of the whole British state. As Conor Cruise O'Brien has well suggested, Burke was putting forward Catholicism as a bastion of order while, conversely, Protestantism in its more militant form was the seedbed of Jacobinism.[72] In an Irish context, it was an Anglican establishment rather than radical Protestantism that barred the way to the resettlement Burke wanted. Hence the practical necessity of diluting the unrepresentative Anglican supremacy in Ireland, a position which by the Fitzwilliam viceroyalty of 1795 had taken him as far as arguing that the three principal Churches in the British Isles, 'in subordination to the legal establishments as they

---

[67] 'The Making and Undoing of a Confessional State: Ireland, 1660–1829', *Journal of Ecclesiastical History* (*JEH*), 44 (1993), 506–13, at 507. See also E. P. Thompson's review in *Times Literary Supplement.* 'In the Gentlemen's Cause', 4 Dec. 1992, and O'Brien's reply, 18 Dec. McCormack (*Ascendancy and Tradition*, 61 ff.) is more measured than O'Brien, and the position is brilliantly summarized by McDowell (ed.), *Writings and Speeches*, ix. 410, where Burke is convincingly depicted as 'A convert to the Catholic cause, although not to Catholicism'.

[68] R. B. McDowell, *Ireland in the Age of Imperialism and Revolution 1760–1801* (Oxford, 1979), 393.

[69] See 'Letter to a Peer of Ireland', [Lord Kenmare] 21 Feb. 1782, and 'A Letter to Sir Hercules Langrishe on the Subject of the Roman Catholics of Ireland', in McDowell (ed.), *Writings and Speeches*, ix. 564–79, 594–639.

[70] McCormack (*Ascendancy and Tradition*, 50) well summarizes the complexities of Burke's position. Plans for Burke to receive an honorary degree from Trinity College in thanks for the *Reflections* were jeopardized by his 'warm part' on behalf of the Irish Catholics: *The Beauties of the late Right Hon. Edmund Burke* (2 vols.; London, 1798), i, p. cxxxi; to John Hely-Hutchinson, 18 Dec. 1790, *Correspondence*, vi. 192–3.

[71] *Correspondence*, viii. 132; ix. 121, 162, 256–7.

[72] O'Brien (ed.), *Reflections*, introduction, p. 38.

stand in the several countries', should all be recognized.[73] Irish Catholics were the first line of defence against Jacobinism, and the state should invest in clerical education as the best antidote to revolutionary contagion.[74] Such recommendations struck at the heart of the enduring Protestant myth that Irish papists existed to be converted, not to have their religious persuasion actually confirmed by further legal recognition.[75]

To a large swathe of moderate Anglican opinion, Burke's viewpoint was not without its merits. Archbishop George Stone of Armagh, primate from 1747 to 1764, had advocated a degree of toleration as long ago as the 1750s,[76] and a limited Catholic relief bill subsequently passed through the Irish Parliament in 1782,[77] the precursor of further substantial concessions in 1792 and 1793. Those Catholic Relief Acts were pressed strongly on Dublin Castle by Pitt's cabinet, and were broadly acceptable to High Church bishops in England like Horsley as a worthwhile concession to an orthodox creed that would have security benefits for Britain as it entered on war with France. They nevertheless sent ripples of concern through the Church of Ireland and Dublin Castle, enough to trigger a significant backlash against any more pro-Catholic measures, for which the rallying cry was 'Protestant Ascendancy'.[78] For worried Irish Anglicans, Burke's crusade on behalf of papists was both unnecessary and unsettling. He offended by going so far towards appeasing the religious majority that the Irish Protestant establishment would become meaningless; from this angle, the increasing appeal to Burke of the Irish Catholic Church as a primitive Christian model appeared quite eccentric even to Protestant moderates.[79] Burke's extreme emollience towards Irish Catholics (which went further than the political rights the British government was ready to concede) thus limited his usefulness to Anglican leaders

[73] To William Smith, 29 Jan. 1795, in McDowell (ed.) *Writings and Speeches*, ix. 662–3.

[74] *Memoirs of the Life and Times of the Rt. Hon. Henry Grattan* (5 vols.; London, 1849), iv. 155. See his letter to Grattan, Sept. 1794.

[75] See the interesting comment arising from a conversation of c.1790. 'It, however, appeared to me evident, that he was convinced we had the best of reasons for not conforming to what is called the Established Church' (*An Account of a Conversation between the Rt. Hon. Edmund Burke and the Rt. Rev. Dr. Gibson* (Manchester, 1819), 9).

[76] Mahoney, *Burke and Ireland*, 359. See also Bishop Frederick Hervey's efforts in the late 1760s: Thomas Bartlett, *The Fall and Rise of the Irish Nation: The Catholic Question 1690–1830* (Dublin, 1992), 79–80.

[77] For Burke's involvement in the Act's origins, see Mahoney, *Burke and Ireland*, 111–18.

[78] 'Protestant Ascendancy' was a relatively new term in the early 1790s. See Jacqueline R. Hill, 'Popery and Protestantism, Civil and Religious Liberty: The Disputed Lessons of Irish History 1690–1812', *Past and Present*, 118 (1988), 96–129, at 125. She notes that it was via Bishop Woodward's *The Present State of the Church of Ireland* (1787) that the term in effect entered the public domain. See also her 'The Meaning and Significance of "Protestant Ascendancy", 1787–1840', in *Ireland after the Union* (Proceedings of the second joint meetings of the Royal Irish Academy and the British Academy, London, 1986; Oxford, 1989), 1–22, at 3, 7–8, and McCormack, *Ascendancy and Tradition*, 68–75, 94–5.

[79] Mahoney, *Burke and Ireland*, 319; McDowell (ed.), *Writings and Speeches*, ix. 408.

by the mid-1790s. It again showed the risks attendant on having such an original character speaking out on the Church of England's behalf and, for High Churchmen particularly, raised questions about the Portland Whig commitments to Anglicanism, especially after the fiasco of Lord Fitzwilliam's tenure of the Irish viceroyalty early in 1795. Their misgivings would have been confirmed had they had access to Burke's correspondence with Richard Burke junior, who acted first as the principal agent of the Catholics in Ireland and was later made their representative in England.[80] At one point, his father confessed that 'Much nearer his heart' even than the strength and security of the established Churches in both England and Ireland was Catholic emancipation in Ireland. He told his son that a man must be a strange Christian and a strange Irishman 'who would not see Ireland a free, flourishing happy Catholic country, though not one Protestant existed in it, than an enslaved, beggared, insulted degraded Catholic country, as it is, with some Protestants scattered through it, for the purpose, not of instructing the people, but of rendering them miserable'.[81]

The statement depicted Burke at his most extreme on Ireland, but gives an accurate reflection of his political frustrations rather than his confessional priorities.[82] The French Revolution confirmed Burke in his contention that the Irish Anglican ascendancy could no longer continue unchanged without endangering its own survival and, by implication, the British state as a whole. He could not appreciate the position of most Anglicans on both sides of the water that the price of improving the civic status of Irish Catholics must entail a diminution of Church of Ireland privileges. Instead, Burke warned that root-and-branch change in that Church's relationship with the Irish Catholic majority could not in safety be long delayed, and his views on this fundamental question were not lost on its leaders. He had known the archbishop of Armagh, Richard Robinson (first Lord Rokeby), for several years before they met again at Bath in 1792, where Burke expressed himself with openness and was not unsympathetically heard.[83] Not every Irish prelate won such respect. Privately, to his son, Burke castigated one of the leading champions of 'Protestant Ascendancy', Archbishop Charles Agar of Cashel, as 'a Jackanapes in Lawn Sleeves' for his disparaging

---

[80] Bartlett, *The Fall and Rise of the Irish Nation*, 140–1, for the anger of the Lord-Lieutenant, Lord Westmorland, and the Chief Secretary, John, Lord Hobart, with the Burkes. For Hobart, see R. G. Thorne (ed.), *The History of Parliament: The House of Commons 1790–1820* (5 vols.; London, 1986), iv. 208.

[81] *Correspondence*, iii. 451–5, 23 Mar. 1792. Mahoney well notes, 'Should this letter have fallen into other hands, there can be no doubt that it would have done incalculable harm to him' (*Burke and Ireland*, 190). Cf. Cobban, *Burke*, 103–4.

[82] He insisted 'not one of those zealots for a Protestant interest, wishes more sincerely than I do, perhaps not half so sincerely, for the support of the established Church in both these Kingdoms' ('Letter to Richard Burke' in McDowell (ed.), *Writings and Speeches*, ix. 649).

[83] Mahoney, *Burke and Ireland*, 202.

reference to the majority of the Irish.[84] It was an expression of frustration at the Church of Ireland's dilatoriness and complacency that led Burke by 1795 to strike a strident, almost anti-Anglican note in criticizing: 'A religion that has for one of its dogmas, the servitude of all that do not belong to it—is a vile Heresy.'[85]

This acerbic note of disappointment was never far away when Burke wrote about religion in Ireland during the last two years of his life.[86] He saw inertia and misrepresentation operating at the very highest levels of the Anglican establishment. Thus in his last letter to Fitzwilliam while the earl was in Dublin, he expressed his alarm that the emancipation both men wanted would be insidiously prevented by conservative prelates. He took seriously the rumour that Archbishop Moore of Canterbury had talked with the King and given him 'an alarm that if the bill should pass the Church could not exist'. Such rumours of malign and secret influence in the closet touched Burke's rawest political nerve, but there was another side to it: if such reports were correct, they amounted to an unwarranted interference by 'another Church, wholly without jurisdiction civil or ecclesiastical in the Country to curtail the civil rights of the far greater part of the King's subjects there'.[87] These sentiments remind us of the limits to Burke's Anglican identity, scarcely disguised by his idiosyncratic claim that mistreatment of Irish Catholics was inconsistent with the principles of the Glorious Revolution.[88] Thus his letter to French Laurence of November 1796, where he declared that Irish 'Protestantism, as things stand now, is no description of a religion at all, or of any principle, religious, moral, or political, but is a mere negation' since Irish Anglicans were not required to take any tests whatsoever, with the clergy of the established Church even excused signing the Thirty-nine Articles. An earlier willingness to give the Irish Church some time to pacify the Catholic majority had gone by this date, and in its place had come a bilious disdain for what Burke dismissively called the 'party of the Established Church'.[89]

Burke's Anglican sympathies must be viewed in relation to a wider spectrum of Christian affinities. These included not merely Irish, but French Roman Catholics, and his work on behalf of the Gallican refugees who crossed to

---

[84] Bartlett, *The Fall and Rise of the Irish Nation*, 135; Burke to Richard Burke, 23 Mar. 1792, *Correspondence*, vii. 118.

[85] Ibid.

[86] McCormack well refers to 'the gathering darkness' of Burke's utterances on Ireland (*Ascendancy and Tradition*, 49).

[87] 13 Mar. 1795, *Correspondence*, viii. 192–3. Both Archbishop Moore of Canterbury and Bishop Porteus of London felt emancipation would violate the coronation oath: Mahoney, *Burke and Ireland*, 269; Bartlett, *The Fall and Rise of the Irish Nation*, 204.

[88] Mahoney, *Burke and Ireland*, 320.

[89] 'Burke insists that Protestantism [in an Irish context] is *interest*, nor religion' (McCormack, *Ascendancy and Tradition*, 55). See also 'Letter to Richard Burke' in McDowell (ed.), *Writings and Speeches*, ix. 647. As Grayson Ditchfield has pointed out to me, his position here may be compared to Gladstone's in 1868–9.

England in poverty and bewilderment during 1791–2 is deservedly well known.[90] He was by no means alone among the Portland Whigs in supporting Wilmot's Committee for Emigrant Relief: Fitzwilliam and Windham joined the Pittite marquess of Buckingham as members, and Burke's protégé Walker King sat alongside the government loyalists, Bishops Barrington of Durham and Horsley of Rochester.[91] Once again, there is no question of Burke unconsciously aligning himself with his preferred religionists. Historically, the Gallican Church had long represented to High Church Anglicans the tolerable side of popery,[92] and this empathy had not diminished during the second half of the century. Attention has focused on the immediate, post-Revolutionary background in explaining the sympathetic reception accorded by 'orthodox' Anglican clergy to the *émigré* priests from France in the early 1790s, but this emphasis neglects the evolving perception among clergy who looked to bishops like Horsley and Horne for leadership that the Church of England no less than its estranged Gallican sister was similarly confronted by the related perils of heterodoxy and unbelief.[93] They shared Burke's anxieties that the Revolution had been incited by a 'cabal' of philosophers, deists, or materialists to a man, discontented with the aristo-cratic order and ready to strip the Church of political and landed power.[94]

Burke's involvement in relieving the distress of the Gallican exiles was prompted by charitable and humanitarian sentiments, and rekindled the admi-ration felt for him by High Churchmen. In Ireland, his pro-Catholic lobbying could be deemed as ill advised and undermining the established faith; in France, Gallicanism *was* the established faith, whose recognition was essential if the revolutionary republic was to be overthrown. Most Anglicans might deplore Burke's insistence that in Ireland the Catholic religion 'should be upheld in high respect and veneration',[95] but in a French context they could hardly disagree: the Gallican Church and the monarchy went together, and should be restored together. Burke was happy to extol the exiles' principles and tell the public of their endurance, as in his *Case of the Suffering Clergy of France* (September 1792), where he appealed to the generosity of all 'right-thinking men' and hoped 'that a difference in religious persuasion will not shut the hearts of the English public

---

[90] Mean figure of 5,000 French exiled clergy on the British mainland in the period 1793–1800: Dom Aidan Bellenger, *The French Exiled Clergy in the British Isles after 1789* (Bath, 1986), 3.

[91] Bellenger, *The French Exiled Clergy*, 15–16; *Correspondence*, viii. 317–23, 396–7.

[92] Anthony Milton, *Catholic and Reformed: The Roman and Protestant Churches in English Protestant Thought, 1600–1640* (Cambridge, 1995); J. Gres-Gayer, *Paris–Cantorbéry: Le Dossier d'un premier œcuménisme* (Paris, 1989).

[93] Nigel Aston, 'The Dean of Canterbury and the Sage of Ferney: George Horne Looks at Voltaire', in W. M. Jacob and Nigel Yates (eds.), *Crown and Mitre: Religion and Society in Northern Europe since the Reformation* (Woodbridge, 1993), 139–60.

[94] Harris, 'Paine and Burke', 56n., 58.

[95] To William Smith, 26 May 1795, *Correspondence*, viii. 243–5.

against their suffering brethren, the Christians of France'.[96] His energetic lobbying for the exiles indicates just how much Burke's outlook had changed since 1776, when the fate of the American Episcopalian clergy similarly hung in the balance and fuelled High Church anxieties in England sufficiently to cause them to open a relief fund. Episcopalian survival was not a priority to Burke in the mid-1770s; by the early 1790s nothing mattered more to him.[97] Where he could bring his influence to bear on their behalf, he did so. Indeed, he had no hesitation in appealing to the greatest Anglican citadel of all in 1792, to persuade Oxford University to participate unstintingly in the relief of the French clergy.[98]

The *Reflections* had first made publicly clear Burke's admiration for the religious integrity of the Gallican Church, in which his anxieties about an attack on the property of a great corporation within the State merge with broader theological concerns.[99] In the last weeks of the National Assembly, he publicly applauded the principled leadership offered by the French episcopate to the Civil Constitution, for they had made known the advantages which religion derived 'from the alliance of its own proper dignity with the character which illustrious birth and the sentiment of honour gives to man'.[100] Burke's highflown respect was derived only to a limited degree from first-hand familiarity, principally from acquaintance with Bishop J.-B.-M. Champion de Cicé of Auxerre and his sister, Elisabeth-Marie de Cicé, who had befriended Richard Burke junior during his stay in the town.[101] Their sterling character indelibly coloured Burke's view of their Church as one combining grandeur with pastoral concern. The opportunities for meeting such exiles after 1789–especially those who from the start doubted the benefits of the Revolution—confirmed his approval of the Gallican

[96] The publication first appeared in *Evening Mail* (17–19 Sept. 1792) and *The Times* (18 Sept.), and was later distributed in pamphlet form, reprinted in *Annual Register*, and translated into French.

[97] Note, however, that Burke suggested that the rough treatment of the Episcopalians by the dissenters' allies in North America weakened their own claims for toleration. See *Correspondence*, ii. 309–10. I am grateful for Grayson Ditchfield's help on this point. See also his article 'Lord North's Ecclesiastical Policy', in Walsh, Haydon, and Taylor (eds.), *From Toleration to Tractarianism*, 241–3.

[98] To Revd Richard Hughes, 16 Oct. 1792, *Correspondence*, vii. 270. The charitable theme was urgently stressed in Walker King, *Two Sermons Preached at Gray's Inn Chapel* (London, 1793). Burke's most conspicuous relief took the form of a foundation for exiled French children at Penn in 1796. See Ralph M. Robinson, *The Penn Country and the Chilterns* (London, 1929), 62–3; J. Gilbert Jenkins, *A History of the Parish of Penn* (London, 1935), 149–53; F.-X. Plasse, *Le Clergé français réfugié en Angleterre* (2 vols.; Paris, 1866), ii. 57–73.

[99] Dreyer ('Burke's Religion', 211) sees the few references to the Civil Constitution of the Clergy in the *Reflections* as another pointer to Burke's 'latitudinarianism'. Quite apart from overlooking the link between land seizure and institutional reform of the Church, such a view minimizes Burke's admiration for the exiles' attachment to principle on that issue, based on first-hand contact with them.

[100] Dated 15 July 1791, reprinted in the London newspapers. See *Correspondence*, vi. 293–5.

[101] Prior, *Life*, 408, for his charity towards them. Weighed down by Richard's death, Burke had to refuse hospitality in 1794 to the Bishop of Auxerre's brother, Archbishop Champion de Cicé of Bordeaux: to Abbé d'Héral, 30 Nov. 1794, *Correspondence*, viii. 86–9; to Walker King, 30 Nov. 1794, ibid. 89–90; Thomas Macknight, *History of the Life and Times of Edmund Burke* (3 vols.; London, 1858), iii. 612–13.

Church and of its clergy 'as Patterns for Piety, Humility & every Christian virtue',[102] and from discussions with them, as Leslie Mitchell has persuasively argued,[103] was formed his wider view of what was happening in France. *Émigré* clerics soon flocked to Beaconsfield, making it, in Mitchell's words, 'a little court in its own right',[104] an important channel of communication between the exiles and Whitehall.

Two exiled leaders of the Gallican Church became particularly important contacts for Burke, and confirmed his appreciation of its episcopate. He had been in regular contact with the first of them, Boisgelin of Aix (leader of the clergy in the National Assembly), before the archbishop's emigration in the autumn of 1791, with an exchange of letters which deepened their mutual regard.[105] Boisgelin was a gifted administrator whose hopes of high state office had been demolished by events in Paris; there was no political future for him after the closure of the National Assembly. In him, Burke was brought face-to-face with one of the most gifted and representative prelates of the 'generation of 1789', and Boisgelin frequently passed on to him the latest news about revolutionary developments,[106] much of it gleaned from clandestine contacts with clergy who had stayed behind in Paris and Provence. The Burke–Boisgelin association was derided by one radical as indicative of 'the polluted source whence his [Burke's] intelligence is derived',[107] but it did his standing no harm in the sight of High Churchmen.[108] Before the Revolution, Boisgelin's political importance had been much higher than the *de facto* leader of the French clergy exiled in Britain, the former army officer, Bishop Jean François de La Marche of Saint-Pol-de-Léon in Brittany.[109] Arguably, it was less La Marche's theology that impressed Burke

---

[102] *Extracts from Mr Burke's Table-Talk*, 10. Burke claimed he appreciated the prejudices operating against them, and accepted that compassion could be worn out.

[103] *The French Revolution*, ed. Mitchell, 2; Plasse, *Le Clergé français refugié*, ii. 51. cf. Colin Lucas, 'Edmund Burke and the Émigrés', in Furet and Ozouf (eds.), *The French Revolution and the Creation of Modern Political Culture*, iii. *The Transformation of Political Culture 1789–1848*, 101–30, esp. 106–7.

[104] *The French Revolution*, ed. Mitchell, 2. Cf. Lucas (Edmund Burke and the Émigrés, 113), who contends that 'the relationship between Burke and the émigrés seems to have been curiously sterile.'

[105] *Lettre de M. Burke à M. l'archevêque d'Aix* (Paris, 1791). See generally E. Lavaquerie, *Le Cardinal de Boisgelin, 1732–1804* (2 vols.; Paris, 1921). Rougane, a parish priest from the Auvergne, warned Burke against Archbishop Boisgelin's earlier willingness to support revolutionary legislation such as the civic oath of 4 Feb. 1790: *Plaintes à M. Burke sur sa lettre à M. l'archevêque d'Aix* (Paris, n.d.).

[106] To Rcd. Burke, 11 Nov. 1793, for a visit by Archbishop Boisgelin to Beaconsfield, *Correspondence*, vii. 483.

[107] Charles Pigott, *Strictures on the New Political Tenets of the Right Honourable Edmund Burke* (London, 1791), 59.

[108] Burke did not neglect the Gallican lower clergy. In spring 1793 he introduced two French priests into the Commons and sought the Speaker's permission to allow them to sit under the gallery. The action was criticized in *Lloyd's Evening Post*, 15–17 May 1793. For the Burkes bringing Abbé Foulon to dinner with Mrs Montagu, see her letter of 20 Dec. 1790, in Reginald Blunt (ed.), *Mrs. Montagu, 'Queen of the Blues': Her Letters and Friendships from 1762 to 1800* (2 vols.; London, 1923), ii. 252.

[109] Boisgelin and La Marche were his two most prestigious contacts among the prelates who had emigrated to England. Burke knew and commended other leading opponents of the Civil Constitution,

when he received him at Beaconsfield than his reputation for pastoral concern[110]—and his stubbornness. As his biographer, Kerbiriou, aptly pointed out, La Marche was essentially a 'Lutteur avant tout', ready as a bishop to defend and assert the privileges of his see, and no less dogged in adversity after the Civil Constitution was passed.[111]

Burke's encounter with Gallicanism in the 1790s was vital in altering his persuasion that clerical authority was an institution of convenience. It also did not diminish the breadth of his religious outlook, or undermine the centrality of its critical but generous Anglican foundations. Yet Burke by temperament and conviction could not help but look out beyond the Church of England, and in so doing transcend the tradition of Anglican political theology at the same time as he restated it and made it central to his own political outlook. Burke—a personal admirer of Pius VI's—always asserted that England had nothing to fear from the papacy.[112] Catholic dogmas commanded his respect, and his knowledge of the religion was exceptionally thorough,[113] and if he never swerved from acceptance of the Church of England as a Protestant establishment, it did not lessen his conviction that its survival was inextricably and honorably linked in revolutionary times to the Roman Catholic Church across Europe. As he told Mrs Crewe:

How is it possible to support [the view] that if the Catholic Religion were destroyed, the Protestant Religion could alone be able to support Christianity! The numbers are on the side of Catholics in Europe—Jacbins, therefore, persecute Catholics more than any other sect, they know that to hew down the Trunk out of which the branches shoot, is their best Policy![114]

Such an attitude was far from making Burke 'a Catholic in a Canterbury cap',[115] for a conciliatory approach to Catholics had grown significantly from the 1760s within élite Anglicanism, and was by no means exclusively confined to adherents of the High Church tradition; the events of the Revolutionary war made many more Anglicans conclude that the power of the papacy had waned

especially the redoutable Abbé Maury, 'a valiant Champion in the cause of honour, virtue, and noble sentiments; in the cause of his King and his Country; in the cause of Law, Religion and Liberty'. To John Woodford, 11 Feb. 1791, *Correspondence*, vi. 223–6.

[110] Prior, *Life*, 352. Burke's admiration for La Marche had been conveyed to Boisgelin as early as July 1791: Louis Kerbiriou, *Jean-François de La Marche, évêque-comte de Léon, 1729–1806* (Paris, 1924), 356. For Burke and La Marche dining with Sir Joshua Reynolds in Sept. 1791, see *The Journals and Letters of Fanny Burney*, ed. Joyce Henlow (12 vols.; Oxford, 1972–84), i. 63–4.

[111] See A. Mathiez's critical review of Kerbiriou in *Annales historiques de la Revolution francaise*, 2 (1925), 86–7.

[112] Mahoney, *Burke and Ireland*, 318–19.

[113] Ibid. 316.

[114] See *Extracts from Mr Burke's Table-Talk*, 8.

[115] Dryer's telling phrase ('Burke's Religion', 200) critical of Stanlis. The latter also wildly calls Burke's religious convictions 'Catholicism qualified by British nationalism' (*Burke and the Natural Law*, 201).

strikingly in the course of the century, and finally prompted them to set aside their conventional view that Rome and Antichrist were synonymous.[116] Not all of them would have obtained the same comfort as Burke did that the Church of England held fast to the major doctrines of the Roman Catholic faith,[117] but the loyal behaviour of English Catholics over the last half century formed another kind of reassurance. It had secured the passing of the Quebec Act of 1774 and the Savile Catholic Relief Act of 1778, and the intervening years had only increased the belief of most parliamentarians that the Church of England had nothing to fear from the removal of further civil disabilities from papists.[118]

Thus within Britain, the further reduction in anti-Catholic legislation continued when the Relief Bill of March 1791 had an unopposed passage in the House of Commons.[119] It was a relatively generous concession and, since Catholic orthodoxy was beyond reproach, they were exactly the sort of allies that Burke was anxious to secure in the interests of shoring up Anglican political supremacy. As in 1773, he was ready to promote the toleration of conscientious citizens in the interests of the State, so long as he was confident that such concessions would strengthen the established Church.[120] By the 1790s such a viewpoint was firmer than ever, hence his impatience with those Irish Anglicans who resisted improving the legal status of Catholics in the belief that the Church of Ireland's foundations would be fatally undermined. There was no question for Burke in an English context of anything other than specific measures to benefit Catholics, with religious freedom founded on grounds of conscience and prudence rather than any pretended 'Rights of Man'.[121] Nevertheless, the abolition of the French monarchy and the outbreak of war in 1792–3 confirmed the good sense of such a timely gesture as the 1791 English Relief Act: as Burke saw it, a militant and dechristianizing French polity could be resisted only by orthodox Christians putting aside differences that just diverted them from the fundamental challenge to their common heritage and the preservation of the British state.

A common front was a necessity, not from any expectation that it would lead eventually to the recognition of mutually held religious truths (such universalist expectations were quite alien to Burke), but simply to preserve the variations in

[116] Andrew Robinson, 'Identifying the Beast: Samuel Horsley and the Problem of Papal AntiChrist', *JEH* 43 (1992), 592–607.

[117] Mahoney, *Burke and Ireland*, 318. In his last published essay, Burke argued that the only difference between the Roman and Anglican Churches was that the latter denied certain tenets of the former. To Unknown, in McDowell (ed.), *Writings and Speeches*, ix. 679–80.

[118] Discussed in R. R. Fennessy, *Burke, Paine and the Rights of Man: A Difference of Political Opinion* (London, 1963), 58–9.

[119] R. B. Barlow, *Citizenship and Conscience: A Study in the Theory and Practice of Religious Toleration in England during the Eighteenth Century* (Philadelphia, 1964), 282–3.

[120] 'Speech on a Bill for the Relief of Protestant Dissenters (1773)', *Works*, ii. 470.

[121] Frederick Dreyer, 'Edmund Burke: The Philosopher in Action', *Studies in Burke and his Time*, 15 (1973–4), 121–42, at 125–6.

the expression of the Christian faith that were an inevitable feature of mankind's flawed, earthly state.[122] He accepted that most men found it easier to identify what divided them from their Christian brethren, rather than accept that in essentials only minor points separated them:

The weakness (if it be weakness) of men is such, that very few indeed are attached to the great fundamental parts of Religion in which most Christian Sects are agreed, who do not entertain a marked regard to those distinctive Tenets, Rules, or practices, which characterise their particular denomination. To render them indifferent to the latter will render them indifferent, or perhaps worse than indifferent to the former.[123]

Burke thus set himself the task in the 1790s of reminding Anglicans that far more than their own religious heritage was imperilled; the whole Christian commonwealth that constituted European civilization,[124] of which the Churches of England and Ireland formed but a small part, was threatened with undoing, and a generous response to Catholics was part of the strategy of survival. The essential imperative behind Burke's religious politics in the 1790s was thus his fundamental appreciation, in Jonathan Clark's words,[125] that 'The great conflict was no longer between Popery and Protestantism or Anglicanism and Dissent, but between Christianity and Jacobinism.' He lived long enough to see his conviction adopted by a large proportion of English and (to a much lesser degree) Irish Anglicans in a remarkable extension of sympathy to Roman Catholicism and its plight in the revolutionary decade, the last fruits of an emollience that had progressed for half a century.

Beneath Burke's public concern for the security of orthodox Christianity in its various manifestations lay an intensely private faith based on scripture and a 'vivid consciousness of the working of divine Providence in the affairs of the world'.[126] In fact his own trust in God's concern for himself and the wider world prompted the overarching political theology considered in this essay: he took comfort from 'thinking it great presumption to reject wholly what so many of the first men of all nations had adopted with the greatest zeal'.[127] The precise nature

---

[122] 'The "truth" of particular religions was something (like the origins of society) over which a discreet veil should be thrown' (F. P. Lock, *Burke's Reflections on the Revolution in France* (London, 1985), 15).

[123] To Earl Fitzwilliam, 10 Feb. 1795, *Correspondence*, viii. 146.

[124] See Peter J. Stanlis, 'Burke, Rousseau, and the French Revolution', in Steven Blakemore (ed.), *Burke and the French Revolution: Bicentennial Essays* (Athens, Ga., 1992), 97–120, at 101–5.

[125] Clark, *English Society*, 252; see also 'Letter to Richard Burke', in McDowell (ed.), *Writings and Speeches*, 647–8; Carl B. Cone, *Burke and the Nature of Politics: The Age of the French Revolution*, (Kentucky, 1964), 477.

[126] His was not an uncritical or passive acceptance of scripture: 'It is necessary to sort out what is intended for example, what only as narrative, what to be understood literally, what figuratively, where one precept is to be controlled and modified by another—what is used directly, and what only as an argument ad hominem—what is temporary, and what of perpetual obligation—what appropriated to one state and to one set of men, and what the general duty of all Christians' ('Speech on the Acts of Uniformity (1772)', *Works*, ii. 469). See also Cobban, *Edmund Burke*, 94.

[127] *Extracts from Mr Burke's Table-Talk*, 53.

of his faith was a matter on which he was reticent to an extraordinary degree, but that reserve should not be interpreted as a sign that faith had a subordinate, even unimportant place in Burke's personal identity.[128] Its habitual expression took the form of his regular attendance at the Sunday services in his home parish of Beaconsfield,[129] and in his charitable giving.[130] There are, however, occasions in his life when faith can be discerned struggling for public utterance, and during the 1790s it was nowhere better glimpsed than in Burke's reaction to the premature death of his son Richard in June 1794. The tragedy turned Burke into a recluse, 'lonely and disconsolate',[131] at Beaconsfield, reluctant to enter the church in which his son was buried,[132] and keeping in touch with the wider world only through correspondence with trusted friends, particularly French Laurence, Lord Fitzwilliam, and William Windham, Consumed by a sense that he had been less than just to his son,[133] Burke assumed a penitential character that never thereafter deserted him, as he struggled to retain hope in his own—and the world's—eventual redemption: 'I lie like one of those old oaks which the late hurricane has scattered about me; I am stripped of all my honours; I am torn up by the roots, and lie prostrate on the earth! There, and prostrate there, I must unfeignedly recognise the Divine justice, and in some degree submit to it.'[134] The Burke of 1794–7 was irreparably marked by personal loss,[135] and the mourning for Richard became part of a threnody for an ordered world that was also passing, a note struck in all the late writings, as Burke struggled to keep the faith, helped in the last months of his life by such writings as Wilberforce's *A Practical View*

---

[128] See ibid. 54. Burke's thoughts on the psychology of faith as expressed to his wife are briefly discussed in Jeffrey Hart, 'Burke and Pope on Christianity', in *Studies in Burke and his Time*, 8 (1967), 702. Burke's capacity for reverence is well expressed in the *Reflections*: 'It has been the misfortune (not, as these gentlemen think it, the glory) of this age that everything is to be discussed'. There are some illuminating comments on Burke's tendencies to mysticism in Robert H. Murray, *Edmund Burke: A Biography* (Oxford, 1931), 167, and a useful discussion of his view of human nature in Stanlis, *Burke and the Natural Law*, 182 ff.

[129] S. C. Carpenter, *18th Century Church and People* (London, 1959), 165; Minto (ed.), *Life and Letters of Sir Gilbert Elliot*, 10 Apr. 1792, ii. 10.

[130] For Burke's generosity to the poet George Crabbe, see John Timbs, *Anecdote Biography: William Pitt, Earl of Chatham and Edmund Burke* (London, 1860), 238, 331–3; F. E. Reynolds, *Edmund Burke: Christian Statesman* (London, 1948), 48–9.

[131] *Correspondence*, viii. 81, 250; ix. 85.

[132] Copeland, *Edmund Burke*, 83.

[133] Carl B. Cone is rightly critical of Lord Acton's allegation that Burke's religious belief was insincere: *The Age of the French Revolution*, 326.

[134] 'Letter to a Noble Lord', in McDowell (ed.), *Writings and Speeches*, ix. 171; Hole, *Pulpits, Politics and Public Order*, 140–1.

[135] For Burke weeping 'Like a child', see Laurence French to Mrs Haviland, 7 Aug. 1794, MS in Yale University Library, quoted in Cone, *Burke and the Nature of Politics*, 444. The bishop of Ossory, Thomas Lewis O'Beirne, noted after Richard's death how much his father's face showed traces of decay and extreme mental anguish, his chest had sunk, and he appeared bowed down in frame and spirit: Timbs, *Anecdote Biography*, 292, 316–18; cf. the response of Arthur Young to the death of his 14-year-old daughter Martha ('Bobbin') in 1797: *The Autobiography of Arthur Young*, ed. M. Bentham-Edwards (London, 1898), 263–99. I am grateful to Brian Young for this ref.

of the Prevailing Religious System of professed Christians. He could not lose his overwhelming sense that God's heavy hand was lying on him as if for some personal failure; 'nothing but gloom covers any part of the horizon', he wrote,[136] but set against it a resignation to 'a Disposer whose power we are little able to resist and whose wisdom it behoves us not at all to dispute'.[137] Even so, the Christian promise of immortality was not enough to dissipate the clouds in the last three years of Burke's life,[138] and the shock of loss almost certainly hastened his own end. His reading, interestingly, during this time of trial, did not send him, as it would have done the High Churchmen of the 1790s, to the Fathers, the Caroline divines, and the Nonjurors. His preference for Addison and Milton at this time of supreme trial remind us yet again that he had a spiritual eclecticism that defied ready labelling in church-party terms. Sympathetic though he was to orthodox Anglicans, secure in his membership of the same Church as theirs, they did not drink from the same fountainheads; his Whiggish, moderate sympathies had not been entirely destroyed under the pressure of events.[139]

Burke continued in his Protestant allegiance to his death and in the 'manly, rational, solid, and at the same time humble piety' best nourished by the Church of England.[140] Even in his last illness he made clear his preference for the Thirty-nine Articles,[141] so upholding to the end that individual profession of faith he considered inseparable from the health and survival of the British kingdom. In these last years he had moved further away from any Warburtonian concept of Church and State than at any point in his life. Whatever survived of his Erastianism was heavily qualified.[142] As he noted in his speech on the Unitarians' petition of 1792, 'in a Christian commonwealth the Church and the State are one and the same thing; being different integral parts of the same whole'.[143] It was a high Hookerian note, not far removed from the most uncompromising High Church apologists of the decade. Nevertheless, as this chapter has attempted to show, to consider his political zeal for Christianity exclusively in

---

[136] To Mrs. Crewe, *c.*22 Nov. 1794, *Correspondence*, viii. 81.

[137] 'A Letter to a Noble Lord', in McDowell (ed.), *Writings and Speeches*, ix. 171.

[138] Fanny Burney reported to her father on 21 July 1795 that Burke 'had still sometimes *gleams* of himself' (*Journals and Letters*, ed. Hemlow, iii. 144).

[139] Cf. Stanlis, *Burke and the Natural Law*, 133, 180, 202–4; French Laurence, *Maxims, Opinions and Characters, Moral, Political, and Economical from the Works of the Rt. Hon. Edmund Burke* (2 vols.; London, 1811), i. xviii.

[140] 'Speech on the Petition of the Unitarians (1792)', *Works*, ii. 478–9.

[141] Bisset, *Life*, 57–8. Conor Cruise O'Brien's suggestion that Burke sent for a Roman Catholic priest on his deathbed is unpersuasive speculation: *The Great Melody: A Thematic Biography of Edmund Burke* (London, 1992), 590–1.

[142] Dinwiddy claimed that 'his [Burke's] remarks on religion leave an erastian after-taste that probably restricted their appeal, as compared with the headier impact of Evangelicalism' ('Interpretations of Anti-Jacobinism', 45). Cf. Nockles, *Oxford Movement*, 67.

[143] See 'Speech on the Petition of the Unitarians (1792)', *Works*, ii. 475, and NRO, Fitzwilliam MSS, A. xxvii, draft for 1792.

terms of his conviction of its importance to the State will not suffice. What lies behind it is his persuasion of the faith's intrinsic importance that outweighed considerations of political utility, and was based on his own capacity for deep religious feeling. In mature life, he took for granted the truth of Christianity, and sought to show both its usefulness to society and its conformity to human nature. The French Revolution intensified his conviction that it was 'one of the great bonds of human society', a vital source of social stability and civilized values. He was content, like the majority of men, to take his religion on trust, and this view was reflected in what he deemed the Church's essential purpose, one which left unspecified individual rights of participation—or not: 'A Church is no society for free enquiry—or for any enquiry—it is founded for quite other purposes. A Church is a society of men joined together for worshipping God upon some principles which they have in common—The end is worship not speculation.'[144] The fact is that the hope of salvation mattered more to Edmund Burke than historians have admitted'[145] and he looked forward to the life to come with an appropriate humility: 'I hope I may be saved some way or other among that great multitude of Christians.'[146]

There is much work to be done before Burke's theology can be fully reconstructed, and we can at last move away from defining it in terms of what it is against, for instance, its well known anti-deism.[147] Burke's own Christianity was complicated. It rested on the Bible, but recognized the need for its discriminating interpretation: 'If we do not get some security for this, we not only permit, but we actually pay for, all the dangerous fanaticism, which can be produced to corrupt our people, and to derange the public worship of the country. We owe the best we can (not infallibility, but prudence) to the subject, first sound doctrine, then ability to use it.'[148] He rose above confessional religion to an extent remarkable in his day[149]—and his own Anglican loyalism was never reducible to either a High Church or a latitudinarian core. As he lay dying at Beaconsfield, he

---

[144] 'Speech on the Petition of the Unitarians' (1792), *Works*, ii. 475; NRO, Fitzwilliam MSS, A. xxvii. 49. Cf. his comment of 1760 that Christianity was 'not a speculative science but a practical obligation', quoted in Cone, *The French Revolution*, 325.

[145] See Burke's hope for divine mercy obtained through the blessed Redeemer 'whose intercession he had long sought with unfeigned anxiety and to which he looked with trembling hope'. Such deathbed preparation bears a close resemblance to Johnson's in 1784, Quoted in Timbs, *Anecdote Biography*, 318, See also the pious wording of his will.

[146] *Conversation between Burke and Gibson*, 9.

[147] Harris, 'Paine and Burke', 48; id. (ed.), *Edmund Burke: Pre-Revolutionary Writings* (Cambridge, 1993), pp. xvii–xviii, xx.

[148] 'Speech on the Acts of Uniformity', ii. 469.

[149] Burke's appreciation of diversity within the Churches is at all times more pronounced than references to it as an artificial contrivance made by man. Cf. Frederick Dreyer, 'Edmund Burke and John Wesley: The Legacy of Locke', in James E. Cribbins (ed.), *Religion, Secularization and Political Thought: Thomas Hobbes to J. S. Mill* (London, 1989), 111–29, at 120.

frequently declared his attachment to the Christian religion, and his veneration for true Christians of all persuasions.[150] He rejoiced in the richness of this heritage, and was not frightened of looking positively at the Anglican Church's relation to Roman Catholicism. While uncompromising in his defence of the privileges of the religious establishment (at least in England), to the delight of conservative opinion across the country, there was a generous sympathy with the predicament of the French Church in 1790–1 as no less socially useful than its Anglican counterpart.[151] The rehabilitation of Catholicism was part of Burke's intention, an essential dimension of his plan for Europe's survival against revolutionary contagion. His appreciation of Gallicanism, though not unusual among members of the Church of England, was particularly acute, and played a neglected part in the making of his mature religious character, enriching a sophisticated but never artificial Anglicanism, one always marked by generous sentiments to other adherents of Trinitarian orthodoxy. From that fundamental proviso, he never shifted and it must be set against any suggestion that he was as ready as Erasmus to sacrifice truth in the Church to peace.[152]

The impact of public events in the 1790 both tested faith sorely and confirmed it. The experience left Burke in no doubt that the apostasy and unbelief of the Revolutionaries and their sympathizers would be utterly destructive of European civilization. He could not, in his own life, play into their hands, by wavering in his own attachment to Christianity. Hard though it was for him to discern the hand of God in contemporary events, the darker the horizon the more insistent he became on insisting on faith's indispensability, and the stark warning of his favourite passage from Isaiah (55: 8): 'My thoughts are not your thoughts, neither are your ways my ways, saith the Lord.' The death of his son was the supreme test of these convictions, and there is no doubt that a gloom descended on Burke that never afterwards lifted, a gloom that Christian belief was powerless to dissipate,[153] but which itself was never threatened by the pain of bereavement: the note of suffering was never far away from Burke's speeches and writings of the 1790s, and his personal agony was a reflection of that visited on the wider

---

[150] As he had earlier told his son: 'The body and substance of every Religion I regard much more than any of the forms and dogmas of the particular sects' ('To Richard Burke', in McDowell (ed.), *Writings and Speeches*, ix. 656). Cf. Jonathan Clark's comment that for Burke 'Anglican Christianity was established not merely because it was expedient but because it was true' (*English Society*, 251–2). One could just as easily substitute Gallican for Anglican. Stanlis has a useful note on Burke and the mixed ecclesiastical constitutions of Europe: *Burke and the Natural Law*, 226–8.

[151] But Dreyer, 'Burke's Religion', 210, goes too far in reducing state religion for Burke to a matter of 'secular convenience'.

[152] Murray, *Burke*, 198.

[153] 'God knows how long the Church Establishment, on which these people exist, and to which such multitudes are now breeding up, is likely to last. But whenever that goes it will go with everything else' (To Lord Chancellor Loughborough, 19 Oct. 1794, *Correspondence*, viii. 44).

world.[154] In such unpropitious circumstances, where change threatened to scythe down institutions and individuals alike, the protection of an entire Christian order never ceased to be Burke's overriding public priority. The Church was no longer the mere voluntary society of the 1770s, but an institution that demanded obedience to its rules, and whose survival was bound up with the securing of civilization: there could be no higher duty for the civil magistrate than the maintenance of confessional structures as a supreme interest of State.[155] It was the decisive evidence of change in his intellectual outlook under the impact of the Revolution, change nourished and sustained by his mature religious convictions. Burke was his own emblem of how the polity could survive under stress, with the British state (including Ireland)—and eventually the whole European continent—secured and safeguarded by the religious fidelity and integrity of those who composed it.

[154] To go one step further, and claim that Burke 'went to his grave a bewildered and demoralized man', overlooks the considerable evidence that Burke's faith survived the strain: O'Gorman, *Edmund Burke*, 136, 156.

[155] Peter N. Miller, *Defining the Common Good: Empire. Religion and Philosophy in Eighteenth-Century Britain* (Cambridge, 1994), 6.

10

The Kirk, the French Revolution, and the Burden of Scottish Whiggery

COLIN KIDD

The prophylactic role played by religious institutions and ideologies is a staple, though much-debated, feature in discussions of how Britain successfully avoided a revolution during the anxious years of the 1790s. The effects of the French Revolutionary threat on Britain's two national religious establishments, the Church of England and the Church, or Kirk, of Scotland, differed substantially, however. The Church of England had at its disposal a powerful conservative political theology which, even though the diverse ranks of the clergy were by no means tied to a rigid ideology, could nevertheless be deployed unreservedly against the Jacobin menace.[1] In Scotland, attitudes to the crisis were complicated by the embarrassment attaching to the presbyterian Kirk's radical pedigree. Earlier generations of presbyterians had woven a fine web of qualified allegiance to the civil magistrate. Worse, during a turbulent seventeenth century of rebellion and assassination, aery speculation had all too obviously become political practice. For eighteenth-century Kirkmen this legacy was both a definitive part of their heritage as presbyterians and a millstone. Thus, although the Kirk proved to be a vital prop in the defence of the existing order of government, the French Revolution was to exacerbate existing pressures on the Church of Scotland to shed its historic Whiggish commitments and its distinctive Scottish identity. For Scots presbyterians, the 1790s were traumatic not only because they witnessed the emergence in France of a dangerous brand of irreligious radicalism which appeared to threaten the whole fabric of Christendom, but also because of the effects on the Kirk of the conservative reaction which ensued in Britain. The Kirk's considered response to both sets of pressures marked the culmination of a long struggle to evade the burden of presbyterian history.

I should like to thank Nigel Aston and John McCaffrey for comments on an earlier draft of this essay.

[1] R. Hole, *Pulpits, Politics and Public Order in England 1760–1832* (Cambridge, 1989), 11–31, 97–173. But for a sceptical view of the Church's effectiveness, see I. R. Christie, *Stress and Stability in Late Eighteenth-Century Britain: Reflections on the British Avoidance of Revolution* (Oxford, 1984), ch. vii.

The Kirk's keen awareness of its difficult political heritage dawned with the re-establishment of a presbyterian system of discipline in Scotland at the Revolution of 1688–90. At the Kirk's foundation in 1690, King William blocked any reference to *ius divinum* ecclesiology in the legislation establishing presbyterian government.[2] William, a hard-headed *politique* who did not care to be distracted from his wider continental campaigns by the vexed politics of his Scottish periphery, also warned the new Kirk that it enjoyed its privileges on sufferance, and enjoined moderation on the presbyterian regime.[3] Furthermore, the episcopalians, ousted after the refusal of their bishops to abandon the doctrines of non-resistance or to switch allegiances, mounted a vigorous propaganda campaign designed to destabilize the new regime in the Church. By dwelling upon the dangers of presbyterian radicalism, episcopalian pamphleteers hoped that the presbyterians might be seen by the monarchy and the English political élite as a liability which posed an even greater threat to stability than their own all-too-passively-obedient co-religionists.[4] Presbyterian pamphleteers resorted to a degree of trimming and self-censorship in an effort to erase the stigma of rebellion.[5]

However opportunistic, episcopalian arguments conveyed a difficult truth about the Scots presbyterian tradition. Resistance theory had long been the marrow of presbyterian politics. John Knox (?1514–72), the founding father of the Scottish Reformation, though in many respects a cautious revisionist, had none the less played an important role in refashioning Calvin's account of the obligations of obedience into a 'Calvinist' theory of revolution.[6] Less ambiguously, George Buchanan (1506–82) advanced a theory of an elective and accountable Scottish monarchy in his *Historia rerum scoticarum* (1582) and his resistance tract *De iure regni apud scotos* (1579). The leaders of the reformed Kirk also adopted a two-kingdom ecclesiology which explicitly repudiated the supremacy of the civil power over Christ's kingdom, though assigning it a limited role as its temporal nursing father. Andrew Melville famously informed King

[2] 'The government of the Church in this Kingdom established by law', King William to the Earl of Melville, 22 May, 1690, in *Leven and Melville Papers* (Edinburgh, 1843), 437; 'the only government of Christ's church within this kingdom', Act establishing presbyterian government (1690), in G. Donaldson (ed.), *Scottish Historical Documents* (Edinburgh, 1970), 260.

[3] 'His Majesty's gracious Letter to the Assembly' (1690), in *Acts of the General Assembly of the Church of Scotland 1638–1842* (Edinburgh, 1843), 222.

[4] T. Maxwell, 'The Presbyterian–Episcopalian Controversy in Scotland from the Revolution Settlement till the Accession of George I', Ph.D. thesis (Edinburgh, 1954).

[5] C. Kidd, *Subverting Scotland's Past: Scottish Whig Historians and the Creation of an Anglo-British Identity, 1689–c.1830* (Cambridge, 1993), ch. iv.

[6] Q. Skinner, *The Foundations of Modern Political Thought* (2 vols., Cambridge, 1978), ii, ch. vii; but for a more cautious view, see R. Mason (ed.), *Knox on Rebellion* (Cambridge, 1994), 'Introduction'; R. Kingdon, 'Calvinism and Resistance Theory, 1550–1580', in J. H. Burns and M. Goldie (eds.), *The Cambridge History of Political Thought 1450–1700* (Cambridge, 1991), 194–200.

James VI that 'Thair is Christ Jesus the King, and his kingdome the Kirk, whase subject King James the Saxt is, and of whase kingdome nocht a king, nor a lord, nor a heid, bot a member.'[7] The Covenanting movement of the mid-seventeenth century further damaged the reputation of Scots presbyterianism. Hitherto its targets had been confined to Scotland, but the Solemn League and Covenant of 1643 involved a pledge to extirpate episcopal government throughout the British Isles. Samuel Rutherford (1600–61), the most sophisticated mouthpiece of the Covenanting cause, attempted to carve out a niche for presbyterian politics which differentiated them not only from the passive obedience sanctioned by episcopalians but also from the radical resistance theories espoused by the Jesuits. However, his masterpiece *Lex, rex* (1644) contained explosive material, including the argument that the people were justified in resisting even parliamentary institutions when the latter failed to uphold the standards of godly reformation.[8]

The intellectual leaders of the later Covenanters who struggled against the episcopal discipline established at the Restoration further escalated the radicalism of presbyterian politics. Such works as *Naphtali* (1667), *Ius populi vindicatum* (1669), and *A Hind Let Loose* (1687) not only inculcated principles of secession from a state which failed to maintain its religious obligations, but also sanctioned the right of individuals to prosecute the divine will by executing enemies of the work of reformation.[9] Since the principles of godly assassination appeared to have been applied with the bloody murder in 1679 of Archbishop James Sharp of St Andrews and in the manifestos of the Cameronians of the south-west (who denied the authority of the uncovenanted Restoration state), it was hardly surprising that the restored monarchy, already anxious on the score of the Exclusion threat, should attempt to suppress the noxious doctrines emanating from north of the Border. In 1683 the canonical texts of Scots presbyterian resistance theory were burnt, along with other subversive works, under the auspices of the Oxford Decrees.[10] However, even in the aftermath of the Glorious Revolution, Scotland's radical Covenanting heritage remained significantly out of step with the mainstream of English political culture. For the Revolution of 1689 in Scotland was not accompanied by the sort of anguished fudges on the subject of armed resistance to legitimate monarchs which marked English

---

[7] Quoted in J. Wormald, *Court, Kirk, and Community: Scotland 1470–1625* (London, 1981), 148.

[8] J. Ford, 'Lex, rex iusto posita: Samuel Rutherford on the Origins of Government', in R. Mason (ed.), *Scots and Britons: Scottish Political Thought and the Union of 1603* (Cambridge, 1994); Samuel Rutherford, *Lex, rex* (London, 1644), 151–2, 257–65.

[9] [James Steuart and James Stirling], *Naphtali, or the Wrestlings of the Church of Scotland for the Kingdom of Christ* (n.p., 1667); [James Steuart], *Ius populi vindicatum, or the People's Right to Defend Themselves and their Covenanted Religion, Vindicated* (n.p., 1669); Alexander Shields, *A Hind Let Loose* (n.p., 1687).

[10] The Oxford Decrees can be found in D. Wootton (ed.), *Divine Right and Democracy: An Anthology of Political Writing in Stuart England* (Harmondsworth, 1986), 120–6.

political debate. Instead the Scots Claim of Right explicitly declared James VII to have 'forefaulted' the throne.[11]

The Union of 1707 exacerbated the anxious position of the Kirk as a threatened particularism. The British state constituted by the Union involved, in defiance of contemporary political wisdom, a peculiar experiment in Church–State relations. Within this monstrous hybrid Britain's two distinct societies retained their respective legal systems and established Churches, yet political authority resided in a united crown-in-parliament whose legislative competence was only loosely trammelled by the Articles of Union and by the accompanying Acts for the security of the Churches of England and Scotland. Despite these constitutional safeguards for ecclesiastical pluralism, the Anglican Parliament displayed scant sensitivity to the range of the Kirk's privileges. The Tory administration of 1710–14 passed legislation which granted toleration to Scots Episcopalians, flouted the Kirk's approach to holy festivals, and, most controversially, reintroduced lay patronage into a Kirk which subscribed in theory to a rigorous two-kingdom ecclesiology.

Patronage was to be the issue which ultimately rent asunder an institution already torn between its inherited principles and the external constraints acting upon the established Church of a junior province within Britain's mixed-unitary state. As the Kirk attempted to project itself as a civil religion in accord with the values of Hanoverian Britain, it found itself particularly troubled by the antinomian implications of ultra-Calvinist rectitude. In the eyes of traditionalists, the Kirk appeared to be governed by a pusillanimous pragmatism. Was not the strong beer of predestinarian theology being watered down into an insipid secular morality? *The Marrow of Modern Divinity* was sifted for 'antinomian paradoxes'; the Assembly condemned the Auchterarder creed—the supplementary articles required of ministerial candidates by the zealous presbytery of Auchterarder, which included the worrying formula 'I believe that it is not sound and orthodox to teach that we must forsake sin in order to our coming to Christ'; meanwhile the Arminianism taught in the lectures at Glasgow University by John Simson (1667–1740) at first earned only a rebuke.[12] Furthermore, traditionalists considered lay patronage to have usurped Christ's headship of the Church. The Kirk had acquiesced, albeit very reluctantly, in this unwarranted intrusion, by legislating to smooth the internal operation of the illegitimate patronage system. If a presentation were not made by a patron within six months of a vacancy, then the right of appointment devolved on this occasion to the

---

[11] See Donaldson (ed.), *Scottish Historical Documents*, 255.

[12] J. K. Cameron, 'The Church of Scotland in the Age of Reason', *Studies on Voltaire and the Eighteenth Century*, lviii (1967), 1939–51; W. Ferguson, *Scotland 1689 to the Present* (1968; Edinburgh, 1987), 115–21.

Kirk. In 1732 the Kirk passed legislation which restricted the 'call' under this *ius devolutum* to the elders and Protestant heritors of the parish.[13] This act, which appeared to be a restriction on the rights of congregations as a whole, was the immediate trigger for the Secession.

The pressures which had been building up in response to perceptions of theological and ecclesiological backsliding now found release in the withdrawal from the Kirk in 1733 of the Revd Ebenezer Erskine (1680–1754) and his followers. Tellingly, Erskine unmasked the double life of the Kirk: 'There is a difference to be made between the Established Church of Scotland and the Church of Christ in Scotland, for I reckon that the latter is in great measure driven into the wilderness by the first.'[14] In 1743, as if to emphasize this distinction, the Seceders renewed the Solemn League and Covenant. However, the thorny question of allegiance to an uncovenanted civil power remained troubling. The Seceders issued a generous, but carefully qualified, statement of loyalty to the British state: 'We desire to be humbled for the dangerous extreme that some have gone into, of impugning the present civil authority over these nations, and subjection thereunto in lawful commands, on account of the want of those qualifications which magistrates ought to have, according to the word of God and our covenants.' The zealotry of 'propagating religion by offensive arms' was condemned; defensive arms, however loosely defined, presumably remained a legitimate option for Seceders, who acknowledged only the 'lawful commands' of the defective state.[15] Political pressures produced another division in the presbyterian tradition when, in 1747, the Secession itself split in two over the taking of the Burgher oath, required by the state of all office-holders. Henceforth, as a result of this Breach, the Secession had two wings: the Burghers, who accepted the oath, and the hyper-sensitive Anti-Burghers. It is important to note that neither body was opposed to a religious establishment in principle; each saw itself as the true-Kirk-in-waiting.

The Kirk proper, on the other hand, had lost some of its malcontents, but not its reputation. Presbyterian politics retained an unwanted aura of subversion. Given Scotland's outspoken brand of Revolution principles, it was not easy to jettison resistance theory, and the need to take up arms against Jacobite pretensions further complicated matters. For instance, in April 1747 with the 1745 rebellion still a vivid memory, the Revd Robert Monteith (1707–76) preached the opening sermon at the synod of Merse and Teviotdale on *The Right of the Clergy to Appear in Defence of the Liberties of their Country*. Monteith felt compelled to remember the 'glorious appearance' made by the Covenanters in the

[13] Ibid. 122.   [14] Quoted in A. Herron, *Kirk by Divine Right* (Edinburgh, 1985), 57.
[15] Quoted in John M'Kerrow, *History of the Secession Church* (rev. and enlarged edn., Glasgow, 1841), 184–5.

mid-seventeenth century: 'roused by their ministers, [they] invaded England with thirty thousand men, revived the drooping spirits of their fellow-Protestants, and compelled an arbitrary prince to withdraw his oppressive influence.'[16] It was hard to disown outright the Kirk's turbulent history.

Nevertheless, the old unapologetic doctrine of resistance was gradually being watered down into a more refined Whiggish constitutionalism, a process which was accelerated by the rise of the Moderate party in the Kirk during the 1750s. Just as North-Britons-on-the-make repented their Scotticisms, so a distinctive Scots presbyterian dialect gave way within the ranks of the Moderates to the bland voice of a common protestantism. The ideology of the Moderates has been usefully characterized as 'whig–presbyterian conservatism',[17] though each component of this description requires a measure of qualification: the Moderates repudiated much of the Kirk's Whig-presbyterian heritage, yet their espousal of the Enlightenment did infuse the institution with a new stream of liberal values. William Robertson (1721–93), the intellectual leader of the party, set about writing a detached 'philosophical' reappraisal of the Kirk's dubious past, concentrating his revisionist energies on the question of how much respect modern presbyterians owed to the traditions established by their ancestors. Were Scots presbyterians tethered for all time to the authority of Reformation principles? Was it incumbent upon the present generation to maintain the radical political theologies of the past? Robertson set the Scottish Reformation and its founding fathers in their proper historical context, a violent and unsettled sixteenth century whose values were alien to the 1750s. Resistance theory, in particular, had emerged in an altogether different set of circumstances from those which now prevailed in an improved Scotland of commerce and refinement.[18] In other words, modern presbyterians could quite legitimately reject aspects of the Kirk's bloody history which detracted from the Moderate vision of an enlightened civil religion supportive of the polite culture and liberal state of Hanoverian Britain, but also secure enough in its privileges to be sturdily independent of political faction. Nevertheless, from the 1780s, following Robertson's retirement, the Moderate party under the leadership of Principal George Hill (1750–1819) of St Mary's College, St Andrews, sacrificed the prized apolitical freedom of the original generation of Moderates for a cosier relationship with the government of Pitt and Dundas.[19]

---

[16] Robert Monteith, *The Right of the Clergy to Appear in Defence of the Liberties of their Country Asserted and Vindicated* (Edinburgh, 1747), 15.

[17] R. B. Sher, *Church and University in the Scottish Enlightenment* (Edinburgh, 1985), 17, 53–4, 189, 327–8.

[18] William Robertson, *The History of Scotland* (2 vols.; London, 1759); J. H. S. Burleigh, 'The Scottish Reformation as Seen in 1660 and 1760', *Records of the Scottish Church History Society*, xiii (1959), 241–56; Ferguson, *Scotland 1689 to the Present*, 226.

[19] I. D. L. Clark, 'From Protest to Reaction: The Moderate Regime in the Church of Scotland, 1752–1805', in N. Phillipson and R. Mitchison (eds.), *Scotland in the Age of Improvement* (Edinburgh, 1970);

The Evangelicals, or Popular Party opponents of the Moderates, were less conformist than the Moderates, but could scarcely be classed as immovable guardians of the Kirk's traditions. For the Kirk drank deep at the spring of Enlightenment, and the Evangelicals too absorbed its influence. Nor were the evangelicals immune to the pervasive language of English Whig constitutionalism. Friedhelm Voges believes that, so far as matters temporal were concerned, late-eighteenth-century Moderates and evangelicals shared the same anglicized political creed. Ned Landsman, who has done most to recover the lost world of evangelical Enlightenment, has noted a crucial transformation in the political language of Scottish evangelicals in the second half of the eighteenth century. They too were ready to replace the embarrassing rhetoric of the covenanting past with encomiums upon British constitutional liberty.[20]

The trauma of the 1790s was immediately preceded by the centenary of the Williamite Revolution of 1688. The Revolution principles articulated in the overtly political sermons delivered on this anniversary provide an illuminating point of comparison for later reactions to events in France. The centenary of the Glorious Revolution (celebrated in Scotland in 1788 though its own Revolution had taken place in 1689) could have been a moment of uncritical celebration for the Kirk. However, a new strain of self-confidence was tempered by the traditional suspicions endemic within a compromised institution. Might not the centenary of the Revolution turn out to be a trap for unsuspecting clergy? An overenthusiastic and unqualified endorsement of Revolution principles might act as a reminder of the Kirk's political reputation. Given its habitual caution, it is hardly surprising that the Kirk did not celebrate the centenary with one voice. Casuistry, equivocation, and revisionism counterbalanced the undiscriminating triumphalism of the unwary.

After all, the old taunts about presbyterian resistance and disloyalty were still part of the currency of a rehabilitated episcopalianism. In 1788 John Skinner produced an Episcopalian version of Scotland's ecclesiastical history which rekindled old criticisms. The sympathies of Episcopalians for the Jacobite cause remained a sensitive point; nevertheless, Skinner pointed out that Episcopalians had generally remained quiet and obedient, despite their misgivings about the

---

Ferguson, *Scotland 1689 to the Present*, 227. Principal Hill and his family came to exert a powerful grip on preferment at St Andrews. S. J. Brown (*Thomas Chalmers and the Godly Commonwealth* (Edinburgh, 1982), 5) remarks that Psalm 121—'I will lift up mine eyes unto the hills, from whence cometh my help'—acquired a special resonance.

[20] F. Voges, 'Moderate and Evangelical Thinking in the Later Eighteenth Century: Differences and Shared Attitudes', *Records of the Scottish Church History Society*, xxii, pt. 2 (1985), 153–6; N. Landsman, 'Presbyterians and Provincial Society: The Evangelical Enlightenment in the West of Scotland, 1740–1775', in J. Dwyer and R. B. Sher (eds.), *Sociability and Society in Eighteenth-Century Scotland* (Edinburgh, 1993), 203.

Revolution of 1688–9, whilst presbyterians, though Whiggish, were false friends of the Hanoverian monarchy: 'let them not charge our religion with abetting rebellious principles, till they can assure us that they have renounced the principles of their predecessors who avowedly preached up the lawfulness of fighting for their religion against any kind whatever.'[21]

Officially, the Kirk commemorated the events of 1688 with an unabashed Whiggery. The General Assembly noted in its address to the crown on the occasion of the centenary that the events of 1688 had fixed a constitution 'which has hitherto had force sufficient to repair its internal disorders, as well as to repel external violence'. The Act of Assembly appointing a national thanksgiving in Scotland in commemoration of 1688 advanced the conviction that 'the principles of the Revolution settlement [were] the only foundation on which the security of the throne, and the happiness of the subjects, can be permanently established'. Nor was it seen as improper to mention that the Revolution had 'set proper bounds to the royal prerogative'. The thanksgiving was justified, in part, as a means of impressing on the Kirk's flock the value of the liberties won in 1688 and of exhorting its charges 'by every constitutional means, to preserve and transmit them inviolate to the latest posterity'.[22]

The Scottish Revolution of 1689 was disinterred, when it might have been more convenient to blur its radical message in a commemoration of England's constitutional settlement. Although most interpretations stressed the role of providence in the success of the Revolution, some ministers remembered that James had been 'dethroned' and that the Claim of Right 'drawn up by the Convention of Estates, and containing the principal grievances of the nation at that time, which were required to be redressed by King William and Queen Mary' was 'the indispensable condition of their wearing the Crown of Scotland'.[23] William Robertson also used the occasion of the centenary to expound an optimistic liberal thesis about the spread of enlightened and Whiggish principles throughout the nations of Europe.[24]

However, the other 'revolution'—the crisis of the 1640s—remained a troubling spectre. The Revd Alexander Ranken (1755–1827) sought to detach the commemoration of 1688 from the revolution principles of the mid-seventeenth

[21] John Skinner, *An Ecclesiastical History of Scotland* (2 vols.; London, 1788), ii. 662–3.

[22] 'An Address by the General Assembly to his Majesty, on the Proposed Commemoration of the Glorious Revolution' and 'Act Appointing a National Thanksgiving in Commemoration of the Revolution in 1688', both 29 May 1788, in *Acts of the General Assembly*, 827, 829.

[23] John Robertson, *Britain The Chosen Nation, A Thanksgiving Sermon, Preached, November 5th, 1788* (Kilmarnock, 1788), 12; William M'Gill, *The Benefits of the Revolution, A Sermon, Preached at Ayr, On the 5th of November, 1788. To which are added, Remarks on a Sermon, Preached the same day, At Newton upon Ayr* (Kilmarnock, 1789), 8–9.

[24] R. B. Sher, '1688 and 1788: William Robertson on Revolution in Britain and France', in P. Dukes and J. Dunkley (eds.), *Culture and Revolution* (London, 1990), 100–2.

century, with which presbyterianism was embarrassingly linked. For the legitimate resistance and defensive arms which had once been central to the presbyterian heritage, he substituted a cautious doctrine of providential deliverance which verged on a passive de-facto-ism:

In the year 1649, the people subdued and finally beheaded their King, but they remained as distant as ever from the great object of their zeal. They experienced and strikingly exemplified to us, that no human means however vigorous, can prove effectual without the immediate direction and blessing of Providence; that the great Ruler of the world abhorreth the bloody and deceitful, but that he will make his way straight before the face of those who sincerely desire to advance his glory, and the best interests of men.

In the year 1688, by means unaccountably easy, almost without bloodshed, or any struggle, the oppressor yields; the iron sceptre drops from his hand; he vanishes like a dream; the morning of liberty shines forth splendid and beautiful: The people advance soberly and firmly with their claim of political privileges: It is heard and regarded with mildness and wisdom: 'And God said, Let Britain be free, and it was so.'[25]

Another minister passed over the seventeenth century as 'an unhappy contest with episcopacy'.[26] The Kirk's heritage of Reformation principles and heroes could also cause discomfort. Ranken mentioned Knox in a roll-call of figures 'sufficient to recall to our memory the turbulence, the political weakness, and slow improvement' of the independent Scottish kingdom.[27]

The centenary even provoked a bitter squabble in Ayrshire over the propriety of questioning defects in the Revolution establishment. The Revd William Peebles (1753–1826) of Newton-upon-Ayr thought it would have been 'unfair and uncandid to pass over some of those grievances, under which we still labour', namely patronage.[28] This earned a stern rebuke from the Revd William M'Gill of Ayr (1732–1807), who put forward the specious argument that opposition to the law of patronage was not a Revolution principle. Patronage was not formally denounced in the Claim of Right: indeed, it was 'a well known fact, that the law of patronage was in force at the period we commemorate, as it had been in former times; and it was not mentioned among the grievances of the nation, at a time when men of ability were appointed to state those grievances in full length'.[29] M'Gill's revisionism is symptomatic of a certain dishonesty in facing up

[25] Alexander Ranken, *A Discourse on the Advantages of the Revolution 1688. Delivered, Nov. 5th, 1788, in the North-West Church* (Glasgow, 1788), 30–1.

[26] M'Gill, *Benefits of the Revolution*, 10.   [27] Ranken, *Advantages of the Revolution*, 14.

[28] William Peebles, *The Great Things which the Lord hath done for this Nation, Illustrated and Improved; In Two Sermons Preached on the 5th of November, 1788, The Day Appointed by the General Assembly of the Church of Scotland, for a National Thanksgiving, in Commemoration of the Revolution, 1688. To which is Subjoined An Ode to Liberty* (Kilmarnock, 1788), 40.

[29] M'Gill, *Benefits of the Revolution*, 17–18. M'Gill's pamphlet provoked a satirical response: *Modern Moderation Stated and Defended* (Edinburgh, 1790). Despite his cautious Moderatism on this occasion, M'Gill was also the controversial author of *A Practical Essay on the Death of Jesus Christ* (Edinburgh, 1786), which was denounced as Socinian.

to the Kirk's variegated heritage. For patronage had lasted only until 1690 before its speedy abolition at the hands of the new regime.

Nor was there any consensus among the Seceders as to the most appropriate mode of remembrance. The Burgher synod evinced no scruples about commemorating the Revolution.[30] Within the ranks of the Anti-Burghers, however, the centenary provoked a debate about the significance of 1688. The synod, in spite of some ultra-diehard opposition, approved a solemn thanksgiving for the Revolution. The majority felt it 'necessary to commemorate in this manner, that, when our forefathers, in the period previous to the time referred to, were on the point of being swallowed up in the dreadful gulph of popery and tyranny, the Lord brought deliverance to us'. The synod's endorsement was tepid, if not cooler, highlighting a reluctance to identify the overthrow of episcopacy at the Revolution as an authentic landmark within presbyterian tradition:

They do not judge that the defects of the Revolution settlement, frequently testified against in former acts of this synod, should abate our thankfulness for the great and invaluable blessings bestowed upon us in, and resulting from, that wonderful deliverance; though our thankfulness ought to be accompanied with lamentation, because of the said defects, and our woful abuse of that signal interposition of Providence.

This careful mixture of hesitancy, equivocation, and outright criticism was insufficient to appease the backwoodsmen among the Anti-Burghers who petitioned the synod to explain itself. Embarrassingly, the synod was forced to issue a further declaration as a gloss on its original resolution. This apology involved an element of retreat, including a passage which suggested an equivalence between humiliation and thanksgiving.[31] Indeed, the established Kirk's commemoration of the Revolution provoked a caustic response from the leading dissident Anti-Burgher and unprompted conscience of the wider presbyterian community, the Revd Archibald Bruce (1746–1816). Bruce expressed alarm at the failure of the Assembly to distinguish 'between the deliverance of the Revolution, and the principles and settlement of the Revolution—between the work of God and that of men in this matter'.[32] As the Revolution settlement had upheld neither the Covenants, nor an anti-Erastian ecclesiology, it had been a signal betrayal of the Kirk.

The centenary did blow away some of the cobwebs of ultra-cautious Kirkmanship. In 1790 a liberal Moderate, the Revd Thomas Somerville of Jedburgh (1741–1830), launched a campaign for the repeal of the English Test Act (1673) as it applied to members of the Church of Scotland resident in

[30] M'Kerrow, *Secession*, 566–8.   [31] Ibid. 344–6.

[32] Archibald Bruce, *Annus secularis, or, the British Jubilee; or a Review of the Act of the General Assembly, Appointing the 5th of November, 1788, As an Anniversary-Thanksgiving, in Commemoration of the Revolution in 1688* (2nd edn., Edinburgh, 1812), 227.

England. The movement received its first official sanction at the local level from the presbytery of Jedburgh, which denounced the requirement upon members of the Church of Scotland who held office in England to take the Test—Anglican communion—as a profanity, and, moreover, as a measure 'inconsistent with the doctrines and worship of presbytery established in Scotland at the Revolution and confirmed by the Union'.[33] The reform campaign won support from the Synods of Angus and Mearns, and Dumfries, and from the presbytery of Dundee. It was debated, and passed without a vote, in the General Assembly on 27 May 1790. The Popular Party supported repeal, as did an influential cadre of Moderates, including Dr Walker of the Canongate parish and William Robertson junior, son of the party's erstwhile leader.[34]

However, the plan also provoked considerable opposition from within the ranks of the Moderates. Their opposition points up the neurosis still gripping parts of the Kirk a century after the Revolution. For the campaign prompted further exhibitions of the Kirk's well-rehearsed deferential cringe to the imagined susceptibilities of the Church of England. George Hill warned that the Kirk's disparagement of the Test Act might be interpreted south of the Border as a slur upon the Church of England. The Revd Alexander Carlyle (1722–1805) went much further than Hill, demonstrating the extent to which a leading minister had imbibed the Kirk's culture of self-censorship and diffident self-abasement in the face of Anglican power:

The Test Act has confirmed the Union. The Test Act has cured Englishmen of their jealousy of Scotsmen, not very ill-founded. The Test Act has quieted the fears of the Church of England. The Test Act has enlarged and confirmed the principles of toleration . . . The Test Act, sir, has paved the road to office and preferment.

Indeed, rhapsodized Carlyle, there was 'no end of its praises'.[35]

The small window of self-expression which had opened in 1788 was firmly closed and shuttered by 1793. The Revolution in France had auspicious beginnings, and was warmly welcomed by the intellectual leaders of a Kirk buoyed in self-confidence by the recent commemorations of 1688.[36] Indeed, the early, superficially 'Whiggish' phase of the French Revolution seemed almost providential,

[33] G. M. Ditchfield, 'The Scottish Campaign against the Test Act, 1790–1791', *Historical Journal*, 23 (1980), 38–9.

[34] Ibid. 40–2.

[35] Quoted in *The Autobiography of Dr. Alexander Carlyle of Inveresk 1722–1805*, ed. J. H. Burton (London, 1910), 'Supplementary Chapter', 580; Ditchfield, 'Scottish Campaign', 46.

[36] E. Vincent, 'The Responses of Scottish Churchmen to the French Revolution, 1789–1802', *Scottish Historical Review*, 73 (1994), 192–3; Thomas Somerville, *The Effects of the French Revolution, in Respect to the Interests of Humanity, Liberty, Religion and Morality* (Edinburgh, 1793), 30. The September Massacres of 1792 were a significant turning-point: Thomas Somerville, *My Own Life and Times* (Edinburgh, 1861), 264.

following so swiftly in the wake of the British centenary celebrations. However, as the Revolution in France slipped its familiarly Whiggish moorings, it 'made the very name of revolution, for the time, odious'.[37] Worse, the contagion appeared to have reached Scotland. In the spring of 1792 there were riots at which Pitt's political manager for Scotland, Henry Dundas, was burnt in effigy, and, in the course of the year, Societies of the Friends of the People were established north of the Border.

The Kirk was a willing bastion of loyalism. Ministers were quick to denounce the errors of Jacobin infidels, stressing in particular the necessity of religious establishments to curb the passions of fallen man.[38] A rhetoric of declension and divine judgement shaped the presbyterian response to the horrors of the French republican experiment.[39] On the other hand, Kirkmen had few scruples about upholding the unreformed Hanoverian regime.[40] Nevertheless, such enthusiastic loyalism should not obscure the Kirk's predicament.

During the 1790s the 'whig-presbyterian conservatism' of the Moderates was further melted down into the common currency of British loyalism, leaving few distinctive features. The Assembly boasted of the Kirk's role in countering sedition, declaring that they were 'attached by the genius of presbyterian government to good order, no less than to freedom'. Yet, some of the 'dangerous principles' which the Kirk reckoned had 'deluded'[41] the Friends of the People were no more radical, indeed in certain respects less so, than the political ideas of the later Covenanters who had upheld presbyterian resistance to the episcopalian regime of the Restoration era. The Kirk retreated into a loyalist sycophancy, which precluded the expression of political sentiments which had been accept-

[37] Somerville, *My Own Life and Times*, 256.

[38] See e.g. George Hill, *Instructions Afforded by the Present War, To the People of Great-Britain. A Sermon Preached at St. Andrews on Thursday the 18th of April 1793* (Edinburgh, 1793); Robert Duncan, *Infidelity the Growing Evil of the Times, A Sermon Preached at Dundonald, On the 27th February, 1794* (Ayr, 1794); George Skene Keith, *A Caution Against Irreligion and Anarchy. A Sermon, From 1 Kings, xx. 23, 24. Preached in the High Church of Edinburgh, Sunday, May 18th, 1794, Before His Majesty's High Commissioner, and the General Assembly of the Church of Scotland* (Edinburgh, 1794).

[39] See e.g. John Erskine, *The Fatal Consequences and the General Sources of Anarchy. A Discourse on Isaiah xxiv. 1–5 the Substance of which was Preached in the Old Grey-Friars Church, before the Magistrates of Edinburgh, 2nd September 1792* (Edinburgh, 1793); Laurence Moyes, *Gratitude to God: A Sermon, on Jeremiah vi. 17 Preached in the Church of Larbert, Upon A Day of Thanksgiving, Appointed by the Synod of Perth and Stirling* (Falkirk, 1794); Robert Walker, *Patriotism and Courage in Arduous Times Exemplified in the Conduct of Nehemiah: A Sermon Preached on Occasion of the National Fast, March 9, 1797* (Edinburgh, 1797), 23–7.

[40] See e.g. Somerville, *Effects of the French Revolution*, 83; Robert Walker, *The Sentiments and Conduct Becoming Britons in the Present Conjuncture. A Sermon Preached in the Church of the Canongate on Occasion of the General National Fast, Feb. 27, 1794* (Edinburgh, 1794), 42; Thomas Hardy, *Fidelity to the British Constitution, the Duty and Interest of the People. A Sermon Preached in the New North Church, Edinburgh, on Thursday Feb. 27, 1794 Being the Day Appointed by His Majesty for a General Fast* (Edinburgh, 1794); Duncan, *Infidelity the Growing Evil of the Times*, 29.

[41] 'The General Assembly's Dutiful Address to his Majesty on the Subject of the Present War', 18 May 1793, in *Acts of the General Assembly*, 841.

able only four years previously. Even the aged retired leader of the Moderates, William Robertson, was wrongfooted by the sudden volte-face in political orthodoxy. His unpublished centenary sermon of 1788 had become an albatross. Robertson's theme—the significance of the Glorious Revolution for the liberties of modern Europe—had turned out to be topical, almost prophetic, but the sentiments expressed now reeked of potential subversion. After Robertson's death in 1793, the family suppressed this sermon to preserve his reputation.[42]

Self-censorship was also a feature of evangelical politics, despite the links between the Popular Party and the Foxite Whigs. The Popular leader, the Revd John Erskine (?1721–1803) moved to the conservative end of the Whig spectrum, explicitly repudiating the Covenanting era. Erskine warned that, in the seventeenth century, radical action had produced unintended outcomes including the reinvigoration of absolute monarchy:

Ill-judged and unconstitutional measures, in the last century, for redressing real grievances, and checking the usurpations of the prince, inflamed the evils they meant to remove; introduced a new form of tyranny; paved the way for restoring monarchy; and gave the monarch signal advantages, for acquiring, and transmitting to his successors, absolute and unlimited authority.[43]

There was a marked disjunction between inner belief—about the nature of the true Church—and its public expression. Patronage had not become a moot point. Violent intrusions of presentees continued throughout the late eighteenth century.[44] Yet somehow the unwelcome burden of lay patronage was airbrushed out of the picture presented by loyal presbyterians of Britain's spotless constitution. Hyperbolic praise was used to conceal blemishes upon the free practice of presbyterian religion. Principal George Hill, the leader of the Moderates, deluded himself that the Kirk possessed, 'under the protection of government, the faith which was once delivered to the saints'.[45]

On occasions the Kirk's vestigial Whiggery was obscured by a full-blown Toryism. Pamphlets and sermons appeared replete with the standard scriptural references once used to uphold Tory doctrines of non-resistance and passive obedience.[46] The worst offender was the Revd James Wemyss (1750–1822), who

---

[42] I. D. L. Clark, 'Moderatism and the Moderate Party in the Church of Scotland 1752–1805', Ph.D. thesis (Cambridge, 1963), 14–15; Sher, '1688 and 1788', 102–3; Sher, *Church and University*, 306.

[43] Erskine, *Fatal Consequences and General Sources of Anarchy*, 9; W. L. Mathieson, *Church and Reform in Scotland: A History from 1797 to 1843* (Glasgow, 1916), 88. See also William Dalgleish, *The Excellence of the British Constitution and the Evil of Changing It, Demonstrated in Two Sermons* (Edinburgh, 1793).

[44] There were at least twenty-one instances of violent intrusion in Scotland between 1780 and 1815: see Vincent, 'Responses', 203.

[45] George Hill, *The Present Happiness of Great Britain. A Sermon Preached at St. Andrews, Oct. 7th, 1792. And in the High Church of Edinburgh, Nov. 18th, 1792* (Edinburgh, 1792), 9–10.

[46] Vincent, 'Responses', 199, 206; James Wemyss, *A Scriptural View of Kings and Magistrates; And the Subjection and Obedience All Christians Ought to Yield Unto Them. A Sermon: Preached at Burntisland, On*

also appropriated the arguments of Anglican political theology. Wemyss was conscious of how far he had overstepped the bounds of Whiggery. Since Toryism was a dead letter, he argued, he could safely defend monarchy without 'reviving any of the old disputes about passive obedience, and arbitrary power, both long since laid in their graves'.[47] Similarly, the Revd Stevenson MacGill (1765–1840) denied that the case for political meekness was a manifestation of 'the spirit of passive obedience'; rather it was an expression of 'wisdom and brotherly love'.[48] However, the new Kirkmanship did bear a remarkable resemblance to old Toryism. Whereas once it had been incumbent upon presbyterians to resist uncovenanted authority, 'subjection to the civil magistrate' was now declared to be a 'moral duty'.[49] According to Wemyss, it was not only 'wicked' to 'injure government', but even to 'murmur against it, though attended, like all human things, with many imperfections'.[50]

Patriotism was an important weapon in the propaganda effort. In Scotland a prudent amnesia enabled 'the love of our country' to become a staple theme of political sermons. The Revd James Robertson (d. 1812) decried 'excessive praise bestowed on another country' as 'the next step of political depravity';[51] by which, he meant the radical adulation of Jacobin France. But which was '*our* country'? Presbyterian patriotism was riddled with unconscious ironies, unusual silences, and dubious historical appropriations. Scottishness was at least muted if not elided. The presbyterian past was erased from the communal memory, and England rather than Scotland became the fount of a legitimate Anglo-British patriotism. Indeed, the excesses of the French Revolution had closed down what little scope there had been within the lexicon of British patriotism for the weasel words of conditional loyalty traditionally associated with Scots presbyterian politics. An intense filiopietism might have been expected of Thomas Hardy (1747–98), Professor of Church History at the University of Edinburgh. On the contrary, Hardy's suggestively titled pamphlet *The Patriot* revealed an unbridled Anglomania, summed up in his anti-Jacobin slogan 'Nolumus leges Angliae mutari'. 'English history', he informed his 'countrymen', was the source of their

the National Fast, On Thursday Feb. 27th, 1794 (Edinburgh, 1794), 9–10, 21–4; William Cameron, *The Abuse of Civil and Religious Liberty: A Sermon Preached at the Opening of the Synod of Lothian and Tweeddale, On November 13th, 1792* (Edinburgh, 1793), 21–7; Hugh Blair, 'On the Love of Our Country', preached 18 April 1793, on the day of a National Fast appointed by government, on occasion of the War with the French Republic, in Blair, *Sermons* (2 vols.; Edinburgh, 1824–5), ii. 385–7.

[47] Wemyss, *Scriptural View*, 6.

[48] Stevenson MacGill, *The Spirit of the Times: Considered in an Address to the People of Eastwood* (Glasgow, 1792), 11.

[49] Wemyss, *Scriptural View*, 6.

[50] Ibid. 12.

[51] James Robertson, *The Love of Our Country, and the Duties Arising from that Principle: A Sermon, Preached at Callander, on Occasion of the National Fast, 26th February 1795* (Edinburgh, n.d.), 6; Vincent 'Responses', 205–6.

liberties: 'It was to this constitution, matured in some of its branches by the wisdom of ages, and perfected by the Revolution settlement, in the legal limitations of the monarchical branch, that our ancestors submitted themselves and their posterities for ever.'[52] Hardy was not alone in locating his political ancestors in the English past. Carlyle too had the English in mind when he contemplated 'the noble fabric of our constitution, the work of ages, the result of the wisdom and courage of our forefathers'.[53] Constitutional patriotism could not but be Anglo-British. But was there no outlet for a Scoto-British patriotism? Professor Hugh Blair (1718–1800) delivered a potent sermon critical of Jacobin universalism which urged his auditors to 'love our country as the seat of true religion'. His endorsement of 'true religion' was, however, somewhat tepid: 'The church that has been established by law, in the two separate divisions of our island, is suited to the genius and dispositions of the people in each.'[54] Scotland's violent Revolution of 1689 also disappeared from view. Hill helped to collapse the memory of the two distinctive Revolutions of 1688–9 into a single English version: 'through the special favour of heaven, without the tumult and massacres, which, in other countries, have generally attended a change of government, there was calmly accomplished, in both parts of this island . . . the Glorious Revolution.'[55]

The Kirk had long been in thrall to an Anglo-British interpretation of history, a spell which events during the 1790s did nothing to break. The Revd Thomas Somerville published two volumes of history in the course of the decade which together provided a compelling thesis about the foundations of the modern British state between the Restoration and the reign of Queen Anne. Reciting a litany of abuses, Somerville argued that seventeenth-century Scotland had been a scene of economic and political desolation. He was also critical of the illiberality of the Scottish Reformed tradition and its high-flying presbyterian offshoot: at the Revolution his forebears had been 'more anxious to establish their own power and religion, than to extend and confirm the liberties of the nation'.[56] Despite the force of his views, Somerville was in the mainstream of presbyterian opinion. In 1798 he was offered, but declined, the chair of church history at Edinburgh, and

[52] Thomas Hardy, *The Patriot. Addressed to the People, on the Present State of Affairs in Britain and in France. With Observations on Republican Government, and Discussions of the Principles Advanced in the Writings of T. Paine* (2nd edn., Edinburgh, 1793), 9–10, 16.

[53] Alexander Carlyle, *The Love of Our Country Explained and Enforced in a Sermon for Psalm cxxxvii. 5, 6. Preached in St. Andrews Church Edinburgh, March 19 and in Dalkeith Church, April 2, 1797* (Edinburgh, 1797), 7. See also Alexander Carlyle, *A Sermon on the Death of Sir David Dalrymple, Bt., Lord Hailes* (Edinburgh, 1792), 25–32.

[54] Blair, 'Love of Our Country', ii. 379.

[55] Hill, *Present Happiness of Great Britain*, 6.

[56] Thomas Somerville, *The History of Political Transactions and Parties, from the Restoration of King Charles II to the Death of King William* (London, 1792), esp. 242–3, 245, 459, 467–70, 588; Somerville, *The History of Great Britain during the Reign of Queen Anne* (London, 1798), esp. 147–8, 169–70, 210.

his verdict on the Scottish past was endorsed in the Revd Ebenezer Marshal's *History of the Union* (1799).[57] Moreover, presbyterian sermons frequently depicted the independent kingdom of Scotland as a feudal wasteland.[58]

Although the Kirk's heritage was further compromised during the 1790s by the long-standing embarrassment of its political heritage, there was no anguished debate about presbyterian identity, and indeed very little evidence of the sort of radical presbyterianism which surfaced in Ulster during this era.[59] The Revd William Dunn of Kirkintilloch (1745–98), imprisoned for three months in 1793 for having removed three incriminating pages from the minutes of his local society for reform, was highly atypical. In October 1792 Dunn preached a highly controversial political sermon at the opening of the Synod of Glasgow and Ayr. The text was from Rev. 21:5: 'Behold, I make all things new', and in its published version the sermon was dedicated to 'the Friends of the Constitution in Church and State, and of the People'. In his sermon Dunn did not shrink from emphasizing the political differences between the democratic practices of the Kirk and the corrupting influences of the court on the Church of England. Furthermore, he traced the providential hand of perfectibility in all spheres of human history—the mechanic arts, religion, and politics: God had 'interwoven into the frame of human affairs an active energy, which, by incessant successive exertions, is productive of a continual train of perfective alterations, not overthrowing or changing fundamental principles, but unfolding their tendency'. As there were often human bottlenecks to the divinely sanctioned process of improvement, it was sometimes necessary to remove such obstacles, in the political sphere by taking up arms.[60] This was not so far removed from the providentialism and exceptional resistance of Revolution principles, but it was now unacceptably radical to a civil religion chameleon-like in its conformity to the changing environment of British politics.

The real debate over the meaning of the Scottish Whig–presbyterian tradition took place within the ranks of the Seceders, whose numbers contemporaries reckoned at around 50,000 each for Burgher and Anti-Burgher communities,

---

[57] Hew Scott, *Fasti ecclesiae scoticanae* (new edn., 7 vols.; Edinburgh, 1915–28), ii. 128; Ebenezer Marshal, *The History of the Union of Scotland and England* (Edinburgh, 1799), pp. ii–iii, 63, 89, 195–6, 199, 208–10, 228.

[58] MacGill, *Spirit of the Times*, 20–1, 27–8; Hardy, *Patriot*, 18, 20. Cf. the marked anti-feudalism of certain Centenary sermons: M'Gill, *Benefits of the Revolution*, 8, 13; Ranken, *Advantages of the Revolution*, 8.

[59] I. McBride, ' "Scripture Politics": The Religious Foundations of Presbyterian Radicalism in Late Eighteenth-Century Ireland', Ph.D. thesis (London, 1994).

[60] Scott, *Fasti ecclesiae scoticanae*, iii. 483; William Dunn, *A Sermon, Preached at the Opening of the Synod of Glasgow and Air, at Glasgow, 9 October, 1792* (Glasgow, 1792), 6, 10–11, 13–16. Dunn's sermon was answered by Adam Whyte, *Political Preaching: or the Meditations of a Well-Meaning Man, on a Sermon Lately Published; in a Letter Addressed to the Rev. Mr. William Dunn, minister of Kirkintilloch* (Glasgow, 1792).

though a recent estimate puts the wider body of dissenters at 20 per cent of the Lowland population.[61] The Secession Churches confronted a magnified version of the same dilemma which troubled the Kirk. The difficulties of reconciling principle and loyalty were compounded within the Secession by the weightier commitments imposed by tradition, which, in turn, loaded Seceders with a heavier burden of potential disloyalty. The authorities needed to be convinced that these radical Covenanters were not a threat to the State. Yet any demonstration of whole-hearted allegiance risked a betrayal of the good old cause. Furthermore, there was no consistent pattern to the political allegiances of Secession ministers during the confrontations of the 1790s. Some penned pro-government pamphlets, others were active in the radical cause.[62]

The Burghers produced both types of activist. The Revd Alexander Shanks (1732–99) urged the Burgher community to conform to the demands of loyalism: 'Give none occasion to the world who observe you, to call you an ill-humoured and ill-principled sectary, disaffected to the welfare and prosperity of that country in which you are fed and protected.' Shanks went to conservative extremes, importing into his sermons the familiar texts of Tory political theology. He revived a patriarchalist defence of royal authority on the back of a broad interpretation of the fifth commandment. Not only were the old shibboleths of Covenanting resistance theory now taboo, but so too was speaking ill of the monarch. Shanks invoked Ecc. 20:20—'Curse not the King'—to proscribe any hint of sedition. His recommendations left little scope for the circumscribed plain-speaking loyalty once practised by the likes of Melville and Buchanan: 'Honour the King. Respect the person, rank, and authority, of the chief ruler; and yield, in every thing lawful and just, a ready obedience to them who are over you, in his name, for the good of the realm.'[63] Yet the Burgher Professor of Divinity and minister of Selkirk, Dr George Lawson (1749–1820), had no truck with such advice. Lawson was involved with the Scottish Society of the Friends of the People, as were some of his ministerial colleagues, including Ebenezer Hislop, 'the Reverend Democrat'.[64] Eventually the Burghers appear to have resolved their political dilemma, for in 1798 the Synod felt able to approve a loyal address to the crown.[65]

[61] H. W. Meikle, *Scotland and the French Revolution* (Glasgow, 1912), 198; C. Brown, *The People in the Pews* (Economic and Social History Society of Scotland, 1993), 13.

[62] J. Brims, 'The Covenanting Tradition and Scottish Radicalism in the 1790s', in T. Brotherstone (ed.), *Covenant, Charter and Party: Traditions of Revolt and Protest in Modern Scottish History* (Aberdeen, 1989), Cf. J. Brims, 'The Scottish Democratic Movement in the Age of the French Revolution', Ph.D. thesis (Edinburgh, 1983), which remains the standard modern treatment of this period.

[63] Alexander Shanks, *The Admonition against Cursing the King and the Rich, Illustrated and Commended in the Associate Congregation of Jedburgh, December 7, 1794* (Edinburgh, 1797?), 27; Shanks, *Peace and Order Recommended to Society, in an Address to the Associate Congregation of Jedburgh, from Jeremiah xxix. 7* (Edinburgh, 1793), 8.

[64] Brims, 'Covenanting Tradition and Scottish Radicalism', 53.

[65] Meikle, *Scotland and the French Revolution*, 199.

However, the tensions generated by the French Revolution were even more pronounced within the more traditionalist Anti-Burgher Synod, where the differences between theological conservatives and prudential, political conservatives flared up into a heresy hunt. The case of the Revd John Young of Hawick (1743–1806) demonstrates vividly the problems faced by Seceding ministers in constructing a position on the British constitution which met both escalating demands for unambiguous loyalty and the standards of the Anti-Burgher testimony. In his *Essays on Government* (1794) Young engaged in a public-relations exercise on behalf of the Seceders; but his loyalism appeared to compromise the principles of his co-religionists. As a result, Young found himself under investigation for his defence of the political status quo. At the Synod in May 1795 a formal complaint was brought against Young which sparked a new round of the perennial presbyterian debate on the authority of the civil power. Could members of the Anti-Burgher synod conscientiously swear such whole-hearted approbation of the British constitution? The presbytery of Perth identified the 'snares and dangers' lurking in such declarations. Although no action was taken to punish Young, the Anti-Burghers condemned 'all declarations or subscriptions expressive of an unqualified satisfaction with government',[66] which was taken to include the Anglican Church. Somehow the Anti-Burghers felt that they were able to square the circle, testifying against the grievous defections in the British constitution whilst also acknowledging a dutiful subjection to it in all 'lawful commands'.

The Revd Archibald Bruce, who presided at the head of this old guard, exemplifies the difficulties in upholding presbyterian traditions in the 1790s. Out of touch with the culture of modern presbyterianism, Bruce, who was the Antiburgher Professor of Divinity, remained thirled to an older age of arid and prolix Calvinist scholasticism. He had no truck with the literary fashions of the new refined breed of enlightened presbyterians, whose published sermons and treatises conformed to the secular standards of classical rhetoric and contemporary *belles-lettres*. His many works are characterized by a 'great diffusiveness', such was 'the effort of a mind filled to overflow' which, having striven to 'disburden itself of its vast stores of information', remained so fixed on the sacred matters at hand that 'it continued to pour out its riches without pausing to reflect that already a superabundance of argument and illustration had been forthcoming, and that more would but cloy'. Bruce also had considerable difficulty in finding outlets for his radical views. Yet conscience demanded that the voice of true presbyterianism be heard. Bruce overcame this dilemma by buying a printing

---

[66] John Young, *Essays on the Following Interesting Subjects: viz. I. Government. II. Revolutions. III. The British Constitution. IV. Kingly Government etc.* (Edinburgh, 1794); M'Kerrow, *Secession*, 373.

press in Edinburgh and having it delivered to Whitburn, where he secured the services of an old printer. In this way Bruce's interminable jeremiads found their way into print, albeit of inferior type.[67]

However, Bruce's major problem was his disregard for the texture and demands of contemporary political culture. He argued with a reckless casuistry that, because the Treaty of Union guaranteed full Scots presbyterian privileges, the laws of treason and sedition did not extend to criticism of the constitution or monarchy when such attacks were derived from sound presbyterian principles.[68] As was his vaunted right, Bruce carelessly disaggregated British Protestant identity into two ill-matched national traditions, a Scottish commitment to liberty and democracy and an English 'Caesaro-papistry'. Whereas in Scotland the Reformation had 'produced a very remarkable struggle for civil rights, and popular liberty', the English Reformation had not been 'accompanied with any sensible accession of or advantages to civil liberty' but had augmented the authority of the crown with the former powers of the papacy. The Hanoverian monarchs retained an antichristian supremacy over the Church of England which rendered the king, in Bruce's satirical phrase, an 'English *pontifex maximus*'.[69] It is little wonder that Bruce regretted the 'boundless panegyric and vague declamations upon the excellence of the British government, without discriminating the good from the evil, such as have lately been poured upon the public from pulpits and presses'. He contended that this unthinking loyalism was aimed at the inculcation of 'an undefined loyalty' far removed from the 'conscientious loyalty' of authentic presbyterians whose adherence to the civil power was necessarily overridden by their higher duties.[70] 'Are all British laws without exception to be held sacred?' demanded Bruce.[71] Prelates sat in the House of Lords, defying the injunction against confusing the temporal and spiritual kingdoms. How could an honest presbyterian homologate such usurpations on Christ's rights?

On the other hand, could the Hanoverian monarchy rest easy with such expressions of loyalty? Bruce thought it could. The Revolution settlement with

---

[67] 'Memoirs of the Reverend Dr. Wylie', quoted in D. Scott (ed.), *Annals and Statistics of the Original Secession Church: Till its Disruption and Union with the Free Church of Scotland in 1852* (Edinburgh, 1886), 520–1.

[68] A North British Protestant [i.e. Archibald Bruce], *Reflections on Freedom of Writing* (1794), 80–1, 94–105; Bruce, *A Historico-Politico-Ecclesiastical Dissertation on the Supremacy of Civil Powers in Matters of Religion, Particularly the Ecclesiastical Supremacy Annexed to the English Crown* (Edinburgh, 1802), pp. ix–x, 148–51.

[69] [Bruce], *Reflections on Freedom of Writing*, 6–9; Bruce, *Historico-Politico-Ecclesiastical Dissertation*, pp. xi, 87–8.

[70] [Archibald Bruce], *The Principal Difference between the Religious Principles of those Commonly called the Anti-Government Party and of other Presbyterians especially those of the Secession in Scotland on the Head of Magistracy Briefly Stated* (1797), 21.

[71] [Bruce], *Reflections on Freedom of Writing*, 67.

King William had been defective, a mere 'covenant of allegiance'. It was this rope of sand which bound the Seceders to the crown. However, Bruce did not see things in such negative terms. A Covenanted magistracy was not essential to lawful government, only to its *bene esse*: 'There is no need either for denying or extenuating the evils of the British government in order to establish the obligation to limited obedience to it, while supported by the people at large.'[72] Yet in the 1790s such were the new requirements of political correctness that this increasingly formulaic language of passive rebuke was liable to be misconstrued. There was a very real danger that conservative Covenanting might be mistaken for radicalism.[73]

This problem was exacerbated by the New Licht controversy which raged in the Anti-Burgher synod from 1791 and among the Burghers from 1795. The New Lichters were so called because they attempted to redefine the extent of their obligations to the standards of earlier generations. The dispute began in 1791 with the scruples of two licentiates awaiting ordination about certain passages in the Westminster Confession of Faith which appeared to give the civil magistrate unwarranted powers in religious matters. This introspective revisionism soon spread to other areas of the Anti-Burgher testimony, including the authority of the Solemn League and Covenant. In 1795 the Revd John Fraser of Auchtermuchty (1745–1818) inaugurated a similar bout of soul-searching among the Burghers.[74] What was ultimately at stake in these scholastic wranglings was whether the Seceders would move towards a voluntaryist position or retain their theoretical commitment to a state Church. Unfortunately, the issue was threateningly phrased in terms of the authority of the civil magistrate.

As a result, these controversies were to leave a further taint of disloyalty upon the Seceders, which the Burgher synod of 1799 attempted to dispel:

> The controversy among us, indeed, respects the power of the civil magistrate. It is not, however, a political, but an ecclesiastical dispute. It respects not the power which the civil magistrate actually possesses by the constitution of Britain; but the power which is supposed by some to be ascribed to him doctrinally in our standard-books; and it respects even this, only in reference to matters of religion.[75]

This was not enough to convince the Revd William Porteous (1735–1812), a minister of the established Kirk and a correspondent of Dundas. A mischievous Porteous wondered why the New Licht had suddenly illuminated the con-

[72] [Bruce], *Principal Difference*, 4, 15–16, 20. See also Bruce, *A Brief Statement and Genuine Declaration of the Genuine Principles of Seceders, Respecting Civil Government, the Duty of Subjects, and National Reformation and a Vindication of their Conduct in Reference to Some Late Plans and Societies for Political Reform, and the Public Dissensions of the Time* (1799).

[73] Mathieson, *Church and Reform*, 60.

[74] M'Kerrow, *Secession*, chs. xiii and xvii; Herron, *Kirk by Divine Right*, 78–83.

[75] M'Kerrow, *Secession*, 598.

sciences of the Burghers at the very moment when the people were 'agitated' by the dissemination of Jacobin principles, and the British army had been forced to cede Holland to the French: 'THEN, the Associate Synod grasped at the first opportunity of questioning the extent of the magistrate's power, and of inviting public attention to such topics.' As 'Lords of conscience', the Associate Synod had changed their standards unilaterally. Where would it end? Porteous had an inkling of the destination: 'today they may admit Democrates, and tomorrow Atheists.'[76] These smears triggered a further bout of defensiveness. The Revd James Peddie (1758–1845) issued a pamphlet repudiating Porteous's attempts to read seditious politics into the New Licht, but several ministers also went so far as to enlist the Lord Advocate as their counsel in an attempt to clear the New Lichters of the taint of disloyalty.[77]

As well as raising the old spectre of presbyterian disloyalty, the New Licht further divided the Seceders. In 1799 the Burghers split into Auld and New Lichters, and in 1806, after a decade and a half of debate, Bruce led away the Auld Licht Anti-Burghers—a body 'seeking to be more true to the standards of the past than the past itself had been'[78]—from the misguided New Licht Anti-Burghers.

'Everything rung, and was connected with the Revolution in France . . . Everything, not this or that thing, but literally everything was soaked in this one event.'[79] Henry Cockburn (1779–1854) did not misremember the events of his youth. The French Revolution curtailed the free-thinking about society and politics which had been such a characteristic feature of the Scottish Enlightenment. The anxious reaction to the Revolution also put a stop to the burgh reform movement which had arisen in Scotland during the 1780s. Nevertheless, the novelty of the 1790s should not be exaggerated. One of the hallmarks of eighteenth-century Kirkmanship had been a reluctant conformity to the demands of the British state. The long and gradual process of British integration initiated by the Union of 1707 involved the negotiation of a workable relationship between a presbyterian Kirk haunted by its legacy of radicalism and resistance, and a British state whose identity was predominantly Anglican and Erastian. Kirkmen were riven in their consciences, acknowledging the ancestral call of traditional Scots presbyterian values, yet aware too that the preservation of

[76] William Porteous, *The New Light Examined; or, Observations on the Proceedings of the Associate Synod against their own Standards* (Glasgow, 1800), 49, 54.

[77] James Peddie, *A Defence of the Associate Synod against the Charge of Sedition: Addressed to William Porteous, D.D.* (Edinburgh, 1800), esp. 15, 35–6, 46–9, 72–7; Meikle, *Scotland and the French Revolution*, 201 n; M'Kerrow, *Secession*, 600–2.

[78] Herron, *Kirk by Divine Right*, 83.

[79] Henry Cockburn, *Memorials of his Times* (Edinburgh, 1856), 80.

the Kirk's standing as an established Church necessitated some elision of its heritage. The irruption of the French Revolution into presbyterian politics reignited old worries about the Kirk's dubious identity, provoking a new round of compromises. Kirkmen responded with a mundane conservative loyalism whose Scots presbyterian accent was barely audible. However, such adaptation was by now almost second nature to the Kirk's leaders.

The real anxieties were those of the Seceders who had until the 1790s been able to wallow, untroubled by Kirk or State, in an uncompromising and unrealistic pseudo-Kirkmanship. In the tense atmosphere of the 1790s the State needed more convincing of the loyalty of such radical subcultures, especially since the Seceders seemed so preoccupied with probing the authority of the civil magistrate. As a result, many Seceders succumbed to pressures for an expedient cringe. Although Bruce arose as a Jeremiah to denounce such flagrant defections from sacred covenanted principles, his valiant display of filiopietism served only to highlight the incompatibility of traditional presbyterian standards with the expectations of a suspicious British state.

11

Religion according to Napoleon:
The Limitations of Pragmatism

Geoffrey Ellis

What *was* Napoleon's religion? The question may well strike some readers as almost redundant. *Of course* Napoleon did not have a religion in any conventional sense implying personal belief in formal doctrinal tenets of some kind, in a spiritual life, or in the salvation of the soul. On the contrary, the evidence of his writings and recorded utterances suggests that he had a pragmatic, utilitarian, and at times even rather cynical attitude towards not just Roman Catholicism, the formal faith into which he was born, but indeed towards *all* institutional religions. As he once famously said, in 1800, 'it was by making myself a Catholic that I won the war in the Vendée, by making myself a Moslem that I established myself in Egypt, by making myself an ultramontane that I turned men's hearts towards me in Italy. If I were to govern a nation of Jews I would rebuild the Temple of Solomon.'[1]

Several other of Napoleon's often-quoted remarks seem to strike the same note. Around the time of the Concordat of 1801, for instance, he declared that 'the people must have a religion; this religion must be in the control of the government',[2] and again that

society cannot exist without religion. When a man is dying of hunger alongside another who gorges himself, it is impossible to make him accept this difference, if there is no authority to say to him: 'this is God's will, there must needs be poor and rich people in the world, but afterwards, and for eternity, the division of lots will be different.'[3]

His announcement to the council of state in 1806 is perhaps even better known: 'in religion I do not see the mystery of the Incarnation but the mystery of the

---

[1] Cited in E. E. Y. Hales, *Napoleon and the Pope: The Story of Napoleon and Pius VII* (London, 1962), 7–8; from P.-L. Roederer, *Autour de Bonaparte: Journal du comte Roederer*, ed. Maurice Vitrac (Paris, 1909), 16.

[2] Cited in John McManners, *The French Revolution and the Church* (Westport, Conn., 1982), 140.

[3] Cited in Jacques Godechot, *Les Institutions de la France sous la Révolution et l'Empire* (3rd edn., Paris, 1985), 713.

social order.'[4] According to Napoleon, then, religion had little to do with divine revelation or spiritual redemption; its essential function was to sanction his own perception of the social order, along with all the material inequalities thereby implied. As far as the common people at least were concerned, this meant that the Church had a useful role to play in French society, provided it was kept under firm political control.

Yet the difficulty with these and so many other remarks which might be cited on the same theme is that they served the official purposes of Napoleon's exercise of power, or else his later reminiscences about power. As such, they are associated above all with the temporal aims of his rule. Whether they were made at the time of the Consulate and Empire, or during his years of exile on St Helena, such declarations seem inseparable from his religious *policy*, and from his dealings with Pope Pius VII in particular. In either case, there was a need to assert his intentions, to justify his actions rather than reflect on their moral implications. In this respect, the St Helena record is especially deceptive, since it was of course intended to present the fallen emperor in the best possible light. He had to be shown as a man of vision and principle, who in his religious policy, like all his other policies, had always tried to work for the good of all his subjects.

Now, it is not my purpose here to offer any startling new definitions of 'religion' or 'faith' in order to fit Napoleon into some secular variant of them. That he repeatedly declared his belief (however abstract) in a 'God' or 'Creator' common to all mankind is clear, and the influences which may have shaped such a conviction have been variously attributed. For some writers, Rousseau is supposed to have been the lay 'guru' behind his early deference to a natural religion, one experienced through human *sensibilité* rather than formulated by philosophical reasoning. For others, he was influenced more by the rationalist and scientific thinkers of the eighteenth-century Enlightenment. Christopher Herold, for example, in the introduction to his fascinating selection from the written and spoken words—the 'mind'—of Napoleon, claims that 'privately, he remained a Voltairian deist throughout his life'.[5] Others, again, think that his only consistent 'religious' conviction was an instinctive belief in Destiny, rooted in his native Corsican mentality, and that this owed more to classical precepts gleaned from his voracious but highly impressionistic reading of ancient historical texts.[6]

However one interprets Napoleon's attitude to religion in general, or to

---

[4] *The Mind of Napoleon: A Selection from his Written and Spoken Words*, ed. and trans. J. Christopher Herold (New York, 1955), 105; from Pelet de la Lozère (ed.), *Opinions de Napoléon sur divers sujets de politique et d'administration recueillis par un membre de son Conseil d'État* (Paris, 1833), 223.

[5] *Mind of Napoleon*, ed. Herold, pp. xxi–xxii.

[6] Ibid., *passim*, where a number of important original passages are included. Napoleon's view of Destiny is also discussed in many secondary accounts: see e.g. the works cited in nn. 9 and 10 below.

particular religions, it is clear that he did not hold with formal, institutionalized professions of faith—for *himself* at any rate. He was particularly scathing about theology, which in an early manuscript, his 'Discours sur le bonheur' of 1791, he bluntly dismissed as 'that sink of prejudices and errors of all kinds'.[7] He saw formal religious instruction and worship as, at best, a necessary and useful social anodyne for the popular classes, as a means of exhorting them to respect established authority, and so also to acquiesce peaceably in his regime. He regarded such religious observance as particularly important for girls, who might thus be taught their proper place in the patriarchal society he considered both natural and desirable. His note written at the castle of Finkenstein on 15 May 1807 will surely not commend itself to many modern readers:

what we ask of education is not that girls should think, but that they should believe. The weakness of women's brains, the instability of their ideas, the place they will fill in society, their need for perpetual resignation, and for an easy and generous type of charity—all this can only be met by religion, and by religion of a gentle and charitable kind.[8]

In short, if I have raised a question to which the simple answer seems so abundantly clear, it is mainly because earlier writings on Napoleon's personal morality have not given enough attention to his inner motivation. It has so often been assumed that everything ultimately came down to an overriding belief in himself and his own destiny, in other words to his egotism and fatalism, and that the pursuit of unbridled power was its natural extension in the secular world. Any spiritual or moral arbiter external to himself seems remote here. Fortunately, we now know much more about Napoleon's youth, an important formative stage in his education, thanks to the illuminating research of Dorothy Carrington and other historians of Corsica.[9] The pioneering work of Harold T. Parker on the formation of Napoleon's personality during the years which preceded his assumption of power, and on his evolving code of values, has also cast new light on those difficult and elusive subjects.[10] At the time of the *coup d'état* of 18–19 Brumaire Year VIII (9–10 November 1799), Napoleon was 30 years old, his

[7] Ibid. 31; from *Napoléon: Manuscrits inédits, 1786–1791*, ed. Frédéric Masson and Guido Biagi (Paris, 1910), 560.

[8] *Letters of Napoleon*, selected, trans., and ed. J. M. Thompson (Oxford, 1934), 194–5.

[9] See esp. Dorothy Carrington, *Napoleon and his Parents: On the Threshold of History* (London, 1988); see also Thadd E. Hall, Dorothy Carrington, Jean Defranceschi, John M. P. McErlean, and Harold T. Parker, 'Corsica and Corsicans during the Revolutionary Era (1755–1815)', in *The Consortium on Revolutionary Europe: Proceedings 1986* (Athens, Ga., 1987), 48–95.

[10] Harold T. Parker, 'The Formation of Napoleon's Personality: An Exploratory Essay', *French Historical Studies*, 7 (Spring 1971), 6–26; 'Napoleon's Changing Self-Image to 1812: A Sketch', in *The Consortium on Revolutionary Europe: Proceedings 1983* (Athens, Ga., 1985), 448–63; 'Napoleon Reconsidered: An Invitation to Inquiry and Reflection', *French Historical Studies*, 15 (Spring 1987), 142–56; and 'Napoleon and the Values of the French Army: The Early Phases', *Proceedings of the Annual Meeting of the Western Society for French History*, 18 (1991), 233–42.

character more or less formed. In so far as his regime was based on an essentially *personalized* concept of power, and on the public manifestation of a *personalized* heroic ethic, we need to know what motivated the man if we are to understand the nature of his political system. We also need to recognize that its religious dimension was part of a much wider social design. It was only one function of his attempt to organize society on authoritarian, hierarchical, uniform, and centralized principles of government in a much more comprehensive way.

This chapter addresses its subject in three parts. The first covers the years up to Brumaire and considers the evidence on what sort of religious upbringing Napoleon had, and how he reacted to it. The second concentrates mainly on his policy towards the Catholic Church, and also much more briefly discusses his treatment of the other religions in France, during his years of power. The third deals with the St Helena record, the product of what might be considered his more reflective years, and assesses how far it is consistent with those earlier attitudes and policies towards the various religious communities over which he had ruled.

The formal record of Napoleon's religious upbringing is now less sketchy than it used to be. The society into which he was born in Ajaccio on 15 August 1769 was significantly different from that of the French mainland. The history of the Catholic Church in Corsica had long preceded the French annexation of the island in 1768. At different times in its past, it had evolved under the rule of the bishops (later the archbishops) of Pisa, the kings of Aragon, and of course the Genoese, who had ceded Corsica to France. Over those preceding centuries, the Church had had to minister to a people among whom implacable vendettas, banditry 'of honour', and pagan customs going back to megalithic times were still endemic, notwithstanding the official pronouncements of the Council of Trent. The concept of 'honour' itself was identified above all in the family, in clannish instincts, whose 'gender roles' (as it is now fashionable to call them) were deeply rooted and fiercely defended. The main recurring theme of Frédéric Masson's monumental work on Napoleon and his family, the most detailed study of the subject ever attempted, is that their survival in the often difficult years before Brumaire and their evolving dynastic ambitions under the Empire fundamentally reflected the interests of their clan.[11]

The Church in Corsica had had to accept and adjust itself to such overriding loyalties in a society of clans whose total population at the time of the French annexation was around 120,000.[12] There was little in Napoleon's early upbringing to encourage any profound religious sentiment. His father, Carlo, was by all

---

[11] Frédéric Masson, *Napoléon et sa famille (1769–1821)* (13 vols.; Paris, 1897–1919).
[12] Dorothy Carrington, *Granite Island: A Portrait of Corsica* (Harmondsworth, 1984), 87.

accounts a pleasure-loving and irreverent man, whose view of religion had been adversely influenced by his studies at the Jesuit college in Ajaccio, and who poured his scorn for the Church into a number of scurrilous anticlerical writings during his later years. His mother, Letizia, had not yet found solace in the piety which was to characterize her own later life, and in his early years seems to have had rather materialistic priorities and to have treated religious observance as a matter of social form. Dorothy Carrington's minute investigation of the dotal records suggests that the marriage of Carlo and Letizia in 1764 was in all probability not solemnized by any religious service, least of all in church, but contracted and consummated without such ceremony in the bride's home. Although officially frowned on by the Church, that practice was not untypical of Corsican custom, and in this particular case Carlo appears to have been the one who balked at a proper clerical blessing, then or afterwards.[13]

A precedent had thus been set by Napoleon's parents for raising their family in the earliest years according to customary ways rather than by strict adherence to Catholic rites. It is true that Carlo's uncle, Luciano Bonaparte, who rose to become archdeacon of Ajaccio cathedral in September 1779, and Letizia's uncle, Francesco Ramolino, were both in holy orders. Joseph Fesch, moreover, Letizia's half-brother by her mother's second marriage, was also destined for the priesthood. None of these relatives radiated much spiritual conviction, however; Luciano and Fesch in particular were wordly men who regarded, and indeed used, the Church as a vehicle to further their own careers in the material world. With Napoleon's later patronage, Fesch was to be appointed as archbishop of Lyons under the Consulate, to receive a cardinal's hat, and also to serve for a time (and rather ineptly) as French ambassador to Rome during the early Empire. While it was also the family's initial intention that Joseph, Napoleon's elder brother, should take holy orders, the plan foundered a few years after he began his studies at the College of Autun in January 1779.

On the other hand, Carlo's growing political ambitions in due course required official demonstrations of a more orthodox kind, such as might be expected of a petty noble family with hopes of rising to prominence under their new French governors. In furthering his career in the Corsican Estates, he understood the need for outward conformity with the Church. It is more than likely that he took advantage of his position as an *assesseur* (assistant judge) to make a fraudulent entry in the municipal register of Ajaccio, sometime after September 1771, when the family's nobility was recognized under French law, in order to pass his marriage off as a religious ceremony properly conducted in the cathedral.[14] Similar doubt also surrounds the circumstances of Napoleon's baptism on 21

---

[13] Carrington, *Napoleon and his Parents*, 18–22.   [14] Ibid. 19–20.

July 1771, along with Maria Anna, his sister born a week earlier, but who died only four months later. The occasion itself gave little evidence of firm Christian convictions on his parents' part. It appears that the baptism took place in the *casa* Bonaparte, an act also quite typical of Corsican custom, and that Luciano probably conducted the private ceremony. The story later put about that Napoleon had been christened in Ajaccio cathedral was then certainly convenient, but just as certainly false.[15]

Such were the circumstances in which Napoleon, at the age of not quite 2, was put through his first 'Catholic' formality, and we know too that as a young boy he also attended a small mixed school run by nuns. As both he and his mother much later recalled, Letizia had to drive him to Mass by slaps and blows during the first nine years of his life, and beat him for his frequent misbehaviour there.[16] His nickname of 'Ribulione', the troublemaker, was by all accounts thoroughly deserved. He appears to have received his first communion from the village priest while he was a royal scholar at the military school of Brienne, sometime in 1781 or 1782, when he was 12. He was certainly also confirmed on 15 May 1785 by the archbishop of Paris, during his time at the École Royale Militaire in the French capital, where religious observance was much more strictly enforced.[17] On the occasion of his confirmation, according to an anecdote Napoleon later acknowledged to be true, Archbishop de Juigné expressed astonishment at his name, which was altogether unknown in the calendar of saints. The young cadet quickly replied that that could be no rule, since there were an immense number of saints and only 365 days of the year.[18]

These events occurred at a relatively early stage of Napoleon's education, when he was devouring his favourite classics, most notably Plutarch's *Parallel Lives*, which he read in Amyot's celebrated translation, and also beginning to espouse the fashionable deism of the Enlightenment. The Minims of Brienne, a Franciscan establishment not particularly noted for its piety or academic distinction, had no doubt tried to give the young Napoleon a decent Catholic education, according to their lights. Yet the regime of the school was spartan, its ethos aggressively competitive, as the boys were put through their exercises in and outside the classroom. This was hardly the ambiance in which to learn the spiritual blessings of contrition, of humility, or of turning the other cheek. Remembering these turbulent and unhappy years while on St Helena, Napoleon gave the following account of that phase of his schooling:

---

[15] Ibid. 64–6.   [16] Ibid. 90–1.   [17] Ibid. 153, 180.
[18] Emmanuel de Las Cases, *Mémorial de Sainte Hélène: Journal of the Private Life and Conversations of the Emperor Napoleon at Saint Helena* (Eng. edn., 4 vols.; London, 1823), i (pt. 1), 120 (entry for 31 Aug. 1815).

[Reason] exclaims, O religions, religions! The children of man! We very properly believe in God, because every thing around us proclaims him, and the most enlightened minds have believed in him; not only Bossuet, whose profession it was, but also Newton and Leibnitz [*sic*], who had nothing to do with it. But we know not what to think of the doctrine, that is taught us, and we find ourselves like the watch which goes, without knowing the watchmaker that made it. And observe a little the stupidity of those who educate us; they should keep away from us the idea of paganism and idolatry; because their absurdity excites the first exercise of our reason, and prepares us for a resistance to passive belief; and they bring us up, notwithstanding, in the midst of the Greeks and Romans, with their myriads of divinities. Such, for my own part, has literally been the progress of my understanding. I felt the necessity of belief; I did believe, but my belief was shocked and undecided, the moment I acquired knowledge and began to reason; and that happened to me, at so early an age as thirteen.[19]

Napoleon's alienation from most of his schoolfellows at Brienne, the sons of French nobles and nearly all his social superiors, who regarded him as a weird outsider and a vulgar upstart, also reinforced his Corsican identity and his early sense of a personal destiny to free his homeland from French rule. While his social life at the École Royale Militaire was by all accounts much easier, the Corsican dream remained strong. It did not evaporate until his rupture with the Paolists (the implacable champions of Corsican independence who regarded the Bonapartes as renegade 'francisés' and traitors to the patriotic cause) forced Napoleon's family to seek refuge on the French mainland in June 1793.

Whatever the reasons, there is no doubt that the physical and secular strands in Napoleon's education, to a large extent self-taught, had worked through more strongly when, as a soldier of the Revolution, he first gained prominence in France. In an earlier manuscript of 1786, composed when he was 17, he had already set out his objections to the adoption of Christianity as a civil religion, and in terms which might as well have been copied straight out of Rousseau's *Du contrat social* (1762).[20] It did his military career no harm to be associated with the official anticlericalism of the Jacobin government and then of the Directory which eventually followed, after some anxiety over his future during the Thermidorian interlude. There is no evidence that he was ever actively involved in any of the excesses of the 'dechristianization' campaign of 1793–4. On the contrary, his opposition to it can be inferred from his later reaction to the continuing problem of *chouannerie* in the western provinces. His personal indifference to religion during the 1790s is plain. As far as we know, and no doubt in the interests of his military career, he did not attend the permissible services of the Constitutional Church, let alone those of the refractory Church, whose legal

[19] Ibid. iii (pt. 5), 200–1 (entry for 17 Aug. 1816).
[20] *Manuscrits inédits*, ed. Masson and Biagi, 9–10.

status remained precarious even after the National Convention's proclamation of 'the liberty of cults' on 21 February 1795. His marriage to the widowed Josephine de Beauharnais on 9 March 1796 was not solemnized by any religious ceremony; it was contracted under the civil law of the Revolutionary Republic.

In dealing with Pope Pius VI and the conquered Italians during his spectacular campaign of 1796–7, Napoleon treated their religious sensitivities in a wholly pragmatic way, as a means of establishing *his* peace and *his* order, weighing up the political advantages of severity or magnanimity, unmoved by any talk of the wrath of God. To Cardinal Mattei, who had opposed the anti-papal revolt which enabled Napoleon to incorporate Ferrara into the Cispadane Republic, he wrote on 26 September 1796 that 'your character, which is a cause of congratulation to all who know you, induces me to allow your return to Ferrara, and to throw a veil of oblivion over your behaviour during the last month'. But in the same letter he pointedly added: 'go back to your diocese . . . but never again meddle in State affairs. And be assured that the clergy, and all who are in the service of the church, will be under the special protection of the French Republic.'[21]

That, in all essentials, was also his policy towards the Islamic authorities during his Egyptian campaign of 1798–9. Writing to the divan of Cairo on 21 July 1799, his opening shot that 'there is no other god but God, and Mahomet is his prophet!' was general, but his second more personal: 'To the Divan of Cairo, Chosen amongst the Wisest, the most Instructed, and the most Enlightened! May the Salutation of the Prophet be upon them!' Then came the real purpose of the letter: 'after occupying the Natroun lakes, and passing through Bahyreh, to punish my enemies and to restore tranquillity to that unhappy people, we have betaken ourselves to El Rahmânyeh. We have granted a general pardon to the province, which is now in a state of perfect tranquillity.'[22] Clearly, when it came to pacifying the *chouans* and drawing the new pope into a formal reconciliation much nearer home, Napoleon had already learnt a few lessons in the political advantages of quasi-religious overtures to influential clerical figureheads. In that respect at least, his republican loyalties were probably weakening even before Brumaire.

As first consul from November 1799 to May 1804, a period which, of course, included the life consulate as from 4 August 1802, Napoleon was the head of a regime which, officially at least, was still republican in form. While the more outspoken anticlericals who had served in the governments or assemblies of the Revolutionary Republic were in eclipse, a good many had survived the *coup* of Brumaire and continued to matter in the political life of the early Consulate.

---

[21] *Letters of Napoleon*, ed. Thompson, 33.   [22] Ibid. 60.

They included some notable spokesmen in the council of state, in the legislative body and the tribunate, for instance, and they proved a troublesome lobby when the first drafts of the Concordat were presented there. For them, any such reconciliation with the pope seemed a retrograde step, indeed a betrayal of republican principles. They saw it as an unscrupulous concession to the sort of religious 'fanaticism' which had not only wrecked the Constitutional Church and produced schism among the clergy themselves, but also inspired counter-revolution and the Vendéan civil war in France. Their public opposition to the Concordat was one of the factors which prompted Napoleon to 'purge' the membership of both legislative chambers during the early months of 1802.[23]

Why, then, did Napoleon want a Concordat? Background pressures, for a start, were conducive to the agreement in a wider popular sense. Even before Brumaire, there had been growing signs of a religious revival in France, helped by the State's official neutrality towards all cults after the decree of 3 Ventôse Year III (21 February 1795), and notwithstanding the Directory's new wave of anticlerical and anti-royalist measures which followed the *coup* of 18 Fructidor Year V (4 September 1797). The evidence of Professor John McManners suggests that the Constitutional Church itself had gained an unlikely new lease of life in the years 1795–7, thanks in large part to the efforts of Henri Grégoire, constitutional bishop of Blois, but that this had petered out after the Fructidor *coup* and ended in still greater demoralization.[24] In the period which had immediately followed, 'the Constitutional Church stood revealed as an historical accident, neither the Church of a nation nor the Church of a reformation'.[25]

By comparison, the revival also under way in local communities loyal to the refractory Church around the same time proved much more resilient and enduring, as the valuable research of Olwen Hufton on the years 1796–1801 has shown.[26] The revival was more evident in some provinces (notably the west country of France) than in others; it was stronger in the rural areas than in the larger towns; and it was more common among French women than their menfolk. Yet, such as it was, it had encouraged many refractory priests to come out of hiding and minister to their congregations more openly. It had led to a significant restoration of church fabrics, even if the public display of bells and other external signs of religion remained technically illegal under the terms of the Ventôse decree. Above all, perhaps, it had created an expectation among the orthodox Catholic laity that something would be done to restore their Church to

[23] Irene Collins, *Napoleon and his Parliaments 1800–1815* (London, 1979), 63–4, 69–71.
[24] McManners, *French Revolution and the Church*, 123–5.
[25] Ibid. 125.
[26] Olwen Hufton, 'The Reconstruction of a Church 1796–1801', in Gwynne Lewis and Colin Lucas (eds.), *Beyond the Terror: Essays in French Regional and Social History, 1794–1815* (Cambridge, 1983), 21–52.

its rightful place in the French state. In short, it had prepared the ground for Napoleon's reconciliation with Rome. At a more aesthetically refined level, Chateaubriand was another who had sensed that the time was ripe for, and that the educated Catholic faithful would be receptive to, the publication of his *Génie du christianisme* in 1802.

It is clear, all the same, that in making his insistent and at times rather threatening approaches to the new pope, Pius VII, elected in March 1800, Napoleon was acting not from personal religious convictions, but from motives carefully calculated to strengthen his regime. As McManners again has fairly commented, 'Bonaparte's own religion, a blend of sentimental memories and the soldier's fatalism, was real, but was only incidentally involved in his decision to negotiate with Rome'.[27] He had an instinctive sense that there was a new public mood in France which his government could satisfy—to its own advantage—and that popular religiosity among the Catholic laity, if formally recognized, could be harnessed to serve his political purposes. The Consular *arrêté* of 30 December 1799, one of his earliest official acts, had stipulated that Pius VI, who had died in French hands at Valence in the preceding August, should be given proper funeral honours. In another shrewd tactical move, he appointed the Abbé Bernier, the former *chouan* leader, to act as his main agent in the negotiations with Rome, which began in earnest after his victory over the Austrians at Marengo in June 1800.

The Concordat was originally agreed in secret and formally signed on 16 July 1801, after a year of difficult negotiations, and then ratified in Rome on 15 August and in Paris on 10 September following. It was not, however, published until Easter Sunday (8 April) 1802, a delay which was itself an ominous sign of Napoleon's real intentions. For, in the meantime, he had unilaterally added the so-called Organic Articles, without consulting Pius VII, and these were published at the same time, as if to imply mutual agreement. They imposed a much more obviously caesaro-papist formula on Church–State relations, which denied the pope's authority to intervene in many areas of the French Church, and at the same time strengthened the first consul's executive power to do so, not least through a whole battery of special and deliberately vague police regulations. All papal communications with the French clergy, as well as the training of priests, were thus to be brought under the strict control of the government.

By the terms of the Concordat, as published, Napoleon gained formal papal recognition of his *coup*, which he rightly assumed would effectively disarm the scattered remnants of the 'Catholic and Royal Army' in the western departments. Having rejected the idea of an official religion of State or a fully established

---

[27] McManners, *French Revolution and the Church*, 140.

Church, in the sense of an institution with vested constitutional privileges, he merely recognized Roman Catholicism as 'the religion of the vast majority of French citizens', a clause based on descriptive observation rather than prescriptive principles. At the same time, he obliged the pope to give a solemn undertaking that the Church accepted the loss of its alienated property, once and for all. Incumbent bishops were required to resign, although not necessarily excluded from reappointment, and their concordatory successors to swear a new oath of loyalty to the Consular government. The pope's canonical right of investiture was recognized, but the particular choice of bishops and archbishops had to be approved by the first consul.

Here, already, there was a potential minefield for disputes between the temporal and the ecclesiastical authorities. The rights of bishops over their parish clergy were also formally recognized, but the latter had again to be acceptable to the first consul, and they too were required to swear an oath of loyalty to his regime. The whole diocesan and parochial structure of the enlarged French Republic was to be redrawn, to the satisfaction of both contracting parties, and the reduced number of dioceses which eventually emerged were themselves grafted into the administrative structure of the civil state. All official salaries of the Catholic clergy, high and low, were to be paid by the State. In the event, however, only the incumbent *curés* of the chief towns of cantons, about one-fifth of the total parish clergy, were to enjoy assured tenure. All the rest (*desservants*), ministering in subsidiary stations (*succursales*), were considered provisional servants of the State and were removable at their bishops' pleasure. The bishops might establish cathedral chapters and seminaries in their dioceses, but these were not to enjoy any guarantee of State subsidies, and at the same time the government washed its hands of any obligation to maintain church fabrics. Finally, it is worth noting that the Concordat made no provision, officially at least, for the restoration of the old regular orders which had been suppressed by the Revolutionary laws.

While Napoleon's ecclesiastical policy was aimed primarily at regulating the Catholic Church, he extended it in due course to other religious communities in France, a further indication that no one cult would be allowed any exclusive privileges in his state. The Organic Articles for the Protestant sects, also published on 8 April 1802, were at once a declaration of his religious toleration towards them and an assertion of his administrative control over the Calvinist congregations and the Lutheran directories thereby formally established. There were then some 480,000 Calvinists and 200,000 Lutherans in France. As from 1804 their pastors also became salaried servants of the State.[28] If this last provision was never extended to the much smaller Jewish communities, which were

---

[28] Daniel Robert, *Les Églises réformées en France, 1800–1830* (Paris, 1961).

sometimes also the butt of Napoleon's crudest prejudices, his public policy towards them became gradually more conciliatory. In 1806 he brought their newly formed consistories under the same centralized control, and in the following year, by an agreement with their leaders, he created the Grand Sanhedrin of European rabbis.[29] This was again consistent with his general aim that all permissible religions would be organized from the top under the auspices of his government, and that their toleration would be conditional on their obedience to it.

In spite of Pius VII's growing anxiety over the terms and implementation of the Organic Articles, the Concordat achieved its purpose well enough in the early years. It enabled Napoleon to claim that he had 'pacified the Vendée', healed the schism in the French Church, and dissociated the papacy from the royalists in exile. It was, as McManners puts it, 'the supreme example of his genius for synthetic conciliation'.[30] It was a major factor in prompting the proclamation of the hereditary Empire by a *senatus-consultum* on 18 May 1804. Moreover, Pius was later persuaded to come to Paris for the Imperial coronation in Notre Dame on 2 December that same year. (Letizia, incidentally, now graced with the official title of 'Madame mère de l'Empereur', who was then in Rome, did not attend the ceremony and in fact disapproved of it: 'et si ça dure', as she once wryly commented.) As is well known, Napoleon insisted on crowning himself and then, in an act immortalized on canvas by Jacques-Louis David, his empress, while the pope sat stoically by. On the previous day, the emperor and Josephine had attended some sort of private ceremony conducted by Cardinal Fesch (but without other witnesses), which was intended to regularize their marriage according to Catholic rites; but the coronation itself passed without the celebration of any formal religious service. Some *sacre*!

Thus far, it seemed, Napoleon had succeeded in bending the pope to his will. His formula for Church–State relations was intended to ensure the obedience and subservience of the Catholic clergy to his own executive authority. That authority was to be transmitted down to the prefects at departmental and to the mayors at local level, all of whom he appointed himself, and this intrusive regulatory apparatus was further reinforced by his chosen police agents. For these reasons, the bishops have sometimes been likened to 'prefects in purple', the tenured parish clergy to 'mayors in black'—and all on appreciably lower salaries than their lay homologues. Presented in such terms, Napoleon's secular aims were clear and unamusing; but in taking his policy further, by his evident desire to combine the religious obedience of his subjects with his own heroic cult, he

[29] Simon Schwarzfuchs, *Napoleon, the Jews and the Sanhedrin* (London, 1979); Bernhard Blumenkranz (ed.), *Le Grand Sanhédrin de Napoléon* (Paris, 1979).
[30] McManners, *French Revolution and the Church*, 143.

sometimes achieved a rather more comical effect. By instituting 'Saint Napoleon's Day' in place of the traditional Feast of the Assumption on 15 August, his own birthday, he flaunted a sort of personal canonization by decree. The Imperial Catechism which the young were required to recite at their Sunday Schools as from May 1806, and which the pope never officially approved, contained the following remarkable clauses:

QUESTION. Are there special reasons why we should have a particular loyalty to Napoleon I, our emperor?

ANSWER. Yes there are; for God raised him up in difficult times to re-establish the public practice of the holy religion of our ancestors, and to protect it. He restored and preserved public order by his deep and active wisdom; he defends the state by the strength of his arm; he has become the Lord's Anointed by the consecration he received from the Sovereign Pontiff, the head of the Church Universal.

QUESTION. What ought one to think of those who fail in their duty towards our emperor?

ANSWER. According to the Apostle Saint Paul they are resisting the order established by God Himself and making themselves worthy of eternal damnation.[31]

The rupture in Napoleon's relations with Pius VII had a number of causes, of which some directly concerned the pope's temporal rights in Italy. The potential conflict between these two quite different personifications of sovereignty, already a cause of growing concern to the pope in his dealings with the French state, extended soon enough to the peninsula itself. In March 1805 the emperor created the satellite kingdom of Italy, centred on Lombardy, and shortly afterwards appointed his stepson, Eugène de Beauharnais, to rule as his viceroy there. While Napoleon was in Milan for his coronation in May that year, he gave an earnest of his intention to introduce the French Civil Code of 1804, with its provisions for divorce without the Church's approval, and also to reduce the influence of the clergy in schools throughout the new kingdom, in whose territory the papal Legations of Bologna, Ferrara, and Ravenna were now stranded.

If the old bogy of enforced secularization had thus returned to trouble Pius VII, as it had once alienated his predecessor from the French Republic, still more alarming developments much nearer home soon followed. Towards the end of 1805 French military occupation of the other Papal states began. At first, the process was limited, but over the next three to four years it was progressively extended, especially during 1808. Among other things, Napoleon simply imposed his Continental Blockade against British trade on the occupied territories. The papal legate to Paris, Caprara, ironically a conciliatory voice who had tried hard to prevent the breach, was recalled in 1808. What remained of the Papal states was annexed to the French Empire on 17 May 1809. It seems that

---

[31] Cited in Hales, *Napoleon and the Pope*, 89–90.

Napoleon had held back from outright annexation for at least two years, anticipating the stigma which would attach to the likely retribution of excommunication. Pius, for his part, also appears to have delayed wielding this ultimate
weapon for much the same time. But with the official annexation of his lands—
Rome itself was to be fully incorporated into the Empire on 17 February 1810—
there was no need for further restraint, and the bull of excommunication was
formally issued on 11 June 1809.

And so the die was cast. The conflict in Church–State relations, already
implicit in the manner of the Concordat's publication in April 1802, had now
deteriorated into an open rupture for all to see. The five years of deadlock which
followed mark one of the most extraordinary conflicts between temporal power
and spiritual authority history has ever known. Earlier writers have often compared it to the 'classic' confrontations of medieval times—of the Emperor Henry
IV against Gregory VII, or of King Henry II against Thomas Becket, for
instance—even if, in this new episode, there were to be no penitential visits to
Canossa and no murders in the cathedral. During the course of the conflict, and
certainly *without* Napoleon's specific orders in the first instance, Pius VII was
forcibly taken into exile. After the initial confusion, he was removed to Savona
(1809–12) and then to Fontainebleau (1812–14), an unyielding prisoner of the
excommunicated emperor.

The particular issues which had divided emperor and pope multiplied in due
course. Pius would not give his consent to Napoleon's divorce from Josephine,
which was officially announced by a *senatus-consultum* of 16 December 1809,
and then confirmed by an ecclesiastical court in Paris (the *Officialité*) on 14
January 1810. He would not attend the religious ceremony by which Napoleon
and Marie-Louise of Austria were married in Paris on 2 April 1810. He stood by
the thirteen 'black cardinals' who, having also absented themselves from the
ceremony, were stripped of their red robes and publicly humiliated by Napoleon
at an Imperial reception in the Tuileries shortly afterwards, and then taken into
custody. He would not give way on the crucial issue of investiture of new
bishops. Later, he retracted the agreement he had initially given to a new
concordat at Fontainebleau early in 1813. In the midst of the most abject
physical deprivation and humiliation, and in ailing health, his resolve held firm.

In the face of such determined opposition, Napoleon played and exhausted his
temporal hand, but ultimately lost his battle with the pope. It is clear from his
letters and utterances at the time that he simply did not understand the mind of
his captive. Over and over again he was frustrated by what he saw as the most
intransigent obstinacy. His conduct throughout the whole affair oscillated between despotic methods, rough-handling of the crudest sort, and more subtle
political intrigues, but all to no avail. Bullying tactics, including a blunt demand

towards the end of 1811 that the pope should resign and make way for someone 'with a stronger head', got him nowhere. More restrained formal gestures produced momentary hopes of a reconciliation, but never resolved the fundamental conflict of principles. Pius was powerless to resist the loss of his lands, his own imprisonment, and the physical dispersal of the papal curia (along with its archives and secretariat) in 1810, but he never renounced his canonical authority. Napoleon, who assumed that his temporal power would finally prevail, as it so often had on the battlefield, would not accept any spiritual authority which did not conform to his personal sovereignty. His own view of the proper submission of Church to State, by which Caesar was in effect empowered to define God's due, was altogether uncompromising.

Nowhere is this irreconcilable conflict better illustrated than in the investitures dispute. By 1811 a number of bishoprics in the French Empire had fallen vacant, and Pius VII would not accept any of Napoleon's nominees to fill them. To get round the difficulty, the emperor summoned a national council of French and Italian bishops to meet in Paris in June that year. He believed it would approve his plan that, in the event of continued papal refusal, the investiture of new bishops might be conducted by French metropolitans instead. After some initial doubt, Pius had already made his opposition to this proposal known, and indeed had also refused to recognize the validity of the council itself. Presented thus with a clear choice, the council duly swore an oath of allegiance to his canonical authority on the matter, and as a result several of the bishops were imprisoned.

In September 1811, however, Pius seemed to make a very significant concession. In a brief addressed to 'the Bishops of the Empire', he signalled his agreement to the proposal that French metropolitans might after all invest new bishops if the pope had not himself done so after a delay of six months. Napoleon's reaction, conveyed through his minister of cults, was to reject the overture out of hand, on the grounds that the pope had never recognized the council of Paris and had given no assurances on the status of bishoprics in the papal states. Some historians think that this was the vital moment when the only possible chance of a workable compromise was lost. The verdict of E. E. Y. Hales, for example, is clear:

Napoleon did not realize that by his intransigence, at this moment, he had overstepped the mark, had ruined the chance of a settlement that would have meant much to him. It was the cardinal error in his whole ecclesiastical policy, one of the great errors of his career, contributing as much as any to his eventual downfall.[32]

The personal and often dramatic nature of the rupture between emperor and pope has its own fascination, but it may disguise the underlying structural

---

[32] Ibid. 163–4.

difficulties which also hampered the smooth implementation of the Concordat after 1802. These, too, tell us something about Napoleon's views on the proper role of the Catholic Church within his civil state. The subject has been skilfully analysed by Jean Godel in a digest of his own more detailed research on the concordatory diocese of Grenoble (department of the Isère).[33] According to this author, Napoleon had some understanding of the disputes which had often troubled the Church under the old regime, as well as of their political implications, and was determined to prevent their recurrence under his regime. If he fundamentally approved of the episcopal principle, which was consistent with his own concept of strict hierarchical authority within the Church, he was as firmly hostile to any suggestion of ultramontane loyalties. On the other hand, his assumed gallicanism had no place for the advocates of presbyterian principles, most notably among the lower clergy of the eighteenth century, who had themselves been influenced by the earlier Richerist belief that the Church should be governed by the whole community of its clergy. His preferred model here was Bossuet, who had preached the unity and obedience of the Church, formulated the celebrated Gallican Articles of 1682, and supported Louis XIV in his dispute with Innocent XI. What Napoleon wanted was to strengthen the episcopal structure in the concordatory Church, while detaching it from papal influence and interference, and to reassert the historic Gallican liberties, but without their earlier Jansenist associations.

By such a selective formula, Napoleon tried in effect to combine those elements of the episcopal and Gallican traditions of the French Church in ways that would most effectively serve his civil rule. This, in essence, is what he aimed to achieve through the Organic Articles. He had not reckoned with the pope's resolute defence of his canonical authority, and with the reluctance of the French bishops to render everything unto Caesar. Moreover, by involving Pius VII as an official signatory to the Concordat, he had ensured from the start that the agreement could not work well without the pope's continued blessing. Godel thinks that the very subservience Napoleon had tried so hard to drum into the French episcopate was ultimately bound to transfer to Rome, especially when the secular master had fallen not only from grace but from power. Even his eventual release of the pope and vague talk of restoring the Papal states to their historic ruler in 1814 were hardly signs of contrition. They were a calculated but failed attempt to play the pope off as a pawn against Murat, the satellite king of Naples, who had entered into treacherous dealings with the Allies in the hope of saving his throne and incorporating the Papal states into his kingdom.

    [33] Jean Godel, 'L'Église selon Napoléon', *Revue d'histoire moderne et contemporaine*, 17 (1970), 837–45; see also his *La Reconstruction concordataire dans le diocèse de Grenoble après la Révolution (1802–1809)* (Grenoble, 1968).

In short, Napoleon had wanted a Gallican Church reconstructed under his secular authority; what he got, ironically, was an ultramontane Church whose allegiance to the pope was if anything stronger than before. In this way, Napoleon had indirectly and unintentionally contributed something to the Catholic revival of the nineteenth century. Indeed, his brutal treatment of Pius VII and his loyal cardinals, as well as his crass handling of the French bishops, had ensured that that revival would have an ultramontane focus, which we see in the writings of Joseph de Maistre, Louis de Bonald, and Lamennais, among others. The pope's release from captivity and triumphant return to Rome were their own vindication of his spiritual authority. The final peace settlement at the Vienna Congress in 1815 restored his temporal rights over the Papal states in Italy.

The various writings which together constitute the St Helena record of Napoleon's final exile do not on the whole suggest that the fallen emperor, even in his more reflective moments, had too many regrets about what he had actually done, although he had many about the still greater ambitions he had not been able to fulfil. He had never been one to admit his own mistakes while in power, and he was not much more disposed to do so in the nemesis of captivity. However reluctantly, he came of course to realize that the disaster of the Russian campaign of 1812 and the drain of the Peninsular War had seriously weakened him in the closing years of the Empire. But then he was, after all, a military realist who did not spare himself the same tough tactical analysis he applied to enemy commanders. More significant for our present purposes is that he returned many times during his conversations with Las Cases, Gourgaud, Bertrand, Montholon, O'Meara, and Antommarchi to his former relations with Pius VII, and *was* prepared to acknowledge that his ecclesiastical policy had ultimately undermined his own position. As usual, he was inclined to lay the blame on others, and to claim that his beneficent and peaceful intentions had always been misunderstood by his opponents.

In the course of these reminiscences, Napoleon often revealed a surprisingly wide knowledge of ecclesiastical history, which he again always interpreted in relation to his own policy towards the Church, and in a blatantly partisan way. The extended passages which now follow capture the flavour of one such conversation, among the longest and perhaps the most important of all, as recorded by Las Cases on 17 August 1816:

When I seized on the helm of affairs, I had already fixed ideas of all the primary elements by which society is bound together; I had weighed all the importance of religion; I was convinced, and I determined to re-establish it. But the resistance I had to overcome, in restoring catholicism, would scarcely be credited. I should have been more willingly followed, had I hoisted the standard of protestantism. This reluctance was carried so far, that in the Council of State, where I found great difficulty in getting the Concordat adopted, several yielded only in forming a plan to extricate themselves from it. . . .

By the help of catholicism I attained, much more effectually [than by protestantism], all the grand results I had in view. In the interior, at home, the smaller number was swallowed up by the greater, and I relied upon my treating the former with such an equality, that there would be shortly no motive for marking the difference. Abroad, the Pope was bound to me by catholicism; and with my influence, and our forces in Italy, I did not despair, sooner or later, by some means or another, of obtaining for myself the direction of that Pope, and from that time, what an influence! What a lever of opinion on the rest of the world![34]

So far, at least, we may go along with the account as an honest enough statement of Napoleon's *intentions*. But his version of the *effects* of his ecclesiastical policy seems a fairly typical case of selective amnesia:

When the real particulars of my disputes with the Pope shall be made public, the world will be surprised at the extent of my patience, for it is known, that I was not of a very enduring temper. When he left me, after my coronation, he felt a secret disgust at not having obtained the compensations he thought he had deserved. But, however grateful I might have been in other respects, I could not, after all, make a traffic of the interests of the empire by way of acquitting my own obligations, and, I was, besides, too proud to exhibit a seeming acknowledgement, that I had purchased his kindnesses. He had hardly set foot on the soil of Italy, when the intriguers and mischief-makers, the enemies of France, took advantage of the disposition he was in, to govern his conduct, and from that instant every thing was hostile on his part. He no longer was the gentle, the peaceable *Chiaramonti*, that worthy bishop of Imola, who had at so early a period shown himself worthy of the enlightened state of the century. His signature was thenceforth affixed to acts only which characterized the Gregories and Bonifaces more than him. Rome became the focus of all the plots hatched against us. I strove in vain, to bring him back by the force of reason, but I found it impossible to ascertain his sentiments.[35]

The conversation of 17 August 1816 ended with a counter-historical hypothesis that can only be described as fantastic. Speculating on what he would have done had the Russian campaign turned out differently, and if Pius VII had not retracted his agreement to the concordat of Fontainebleau, Napoleon conjured up this most unlikely scenario:

What then would have been the result, had I returned victorious and triumphant? I had consequently obtained the separation, which was so desirable, of the spiritual from the temporal, which is so injurious to his Holiness, and the commixture of which produces disorder in society in the name and by the hands of him, who ought himself to be the centre of harmony; and from that time, I intended to exalt the Pope beyond measure, to surround him with grandeur and honours. I should have succeeded in suppressing all his anxiety for the loss of his temporal power; I should have made an idol of him; he would have remained near my person. Paris would have become the capital of Christendom, and

[34] Las Cases, *Mémorial de Sainte Hélène*, iii (pt. 5), 201–2, 202–3.   [35] Ibid. 211–12.

I should have governed the religious as well as the political world. . . . I should have had my religious as well as my legislative sessions; my councils would have constituted the representation of Christianity, and the Popes would have only been the presidents. I should have called together and dissolved those assemblies, approved and published their discussions as Constantine and Charlemagne had done . . .[36]

Now, it would have been interesting to know what Pius VII's reaction to such a reconstruction of his relations with Napoleon might have been. He died in 1823, the same year in which Las Cases published his *Memorial of St Helena*. We know that he bore the former emperor no lasting grudges, and that he intervened officially on at least one occasion to persuade the British government to ease the physical conditions of his captivity. He seems also to have remained genuinely grateful for what Napoleon had done, by the Concordat, and in spite of their later rift, to improve the lot of the Catholic laity in France.

But, on the specific matter of the text cited above, Pius would surely have found Napoleon's recollection of the negotiations which had led to the short-lived concordat of Fontainebleau a gross distortion of their real encounter. While it is true that the exact terms of the week-long talks between emperor and pope in January 1813 are not known, since no detailed formal record of them has survived, some facts at least are clear. A confidential document, signed by Pius under persistent pressure, was certainly produced on 25 January. News of it, though not its specific terms, was also published in the *Moniteur* two days later, apparently in breach of Napoleon's assurance that the secrecy of the discussions would be respected. The pope, who felt he had been deceived and immediately regretted having signed the agreement, announced his retraction in a letter to the emperor soon afterwards. Napoleon chose to ignore this letter and, for the next year, pretended that the new concordat was still in force.

In any event, there was never any doubt that Pius had resolutely opposed the suggestion that the Holy See might be removed from Rome to Paris, or to Avignon, as had also apparently been mooted by Napoleon. It is equally improbable that he, of all popes, who had already suffered the privations of prolonged exile in defence of his spiritual authority, would have consented to Church assemblies at the emperor's pleasure, and to a merely formal presidential role in them. Nothing in his life or work suggests that the prospect of being set up as an 'idol' on Napoleon's terms, surrounded with 'grandeur and honours', would have attracted him in the least. The whole idea, frankly, would surely have appalled him. In suggesting otherwise, Napoleon was not reconstructing any plausible version of the past, even as it might have been; he was anticipating one of the more fanciful myths of his future legend.

---

[36] Ibid. 214.

Apart from such musings about his ecclesiastical policy, Napoleon also had ample time on St Helena to redefine his attitude to religion in a more general way. Thus, on 7–8 June 1816, for example, he told Las Cases: 'I am assuredly very far from being an atheist, but I cannot believe all that I am taught in spite of my reason, without being false and a hypocrite.'[37] Two months later, in the same important conversation of 17 August referred to earlier, he returned to the subject with a rather different emphasis: 'the absence of religious faith has never . . . influenced me in any respect, and I never doubted the existence of God; for, if my reason was inadequate to comprehend it, my mind was not the less disposed to adopt it. My nerves were in sympathy with that sentiment.'[38] After the expulsion of Las Cases from St Helena in December 1816, Napoleon had to turn to other—less trusted—companions. Particular interest attaches to the memoirs of Francesco Antommarchi, a fellow Corsican, whom he did not like, but who served as his physician during the last eighteen months of his life. To this witness we owe the record of Napoleon's celebrated statement in April 1821, only three weeks before his death, that 'wanting to be an atheist does not make you one'.[39] The first sentence of Napoleon's last will, dated 15 April 1821, formally announced that 'I die in the apostolic and Roman faith, in whose bosom I was born more than fifty years ago.'[40] Four days later, he gave the following instructions to his confessor: 'when I am dead, you will place your altar at my head, in the room where I lie in state. You will continue to say Mass, you will perform all the customary ceremonies, you will not cease until I am in the ground.'[41] Here, at the end of his life, there was at least a stricter outward conformity with Catholic rites than there had been at his birth and baptism.

And so, what finally may be said about the nature of Napoleon's religion? Somehow or other, the definition would have to include the terrible logic of human sacrifice which, as a military commander, he had never allowed to trouble his conscience. It would have to include the nostalgic sentimentality which so often throughout his life drew him back to the remembered past of his youth in Ajaccio—how, much later, he could still be moved by the sound of church bells floating across a meadow. It would have to include his intuitive understanding of the force of popular religiosity—when, for instance, as a conquering hero on his first Italian campaign, he saw the common people process to Mass, women to the fore. It would have to include the calculated pragmatism of his Concordat with Pius VII, as well as the impelling belief in his own ability, and in imperious defiance of his excommunication, to browbeat the pope into submission when

---

[37] Ibid. ii (pt. 4), 130.   [38] Ibid. iii (pt. 5), 201.

[39] *Mind of Napoleon*, ed. Herold, 31; from F. Antommarchi, *Mémoires; ou, Les Derniers Momens de Napoléon* (2 vols.; Paris, 1825), ii. 118.

[40] *Mind of Napoleon*, ed. Herold, 34.   [41] Ibid.; from Antommarchi, *Mémoires*, ii. 118–19.

that initial agreement later turned sour. It would have to include his intellectual doubts about formal religious doctrines, but at the same time his innate belief in God, which never deserted him. It would have to include his almost superstitious belief in Destiny, and more especially in his own destiny, which he thought lay within his power to control or let slip—when, for example, faced with the knowledge on 23 October 1812 that Kutuzov had cut off his retreat along the Maloyaroslavets road, he asked not whether luck had let him down, but whether *he* had let down his luck.[42] And it would have to include an instinctive respect for family decorum, and most of all for the mother he always revered, which led him at the end to choose a proper Catholic burial.

[42] P.-P. de Ségur, *Un aide de camp de Napoléon: Mémoires du comte de Ségur*, ed. Louis de Ségur (3 vols., Paris, 1894–5), ii. 219–20.

12

Religious Reactions in Post-Revolutionary French Literature: Chateaubriand, Constant, Mme de Staël, Joseph de Maistre

Richard Fargher

For again, everything is connected. Inconstancy or staleness in love, religious unbelief in countless forms, drab or terrifying, servility in politics are symptoms of our age. A sorry epoch, in which the decrepitude of civilisation has killed nature, and in which man is bereft of hope in heaven, dignity on earth, and refuge in his own heart.[1]

In this draft for a preface for the second edition of his bleak novel *Adolphe*, written the year after Waterloo, Benjamin Constant, his political career apparently ruined, his emotional life in turmoil, bewails the degradation of occupied France. Reactions to the Revolution had been varied. Burke, in 1790, set the standard for frenzied vituperation of its horrors:

the sanctuary of the most splendid palace in the world, which they left swimming in blood, polluted by massacre and strewed with scattered limbs and mutilated carcasses . . . their heads were stuck on spears, and led the procession; whilst the royal captives who followed in the train were slowly moved along, amidst the horrid yells, and shrilling screams, and frantic dances, and infamous contumelies, and all the unutterable abomination of the furies of Hell, in the abused shape of the vilest of women . . . but if, in the moment of riot, and in a drunken delirium from the hot spirit drawn out of the alembick of Hell which in France is now so furiously boiling . . .[2].

I am grateful to Dr Joanna Kitchin of the University of Edinburgh for her comments on this essay.

[1] Benjamin Constant, *Adolphe*, ed. G. Rudler (Manchester, 1919), Preface, p. xiii n. Not in later editions. Cf. F. R. de Chateaubriand, *Mémoires d'outre-tombe* (3rd Pléiade edn., 2 vols.; Paris, 1957) (hereafter *MOT*), ii. 493: 'There are men who, after swearing an oath to the Republic one and indivisible, to the Directoire in five persons, to the Consulat in three, the Empire in one only, to the first Restoration, to the Additional Act to the Constitutions of the Empire, to the Second Restoration, have still something left to swear to Louis-Philippe.' All translations are mine.

[2] E. Burke, *Reflections on the Revolution in France*, ed. Conor Cruise O'Brien (Harmondsworth, 1969), 164–5, 189.

André Chénier, not long before his own decapitation, bid us be sick at the thought of the *voyeurs* surrounding the guillotine:

> Pour moi, j'ai voulu que leur noble mémoire
> Allât faire vomir un jour
> L'érudit qui lira cet hymne de leur gloire,
> Monument d'estime et d'amour.[3]

Mockery of Christianity, in more than Voltairian fashion, continued. Parny achieved notoriety with *La Guerre des Dieux* (the Norse dog Fingriss snaps up the Holy Pigeon, and the Gods mistake the Virgin for Venus), but in 1799 such scurrilities were superfluous: the death of Pope Pius VI in that year, a prisoner in French hands, gave enemies of the Church reason to believe that the papacy, and Christianity itself, were finished. Anticlerical journalists seized with glee on Chateaubriand's infelicities in *Atala* and *Le Génie du Christianisme* (Father Aubry's aquiline nose and long beard sublime in their quietude, and aspiring towards the tomb by their natural inclination towards the ground; the loving-kindness of God demonstrated by the crocodile's egg). Catholic writers were satirized by Marie-Joseph Chénier (anti-*philosophe* propagandists referred to his brother André as Abel) in *Les Nouveaux Saints*, which included Mme de Genlis, formerly mistress of Philippe-Egalité, and now a pious zealot. But the Church was now safe, restored to France by General Bonaparte, on his own terms, it is true. The irreligion of the *philosophes* was succeeded by loss of faith in the Enlightenment, whose fruits seemed so bitter.[4] There were spectacular recantations, such as that of La Harpe. Joubert 'returned to prejudices' in 1792, commented that 'the Revolution drove my mind out of the real world which it made too horrible for me', and occupied himself with piety and an aesthetic quest. (This did not stop him from remarking in his *Carnets* that Parny's poems were 'honeyed blasphemies, or rather varnished filth. He has a eunuch's heart and soul, but his impotence has some grace.'[5]) Senancour's *Oberman*, in 1804, analytically, and often hauntingly, rejects all consolation whether in religion, nature, society, art, or love:

I review the sad memory of long lost years. I observe how the future, always alluring, changes and shrinks as it draws near. Smitten by a whiff of death in the ghastly glimmer of the present, it pales at the very moment when it should be enjoyed; leaving behind it the allurements which masked its already aged glamour, it passes, solitary, forlorn,

---

[3] A. Chénier, *Poèmes*, ed. F. Scarfe (Oxford, 1961), 101.

[4] *La Décade philosophique*, the organ of the Idéologues, still campaigned violently against the Church from 1794 to 1801, then less stridently until its suppression by Napoleon in 1807.

[5] La Harpe's *Mélanie*, an attack on convents (1778), was banned. *Du fanatisme dans la langue révolutionnaire* (1797) was a violent attack on the *philosophes*. See D. P. Kinloch, *The Thought and Art of Joseph Joubert* (Oxford, 1992), 23–4; *Pensées de Joubert* (Paris, 1928), 338. Joubert's friend Fontanes provided him with a post as *inspecteur-général* in Napoleon's state education system.

dragging with it its hideous and exhausted spectre, as though insulting the weariness caused by the sinister gliding of its eternal chain.[6]

There were, however, voices which discerned, in the cataclysmic energies un-leashed by the Jacobins, the beginning of a new stage in history, and the possibility, however remote, of better things. Chateaubriand's perfervid style is not that of a passive victim:

Where are they living, these puny minds, who pertinently calculate what should have been done by what was done before, and who see in the present struggle only battles lost and won, and not the Spirit of France, in the convulsions of a crisis brought on by force of circumstance, rending asunder, like Hercules on Mount Oeta, those who dare ap-proach it, hurling their bloody limbs upon the pallid plains of Italy and Flanders, and about to turn upon itself its frenzied hands? One might surmise that there exist epochs, uncharted but regular, when the face of the earth is renewed. We have the misfortune to be born at the time of one of these great revolutions: whatever be its result, happy or unhappy for men unborn, the present generation is lost: so was it in the Vth and VIth centuries, when the peoples of Europe, like rivers, burst forth from their courses.

From the depths of grief, Mme de Staël ponders on a providential future:

Man is astray in life, like a being launched into an alien element . . . By sorrow alone he is aware of himself, and the continuity of sorrow is all that remains to link our days. Shall we . . . see virtue in power, crime contemned, innocence at peace? Alas, Providence alone knows in what epoch this future will begin for us.

Joseph de Maistre finds a message of hope in St Paul:

There is only violence in the universe; but we have been spoiled by modern philosophy, which said that all is well, whereas evil has sullied everything and, in a very true sense, all is evil, since nothing is in its right place. '*All creatures groan* (St Paul to the Romans, VIII, 22 *et seq.*), and strive, with effort and pain, toward another order of things.[7]

Chateaubriand was familiar with political and religious change. Two years before the Revolution he had been tonsured by the bishop of Saint-Malo, as a prelimi-nary to an eventual income of 200,000 *livres* a year from the Knights of Malta. The Revolution abolished such ecclesiastical abuses. In 1791 he was in Protestant America, where he observed not only the 'Philadelphia Quakeresses with their grey frocks, little uniform hats, and pale faces', but also acquired some first-hand acquaintance with religious practices of the Native Indians. In 1794, invalided out of the Army of the Princes, an impoverished refugee, he was given hospitality

---

[6] É. de Senancour, *Oberman*, ed. A. Monglond (2 vols.; Paris, 1979), i. 175.

[7] F. R. de Chateaubriand, *Essai sur les Révolutions* (Paris, 1978), i. 153–4; Mme de Staël, *Des circonstances actuelles qui peuvent terminer la Révolution et des principes qui doivent fonder la République en France*, ed. L. Omacini (Paris, 1979), 2–3. Joseph de Maistre, *Considérations sur la France* (Lyons, 1852), 2–3. The *Essai* was first published in London in 1796; *Des circonstances* was written in 1798–9, but was overtaken by events; the *Considérations* was published in Basle in 1797.

by the Revd Mr Ives at his house in Bridge St, Bungay, in Suffolk. His gratitude to certain Anglican clergy, 'wise, learned, philosophical, generous men', caused him 'to deplore, from the bottom of his heart' the inevitable ruination which he predicted for the Anglican Church in his *Essai sur les Révolutions* on which he had set to work the year before. Part II of the *Essai* surveys political and religious change from Alexander the Great to the Revolution, and speculates on what religion would replace Christianity. In 1801 General Bonaparte restored the French Church, as 'the religion of the majority of Frenchmen', by a Concordat with Pope Pius VII. On the Wednesday before Easter 1802, Chateaubriand's *Le Génie du Christianisme ou Beautés morales et poétiques de la religion chrétienne* was published. In gratitude for this pro-Concordat propaganda, Bonaparte appointed him secretary at the French embassy in Rome, where in 1803 he was presented to Pius VII, 'pale, sad and religious, the true pontiff of tribulations'. Six years later this same pontiff, like his predecessor, was arrested by the French, and on the orders of the Emperor Napoleon imprisoned, first at Savona, then at Fontainebleau. Chateaubriand's *Les Martyrs ou le Triomphe de la religion chrétienne* was begun in 1804. Among numerous other things, it gives a sympathetic portrait of Greek paganism in the early days of Christianity, and tells a lurid tale of the expiring Druid cult in his native Brittany.[8]

For an assessment of the appropriateness to its times of *Le Génie*, its possible influences, and its weaknesses, one can do worse than read Chateaubriand himself, in Part 2, Book 13, 10, of his *Mémoires d'outre-tombe*. It would be tedious to attempt here a summary of its 907 chapters. Without denying any Catholic doctrines, Chateaubriand envelopes them in an aura of mystery, sentiment, and mythology, in his attempt, should conversion be impossible, to arouse a comfortable and benevolent attitude to religion in the hearts of his readers, who had been brought up in an epoch when irreligion was the fashion, had lived through the years when the ancient rites were abolished, or driven underground, and who now, with the Treaty of Amiens signed, could hope to enjoy peace and reconciliation. The strictly theological discussions tend to be presented in an authoritative language, as though urging the reader, dazzled by the author's inexhaustible learning, to skip them and turn to more palatable fare. Thus Part 1, Book 1, 7, does contain the words *Hoc est corpus meum* and 'the direct mystery of the real presence of God in the consecrated bread'. It dispatches in seven sentences the doctrines of the fall, the incarnation, and the redemption. Then, after a not altogether transparent gloss ('the Word, concealed under the emblem of bread, is for the eye of the body a perceptible object, whereas it remains an intellectual object for the eye of the soul . . .'), he continues: 'If this lofty and

---

[8] Chateaubriand, *MOT* i. 158, 220, 449; *Essai* (Pléiade edn., 1978), i. 420.

mysterious philosophy of which we have merely outlined a few features should terrify readers, let them nevertheless consider how luminous this metaphysic is compared with that of Pythagoras, of Plato, of Timaios, of Carneades, of Epicurus.' (There is evidence that the young Chateaubriand was not without a wicked sense of fun.) The chapter also speaks of the delicate souls and innocent tongues of first communicants, the spring countryside, seedtime and harvest, and the high value of Christian rites proven because 'they were practised by our fathers, the mothers who rocked our cradles were Christian, and religious chants accompanied the coffins of our forefathers and wished peace to their ashes'. Part 4, Book 1, Chapters 5 and 6 (*Explication de la messe, Cérémonies et prières de la messe*) link the Mass with ancient traditions of sacrifice, extol the aesthetic attractiveness of the liturgy, and give as specimens of the Gospel at Mass the woman taken in adultery, the good Samaritan, and 'suffer the little children to come unto me'. The Creed is reduced to *Credo in unum Deum* and belief in a God who gives us such examples as these Gospels. The words of consecration are omitted, but there is an approximate translation of the *Supra quae propitio ac sereno vulto* . . . and *Supplices te rogamus* . . . , followed by 'At these words the mystery is accomplished, the Lamb descends to be sacrificed'. For those unable to accept this, Chateaubriand supplies, with the assurance 'that they depict with the utmost exactitude the Christian sacrifice', twenty lines from a poem on All Souls Day by his friend Louis de Fontanes:

'O solemn moment! this congregation bowed low, this church with its mossy porches, this bronze lamp which, in ancient times the symbol of the sun and eternity, gleams before the Most High, suspended there day and night; the majesty of a God come down amongst us, the tears, the vows, the incense rising toward the altar, and the young beauties who, under the maternal eye, make even sweeter by their innocent voices the touching pomp of religion; this organ, now silent, this pious quietude, the invisible union of earth and heaven, all kindle, swell, move the man of feeling; he as it were crosses into that inaccessible world where, on harps of gold, the immortal Seraphim chant hymns without end at the feet of Jehovah. Then on all sides, a God is heard speaking; he hides himself to the learned, reveals himself to the tender heart. Rather than be proved, he must be felt'.

Fontanes became *grand maître de l'Université*—head of the Emperor Napoleon's state education system—in 1808.

Bird migration, Dido, maternal crocodiles, *Paradise Lost*, Gregorian chant, the virgin of the last love, the road to Compostela, the ruins of Palmyra, village craftsmen, Midnight Mass, Twelfth Night, the Fathers, Fingal's Cave, country churchyards, storms, French missionaries in Canada lost to the English and in Louisiana not yet sold to the States, sisters of charity, the Middle Ages—there is an endless torrent to prove that Voltairianism was bad and that Christianity is aesthetically attractive, morally uplifting, civililizing, and socially and economically useful. No argument is unworthy of his holy task:

In the very interest of her beauty a woman must be pious—Woman, who has a natural instinct for mystery, who never uncovers more than half her graces and her thought, who can be divined but not known, who as mother and maiden is full of secrets, who pleases above all by her ignorance, who was formed for virtue and the most mysterious sentiment, shamefastness and love; will this woman, renouncing the gentle instinct of her sex, seek with a weak and reckless hand to lift the thick curtain which conceals the Divinity? . . . What man of good sense would wish to wed an impious helpmeet?

(Chateaubriand did, in 1834, hope for the legal emancipation of women.) One comes with relief to a paraphrase of Burke:

The conjuring up of spirits, necromancy, are merely the religious instinct among the people, and one of the most striking proofs of the need for a religion. Men are very close to believing anything when they believe nothing: there are soothsayers when the Prophets are gone, magic spells when religious rites have been abandoned, and the dens of the sorcerers are opened when the temples of the Lord are shut down.[9]

The sincerity of Chateaubriand's religion has been much debated. His claim that the news of his mother's death inspired him to write a Christian work—'I wept and I believed'—does not coincide with known facts. He certainly intended that *Le Génie* should help his career. But he was not one of those time-serving hypocrites denounced by Constant. The First Consul, to whom he dedicated the second edition, was seen by some Royalists as a new General Monk—the Cromwellian who, with an army at his command, brought back Charles II. When Bonaparte murdered the duc d'Enghien in 1804, Chateaubriand resigned his new appointment as minister in the Valais. In 1807, at more than slight personal risk—Joubert reports that 'the Thunderbolt in person warned Fontanes that if his friend did it again he would be struck'—he published his famous article in the *Mercure*:

When, in the silence of abjection, only the chains of the slave and the voice of the informer ring in the ear; when all trembles before the tyrant, and it is as dangerous to incur his favour as to merit his disgrace; the historian appears, charged with the vengeance of the peoples. In vain does Nero prosper, Tacitus has already been born in the Empire.

It is plain why Mme de Staël, to whom he was not always kind or fair, addressed him (in English) as 'my dear Francis'. There can be no good reason to reject his statement that his pious mother's influence remained with him, that he alter-

---

[9] Chateaubriand, *MOT* i. 1051; *Génie du Christianisme* (Pléiade edn., 1978), iii. 356; Burke, *Reflections*, 187–8.

nated between doubt and faith, and that 'there was no Christian more believing, and no man more unbelieving, than himself'.[10]

The *débutant* presented at Court in 1787, the 2nd lieutenant in the Regiment of Navarre, survived into the age of railways and radicalism. He had been minister of state, minister plenipotentiary at Berlin, ambassador in London, ambassador in Rome. He had kept his oath to the king, just as, whatever his shortcomings, literary and personal, he had defended his Church. He knew that the Bourbons were out of place in the changed world of 1830, but he refused to serve the Orléanist usurper Louis-Philippe. His own political career was ended, but he knew that, to survive, the Church of Rome, 'stable in its doctrines, mobile in its enlightenment', must adjust itself to change. 'Far from being at its end, the religion of the liberator has barely entered its third period, its political period, liberty, equality, fraternity.' He had hoped, while still in office, to guide France at the head of 'la grande levée du genre humain', the mobilization of mankind for 'innovation, enterprise, discovery'. (De Gaulle was an admirer of the *Mémoires d'outre-tombe*, as was Proust.) But he also doubted whether industry would really produce a desirable prosperity, or whether, 'the barren dream of sterile minds', it would destroy the imaginative faculty, poetry and the arts, reducing men to 'cogs in a machine, atoms in organized matter'. He was horrified by a society in which some individuals had millions, and others subsisted in filth and squalor. In 1831, on the road to the Simplon in the service of the Bourbons, he encountered 'a little girl, half naked, who was dancing with her goat, seeking alms from a rich, well-dressed young man who was travelling post, a uniformed courier ahead, two footmen sitting at the rear of his carriage. Do you think that such a distribution of property can continue? Do you think that it does not justify popular uprisings?' He describes the avid bourgeois under Louis-Philippe as 'a stunted herd, without conviction, with no political or religious faith, grasping at money and office like paupers at a distribution of free food'. The Saint-Simonians, the Fouriéristes, the Owenites, the socialists, the Communists, even his friend Lamennais now that he had broken with Rome, failed to convince him. He speculates on the disadvantages of a future world state, on the possible colonization of other planets. He foretells that the search for a just society will produce catastrophe and bloodshed, because 'the law of blood and sacrifice is everywhere; God submitted his son to the nails of the cross to renew the order of the universe'. 'All philanthropic acts, all progressive ideas, whatever their name, whatever their imperfections, are the Word made flesh.' The seed may fall on stony ground, but if one seed remains, it will spring up, and a second incarnation

[10] Joubert, *Correspondance*, ed. P. de Raynal (Paris, 1924), 165; Chateaubriand, *MOT* i. 570; ii. 735, 932.

of the Catholic spirit will renew society. Ages may elapse, civilizations may disappear, Christianity may be driven back into the desert. If there is to be a future, powerful and free, it is far below any visible horizon. It can only be attained by help of 'this Christian hope, whose wings extend as all seem to betray it, a hope longer than time and stronger than adversity'.[11] Chateaubriand died in 1848, the year of revolutions and the *Communist Manifesto*.

Benjamin Constant's preoccupation with religion and the study of religion presumably derives from his own emotional needs. His use of the mantra l.v.d.D.s.f. (the will of God be done) in his *Journaux intimes* may have been a refuge from his inability to accept his own decisions, or, even, himself. He was addicted to gambling, in which chance took control. He had an obsessive horror of death: 'Each one of us knows that this hour will be terrible, accompanied by convulsions of dire portent, and by pains unknown which none has been able to describe and which no being alive can conjecture. These pains, these convulsions, after a last effort, are followed by a silence which will never be broken.' Adolphe is astounded that any man should think himself strong enough to dare reject religion: 'in the dense darkness that enshrouds us, is there a glimmer which we can reject? amid the torrent that bears us away, is there a branch which we refuse to grasp?'[12] But whatever positive beliefs his incisive intellect allowed him to hold—he was too sceptical to embrace atheism, the word agnostic had not been invented, and he claimed Protestant Christian affiliation—as a writer he was, according to his own statement, 'merely the mouthpiece for prevailing ideas'. An exaggeration, no doubt, but certainly in *De l'esprit de conquête et de l'usurpation dans leurs rapports avec la civilisation européenne*, published in Hanover in January 1814 two months before Napoleon's first abdication, his socio-religious message ('For again, everything is connected') is part of his political campaign. His apparently counter-revolutionary dislike of Republican centralization with its hectares and myriametres, his approval of local traditions, usages, and languages, his discovery of something miraculous, mysterious, venerable in legitimate monarchy and an ancient hereditary aristocracy, are part of his denunciation of Napoleon's system of rule.[13] In the chapter 'Religion under Arbitrary Government', Constant, the former disciple of the Enlightenment, uses the rhetoric of the anti-*philosophe* propagandists whose fashionable success he elsewhere deplores. The despot has demeaned the Church, 'that divine power come down

---

[11] Ibid. ii. 482–4; *Revue des deux mondes* (15 Apr. 1834), in ibid. ii. 1047–52; ibid. ii. 765; *Vie de Rancé*, in *Œuvres romanesques*, i. 1067, 1390; *MOT* ii. 916–33.

[12] B. Constant, *De la religion, livre premier, suivi d'extraits des autres livres*, ed. P. Deguise (Lausanne, 1971), 178; *Adolphe*, 94.

[13] B. Constant, *De l'esprit de conquête*, ed. Alfred Roulin (Paris, 1957), 1014–20, 1017, 1031–4.

from Heaven to astound or reform the earth'; its ministers, sullying the sublimity
of its sacred books with the sophism of politics no longer, like Bossuet, make the
ancient vaults resound with the accents of courage and conscience, but stammer
mutilated words at the foot of its enslaved altars, bless Heaven for the achievements of crime, and blaspheme against the divine will by accusing it of complicity. Better the yoke of religion, a nation bowed down under superstition, for at
least it is sincere in its errors, than political despotism, served by intelligent,
enlightened unbelievers, a breed which, in its voluntary degeneration, denies the
Gods but crawls and trembles before a man who, from the height of his throne,
throws them a salary. 'Such a breed has fallen from the rank which Providence
assigned to the human race.'[14]

But his emotion was more than political. From the 1780s onwards,
intermittent research into comparative religion was, for Constant, a way to find
himself. 'It is by delving into facts . . . and coming up against the innumerable
obstacles which they put in the way of unbelief, that I found myself compelled
to withdraw into religious ideas.'[15] His *De la perfectibilité de l'espèce humaine*,
published in 1829, outlines his hope for moral and social progress. The five
volumes of *De la religion* appeared between 1825 and 1831. The evolution over
the years of his religious writings is extremely complex, and still in parts obscure.
Religious sentiment, he argues, which seems to reveal an infinite creator, is an
inherent quality of our nature, placed there by God; in this sense it is revealed,
even though religious ideas reach us through the senses. It is the source of virtues,
sympathy, pity, justice, which have been degraded by self-interest and economic
calculation. Religion is not a penal code, an ally of governments, it is a relationship with the Divinity, with what makes man a moral being. Morality, emanating from God, like religious sentiment, is in the heart of man, and unveils itself
to them as they become enlightened. But l'*esprit*—the *wit* of the eighteenth
century—becomes 'the vilest of instruments when it is separated from conscience, disporting itself elegantly amid the general degradation'. Liberty,
progress, and religious sentiment are linked with perfectibility. Perfectibility, the
progressive improvement which connects the generations, demands self-abnega-
tion, disinterestedness, sacrifice, enthusiasm. Man's faculty for self-sacrifice is the
indestructible seed of perfectibility. Pain is holy; it is a source of strength, a
means of progress lavished on us by Providence. Though priestcraft may pervert
its use, and though the theory of expiatory sacrifice and the efficacy of bloodshed
is unacceptable, pain is the source of our noblest and most tender qualities; it
teaches us to struggle for ourselves and to feel for others.

[14] Ibid. 1072–5.
[15] Letter to Hochet, dated 11 Oct. 1811, B. Constant and Mme de Staël, *Lettres à un ami*, ed. J. Mistler
(Neuchâtel, 1948), 194–5.

The Revolution, Constant predicted, will be followed by other destructive periods, but these will denote eventual deliverance. There is already in Germany, in Switzerland, in England among the Methodists, in France even, a mysterious stirring, a wish to believe. Man, yearning to transcend the visible nature of which he is master, thirsts for an invisible, boundless nature. The imagination needs to burst its bonds; the 'suffering and agitated part of our nature', the 'dream-like and melancholy part of religious sentiment', seek a sphere which it can embellish at its will. No society can be content with the denial of powers higher than man, of communication with this power, of appeal to its goodness and justice. Religious sentiment is not an iron band: doubt, as distinct from dogmatic unbelief, may be more infused with religious sentiment than some religions, and may be a factor in religious progress, since progress, which is a law of nature and of man, must apply also to religion. Dogmas, beliefs, rites, and ceremonies are notions of the Divinity conceived by man: they must change when these notions become less crude, and be discarded when religious sentiment no longer expresses itself in them. All religions which attract public veneration are worthy of respect; error is better than no religion. When existing religious sytems are discredited, men hurl themselves into the most terrifying superstitions. There should be no sudden changes by government order, since religious forms, names even, are rightly important through habit and belief, and reassuring to the timid. But when institutions delay the abolition of outworn creeds, their prolongation is artificial; enthusiasm departs, all that is left are forms of words, practices, and priests. It cannot be a crime to use the critical faculty which Providence has bestowed on man. The more one believes in the goodness and justice of Providence, the more natural it is to admit that this beneficent Providence proportions its teaching to the state of intelligence destined to receive it.[16]

Mme de Staël incarnates the ardours, ambitions, intellectual ferment, suffering, and religious feeling of her age. Passionately engaged in moderate Republican politics in the 1790s, exiled by Napoleon, perhaps as much for her overwhelming personality as for her unremitting espousal of liberal ideals, in 1814 she unsuccessfully attempted, with Benjamin Constant, to replace the Empire with the rule of Bernadotte, the new Protestant king-elect of Sweden. After Waterloo she made obeisance to Louis XVIII at Hartwell House, and appealed against the slave trade to the allied sovereigns in Paris with their armies of occupation. In her château at Coppet she presided over a kind of cultural centre for prominent European intellectuals. Byron said of it: 'she has made Coppet as agreeable as

---

[16] B. Constant, *De la Perfectibilité de l'espèce humaine*, ed. P. Deguise (Lausanne, 1967), 9–34, 35, 37, 42, 51–4; *De la religion*, 14, 21, 24–5, 30, 36, 38–9, 42–7, 56–7, 61, 65, 72, 84, 216, 233–6, 268, 269.

society and talent could make any place on earth.'[17] Conscious of her own mission, and convinced that the talent for writing is inseparable from energy of soul and character, she believed that, since the invention of printing, thinkers are more powerful than generals, books than bayonets.[18] The essentials of her moral and religious thought are already clear in *De l'influence des passions sur le bonheur des individus et des nations* of 1796, and in *Des circonstances actuelles*, planned as its sequel, written two years later. There is a contrast between personal sadness and hope for the eventual transformation of society. Love cannot bring happiness, since 'its celestial nature is at odds with all human destiny'. The yearning for glory and for greatness of soul is unassuageable. Her feminism is defeatist: even the most exceptional woman, she believes, cannot escape from the 'insurmountable weakness of her nature and her situation in the social order'.[19] She urges hatred of fanaticism, both religious and political, stoic self-control, and the absolute liberty of the moral being.

Deep thought about 'the most metaphysical conceptions', contemplation of infinity, and instinctive morality all lead to the rejection of materialism and suggest the spirituality of the soul and immortality. Aware of Condorcet, whose *Esquisse d'un tableau historique des progrès de l'esprit humain* was published the year after his death in a Republican prison cell, and of Godwin, whose *Enquiry Concerning Political Justice and its Influence on General Virtue and Happiness* Constant had translated, and firm in her attachment to reason and Enlightenment, she believes that the application of mathematical principles and social sciences can discover what is best for the greatest number, but that the understanding of the inner soul and spiritual existence is still undeveloped. Pity is essential to governments; the minority must not be sacrificed to the majority, and generosity, enthusiasm, and moral sentiment are necessary for the social and spiritual regeneration of France. Providence, which each year decks the earth with flowers, will not for ever consent to injustice and cruelty. But a contemporary of the *Illuminati* as well as of Condorcet, she conjectures that, 'in the great mystery whose secrets are unknown to us, Providence may have introduced barbaric acts and cruel men as agents of its general will'. *De la littérature considérée dans ses rapports avec les institutions sociales* reiterates her belief in perfectibility, which, she says, has been the doctrine of enlightened philosophers for the previous half century: Adam Ferguson, Turgot, Kant,

---

[17] Byron's *Letters and Journals*, ed. L. A. Marchand (11 vols.; London, 1973–9), iv. 109. Byron described Mme de Staël as 'certainly the cleverest, though not the most agreeable woman I have ever known' (ibid. iii. 244). For comments on Our Lady of Coppet, see iii. 210, 218, 256; vii. 161.

[18] Mme de Staël, *Des circonstances*, 272–3.

[19] See J. Kitchin, 'La Littérature et les femmes selon *De la littérature* de Mme de Staël', in *B. Constant, Mme de Staël et le groupe de Coppet* (Oxford, 1982), 401–25.

Condorcet, Godwin.[20] She now ascribes the atrocities of the Revolution to 'men of the class of the people' who had seized power. 'The conquerors must be educated', to eradicate vulgarity and savagery. She denounces the economic doctrine of self-interest, and pleads for respect of human dignity: 'the existence of man, sacred for man'. The book is in part an appeal and warning to General Bonaparte, who was already master of France when it was published. Courage was one of Mme de Staël's many virtues.

Her two novels, *Delphine*, of 1802, and *Corinne ou l'Italie*, of 1807, are frenzied, woebegone, improbable, and sentimental, though less so than *La Nouvelle Héloïse*. Their theme is the suffering inflicted on two chaste, intelligent, talented, passionate young women by Providence and by the artificial social codes which deny them happiness by marriage to men worthy of them. The novels also deal, at greater length than the previous works, with Mme de Staël's religious beliefs, which are rooted in eighteenth-century deism, the sentimental sub-Christianity of Rousseau, Geneva, and the writings of her revered father Necker.[21] His *De l'importance des opinions religieuses*, of 1788, and his *Cours de morale religieuse* are not specifically Christian but regard Christian revelation as a help to natural religion. His daughter's two novels teach the existence of God, immortality of the soul, and morality, personal and social, but not Christian revelation. 'Religious sentiment unites man, when self-love and fanaticism do not make it an object of jealousy and hatred. Praying together, in whatever rite it be, is the most touching fraternity of hope and sympathy which men can experience on this earth.' The enthusiasm and imagination of the heroines pervade the novels. Both are priestesses. On her deathbed, the deeply repentant Mme de Vernon, the treacherous destroyer of Delphine's happiness, rejects the priest, confesses to Delphine, and chooses Delphine as mediatrix: 'This angel whom I have offended will intercede for me with the Supreme Being.' When the Royalist Léonce, her beloved, is about to be shot by the Republicans, Delphine again replaces the priest. Corinne is described as 'the inspired priestess, who joyfully consecrated herself to the cult of genius'. Mme de Staël's Protestantism is still present in *Corinne*. There is a portentously reverential description, curious in a French book published two years after Trafalgar, of divine service on board a British man-o'-war anchored off Naples. But Corinne, half British, half Italian, glories in the name of Roman. The aesthetic and emotional allurements of Catholic architecture, practices, beliefs, and folklore are described, at great length, throughout the novel. When Corinne kneels before the image of the

---

[20] Mme de Staël, *De la littérature considerée dans ses rapports avec les institutions sociales* (Geneva, 1959), i. 11–13.

[21] See F. P. Bowman, 'Necker et l'apologétique', *Cahiers staëliens*, 36 (1985), 30–52; H. Perrochon, 'Les Sources suisses de la religion de Mme de Staël', in *Mme de Staël et l'Europe* (Colloqe de Coppet; Paris, 1970), 145–56.

Virgin at the Santa Casa at Loreto, 'the image of goodness, the symbol of celestial sensibility', the Protestant Oswald asks Corinne 'how a person of such superior intelligence could accept such popular practices', and is enraptured by her not wholly convincing explanation. They visit Milan cathedral, where 'the light filtering through the coloured windows, the singular shapes of the Gothic architecture, indeed the whole aspect of the church is a silent image of the infinite that one feels within oneself without ever being able to free oneself of it or to understand it'. When Corinne is dying, stricken by the love which in heroic self-sacrifice she has forgone, she asks the priest, 'a venerable old man', to replace the portrait of Oswald by a crucifix, 'the image of Him who descended upon earth not for power, not for genius, but for suffering and death'. The moment before she expires, she points out to Oswald the same cloud-covered moon which they had seen over the bay of Naples.

Clearly, *Le Génie du Christianisme* was not unique in portraying sentimental religiosity. Scott, internationally famous, inserted an *Ave Maria* into canto 3, XXIX, of *The Lady of the Lake*:

> Ave Maria! maiden mild!
> Listen to a maiden's prayer!
>
> .   .   .   .
>
> Maiden, hear a maiden's prayer.
> Mother, hear a suppliant child!
>   Ave Maria!

Byron disapproved, but he too, in canto III, 101–3, of *Don Juan*, followed a trend:

> Ave Maria! 'Tis the hour of prayer!
> Ave Maria! 'Tis the hour of love!
> Ave Maria! May our spirits dare
> Look up to thine and to thy Son's above?
> Ave Maria! Oh that face so fair!
> Those downcast eyes beneath the almighty dove—
> What though 'tis but a pictured image—strike.
> That painting is no idol, 'tis too like.[22]

Burke, in 1790, had robustly pointed out the attractions of an undemanding religion for the rich and the great, whose cares and anxieties 'range without limit, and are diversified by infinite combination in the wild and unbounded regions of imagination', and who need 'something to relieve in the killing languor and over-laboured lassitude of those who have nothing to do'. He also realized that a non-dogmatic benevolence towards religion offered a bulwark against revolution.

---

[22] Cf. Byron, *Letters*, ix. 119: 'I am no enemy to religion, but the contrary. I incline, myself, very much to the Catholic doctrine.' There are several other remarks in the same vein.

Truly tolerant men 'would reverently and affectionately protect all religion, because they love and venerate the great principle upon which all agree. They begin more and more plainly to discern, that we all have a common cause, as against a common enemy.'[23]

When he was not ranting, Romanizing and vaticinating, Joseph de Maistre seems to have been an affable, amiable, urbane man, with a delicate sense of humour and a self-deprecatory charm. To save an English vice-admiral the trouble of replying in French to a letter, he explains: 'my eyes know English perfectly well, although my ears are unaware of the fact.'[24] To a young relative, 'mon cher Nicolas', he tells, with doubts about its veracity, a very Russian story: at a combined mass baptism and blessing of the waters round a hole in the ice on the Neva, the archbishop, having let an infant slip from his frozen hands, said 'davai drugoi' (give me another) and went on baptizing.[25] His letters to his wife and family reveal tender, loving, wistful emotions during his fourteen years of exile in St Petersburg, where he had gone in 1803 as envoy extraordinary and minister plenipotentiary of the king of Sardinia. But beneath a cosy, melancholy, Charles Lamb-like letter to a lady, an obsessive horror emerges:

After 9 o'clock I give orders to be driven to some lady's, because I always prefer women. I am aware, Madame, that you take a different view, but no matter, everyone to their taste. Here, or there, I try to recover a little of that native gaiety which has preserved me until now: I blow on the fire like an old woman lighting her lamp from yesterday's embers. I attempt to call a truce to dreams of severed arms and shattered heads which trouble me unceasingly; then I take supper, like a young man, then I sleep like a child, and then I wake up like a man, I mean early in the morning; and then I begin again, turning in the same circle, placing my foot in the same place, like an ass turning a mill. [26]

He is chiefly remembered, not unfairly, as the apologist for capital punishment, 'l'ami du bourreau':

They throw him a prisoner, a parricide, a sacrileger: he seizes him, stretches him out, binds him to a horizontal cross, he lifts his arm: then amidst a horrible silence, the only sound is of bones breaking beneath his rod, and the howls of the victim . . . Is he a man? Yes: God receives him in his temples and allows him to pray. He is not criminal, yet no language consents to say that he is virtuous . . . And yet all grandeur, all subordination rests on the executioner: he is the horror, and the bond of all human association. Remove from the world this incomprehensible agent; at that very moment order yields to chaos, thrones tumble and society disappears.[27]

---

[23] Burke, *Reflections*, 201, 259. See C. C. O'Brien's remarks on p. 47.

[24] J. de Maistre, *Lettres et Opuscules* (2 vols.; Paris, 1853), i. 84.

[25] Ibid. 73.

[26] Ibid. 80–1.

[27] J. de Maistre, *Les Soirées de Saint-Petersbourg, ou entretiens sur le gouvernement temporel de la Providence*, ed. L. de Grémilly et P. Mariel (Paris, 1960), 40–1.

His system of thought is an attempt to explain how the evils of the Revolution came about (for he sees no immediate good results) and how they may lead to good. In *Considérations sur la France*, of 1797, he proclaims that the sinfulness of the Enlightenment, the moral degradation of the French aristocracy, and the weaknesses of the clergy brought on divine punishment, but in order to regenerate. The Revolution, which outstepped the normal circle of crime, was satanic in character. The infernal genius of Robespierre and the Jacobins preserved France from foreign invaders. Throughout history a divine Providence has been visible, working for mysterious ends. 'We are bound to the throne of the Almighty by a supple chain; free and slaves, we operate voluntarily and necessarily.' Man, therefore, is responsible for evil; wicked and innocent alike incur punishment, since punishment, expiation, sacrifice, war, bloodshed, are the law. But society is not helpless. What God is to mankind, kings are to nations. Evil can be diminished by following traditional wisdom, that is, monarchy and the Church. A new outpouring of the spirit may be awaited. The schismatics will unite with Rome; there will be a theocracy with an indefectible pope as moderator and supreme court of appeal for Christian monarchs.[28]

All this is repeated and elaborated in *Les Soirées de Saint-Pétersbourg*. Three friends, the count, a Russian senator, and a young French chevalier are being rowed along the Neva on an idyllic evening in July 1809, with all the splendours of the imperial city in view. But the sinister touch is there: 'the sun, shrouded by reddish mists, passes like a fiery wain over the dark forest crowning the horizon, and its beams, reflected in the palace windows, offer the spectacle of a huge conflagration.'[29] Throughout the *Soirées* relaxed and sometimes deeply personal sad interludes contrast with Maistre's heavy, relentless hammer-blows. Yet, even when most virulent, he can still mock himself. At the end of an inordinately long and savage diatribe against Voltaire—'other cynics astounded virtue, Voltaire astounds vice. He plunges in the mire, he wallows in it, he slakes his thirst in it; he abandons his imagination to the enthusiasm of Hell—the lowest of men after his admirers . . . Sodom would have banished him . . .'—the chevalier interjects, 'Citizen, your pulse?'[30] The ferocity of the times is reflected in his prose. Sometimes his powerful intellect and subtle reasoning predominate. But on and on it goes. Pain is the remedy for disorder. Ancient blood sacrifices were a prophetic cry of mankind announcing salvation by blood. Christianity, a God who causes a God willingly to die, explains to man what he is, 'the enormity of the crime demanded such an expiation'. Reversibility, whereby the sufferings of the righteous counterbalance the evil done by others, is 'the great mystery of the universe': 'on the one side all the crimes, on the other all the satisfactions; on this side the

---

[28] Maistre, *Considérations sur la France*, 1–30, 40–7.   [29] Maistre, *Les Soirées*, 21–2.
[30] Ibid. 118–19.

good works of all men, the blood of the martyrs, the tears of the innocent, accumulating without respite to balance the evil which, from the beginning, has poured out its poisonous torrent on the other side.' Those of us who, like the Psalmist, do not exercise ourselves in great matters, which are too high for us, Maistre leaves to our fate: 'When the cleverest of men lacks the religious sense, not only can we not convince him, but we have no means of making ourselves understood by him, which proves nothing except his own misfortune.'[31] What he incontrovertibly and copiously insists on is the fact of war, the blood of the guilty and the innocent alike, continuously shed, with brief respites in some places. All life, in nature, is linked with slaughter. Man's destructive hand spares nothing alive. 'The whole earth, continually drenched with blood, is but an immense altar, where all that lives must be sacrificed, without end, without measure, without respite, until the consummation of things, until the death of death.' Then follows a sevenfold litany: 'War is therefore divine . . . War is divine by . . . War is . . .'[32]

The union of the Protestants with Rome is another of his obsessions. By Protestant he means all non-Roman. He denies the term Orthodox to the Russian and Greek Churches, which, in his overbearing and arrogant fashion, he dubs Photian. Indeed, he considers them further from Rome than Western schismatics, since the latter in his view have gone the whole circle of error, whereas the Orthodox are just beginning. He privately mocks the Czar Alexander I's transcendental leanings and his Holy Alliance in the Name of the Most Holy and Indivisible Trinity, which, Maistre says, 'has made all *religious* Europe guffaw'. In any case, when the serfs are liberated, suspect influences will ensure that 'they pass brusquely and infallibly from superstition to atheism'. Germany is dangerous: 'revolutionary principles linked with German fanaticism will make all Europe tremble.' He amuses himself with gibes at the Church of England. 'Where there is no sacrifice of the mass there can be no priest. An Anglican minister is a man dressed in black who goes into a pulpit on Sundays to make moral observations.' If he says he believes, his audience will ask 'Qui sait si ce Fellow—who knows if this fellow believes all that he is going to tell me?' He applies to the English bishops ('say of these bishops all the good things you can, you will never say more than I think') the eulogy of the virtuous Saracen in the abhorred Voltaire's *Zaïre*:

> Généreux, bienfaisants, justes, pleins de vertus
> Dieu, s'ils étaient chrétiens, que seraient-ils de plus?

Nevertheless, it is the king of England, already Defender of the Faith, and the restored king of France, who shall lead Europe, and the world, to unity. French

---

[31] *Les Soirées*, 266–74.   [32] Ibid. 218–24.

is the international language. The exiled French clergy are implanting the French language in England, and the French themselves are learning foreign tongues. Protestantism is slowly dying: 'everything heralds a general change, a magnificent revolution of which the French revolution was but the terrible preliminary.' The English are unsurpassed by any nation in unity, strength, national glory; Catholic emancipation is imminent; a magnificent Catholic church is being built in London. 'Ah! if ever the same faith spoke only English and French, in the twinkling of an eye obstinacy against this faith in all Europe would become ridiculous, why should I not say it? *bad form*.' 'Noble English! you were once the first enemies of unity; it is upon you that the honour has fallen of restoring it to Europe.' Then the popes would be hailed as supreme agents of civilization, creators of European unity, conservators of learning and the arts, founders, protectors of civil liberty, destroyers of slavery, enemies of despotism, indefectible supporters of sovereignty, benefactors of humanity. 'Once the separated clergy enters into legitimate unity, it will ascend immediately as though by enchantment to that high degree of dignity from which it recognizes that it has fallen. With what good will, with what joy we should carry you there with our own hands! Our respect awaits them.' Exactly what would happen when the laymen in black and their wives had obeyed their ex-supreme governor and cried O Sainte Église de Rome in their Anglo-French is not specified. They are assured that Rome is very tolerant about local usages, 'and will satisfy princes in all that is christianly possible'.[33]

Joseph de Maistre had courteous relations with Mme de Staël, 'a Protestant lady of great wit and judgement'. He recalls theological and political arguments with her which reduced both of them to helpless laughter. He dismisses Chateaubriand as 'a very great colourist and above all a very clever man who looks after his own successes', and he reproves a young correspondent who told him that Chateaubriand was created by God to guide the world. On one point at least he agrees with Constant: 'Ah! quelle chienne d'époque.'[34]

Henri-Benjamin Constant de Rebecque's Germano-Helvetic meditations on the sanctity of pain and the celestial yearnings of melancholy souls are more akin to various poems of Alphonse de Lamartine and Alfred de Musset than they are to nineteenth-century liberal thought. Nevertheless, his lucid style notwithstanding, Constant's ideas on religious change may perhaps seem valid in some

---

[33] J. de Maistre, *Lettre à un gentilhomme russe sur l'Inquisition espagnole* (Paris, 1821), 5ᵉ Lettre, p. 139; 6ᵉ Lettre, pp. 155–6; *Du pape* (2 vols.; Lyons, 1830), i. 1–13, 25, 74, 79, 168, 187, 197–9; ii. 97–100, 103, 109–11, 120–4, 183, 229, 241, 325, 329, 343, 346–7. *Examen de la philosophie de Bacon* (Lyons, 1860), ii. 334–5.

[34] J. de Maistre, *Du pape* (2 vols.; Lyons, 1830), i. 74; Maistre, *Lettres et opuscules*, i. 82, 91–2; ii. 88, 399–400.

theological circles today. Certainly, events in Europe since 1917 have given renewed scope for that servility in politics which he so deplored. Mme de Staël remains an exemplar of resistance to oppression, as well as a pioneer of feminism, literary sociology, and German–French understanding. The aesthetic–antiquarian religious sentiment of *Le Génie du Christianisme* is still with us in various forms. (The greatness of Chateaubriand's *Mémoires d'outre-tombe* was not fully appreciated until our own times.) And, in spite of his atrocious doctrines, survivors into our own declining century must have some slight fellow feeling for Joseph de Maistre, with his wars, and his violence, and his interrogative disculpation of soldiers: 'Explain why what is most honorable in the world . . . is the right to shed innocently innocent blood?'[35]

[35] Maistre, *Les Soirées*, 212.

13

A Not Exclusive Truth: An Early Nineteenth-Century Pastoral Theology and Erasmus

BRUCE MANSFIELD

In 1820 there appeared in Lucerne an edition of Erasmus's *Paraclesis*, a German translation and the Latin original. Accompanying it was a collection of twelve essays on theological subjects loosely related to the *Paraclesis*. Their author, and the editor and translator of Erasmus's text, was Joseph Widmer, at the time Professor of Moral and Pastoral Theology at Lucerne.

The conjuncture seems a strange one: Erasmus and Widmer. At least it arouses curiosity. The *Paraclesis ad lectorem pium* was among the most open of Erasmus's works.[1] It was part of the prefatory material to his edition of the New Testament (1516). It was a plea for making the scriptures more accessible to the people, not least through vernacular translations. 'Ideally', says Erika Rummel, 'he would have liked to involve all Christians in his work, for he firmly believed that everyone ought to be able to acquire a firsthand knowledge of God's word and not only to read it, but also to ponder it, interpret it, and discuss its significance.'[2] The *Paraclesis* also offered studied, if restrained, criticism of religion that was too ceremonial, legalistic, and institutionalized, and of theology that was too bound by scholastic formulas. It expressed a piety centred on the person of Jesus, a piety at once inward, ethical, and social.[3] It was, like the

---

I wish to thank the Inter-Library Loans section of the University of Sydney Library for much assistance; the microfilm copy of the *Paraklesis* was supplied to Macquarie University Library by the Gemeentebibliotheek, Rotterdam.

[1] Lat. text, *Desiderius Erasmus Roterodamus: Ausgewählte Werke*, ed. H. Holborn (Munich, 1933; repr. 1964) (hereafter Holborn), 139–49; Eng. trans., *Christian Humanism and the Reformation: Selected Writings of Erasmus*, ed. J. C. Olin (3rd edn., New York, 1987) (hereafter Olin), 97–108.

[2] E. Rummel, *Erasmus' Annotations on the New Testament: From Philologist to Theologian* (Toronto, 1986), 26.

[3] J. Étienne, *Spiritualisme érasmien et théologiens louvanistes: Un changement de problématique au début du XVIᵉ siècle* (Louvain, 1956), 20–2.

whole edition, 'part of a grandly conceived plan for the renewal of church, culture, and society'.[4]

The incipient radicalism of the *Paraclesis* did not go unremarked by the conservative and even the prudent. In his own cautionary advice on the vernacular Bible, Fénelon at the beginning of the eighteenth century recalled that the Faculty of Theology at Paris had censured Erasmus on this question during his lifetime, and the clergy of France had approved that censure in 1661.[5] Joseph Widmer quoted Fénelon at some length.[6]

Widmer appears to belong to the Catholic reaction of the post-Napoleonic era. His views have been called 'ultramontane'.[7] In the political and religious struggles of his native land, Lucerne, his associations were with the traditionalists, the opponents of the Enlightenment, the defenders of the Church, its independence, and even its dominance. At least at first glance he seems to have stood with those who, since the sixteenth century, had been severe critics of Erasmus, for the very openness of works like the *Paraclesis* and his corrosive effect generally on the structures and standing of the Church. There is a puzzle in the conjuncture of Erasmus and Widmer; its solution requires a closer look at Widmer and his world and a study of his text, its intellectual debts and associations and its place in the history of Erasmus interpretations.

Joseph Widmer was born at Waldisbühl in the old Catholic canton of Lucerne in 1779.[8] When in 1802 he went to study theology at the University of Landshut in Bavaria, he took, on his own account, a mind formed by the late Enlightenment, by Kant, and a spirit aroused by the revolutionary storm which had passed over Switzerland as well as France.[9] Widmer had been attracted to Landshut and the thought of studying theology by reading the *Gebetbuch* of Johann Michael Sailer (1751–1832), who was Professor of Moral and Pastoral Theology there. He persuaded a younger comrade, Joseph Heinrich Alois Gügler (1782–1827), to accompany him. Their destinies were to be connected for the next twenty-five years, at Landshut and Lucerne. The transfer of the university from Ingolstadt to

[4] H. J. de Jonge, '*Novum Testamentum a nobis versum*: The Essence of Erasmus' Edition of the New Testament', *Journal of Theological Studies*, NS 35 (1984), 406; cf. J. H. Bentley, *Humanists and Holy Writ: New Testament Scholarship in the Renaissance* (Princeton, 1983), 124.

[5] 'Lettre à l'évêque d'Arras sur la lecture de l'écriture sainte en langue vulgaire', *Œuvres complètes*, ii (Paris, 1848), 194–5; the Sorbonne's censures and Erasmus's replies in his *Declarationes ad censuras Lutetiae vulgatas sub nomine Facultatis Theologiae Parisiensis, Opera omnia* (Leiden, 1703–6), ix. 870F–875F.

[6] J. Widmer, *Paraklesis des Erasmus von Rotterdam, oder Ermahnung zum Studium der christlicher Philosophie. Als Grundlage zwölf theologischer Abhandlungen* (Lucerne, 1820) (hereafter Widmer), 98–101.

[7] *Dictionnaire historique et biographique de la Suisse* (7 vols.; Neuchatel, 1921–33), vii. 305.

[8] Biographies: *Dictionnaire historique*, vii. 305; *Allgemeine Deutsche Biographie* (hereafter *ADB*) (56 vols.; Munich, 1875–1912), xlii. 361–2 (Widmer), x. 95–9 (Gügler); *Lexikon für Theologie und Kirche* (hereafter *LThK*) (2nd edn., 10 vols.; Freiburg im Breisgau, 1957–65), x. 1094–5.

[9] *Allgemeiner Religions- und Kirchenfreund*, xx (1847), quoted in B. Lang, *Bischof Sailer und seine Zeitgenossen* (Regensburg, 1932), 132.

Landshut in 1800 was one of the Bavarian administration's plans for moderniz-
ing the state in the spirit of the Enlightenment. Ironically, academic developments at Landshut took the university off in other directions, not least towards
a Catholic resurgence.[10] For that twist, Sailer takes a large share of the
responsibility.

Almost certainly, he is also the key to understanding Widmer. The key does
not turn easily; assessing Sailer himself is, historiographically, a complex task.
Nevertheless, for us what matters is his function at a critical moment in
Widmer's development. Of Sailer, this much at least should be said: from Philipp
Funk's monograph of 1925, *Von der Aufklärung zur Romantik*, scholarship has
seen Sailer not, as had once been the case, as the last word of the Enlightenment,
but as the beginning, in large part the creator, of the Catholic restoration.[11] We
might enlarge a little. When Widmer and Gügler became his students in 1802,
he had a prominence unusual for a Catholic intellectual at that time. Scholasti-
cally trained for the Jesuit Order, he was released by the Order's suppression in
1773. In giving his theology biblical and patristic foundations, he made use of
Protestant scholarship. His interest in mysticism did not exclude the pietists. On
ethics he came to terms with Kant, in education with Pestalozzi. His mind was
eclectic, his disposition irenic, but centrifugal tendencies were contained. In
understanding the Enlightenment, it has been said, he overcame it.[12] His writings
on pastoral theology and education sought a faith living and realized, 'the
merging of spontaneity and given grace'.[13] A modern commentator finds in the
expression 'lived faith' the summation of his thought and influence.[14] Sailer's
teachings on the incarnation and the cross, and on the Church as indispensable
to faith and salvation, checked any tendency to subjectivism.

Widmer lived in Sailer's house when he first came to Landshut. In conversation on daily walks Sailer gradually detached the young Swiss from his Kantian
philosophy and dissuaded him from abandoning Landshut for the Enlightenment atmosphere of Munich. Sailer was patient, never pressing or confronta-
tional, almost indirect. He followed the prescriptions of his own pastoral
theology as Widmer describes it, in introducing 'the instructive and edifying

---

[10] P. Funk, *Von der Aufklärung zur Romantik: Studien zur Vorgeschichte der Münchener Romantik*
(Munich, 1925), 41; C. E. McClelland, *State, Society, and University in Germany 1700–1914* (Cambridge,
1980), 103, 107–8.

[11] For summative accounts, *Dictionnaire de théologie catholique* (15 vols.; Paris, 1930–50), xiv, pt. 1,
749–54; *LThK* ix. 214–15.

[12] H. Jedin (ed.), *Handbuch der Kirchengeschichte*, vi. *Die Kirche in der Gegenwart*, pt. 1. *Die Kirche
zwischen Revolution und Restauration*, R. Aubert, J. Beckmann, J. Corrish, and R. Lill (Freiburg, 1971),
266; cf. J. Vonderach, 'Bischof J. M. Sailer und die Aufklärung', *Freiburger Zeitschrift für Philosophie und
Theologie*, 5 (1958), 257–73, 384–403. B. Meier, *Die Kirche der wahren Christen: Johann Michael Sailers
Kirchenverständnis zwischen Unmittelbarkeit und Vermittlung* (Stuttgart, 1990), 50–9.

[13] A. Dru, *The Church in the Nineteenth Century: Germany 1800–1918* (London, 1963), 44.

[14] J. Hofmeier, 'Sailer heute: Wegweiser und Wegbegleiter zu gelebtem Glauben', *Theologie und
Glaube: Zeitschrift für den katholischen Klerus*, 73 (1983), 36–46. Cf. Meier, *Die Kirche*, 179–81.

things the most gifted Christians of past and present have written or said about passages and texts of holy scripture or about the relations and circumstances of human life'.[15] Sailer's advice was never to become the prisoner of any human system and, amid the flux of human affairs so apparent in their time, to hold fast to the Church as the pillar of truth, and unchangeable.[16]

Widmer and Gügler took this injunction into the ecclesiastical struggles of Lucerne when they returned home in 1804. Sailer's influence remained in their theological and pedagogical work, and we will seek traces of it in Widmer's Erasmus edition. He had a special affection for his Swiss students and visited them regularly, Widmer acting, as he jokingly put it, as his 'personal coachman'.[17] He called Widmer and Gügler the 'most accomplished and capable fellows' among his pupils.[18]

In 1804 Widmer was ordained priest at Constance by I. H. von Wessenberg, vicar-general of the diocese of Constance, which then embraced much of Switzerland, including Lucerne. The encounter had its overtones and ironies. Wessenberg (1774–1860) was himself a pupil of Sailer's from an earlier time and shared his pastoral and pedagogical concerns, but he had an essentially Enlightenment understanding of the Church as educator and guide and no taste for 'mysticism'.[19] Widmer and Gügler both received appointments in the Lucerne Lyzeum or theological faculty, Widmer in philosophy, Gügler in exegesis.

The Lucerne to which the two theologians returned was under the Napoleonic Act of Mediation (1803–14), which moderated the attempt of the preceding revolutionary regime at a 'religionless state',[20] but without securing a lasting settlement. Government, clergy, and community were divided between the Tridentine Catholicism dominant in Lucerne since the sixteenth century and the Enlightenment in various guises, including Josephist ideas on state administration of the Church. Such ideas were influential in Lucerne before the Revolution and French occupation. After 1798 they were represented above all by Thaddäus Müller (1763–1826), commissary of the bishop and Wessenberg's lieutenant, active especially in educational reform.[21] The country folk were traditionalist.[22]

---

[15] Quoted in Lang, *Bischof Sailer*, 134. Cf. H. Schiel (ed.), *Johann Michael Sailer: Leben und Briefe*, i (Regensburg, 1948), 346–7, 358.

[16] Lang, *Bisch of Sailer*, 137.

[17] Ibid. 173; cf. Funk, *Von der Aufklärung*, 174, Schiel, *Sailer*, i. 650.

[18] Quoted in A. Härdelin, 'Kirche und Kult in der Luzerner theologischen Romantik: Alois Gügler und Joseph Widmer', *Zeitschrift für katholische Theologie*, 89 (1967), 142 n.

[19] *LThK* x. 1064–6.

[20] A. Staehelin, 'Helvetik', *Handbuch der Schweizer Geschichte*, ii (Zurich, 1977), 828.

[21] *ADB* xxii. 675–7; P. Kaspar, *Alois Gügler 1782–1827: Ein bedeutender Luzerner Theologe im Spannungsfeld von Aufklärung und Romantik* (Schüpfheim, 1977), 58–61.

[22] J. Droz, *Le Romantisme allemand et l'état: Résistance et collaboration dans l'Allemagne napoléonienne* (Paris, 1966), 287–92; *Dictionnaire historique*, iv. 575–7, 588.

What role Widmer and Gügler were to play in this situation was initially misunderstood. The nuncio, and even the pope, suspected them, as Sailer was from time to time suspected of threatening Church dogma and Church authority.[23] In fact, they represented a new force distinct from Tridentine traditionalism and the Enlightenment theology of Wessenberg and Müller, a new kind of clerical activism, a new piety and theology, come from Sailer and his associates, and later dubbed 'romantic'.[24]

Open dispute arose between Gügler and Müller in 1809–10, and the government was drawn in. The executive, or Small Council, acted on its Josephist principles and deposed Gügler, but agitation among the students, a popular movement in Gügler's support, and Widmer's embarrassing resignation in solidarity with his colleague forced his reinstatement.[25] Nevertheless, the administration remained inclined towards Wessenberg and Müller, and Gügler and Widmer were in opposition until the Restoration. Then there was an adjustment in the balance of forces, if not a complete change. The patrician order of the eighteenth century returned in Lucerne, bringing with it, ostensibly, a Catholic restoration. The nuncio returned to the city. Church and government succeeded in detaching Lucerne from the diocese of Constance, but disagreements quickly followed, over the new diocesan structure and the independence of the Church from the regime, on the one hand, and from Rome, on the other.[26] Once again, the seminary and the theological faculty registered changes in the prevailing atmosphere: in 1814 a rationalist exegete was dismissed; in 1819 a mentor of Widmer and Gügler, Franz Geiger (1755–1843), was removed from his chair of theology for 'principes ultramontains'.[27] In the midst of these struggles, Widmer, appointed to the chair of moral and pastoral theology in 1819, produced his edition of the *Paraclesis*.

The struggles became more embittered in the last fifteen years of Widmer's life. He did not live to see the catastrophe. After the revolutions of 1830 there was a liberal and anticlerical regime in Lucerne. It capped secularizing measures within the canton with adherence to the so-called Baden articles of 1834, agreed to with like-minded cantons. The articles were rejected in Rome, contested by

[23] Kaspar, *Alois Gügler*, 67–71; R. Pfister, *Kirchengeschichte der Schweiz*, iii (Zurich, 1985), 154.

[24] Härdelin, 'Kirche und Kult', 139–40. On another Catholic canton, Fribourg, during the revolution and under the Act of Mediation, with a comparable appearance of clerical activism, see P. Python, 'De quelques effets de la Révolution dans la diocèse de Lausanne (1789–1818)', in B. Plongeron, P. Lerou, and R Dartevelle (eds.), *Pratiques religieuses, mentalités et spiritualités dans l'Europe révolutionnaire (1770–1820)* (Turnhout, 1988), 147–56.

[25] Kaspar, *Alois Gügler*, 75–88, 277; *ADB* x. 96–7; Droz, *Le Romantisme allemand*, 289–90.

[26] J.-C. Biaudet, 'Der modernen Schweiz entgegen', *Handbuch der Schweizer Geschichte*, ii. 900, 902; Pfister, *Kirchengeschichte*, iii. 160–1; J. Dierauer, *Geschichte der Schweizerischen Eidgenossenschaft*, v, pt. 2 (Gotha, 1922; repr. 1967), 468–73.

[27] *Dictionnaire historique*, iv. 588; *LThK* iv. 606; Kaspar, *Alois Gügler*, 156; Pfister, *Kirchengeschichte*, iii. 154.

the clerical party, which was organizing itself strenuously, and resisted by the Catholic majority in Lucerne.[28] Probable drafter of the Baden articles, with their national, synodal, and Josephist elements, was a volatile liberal priest, Christopher Fuchs (1795–1846).[29] In 1833–4, Fuchs was to Widmer what Thaddäus Müller had been to Gügler a quarter-century before. For his opposition, not least to the liberals' proposed revisions of the federal constitution, the government removed Widmer from his chair in 1833, and Fuchs took his place. Agitation surrounded these events, which brought theological teaching near to collapse.[30] In his last years, Widmer's old teacher, J. M. Sailer, now bishop of Regensburg in Bavaria, had also been fighting for what the Catholic movement called the 'freedom of the church' against unwanted state intervention, while remaining opposed to the Ultras or 'hyperorthodox'.[31]

Widmer's reinstatement took eight years. It followed a political reversal in Lucerne, part of a conservative reaction set off by the controversy over D. F. Strauss in Protestant Zurich. The political leader of the conservative Catholics in Lucerne was the landowner Joseph Leu von Ebersol (1800–45), who saw what use could be made of the Catholic voting majority in the canton. He stood for a 'clerical democracy', a mixing of conservative Catholic ideology and popular sovereignty.[32] Joined with him in the leadership was Constantin Siegwart-Müller (1801–69), a leading liberal, or liberal Catholic, administrator of the 1830s and friend of Christopher Fuchs. The Strauss affair restored Siegwart-Müller without subtraction or qualification to the Catholic faith of his childhood.[33] Fuchs, who had, long after Widmer, been a pupil of Sailer's at Landshut, now took the same path as his friend.[34] The voters rallied to the conservative regime with a crushing majority in May 1841. In this atmosphere Widmer was restored to a chair and, in the following year, appointed provost of the ancient chapter of Beromünster. In the last year of his life, the new administration took, despite the reluctance of the Jesuit general and Widmer's own doubts, the fateful step of bringing the Jesuits back to Lucerne and delivering the seminary and theological teaching into their hands. On Siegwart-Müller's part, it was a deliberate challenge to Protestant and liberal Switzerland and a policy of high risk.[35] Already the Catholic

---

[28] Biaudet, 'Der modernen Schweiz entgegen', 935–7; Dierauer, *Geschichte*, v, pt. 2, 619–26; M. Salamin (ed.), *Documents d'histoire suisse 1798–1847* (Sierre, n.d.), 103–4.

[29] A. Stoecklin, 'Constantin Siegwart-Müller: Ein Übergang vom liberalen zum ultramontanen Katholizismus', *Schweizerische Zeitschrift für Geschichte*, 39 (1989), 16, 28; *ADB* viii. 159–62; *Dictionnaire historique*, iii. 285.

[30] *Dictionnaire historique*, iv. 579; Lang, *Bischof Sailer*, 173–4.

[31] Funk, *Von der Aufklärung*, 184, 191–2.

[32] Pfister, *Kirchengeschichte*, iii. 164; Biaudet, 'Der modernen Schweiz entgegen', 938; Dierauer, *Geschichte*, v, pt. 2, 667–71.

[33] Stoecklin, 'Constantin Siegwart-Müller', 7–8.

[34] Ibid. 19 n.

[35] Ibid. 13; Pfister, *Kirchengeschichte*, iii. 165; Biaudet, 'Der modernen Schweiz entgegen', 949–50; Kaspar, *Alois Gügler*, 238, 380.

cantons were meeting separately, and the *Sonderbund* was in more than embryo. When, after two strokes, Widmer died on 10 December 1844, two days after a failed radical coup in the city, Switzerland was on the way to civil war and the ultramontane party to disaster.

Widmer's career was thus intertwined with the history of the Catholic restoration in Lucerne. More than once his position in the theological faculty put him in the front line of the battle. His treatment by liberal regimes, his confrontations with Thaddäus Müller and Christopher Fuchs, his reinstatement in times of reaction or restoration associated him in contemporaries' minds, the minds of both friends and foes, with the conservative forces.

A pattern has been found in the history of the Catholic revival between 1800 and 1860. The relatively open, irenic, pietist, or mystical movement coming from Sailer and Landshut gave way, it is said, to a more reactionary, ultramontane, politicized Catholicism.[36] In Mainz, for example, the seminary returned to scholastic forms of teaching, the influence of the French counter-revolutionary and ultramontane thinkers, Maistre and Bonald, was more apparent, and there were the beginnings of a ghetto mentality.[37] Already in *Von der Aufklärung zur Romantik*, Funk had suggested a change of mood with the gathering of a new circle of Catholic publicists around Joseph Görres (1776–1848) in Munich after the succession of King Ludwig I in 1825 and the transfer of the university from Landshut to Munich.[38] 'The political character of the century, the attractions of power, the links with the monarchy in Bavaria and, last but not least, the policy of Rome, gradually obscured the ideals of Sailer, and brought Mainz to the fore.'[39] Lucerne, however provincial, was not on the margins of these struggles. Its Catholic revival was of European significance, and Widmer was a major figure in that revival. His experience and Lucerne's, we can tentatively conclude, do not conform to the model. The two stages or, better, the two aspects of Catholic revival, the spiritual and the political, the positive and the reactionary, are not in sequence with him, or at Lucerne, but go together. Is it that the battle with Müller and Wessenberg on the arena of the extended bishopric of Constance and the intervention of governments wedded to Josephist ideas made the Sailer movement immediately and irrevocably political in Lucerne?

The combination of spiritual freshness or openness and political reaction and intransigence—suggested by Widmer's long and continuing connection with

---

[36] Dru, *Church in the Nineteenth Century*, esp. chs. 6, 7.

[37] Jedin, *Handbuch*, vi, pt. 1, 268–9; F. Schnabel, *Deutsche Geschichte im neunzehnten Jahrhundert*, iv. *Die religiösen Kräfte* (2nd edn., Freiburg, 1951), 78–92; on Maistre, see B. Plongeron, *Théologie et politique au siècle de lumières (1770–1820)* (Geneva, 1973), 307.

[38] Funk, *Von der Aufklärung*, 183–4, 192.

[39] Dru, *Church in the Nineteenth Century*, 107; cf. Schnabel, *Deutsche Geschichte*, iv. 62.

Sailer, on the one hand,[40] and his political associations in Lucerne, on the other—must be built into any attempt to solve the puzzle of the conjuncture of Widmer and Erasmus. The next step is to consider the use Widmer makes of Erasmus in his twelve essays.

There are direct references to Erasmus scattered through the text. Widmer describes his work as a kind of *raisonirender Eklektik*,[41] and it appears as a series of reflections triggered by the *Paraclesis*, which seems often to fall from view. Erasmus is quoted as but one author among many. The direct references are, however, enough to anchor Widmer's discourse, if on a long line, back into the *Paraclesis*. Thus, in his first chapter, on the eloquence of the preacher, Widmer quotes Erasmus's opening declarations on the simplicity and urgency of Christ's eloquence compared with that of poets and orators in every age.[42] On the dispositions necessary in the theological candidate, he refers to Erasmus's more extended treatise, *Ratio seu compendium perveniendi ad veram theologiam*, which had also begun as a preface to the New Testament.[43] Widmer opens his long central chapter on 'Der Geist des Christenthums im Regenten, Priester und Erzieher' with Erasmus's remarks in the *Paraclesis*, and of course elsewhere, on the service rulers, priests, and pedagogues can give to the renewal of Christian society and to peace. On education and the educators, where, as we shall see, Widmer is more sharply polemical than anywhere else, he quotes Erasmus on the imbuing of teachers with Christian principles, which is possible only through the inspiration of divine love.[44] As for children, they should, as Erasmus says, take in Christ's simplest teachings with their mother's milk.[45] Widmer brings Erasmus in on the relation between doing and knowing; he gave priority to the former, since Christian wisdom came from the disposition and heart (*im Gemüthe*) rather than from the intellect (*im Verstande*), Jesus himself saying: 'Whoever has the will to do the will of God shall know whether my teaching comes from him' (John 7: 17).[46] Two late chapters are headed by consecutive sentences of the *Paraclesis*: 'Moreover, what else is the philosophy of Christ, which He Himself calls a rebirth, than the restoration of human nature originally well formed? By the same token, although no one has taught this more perfectly and more effectively than Christ, nevertheless one may find in the books of the pagans very much which does agree with His teaching.'[47] Finally, there are divergences, suggested

---

[40] Sailer edited Widmer's *Der katholische Seelensorger in gegenwärtiger Zeit* (Munich, 1819); Widmer edited Sailer's works (41 vols.; Sulzbach, 1830–45).

[41] Widmer, p. xi.

[42] Ibid. 51; Holborn, 140; Olin, 98–9.

[43] Widmer, 75–8; Holborn, 178–80.

[44] Widmer, 158–9, 215, 228; Holborn, 143–4; Olin, 102–3.

[45] Widmer, 331; Erasmus, *De pueris instituendis*, in *Collected Works of Erasmus* (Toronto, 1974–), xxvi. 298–9.

[46] Widmer, 238.   [47] Olin, 104; Holborn, 145.

rather than elaborated, from Erasmus's views on scholasticism and the place of scripture,[48] and to these we will return.

The correspondence between the two texts is actually greater than the direct references to Erasmus might suggest. Without being explicit about it, Widmer, through his twelve chapters, follows the pattern and sequence of the *Paraclesis*. Thus both works begin with the question of eloquence and locate it in a kind of inspired simplicity. Widmer commends to the preacher simplicity of utterance rather than high style. All depends on the inspiration of the Holy Spirit; the education of preachers should then be mostly negative, to remove what stands in the way of the Spirit's action.[49] His second chapter, on theological education, condemns those who enter on the study of theology routinely, or for mundane reasons, and this corresponds loosely to Erasmus's criticism of contemporaries of his who, in their enthusiasm for the classics, neglect Christian studies, despite what they richly and uniquely offer. Widmer's attack is on the clergy of the state Churches, prepared 'with a few mechanical skills acquired through witless practice'.[50] Only the interaction of *Glauben* and *Wissen*, faith and knowledge, can make the theologian: 'What weakens faith lessens, what strengthens faith of necessity increases the tendency to a study whose subject is precisely the content of that faith.'[51]

In his third chapter Widmer rejects or heavily qualifies Erasmus's famous call in the *Paraclesis* for the vernacular Bible: 'Christ wishes His mysteries published as openly as possible. I would that even the lowliest women read the Gospels and the Pauline Epistles. And I would that they were translated into all languages so that they could be read and understood not only by Scots and Irish but also by Turks and Saracens.'[52] What are we to think of this, asks Widmer, and of the work of the Bible societies against which a papal warning was already out?[53] The Church has never deviated in its support for the 'well-regulated' reading of the scriptures, but, like a good mother, it has sought to safeguard the fine fruit against corruption. Scepticism about the efficacy of the written word comes ultimately from Plato, and the oral character of the Apostolic witness confirms what Christ himself made clear, that his people were to be guided, not by their own perusal of written documents, but by the teaching office of the church (*heilige und bleibende Lehramt*).[54]

The substantial fourth chapter on the relation of philosophy and theology has the narrowest base in the *Paraclesis*, in Erasmus's remark that the Apostles and the Fathers did not teach the subtleties of the philosophers, even if they knew

---

[48] Widmer, 325–8, 341–6.   [49] Ibid. 54–5.   [50] Ibid. 62.   [51] Ibid. 74.

[52] Olin, 101; Holborn, 142.

[53] Briefs of Pius VII, June, Sept. 1816. Jedin, *Handbuch*, vi, pt. 1, 114.

[54] Widmer, 97, 108, 111.

them, but Widmer well knew of Erasmus's critique of scholasticism and, in fact, another throwaway line late in the *Paraclesis* gives him a chance to return to that subject (chapter 10), as we shall see. Widmer begins with a condemnation of the sophists, who turn what genuine philosophers treat with a certain awe into frivolous games. But the philosophers themselves are tempted to make universal claims for partial, time-bound systems. Widmer is philosophically irenic or eclectic: the discipline rightly takes many different and seemingly contradictory forms. This multiplicity is, in fact, a sign as much of philosophy's weakness as of its richness. Widmer returns to the dependence of *Wissen* on *Glauben*. Each philosophical system represents but a fraction of eternal truth; the relative value of the fractions can be assessed by the standard of revelation. Philosophy's best service is preparatory to, and explanatory of, positive or revealed religion.[55] That is the position of Augustine and Clement of Alexandria.[56]

In his tenth chapter, on scholasticism, Widmer adds: in its healthy aspects scholasticism plays such a supporting role. It arose and arises from the natural and necessary struggle to understand and to harmonize the Christian faith with other branches of knowledge. The medieval theologians applied a rare acumen to this problem. Even in modern times *christkatholische Theologie* can use the language of contemporary philosophers—Kant, Fichte, or Schelling—without a betrayal of the fundamentals.[57] Widmer considered that in these matters Erasmus's position was more absolute than his own. Indeed, Erasmus's references to the scholastics in the *Paraclesis* are sceptical, if prudent. In comparison with the Gospels and the Apostolic letters, he says, 'these other writings do not seem holy'.[58] For Erasmus, says Widmer, the divine revelation must be explained out of itself without any human admixture. Widmer's defence of scholasticism and its seeking to 'put philosophy in all its branches with theology in a true and lasting unity' makes him more open to the contemporary philosophical culture than Erasmus himself.[59]

Around the middle of the *Paraclesis*, Erasmus writes: 'For upon these three ranks of men principally the task of either renewing or advancing the Christian religion has been placed: on the princes and the magistrates who serve in their place, on the bishops and their delegated priests, and on those who instruct the young eager for all knowledge.' If these respectively demonstrated, inculcated, and instilled the basic Christian teaching which the sophisticated call vulgar (*plebeia*), then Christendom would be spared controversy, war, and depredation, and, 'finally, we would not differ from those who do not profess the philosophy of Christ merely in name and ceremonial'.[60] This is the trigger in the *Paraclesis*

---

[55] Ibid. 116, 124–7, 149–51.   [56] Augustine: Widmer, 127–9; Clement: Widmer, 147.
[57] Widmer, 321–4.   [58] Olin, 106–7; Holborn, 147–8.
[59] Widmer, 321, 325, 327.   [60] Olin, 102–3; Holborn, 143–4.

for Widmer's discussion of 'the spirit of Christ in the ruler, priest, and pedagogue' (chapter 5), which is central to his book. The controlling impulse in the service rendered by princes, priests, and educators, and the controlling idea in the three sections of Widmer's chapter, is 'holy love'. Love stands, as in the incarnation and the redemption of the human race, as the 'mediator of opposites' (*Vermittlerinn der Gegensätze*), 'reconciling all contradictions and completing the imperfect'. It holds in tension diversity or multiplicity and unity.[61] It gives temporal rule a personal and paternalistic character. The ruler directed by divine love cannot use people as mere means to an end; each is an end in himself (*Selbstzweck*) and deserves protection, without which his being an end in himself is inconceivable. Protection extends to the communities and corporations through which *Selbstzweckheit* is expressed. The ruler will be the 'shepherd and father of the people', not satisfying their every demand but, like a wise parent, resisting what corrupts and, above all, cultivating *Religiosität*, the seedbed, not only of good order, but of humanity itself. There is an absolute right, unaffected by time or place, independent of individual wills and the general will, towards which rule and temporal justice should be directed. It excludes both arbitrary rule or despotism and the revolutionary distemper which has corrupted or destroyed all truly human relationships.[62] This vision of Widmer's is profoundly conservative but not nostalgia for the patrician or territorial administrations of the old regime or for enlightened despotism. We will track it more closely when we separate out his references to his contemporaries.

Priestly organization, Widmer says in his second section, is a hierarchy. An unnamed ultramontane writer attributes to it 'the unity of the patriarchal government of a family'. This is not a collegial unity (as Gallicans or Febronians might claim) but a personal one centred on Peter and his successors. Hierarchy must, above all, be understood organically. Widmer here demonstrates his affiliation to the romantic thinkers from Herder on. Love come from Christ is, for priests as for rulers, the *organisirendes Prinzip*, the root from which the whole plant springs.[63] When Widmer applies the metaphor to Church–State relations, the picture becomes cloudy: the relationship is neither a unity nor a separation but 'rests on an organic union of both by which they are necessarily different in their unity and necessarily one in their difference'. He tries another metaphor which is ultramontane enough: the Catholic Church is over the states as their inspiring principle but does not remove their independence any more than the sun removes that of the planets.[64] Widmer's historical and contemporary references are plainer. He rejects the idea of a national Church, which Wessenberg

---

[61] Widmer, 161–3. Widmer quotes Aristophanes in the *Symposium* on the healing powers of love (pp. 161–2).

[62] Ibid. 170–7.   [63] Ibid. 209–11.   [64] Ibid. 223–4.

wanted for Germany and the Restoration regime in Lucerne for Switzerland. In that way the Church would lose its character 'as the objective expression or the essential form of the eternal and unchangeable religion'. The romantic idealist language was close to Gügler's in his theological work. Neither the theocratic system, which had, Widmer said, few supporters in his day, nor the territorial, which subordinated priests to rulers at every point according to the principle of *cujus est regio ejus est de religione dispositio,* was acceptable. The latter, the bureaucratic and police methods of dealing with the Church, must be resisted. 'Freedom' has that meaning for Widmer.[65]

Divine love expressed through rulers, priests, and then teachers—the last must be a favoured subject for a disciple of Sailer's. Widmer picks up momentarily the liberal, individualist, and empirical psychology of Erasmus, which J.-C. Margolin links to John Locke's: education thrives as a work of love which cultivates the powers and aptitudes of the educated.[66] But soon we are returned to the world of the Restoration, to the post-Revolutionary world. Widmer says that the educators of the Enlightenment, above all Pestalozzi, had an imperfect understanding of original sin. Christian educators, by contrast, began from that assumption (*Voraussetzung eines Radikalbösen*). Widmer's unnamed target was Pestalozzi's disciple, the Franciscan Jean Baptiste or Grégoire Girard (1765–1850), the 'Catholic Pestalozzi', who was under attack in Fribourg for promoting irreligion by his teaching methods and who was to teach in Lucerne itself between 1823 and 1834.[67] Widmer quotes with relish the attack on Pestalozzi and on J. B. Basedow (1724–90), 'leading representative of Enlightenment pedagogy in Germany', by a conservative Protestant writer: in the well educated, evil but takes a more sophisticated form; while true religion remains among the people, irreligion is the province of the educated. If religion and education are to work together as they must, then the educator must be under the oversight, not of the state, but of the priest.[68] The resonances in this long chapter are of the controversies of Widmer's own time and place; the *Paraclesis* can fairly be described as at best a 'trigger' for Widmer's contemporary reflections. Nevertheless, at the deepest level there was, to use the organic metaphor, a root, common to Widmer and the *Paraclesis*, in 'holy love'.

In what follows, chapter six on the relation of knowing and doing and chapter seven on rebirth as a fundamental Christian teaching, Widmer is close to the heart of Erasmian doctrine. On the first issue, the point is made aphoristically in

---

[65] Ibid. 217–19, 224; on Gügler, see Härdelin, 'Kirche und Kult', 150 and *passim.*
[66] Widmer, 229; J.-C. Margolin, *Erasme: Declamatio de pueris statim ac liberaliter instituendis: Étude critique, traduction et commentaire* (Geneva, 1966), 43–6.
[67] Widmer, 230; on Girard, see Pfister, *Kirchengeschichte,* iii. 62–6; *LThK* iv. 900–1.
[68] Widmer, 231–6; on Basedow, see *Neue Deutsche Biographie* (hereafter *NDB*) (Berlin, 1953–), i. 618–19.

the *Paraclesis*. 'Life means more than debate, inspiration is preferable to erudition, transformation is a more important matter than intellectual comprehension.'[69] Widmer expresses it appropriately for a post-Kantian age: there is no fast dividing-line between theoretical and practical reason (*Vernunft*) or between the will and the intellect; if the will is fallen, then the intellect is corrupt.[70] On the second issue, he takes the idea of rebirth as summary of the whole Christian teaching: creation, fall, redemption. He describes the creation and the fall, partly in organic, partly in Platonist terms: in the original order, communication between Creator and created was like that between members of a healthy organism; in the corrupted order, human works and plans betray the sense of an order that is lost, the world of appearances standing far beneath the *Idealwelt*.[71] The enemies of Christianity always attack the doctrine of the fall; redemption comes not, as they in these days believe, from enlightenment but from the Christian religion alone. In rebirth, man steps from one order to another, in reality as well as in appearance. Basing himself on the Tridentine decree on justification, with its assumed cooperation of grace (the sowing father-principle) and free will (the receiving mother-principle), Widmer teaches a kind of Christian perfectionism: the redeemed person 'nicht nicht Gutes wirken kann'.[72]

All this, if one sets aside the idealist romantic expression and discounts the emotional intensity of the post-Revolutionary time, is not far from Erasmus. The starting-points of the next two chapters, Erasmus's account of the relation of the pagan philosophers to Christian teaching and his criticism of devotion paid to human, especially monkish, rules, pose a greater challenge to Catholic exclusiveness. The truths of the pagans are, says Widmer, but fragments, gathered up and united in Christianity 'like the different forms of organic nature in the figure of humanity'.[73] As for the rules written by men, by Benedict or Augustine or Francis, which some, Erasmus says, treasure ahead of the Gospel writings themselves, Widmer puts them in the same category as all positive laws and personal and communal maxims which are not, unlike the divine law, eternal and immutable, but deserving of honour nevertheless, so long as they derive from or participate in that law. The religious Orders are 'particular and proper organs in the Christian organism'. Like Erasmus, one wishes, Widmer says, that among them, too, all traces of the merely human could be blotted out; yet every law and rule can be 'a lodestar for man, through which he reaches his goal in the shortest way'. Widmer is not intransigent: 'Omne nimium vertitur in vitium. . . . In medio stat virtus.' Virtue is in the middle path; it is unjust to give human rules the same observance as the divine, but unreasonable to deny them value without discrimination.[74]

---

[69] Olin, 104; Holborn, 144–5.   [70] Widmer, 240.   [71] Ibid. 261, 264–9.
[72] Ibid. 273, 276, 282, 286, 288.   [73] Ibid. 308.   [74] Ibid. 310–17.

After a brief return to the relation of teacher and pupil, which prompts Widmer to a long quotation from Sailer's *Pädagogik*,[75] the *Paraclesis* ends with remarkable expressions about the New Testament: 'These writings bring you the living image of His holy mind and the speaking, healing, dying, rising Christ Himself, and thus they render Him so fully present that you would see less if you gazed upon Him with your very eyes.'[76] Thus, Widmer has again to face the challenge of Erasmus's elevation of scripture. He replies: scripture cannot contain the whole Christ; the finite (words) cannot contain the infinite, or the temporal the eternal. The scriptures report but a small part of what Christ said and did. Besides, they are prone to misinterpretation and cannot defend themselves against error. The first Christians found Christ only in the Church he established, whose body is scripture, whose soul is the living word of oral tradition, whose spirit is the presence of the Holy Spirit. Widmer finishes his long work with an argument, based on Augustine's *De doctrina christiana* in particular, that these three must be held together if Christ is not to be divided: isolated, the letter of scripture kills rather than enlivens; tradition advancing things foreign to scripture is deceptive; claims to the spirit outside scripture or beyond the leading of the living word risk ending in a labyrinth of vain enthusiasm (*Schwärmerey*) and confusing the divine with the human spirit.[77]

Widmer was then engaged with the *Paraclesis* and with Erasmus through his text. Sometimes he is in controversy with Erasmus himself, even sharply. Sometimes he uses Erasmus to reinforce his own contentions in contemporary debates. At many points, contemporary controversies are on, or not far below, the surface. Above all, there is for Widmer the question of how pastors should be formed for guiding the people of the post-Revolutionary era. What is not clear is why Widmer should choose Erasmus and his brief, open, and rhetorical text to serve his purpose. What in his own situation pointed him back to Erasmus? Two approaches might help in answering this question. One is to identify the more important contemporary references in his work and thus map his intellectual world. Who are Widmer's chosen authors, and what does he take from them? The other is to locate him in the long history of Erasmus interpretations. Where does Widmer locate Erasmus himself in the history of Christian thought and piety?

Sailer predictably receives filial reference and deserves mentioning first. From his *Pastoraltheologie* Widmer takes the claim that reason is better served if philosophers turn, for their views on God and religion, to revelation in scripture than if theologians cut the cloth of biblical truth to the measure of philosophical

---

[75] Holborn, 148; Olin, 107–8; Widmer, 334–5.   [76] Olin, 108; Holborn, 149.
[77] Widmer, 341–51.

opinion. Widmer's other references are to the *Pädagogik*. Education is, in Sailer's image, a guardian angel (*ein übermenschlicher Genius*) who nurtures the tender, growing humanity in the child, bringing it to the stage where it can, not so much dispense with its guardian, as govern itself in his spirit. Children are capable of religious feeling and moral feeling, but, without education, these will be lost. Education brings the person through the three stages of childhood, youth, and adulthood, and to each there corresponds both a pedagogical and a religious form: the first is the realm of dispositions, the second of emerging concepts, the third of fully fledged ideas. Religious feeling needs strengthening through all three stages. Yet, Sailer, like Widmer, holds that education can turn to evil as readily as to good.[78] The picture of Sailer suggested by Widmer's selections is finely balanced: his is a biblical, not a speculative, theology but he insists on the primacy of revelation; he assumes educable qualities in the child but holds to the doctrine of original sin. The liberal Sailer, the sympathetic pastor, the acquaintance of Pestalozzi, the enemy of the hyperorthodox, is certainly present.

At the same time Widmer draws much on major apologists and ideologues of Catholic restoration. From Friedrich Schlegel there is a brief quotation—a criticism of *Sophistik*[79]—but Adam Müller and Franz Baader (to mention the best known) bulk large. There are others. The first to be mentioned was hardly a conventional Catholic, though much used by Catholic apologists. Louis Claude de Saint-Martin (1743–1803), who dubbed himself *le philosophe inconnu* and whom Widmer in emulation called *der allzuwenig Gekannte*,[80] was introduced to the occult by the Portuguese Jew Martinez de Pasqualis, read Swedenborg and Protestant enthusiasts like J. C. Lavater, was drawn into the borderlands between science and mysticism, with his interest in vitalism, magnetism, and mesmerism, and, as his translator, became the channel for the Lutheran mystic Jakob Böhme to enter intellectual and religious life at the turn of the nineteenth century.[81] But he also confronted the Revolution, in his *Lettre à un ami, ou considérations politiques, philosophiques et religieuses sur la révolution française* (1795), which, like other works of his, was, within a generation, translated into German. 'The excesses of the revolution grieved him . . . but he acknowledged the greatness of the movement and the beauty of the aim.'[82] What Widmer takes from Saint-Martin is, first, a doctrine of creation: as in creation

---

[78] Ibid. 131–2, 228, 234–5, 334–5.   [79] Ibid. 117.   [80] Ibid. 171.

[81] J. C. F. Hoefer (ed.), *Nouvelle biographie générale* (Paris, 1853–66), xliii. 62–70; *Die Religion in Geschichte und Gegenwart* (3rd edn., 6 vols.; Tübingen, 1957–62 v. 1316–17; L. C. de Saint-Martin, *Mon portrait historique et philosophique (1789–1803)*, ed. R. Amadou (Paris, 1961), pp. ix–xvii, 75, 184 (Pasqualis, Böhme), 93–4 (Lavater) 107 (Pasqualis), 135 (Swedenborg), 143, 155 (Böhme); Droz, *Le Romantisme allemand*, 14; on Saint-Martin and Böhme, *Theologische Realenzyklopädie* (hereafter *TRE*), ed. G. Kravse and G. Müller (Berlin, 1976–), vi. 752.

[82] Hoefer (ed.), *Nouvelle biographie générale*, xliii. 66.

humanity participates in the godhead's perfection, being an image of it or reflecting it as in a mirror, so nature participates in the same perfection through humanity; all is enfolded in the divine completeness and perfection. With the fall, for both Saint-Martin and Widmer, the pattern is broken, first for humanity and then for nature. Men, everywhere in chains, should, in explaining their condition, look beyond social restrictions to the original misfortune.[83] From these premisses, Saint-Martin and Widmer in his train draw political conclusions. The order sadly lost, though still traceable in both men and nature, cannot be restored by seeking a general will in the human collective or an accumulation of individual wills. Only a general will grounded in the divine wisdom, pre-existent in the mind of God, can heal the sickness of human society. [84]

More directly political is what Widmer, in his section on Church–State relations, takes from Christian Friedrich Schlosser (1782–1829). Christian Friedrich and his brother Johann Friedrich Heinrich (1780–1851), from a prominent Frankfurt family, were Catholic converts (one in 1812 and the other in 1814) and publicists for the Catholic movement under the Restoration; J. F. H. Schlosser was Frankfurt's representative at the Congress of Vienna and belonged to the circle around Friedrich Schlegel and Clemens Maria Hofbauer, the first German Redemptorist, which sought, under Metternich's suspicious eye, to dismantle the Josephist state. Christian Friedrich, a nervier individual than these more robust natures, was best known for his campaign for the constitution of orders and estates and his book *Ständische Verfassung, ihr Begriff, ihre Bedingung*, published in 1817; in the same year Stein employed him on setting up provincial estates in the Prussian Rhineland. His views on estates were shared by the Vienna circle.[85]

Widmer draws on Schlosser's notes to the *Correspondance politique et administrative* of Joseph Fievée (1769–1839), one of the leading theorists of that time on state administration, a prefect at the end of the Empire and an ideologue, successively, of the Ultras and the liberals under the Restoration.[86] The independence of the Church, a crucial principle for Widmer and his associates, rests, Schlosser says, on its exclusive responsibility for the inner life. Its power lies in the hold faith and conscience have over men. By contrast, the State acts only on

[83] Widmer, 264–7, 271.   [84] Ibid. 171–2.

[85] Christian Friedrich Schlosser should not be confused with the *Aufklärer* historian, Friedrich Christian Schlosser (Widmer states the given names in that order). See *ADB* xxxi. 541–7, for various relevant members of the Frankfurt Schlosser family; cf. Droz, *Le Romantisme allemand*, 182, 250, 270. Droz confuses the two brothers at one point and one or other of them with their uncle Johann Georg, Goethe's brother-in-law (p. 250). On the Vienna circle, see Droz, *Le Romantisme allemand*, 248, 251–3; Jedin, *Handbuch*, vi, pt. 1, 264–5.

[86] *Dictionnaire de biographie française* (Paris, 1933–), xiii. 1315–16; Hoefer (ed.), *Nouvelle biographie générale*, xvii. 664–6; *Correspondance politique et administrative, commencée au mois de mai 1814* (15 parts; Paris, 1815–19).

the outward and visible. The constitutional and administrative relationship between Church and State is not fixed; it may change as circumstances change. What the Church can never accept is the State's intrusion into its own inner life. Worldliness, in selecting its bishops, for example, is, as recent history has shown, its danger and destruction. Josephism and the state Church remain the enemy, as Schlosser's concluding reference to the Church, 'through promise and history bound sacramentally to its highest head', suggests.[87]

It was not a long step from Schlosser's system of estates to the more comprehensive political and social philosophy of Adam Müller (1779–1829).[88] He, too, was a convert to Catholicism, in Vienna in 1805 with the support of his friend Friedrich Gentz, the counter-revolutionary publicist, who remained a Protestant. By the time of the book on which Widmer drew, *Von der Nothwendigkeit einer theologischen Grundlage der gesammten Staatswissenschaften und der Staatswirtschaft insbesondre* (Leipzig, 1819), Müller had shed the pantheism which, with its universe of unresolved antinomies, sat uneasily with his new faith.[89] He could define his social philosophy then as wholly Christian and Catholic: the social order must rest on the Christian religion, on the divine imperatives. Widmer echoed this appeal to theocratic principles, but he also accompanied Müller into other regions of his social thought, his medievalism and admiration for the decentralized state, his assault on absolutism and Jacobinism and liberal political economy, his patriarchalism and positive jurisprudence, his organic thinking. Through the press, Müller promoted his views in Napoleonic and post-Napoleonic Europe. In Berlin in 1810, without completely antagonizing the Prussian government, he had attacked Hardenberg's reforms aimed at restricting the nobility and moving Prussia towards a liberal economy. In the last years of the Empire, he joined the Vienna circle and moved into Austrian service; after 1815, he was a publicist in Germany for the Restoration as Austria understood it. The combination of roles, publicist and social philosopher, Austrian and Catholic, was not without contradictions and tensions. Widmer did not dwell on that; he called Müller 'one of the most profound and on every count most estimable of German jurists'.[90] The passage from Müller— not word for word, but following the main trends—is the longest from any author in his book.

Following Burke, his mentor, Müller, as Widmer presents him, rejects the attempt to shape society to an abstract ideal, especially an ideal of equality. In the

---

[87] Widmer, 225–7.

[88] A. Müller, *Kritische/ästhetische und philosophische Schriften*, ed. W. Schroeder and W. Siebert, ii (Neuwied, 1967), 'Biographische Einführung', 301–11; 'Die Adam Müller-Forschung im 20. Jahrhundert', 382–95; *ADB* xx. 501–11; *LThK* vii. 671–2.

[89] Droz, *Le Romantisme allemand*, 68.

[90] Widmer, 201.

Kingdom of God, known by revelation and faith, equality comes by the way of abnegation, not by the way of abstraction. Towards God all have an equal obligation; in human societies responsibilities are different and unequal. The true state of affairs, morally speaking, can be discerned only through the combination of theology and jurisprudence.[91] The true model of the State, furthermore, is not an abstraction of any kind, but an organism. Organic thinking allows Müller to encompass two of the dialectics that are characteristic of his thought.[92] First is the dialectic of dependence and independence: like parts of a body, members of a State are both independent of and dependent on one another. In recent centuries force has replaced faith as the shaper of societies, and absolutism has denied a place to corporate bodies and estates, the 'states within the state'. In reaction has been raised the cry of freedom, but an abstract freedom, not that positive freedom 'where each can be a lord within his own God-given sphere'.[93] For Müller there is no freedom, only freedoms.[94]

The second dialectic is that of movement and stability. Human societies cannot remain static (*beym bloss Gegebenen*); here Müller and Widmer, following him, diverge from the merely backward-looking, authoritarian type of Restoration thought. Organisms grow and develop. So law, which represents what is, and the intelligence, shrewdness, and insight (*Klugheit*) for guiding change must balance one another.[95] In contemporary politics they are dangerously divided, the Ultras standing on legitimacy alone, the liberals seeking only the utilitarian. This conflict between those who see in the future only ruin and those who see in the past only abuse can be resolved, say Müller and Widmer, in Christianity alone.[96]

There follows the statement of a Christian social philosophy and a critique of liberal political economy and individualism. Human beings and groupings all have a distinct existence. Their model is the family and household. Müller's thought is personalist and patriarchal. 'How the living nature of the state is expressed in the natural constitution of the family common to all the peoples on earth' was a chapter heading in his earlier work (1809), *Die Elemente der Staatskunst*.[97] Now the cash nexus has replaced personal relationships, men are

---

[91] Widmer, 182, 193–4.

[92] Thus, in his early work *Die Lehre vom Gegensatze* (1804): 'die Fragen nach einer Realität über das Verhältnis, über den Gegensatz hinaus in sich widersprechend, unsinnig und leer sind' (*Kritische/ästhetische und philosophische Schriften*, ii. 203).

[93] Widmer, 186–9.

[94] Ibid. 180–1.

[95] Just as the nobility (the settled, feminine element) and the bourgeoisie (the progressive, masculine element) must balance one another (*ADB* xxii. 507).

[96] Widmer, 190–2.

[97] *Die Elemente der Staatskunst* (Berlin, 1936, repr. 1968), ch. 5, 59–70, esp. 65, 69.

treated as more or less usable machines and have become slaves to things or money. Human nature has shrunk, to be restored by Christian faith and love alone.[98]

Baader, like Müller, observed the alienation of what his generation was coming to call the 'proletariat' and looked for workers' organizations led by the Church.[99] Widmer did not pick him up at that point. Baader (1765–1841) was a polymath: medico, mineralogist, administrator.[100] Many of the spiritual tendencies of the age found heightened, if fragmentary, expression in him. He was, as a young man, close to Sailer; he shared with Saint-Martin a preoccupation with Böhme; he was, for a time, a friend of Schelling, influencing the evolution which brought Schelling 'from system to mysticism, from understanding to will', as shown in his *Essay on Freedom* (1809).[101] He also looked beyond his contemporaries to older traditions: the mystical, the gnostic, the scholastic—before the scholastic revival, he was the student of Aquinas. He acted on a broad stage, as publicist for the Holy Alliance and the reunion of Churches, including the Russian Orthodox.[102]

Widmer's selection, taken from Baader's most recent work, *Sätze aus der Bildungs- oder Begründungslehre des Lebens* (Berlin, 1820), demonstrates what modern scholarship has accepted, that Baader is centred on Christian revelation.[103] His formula—*Cogitor [a Deo] ergo cogito et sum*—was a challenge to subjectivism and human claims to autonomy. Widmer quotes Baader at the end of his chapter on the doctrine of rebirth: as, in nature, lower forms are drawn to a new stage by the attracting power of higher forms, so the grace of God elevates and enlivens the fallen human spirit. This is an act of procreation and incorporation, so that the divine gives to the human nature life, foundation, new birth; Baader quotes the eucharistic discourse in John's gospel: 'he who eats me shall live because of me' (John 6: 57).[104]

Widmer accompanies Baader, whom he praises as *der christlicher Theosoph unter den Philosophen*, to the wider horizons, or the darker regions, of his thought.[105] The powers which come through his new relationship with God

---

[98] Widmer, 195–9; on Müller and Adam Smith and his disciples, *Elemente der Staatskunst*, 230–2; F. Heyer, *The Catholic Church from 1648 to 1870* (London, 1969), 170.

[99] Ibid. 170; Droz, *Le Romantisme allemand*, 286; F. von Baader, *Gesellschaftslehre*, ed. H. Grassl (Munich, 1957), 45–8.

[100] *NDB* i. 474–6; *TRE* v. 64–7.

[101] T. F. O'Meara, *Romantic Idealism and Roman Catholicism: Schelling and the Theologians* (Notre Dame, Ind., 1982), 79.

[102] *Gesellschaftslehre*, 26–34, 48–55.

[103] *TRE* v. 66.

[104] Widmer, 292–4.

[105] For the 'dark' elements in romantic theology, see Härdelin, 'Kirche und Kult', 155–6; cf. D. Baumgardt, *Franz von Baader und die philosophische Romantik* (Halle, 1927), 337–47.

extend to man's associations with the material world: clairvoyance and miracle-working become possibilities. The natural world, darkened by the fall and now in travail, as Paul says (Rom. 8: 22), remains obscure to those outside the new creation in Christ but will reveal its hidden spirit to those within.[106] Rebirth is an associative experience, binding individuals, communities, and the natural creation.

The ecumenism, which in Baader took a Slavophil and anti-Roman form, was present in various forms in the first quarter of the nineteenth century.[107] Whatever the 'ultramontanism' of his associations in Lucerne, Widmer demonstrates that ecumenism in the use he makes of Protestant authors. Before quoting J. A. Kanne (1773–1824), an idiosyncratic mythologist, linguist, and pietist from the Reformed camp, he notes the Pauline admonition: 'Prove all things; hold fast that which is good' (1 Thess. 5: 21). Catholics, he says, will read with profit and joy Kanne's declaration that our return to God depends on his first coming down to us, as angels descended and ascended on Jacob's ladder.[108]

Similarly, Widmer, at the end of his chapter on philosophy, introduces the Heidelberg theologian Carl Daub (1765–1836) with the remark that, though a Protestant, he deserves commending to Catholic theologians for his argument that, without philosophy, theology in the scholarly sense is impossible; only speculatively, not empirically or historically, can theology have knowledge of religion's absolute ground.[109] The language is Schelling's, and the passage belongs to a work from Daub's time of closest association with Schelling, the *Einleitung in das Studium der christlichen Dogmatik aus dem Standpunkte der Religion* (1810). Earlier Widmer had quoted the same work on how theological studies may be hindered by moral failings, of which vanity is the first. It is ironical that Widmer should include among the vanities abstract intellectual systems when Daub was in time to become the chief proponent of associating theology with the Hegelian system.[110]

Towards Schelling himself Widmer seems reserved: did what he said about theology in his lectures on academic studies (1802) not undervalue faith and put too much trust in ontological knowledge, in mind at the expense of spirit (*der Verstand auf Kosten des Gemüthes*)?[111] Widmer finds the corrective in Schelling's Lutheran supporter, A. C. A. Eschenmayer (1768–1852). Eschenmayer was Professor of Medicine and Natural Philosophy at Tübingen from 1811 and, like Schelling and others of his circle, put scientific knowledge in the framework of idealist philosophy.[112] Widmer quotes from his *Religionsphilosophie* his account

---

[106] Widmer, 291, 296–9.   [107] Jedin, *Handbuch*, vi, pt. 1, 137–9.
[108] *NDB* xi. 105–6; Widmer, 279–82.
[109] Ibid. 157.
[110] Ibid. 80–1; *NDB* iii. 522; *ADB* iv. 768; O'Meara, *Romantic Idealism*, 5, 56.
[111] Widmer, 138.   [112] *NDB* iv. 644.

of the idealist transformation of European thought: the ideas, unchangeable and universal, have, like the Copernican sun, rightly taken the central position, usurped in the previous epoch by the intellect (*Verstand*), whose command actually extends only to the particular and the changeable.[113] Eschenmayer, with Widmer's acclaim, breaks free from the common ground of idealism: 'At the limit of the idealist system is faith, and God is at the limit of faith.'[114] *Glauben* is superior to *Wissen*, which brings no revelation. Faith is the one transcendent capacity of the soul, but it is not an active but a receptive capacity, a capacity for receiving the divine light. Here Eschenmayer adds a Lutheran element to the idealist structure. Widmer, however, uses what Eschenmayer says about knowing and believing for his own purposes, to promote the movement from Enlightenment theology to the theology of Catholic restoration.[115]

Tracking Widmer's references has brought us a long way. We can take one further step. Widmer draws even on those beyond the Christian camp or those whose Catholic orthodoxy was contested. He takes F. H. Jacobi (1743–1819), a meeting-point of many tendencies of the late Enlightenment and early romanticism, as a demonstration of how philosophy can stand in the way of adherence to Christian revelation, even when the individual is receptive and sympathetic.[116] More strikingly still, Widmer quotes approvingly the advice to students of a theologian who was already suspect in Catholic pietistic circles and among strictly orthodox theologians: accompany doubters in their wanderings, in order to help them; ensure that there is no contradiction between what you say and what you believe; bring everything into a system, so that new issues can be accommodated.[117] Georg Hermes (1775–1831) of Bonn sought to make assent to the truths of Christianity a rational necessity, building a Catholic theology on a Kantian foundation. Critics pursued him from the publication of the work quoted by Widmer, *Einleitung in die christkatholische Theologie* (1819), and in 1835 Rome condemned him.[118]

What light does this constellation of authorities, from Sailer to Müller to Hermes, throw on Widmer's position and, in particular, on his choice of Erasmus's *Paraclesis* to be the launching-pad for his thoughts on the whole range of topics, pedagogical, pastoral, theological, and socio-political, covered in his

---

[113] Widmer, 140–1.   [114] O'Meara, 64.

[115] Widmer, 141, 146–7. In an ecumenical extension (pp. 142–6), Widmer praises Bacon's distinction between natural theology accessible to reason and the divine mysteries known only to faith: Bacon, *De dignitate et augmentis scientiarum libri IX* (1623), iii. 2, ix. 1, in *Works*, viii (London, 1827), 158–9; ix (London, 1828), 117.

[116] Widmer, 132–4; on Jacobi and Christianity, see *TRE* xvi. 434–8; *NDB* x. 222–4; Funk, *Von der Aufklärung*, 53–4.

[117] Widmer, 91–2.

[118] *NDB* viii. 671–2; Schnabel, *Deutsche Geschichte*, iv. 65; Jedin, *Handbuch*, vi, pt. 1, 293.

book? First, he is irenic, even eclectic. He treats Protestant authors with respect and includes authors, like Saint-Martin and Hermes, whose relation to Catholic orthodoxy was uncertain or debatable. This relative openness would make Erasmus attractive to him.

Secondly, there is a central core to which he is bound. Sailer belongs to it, and also Adam Müller and even Baader. The link Widmer makes between these thinkers is their sense of Christian community, of the Church as the unique channel for the dispensing of God's love to the world and, consequently, as the pre-eminent source of the values that make civilization and human society possible. The connection to philosophical idealism and to early romanticism, in its power and freshness, is apparent. In political terms, what matters most is the freedom of the Church, its loose fit to State structures, the end of bureaucratic ways of handling religious issues. The Widmer of 1820 is distant also from the kind of ultramontanism that sees the Church primarily as structure, bureaucracy, authority. There are backward-looking elements in what Widmer says in this book, even narrowing and confining ones, but there is also a sense of revival, of the relaying of foundations, of a creative moment in Christian history.

Widmer knows that he cannot shape Erasmus entirely to his own purposes; hence his at times sharp criticisms of and divergences from his subject. A gap remains between Erasmus's *Paraclesis* and Widmer's *Paraklesis*, just as a gap remains between the Widmer of the *Paraklesis* and the Widmer of the struggles in Lucerne, which we have tried to explain above. Yet Widmer sees in Erasmus the prophet of a society whose values, habits, practices, and structures are shot through with divine love. Erasmus can justly be taken as guide to a Church which, through its educational and pastoral practice and—to a degree—through its political action, works to shape such a society and civilization.

In the 300 years between Erasmus's publication of his *Paraclesis* and the appearance of Widmer's *Paraklesis*, Erasmus's reputation had gone through many vicissitudes. Among both Protestants and Catholics, there were hard and and soft judgements about him. On the Catholic side there was an especially virulent Jesuit tradition against him, which makes a curious counterpoint to Widmer's career and attitude to Erasmus. To the hard school of thought the great humanist was a destructive force through his sceptical temper, his mockeries, his abrasive criticism of popes and bishops, his eroding of the credit of monks and theologians, his subversive revision of the texts on which the doctrinal edifice rested. To the other side he was essentially orthodox, soberly devout, applying his literary and scholarly skills to cleansing the Church of its abuses and to restoring the texts from which Christian living and Christian culture drew their life's blood.[119]

---

[119] See my *Phoenix of His Age: Interpretations of Erasmus c.1550–1750* (Toronto, 1979) and *Interpretations of Erasmus c.1750–1920: Man On His Own* (Toronto, 1992).

Widmer's choice of the *Paraclesis* and his use of Erasmus suggest that by and large he takes the softer line, and what he writes about the man himself confirms this. There are, Widmer says, some dangerous expressions in his writings, but these must be read in the light of the times. He combined Catholicity, an unusual learning, and warm piety, and his aim was to purify theology and lead it back to its divine sources. To the present time (the unsteady post-Revolutionary world, the battleground of liberals and Ultras), he shows how faith in Catholic doctrine and submission to authority can be combined with intellectual capacity and freedom of spirit.[120]

There are, says Widmer, three conflicting theological parties: the supernaturalists, who base themselves on the unchanging word of God; the rationalists, who emphasize human autonomy and progress; the mystics, less bound to tradition than the first and less trustful of reason than the second, who are centred on the living light and fire of revelation in man's inmost being. Each has a truth, but not an exclusive truth. The classic theological writers, of whom Erasmus is one, hold together true doctrine, intellectual clarity, and piety.[121] So Widmer locates Erasmus in the span of theological history, so he locates himself amid the turbulences of the post-Revolutionary world.

[120] Widmer, pp. ix–xi.   [121] Ibid. pp. iii–ix.

14

The Office of Chief Rabbi: A Very English Institution

Aubrey Newman

During the three and a half centuries following the 'Resettlement' of Jews in England in the middle of the seventeenth century, Anglo-Jewry[1] has developed an almost unique structure of secular and religious organization. Jews came into England at a time when the state was becoming increasingly a 'confessional' state. The application of the Test Acts confined many of the offices within the state to communicant members of the Church of England, imposing many restrictions on nonconformist Protestants, Roman Catholics, and of course the Jews. And yet, unlike the situation in virtually every other state and principality in Europe, government permitted these Jews to enter the country and take up residence with no restrictions on where they could live nor on the numbers who could enter, a factor which in itself must throw doubts upon the extent to which Britain could be regarded as a genuine 'confessional state'.[2]

The impact of this confessional state upon the Jews of England was surprisingly minimal. Whatever their family origins, those Jews who were born in England were regarded as full British subjects with all the privileges of their countrymen. The only restrictions imposed on them were those which affected all who were not members of the Church of England and who therefore could not produce a 'Sacrament Certificate'. On occasion they were even given special privileges. In 1753, for instance, when Lord Hardwicke's Marriage Act imposed restrictions on the circumstances under which marriages could be solemnized, insisting that virtually all weddings had to be conducted under the auspices of the

[1] This is the term traditionally (if inaccurately) used to describe the community of Jews in the United Kingdom. Jewish communities in Scotland and Northern Ireland developed later than those in England, and are usually regarded as offshoots of 'Anglo-Jewry'.

[2] It is noticeable that in his discussion of England as a 'confessional state', J. C. D. Clark (*English Society, 1688–1832* (Cambridge, 1985)) ignores the existence of a Jewish community, nor does he refer to any of the privileges which that state saw fit to permit. For a discussion of these and other issues, see also, however, D. S. Katz, *The Jews in the History of England, 1495–1850* (Oxford, 1994), and Israel Finestein, *Jewish Society in Victorian England* (London, 1993), ch. 2, 'The Jews and English Marriage Law during the Emancipation'.

Church of England, it was only the Jews and Quakers who were given authority to conduct their own weddings under their own regulations. Presumably it was felt that it would be almost impossible to enforce obedience to the law, and that the problems of doing so were not worth the trouble involved. The status of these native-born Jews was in no way affected by the 'Jew Bill' of 1753, under which foreign-born Jews who sought naturalization through the passage of a private Act of Parliament were exempted from the necessity of producing a 'Sacrament Certificate', which would, of course, have been an impossibility for them. The Act aroused a great deal of opposition and was hastily repealed in the following session of parliament. It is not clear whether this was an example of antisemitism or xenophobia, repeating antagonism at other times during the century to the various attempts at general naturalization of foreign-born Protestants, such as in 1746 and 1751.

The community consisting originally of a handful of independent congregations, at first largely Sephardi (Spanish and Portuguese) in origin, with a small number of Ashkenazi (German–Polish) Jews, had by the early twentieth century become a much larger community, overwhelmingly Ashkenazi in ritual and traditions. At the same time that community came to owe an ecclesiastic 'allegiance' to a unified chief rabbinate, very much under his direct guidance if not absolute control. This chief rabbinate has become almost unique not only in Europe but in most parts of the world, not merely because of its existence but because it emerged by custom and consent from within the community itself. The pattern in central and Eastern Europe had been that very often the secular, non-Jewish authority had demanded that its Jewish community should be represented by an 'ecclesiastical' official who was often designated rabbi or *Landrabbiner*. Sometimes that official was even chosen by such external, secular authority, and the last factor in the mind of those making such a choice was the possible rabbinical scholarship of the incumbent. As a result, many of those subjected to the 'rule' of such an official rabbi imposed from above by the 'host' non-Jewish society in which Jews were living had the lowest possible opinion of his capabilities and had nothing but contempt for his religious rulings.[3]

The existence of such a chief rabbinate in Britain was in consequence a particularly Anglo-Jewish institution which developed its own characteristics. One of these was the way in which in many aspects it came to model itself in many ways on the habits of the host society. The most obvious parallel was between the office of chief rabbi and a bishop of the Church of England. It was suggested that one chief rabbi went so far as to adopt 'clerical gaiters', and if he did not actually wear an ecclesiastical hat with appropriate rosettes he came close

---

[3] See *Encyclopaedia Judaica* (Jerusalem, 1971–1974), vol. x, cols. 409–10.

to so doing. Several of them insisted on being termed 'Very Reverend the Chief Rabbi', and at various stages, when there was a search for a successor chief rabbi, the 'job-specification' that was developed included the statement 'the visitation of Provincial Synagogues and Schools is exclusively the function and duty of the Chief Rabbi, as is the visitation of a diocese by its Bishop'.[4]

An even closer parallel was to be found in 1848 when the Great Synagogue felt the need to establish a 'branch' synagogue in the West End of London. When it was ready for consecration, proclamation was made from the reading desk that 'notice is hereby given that this building now about to be consecrated is a Branch of the Great Synagogue situate in Duke's Place, in the parish of St James' Aldgate'. No marriages could be solemnized in it, its honorary officers were appointed for it by the parent congregation, and its financial affairs were strictly controlled by the Great Synagogue. It was the nearest equivalent which could be found to a 'Chapel of Ease' within the Church of England, and the lawyers responsible for this formula might well have consulted Canon Law.[5]

The reasons for this development lie partly within the ways in which the community as a whole gradually changed during the late eighteenth and early nineteenth centuries. Above all they are to be found in the way in which the Jewish community and the 'host', non-Jewish, community interacted with each other. The latter had a considerable impact upon the Jews of England, certainly with the leading members of Jewish society. There was a desire by many within the Jewish community to 'acculturate' themselves to the ways of their hosts, especially in such 'obvious' matters as the organization of their religion, and the extent to which strict religious observances might mark them out as being distinctive from the surrounding society. Sampson Gideon, for example, was so keen to establish his family within the English peerage that he married out of the faith and had his children baptized at birth. When his son, at the age of 13, was awarded a baronetcy, Sampson wrote to him that his further advancement would have to be on his own merits; the son, also Sampson, changed his surname to Eardley and eventually became an Irish peer.[6]

While Anglo-Jewry had never been known as particularly 'religiously observant', unlike, for example, many of the communities of central and Eastern Europe, many of those who came as religious leaders into one or other of the London congregations were particularly scathing about the standards of religious observance amongst those to whom they were supposed to minister and give spiritual guidance. One of them, Rabbi Zvi Hirsch Levin, who served in London

[4] See my 'The Chief Rabbinate and the Provinces, 1840–1914', in J. Sachs (ed.), *Tradition and Transition: Essays Presented to Chief Rabbi Sir Immanuel Jakobovits* (London, 1986), 220.
[5] See my *The United Synagogue, 1870–1970* (London, 1977), 3.
[6] L. S. Sutherland, *Politics and Finance in the Eighteenth Century* (London, 1984), 396–7.

from 1756 until 1764, attacked his members for dressing like gentiles, for associating with English people even on Christian feasts, for even having their letters opened for them on the Sabbath in front of the Post Office by passing strangers. He complained in one sermon that 'The shaving of the beard, a non-Jewish custom, strictly and repeatedly forbidden . . . you regard as minor matters. . . . You direct a non-Jewish servant to light the fire, to make fresh tea or coffee on Sabbath. Do not forget the punishment for this sin is that fire breaks out in your houses.'[7]

Levin left after only eight years, while others who stayed longer still spent much of their time complaining about the way they were treated by their congregations. Gradually, however, a sort of organizational discipline imposed itself upon the community as a whole during the second half of the eighteenth century and the early part of the nineteenth. Small groups grew up in various parts of the country, later to be the nucleus of a number of provincial communities. Many of their members had come originally from London and they tended to look to one or other of the London Ashkenazi congregations for such religious guidance as they required. Over and over again rabbis from London found officials who could provide circumcision or the supply of ritually acceptable food. Increasingly, however, it was to one synagogue to whom these smaller communities turned, that in Duke's Place, the so-called Great Synagogue, and increasingly its rabbi came to be regarded as THE rabbi, the chief rabbi.[8]

Another development within the community came in 1760, on the accession of George III, when the leaders of the Sephardi congregation presented him with a loyal address of congratulation on this occasion; the Ashkenazi leaders expressed annoyance to the Sephardi leaders that they had not been invited to participate, whereupon it was agreed that in future 'each nation should communicate to the other what they were doing in public affairs'. It was this decision which has been taken as the establishment of the London Committee of Deputies. The name itself, however, indicates the parallels which must always be made between the London Jewish community and its non-Jewish hosts. For in 1732, when the various Protestant nonconformist bodies in and around London had wanted to make joint representations to the principal ministers of the day, they had formed themselves into the London Board of Dissenting Deputies. In practice there were few occasions for meetings of this new Jewish body, and it was not until the second and third decades of the nineteenth century that the body was to assume a much greater significance.

---

[7] Quoted C. Duschinsky, *The Rabbinate of the Great Synagogue London, from 1756–1842* (London, 1921), 11–12.

[8] See C. Roth, *The Rise of Provincial Jewry: The Early History of the Jewish Communities in the English Countryside, 1740–1840* (London, 1950), and his *History of the Great Synagogue, 1690–1940* (London, 1950).

In 1802 Rabbi Solomon Hirschell was appointed rabbi in the Great Synagogue, and he was probably the first to whom the title chief rabbi could be awarded without any real dispute. It was probably less due to the force of his own personality as to the lack of any equivalent minister in the other main London synagogues, but his willingness to take great pains must also have been relevant. Certainly his letter books show him in correspondence with individuals and congregations throughout England, while there is evidence of his being involved with communities being established in the Antipodes. It could well be claimed that he was regarded as the spiritual head of Ashkenazi Jews not only in England but over the British Empire as well, and on his death there was, for example, a memorial sermon preached by a non-Jewish clergyman at Portsmouth in which Hirschell was referred to as 'The Chief Rabbi of the German and Polish Jews in the British Dominions'.[9]

It was in 1836, towards the end of his period of office, that the first major accession of authority from outside arrived, just as it was in 1840, near its end, that the first major split developed within the community. The enhancement of the chief rabbinate's status arose out of the activity of the secular, non-Jewish state, and above all the authority which this state gave, almost by accident, to a lay Jewish leadership which itself was determined to maintain the religious authority of the ecclesiastics. The introduction of registration of marriages under the 1836 and 1837 Marriage Acts, regulating the licensing of places of worship for the purposes of conduct and registration of weddings, made provision for the continuance of the earlier autonomy of Jewish congregations. The (lay) president of the Board of Deputies of British Jews was given the authority to certify individual congregations as being Jewish, and therefore having permission not only to conduct marriages but, like Anglican Churches, to hold their own Wedding Registers, thus obviating the need for the intervention of lay registrars. The president was unwilling to exercise that authority on his own account, and chose instead to turn to the relevant 'ecclesiastical authorities' to certify in turn to him that they themselves recognized such congregations. All that was demanded from such congregations was that they acknowledged the spiritual authority of this chief rabbi. As a consequence, therefore, secular authority, Jewish and non-Jewish alike, gave a status to the chief rabbinate which otherwise it might never have achieved, and it was thus that the chief rabbinate could secure authority not only over any new congregations but over any minister which any congregation might seek to appoint.[10]

The extent of the authority which this had given the chief rabbi was illustrated during the controversy over the emergence of a 'Reform' community in London

---

[9] H. A. Simons, *Forty Years a Chief Rabbi* (London, 1980), 110.
[10] See 'Chief Rabbinate and the Provinces', *passim*.

during the 1840s. The existing synagogues were all situated on the eastern side of the City of London but various members who had moved out to the West End sought permission to hold services nearer their homes. The regulations of their mother congregations forbade such prayer meetings, so the decision of these individuals to proceed and establish their own place of worship—the West London Synagogue of British Jews—involved their exclusion from the existing congregations and was followed by a refusal of the president of the Board of Deputies to certify this synagogue as 'Jewish' within the meaning of the Registration Acts. It was not until 1856, when this 'Reform' congregation secured an Act of Parliament specifically to permit it to conduct marriages, that the problem was overcome, but not with the permission of the chief rabbi.

Hirschell died in 1842 and the Jewish weekly, the *Voice of Jacob*, the only such in existence in the community at that time, commented on the office of chief rabbi and on the particular qualities to be looked for in the new incumbent:

> Though forty years since a Chief Rabbi was the functionary of that congregation exclusively [i.e. the Great Synagogue] yet two other metropolitan congregations . . . from sheer necessity, have looked up to the Great Synagogue Rabbi. The provincial and colonial synagogues, scarcely one of which had, forty years ago, a status in the Jewish world, have since grown into importance, and they have found reference and subordination indispensable in Shehita, marriages, divorces etc., and hence, not from design or system but from inevitable necessity the late Chief Rabbi was recognised as the spiritual head of most Jews claiming British origin.[11]

Hirschell's successor, Nathan Marcus Adler, was appointed in 1845 by a committee which had claims to represent the five existing Ashkenazi communities in London as well as a wide spectrum of provincial congregations—nineteen in all—and he lost no time in seeking to establish wide recognition of his status. The following year, in 1846, he launched a searching series of questions to all the congregations in Britain, and indeed to several in the colonies as well. In 1847 he published a volume, *Laws and Regulations for all the Ashkenazi Synagogues in the British Empire*, which included the section 'The erection of a new synagogue must have the sanction of the Chief Rabbi; and the formation of a new Congregation must have the sanction of the Chief Rabbi, besides that of the Board of Deputies.' Technically, that was incorrect, in that he could not stop the building of a synagogue, but if such a congregation wished to conduct marriages within it and to hold its own marriage register it could do so only if those two had approved the congregation and its officiants in the first place.

A measure of the control which began to be exerted is to be seen in the ways in which he reacted to requests from congregations for help in finding suitable

[11] 11 Nov. 1842.

officiants. What was new in this was an insistence that, even when a potential incumbent had been found independently, he had to secure the chief rabbi's approval. There were difficulties in Manchester, for example, when the chief rabbi insisted on rejecting various attempts at local autonomy. After his death, the committee appointed to find his successor drew attention to the way in which the provincial communities

are constantly calling upon the Chief Rabbi to use his influence in the collection of funds towards building new synagogues inviting him to consecrate their edifices and to examine their schools . . . they write to him continually concerning their local affairs; they invoke his decision on religious questions; they rely on him to find and examine suitable officials as Preachers, readers, teachers, and shochtim [ritual slaughterer], and they appeal to him for his advice on every conceivable occasion.[12]

The extent to which his authority had extended—and the community as a whole had grown in the provinces—can be indicated by the fact that the committee appointed to consider the question of his successor was attended by the representatives of thirty-two provincial communities.

It was during the office of Nathan Marcus Adler (from 1846 until his death in 1890) and that of his son and successor, Hermann Adler (from 1891 until his death in 1911) that there can be seen the most extreme statements of authority and the widest expressions of discontent with it. Much of this discontent arose as a result of the 'great migration' out of Russia and Eastern Europe generally (i.e. 1880–1914) and the very obvious and very marked antagonism to the concept of a chief rabbinate from these newer arrivals. They were used to the existence of such an office as imposed by the state, and therefore to doing their best to evade and circumvent its decisions and wishes. A further complication arose out of the concentration of many immigrants into provincial centres. Previously, even in terms of numbers alone, London could claim an ascendancy over the provincial centres, but now the growing provincial communities could demand to be allowed their own active religious lives, drawing upon sources of religious authority independent of the chief rabbi and the London-based lay oligarchy. These religious leaders, both in dissident congregations within London and in the provinces, followed their own ways of life, and they often found themselves in conflict not only with the Anglo-Jewish establishment but also with the secular law. In seeking to establish their own marriage and divorce practices without regard to the decisions of the chief rabbi they ignored the demands of the secular law. While the chief rabbi tried valiantly to expedite the process of 'Anglicization', there were many congregations with little desire to try and assimilate into Anglo-Jewry. The result led many, on the death in 1911 of Hermann Adler

---

[12] 'Chief Rabbinate and the Provinces', 222.

[Nathan's son and successor], to reassess the importance of the institution. One leading provincial rabbi declared: 'The Chief Rabbinate in its present form has outlived itself . . . The Chief Rabbinate has crippled the community, has destroyed the sense of responsibility in congregation and minister alike.'[13]

That argument was not accepted; the Anglo-Jewish establishment felt at home with a chief rabbi, and so a man was appointed who had, on the one hand, every desire for the full authority possessed by his predecessors but who also had sympathy with and a clear view of the needs of Anglo-Jewry, including its new members who had been there longer. While he might have agreed with them that there had to be some measure of change, the one thing he would never accept was any lessening of the powers of his office. But, with Joseph Herman Hertz, Anglo-Jewry had chosen a man who found himself in conflict with the very establishment which had been responsible for his election.

The problem was that there had developed weaknesses within the narrow circle of families which had run the community for over 100 years. While their own religiosity had been wearing thin, Hertz had become increasingly aligned with a more religious wing. The result was a series of clashes. Hertz was well known as pugnacious—'always prepared to follow a peaceful path when all others had failed'—while his opponents were led by Sir Robert Waley-Cohen, a man who made it clear that, while all spiritual matters were under the absolute control of the chief rabbi, secular matters were under his own equally absolute discretion—and that he himself decided what was spiritual and what was secular. For almost twenty years the clashes between these two points of view continued, and when Chief Rabbi Hertz died the major aim of the lay leadership was to find a candidate who could be at once spiritually acceptable and at the same time more accommodating. The irony was that the candidate who was chosen as fulfilling these criteria was to end as the centre of bitterness even deeper than there had been with his predecessor.[14]

The appointments which have covered the period after 1914 have left problems. The issues which have emerged involve to a considerable extent the movement of large numbers to either the religious left or the religious right—both of which refuse to recognize any specific authority in the office of the chief rabbi. Indeed, the extent to which the 'host society' has welcomed the intervention of successive chief rabbis in its politics—even to the extent of awarding one of them a seat in the House of Lords—might well in itself have weakened the status of the chief rabbinate within the Jewish community itself. And the extent to which the state has turned to the chief rabbinate and regarded it as the official

---

[13] *Jewish Chronicle*, 23 June 1912.

[14] A. Newman, *Commemoration of the Centenary of the Birth of Chief Rabbi Dr Joseph H Hertz* (London, 1973).

spokesman of the community has further alienated those groups within the community who are unhappy about many of its aspects.

The chief rabbinate is a very English institution. Certainly its development and growth would have been unlikely in any other country or in any other circumstances. The links between spiritual and secular authorities within the community were paralleled by links between the community and the non-Jewish host society. Just as in the host society Church and State were on occasion in a state of tension, so within the Jewish community similar strains can be perceived. There were times when it was argued that the Jewish ecclesiastical leaders were the tools of secular leadership, that the chief rabbi and his associates were merely representing the wishes of a secular establishment. In practice, the chief rabbinate was never a tool of any of the secular groups, but it is interesting to see how often the wishes of secular and religious leaders paralleled each other. The twentieth century illustrated clearly the occasions when they worked together as well as those when they were at odds with each other.

15

'A footing beyond Time': Church, State, and the Individual in Carlyle's Historical Writing

Laurence Le Quesne

One of the great themes of the Romantic, and of the liberal, imagination is the image of the heroic individual in resistance to the forces of impersonal power. It is an image which takes many forms: Antigone resisting the State in the name of family piety, Prometheus bringing fire to men in defiance of the gods, Luther challenging the Diet of Worms because his faith gave him no option, Silvio Pellico's long martyrdom at the hands of the Austrian authorities in the Spielberg, down to the heroic resisters of totalitarianism in our own day, from Dietrich Bonhoeffer in Germany to Irina Ratushinskaya in the USSR. He or she is the figure of powerless justice: the forces of Church and State may bear them down, but they can resist them to the point of martyrdom because they take their stand on values more permanent than those of the contingent world which oppress them—because they have a footing beyond time.

'A footing beyond Time': the phrase is Thomas Carlyle's; it comes from his extraordinary description of the fall of the Bastille in his *History of the French Revolution*, from a passage in which he is describing the dilemmas confronting the unfortunate marquis de Launay, the governor of the Bastille, with the crowd thundering at his gates. The heroic option is available to de Launay: he could fire the magazine, and blow himself, the Bastille, and the crowd to destruction together. And yet, says Carlyle, he could not, because the clamour and the massed emotion of the crowd bear him down. 'Great is the combined voice of men; the utterance of their *instincts*, which are truer than their *thoughts*: it is the greatest a man encounters, among the sounds and shadows which make up this World of Time. He who can resist that, has his footing somewhere beyond Time.'[1] The individual confronts the mass; and indeed, if ever a historian was preoccupied with the theme, who more than Carlyle, who so emphatically identified the heroic individual as the motive power of history? If the defiant hero

---

[1] *The French Revolution*, i. 194. (All references to Carlyle's works are to the Centenary Edition of 1896–9.)

is one of the classic images of European Romanticism, who might be expected to employ it better than Carlyle, the supreme exemplar in English of the Romantic imagination applied to the task of historical writing?

So we might expect; but as we look more closely at Carlyle's historical writings, doubts arise. They may be aroused even by the brief passage just quoted. For de Launay is defined, not by his heroism, but by his lack of it, by the fact that he lacks the 'footing beyond Time'—representative in this of an age and a class fatally adrift from their moorings—with the result that the crowd, and the Revolution, roll over him and them. And it is not Church and State, nor even the unjust power of the gods, that de Launay fails to withstand, but a crowd that, to Carlyle, represents the force of History itself.[2] There *are* heroes in *The French Revolution*; but they do not withstand the crowd—they lead it, if only for a time. There is a dialectic here; but it is not the classic liberal dialectic of Might and Right. The difference seems worth exploring, and this is what I shall try to do in this chapter.

We should start with the philosophical idealism that Carlyle had derived from his readings in the literature of the German philosophical renaissance, ultimately from Kant. From this source Carlyle derived the distinction between a contingent world of phenomena, governed by the categories of space and time—for the great majority of mankind, the only world there is—and the world of realities that underlies it, occasionally breaks through into it, and whose presence is sensed and proclaimed by only an enlightened few—Fichte's 'learned men', Carlyle's own prophets and heroes—whose footing is indeed 'beyond Time'. It was with the recognition and the celebration of that few that Carlyle was to become increasingly preoccupied in his later writings. But what was the nature of their interaction with the institutions of Church and State?

We should note at the outset that Carlyle had little patience with institutions: much more often than not, his inclination was to dismiss them out of hand as mere 'machinery'. The note was first struck in his two great essays, *Signs of the Times* (1829) and *Characteristics* (1832), that mark his transition from the field of literary to that of social criticism. Both express forcefully Carlyle's preference for the inward, the dynamic, and the spontaneous, rather than the outward, the mechanical, and the calculated, and both condemn the present age for its precise reversal of this estimation. 'It is the noble People that makes the noble Government; rather than conversely',[3] he says in *Signs of the Times*; and in *Characteristics*

---

[2] A confrontation with eerie echoes in the recent history of central and Eastern Europe, as those will recollect who remember the pictures of East German bureaucrats on their balconies, helpless in the face of crowds hundreds of thousands strong, and their unanswerable chant of 'Wir sind die Volk' ('We *are* the People').

[3] *Critical and Miscellaneous Essays*, ii. 72.

it is the formation of society by the force of a common idea 'generated, or say rather heaven-kindled, in the solitary mind' which 'awakens its express likeness in another mind, in a thousand other minds, and all blaze-up together in combined fire',[4] which so evidently fires Carlyle's own imagination, and not at all the journeyman task of giving that idea institutional form, necessary though Carlyle recognizes that to be. It is the spirit that drives the institution, and not the form of it, that matters: the implication is that, if the spirit is living, it can find expression through almost any institution, and if the spirit is dead, no institutions can avail. It is worth noting, too, the source and the channel that Carlyle anticipates for the all-important inspiring idea. It is 'generated, or say rather heaven-kindled'—the ambiguity as to whether this is a natural or a divine process is characteristic of a deeper-lying ambiguity in Carlyle's own mind as to how, and whether, the philosophical Idealism he had derived from his German mentors was to be reconciled with his sternly Presbyterian upbringing; but so is the final resolution in favour of the divine. And this original kindling is generated in the *solitary* mind, from which it flashes to the thousand other minds: already there is there by implication the emphasis on the crucial role of the inspired individual, the 'prophet' and the 'hero' to come, and the merely secondary role of the crowd.

This is not to say that Carlyle had no appreciation of the importance of institutions. When, in the mid-1830s, he started work on *The French Revolution*—his first major work of history—he set out his understanding of the role of Church and State as early as its second chapter, revealingly titled 'Realised Ideals'. They are there presented as the central symbols which meet man's two deepest needs, the need to believe and the need to obey, and as such they are of vital importance to the well-being of every human society. But it is important to note here the very peculiar form that the political need takes in Carlyle—a form far removed from the idea of the social contract which was its equivalent in the dominant tradition of eighteenth-century political thought, a tradition which Carlyle swept aside with contempt—'Theories of government! Such have been, and will be; in ages of decadence.'[5] In fact he rejects not merely the notion of contract, but even the word 'state', identifying the two key symbols not as Church and State, but as Church and Kingship, and seeing French kingship reach its apogee in Louis XIV and his declaration 'L'État, c'est Moi'—the State not as an institution, but a person.[6] If the need is obedience (to obey, not to be obeyed) rather than community, or mutual security, it is best met not by an institutionalized society, but by a personalized one; and in such a context, the classic conflict between the heroic individual and the State could scarcely arise.

---

[4] Ibid. iii. 11.   [5] *The French Revolution*, i. 54.   [6] Ibid. 9.

For Carlyle, the heroic individual does not typically withstand the State, or even serve it: he *is* the State.

But if Carlyle rejects the symbol of the State, he accepts that of the Church. The Church, in its origin at least, was precisely the channel for the transmission of the divine idea—in addition, it does not take a very profound knowledge of Scottish history to understand how, to a youth reared in the tradition of Presbyterian piety, the Kirk might very well seem a far more sublime institution than the State. But the Church too was an institution, to which the divine word came only through the inspired individual, and, as an institution, it was fatally liable to the dangers of ossification, of ceasing to be a true medium for the word, and of becoming a mere hollow sham, that beset all institutions. In the recurrent conflicts between the institutional Church and the voice of antinomianism that have bedevilled ecclesiastical history, Carlyle's commitment is unequivocally to the rebel voices, the Luthers and the Knoxes. The rival Catholic view of the institutional Church as itself the inerrant voice of God was one, in both its Roman and its Anglo-Catholic form, that he violently rejected. And again it is easy to relate this to the influence of the religious background of his youth; and not only to the mainstream tradition of Scottish Presbyterianism, based as it was on memories of defiance of an institutionalized Catholic Church in the sixteenth century and of an institutionalized episcopal Church in the seventeenth, but also in Carlyle's case to his family's membership of the Burgher Secession Church, which had seceded from the institutionalized Church of Scotland in the eighteenth century.

In France before 1789, however, Carlyle suggests that both the need to believe and the need to obey go miserably unmet. Both Church and Kingship are eaten hollow from within, the Church by wealth, ease, and a fashionable scepticism that makes a mockery of its own professed beliefs, the monarchy by indolence, frivolity, and a progressive blindness both to its own responsibility to rule and provide for its people and to the realities of bankruptcy and revolution that loom more and more menacingly through the tissues of the court life of Versailles. Such spectres were no strangers to Carlyle. 'I had been at Mrs Austin's,' he wrote in his journal in the summer of 1835, while he was struggling to rewrite *The French Revolution* after the destruction of the original manuscript; 'heard Sydney Smith the first time guffawing, other persons prating, jargoning. To me through these thin cobwebs Death and Eternity sate glaring.'[7] It echoes the confrontation that Louis XV experienced one day when out hunting with 'a ragged Peasant with a coffin: "For whom?"—It was for a poor brother slave, whom Majesty had sometimes noticed slaving in these quarters. "What did he die of?"—"Of hun-

---

[7] J. A. Froude, *Thomas Carlyle: A History of his Life in London* (London, 1884), i. 54.

ger":—the King gave his steed the spur.'[8] Like so many of the images in *The French Revolution*, the incident works on more than one level: it is a reminder both of Louis's own mortality, which he dreaded, and of the sufferings which his neglect of his duties has brought upon his subjects, and which revolution will finally avenge. There is a third, fainter, echo too: of the failure of another ruling class, the British, to attend to the needs of its subjects in Carlyle's present, and of the judgement that he sees hanging over that also. The reading of *The French Revolution* called for a sensitive ear.

In *The French Revolution*, accordingly, a Church that has ceased to believe and a State (or, rather, a monarchy) that has ceased to enforce obedience both go down to a proper destruction by a volcanic outburst of intolerably deprived and frustrated human nature, the force which Carlyle christens 'Sansculottism', a force—to adapt a supremely appropriate Carlylean phrase from a a different context—'worthy of horror, worthy of worship',[9] and which, being a spontaneous, natural thing (the categories of Romanticism start brilliantly to life under Carlyle's handling) sweeps away the flimsy shams of the French Church and the French state, and indeed the successive paper constitutions of the early years of the Revolution. Individuals—like de Launay—are swept helplessly before it, all except those few who retain a 'footing beyond Time'; and in *The French Revolution* even they can do nothing more than stem the torrent momentarily. *The French Revolution*, unlike all Carlyle's later books, has no masterful hero imposing order on the natural chaos of events. It has two protagonists, Mirabeau and Danton, on whom Carlyle seems to confer heroic status, but both in the end go down before the onrush of the Revolution, which is irresistible until its destructive force has worked itself out: when that time comes, it can be quelled easily by General Bonaparte's 'whiff of grapeshot' on 5 October 1795. Even he is no more to Carlyle than the right man in the right place at the right time: in *The French Revolution*, individuals are less the masters of history than its victims. What is right for man, says Carlyle in *Heroes and Hero-Worship* (published three years after *The French Revolution*), is 'co-operating with the real Tendency of the World'.[10] No individual in *The French Revolution* succeeds other than briefly in conforming with this classic definition of historicism: if anything does, it is the Mob, the incarnation of 'Sansculottism', and the primal force of Nature at its most spontaneous. 'When so much goes grinning and grimacing as a lifeless Formality, and under the stiff buckram no heart can be felt beating, here once more, if nowhere else, is a Sincerity and Reality. (Your mob is a genuine outburst of Nature; issuing from, or communicating with, the deepest deep of Nature).'[11] Even 'battles ever since Homer's time, when they were Fighting Mobs, have

[8] *The French Revolution*, i. 19.   [9] Froude, *Thomas Carlyle*, i. 19.
[10] *Heroes and Hero-Worship*, 63.   [11] *The French Revolution*, i. 251.

mostly ceased to be worth looking at, worth reading of or remembering', war having become mechanical, 'with the slightest possible development of human individuality or spontaneity'[12]—a point on which Carlyle was later to change his mind.

This emphasis on the spontaneous, the uncontrollable, and the unpredictable lies right at the heart of Carlyle's interpretation of history in *The French Revolution*: history is a mass of red-hot, heaving, dynamic matter, which drives Carlyle repeatedly to volcanic images, and of which the mob is the human expression. This is an intensely Romantic (and an intensely historicist) conception of history. It is one which devalues institutions such as Church and State to the point of insignificance, because they purport to impose fixed forms on what is by its nature plastic and uncontrollable. As for individuals, the great mass of them are swept along by the tide, insignificant atoms in the mob. The heroic few, with their footing outside time, have not Church and State to contend with, but the naked forces of Nature itself, and against them they cannot prevail: they can at most sense them, check them momentarily, or divert them a little.

Periods such as the French Revolution, when history as it were turns molten (as it did in Eastern Europe in 1989), are—like volcanic eruptions—not the norm, but the exception: frequently the catastrophic exception, in which formal institutions which have lost their meaning and formulas of belief which have become hollow are swallowed up. But forms and formulas alike did once have a vital meaning: there was a time when they truly incarnated man's need to believe and his need to obey, and, the molten phase once ended, new forms and new formulas will shape themselves to fit the changed realities of religious belief and political power. *The French Revolution* ends precisely at the point where the lava sets and begins to harden—the transition is marked by the 'whiff of grapeshot'. It is the only one of Carlyle's histories that is concerned with one of the molten phases of history: his later books (*Past and Present*, the *Letters and Speeches of Oliver Cromwell*, and the *History of Frederick the Great*) are concerned either with periods of living religious faith, in which heroic leadership becomes possible— these, for Carlyle, are the golden ages of human history—or, in the paradoxical case of *Frederick the Great*, with a period in which all living faith, all contact with the divine realities, has been lost, and scepticism, indifference, and frivolity reign supreme (the identical world, in fact, with that of the first chapters of *The French Revolution*), and yet somehow it is still possible for Frederick the Great, the 'last of the Kings', to demonstrate heroic virtue.

What, in these changed circumstances, becomes of Church and State and of the individual in his relationship with them? The answer is that much changes,

---

[12] Ibid.

but that these changes are largely concealed under a superficial continuity of concepts and language, which make any wholly coherent systematization of Carlyle's ideas impossible—all the more so because Carlyle himself was apparently unaware of how far he had shifted his ground. The basic idealist concepts, of a world of appearances and a superior world of realities, with which, sooner or later, the world of appearances must conform, and of the gifted few who alone have the insight to translate the demands of the real into the language of the phenomenal world—these persist; but the notions of what constitutes reality, and of the role of the gifted élite, subtly change, and Carlyle's use of language was never rigorous enough to force him to recognize the change, or to make it self-evident.

We have seen that there are no true heroes, in the later Carlylean sense, in *The French Revolution*: no leaders who succeed in mastering their time, but at most the two quasi-heroes, Mirabeau and Danton, who for a short and precarious time triumphantly ride the crests of the breakers of the Revolution, only to be flung off and left behind broken in the trough. The true dynamic of *The French Revolution* is in the storm itself. With *Heroes and Hero-Worship*, published in 1841 four years after *The French Revolution*, we are in a different world, in which the idea of the hero for the first time assumes the central place in Carlyle's understanding of history, and of the processes of history. In this book Carlyle identifies six different types of hero—the divinity, the prophet, the poet, the priest, the man of letters, and the king—and all are achievers, shapers of their times. Beneath the apparent diversity of types, there is a unity: what makes all these types, and the examples that Carlyle gives of them, heroic is their Fichtean quality, their ability to make the world of reality and its demands apparent to the world of men. This religious, or quasi-religious, function is most obvious in the case of the divinity (this is the divinity *incarnate*: Carlyle's example is Odin, for whom he imagines a human original), the prophet (Mahomet), and the priest (Luther and Knox); but for Carlyle, all true poetry and indeed all true literature shared this function. All these men are shapers. They do not merely bear witness to a people of deaf ears; they compel them to hear them. The man of letters is a particularly interesting category, because clearly it included Carlyle himself, and he cannot have been unaware of it. It can hardly be accidental that in this one instance, Carlyle's examples—Johnson, Burns, and (surprisingly, given his detestation of political theorizers and introverted autobiographers) Rousseau—are of men who were less than wholly successful in compelling the world's recognition in their own lifetimes: for by the 1840s Carlyle was becoming increasingly conscious of himself being a prophet unheard. But the final heroic type, the king, returns more emphatically than ever to the image of the hero as maker and shaper. Carlyle's two examples are Cromwell and (with considerable reservations) Napoleon: men who transformed their worlds, irruptions of the real into the phenomenal, upthrusts of living rock through the blanketing clays and drifts of the here and now.

It is apparent that the authority of these men is a quality of their personalities and is not mediated through institutions. Church and State scarcely figure in *Heroes and Hero-Worship*, or figure in purely negative roles. The Church of the seventh century is contrasted very unfavourably with Mahomet's inspired role —on the one hand, 'those miserable Syrian Sects, with their vain janglings about *Homoiousion* and *Homoousion*, the head full of worthless noise, the heart empty and dead'; on the other, 'this wild man of the Desert, with his wild sincere heart, earnest as death and life, with his great flashing natural eyesight'.[13] The man is contrasted with the institution, to the unequivocal advantage of the man. Luther's role is identical: at the Diet of Worms, he confronts the powers of both Church and State—'the world's pomp and power sits there on this hand: on that, stands-up for God's Truth, one man, the poor miner Hans Luther's son'.[14] Here, for once, Carlyle's vision of the heroic individual confronting the massed powers of Church and State seems to coincide with the liberal version. But note the difference: because Luther has his footing beyond time, because he stands for the transcendental realities that the Church and State of his time are blind to, they are weak and he is strong, and it is he who triumphs. As for the State, we have seen already that Carlyle denies it legitimacy, recogniz-ing only Kingship; and when it comes to the hero as king, the institutional aspect of it is reduced to an absolute minimum by his choice of examples, Cromwell and Napoleon—both of them born totally outside the narrow circles of hereditary kingship, both of them kings in right of their personal qualities alone.

Carlyle's next major work, *Past and Present* (1843), was a diagnosis of the condition of contemporary British society—a condition which Carlyle saw as morbid, infected with many of the same evils as had infected French society before 1789, and threatening to end in the same revolutionary cataclysm. It is in every respect an extraordinary piece of social criticism; but for the present purpose its interest is concentrated especially in its second book, *The Ancient Monk*, in which Carlyle adduces the abbey of Bury St Edmund's in the twelfth century (illuminated through the recent publication of Jocelin of Brakelond's chronicle of the abbey[15]) as an example of a healthy society in sharp contrast to the England of his own day. Where eighteenth-century France (and even nine-teenth-century Britain) were for him examples of corrupt societies in which the

[13] *Heroes and Hero-Worship*, 63.   [14] Ibid. 134.
[15] *The Chronicle of Jocelin of Brakelond*, ed. J. G. Rokewood (Camden Society; London, 1840).

institutions of Church and Kingship were no more than rotten shams, twelfth-century England was an example of a healthy one, in which those institutions truly reflected the realities of which they were symbols. The book therefore gives us a positive image of what Carlyle sees as the true roles of Church and Kingship, and of the relation of the individual to them.

It is a relationship in which the merit of the institution lies above all in its capacity to recognize, and to give free rein to, the hero. For Carlyle, twelfth-century society is distinguished from nineteenth-century society partly by this, and partly by its capacity to make the ideal—to Carlyle, the real—world explicit in the phenomenal one of the here and now. It is not at all a mystical or a theological world: it is a world in which the most mundane affairs of daily life take on a hard-edged, crystalline significance because the presence of the transcendent is felt in them all. In such a society, the recognition of the natural authority of the hero, the inspired translator of the will of God to man, is instinctive. The hero in this instance is Abbot Samson (Jocelin of Brakelond's hero also), the great reformer, who finds the abbey of Bury St Edmund's mired in debt, sloth, and corruption, and restores it to discipline, industry, and prosperity. It is worth remarking that the age of Samson was also the age of Francis of Assisi; but St Edmund's is a world very remote from Assisi, and Samson is a figure very different from St Francis. It is true that there is a strain of asceticism in Samson (who always wore a hair shirt next to his skin), but it is not the beauty of holiness in any conventional sense that distinguishes the St Edmund's community when Samson has restored it to health. Samson is above all the hard-working, clear-headed administrator and disciplinarian, remorseless in his exaction of the abbey's rights, fearless in his resistance to baronial bullyings, ready to stand up even to the formidable wrath of King Richard himself; but all is done to the glory of God, and in the light of the obligations that God (as Samson would have said), or the moral order of the real world (as Carlyle might have preferred to put it), lays on every man; and to Carlyle, it is by this kind of intensely practical, but intensely dedicated, work that God is properly worshipped and served. Beside this, the religious movements of Carlyle's own time are empty introspective phantasms—'Methodism with its eye forever turned on its own navel', or the followers of the Oxford Movement, who 'think to save themselves and a ruined world by noisy theoretic demonstrations and laudations of *the* Church, instead of some unnoisy, unconscious, but *practical,* total, heart-and-soul demonstration of *a* Church'.[16] The title of this chapter, 'Practical-Devotional', echoes exactly the title of the parallel chapter in *The French Revolution,* 'Realised Ideals', and both summarize the moral and philosophical

---

[16] *Past and Present,* 117.

foundations on which his whole interpretation of history and of contemporary society rests.

What, then, of the role of institutions in this high medieval society, where the real and the phenomenal, the divine and the human, are brought so closely into the conformity that is proper to them? What, especially, of the Church—for this is the institution within which all Samson's work is done? The Church is omnipresent, but not as an impersonal authority: it is 'unconscious, practical, and total', as we have just seen. It is the natural, instinctive product of a society properly inspired, and above all properly led, and consequently it is not felt as an external force at all. All the immense superstructure of twelfth-century Catholicism is either ignored by Carlyle, or taken wholly for granted as the natural and proper symbol of the society's belief—which is no doubt the light in which he would have seen the abbey of Bury St Edmund's itself, with the grandeur of its buildings, its vast estates, the elaboration of its liturgy, and so on. All these things are healthy as long as they are spontaneous.

But the condition of this spontaneity, and the inevitable product of a society so attuned to the demands of the real, transcendental world, is its recognition of its heroes, and the freedom given to them to work out their instinctive apprehension of its demands in the practical world of the here and now. The Church provides Samson with his sphere of action, but the channel of inspiration is through him to it, rather than through it to him. The confrontation of the heroic individual and the institution is possible only when the institution is diseased, and has ceased to reflect the world of the real—as it had done in Luther's day, and in Knox's, and indeed under Samson's inept predecessor at Bury St Edmund's—and then, by definition, it is lost, until a new hero comes to revivify it.

In *Past and Present*, then, the hero is unequivocally the master of his times. It is worth noting, though, that, by comparison with the examples Carlyle had chosen for *Heroes and Hero-Worship*, Samson represents a narrowing and a hardening of the concept. In the latter book, and indeed in *The French Revolution* also and in all Carlyle's earlier writings, the heroes are charismatic figures: their authority and their success rest on their instinctive community of feeling with their hearers or their readers. There is a certain sense in which this is true of Samson also, for we have seen that his society has the capacity to *recognize* its heroes, and this instinct in the monks of Bury St Edmund's is strong enough to force its way even through the strangely arbitrary processes of a twelfth-century abbatial election. But, once he has been elected, there is not much of the charismatic leader about Samson, who, as had been foretold, 'rages like a wolf' through his easy-going community to whip it back into order: he rules by force of character, by making full use of the authority of his office and the resources of the law. The shift in Carlyle's notion of the hero from the charismatic to the authoritarian has begun, and it has a lot further to go.

The *Letters and Speeches of Oliver Cromwell*, which followed *Past and Present* in 1845, in essence recapitulates the themes of the earlier book. Its subject is one that Carlyle had long been contemplating, and whose appeal for him is natural: here once again, as in Abbot Samson's Bury St Edmund's, he is dealing with a society fired and united by an acute apprehension of the transcendental—a 'very practical world based on Belief in God' (was Carlyle the last writer in English to make sensitive use of initial capitals?), in which 'Cant was not fashionable at all; that stupendous invention of "Speech for the purpose of concealing Thought" was not yet made',[17] and with a hero who demonstrates to perfection that unity of faith and action. Indeed, Cromwell makes a better hero for Carlyle's purposes than Samson had done. For all Carlyle's expressed admiration for the inarticulacy of Samson's faith, it seems to have been *so* silent in him, or so limited to merely formal means of expression, as to leave room for doubt as to how deep it actually was—whereas with Cromwell no such doubt is possible. There is no questioning the reality of his faith, or of his anguished gropings for certainty: it is one of the chief claims to distinction of Carlyle's *Cromwell* that he was the first biographer properly to grasp this profound truth about Cromwell.

It is also true that Cromwell is a more charismatic figure than Samson: the bond of communion between him and the Puritans he commands goes deeper— particularly the bond with the army he speaks for, as against the parliament the sweeps aside, a preference and an act exactly reflecting Carlyle's own contempt for parliaments. That said, however, it is obvious that Cromwell is also a great enforcer of his will—a scourge of parliaments, a Protector who imposes his authority by the military regime of the major-generals, above all a soldier who identifies the will of God with the outcome of the battles he fights—and that in all this Carlyle consistently and vociferously cheers him on, even when it comes to the massacres of Drogheda and Wexford. The Cromwell of the *Letters and Speeches* is the first of Carlyle's *military* heroes—it is very noticeable that, in *Heroes and Hero-Worship*, the heroism of both Cromwell and Napoleon rests not on their military achievements, but on their roles in the domestic histories of their countries. Cromwell is an Abbot Samson with the resources of a nation and the power of a victorious army at his disposal, and with him the image of the hero becomes more than ever that of one who works not by shaping the minds of men but by imposing his own inspired solutions on them. The solutions are not arbitrary: he is still the sensor of reality, the transmitter of the divine will, but increasingly the subjects he rules are his passive, and no longer his active,

---

[17] *Oliver Cromwell's Letters and Speeches*, i. 80.

instruments. Moreover, this shift in the concept of the hero, or of the hero's role, is mirrored by a shift in another key concept—that of reality. In Carlyle's earlier writings, as in the German sources from which they derived, the world of reality is above all a moral order. By the time he came to write the biography of Cromwell, 'reality' is increasingly coming instead to bear its everyday sense of the practical, of what actually works. The contrast is not absolute, because Carlyle had always been troubled by the dichotomy between might and right, and had always argued that the transcendental moral order would, in the end, triumph in the phenomenal world as well (it was in this light that he had interpreted the French Revolution), but it was nevertheless profound.

In this context, institutions are less than ever able to form an effective coun-terbalance to the will of the hero. In the early stages of his career, it is true, Cromwell does play something like the classic defiant role of the individual confronting Church and State, in his clashes with the Laudian established Church and the monarchy of Charles I; but it is, again, a confrontation in which the odds are weighted entirely in favour of the individual. Carlyle's typical attitude is best summed up by a passage on this phase of Cromwell's career, not from the *Letters and Speeches*, but from *Heroes and Hero-Worship*, in which he describes the Puritan rejection of Laudian ceremonial forms of worship: 'Puritans found *such* forms insupportable; trampled on such forms;—we have to excuse it for saying, No form at all rather than such! It stood preaching in its bare pulpit, with nothing but the Bible in its hand. Nay, a man preaching from his earnest *soul* into the earnest souls of men: is not this virtually the essence of all Churches whatsoever?'[18] He never stated more clearly his conviction of the priority of the individual—the inspired individual—to the institution; and of course the Laudian Church and the monarchy of Charles I go down, and Cromwell triumphs.

This shift of values reaches its conclusion in Carlyle's final work of history, the *History of Frederick the Great*, the last and most improbable of Carlyle's heroes. Here, Carlyle returns to that eighteenth-century background against which his views of history had first taken shape—not for him an age of faith, but an age of corroding scepticism, an age in which institutions had long since ceased to perform their functions and to symbolize effectively the transcendent realities they stood for and become mere hollow shams. This return to the landscape of the early chapters of *The French Revolution* (and of such early historical essays as 'Voltaire', 'Cagliostro', and 'The Diamond Necklace') is surprising, and his choice of heroes is hardly less so. With Frederick, the transition in the image of

---

[18] *Heroes and Hero-Worship*, 206.

the hero from the charismatic leader of men to the military despot is complete. Cromwell had at least owed his rise to power to his function as the incarnation of Puritanism, which to Carlyle was one of the three great eruptions of the transcendent into the real world by the medium of the popular will in modern times (the other two being the Reformation and the French Revolution); even Abbot Samson, as we have seen, owed his rise to power to his recognition by his peers, through the medium of election. But Frederick came to power by heredi- tary succession, the least populist of all forms of selection. More than that, he incarnates some of the very tendencies of the eighteenth century which Carlyle rejected most vehemently—notably its religious scepticism and its penchant for what Carlyle persisted in regarding as the airy flimflams of the *philosophes*. What heroic qualities, then, does Carlyle find in him?

Carlyle's central claim for Frederick is that he is 'the last of the Kings'—the last effective monarch, before the eruption of democracy in the French Revolution took the soul out of kingship (or at least out of hereditary kingship) for good. And if we ask what is the test of effectiveness in this context, there is not much doubt about Carlyle's answer—it is above all Frederick's military genius, and his ability, by means of this genius backed by some deft political manœuvreing, to seize the disputed territory of Silesia from Austria and to hold on to it during the Seven Years' War in the face of an almost pan-European coalition against him— the triumph, in other words, of *realpolitik*.[19] The world of the real has become the world of *realpolitik*, and in the process shed the transcendent altogether, and become simply the practical, simply what succeeds.

In this atmosphere, institutions count for very little indeed. As king of Prussia, Frederick is the master of the institutions of both Church and State, and the possibility of conflict with them does not arise: the emphasis is all on the personal nature of his authority, and indeed on his readiness to override merely formal restraints in the pursuit of justice. At bottom, Carlyle's notion of 'Kingship' is incompatible with the conventional notion of the state for precisely this reason: it is fundamentally personal, where the idea of the state is institutional. It might be expected that the choice of a hero whose kingship is hereditary and who rules an institution as powerful as the Prussian state would do something to qualify this attitude; but it does not do so. The earlier image of the hero as the challenger of corrupt institutions has disappeared: they no longer have an existence apart from him.

[19] It is worth remembering in this context Carlyle's exultant support for the German side in the Franco- Prussian War, and for the achievement of German unity which accompanied it, one of the grand acts of *realpolitik*; and Carlyle's acceptance of the Prussian Order of Merit from Bismarck, the grand *realpolitiker* himself.

The choice of such an anomalous figure as the subject of his last (and by far his longest) book has always been puzzling; and the explanation for it must be sought in a major, though for the most part unconscious, change that had come over Carlyle's whole view of history. It is, after all, very hard to see how the heroic Frederick can be fitted into the same set of values as that which had informed the writing of *The French Revolution* and made him say that 'he would not have known what to make of history but for the French Revolution'.[20] The Revolution then had appeared as the divine wind—hurricane, rather—which swept away a rotten society, and opened the way for something better to come—something not very clearly discerned, it must be said. By those values, it is hard to see Frederick the Great's Prussia as anything but part of the rightly doomed old order. The truth is, I think, that, between the writing of the two books, Carlyle had lost his faith in the beneficence of the processes of history. A faith in the spontaneous—which easily translates into a sympathy for unpremeditated mass action, and hence for revolution—had been replaced by a faith in the necessity of authority, which easily translates into a sympathy for despotism. In *Heroes and Hero-Worship*, the hero's task had been defined as 'cooperating with the real Tendency of the World'.[21] This is a classic profession of the historicist faith— that the world has a powerful natural 'tendency' of its own, which will inevitably triumph in the long run, that virtue and wisdom lie in awareness of it and success in cooperation with it. In the 1830s Carlyle had accepted that: like his heroes, he had felt the movement of history, and associated himself with it. By the 1850s he had lost that faith: he had ceased to believe in the triumphant breakthrough of reality into a world of shams, and had become convinced rather that society was plunging deeper and deeper into hollowness, corruption, and hypocrisy—'beer and balderdash', as he once memorably phrased it. This is a note that echoes again and again through his writings of the period. There are grounds for thinking that this was linked with the failure of his own prophetic message to his own nation, expressed most directly in *Past and Present*, the message of repentance or doom, to come true. As the exuberant Palmerstonian self-confidence of the 1850s replaced the social anxieties and the anguished soul-searching of the 1840s, it became very clear that Britain had not repented, and had not been doomed. At that point, Carlyle cut himself loose from contemporary society, and lost his faith in the spontaneous processes of history: the only hope now lies in despotism, in the unfettered authority of the one man with eyes to see. It is not a new suggestion that, in his subconscious at least, Carlyle saw himself in that role. As he lost his trust in the spontaneous and the popular, his heroes cease to

[20] J. A. Froude, *Thomas Carlyle: A History of the First Forty Years of his Life* (London, 1882), ii. 18.
[21] *Heroes and Hero-Worship*, 63.

be charismatic: as he became conscious of British society's increasing rejection of his own message, his heroes become despots.

But neither earlier nor later phases provided fertile soil for the classic type of confrontation between the individual and the forces of Church and State, and the reasons for this may now be apparent. In the first place, Carlyle's depreciation of institutions and his overwhelming emphasis on the role of individuals persisted through both periods; and the State, in particular, never had a chance, since Carlyle replaced it by the concept of 'Kingship'. Secondly, the classic type sees the individual's role as heroic, but tragic—the individual is right, but the institution is all-powerful—and Carlyle had no use for the tragic. *Victrix causa deis placuit, sed victa Catoni*—the gods preferred the winning cause, but Cato the losing one—will always sound to the liberal like a verdict for Cato: to Carlyle, it would have been a condemnation of him, since for him the hero is the one who senses and cooperates with 'the real Tendency of the World'. Admittedly, 'the real Tendency' is open to a variety of interpretations. History, as Herbert Butterfield remarked, has never proved anybody right in the long run, and there is no doubt a sense in which Socrates, Jesus, and Dietrich Bonhoeffer can be said to have sensed the real tendency of history better than those who condemned them, and that is why posterity has been so kind to them. But to Carlyle, it is the tendency of his own time, rather than that of distant posterity, that the hero works with. Consequently, he can find himself in conflict with Church and State only when they themselves are out of touch with that tendency, and hence doomed to defeat in any such conflict. It is true that in his later years, as we have seen, Carlyle lost his faith in 'the real Tendency of the World', and that this might have left room for the classic confrontation of Church and State with the individual: in practice, however, it led Carlyle to a further downplaying of the role of institutions and a further exaltation of the unfettered free will of the hero.

The hero who masters the events of his time was not, of course, uniquely a Carlylean notion. On the contrary, the nineteenth century was fruitful of the type, and very ready to worship it, especially in the heroic makers of nations, whether the charismatics like Mazzini, Garibaldi, and Kossuth, or the contrivers like Cavour and Bismarck. The type has not been extinct in the twentieth century either—it is not too difficult to see Kemal Ataturk, or even Franklin Roosevelt, as Carlylean heroes who mastered their times. But the image of the great man has become much more ambivalent in the century of Hitler and Stalin, even as the State (if not the Church) has become more and more formidably powerful, and it is not very surprising if the image of the passive hero, who tragically confronts the inhuman institutions, has increasingly been the one that liberals have found most attractive. It may be that a Carlyle of the twentieth century would have shared their evaluation. Certainly it is hard to imagine him failing to recognize, in the Dietrich Bonhoeffers and Irina Ratushinskayas of this century, men and women who, unlike de Launay in the Bastille, had their sure footing outside time, and kept it.

16

L'Église, l'État et l'Université: Les Facultés de Théologie Catholique en France au XIXe siècle

Bruno Neveu

> Paris est religieusement la rivale de Rome en France. C'est la Rome des gallicans et des hérétiques, c'est la Rome future de tous ceux qui rêvent d'une religion nationale.[1]

Sous l'Ancien Régime, la société française si bien décrite par John McManners dans sa pénétrante étude sur Angers au XVIIIe siècle[2] ignore la séparation entre l'ordre temporel et l'ordre spirituel: la concorde s'étend jusqu'à l'imbrication. L'Église est dans l'État, l'État se dit et se croit encore le protecteur, le ministre de la religion dans le royaume du christianissime.[3] Comme le proclame le chancelier d'Aguesseau:

> Le Sacerdoce et l'Empire sont deux puissances suprêmes qui procèdent du même principe et ont pour fin commune la gloire de celui qui prononce ses oracles par la bouche de l'Église et les fait exécuter par l'autorité des Rois.

Le régime particulier de l'Église gallicane, présenté fièrement comme une survivance glorieuse du droit commun jadis en vigueur en tout point de l'*orbis christianus*, ne laisse au Saint-Siège, à ses organes de gouvernement et à sa représentation apostolique qu'une influence réduite sur la vie du clergé et des fidèles. C'est ainsi que l'enseignement des sciences sacrées dispensé dans les séminaires diocésains, souvent confiés à des compagnies de prêtres, sulpiciens, lazaristes, eudistes, oratoriens, et même dans les universités et leurs facultés de théologie ou des droits, échappe entièrement au contrôle de Rome dans tous les ordres: nomination des professeurs, programmes et cours, traités et manuels,

---

[1] Lettre de Mgr Parisis, évêque d'Arras, blâmant l'attitude de Mgr Affre envers les jésuites, en date du 1er juillet 1845, éditée dans Lucien Alazard, *Denis-Auguste Affre, archevêque de Paris* (Paris: Ch. Amat, 1905), 538–40.

[2] *French Ecclesiastical Society under the Ancien Regime: A Study of Angers in the Eighteenth Century* (Manchester, 1960).

[3] Voir les analyses de Joseph Lecler, SJ, *L'Église et la souveraineté de l'État* (Paris 1946), bonne synthèse des travaux antérieurs de l'auteur et des études sur le gallicanisme.

examens et thèses, collation des grades (baccalauréat, licence, doctorat et pour les Arts maîtrise). Quand Clément XI, le 18 novembre 1716, décida de punir la *Sacratissima Facultas* de Paris pour être revenue sur son acceptation de la bulle *Unigenitus*, en suspendant tous les privilèges accordés à cette compagnie doctorale par ses lointains prédécesseurs, cet acte pontifical fut supprimé par le Parlement de Paris et le chancelier de Notre-Dame continua en toute tranquillité à remettre *ex auctoritate apostolica* le bonnet aux nouveau docteurs. À l'autonomie de ces institutions universitaires qui avaient pourtant grandi à l'ombre protectrice de la papauté,[4] répondait leur liberté en matière doctrinale, dans l'ordre ecclésiologique surtout. Héritier des maximes de l'École de Paris, que la déclaration du Clergé de France sur la puissance ecclésiastique avait en 1682 cristallisées en ses Quatre Articles, le clergé régnicole professait officiellement sur la primauté du pontife romain, juridiction comme infaillibilité, des thèses opposées trait pour trait à celles des Romains, comme on appelait alors ceux qui deviendront au XIXᵉ siècle les ultramontains. On croyait en France, avec un nationalisme religieux et politique quelque peu naïf et souvent arrogant, que les eaux de la Seine étaient plus pures que celles du Tibre. La science ecclésiastique gallicane, dédaigneuse des subtilités de la scolastique tardive, se vantait de la supériorité reconnue par toute l'Europe savante dans l'ordre de la théologie positive, de l'histoire ecclésiastique, des éditions et des commentaires des conciles et des Pères.[5]

À la fin du XVIIIᵉ siècle cet édifice imposant s'effondra sans crier gare, en moins de cinq ans: les universités, leurs facultés et leurs collèges furent supprimés, l'enseignement interrompu, les séminaires fermés, les bibliothèques dispersées ou confisquées, les bâtiments désaffectés, les grades universitaires privés d'effets par l'abolition du système bénéficial concordataire, les réguliers expulsés, l'Église constitutionnelle imposée par force à la nation bien que schismatique, une bonne partie des prêtres mis hors la loi. Après la persécution sanglante et la loi de séparation du 21 septembre 1795, qui visait ouvertement à réduire la religion catholique à la marginalité d'une secte, le clergé français—désormais amputé de ses ordres religieux masculins, pour certains si actifs dans la transmission et les développement de la haute culture théologique—campa dans un champ de ruines matérielles, intellectuelles et morales que l'application du concordat du 15 juillet 1801, assorti de ses redoutables Articles organiques par la loi du 18 germinal an X, ne releva qu'en partie et peu à peu. On dut parer au plus pressé, l'évangélisation des peuples, la réconciliation des constitutionnels, le recrutement

---

[4] Voir les considérations d'Alphonse Dupront, «Réflexions sur l'histoire de l'Université française», *Revue de l'enseignement supérieur*, 3 (1960), 165–72.

[5] Nous nous permettons de renvoyer à nos propres travaux, en particulier les études recueillies dans le volume *Érudition et religion aux XVIIᵉ et XVIIIᵉ siècles*, Préface de Marc Fumaroli (Paris, 1994).

des ministres du culte. Chaque évêque «pourra», dit comme à regret l'article XI du concordat, entretenir un séminaire, sans dotation de la puissance publique, qui sera placé «sous l'inspection du magistrat politique» et où l'on enseignera les Articles de 1682 et les maximes gallicanes, tout en visant à maintenir l'idéal sacerdotal défini par la Réforme catholique.[6] La formation dispensée dans ces établissements ne pouvait guère être que sommaire: elle visait avant tout à inculquer les vertus morales et le zèle pastoral.[7] Le traumatisme provoqué par la Révolution devait faire sentir ses effets sur l'Église de France pendant plus de cent ans, au-delà de la Séparation de 1905 et au moins jusqu'à la guerre de 1914–18. Ce qui reste de l'esprit gallican, après la disparition de la «religion de Reims» et l'écroulement des institutions civiles et ecclésiastiques de l'Ancien Régime, n'est plus nourri, irrigué par une forte culture savante de couleur historique, patristique et juridique. Il est compromis de surcroît par l'alliance contractée par le gallicanisme avec le jansénisme appelant et l'Église constitutionnelle. Il ne saurait plus animer un clergé séculier qui n'a ni les moyens ni le goût d'acquérir un savoir devenu inutile et suspect. Le succès étonnant dans les presbytères de l'*Encyclopédie théologique* de l'abbé Migne—171 volumes in-quarto de 1844 à 1873, d'un tirage assez restreint du reste—traduit le désir de connaissance qui habite un clergé mal formé, quasi autodidacte. Mais cette vulgarisation aux orientations militante, anti-protestante, ultramontaine, peut s'accorder, par son manque de rigueur critique, avec le catholicisme déclamatoire et provocateur répandu par *L'Univers* et Louis Veuillot, qui font régner avec l'appui de Rome un véritable terrorisme.[8] Ce que l'on appelle «gallicanisme»—terme significativement forgé au XIXe siècle—sera de plus en plus nettement, après la disparition progressive de la génération épiscopale et sacerdotale instruite avant la Révolution, l'apanage d'une élite de laïcs, représentée au sein des assemblées parlementaires, du barreau, de la magistrature, du Conseil d'État, de la haute administration, de l'Université. Ce groupe traditionaliste tendra à se rapprocher, en face de la conquête ultramontaine, soit du libéralisme catholique soit du régime concordataire.[9] Il n'y a plus en tout cas de *schola theologorum* pour

---

[6] Voir le tableau très détaillé présenté par Dominique Julia, «L'Éducation des ecclésiastiques en France aux XVIIe et XVIIIe siècles», dans *Problèmes d'histoire de l'éducation* (Rome, 1988), 140–205, qui fournit de précieux détails sur les pratiques scolaires et le niveau des études, médiocre sauf aux séminaires de Saint-Sulpice de Paris et d'Issy.

[7] Voir Claude Langlois, «Le Temps des séminaristes. La Formation cléricale en France aux XIXe et XXe siècles», dans ibid. 229–55, qui montre la priorité de l'inculcation des valeurs cléricales et du dressage disciplinaire sur la formation intellectuelle, même si la poussée ultramontaine stimule cette dernière à partir des années «soixante», de manière plus polémique que scientifique.

[8] Voir *La Science catholique: L'«Encyclopédie théologique» de Migne (1844–1873) entre apologétique et vulgarisation* [sous la direction de Claude Langlois et François Laplanche] (Paris, 1992).

[9] Il faudrait explorer plus profondément les milieux attachés au «christianisme sévère», rigoriste et parfois jansénisant, évoqués par Léon Séché, *Les Derniers Jansénistes depuis la ruine de Port-royal jusqu'à nos jours (1710–1870)* (3 vols.; Paris, 1891–3), iii; par Jean-Rémy Palanque, *Catholiques libéraux et gallicans*

s'opposer à une autorité romaine sortie renforcée des épreuves infligée par la France à la papauté au cours des années 1796–1814, et les facultés de théologie universitaire, dont on va évoquer ici l'existence singulièrement effacée, n'auraient jamais pu empêcher ou retarder «la victoire du dogme sur l'histoire»—définition du concile du Vatican prêtée à Manning—ni même entretenir une *Gelehrtenhäresie* comme ce fut le cas dans le monde germanique après 1870.[10]

Napoléon, Portalis, le cardinal Fesch, M. Emery, les hommes d'État et les hommes d'Église du nouveau régime furent bien conscients que l'intérêt même d'une nation où le catholicisme était la religion de la majorité des citoyens, qui restaient attachés à ce culte, ne permettait pas à l'ordre politique de négliger la formation morale et intellectuelle d'un clergé encore influent sur la société. S'il n'est plus sérieusement question d'un État théologien comme celui de l'Ancien Régime, alors que le concordat vient de reconnaître au pontife romain des pouvoirs de juridiction jusque-là exorbitants sur les diocèses de France et que les écoles de Sorbonne et les assemblées doctorales ne proposent plus d'*elucidatio doctrinae*, il est convenable d'assurer à l'enseignement des sciences sacrées leurs fondements matériels et de veiller à leur organisation. Les séminaires diocésains vont être dotés. On crée en 1806 des séminaires métropolitains au programme d'études plus ambitieux, qui n'existeront que sur le papier mais qui annoncent la présence de facultés de théologie catholique au sein de l'Université impériale, fondée en 1806 et organisée par le décret du 17 mars 1808, véritable charte de l'Instruction publique restée pour l'essentiel en vigueur jusqu'à nos jours. Il s'agit là d'établissements supérieurs en étroite relation avec le culte catholique, dont le statut singulier va, jusqu'à la fin de leur existence à la fois tourmentée et languissante, entre 1809 et 1885, entretenir des tensions parfois assez vives entre le gouvernement français sous tous les régimes politiques, du Premier Empire à la Troisième République, l'épiscopat national et le clergé séculier doublé d'un clergé régulier en continuelle expansion, le Saint-Siège. Les six facultés de théologie catholique établies à Paris, Aix, Bordeaux, Lyon, Rouen et Toulouse,

---

en France face au concile du Vatican, 1867–1870 (Aix-en-provence, 1962); par Lucienne Portier, *Christianisme, Églises et Religion: Le Dossier Hyacinthe Loyson (1827–1912). Contribution à l'histoire de l'Église de France et à l'histoire des religions* (Louvain-la-Neuve, 1982), qui complète la grande biographie de Loyson par Albert Houtin, parue 1920–24.

[10] Sur l'état de la théologie au XIXe siècle dans l'ensemble du monde catholique, du renouveau d'inspiration romantique à la restauration de la scolastique et au développement des études critiques appliquées à l'Écriture et à l'histoire de l'Église, voir la synthèse du P. Congar, dans *Dictionaire de théologie catholique*, xv (Paris, 1946), 431–44. Le même auteur a remarquablement mis en lumière le processus qui a conduit la pensée catholique au XIXe siècle à s'orienter vers une théologie du magistère: «L'ecclésiologie de la Révolution française au concile du Vatican sous le signe de l'affirmation de l'autorité», *L'Ecclésiologie au XIXe siècle* (Paris, 1960), étude qui précise celle de Roger Aubert, «La Géographie ecclésiologique au XIXe siècle», ibid. 11–55, très instructive. Voir la bibliographie fournie par Philippe Boutry, «Autour d'un bicentenaire: La Bulle *Auctorem fidei* (28 août 1794) et sa traduction française par le futur cardinal Clément Villecourt», *Mélanges de l'École française de Rome: Italie et Méditerranée*, 106/1 (1994), 203–61.

appartiennent comme leurs deux sœurs protestantes à l'Université impériale, puis royale, désignée comme Université de France jusqu'en 1896. Elles font partie organiquement de ce corps enseignant, à l'égard des autres ordres de facultés institués en 1808, droit, médecine, sciences et lettres. Les professeurs, bien qu'il soient statutairement ecclésiastiques, dépendent entièrement, pour la nomination, la carrière, la discipline, le traitement, la surveillance de l'enseignement, du seul grand maître de l'Université, après 1848 du ministre de l'Instruction publique, et des recteurs des académies où se trouvent les facultés, qui demeurent indépendantes les unes des autres (les universités ne seront reconstituées qu'en 1896). Le Saint-Siège n'a pas été consulté sur la création de ces facultés, opérée à l'heure la plus tourmentée du conflit entre Pie VII et Napoléon. Elles ne rentrent en aucune manière dans le cadre concordataire ni dans celui des Articles organiques, et la seule garantie offerte à l'Église à leur sujet est la présentation par l'évêque du chef-lieu de l'académie d'une liste de docteurs en théologie jugés par lui idoines, parmi lesquels le grand maître choisit, nomme et institue le professeur. Les diplômes de grade seront délivrés sous le sceau de l'Université, tout comme pour le droit ou les lettres, et ouvriront, sur le papier en tout cas, à partir de 1835 l'accès à la carrière ecclésiastique concordataire, disposition légale qui soulèvera une forte opposition des évêques et de la cour de Rome. Aucune procédure n'est prévue pour le cas où le professeur s'écarterait dans son enseignement de la doctrine orthodoxe ou se rendrait suspect par sa conduite morale. En revanche la soumission au gouvernement politique est exigée, ainsi que l'obligation d'enseigner les Quatre Articles de 1682, qui demeurera en vigueur jusqu'au bout dans la lettre de la loi, même si elle est tombée en désuétude au cours de la monarchie de Juillet, quand eurent disparu les premiers professeurs des nouveaux établissements académiques, tous formés sous l'Ancien Régime, souvent docteurs de la faculté de théologie de Paris et sociétaires de Sorbonne, donc imbus des maximes gallicanes. L'examen des programmes et des affiches des cours—conservés à partir de la restauration universitaire effectuée par Fortoul au début du Second Empire—invite à nuancer l'affirmation, communément avancée par les défenseurs comme par les détracteurs des facultés, qui ferait de celles-ci la citadelle ou le repaire du gallicanisme, sous la forme mitigée qu'il avait prise au XIXe siècle. En fait les professeurs semblent avoir représenté à peu près tout l'éventail des opinions et des doctrines en circulation dans l'univers catholique: ni avant ni après le concile du Vatican (auquel les facultés ont donné leur adhésion pour les canons promulgués) aucune plainte n'a été élevée par les archevêques sur l'enseignement dispensé au sein de l'Université. Ceci dit, il est évident que le statut des ecclésiastiques devenus professeurs des facultés des académies, membres de la Fonction publique, tout comme la culture profane et sacrée dont ils étaient pénétrés, conduisirent nombre d'entre eux à adopter une attitude beaucoup plus indépendante que le reste du clergé national, plus soucieuse des bons rapports entre l'Église et l'État—qui d'ailleurs a fait de ses facultés de théologie une pépinière d'évêques—plus ouvertement réservée sur les progrès de la centralisation romaine et de la puissance pontificale. Les attaques des ultramontains, leur persiflage contre le corps enseignant des facultés eussent du reste suffi à pousser ou à maintenir les professeurs dans le camp opposé.

L'histoire juridique, canonique et diplomatique de ces facultés de théologie universitaire, de leur création à leur suppression, vient d'être retracée par nos soins, à partir des documents originaux conservés en France, à Rome et dans la Cité du Vatican: cette étude d'ensemble est sur le point de paraître et l'on pourra s'y reporter pour l'exposé des questions de doctrine et des problèmes administratifs que soulevèrent l'existence et le fonctionnement d'établissements publics sans institution canonique et jouissant en revanche du monopole de l'enseignement (jusqu'en 1875) et de la collation des grades en théologie (jusqu'en 1885).[11] En marge de cet ouvrage, on aimerait présenter ici très brièvement quelques observations sur la part que ces facultés, ou plus exactement leurs professeurs—car le nombre des étudiants immatriculés et candidats aux grades demeura toujours très faible—ont tenue durant trois quarts de siècle, dans le mouvement des études théologiques et dans la culture ecclésiastique du XIXe siècle, généralement très décriée par l'historiographie.

En bonne méthode et si l'espace n'était pas strictement mesuré, il conviendrait de présenter un tableau des disciplines enseignées à Paris et en province, des programmes et des cours, des thèses publiées, et de faire défiler le cortège des professeurs et chargés de cours qui ont été attachés aux facultés, réduites *de facto* à cinq dès la monarchie de Juillet par suite du refus de l'archevêque de Toulouse de faire les présentations pour les chaires de la faculté siégeant dans sa métropole.

À vrai dire, l'état de la documentation manuscrite et imprimée ne permet pas d'éclairer de manière complète et précise la vie de ces établissements, surtout durant la première moitié du siècle, où l'administration universitaire resta embryonnaire et ne prit guère soin de ses archives. L'image que l'on parvient à tracer demeure floue, une fois que l'on a relevé le nom des titulaires des chaires, dont le nombre varie de six à huit, Écriture sainte, Hébreu, Dogme, Morale et Discipline ecclésiastique, Droit ecclésiastique, Éloquence sacrée. Tout indique que les professeurs et chargés de cours (ces derniers les plus nombreux dans les facultés en raison de la difficulté persistante à pourvoir les chaires, vu la rareté des titulaires du doctorat en théologie, seuls susceptibles d'être présentés) dispensèrent tout au long du siècle, sous le contrôle à la fois débonnaire et méticuleux du doyen de la faculté, nommé par le ministre, et surtout du recteur

---

[11] Bruno Neveu, *Les Facultés de théologie catholique de l'Université de France (1808–1885)* (Paris, Klincksieck, sous presse).

de l'académie, leur enseignement, assez peu astreignant, presqu'entièrement à leur guise, s'écartant à plus d'une reprise de la matière qui leur était assignée pour traiter d'autres sujets répondant mieux à leurs curiosités personnelles et aux intérêts de leur auditoire. La monographie consacrée à la faculté d'Aix, qui comprend une liste bio-bibliographique du personnel enseignant, l'esquisse historique consacrée à la faculté de Rouen, les programmes de cours conservés et annotés par l'administration de l'Instruction publique invitent à penser que ces établissements plutôt somnolents, en province surtout car la Sorbonne a toujours connu plus d'animation, semblables d'ailleurs en cela aux facultés des lettres et des sciences jusqu'aux années 1880, offraient un honorable asile à des ecclésiastiques souvent distingués, érudits parfois, présentés par l'archevêque en raison de leurs services antérieurs dans le ministère sacré, de leur réputation morale et intellectuelle, voire de la richesse de leur bibliothèque personnelle. Bref une sorte de canonicat universitaire.[12] Certains des professeurs se consacraient à l'histoire locale—une des occupations favorites du clergé d'alors, si actif au sein des sociétés savantes—à l'archéologie, voire à la préhistoire, aux antiquités chrétiennes, aux traditions populaires, à la littérature d'oc. La plupart se livraient à l'intention de leur public d'amateurs, où dames et demoiselles firent bonne figure dans la seconde partie du siècle, à des développements oratoires ou à des considérations apologétiques fort à la mode depuis le renouveau romantique: ils exaltaient la valeur civilisatrice de la religion, la profondeur du dogme catholique, la pureté de la morale et son influence bénéfique sur la société, les splendeurs du culte, les beautés de l'Écriture, des Pères de l'Église, des grands écrivains classiques français. Souvent ils reprenaient les thèses du traditionalisme sur la révélation originelle, dont chaque religion aurait gardé des traces mêlées à des superstitions, et ils développaient parfois les thèmes de l'ésotérisme chrétien, si vivace en France au XIXe siècle, comme l'ont montré les recherches récentes de Jean-Pierre Laurant et de Marie-France James. À Paris le niveau de la faculté fut toujours plus élevé: tout entière formée à ses débuts d'anciens docteurs de la maison et société de Sorbonne, elle conserva pendant deux à trois décennies les traditions savantes de la théologie enseignée sous l'Ancien Régime à de jeunes clercs rompus aux études classiques et à la logique formelle, désireux d'obtenir aux termes d'épreuves exigeantes le grade qui leur ouvrirait la voie des bénéfices et des dignités.

Ce type d'étudiants ecclésiastiques avait complètement disparu après la Révolution et le concordat, et lorsque moururent un à un les vénérables professeurs de Sorbonne de qui les leçons devaient sans nul doute prolonger celles qu'ils avaient écoutées au siècle précédent dans les mêmes lieux, au cœur du Pays

---

[12] Voir Marius-Antoine Chaillan, *La Faculté de théologie d'Aix au XIXe siècle* (Marseille, 1939); F. Bouquet, *L'Enseignement supérieur à Rouen pendant le XIXe siècle, 1808–1895* (Sotteville-lès-Rouen, 1896).

latin, l'enseignement prit un autre caractère, dont on hésite à définir les traits principaux. On distingue aisément parmi les professeurs et les chargés de cours des personnalités qui ont su s'attirer l'estime, parfois même une réputation incontestée. Il ne faut pas se dissimuler pour autant que la formation technique de ces théologiens resta longtemps peu méthodique et peu approfondie. On rencontre assez souvent chez les meilleurs une certaine familiarité avec l'Allemagne savante et son avant-poste français, Strasbourg (où fonctionne une des deux facultés de théologie protestante, d'un niveau assez élevé): un Bautain, un Maret, un Meignan, un Vollot ont fait successivement des séjours dans le monde germanique, ils en connaissent ou en soupçonnent les ressources dans l'ordre de la critique et dans celui de la réflexion spéculative. Mais l'Université de France dans son ensemble—un Victor Cousin et ses disciples mis à part—et le clergé français sont bien loin de mesurer le prix de cette «Wissenschaft» d'outre-Rhin. L'enseignement supérieur se montra longtemps peu exigeant sur les exercices qui sanctionnent des études et ouvrent l'accès au professorat. Évoquons rapidement pour rendre couleur à un passé depuis longtemps évanoui le déroulement ou les suites de deux soutenances de thèse en théologie, l'une devant la faculté d'Aix, en avril 1846, l'autre devant la faculté de Paris, en janvier 1850.

La première est celle d'Auguste Alphonse Gratry, ancien élève de l'École polytechnique, associé de Bautain à Strasbourg entre 1828 et 1840, où il reçut l'ordination sacerdotale en 1832, directeur du collège Stanislas en 1840. Distingué par P. F. Dubois, fondateur du journal *Le Globe*, député de la Loire inférieure sous la monarchie de Juillet, directeur de l'École normale supérieure, il obéit au conseil de ce haut personnage, qui désirait l'appeler au poste d'aumônier de cette grande école, de se rendre à Aix pour prendre ses grades en théologie.[13] En avril 1846 le brillant abbé polytechnicien fit donc en hâte le voyage de Provence, où il obtint tous les grades en quatre jours: reçu bachelier en théologie le 22 avril, licencié le 23, il soutint sa thèse de doctorat le 25 et fut jugé à l'unanimité digne de ce grade supérieur. Les sujets à traiter portaient, pour le baccalauréat, sur: «Dieu, considéré comme auteur de la nature», pour la licence, sur «Dieu, auteur de la grâce», pour le doctorat, sur: «L'accord de la foi et de la raison». Le rapport de la faculté atteste que le candidat a su répondre aux questions de ses juges avec la plus grande distinction. Mais survint un incident, qui ne fut heureusement qu'une tempête dans un verre d'eau: Gratry en a fait lui-même à son protecteur Dubois le récit, qui n'a pas perdu tout son piquant après cent-cinquante ans:

Je viens de soutenir ma quatrième épreuve, ma thèse de doctorat. Je suis donc docteur, je crois. M. le recteur [Defougères de Villandry, professeur à la faculté de droit d'Aix] a eu la bonté de penser à assister à ma dernière thèse et a dit au doyen qu'il y assisterait

---

[13] Voir A. Boucley, «La Soutenance de thèse de l'abbé Gratry ou les tribulations d'un candidat», *Revue universitaire*, 36ᵉ année, n° 6 (juin 1927), 47–9, qui publie la lettre de Gratry à Dubois.

officiellement. Le doyen lui a répondu que la faculté [de théologie] en serait honorée et qu'un siège d'honneur lui serait préparé. Mais M. le recteur a déclaré que son droit était de siéger parmi les juges, sans être juge il est vrai, mais de siéger au milieu des juges. La faculté a pensé que l'application du droit sous cette forme, quant aux facultés de théologie, était douteuse, mais que du moins l'exercice en était inopportun dans un moment où les évêques et le clergé sont d'une si étrange froideur au sujet des facultés. Ces messieurs ont été unanimes à ce sujet et ont fait prier le recteur officieusement, par ma bouche, de ne pas user de son droit en cette occasion. Le recteur m'a répondu que désirant ne pas me mettre dans l'embarras, il acquiesçait à ma demande . . . mais qu'il maintenait son droit, allait écrire au doyen à cet effet et, sur une lettre du doyen qui lui ferait part de la difficulté, s'abstiendrait de paraître et référerait à Paris. Le recteur écrit cette lettre, le doyen lui répond, lui fait part de la difficulté qui consiste, dit le doyen, en ce que la faculté est disposée à différer l'épreuve pour en référer au ministre si M. le recteur veut exercer son droit.

Cet éventuel appel à l'autorité ministérielle n'agréant pas au recteur, celui-ci se ravise et tient bon sur ses privilèges. Gratry, aux abois, obtient du doyen une nouvelle lettre, déposée chez le recteur à *deux* heures, alors que la soutenance est fixée à *trois* heures:

Je cours de nouveau chez le doyen, où je trouve la faculté assemblée. L'abbé Sibour, admirable et bien bon, déclare qu'on ne me laissera pas partir sans diplôme. Je supplie la faculté de se réunir en tout cas, sauf à aviser si le recteur se présente. La faculté y consent, on se rend à la salle des épreuves et je subis ma dernière épreuve, non sans quelques succès, à ce que l'on m'a dit. Je reçois l'accolade et je me précipite de nouveau et de suite chez le recteur, que je trouve assez modéré dans la forme . . . mais prenant au fond la chose comme une affaire scandaleuse, dont la faculté se serait rendue coupable et qui pourrait tout annuler. Je ferai, m'a-t-il dit, mon rapport au ministre; nous verrons ce qui sera décidé.

Que le vétilleux juriste ait ou non averti l'administration de l'Instruction publique, celle-ci se résolut à délivrer le diplôme de docteur en théologie, non sans des retards qui exaspérèrent l'impétrant, désireux d'être installé au plus tôt dans ses fonctions d'aumônier de l'École normale supérieure, où il devait s'opposer vivement à Étienne Vacherot et à son *Histoire de l'École d'Alexandrie*, couronnant sa réfutation par un écrit mordant qui eut un grand retentissement: *Une étude sur la sophistique contemporaine* (1851).

Quant à la thèse de théologie soutenue devant la faculté de Paris par l'abbé Maret, présentée dans des conditions qui n'étaient guère plus strictes que celles de la thèse de l'abbé Gratry à Aix, c'est après la soutenance qu'elle souleva et entretint une polémique assez ardente qu'il est instructif d'évoquer.[14]

Le titre de docteur en théologie de l'Université de France était nécessaire à Henry Maret pour être nommé professseur titulaire auprès de la faculté de Paris,

---

[14] Voir *L'Univers*, 28 juillet 1850: «Protestation de M. le doyen de la faculté de théologie de Paris»; Gustave Bazin, *Vie de Mgr Maret* (Paris, 1891), i. 366–71; Claude Bressolette, *L'abbé Maret* (Paris, 1977), 148–60.

où il enseignait depuis 1841 avec le plus grand succès comme chargé de cours de Dogme. Le ministre lui accorda la dispense des épreuves inférieures, conduisant au baccalauréat et à la licence, eu égard à ses titres de docteur en théologie de Louvain et de Prague. M. Glaire, en sa qualité de doyen de la faculté de la Sorbonne, accepta d'admettre le candidat à soutenir sa thèse, au vu des «positions» de celle-ci, qui tenaient en quatre pages et demi. Il présida la soutenance de la thèse, le 25 mars 1850, concourut à tous les actes complémentaires, et après avoir pris connaissance du certificat d'aptitude délivré par la faculté, le ministre, M. de Parieu, signa le diplôme de docteur en théologie, avant de nommer aussitôt, dès le 1ᵉʳ avril, l'abbé Henry Maret professeur titulaire, sur présentation de l'archevêque de Paris, Mgr Sibour, très favorable au candidat. Mais l'irascible doyen Glaire n'avait pas pardonné à Maret d'avoir exprimé de nettes réserves sur son discours de rentrée universitaire, prononcé le 12 décembre 1842, où était soulignée la nécessité de donner plus de part à l'autorité spirituelle dans le fonctionnement et l'enseignement des facultés de théologie, thèse qui avait provoqué approbations ou critiques, de *L'Ami de la religion à L'Univers*. Le 27 juin 1850, trois mois après la soutenance de cette thèse, qui n'avait été qu'une formalité, imposée par les contraintes administratives et budgétaires, le doyen de la faculté de Paris adressa au rédacteur des *Annales de philosophie chrétienne*, organe du traditionalisme et à ce titre hostile à Maret, une lettre qui fut reprise dans *L'Univers* du 28 juillet 1850. C'était une protestation en règle contre la valeur de l'acte universitaire du 25 mars précédent: le jury spécialement composé ne comptait que deux professeurs titulaires de la faculté, MM. Glaire et Receveur, auxquel on avait adjoints M. Léon Sibour, docteur en théologie et professeur à la faculté d'Aix, et M. Gratry, docteur ès lettres et docteur en théologie (comme on vient de le voir). Le doyen précisait que «la thèse lui avait été remise imprimée, quelques heures seulement avant le moment fixé par M. Maret pour la soutenance». Maret reconnut lui-même, dans une lettre de 1851, que «cette thèse avait été rédigée de mémoire, en une heure de temps, et imprimée avec une telle précipitation que des fautes typographiques nombreuses m'échappèrent». S'érigeant en *laudator temporis acti*, en défenseur des traditions de l'ancienne Sorbonne—dont le mythe ne cessa d'inspirer le XIXᶜ siècle universitaire—en partie préservées jusque-là, l'abbé Glaire allait jusqu'à écrire: «Je conviens que la thèse de M. Maret n'a pour le fonds et pour la forme aucun rapport avec celles qui ont été présentées à la faculté de Paris jusqu'à ce jour». On ne pouvait contester plus nettement et les aptitudes du candidat et la valeur du diplôme de grade à lui délivré. *L'Univers* saisissait aussitôt cette occasion d'enfoncer le clou:

Entretenir le public des misères de sa faculté, c'est nous imposer le devoir de rappeler qu'elle est purement et simplement une faculté de théologie instituée universitairement et pas du tout une faculté de théologie instituée canoniquement. l'Université seule est responsable des docteurs qu'elle fait et de la façon bizarre dont elle les fabrique . . . Les erreurs de M. l'abbé Maret inquiètent M. l'abbé Glaire; mais si elles n'inquiètent pas l'Université, qu'a-t-il à dire? Est-ce que le ministre chef du corps enseignant n'est pas plus compétent qu'un simple doyen de faculté, dès qu'il s'agit d'orthodoxie universitaire?

Et le rédacteur de l'article de renvoyer, avec le talent polémique ordinaire à son journal, les deux professeurs de théologie de l'État dos à dos:

Quant à l'abbé Maret, mettons-le hors de cause, il est dans cette affaire beaucoup plus à plaindre qu'à blâmer. Obligé pour conserver sa position à la Sorbonne de se soumettre à cette parodie ridicule des examens d'autrefois, le docte professeur a dû trouver qu'il payait un peu cher ce titre de docteur en théologie de la faculté de Paris, dont mieux que personne assurément il apprécie la valeur canonique, ce titre conféré par une commission universitaire, comme si cette mission pouvait appartenir à d'autres qu'à l'Église, comme si le droit de conférer les grades théologiques n'était pas le droit exclusif de l'Université et de ceux auxquels elle a donné pouvoir pour cela. . . . Nous voulons demander à notre tour à M. le doyen de la faculté de théologie de Paris comment et par qui il a été fait docteur? De qui il a reçu et ce titre et le pouvoir de le conférer à d'autres? S'il ne peut prouver qu'il les tient de l'Église, force lui sera de convenir qu'ils sont usurpés et qu'ils lui viennent d'une autorité étrangère et illégitime.

Dès le 31 juillet 1850, l'abbé Maret de hâta d'adresser une lettre au rédacteur de *L'Univers*, publiée le 5 août. C'était une réfutation en règle des assertions du doyen Glaire: «Ce n'est point à moi de justifier ces dispenses [des épreuves], ni ma promotion, [laquelle] n'était et ne pouvait être, dans l'intention de l'autorité diocésaine et de l'autorité universitaire, qu'une simple formalité.»

Ici le docteur professeur, tout vicaire général et chargé de cours à la faculté qu'il eût été lors de la soutenance de sa thèse, trahissait peut-être une désinvolture trop marquée envers l'esprit et la lettre des réglements universitaires. Il rejetait avec vigueur le jugement porté sur ses doctrines: «Je ne reconnais pour juges que le Saint-Siège et l'épiscopat», ce dernier s'étant prononcé avec éloge avec la recommandation accordée à la *Théodicée chrétienne* (1844, 2e éd. en 1850) par la plume de Mgr Affre. On pourrait encore faire observer au professeur de dogme qu'il s'agit à présent non de ses ouvrages mais d'un acte universitaire, soumis au seul jugement scientifique des membres du jury de la thèse, pour le fonds et pour la forme. En tout cas le procédé de M. Glaire envers un de ses collègues et le corps de sa faculté fut trouvé déloyal, inconvenant puisqu'il paraissait faire la leçon au ministre. Celui-ci, piqué, écrivit une lettre fort sévère au doyen de la faculté de Paris, sachant que Mgr Sibour, archevêque de Paris, était aussi irrité qu'affligé par ce scandale qui avait ramené l'attention sur la *vexata quaestio* du statut des facultés de théologie en France. La nomination d'un nouveau doyen fut résolue de concert par les deux autorités, universitaire et archidiocésaine, mais Maret, d'abord présenté par Mgr Sibour, fut écarté «pour des raisons de convenance et de délicatesse». Le dossier personnel de l'abbé Glaire, aux Archives nationales aujourd'hui,[15] renferme toute une série de pièces originales relatives à la démission de la charge décanale, que l'on exigeait de lui avec fermeté mais en conservant certains égards que l'on n'aurait peut-être plus aujourd'hui. L'archevêque de Paris n'hésitait nullement à réclamer avec la dernière énergie la révocation du doyen de la Sorbonne:

> Il a manqué à tous ses devoirs à l'égard de mon autorité [écrivait-il au ministre le 25 novembre 1850] en portant publiquement une accusation calomnieuse contre la personne et l'enseignement d'un professeur revêtu du titre de mon vicaire général ... Toujours il y a eu entente entre le ministre et l'ordinaire pour le choix des doyens des facultés de théologie. Leur influence est trop grande, trop décisive pour que l'autorité épiscopale ne tienne pas, avec raison, à voir à leur tête des hommes complètement dignes de son estime. Ce ne sera pas vous, Monsieur le Ministre, dont la piété et le zèle pour le bien me sont connus, qui voudrez rompre cette entente et me mettre dans l'impossibilité de continuer mon concours à une institution qui au point de vue catholique n'existe que par l'autorité de l'ordinaire. Les prêtres qui professent dans les facultés sont sous ma juridiction immédiate. Ils ne peuvent enseigner la théologie qu'autant que je leur en donne la mission. Si j'étais forcé de retirer ce pouvoir au doyen actuel, vous voyez M. le Ministre, quelle serait la situation de M. Glaire et de la faculté elle-même. Ces mesures de rigueur me coûteraient infiniment. Je suis trop jaloux de conserver les meilleurs rapports avec l'Université et avec son chef si digne et si chrétien.

En fin de compte l'abbé Receveur, docteur en théologie depuis 1833 et titulaire de la chaire de morale depuis le 1er mars 1841, fut nommé doyen le 6 décembre 1850, et Henry Maret dut patienter jusqu'au 7 novembre 1853 pour accéder au décanat et le conserver jusqu'au jour de sa mort, survenue à la Sorbonne, où il avait son appartement de fonction, le 16 juin 1884. L'abbé Glaire lui avait encore donné tablature en 1854, à l'occasion de la thèse de doctorat présentée par l'abbé Bargès, lui aussi chargé de cours à la faculté et aspirant au professorat: de nouveau l'ancien doyen déclarait la soutenance, qui s'était déroulée le 29 mai, entachée d'irrégularité, parce qu'il n'y avait dans le jury qu'un seul professeur de la faculté. Le 19 septembre 1854, l'archevêque de Paris se plaignait au ministre de cette opposition systématique du professeur à tous les actes de sa faculté et demandait qu'on mît M. Glaire à la retraite ou tout au moins en disponibilité, car «cette conduite est intolérable». L'administration suivit la proposition de Mgr Sibour et une lettre de Glaire au ministre, en date du 27 septembre, le montre «frappé par le coup terrible qu'est l'ordre de demander un congé de disponibilité». Il interprète la mesure prise contre lui comme «une disgrâce épiscopale». Le ministre Fortoul, si longtemps dépeint par l'historiographie comme un tyran aux vues étroites, se montra bon prince,

---

[15] Archives nationales, F¹⁷ 20848, Dossier Glaire (Jean-Baptiste).

puisque la mise en disponibilité fut accordée aux conditions les plus favorables, l'*intégralité* du traitement, soit 4,000 francs, qui fut versée jusqu'au calcul de la pension de retraite accordée à l'infatigable polygraphe, retiré à Issy jusqu'à son décès, survenu le 25 février 1879.

Ce n'est qu'à partir de 1860 environ que les thèses de doctorat en théologie catholique virent s'élever leur nombre et leur qualité: à la veille de la suppression des facultés, dans les années 1875–85, elles connurent la même évolution que les thèses de doctorat ès lettres, chef d'œuvre valant brevet d'accès à l'enseignement magistral, et certaines attestent une réelle compétence scientifique. Mais dès la Restauration, la monarchie de Juillet surtout, le corps enseignant avait compté des personnalités assez remarquables. Ainsi une récente et savante étude sur l'éloquence sacrée à l'époque romantique a mis en évidence l'intérêt des théories sur l'art oratoire exposées succesivement à la Sorbonne avec talent par des maîtres aussi différents que l'abbé Guillon—connu par ailleurs pour avoir administré les sacrements à Grégoire mourant et devenu «évêque de Maroc»[16]—l'abbé Dupanloup, l'abbé Duquesnoy, l'abbé Cœur (devenu évêque de Troyes et resté ardent gallican).[17] L'abbé Jean-Nicolas Jager mérite une mention spéciale: après une rencontre à Paris avec Benjamin Harrison, «student of Christ Church», hébraïsant, et William Cureton, syriacisant, ce professeur d'histoire et discipline ecclésiastique à la Sorbonne avait adressé à ces «clergymen» de l'Église établie d'Angleterre des *Lettres* qui parurent dans *L'Univers* à partir du 30 août 1834, où il développait courtoisement une controverse apologétique en faveur de la doctrine catholique, où il montrait une connaissance de l'anglicanisme et de ses écrivains théologiques assez rare sur le continent. John Henry Newman s'inséra dans le débat dés la fin de 1834 et c'est avec lui que Jager continua à dialoguer sur des points centraux, «the rule of faith» et le rapport entre Écriture et Tradition. À l'oxonien qui insistait sur le primat de la «Prophetical Tradition» en face de l'«Apostolical and Episcopal Tradition», et affirmait avec les protestants que «Scripture is an authoritative depository, i.e. speaking by inspiration; Tradition is not» le professeur catholique français répliquait en montrant dans ses 4e, 5e, 6e lettres que les anglicans plaçaient en réalité sur bon nombre de points les enseignements de la Tradition avant les énoncés tirés littéralement de la Bible. Jager publia en volume le texte des lettres: *Le Protestantisme aux prises avec la doctrine catholique, ou Controverses avec plusieurs ministres anglicans membres de l'Université d'Oxford* (Paris, 1836, déjà édité en 1835). Il est évident que son argumentation nourrie et serrée ne fut pas sans faire impression sur Newman,

---

[16] Sur Mgr Guillon, voir Paul Poupard, *Correspondance inédite entre Mgr Antonio Garibaldi, internonce à Paris... et Mgr Césaire Mathieu, archevêque de Besançon* (Rome–Paris, 1961), 44–8.

[17] Voir Frank Paul Bowman, *Le Discours sur l'éloquence sacrée à l'époque romantique: Rhétorique, apologétique, herméneutique (1817–1851)* (Genève, 1980), spéc. 16–17; 40–1, 83–6, et *passim*.

alors engagé dans la réflexion historique et doctrinale qui devait dissiper ses préjugés contre «le romanisme» et le conduire à la conversion en 1845.[18]

Le corps professoral de la faculté de Paris à la fin de la monarchie de Juillet, après le ministère Salvandy qui eut d'heureux effets, durant la Deuxième République et surtout sous le Second Empire, compta encore d'autres ecclésiastiques de talent, tels l'abbé Receveur, l'abbé Bargès, orientaliste distingué, l'abbé Bautain surtout, chargé de l'enseignement de la théologie morale et philosophe d'envergure.[19] Le public se pressait dans les étroites et sombres salles de la vieille Sorbonne pour écouter Dupanloup, durant son trop bref passage, Gratry, Cœur, Perreyve, Freppel, Perraud, Maret d'abord, qui attirait parfois deux cents auditeurs et plus par ses réfutations des systèmes philosophiques alors en vogue. Cette assistance de laïcs, où ne manquait pas la jeunesse des écoles, curieux de théologie ou plutôt de connaissances religieuses dans leurs rapports avec la civilisation moderne, invitait les professeurs à ne traiter ni d'érudition ni de spéculation dogmatique selon le mode scolastique mais à confronter à grands traits, au risque de quelques tentations oratoires, les vérités du christianisme catholique aux théories philosophiques et politiques du jour. Bautain allait jusqu'à comparer ces leçons aux «grandes catéchèses chrétiennes comme celle d'Origène et de ses successeurs à l'École d'Alexandrie». Maret parlait de son côté pour la Sorbonne en 1859 encore d'«un haut enseignement chrétien plutôt que d'une faculté de théologie à proprement parler», c'est-à-dire comme il l'avait écrit d'abord «une faculté de théologie qui est plutôt une faculté des lettres chrétiennes et de philosophie chrétienne». Pendant plus de trente ans Henry Maret, devenu évêque *in partibus* de Sura après le refus de Rome de lui accorder l'investiture pour le siège de Vannes auquel il avait été nommé par Napoléon III, et enfin archevêque *in partibus* de Lépante, fut «l'évêque de la Sorbonne» ainsi que le désignait avec ironie son adversaire acharné, Mgr Pie, évêque de Poitiers et futur cardinal, un des chefs du parti ultramontain en France et au concile, qui devait en 1875 obtenir de Pie IX l'érection d'une faculté libre de théologie à Poitiers, confiée à la Compagnie de Jésus, projet mal conçu et qui allait avorter dès 1880.[20] La réflexion théologique en amont et en aval du second concile du Vatican a réveillé l'intérêt pour le théologien en renom que fut Mgr Maret, un des principaux représentants de la

---

[18] Voir Louis Allen, *John Henry Newman and the abbé Jager: A Controversy on Scripture and Tradition (1834–1836)* (London, 1975).

[19] Sur ce normalien élève de Victor Cousin, ami de Jouffroy et de Damiron, d'abord professeur à la faculté des lettres de Strasbourg, prêtre en 1828, accusé de fidéisme à la suite de la publication de sa *Philosophie du christianisme*, reconnu comme orthodoxe après rétractation en 1840, voir Paul Poupard, *Un essai de philosophie chrétienne au XIXᵉ siècle: L'abbé Louis Bautain* (Paris, 1961).

[20] Voir Bruno Neveu, «La Faculté de théologie de Poitiers et la Compagnie de Jésus», *Archivum historicum Societatis Jesu*, lxii (1993), 87–128.

minorité au premier concile du Vatican, où l'on discuta beaucoup son gros ouvrage paru en septembre 1869: *Du concile général et de la paix religieuse*, étude mûrie depuis longtemps par l'auteur à la faveur de son enseignement. Les récentes et remarquables recherches de M. Claude Bressolette ont remis en lumière la carrière et la pensée de Maret jusqu'en 1854 et retracé son évolution religieuse, depuis les débuts mennaisiens, et les luttes qu'il devait mener jusqu'à son dernier souffle pour conjurer la suppression des facultés de théologie catholique et celle du chapitre épiscopal de Saint-Denis dont il était devenu le primicier.[21] L'examen des écrits proprement doctrinaux d'Henry Maret ne révèle pas un théologien profond ou original. Son épiscopalisme de ton irénique s'inspire étroitement des principes développés antérieurement par Bossuet, surtout dans la *Defensio Declarationis*, et repris par le cardinal de La Luzerne: la souveraineté spirituelle est partagée par la volonté du Christ entre le pontife romain et les évêques, et le concours de ces deux organes constitutifs est nécessaire pour l'exercice de l'infaillibilite.[22] En revanche Maret reprend l'avantage sur d'autres points, comme le montrent les soigneuses analyses de M. Bressolette:[23] sa réfutation du panthéisme, sa conception de la société moderne, des rapports que l'Église doit entretenir avec elle en acceptant «les principes de liberté et de progrès proclamés en 1789»—c'est le sujet de son dernier livre, d'une étonnante lucidité—le placent parmi les observateurs pénétrants et ouverts assez rares dans le clergé français de son temps et même chez les laïcs, qui ont généralement excommunié toutes les expressions de la modernité et contribué à faire regarder l'Église comme une force du passé. On peut ranger Maret parmi les meilleurs représentants du «catholicisme bourgeois», sensible aux valeurs civiles et civiques du nouvel ordre social et moral, attentif aux aspirations des élites cultivées, attaché à l'Université, autant de points opposant le doyen de la faculté de théologie de la Sorbonne aux catholiques intransigeants alors dominants, qui contestent violemment toutes les formes de la sécularisation et recherchent non sans générosité les voies d'une action sociale fidèle aux normes religieuses.

En tout cas l'évolution récente de l'ecclésiologie, telle que l'a instaurée le second concile du Vatican, marque sans aucun doute un retour en faveur des thèses de la minorité du premier concile du Vatican, dont Maret fut un des hérauts, voire un des héros. Comme l'évêque de la Sorbonne l'avait annoncé lui-

---

[21] Voir Claude Bressolette, *L'Abbé Maret: Le Combat d'un théologien pour une démocratie chrétienne (1830–1851)* (Paris, 1977); id., «Les Derniers Combats de Mgr Maret pour le maintien de la faculté de théologie de Sorbonne», *Humanisme et foi chrétienne: Mélanges scientifiques du centenaire de l'Institut catholique de Paris* (Paris, 1976), 49–69.

[22] Voir Raymond Thymann, «Le Gallicanisme de Mgr Maret et l'influence de Bossuet», *Revue d'histoire ecclésiastique*, 53 (1957), 401–65; Andrea Riccardi, *Neo-gallicanesimo e cattolicesimo borghese: Henri Maret e il Concilio Vaticano I* (Bologna, 1976).

[23] Ouvrage cité n. 20, Bressolette, *L'abbé Maret*, 241–455.

même, «la minorité a triomphé dans sa défaite»—expression reprise par Margaret O'Gara, *Triumph in Defeat. Infallibility, Vatican I and the French Minority Bishops* (Washington, 1988)—car si la majorité avait en 1870 pensé l'infaillibilité en termes de souveraineté et même de juridiction, la minorité en termes de communion et de témoignage de la foi, c'est cette dernière manière de voir qui s'est imposée, avec les formulations correspondantes, en 1962–5.

Le succès remporté par les leçons publiques de certains professeurs de théologie catholique à Paris été évoqué d'assez heureuse façon pour les années 1865–75 environ par un ancien auditeur assidu, Henry Jaudon, devenu conseiller à la Cour de cassation:

Notre Sorbonne ecclésiastique gardait noble figure . . . Elle m'apparaissait comme une survivance raccourcie de cette Église gallicane dont Bossuet avait célébré les gloires et dont le concile du Vatican allait faire disparaître les derniers vestiges. Lorsque sous les fresques de Philippe de Champaigne et en face du tombeau du cardinal [dans la chapelle], j'y voyais ces professeurs dans leur archaïque costume avec l'épitoge violette, le bonnet carré et le rabat français, je songeais aux soutenances sorbonniques . . . et je croyais entendre une dissertation sur la bulle Unigenitus ou les cinq propositions.

L'évocation se conclut sur ce jugement empreint de nostalgique sympathie:

Il se dégage une pénible impression, celle d'un contraste entre le mérite des professeurs et l'impuissance de leur action. La Sorbonne ecclésiastique a eu des maîtres de choix, tous docteurs ès-lettres, à une époque où ce grade était moins prodigué qu'aujourd'hui, profonds théologiens, savants érudits, orateurs éloquents . . . Ils n'ont pas fait école et n'ont pas eu d'action sur le clergé français. Ils ont eu l'autorité du caractère et du talent; il leur a manqué celle qu'un accord avec Rome aurait pu leur donner.[24]

S'il est bien vrai que les personnalités universitaires dont la présence dans les chaires théologiques de la Sorbonne vient d'être rappelée ont souvent été d'une réelle envergure et d'une incontestable générosité intellectuelle, il reste que la plupart des professeurs des facultés de théologie catholique, jusqu'à leur suppression, n'ont pas été sauf exception des théologiens originaux, spécialistes confirmés et aguerris d'une des branches de la science sacrée, de l'exégèse ou de la dogmatique à l'histoire ecclésiastique ou au droit canonique. Comme les autres représentants de la culture ecclésiastique en France entre 1820 et 1880—quelles qu'aient été durant trois quarts de siècle les inévitables évolutions survenues dans chaque discipline et dont un faible écho a pu se faire entendre dans les enseignements universitaires—ces maîtres ont mérité assez largement les critiques acérées d'Étienne Vacherot dans son article dévastateur de la Revue des

---

[24] Henry Jaudon, «Un centenaire oublié [La faculté de théologie catholique de la Sorbonnel]», *Revue bleue* (15 septembre 1923), 621–3; (6 octobre 1923), 664–6; (20 octobre 1923), 698–701. Quelques mentions aussi dans Dr A. Lebleu, *Vingt-cinq ans de Sorbonne et de Collège de France (1860–1884)* (Paris, 1884).

Deux Mondes du 15 juillet 1868, «La théologie catholique en France»,[25] dont il faut citer quelques lignes au moins. Après avoir laissé de côté «les théologiens protestants [qui] s'inspirent plutôt du sentiment que du dogme», l'auteur pose la question centrale: «Comment conserver le dogme dans son absolue intégrité tout en tenant compte des convenances du siècle et des difficultés créées aux apologistes chrétiens par la science et la critique modernes?» La revue des écrivains ecclésiastiques contemporains et de leurs œuvres indique que les réfutations, en dehors des anathèmes passionnés, n'ont guère eu de portée: Dupanloup, «toujours sur la brèche, attaque beaucoup, plus qu'il ne défend; il invoque les principes de l'ordre social plus que les textes»; Bautain, «esprit fin et délié, [est] plus moraliste que théologien»; Gratry, qui «sait les textes et s'en sert habilement ... conçoit tout avec imagination et juge tout avec passion», «adversaire déloyal ... plus proche de Tertullien que de Malebranche». Maret est mieux traité:

esprit calme, sensé, plus fait pour les analyses et les critiques de longue haleine que pour les vives et amères polémiques. C'est encore plus un philosophe qu'un théologien, qui aime à laisser les questions de critique dogmatique et d'histoire religieuse pour les problèmes de philosophie pure. Il défend le spiritualisme plutôt que la théologie catholique, il réfute le panthéisme et l'athéisme plutôt que l'exégèse allemande ou française. Sa méthode de réfutation est essentiellement philosophique ...

La conclusion de Vacherot est cruelle pour les théologiens de profession: «C'est en général aux corps savants et aux professeurs de l'Université que la théologie française laisse le soin de faire la guerre des textes ... C'est qu'en effet la science, même la science religieuse, est plutôt là qu'ailleurs». La «science des religions» (mot exact pour les recherches de la critique du XIXe siècle) est tout entière à l'analyse historique, «elle s'en tient à la réalité qu'elle constate, décrit, classe, explique, sans sortir des conditions de la connaissance positive [. . .]. L'esprit du siècle est plus historique au fond que philosophique»: c'est dire que l'œuvre d'un Henry Maret ne saurait avoir grande portée, car ce n'est pas l'ordre des réponses qu'on somme la théologie d'offrir à la science nouvelle.

Ces répliques appuyées sur la critique d'érudition, les universités catholiques créées en application de la loi du 12 juillet 1875 ont-elles cherché à les fournir, se sont-elles donné les moyens d'y parvenir?[26] En face des facultés de théologie de l'État, elles-mêmes en transformation mais encore attachées dans l'ensemble à une tradition apologétique plus attentive aux systèmes et aux idées qu'aux sources et aux textes, a-t-on vu en quelques années surgir dans les facultés libres de théologie—plus exactement les écoles de théologie instaurées sur un pied

---

[25] 76: 294–318.
[26] Neveu, *Facultés*, chapitre VI; Claude Bressolette, «La lente Fondation d'une faculté de théologie à Paris», *Revue de l'Institut catholique de Paris*, 36 (octobre–décembre 1990), 23–51.

modeste en attendant prudemment l'institution canonique—un esprit scientifique dont les représentants seraient à même de croiser le fer avec leurs adversaires sur le terrain des disciplines historiques et philologiques, de l'histoire des religions? Il convient sur ce point de se défier des célébrations intéressées à dénigrer les expirantes ou défuntes facultés de théologie universitaires pour mieux exalter le déploiement des hautes études dans les instituts catholiques, voire les grands séminaires.[27] Les mésaventures de Louis Duchesne et d'Alfred Loisy ne sont que les épisodes les plus connus d'une forte résistance aux méthodes critiques appliquées à la théologie positive, et l'on peut dire que la crise du modernisme est déjà en germe dans les incidents assez vifs des années 1880. C'est probablement dans les maisons de formation des grands ordres et congrégations, en dépit de leurs tribulations et expulsions, que le mouvement de recherche a été le plus sensible, l'essor historique et spéculatif le plus net. Les dominicains, franciscains, carmes, jésuites, oratoriens, sulpiciens, ont apporté assez rapidement une contribution de premier ordre à la rénovation des méthodes et de la réflexion fondamentale en théologie.[28] En dépit de leur neutralité agressive, les grands établissements supérieurs publics, Collège de France et École pratique des Hautes Études (avec une section des sciences religieuses à partir de 1886), facultés des lettres et de droit, parvenues à la maturité scientifique, ont compté parmi leurs auditeurs et élèves un nombre de prêtres et de religieux assez constant, qui a su faire le meilleur usage des méthodes et des connaissances acquises. Ainsi se sont réalisés en partie les vœux formés avec autant d'élévation que de perspicacité par Mgr d'Hulst, recteur de l'Institut catholique de Paris, dans son rapport au Conseil supérieur des évêques en date du 18 juillet 1883:

Le plus grand besoin de ce temps, ce sont des prêtres saints et des prêtres savants: il faut au peuple des apôtres . . . , il faut à la société des docteurs . . . Deux choses sont nécessaires: une connaissance approfondie du dogme, et une initiation chaque jour plus complète aux sciences historiques qui éclairent les origines de la révélation. Théologie scolastique, théologie positive, exégèse et philologie, voilà nos armes: mais il faut savoir les manier, et cela demande un long apprentissage; il faut en outre les perfectionner sans cesse . . .[29]

Une fois obtenue en 1875 la liberté de l'enseignement supérieur, suivie de la création de cinq universités (instituts à partir de 1880) catholiques, l'épiscopat et

---

[27] Voir par exemple Louis Baunard, *Un siècle de l'Église de France, 1800–1900*, 3e éd. (Paris, 1902), 371–2: «Les facultés officielles de théologie . . . établissements hybrides rapidement tombés en discrédit»; Alfred Baudrillart, *Le Renouvellement intellectuel du clergé de France au XIXᵉ siècle: Les Hommes, les institutions* (Paris, 1903); id., *L'Enseignement catholique dans la France contemporaine: Études et discours* (Paris, 1910).

[28] Voir le tableau bien documenté de Charles Wackenheim, *La Vie Intellectuelle*, dans *Église et Sociétés* (Paris, 1984), 295–333 (*Histoire du droit et des institutions de l'Église en Occident*, xvii).

[29] Édité par Cl. Bressolette, «La lente fondation», 42–5.

les fidèles eurent encore moins de raisons qu'auparavant de ménager les facultés de théologie catholique de l'Université de France, attaquées avec acharnement par les anti-cléricaux désireux d'effacer toute présence religieuse dans l'État et contraints de s'en prendre aux aumôniers des lycées ou des armées ou aux professeurs de théologie, faute de pouvoir abolir le Concordat. Les Chambres, saisies systématiquement de projets de suppression de ces facultés, dénoncées comme budgétivores et obscurantistes, finirent, en dépit des efforts de l'administration, appuyée par Jules Ferry, par voter la suppression des crédits à affecter aux facultés catholiques, le 13 mars 1885, ce qui entraîna *ipso facto* la disparition de ces établissements.

En application de la loi de séparation des Églises et de l'État, en date du 9 décembre 1905, il fut mis fin à l'existence au sein de l'Université des facultés de théologie protestante (Montauban et Paris, transféré de Strasbourg en 1877) épargnées en 1885 tant en raison de leur rôle majeur dans la formation des ministres des cultes concordataires protestants que de la faveur dont jouissait alors le protestantisme au sein des élites au pouvoir. L'ordre de la théologie, institué le 17 mars 1808 dans l'Université impériale disparut ainsi entièrement. Étendant jusqu'à la sphère intellectuelle son régime de laïcité, la France semble affirmer une incompatibilité entre l'État, avec ses organes d'enseignement supérieur, et les sciences religieuses cultivées et transmises dans le cadre théologique des Églises chrétiennes. On doit donc tenir pour une heureuse surprise que le retour à la patrie, au terme de la première guerre mondiale, de l'Alsace et de la Moselle ait entraîné la décision de restaurer dans une académie l'ordre des facultés de théologie. Dès 1919 la faculté de théologie protestante et la faculté de théologie catholique antérieurement érigées auprès de l'université impériale de Strasbourg furent réorganisées et dispensèrent leurs enseignements assortis de la collation des grades en toute régularité.[30] À l'issue de négociations entre le ministère des Affaires étrangères français et la Secrétairerie d'État du Saint-Siège, un décret du président de la République signé le 30 juin 1924 donna à ces facultés leur statut légal plénier, au sein de l'université de Strasbourg: à l'article 6 étaient réglés les rapports avec l'autorité ecclésiastique, ce qui permettait à la faculté de théologie catholique de jouir d'un statut canonique parfaitement régulier, sous la tutelle de la sacrée congrégation des Affaires ecclésiastiques extraordinaires, et la plaçait ainsi sur le même pied que les autres facultés d'État reconnues par le Saint-Siège.[31]

Ainsi s'est renouée en droit et en fait une tradition universitaire d'État de la

---

[30] Voir *Faculté de théologie catholique de l'Université de Strasbourg: Mémorial du cinquantenaire, 1919–1969* (Strasbourg, 1970); Matthieu Arnold, *La Faculté de théologie protestante de l'Université de Strasbourg de 1919 à 1945* (Strasbourg, 1990).

[31] *Annuario pontificio 1994* (Città del Vaticano, 1994), 1670–3: Facoltà theologiche presso Università di Stato (vingt-sept facultés).

théologie qui semblait à jamais brisée dans une société sécularisée: les professeurs oubliés qui occupèrent au cours du XIXe siècle les chaires des facultés de théologie catholique des académies n'ont sans doute pas contribué de manière éminente à l'essor des sciences sacrées, à leur perfectionnement, mais ils ont affirmé et maintenu, avec résolution et constance, la fécondité pour les deux puissances, l'État et l'Église, d'une présence officielle de la théologie, enseignée dans son cadre dogmatique, parmi les disciplines universitaires.

17

Colonial Church Establishment in the Aftermath of the Colenso Controversy

Peter Hinchliff

John William Colenso, first bishop of Natal in southern Africa, became embroiled in dispute concerning the precise legal and constitutional position of the established Church of England in the British colonies.[1] The Elizabethan Act of Supremacy had asserted that the queen, as supreme governor of the Church of England, possessed jurisdiction over all persons and all causes ecclesiastical as well as temporal (or secular) throughout all her dominions. It is to be noted that it did not say that the queen was supreme head of all religion in all her dominions. She was supreme governor of the Church of England. That supremacy extended over persons and over lawsuits (causes). When the Act was passed it was assumed that there was only one Church in England and that the queen's territories were England and Wales with an Irish dimension and certain other attachments, offshore islands, and the like. By the nineteenth century the English crown had been united with the crown of Scotland; there was a united kingdom with a single parliament but separate and very different religious establishments in Scotland and England; and there was an extensive empire. By that time the Act of Supremacy seems to have been interpreted as applying not so much geographically, to a territory, as personally, to members of the Church of England within a territory. It was held to have established, in other words, a relationship between the crown and certain persons within her dominions beyond the seas.

Furthermore, the nature of the English constitution itself had changed by the development of a parliamentary system. The process was not yet completed by the time Victoria came to the throne but the main features of it were already in

[1] For a fuller treatment of the whole controversy, see Peter Hinchliff, *The Anglican Church in South Africa* (London, 1963), 82 ff., and Peter Hinchliff, *John William Colenso, Bishop of Natal* (London, 1964), 115 ff. See also Peter Hinchliff, *The One-Sided Reciprocity: A Study in the Modification of the Establishment* (London, 1966), 177 ff., and Peter Hinchliff, 'Church–State Relations', in Stephen Sykes and John Booty, *The Study of Anglicanism* (London, 1988), 351 ff. Cecil Lewis and G. E. Edwards, *Historical Records of the Church of the Province of South Africa* (London, 1934), contains extracts from many relevant documents but its interpretation of them is somewhat partisan.

place. The government was in the hands of a cabinet, responsible to the House of Commons, and it was assumed that the monarch would act on the advice of the ministers in office, even in ecclesiastical affairs. In other words the original Henrician concept of a 'temporalty' and a 'spiritualty' envisaged in the Act in restraint of appeals of 1533, each with its own legislature and each governed personally by the crown, had over the centuries given way to a quite different state of affairs in which ecclesiastical matters were ordered by politicians, either directly by Act of Parliament or indirectly by the ministers' advice to the crown, whose prerogative power would more and more be exercised in accordance with that advice. The prerogative power, originally precisely that part of the crown's authority which was independent of Parliament, thus came to be exercised by the cabinet and not by the monarch personally. And as that happened, so the crown's prerogative became more and more a legal abstraction rather than a personal authority, so that there came a time when the law courts could hold that the monarch's prerogative had been illegally exercised. The personal relationship that originally held crown and Church together had become little more than a way in which government and the law could control the Church.

That the colonial religious establishment was nevertheless still *treated* as if it were a personal relationship between the sovereign and some of his or her subjects is shown by certain facts which would otherwise be glaring anomalies. In the first place, in spite of the fact that the colonies were *British* colonies only the *English* Church was normally regarded as automatically established there. Endowment was an entirely separate matter. The Church of Scotland might be given land or provided with government subsidies but so might other denominations. It was not 'established' in the colonies for the difference was that the Church of Scotland, though established in Scotland, recognized no supremacy vested in the crown. Only the Church of England possessed a supreme governor: it was only over Anglican colonists that the crown claimed this jurisdiction. Moreover, it was also clear that the supremacy was regarded as extending over persons rather than over geographically defined territories because it seemed that other Churches could possess the same kind of relationship with the crown as the Church of England. When the Cape Colony was captured from the Dutch during the Napoleonic Wars, the Dutch Reformed Church was given the same position *vis-à-vis* the British government as it had previously possessed in relation to the Dutch administration. The British crown appointed its clergymen, its services were held by permission of the governor, all its former privileges were continued. But none of this implied that the Church of *England* was not by law established in the colony.

The Colenso controversy had, in addition to the constitutional issues arising from this very tangled situation, a theological dimension also. Colenso had gone to Natal as a missionary. He had, soon after his arrival, published a commentary on the Epistle to the Romans which had set out a view of the atonement which urged that Christ's death saved the whole of humanity.[2] He also took a different attitude to African culture and social customs from that of most missionaries. Instead of regarding Zulu society as 'heathen', he urged that missionaries should indigenize Christianity, giving it a Zulu character or dress. And he refused to compel polygamous converts to put aside all but their first wives. He did not *like* polygamy but he saw that it was part of the fabric of African society and that the effect of its destruction on the wives and children, whose legitimacy would be called into question, would be disastrous. His missionary work also raised questions about the Bible, for his converts asked why their own legends and traditions should be regarded as bloodthirsty and wicked when the Old Testament was full of equally savage episodes described as being in accordance with the divine will. Colenso set to work with prodigious energy to produce what became a many-volume work of biblical criticism in which he really sought to prove that, since the Old Testament was not to be regarded as dictated *verbatim* by God, one need not regard its moral standards as unalterable divine commands.[3]

As a result of all these views, then unconventional and controversial, Colenso was tried for heresy in Cape Town in 1863. Robert Gray, bishop of Cape Town, presided at the trial. He was the son of that bishop of Bristol whose palace had been burnt by rioters when he and his brother bishops had voted against the first Reform Bill of 1831. He had inherited his father's old-fashioned Tory High Churchmanship, but he was not a Tractarian, since he had completed his time as an undergraduate at Oxford by 1831, which is to say two years before the Oxford Movement began. He was ordained by his father in 1833, married in 1835, and then spent ten years as an incumbent in Durham until he was invited to become the first bishop of Cape Town in 1848. He had then been issued with royal letters patent, but his diocese had been divided in order to create Colenso's diocese of Natal in 1853, and he had been given new letters patent which purported to make him 'metropolitan'. He sat, with two other bishops, as assessors, found Colenso guilty of heresy, and deposed him from office. Colenso appeared by proxy but only to protest against the court's jurisdiction. When he ignored its sentence, he was formally excommunicated.

As it happened Gray had already been involved in an attempt to exercise the authority which his letters patent appeared to have given him. A clergyman in the diocese refused to obey the bishop's summons to attend a synod. Gray tried to

---

[2] J. W. Colenso, *St Paul's Epistle to the Romans: Newly Translated and Explained from a Missionary Point of View* (Natal, 1861).

[3] J. W. Colenso, *The Pentateuch and the Book of Joshua, Critically Examined*, pt. I (London, 1862), 143–4.

discipline him for contumacious behaviour, but it soon became clear that his letters patent conferred on him no coercive jurisdiction. The courts had ruled in the so-called Eton College case of 1857 that the Church of England could no longer be regarded as established in colonies where there was an independent legislature. The crown, in other words, was held to have limited its own prerogative powers by creating, within its dominions, a body with authority to make law. The law would not recognize the action of the crown. In the case of Gray's contumacious clergyman, an appeal to the Judicial Committee of the Privy Council determined that Gray could exercise only such authority as the members of the Church were willing to give him through the voluntary acceptance of an ecclesiastical constitution regulations.

Colenso sought redress against Gray's action by means of a petition to the crown. This was not an appeal against the decision of the metropolitical court, for that would have implied that Colenso recognized its jurisdiction. It was rather a request for a declaration from the crown that Gray had no right or power to remove another bishop whom it had appointed. The petition was heard by the Judicial Committee of the Privy Council (and is known as '*ex parte* the Bishop of Natal') in 1865. It held that the letters patent of both bishops were void, since the Cape Colony and Natal each possessed its own legislature. Nor did the fact that Colenso had taken an oath of canonical obedience to Gray constitute a voluntary acceptance of his authority or give the metropolitan any right to depose him. On the one hand, the letters patent were held, despite their invalidity, to have created ecclesiastical persons who could not be un-made except by the crown. And, on the other, it was maintained that, because the letters patent could not confer jurisdiction, Colenso ought not to have taken an oath of obedience to a metropolitan who had no legal authority to demand it. Moreover, Gray's letters patent as metropolitan had been issued slightly later than Colenso's as bishop of Natal, a further reason for regarding them as powerless to confer authority on the former over the latter.

The Colonial Bishopricks Fund had withheld Colenso's income after his excommunication and Colenso now sued for its restoration. The case was heard by the Master of the Rolls, Lord Romilly, and is known as 'the Bishop of Natal *v.* Gladstone and others', Mr Gladstone being the treasurer of the Colonial Bishopricks Fund. Romilly decided that ecclesiastical persons created by the crown were corporations capable of holding property in the name of the Church of England. In that sense, in other words, the Church of England as by law established *could* exist, even in a colony with an independent legislature, by means of admittedly invalid letters patent. The lawyers, having allowed documents to be issued, and then having declared those documents worthless, had begun to feel, no doubt, that they had better do something to protect the person whom their muddle had made most vulnerable. But, in reality, the courts had simply come full circle. And the various sets of invalid letters patent—'These baubles!', said Gray—had cost something in the order of £10,000.[4]

It would be unfair, of course, to pretend that the whole situation was invented by the lawyers. If Colenso had not been determined to insist on his right to express opinions which were not contrary to the law, and if Gray had not been equally determined that it was for the Church and not the law to decide what was orthodox doctrine, there would have been no lawsuits in the first place. But the result for Natal was a kind of stalemate: nor were the lawsuits over yet. Colenso took action in the Supreme Court of Natal to gain possession of all the property which had in one way or another been aquired by 'the Church of England'. Thereafter the five parish churches, the cathedral, and all the mission stations save one belonged to Colenso and the Church of England in Natal. A Church Council was constituted to assist the bishop in the conduct of the affairs of this Church of England. Probably two-thirds of the white colonial laity, some of them socially prominent—including Theophilus Shepstone, secretary for Native Affairs in the colonial administration—supported Colenso. But seventeen of the twenty clergy, led by James Green, the dean of the cathedral, who had been declared 'an outlaw' and 'in perpetual contempt' by the Supreme Court, were opposed to the bishop and wished to be part of the voluntary association, the Church of the Province of South Africa, the part of the Anglican Communion over which Gray presided as metropolitan. A new bishop was chosen, W. K. Macrorie, and took the title of bishop of Maritzburg (Pietermaritzburg, commonly thus abbreviated, being the capital of the colony). A majority of the English bishops agreed to inhibit Colenso from officiating in their dioceses. The fact that 'liberals' like Arthur Stanley and Benjamin Jowett came out in his support probably did him little good, for the furore caused by *Essays and Reviews* had not yet died down. Though Macrorie and his supporters had to build new churches in all those places where Colenso had acquired the property of 'the Church of England', they had the moral and financial support of the influential Society for the Propagation of the Gospel in England. The stalemate was typified by the story that Garnet Wolseley, when commanding the army in Natal, invited both bishops to dinner but refused to attend either cathedral.

For Colenso, however, things slowly got worse. In spite of having the income from the Colonial Bishopricks Fund and £300 a year voted by the Natal Legislative Council, there was not enough money to pay the few clergy he had, maintain the mission stations, and keep his family. He was reduced to the humiliating (and unsuccessful) expedient of writing to Gray and begging for

[4] Hinchliff, *Anglican Church*, 97.

money for his sons 'who are guiltless of what in your eyes must seem to be their father's fault'.[5] His greatest difficulty lay in finding suitable clergymen. Most of those who went to join him turned out to be misfits or indolent or undesirable.[6] The pathetic story of the other Robert Gray is typical. No relation of the metropolitan, he came to work for Colenso in the late 1860s, amid many high hopes that he would be able to be dean of the cathedral *and* tutor to the Colenso boys.[7] But his sermons were boring; he was irresponsible with his own money and with the Church's; and he was eventually sent packing after getting into a drunken brawl with a native policeman who struck him with a knobkerrie.[8] The summoning of the first Lambeth Conference in 1867 was partly occasioned by the Colenso controversy, and, though Archbishop Longley was determined to prevent the matter's being discussed, the very fact that Colenso was not among those invited was bound to make it seem that he was not a fully accredited member of the Anglican episcopate.[9] His position was further weakened by hostility arising from his active and heroic championing, first of the Hlubi chief Langalibalele, and subsequently of the Zulu king Cetewayo, which offended Shepstone. The bishop had been made a member of the Natal Native Affairs Commission in 1881, but his advocacy of Cetewayo's cause, so soon after the near disaster of the Zulu War, was the subject of bitter comment in the Natal press. In his last years he was inevitably a lonely figure. His three unmarried daughters (Harriette, Frances, and Agnes) were deeply committed to their father's struggle for the rights of the indigenous people and would continue it after his death in 1883.

Even before he died Colenso seems to have realized that there was little or no likelihood of his having a successor: in effect he had come to see that the lawyers would not repeat their mistakes and, therefore, would not need to extend the protection they had given to their victim. He had told the Church Council in 1882 that, when the crown ceased to issue royal mandates and letters patent, the courts might recognize, as successors to the letters-patent bishops, bishops 'whose consecration has not been authorized by the crown, nor performed directly or indirectly by the Archbishop of Canterbury'.[10] But not everyone could be so

[5] Natal Archives, Pietermaritzburg; Colenso Collection, Correspondence 136, draft letter from Colenso to Gray.

[6] M. A. Hooker ('The Place of Bishop Colenso in South African History', unpublished Ph.D. thesis (Witwatersrand, Johannesburg)) devotes a whole chapter to Colenso's clergy.

[7] Wyn Rees (ed.), *Colenso Letters from Natal* (Pietermaritzburg, 1958), 128.

[8] Natal Archives, Pietermaritzburg; Colenso Collection, Correspondence 136, Colenso to Sanderson, 4 Feb. 1871.

[9] For a detailed consideration of Colenso in relation to the Conference, see A. M. G. Stephenson, *The First Lambeth Conference: 1867* (London, 1967), 120 ff. and 267 ff. and cf. Lambeth Palace Library, F. Temple Papers (Official Letters), vol. 25, fos. 1–14, which strongly support Gray's claim to have received the unofficial support of a considerable majority of the bishops present at the conference.

[10] Lambeth Palace Library, F. Temple Papers (Official Letters), vol. 19, fos. 101–4, printed account of Archdeacon Colley's address to the Church Council of the Diocese of Natal, 3 June 1885.

philosophical. Colenso's daughters, who had invested so much emotional capital in their support for their father and his causes, could not be expected suddenly to accept that the legality for which they had suffered so much in unpopularity, ostracism, and isolation no longer mattered. They were chiefly concerned with maintaining Colenso's mission stations and with his other work for the African people. Their efforts eventually resulted in what came to be known as the 'Sobantu Church', 'Sobantu' or 'Father of the People' being the Zulu name for Colenso. They were—perhaps because their continued possession of the missions depended on it—doughty fighters in the constitutional issue, but, for the most part, that aspect of the controversy was an issue which primarily concerned the white colonists. It was part of their attachment to all things English.

The Church Council made strenuous efforts to secure a successor to Colenso. First it petitioned the crown for the appointment of a new bishop by letters patent. Colenso's prognostication proved entirely accurate and the petition failed. The Council then attempted to persuade the English archbishops and four other bishops to choose a bishop for Natal, thinking that this procedure would at least preserve some obvious signs of its being in communion with the Church of England. The bishops whom it approached were either 'liberals' (like Colenso himself) or evangelicals (who would dislike Colenso's mostly high church opponents). Nevertheless the scheme failed.

The English episcopate had received a warning that it might be asked to intervene in the South African problem. On 4 February 1884, at a regular meeting of the bishops from both provinces,[11] the bishop of Oxford (Mackarness) drew the attention of his colleagues to 'the complications of the present position of the South African Church'.[12] Later in the year,

The Archbishop of Canterbury read a letter from the Bishop of Capetown [William West Jones who had succeeded Gray on the latter's death in 1872] on the position of the Church in South Africa suggesting . . . the issue by the English Bishops of some declaratory statement that the Church of South Africa is in that colony the true and only representative of the Mother Church . . .

It was resolved that in the event of such a question as the Bishop of Capetown anticipates being sent to the Archbishop, he should, if it should appear necessary, summon a special Meeting of Bishops to consider the precise reply which ought to be sent.[13]

There is no record of any such meeting taking place. Perhaps it was judged unnecessary because of the request from Natal addressed to the archbishops and four other bishops.

---

[11] The bishops of both provinces had been meeting together informally for some time, though the earliest records of the meetings only date from 1871 and for the first eight years consist of rough notes, often barely legible, kept by Archbishop Tait himself (Lambeth Palace Library, Bishops Meetings, BM1).
[12] Ibid. BM3, p. 25, 4 Feb. 1884.   [13] Ibid. 43, 20 June 1884.

A meeting of the Church Council was summoned for 3 June 1885 'to receive the reply of the Archbishops of Canterbury and York and the Bishops of Worcester, London, Manchester and Liverpool to a petition and prayer of the Church Council to the Most Rev and Right Rev Prelates for the appointment of a Bishop to the See vacant through the death of the Right Rev J. W. Colenso DD Lord Bishop of Natal'.[14] The most reverend and right reverend prelates declined to do as the Church Council asked.[15]

The Church Council then proceeded in August 1886 itself to elect a successor to Colenso. This was really to admit failure, for its case had always been that an elected bishop (a bishop produced, in effect, by voluntary association) was not at all the same thing as a bishop appointed by letters patent from the crown. Nevertheless, they had little alternative and the person they chose was the Revd G. W. Cox who had long been one of Colenso's keenest sympathizers in England and was actually in the process of writing a biography of the bishop from materials supplied by Mrs Colenso.[16] Cox also claimed to be a baronet (which may have counted for something in colonial Natal), though when the claim was put to the test by Cox's son after his death it would be unsuccesful.[17] The council did its best to regularize its position and to ensure that its candidate would be as much as possible a Church of England bishop by petitioning Archbishop Benson to apply for a royal licence to consecrate Cox. This Benson refused to do, on the ground that Natal had been from the beginning a part of the province of South Africa and that that province would not recognize the election. In the following year an attempt to persuade the crown to compel the archbishop also failed and in answer to a question in the House of Commons on 18 August 1887 a government spokesman said: 'It was decided in 1884 that, having regard to the Report of the Committee of the Privy Council of 24th June, 1873, Her Majesty should not be advised to appoint by Letters Patent a successor to Bishop Colenso, and Her Majesty's present advisers see no reason to depart from that decision.'[18] It was the end of that particular road and the council proceeded no further with 'Sir' George Cox.

An attempt at reconciliation next came from an unexpected quarter—an attempt which is hardly mentioned in any of the secondary sources, perhaps because neither side was particularly taken with either the proposal or the man

[14] Lambeth Palace Library, F. Temple Papers (Official Letters), vol. 19, fos. 101–4, printed account of Archdeacon Colley's address to the Church Council of the Diocese of Natal, 3 June 1885.

[15] Ibid., fos. 105–6.

[16] George W. Cox, *The Life of John William Colenso, DD, Bishop of Natal* (2 vols.; London 1888).

[17] Information supplied by the Home Office shows that at a meeting of the Baronetage Committee of the Privy Council on 9 Nov. 1911, the committe advised King George V that the name of Edmund Charles Cox (George Cox's son) 'ought not to be entered on the Official Roll of Baronets in respect of the Irish Baronetcy of Cox of Dunmanway'.

[18] Lewis and Edwards, *Historical Records*, 349.

who made it. He was Thomas Colley, Colenso's archdeacon of Pietermaritzburg, who had come to feel his position, and that of the Church of England in Natal, to be more or less untenable. In many ways a rather foolish person, Colley had nevertheless been clear and cogent in his attempts to persuade the Natal Church Council of the hopelessness of its case. On the occasion when he had summoned the Council to tell it of the answer of the English prelates he had argued, first, that their plain and negative answer must be accepted because the very fact that the Church Council had appealed to them had implied a recognition that they would be *final* arbiters. Secondly, he had reminded the members of the council of Colenso's address to them in 1882 when he had warned them that the issuing of royal mandates for the consecration of colonial bishops would inevitably cease.[19] He pointed out, thirdly, that there was no real restraint upon what the clergy of the Church of England in Natal might do liturgically. If they chose, they might use copes, candles, and crosses on the altar, the eastward position, and so on. If clergy in England could get away with all those things, then there was no guarantee that a bishop consecrated by the archbishop of Canterbury, or any clergymen of the Church of England serving under him, would be any more acceptable than one of Macrorie's priests. Therefore, he advocated union with the Church of the Province of South Africa and, as a first step, the immediate exchange of pulpits with its clergy.[20]

It is very difficult to decide whether Colley's proposals were taken seriously by either side. Years afterwards a former archdeacon of Macrorie's party was to assert that Colley had done a great work in persuading the Church Council to confer with representatives of 'the Church of South Africa at which the idea of a synod was virtually agreed upon'. Since, however, he thought that Colley's 'greatest triumph' was the decision to appeal to the English prelates, and that by the prelates' decision 'the burden of disloyalty was placed upon the proper persons', his estimate of his fellow archdeacon's contribution appears a somewhat back-handed one.[21] It would not be surprising if the Church Council disliked having 'the burden of disloyalty' placed upon its own shoulders. And Archbishop Benson was said to have deeply distrusted Colley and to have set an example of keeping him at arm's length.[22]

In fact Colley does not appear to have been an attractive character. He had gone to work with Colenso at a time when the bishop had hardly a single clergyman left to him. He had been appointed archdeacon of Pietermaritzburg and canon of the cathedral in September 1879, which was within three years of

[19] See p. 350.
[20] Lambeth Palace Library, F. Temple Papers (Official Letters), vol. 19, fos. 101–4, printed account of Archdeacon Colley's address to the Church Council of the Diocese of Natal, 3 June 1885.
[21] Ibid., vol. 10, fos. 256 ff.
[22] Ibid., vol. 19, fo. 118, letter from A. H. Baynes, dated 20 Sept. 1898.

Colenso's death.[23] He claimed a string of impressive titles which did not amount to anything; claiming to be the senior archdeacon of the diocese (but there may at times only have been one other clergyman in priest's orders); sometimes calling himself 'vicar-general', sometimes 'administrator of the see', and 'president of the Church Council of the Church of England in Natal'. Colley may even have hoped that he might be chosen as Colenso's successor and he did at one time petition the crown to be appointed vicar-general of the vacant diocese of Natal.[24]

In 1888, at the point when it had become clear that no bishop would ever be consecrated for the Church of England in Natal, Colley went back to England and began his campaign to become the person who provided the solution to the problem. He always made it very clear that he had his price and that that price was a Lambeth degree awarded by the archbishop of Canterbury in recognition of his great services and greater sacrifices. He asked first for a DD, then for a BD, and then, as it became clear that successive archbishops were not going to reward him in this way, for a much more modest MA. Why he was so anxious to acquire a Lambeth degree is not clear. He had been an undergraduate at Magdalen Hall, Oxford, but had gone down without taking a degree. Perhaps he had always hankered for the degree he had not earned; perhaps he thought that further preferment depended on his being a graduate. At all events, the records at Lambeth Palace contain any number of letters from Colley pleading for this recognition. No snubs, no rebuffs, no patient explanations, no angry words, ever put him off from demeaning himself once more in the hope that this time he might get some sort of degree from the archbishop. Frederick Temple, when exasperated by endless appeals from Colley, told him, 'You spoil all sacrifices by perpetually asking to be paid for them!'[25]

E. W. Benson was still archbishop when the archdeacon went to England in 1888. It seems that he never visited Natal again—though he often threatened to resume his archidiaconal status from which he claimed that he had 'retired but not resigned'.[26] He wrote to Temple, then bishop of London and, as such, traditionally supposed to have a particular responsibility for the colonial Church, on 8 June, a very characteristic letter with its slightly pretentious, slightly malapropistic language. Perhaps he thought that one high ecclesiastic ought to

[23] Ibid. fos. 112–14, copies of licences issued by Colenso and dated 23 Sept. 1879. The copies were certified true copies by Dr Whitmarsh, vicar of Sandford on Thames, George Moore, vicar of Cowley, and W. M. Merry, vicar of St Michael's and countersigned by the bishop of Oxford certifying that those clergy were beneficed in his diocese and worthy of credit.

[24] Ibid., Fulham Papers (F. Temple), vol. 55, fos. 144–5, Benson to Temple.

[25] Ibid., F. Temple Papers (Official Letters), vol. 21, fos. 351–2, Colley to Archbishop Frederick Temple, date illegible. The archbishop's comment is written on Colley's letter to guide his chaplains when writing the reply.

[26] Ibid., vol. 19, fos. 110–11; Colley to Archbishop Frederick Temple, 19 Sept. 1898.

use that kind of style when addressing another. He told the bishop that he believed that there was an opportunity to bring about Church unity in Natal. The bishop of Cape Town (West Jones) was in England and the bishop of Maritzburg (Macrorie) soon would be.

It is proposed that we should meet in Conference with the Archbishop of Canterbury and endeavour to arrive at some terms of settlement before our return to South Africa.

The Bishop of Maritzburg has already proffered [*sic*] to confirm all candidates presented by me, or through me from any of the six churches of the lapsed diocese of Natal under my administration. But I think more than this will be the result of the conference. For I propose that as the diocesan system of the vacant and virtually lapsed see cannot be carried out, Her Majesty's Ministers shall advise the Government of Natal to favour a measure I have drafted for apportioning to our six churches that have congregations, the property of the Diocese for endowment of the six livings that have never had any endowment—the clergy being supported entirely from the fluctuating offertories—so that under the joint patronage of the several vestries, of myself as Vicar General, and perhaps the Bishop, clergymen of the Church of England from England might in perpetuity be had for each of the remaining churches, who should be subject to the Bishop of Maritzburg and the ecclesiastical system of the Church of the Province of South Africa only to such an extent as they would be subject to the Bishop of any diocese in England.[27]

Temple seems to have passed the letter to Benson. It is not known who, besides Colley, had proposed that he and the two South African bishops 'should meet in Conference with the Archbishop of Canterbury'. Benson told Colley that he was only willing to see him if the bishop of Cape Town were to request it and he told Temple that he had heard no more of the matter after that.[28] There is no record that such a meeting ever took place. Certainly that particular proposal does not seem to have borne fruit, nor is there any trace of its ever having been put to the British or the Natal goverment.

Nor does Colley's earlier and very public *démarche* in Natal appear to have had any effect. He had clearly burnt his boats and, for all that he is an unsympathetic character, one cannot help feeling a little sorry for him. He gave up what was an assured, if unimportant, position to live in England without work or income, doing temporary locums when he could get them, until he became rector of Stockton in 1901. He contrasted his own situation with that of Macrorie, who had been given a canonry at Ely. He had, he said bitterly, always done what archbishops of Canterbury had asked of him, whereas Macrorie had insisted on going out to Cape Town to be consecrated in South Africa 'in the face of the expressed wishes of the English Archbishops and Bishops'.[29]

Yet Colley may, after all, have had some influence on affairs. For in February 1891 Benson came up with a proposal for an 'autocephalous' diocese for the

[27] Ibid., Fulham Papers (F. Temple), vol. 55, fos. 142–3.   [28] Ibid., fos. 144–5.
[29] Ibid., F. Temple Papers (Official Letters), vol. 21, fos. 355–6, Colley to Temple, 10 May 1899.

colony of Natal which would not be wholly part of the Church of the Province of South Africa, nor yet simply a continuation of the letters-patent bishopric which Colenso had held. If it were directly under his own jurisdiction, it might be, he hoped, acceptable to both sides. It is just possible that in coming to this conclusion he may have been influenced by Colley's proposal made to Frederick Temple and shown by him to Benson in 1888.[30] In spite of his doubts about Colley, Benson had spoken quite kindly of his activities, saying, 'I fancy he has been doing his best for the Church.'[31] Colley's proposal for the appointment of clergymen for the Church of England in Natal jointly by himself, as vicar-general, and by Bishop Macrorie, had also been a proposal to create something which would have this dual-purpose character. Those clergymen would have been 'subject to the Bishop of Maritzburg and the ecclesiastical system of the Church of the Province of South Africa only to such an extent as they would be subject to the Bishop of any diocese in England'.[32] And, in effect, there would have been two parallel ecclesiastical systems, under a single bishop, one of which would be subject to the constitution and regulations of the Church of the Province of South Africa and the other under the law of England as it affected the Church of England.

What Benson now proposed would have a similar effect. It was entirely inconsistent with the answer he had given the Natal Church Council on the question of the consecration of Cox, that Natal had always been part of the province of South Africa.[33] There was in reality little or no possibility that any such scheme would ever be acceptable to either side, for the legal complexities had, in effect, created two vested interests and the interests were vested in two diametrically opposed views of what constituted the Church. For the Church of England in Natal, its very existence—and the property upon which, in a sense, that existence depended—rested on its claim to be in every possible legal sense continuous with the Church of England as by law established. The Church of the Province of South Africa, though in full spiritual communion with Canterbury, believed that it dare not surrender its status as a voluntary association lest it find that it had lost the power to control and discipline its bishops and clergy. Moreover, both sides contained people who had been sufficiently badly hurt by events for there to be personal bitterness involved as well as determination to maintain principles.

The bishop of Cape Town made it immediately and comprehensively clear to Benson that there was no chance of the provincial synod or the (by now) thirty clergymen of the diocese of Maritzburg agreeing to his scheme.[34] But Macrorie,

[30] See p. 355.
[31] Lambeth Palace Library, Fulham Papers (F. Temple), vol. 55, fos. 144–5, Benson to Temple.
[32] See p. 355.   [33] See p. 352.
[34] M. H. M. Wood, *A Father in God: The Episcopate of William West Jones* (London, 1913).

having been told that his withdrawal might bring a peaceful settlement nearer, tendered his resignation in June 1891, though he did not actually leave the diocese until the following February. As soon as he knew Macrorie intended to resign, West Jones seems to have told Benson that the diocese of Maritzburg might agree to delegate the choice of a new bishop (a procedure for which the constitution of the Church of the Province of South Africa provided). If it were to delegate the choice to Benson, his nominee—as nominee of the 'Chief Pastor of the Mother Church'—might be acceptable to the Church of England in Natal. At the same time West Jones made it clear that the new bishop might be consecrated in England by Benson, provided that he took an oath of canonical obedience to the metropolitan of Cape Town and not to the archbishop of Canterbury.[35] Benson completely misunderstood the point which West Jones was making and was also mistaken in believing that West Jones had bound himself at his own consecration by an oath of obedience to Canterbury. He therefore assumed that, if he were to choose and consecrate a bishop who took an oath to Cape Town as metropolitan, he would be bound to Canterbury at one remove and thus acceptable to the Church Council.[36]

The council seems to have made yet another attempt to elect a bishop of its own (the Revd William Ayerst, principal of a private hall in Cambridge) and to persuade Benson to consecrate *him*. Benson, however, was determined to proceed with his new proposal, but seems to have given Miss Colenso, Sir Theophilus Shepstone, and the Natal Church Council to believe that the new bishop would head two entirely separate and independent bodies.[37] The plan was, therefore, doomed from the start, because each side had been given an entirely different explanation—two explanations which Benson *thought* were reconcilable but which, in fact, were not. The Church Council had agreed to the proposal provided that the rights, privileges, and properties of the Church of England were guaranteed.[38] The diocese of Maritzburg had agreed provided that the new bishop signed the constitution of the province and took an oath to the South African metropolitan and not to Canterbury. So deep was the divide by this time that the accounts of the events written by Colenso's daughter and Benson's son read almost as if they are describing different things.[39] The man whom Benson chose was his own former chaplain, Arthur Hamilton Baynes; but Baynes had very little chance of success, since he not only had to be a dual-capacity bishop but each of the parties understood each of the two capacities differently. He was consecrated by Benson in Westminster Abbey in September

[35] Ibid. 224.
[36] Ibid. 225, and, for an account of West Jones's oath at his consecration, Hinchliff, *Anglican Church*, 120–1.
[37] H. E. Colenso, *Reply to Bishop Baynes' Explanation* (Durban, 1894), 34 ff.
[38] Wood, *Father in God*, 226.
[39] H. E. Colenso, *Reply*; A. C. Benson, *Life of Edward White Benson* (2 vols.; London 1900), ii. 473 ff.

1893, taking the oath of obedience to the metropolitan of Cape Town and signing the provincial constitution, and arrived in the colony in November of the same year, calling himself, as Colenso had done, the bishop of Natal.

The impossibility of his position was soon revealed. The Church Council asked him to recognize the continuing existence of the Church of England in Natal as an independent body and to make a solemn declaration that he would uphold its constitution and observe its regulations. This he felt he could not do, though he offered a compromise which was, in turn, rejected by the council. The upshot of these manœuvrings was that the council would not recognize Baynes as 'the Church of England Bishop of Natal' in succession to Colenso, though it was willing to treat him as *a* Church of England bishop whose services they could legitimately use. Baynes continued to try to bring the two bodies together in some form which would enable him to preside over them with integrity and he began to win small victories. When Archbishop Benson died in 1896, there were actually two letters from Baynes on their way to England reporting on the latest of these.[40] He wrote again to the new archbishop (Temple) to put him in the picture and to report the most important of his successes. The curators appointed by the Supreme Court of Natal to administer the properties and funds of the Church of England in Natal, who had hitherto done exactly as the Church Council had asked, had agreed to use part of the income of about £700 a year to pay a missionary and the native teachers on one of the mission stations under Baynes's full episcopal authority. And this in spite of tenacious opposition from the Council.[41]

Baynes had begun to hope for a different solution. He believed that many of those who had hitherto belonged to the other party would swing round and support him if he could provide them with a guarantee that there was an ultimate authority outside South Africa which would protect them from unfair or biased treatment at the hands of the provincial tribunals. There was a proposal which was to be put before the Lambeth Conference of 1897, for the establishment of a court of appeal for the whole Anglican Communion. It emanated from the American bishops, who had asked for the creation of a proper organization of the communion as a whole. If that happened and if the provincial synod accepted it as the final court of appeal from the tribunals of the Church of the Province of South Africa, and if the parishes of the Church of England in Natal were to be guaranteed a say in the choice of their clergy, he thought there was every hope that the controversy might come to an end.

In fact some of those parishes had begun to drift towards the Church of the

[40] Lambeth Palace Library, F. Temple Papers (Official Letters), vol. 19, fo. 83, Baynes to Frederick Temple, 30 Oct. 1896.
[41] Ibid., vol. 19, fo. 83.

Province. The vestry of what had been Colenso's cathedral in Pietermaritzburg had actually asked to join, but this had provoked the curators into threatening legal action to test the right of the congregation to continue to use the land and building under those circumstances.[42] By late 1897 Baynes was in England working hard to secure a resolution of the Lambeth Conference setting up a court of appeal for the Anglican Communion. The bishops specifically declined to create an actual court of appeal, which every province would be obliged to recognize. Indeed, it would have been beyond its power to do any such thing. But it did agree to the setting-up of a consultative body (actually to be appointed subsequently by the archbishop of Canterbury) which might be recognized by individual provinces as a final court of appeal.[43] In January of 1898 Baynes sent Temple a draft resolution which he proposed to set before the provincial synod in South Africa which would recognize the consultative body as the court of appeal from the ecclesiastical tribunals of the province.[44] He thought that this proposal would overcome the objections of all but the most obdurate of the Colensoites. Temple asked the bishop of Winchester (Randall Davidson) for his advice. As himself a former chaplain to Archbishop Tait, Davidson was sympathetic to Baynes's situation. He was also frequently consulted on important matters by both Benson and Temple. On this occasion he replied that he believed that there would never be another case like Colenso's and that a pan-Anglican court of appeal would never be needed. Nevertheless, he said, it was so important that '*some* bridge should be built for uniting the South African forces, that I am not disposed to be critical of the bridge-builders' *modus aedificandi*'.[45]

A bridge, in fact, was almost an impossibility. The completely irreconcilable vested interests created by the law were locked into their positions. The only way out of the impasse was for one side to win and, in effect, to destroy the other. This was revealed very clearly by the next initiative to be taken: this time by the legislators, who thought *they* might solve the problem created by the law. In the spring of 1898 Baynes had to go back to his diocese because a bill, which originated with the curators of the Church of England property, was before the Natal legislature. It was widely advertised as 'the final step in the reunion of the divided churches'. It was designed virtually to revive the authority of Colenso's letters patent of 1853 and then to recognize Baynes, the Church of the Province

[42] Ibid., fo. 85, Baynes to Temple, 13 Nov. 1897.

[43] A. M. G. Stephenson, *Anglicanism and the Lambeth Conferences* (London, 1978), 100 ff. The report of a committee of English bishops to consider the question is recorded in Lambeth Palace Library, Minutes of Bishops' Meetings, BM3, 15 Feb. 1896.

[44] Lambeth Palace Library, F. Temple Papers (Official Letters), vol. 19, fo. 86, Baynes to Temple, 3 Jan. 1898.

[45] Ibid., fo. 88.

bishop, as the legal successor to Colenso. It would have vested the properties of the Church of England in Natal in trustees appointed by the courts instead of making them available for the use of the united church as a whole. The bishop thought that it would not please anyone. It would have alienated the members of the Church of the Province, because, in effect, it would have entrenched the legal existence of the former 'Church of England' within the reunited body. The fact that the existence of that body would have been enshrined in an act of the colonial legislature would be tantamount to establishing it by law and thus would also be quite unacceptable to those who, in England, would have been 'dissenters'. The bishop was able to persuade the sponsors of the bill to withdraw it, at least for the time being, and believed that he would have no option but to oppose it, though he feared that Miss Colenso would then say, 'I always said he was not a bishop of the Church of England and now he refuses to be made one.'[46]

Baynes believed that the Natal parliament would not insist on the passage of such a bill in the face of opposition from the bishop and all his clergy, though one of the curators of the Church of England property was a cabinet minister and that might mean that he would be able to arrange for the bill to receive a majority in the house. Back in the colony, Baynes scurried round trying to persuade everyone that it was better not to proceed with the bill but to rely on the proposal for creating a consultative body which could serve as a court of appeal for the Anglican Communion. Leading members of the Natal cabinet were amazed to discover that the bishop had not previously been consulted about the bill. Baynes was equally amazed to find Dean Green was in favour of allowing the bill to proceed in the hope that it could be amended into something useful, though he told Davidson, 'I am so accustomed to find him taking a line opposite of what one would expect that I was not wholly surprised.'[47] The danger with this course of action, the bishop said, was that one would then have to accept whatever emerged from the legislature. He concentrated his energies on persuading the curators to accept the consultative body as an appeal court. The cabinet minister among their number swung round to support the bishop, though there was one curator who remained strongly opposed to him. The cathedral chapter also came round, in spite of Green's objections. In the end the bill was withdrawn.

There can be no real doubt that Baynes was sincere in his desire for a genuine agreement. He shuttled (very slowly because the voyage took a month) between England and South Africa. He pursued English bishops to get their support. 'London has disappeared into space and neither Chaplain nor Butler knows his

---

[46] Lambeth Palace Library, Davidson Papers, vol. 522, fo. 291, Baynes to Davidson, 6 Apr. 1898; fos. 292–311 are a typescript copy of the bill itself. And see also Lambeth Palace Library, F. Temple Papers (Official Letters), vol. 19, fos. 92 ff., letters from Baynes to Frederick Temple.

[47] Lambeth Palace Library, Davidson Papers, vol. 522, fo. 312.

address—a bold stroke for a Bishop of London.'[48] He was now a married man
with a young child, but he soldiered on, sometimes at very real risk to his
health.[49] Gradually he began to make progress. The curators in Natal and two of
the Colenso parishes indicated that, if some sort of court of appeal were established, then there would be no objection to a real and complete reunion and a
total pooling of property.[50] His anxieties were increased by the time Temple took
to appoint the Lambeth consultative body and to define its powers; and he wrote
repeatedly both to the archbishop and to Davidson urging the need for haste. 'It
is really a matter of life and death with us here . . .'[51] But the need to reconcile the
irreconcilable remained. To persuade the Natalians he had to make the consultative body seem powerful: to persuade the province he obtained a statement
signed by the English archbishops and influential bishops making it seem
innocuous.

The Consultative Body appointed in pursuance of Resolution 5 of the Lambeth Conference of 1897 is intended to give information and advice to such National Churches,
Provinces and extra-Provincial Dioceses of the Anglican Communion as may apply to it.
It does not concern itself with the purpose for which either information or advice is asked,
nor with the use to which the answer that is given, is put.[52]

In October 1898 Baynes was able to tell the archbishop that the provincial synod
had agreed to his proposal.[53]

Meanwhile he had also been having considerable success with the parishes of
the Church of England in Natal. There was a growing split between the intransigent members of the Church Council and the parochial laity, and the bishop
had clearly come to believe that there was no further point in trying to find
an impossible compromise. The Council had ceased to ask Baynes to preside at
its meetings because he would not promise to preserve the whole separate
organization of the Church of England in Natal. After three meetings at which
this had happened, Baynes addressed them—as he recalled his own words—as
follows:

As you have, gentlemen, three times over deliberately repudiated your delegation [of the
choice of bishop] and rejected me as your Bishop, I will not intrude further on you. But
if your congregations whom you profess to represent are not of your opinion it will be
open to them to repudiate your action, withdraw their representatives from your body,
place all their affairs in my hands, and I shall be glad to act for them as Bishop.

Within a few weeks, he told Archbishop Temple, all the vestries had passed the
kind of resolution for which he had asked; the Church Council had ceased to

[48] Ibid., fo. 322, Baynes to Davidson, 24 Sept. 1898.
[49] Ibid.   [50] Ibid., fo. 314   [51] Ibid., fo. 315.
[52] Ibid., fos. 324–32, copies of letters from English archbishops and bishops.
[53] Ibid., F. Temple Papers (Official Letters), vol. 19, fo. 126.

meet and its views were no longer taken seriously by the curators of Church of England property; one parish had become a full part of the Church of the Province and two others had declared their acceptance of Baynes's episcopal authority.[54]

It would be foolish to claim that the schism had ended, for there is a body called the Church of England in South Africa, claiming identity with Colenso's Church of England in Natal, which still exists today. But it has no legal continuity with the Church of England as by law established, except, ironically, in so far as it *voluntarily* agrees to be bound by the laws of England as they affect the established Church. What this means in terms of the Acts of Parliament by which there now exist the General Synod and the Alternative Services Book is not at all clear.

The egregious Archdeacon Colley continued his attempts to obtain an honorary degree. He believed that Frederick Temple was particularly likely to look favourably on his case because they were both teetotallers. He wrote to the archbishop from Oxford in 1898 about the work he wished to do now that he had, he said, given up all thought of returning to Natal.

It is the work that as a life-long Abstainer comes to me with over fifty years' conviction of its importance, & my experience of its necessity from what I have seen in India, South Africa and elsewhere . . .

My son is now at Christ Church and . . . I have nothing to do (yet would very much rather work without pay than be without work) . . .

And so, he said, he would like to talk to the archbishop, who was due to visit Oxford in a few days' time, about what he might do in a voluntary way.[55] That the archbishop sent him no reply did not deter Colley in the least from pressing forward with his attempts to secure his favour. Temple addressed a meeting at the union and Colley must have intervened in the discussion which followed. He may even have proposed the setting-up of some kind of undergraduate society, for a few days later he wrote again to the archbishop saying that he had been anxious:

to strike while the iron is hot from the effect of your Grace's speech at the Union & see what can be done touching the proposed Oxford University Temperance Union. My son who is everything a father could wish—athletic yet studious & popular at Christ Church & wherever he goes—will be a great help. And if I might hope for the assistance of your Grace's son at Balliol, these, with others whom I know at different colleges would form a committee to act with me.[56]

---

[54] Ibid., fos. 121 ff.   [55] Ibid., F. Temple Papers (Official Letters), vol. 10, fos. 248–9.
[56] Lambeth Palace Library, F. Temple Papers (Official Letters), vol. 10, fos. 252–3, letter dated 3 Nov. 1898.

Inevitably the letter ends by saying that the writer 'would be most glad of the coveted mark of your Grace's favour . . . I mean the Lambeth BD'.

The plan to involve the young William Temple in the proposed society backfired, in spite of the fact that Colley thought to attract undergraduates by calling it 'the Oxford University *Esoteric* Temperance Union'.[57] At any rate, William evidently wrote to his father saying that Colley's son was attempting to put very unwelcome pressure on him to join the new committee. The archbishop replied:

I am afraid that you will have much trouble from Archdeacon Colley. He is always wanting to do things and always spoiling everything he does.

I should advise you to stand on your right as a freshman and decline to have anything to do with him on the ground that you do not know enough of Oxford to join in any such movement as he wishes to set going. I am obliged to put nil on most of his letters and let Ridge have them to keep.[58]

William must have sent his father a draft of a letter which he intended to write to the younger Colley, for the archbishop wrote again a few days later. 'I see nothing to object to in your letter to Mr Colley. What a bore he is! and his father a greater. But such people are part of the ordinary afflictions of life into which you are entering, dear lad. Be as civil to the young man as you can. He may be much better than his father.'[59]

Colley never obtained the degree which he so much wanted. He was, in fact, one of the ordinary individuals who were casualties of the process by which the crown's relationship with the Church had become an impersonal legal abstraction. Most of those who wished to maintain the constitutional links with the crown did so because they thought of the queen, personally, as one of their most treasured links with England. They wished to think of themselves as *her* people. But the law had created an impenetrable system which no one could operate. Gray lost money which might have been used on missionary work and his health was ruined. Colenso became a lonely, rejected old man. Colley, however mixed his motives may have been, wanted reunion and could not find the way to it through the tangle of vested interests that the law had created. There were no winners except the people who pocketed the legal fees.

---

[57] Ibid., fos. 254–5, Colley to Temple, 17 Nov. 1898.

[58] Family Papers in the possession of the Right Revd F. S. Temple; Frederick Temple's letters to his children; letter to William dated from the Old Palace, Canterbury, 5 Dec. 1898. Ridge was the archbishop's chaplain and 'Nil' was what Temple wrote on letters to which there was to be no reply.

[59] Ibid., letter to William dated 9 Dec. 1898.

18

The British Ambassador and the Funeral of Pope Pius IX

OWEN CHADWICK

Pope Pius IX died in February 1878. He had resisted the Italian Risorgimento to the last breath of a pontificate which had lasted longer than that of any other pope. At his death he was as unpopular in Italy as any pope since the Middle Ages. Yet he was revered by many Catholics throughout Europe and America, as no pope before him—partly because he was the first pope to command the modern media, and partly because he was regarded by many Catholics almost as a martyr. Forced to flee from Rome in 1848 and restored by French force of arms, he had lost most of the historic papal states, and all their prosperous towns, through invasion by the Piedmontese army in 1859–60. He had lost the protection of Austria, one of his two Catholic friends, when the Prussians beat the Austrian army in the war of 1866, and his last protector, the French army, withdrew in the summer of 1870 to meet the Prussian invasion of France. The last of the papal armies was ordered to surrender Rome on 20 September 1870. Pius IX never compromised: he never gave up his claim to independence and legitimate rule of a state, and never modified the demand to be restored to sovereign rights, a demand which certainly was justified by many centuries of history. As part of that refusal to compromise, he continued to denounce the Italian government as usurpers in language that no one could call temperate.

After Rome fell to the Italians, a moderate Italian government, headed by Lanza and Visconti-Venosta, felt it necessary to satisfy the less extreme Catholic opinion inside Italy, and even more necessary to satisfy international Catholic opinion outside Italy, by giving the pope and his office a unique guarantee of spiritual independence. The law of guarantees was fought through parliament in the early spring of 1871. It gave the pope absolute spiritual independence (but neither the free choice of Italian bishops nor the free maintenance of monasteries and nunneries), the honours due to a sovereign, the right to receive and send out ambassadors, the right to enlist papal guards, and a very large sum of money as endowment for his spiritual work. The bill was vehemently opposed on the ground that parliament could make no one 'sovereign', that there was now no conceivable reason for a corps of diplomats at the Vatican, that a right given to one member of the Italian state to enlist a private army must cause chaos in the state, and that two sovereigns in Italy could endanger the precarious Italian unity. Garibaldi thought the bill anathema. The Senate removed an offensive clause, which declared the pope's museums and libraries to be national property. The bill became law on 13 May 1871.

The pope and his supporters regarded it as an insult. He refused to accept the large endowment offered and so caused future problems for the curia. A bill which a parliament could pass by a majority could easily be revoked by a future majority. The guarantees had no security. The law made no difference to the pope's attitude to the Italian state. But it achieved two opposite ends. It largely satisfied much, though not all, of international Catholic opinion. For it was a sort of assurance that the pope was not in the power of the king of Italy; and it enabled Pope Pius IX to abuse the Italian government with impunity. This second part was as important in satisfying international opinion as the first. Catholics outside Italy must not feel that the pope, who now had no state, had become a private chaplain to a usurping monarch. If the pope uttered tirades against the Italians and could not be stopped, that was the clearest of all signs that he was still independent.

But this very situation made the pope, already unpopular in Italy, even more unpopular. He could not prove his independence of Italy to the world without making himself hated by some Italians.

Hence his 'prison' in the Vatican. Legally he was as free to come and go as any other citizen of the state. If he came out, the police were bound to protect him, as they were bound to protect any other citizen—and more than any other citizen, because under the new law he was to be given the protection due to a 'sovereign'. But police can do only what it is possible to do. Passers-by hurled insults at the Vatican windows. If he came out, no one knew what could happen, what pollution of his sacred office. It was a risk not to be taken. The prison was invisible but still a prison.

Pius IX expressed the wish to be buried in San Lorenzo outside the Walls, the other side of the city. The question was, how could this wish be fulfilled? After all that had happened, if he had crossed the city alive, he would have suffered insult certainly and stones probably. If this were true of a live pope, was it also true of a dead pope? Would a mob be more likely to respect the remains than the person? No one could know. Yet the wish of Pius IX for burial at San Lorenzo demanded that his body go out into the city. The question for the Vatican was how was it to be done.

The three cardinals who were executors of the dead pope consulted the chapter of St Peter's. The canons decided that the coffin should go by night, as it were by stealth. They selected the night of 12–13 July 1881. Their secretary and architect, Count Vespignani, acting both for the canons and for the three cardinals, formally asked leave of the prefect of the city to transfer the coffin that night. The coffin would be on a bier without ornament, and would be followed by two or three other carriages only and no other retinue. On this basis—passers-by would not know whose coffin it was, and a couple of carriages would hardly be observed as odd—the prefect gave leave for that unusual thing, a procession in the dark, because he thought that two carriages hardly made a procession. Naturally he ordered the police to take precautions.

But the idea, shared by both canons and prefect, that this solemn event could happen almost unnoticed was naïve. To prepare it with fitting dignity, far too many people in the curia had to know about it. To organize adequate protection, a lot of policemen must know that something unusual was happening. Several days before the event, reported the British diplomat Paget to his foreign secretary Lord Granville, it became known that the reburial would happen on the night of 12 July, and that it 'would be effected with a good deal of pomp and ceremony. This announcement was naturally calculated to excite a good deal of attention, and the execution of the project to arouse no little curiosity, if not other feelings.'[1]

Britain no longer had an envoy at the Vatican. For twelve years, during all the exciting years of the Risorgimento and the ending of the pope's temporal power, they had ('unofficially', for British law did not permit an ambassador to the pope) a true expert at the Vatican, Odo Russell. But Russell proved himself too able to be left in Rome when there was no longer a papal state and during 1870–1 he had been sent on a special mission to Bismarck in the Prussian camp outside Paris and did so well there that he was soon the first British ambassador to the new German Empire (and incidentally ambassador to some of its constituents, Saxony, Weimar, Brunswick, Anhalt, Mecklenburg-Schwerin, and Mecklenburg-Strelitz), where he used his Vatican expertise all through the *Kulturkampf* fight between Bismarck and the Catholic Church. He left behind in Rome as British agent to the Vatican a chargé, Harry Jervoise, whose reports are much duller, but then, since the pope now had no state, he had less to report; moreover, when the capital was moved from Florence to Rome, the reports from the Vatican office ceased to matter to the British government, because they now had a full ambassador in Rome. For four years after Odo Russell had left, Jervoise kept the office to the Vatican going, until questions were asked in the House of Commons what Britain was doing keeping an envoy to a country which no

---

[1] Public Record Office (hereafter PRO), FO 45/430, no. 457.

longer existed? Disraeli accepted the argument, withdrew Jervoise (8 October 1874), sent him off to be in charge of the embassy at Lisbon, and abolished the mission to the Vatican. Henceforth all business from London went to the British ambassador accredited to the kingdom of Italy.

From 1867 the British ambassador to the Italian government in Florence (an envoy rather than an ambassador for his first years) and then in Rome (where he was only made a full ambassador in 1876), was Sir Augustus Paget. He was the son of that Arthur Paget who had a melodramatic career as a British envoy in various posts during the Napoleonic Wars, and a nephew of that Paget who commanded the cavalry at Waterloo and lost the most famous of legs and became the first marquis of Anglesey. He was a professional diplomat who served in Paris when Louis Napoleon seized power. In all his posts he won the praise that, however difficult the situation, he could be relied upon not to make it worse. He had the additional advantage for those days that he had married a Prussian countess. He was, of course, a Protestant. It was his duty *ex officio* to back the government of Italy, where he could, against the claims of a 'government' inside the Vatican which his own government no longer recognized as a government. Thus it was Paget who had to represent to London what happened over the funeral of the pope.

On that night of 12 July 1881 papal devotees assembled to do honour to someone whom they regarded as one of the great popes. When the coffin set out shortly before midnight, after prayers in a St Peter's closed to the public, it was 'on a car of large dimensions covered with red—lit by a torch at each angle and drawn by four horses'. The coffin was clad with the historic red cloth which from 1190 to 1870 covered the loggia from which the pope gave his blessing *urbi et orbi* at Easter. The cortège was escorted at the front by some *carabinieri* and some city guards. Immediately behind the large car 'came a number of persons of both sexes, bearing torches and Bengal lights. After that followed numerous carriages with cardinals, dignitaries of the Church, and other persons, adherents of the Vatican'.[2] The Italian observers reckoned there were about 2,000 people, carrying torches and singing hymns; some journalists said it came to 6,000. As the cortège moved away, there were shouts up to windows that householders should illuminate their windows.

At once the trouble started. Hostile anticlericals, still fewer but enough to be more than a handful, were quick to do their work. In the Piazza Rusticucci a group of youths sang 'inappropriate songs'. The Briton Paget heard that they were only about forty. They were soon joined by the lads of the night, who saw

---

[2] Paget to Lord Granville, ibid. Description by a close observer in *Gazetta piemontese* (future *La Stampa*), 13 July 1871.

fun brewing. There began to be shouts of 'Viva l'Italia', 'Viva il re', 'Down with the pope', 'Viva Garibaldi', and hissing. Then there were other shouts of 'Papa-Re', the pope as king of Italy. At various points there were scrimmages. The police had expected nothing on this scale and their precautions were utterly inadequate. On the bridge over the Tiber the coffin came close to being pitched into the river. There were cries from the crowd, 'To the river' or 'To the sewer'. As the cortège passed the main station at Termini, prelates were spat upon and troops gathered, and the fight was so furious that the coachmen whipped up their horses and the procession went too fast to be solemn. The police did not regain full control until the cortège reached San Lorenzo. There was another scuffle outside the church, but it was of a different kind, for the clergy had locked the doors to ensure a reverent interment, and many of the faithful were left struggling to get inside. The reburial service took place reverently.

Paget reported it moderately to London.

Although the disorder which threatened was quickly suppressed, the group continued to follow the cortège, momentarily increasing in numbers, and repeating from time to time the same cries. At several places during their progress, the police had to interfere in order to protect the procession from the spectators, and some arrests were made; near the station stones were thrown at the carriages of the ecclesiastical dignitaries. In front of the church of the Santo [*sic*] Cuore, the crowd from which the cries and hisses proceeded was finally prevented, by the aid of troops, from following the procession, and many arrests were made. The progress was thenceforward undisturbed.[3]

Paget heard that the soldiers and *carabinieri* had had to draw their swords to prevent the devout scrimmage outside San Lorenzo, and to ring the church with a cordon.

Paget at first heard of 'many arrests'. He exaggerated. The police arrested a few youths. On 14 July six of these youths were brought before the court on a charge of riotously disturbing a religious ceremony. Paget reported that their appearance in court was received with cheers; that the counsel for the accused contended that, though they were accused of disturbing a religious ceremony, their acts

had nothing to do with religion but were the consequence of the strife carried on by the clerical party against the liberty and constitution of the country. In consequence of the outburst of applause following this statement, the Court was cleared for a short time. On the public being readmitted the defence of the prisoners was continued by the argument that the funeral procession was in reality a political demonstration.

The court sentenced three to a month's imprisonment and a fine of 100 lire, and two others to three months and a fine of 250 lire and the sixth to three months and a fine of 100 lire.

[3] Paget to Granville, PRO, FO 45/430, no. 457.

This result, reported Paget,

was followed by a loud manifestation in favour of the prisoners, ending in four more arrests outside the Court.

Subsequently a committeee of four or five persons waited on the Minister of the Interior,[4] to request the liberation of the prisoners. They were received by Commendatore Bolis, who replied that an enqiry should be instituted.[5]

Later the appeal court of Rome reduced the sentences. The anticlerical committee presented gold medals to the culprits. The republican paper *Lega della democrazia* regretted that the 'carcase' had not been thrown into the river. Later a clerical defender of that night was given eight months in gaol because he had carried a long knife.

Here was an incident with international danger. The new Italian foreign secretary was Mancini. He was a brash lawyer and an able parliamentarian with an anticlerical record that made the Curia regard him as an enemy. He had drafted the laws for the unification of Italy, and in the kingdom of Naples was responsible for dissolving the religious orders, seizing the property of the Church, and one-sidedly revoking the Concordat. He advocated a policy opposed to the slogan 'a free Church in a free State', for he believed it necessary for an anticlerical state to control the Church. He disliked the Curia and all it stood for, and the Curia fully reciprocated.

The Italian ambassador in London was Luigi Federico Menabrea. He was a Savoyard who preferred French as his language. After teaching physics and mathematics, he was used as a military engineer and went through the campaigns of 1848. In Cavour's parliament he started as a man of the far left but had moved steadily to the centre as an antagonist of Cavour's extremist church policy. In the fights of 1860 he did well and rose to the rank of general. In 1867 he became prime minister when his predecessor Rattazzi was found guilty of encouraging Garibaldi to a *coup* against Rome, but he resigned about the time that the Vatican Council was opened towards the end of 1869 and had never again sat in parliament. He was looked upon as one who had outgrown the extremisms of earlier days and was quiet and sensible.

All over Europe there was Catholic fury. It seemed as though the Pope was not safe in Rome and was liable to insults. The government in Vienna was under pressure to act, even with force, to protect the pope. The British did not welcome the unsettlement of the Irish (Gladstone at that moment was much engaged on his various plans to pacify the Irish); the Prussians did not welcome the further unsettlement of the Poles (who were already unsettled in the *Kulturkampf*); the

---

[4] Depretis was minister of the interior as well as prime minister.
[5] Paget to Granville, PRO, FO 45/430, 18 July 1881.

insecure French republican government did not wish strength to the royalist/ Catholic cause in France, and in Spain, where the political battle between liberals and Carlists was intense, the 'clerical' newspapers opened up a battery of attack upon the Italian government,[6] with cries that all the Catholic powers should unite to restore by force the temporal power of the pope. Cardinal Moreno,[7] the archbishop of Toledo, was so vehement that the Spanish government had to take action about his abuse of a friendly power. In Germany it was harder to know the truth because in the *Kulturkampf* diplomatic relations between Germany and the Vatican were cut and diplomatic messages from the Vatican to Berlin could only go via Vienna.

The Italian parliament, perhaps fortunately for everyone, was not sitting that day. But a series of questions came from senators—from Marquis Alfieri[8] and Count Cambray Digny,[9] for example—deploring what had happened and demanding to know what measures were taken to maintain order. Cambray Digny wanted to know why, when it was known that the ceremony was to be conducted with a certain amount of ostentation, adequate precautions were not taken. The government should have insisted that the funeral take place in broad daylight, with the full honours due (under the law of guarantees) to a king, and with a proper escort from the army.

The Prime Minister Depretis regretted the disturbances. But that was not the same as an admission of any kind of guilt or negligence. He said that the government had been told that the remains would be transferred without pomp; that only on the morning of the day were they warned that circulars had been sent round 'inviting the Catholic population to take part in the funeral procession'. They then took precautions. He had ordered an enquiry into what happened. He assured the senate that, 'if it should appear that any functionaries had been wanting in the fulfilment of their duties, they would be punished'.[10]

Paget accepted the statement of Depretis that the government was

---

[6] Cf. Graffi at Madrid to Mancini, 21 July 1881, in *I documenti diplomatici italiani* (hereafter *DDI*), ser. 2, vol. xiv, no. 108.

[7] Moreno y Maisonave, of a family which fled from Guatemala, carrying him as a child, when the country took independence. He became an eminent lawyer, but renounced his career for ordination and was a bishop within eight years. When he visited Rome, Pius IX was much impressed, and he became archbishop of Valladolid in 1863, transferring to Toledo in 1875. He steadily fought Spanish regalism.

[8] Married Cavour's niece; a strong liberal and strong Catholic, admiring British institutions and opposed to radical change. Opposed transfer of the capital from Florence to Rome on the basis that the move could affect religious freedom.

[9] Luigi Cambray Digny was of a rich Florentine family and always a moderate Tuscan liberal; an important figure for stability in the Florence disorders of April 1849. In 1859–60 he faced the fact that Tuscany could not continue independent and dedicated himself to Cavour; from 1867 he led the Tuscan right-wing and was always keen on the principles of orthodox finance and a balanced budget. Founded a monarchist association in 1882: 'Re, Patria, Libertà e Progresso'.

[10] Thus Paget to Granville, 14 July, PRO, FO 45/430, no. 298.

led astray by a declaration, received on the part of the Cardinals charged with the execution of the wishes of the defunct Pontiff, that it was intended to conduct the ceremony without any external signs and in the most private manner; but that instead, there were assembled in the Piazza of St Peter's numerous carriages, and an extraordinary number of persons with lighted torches etc etc.

To Menabrea and to others of his ambassadors Mancini played down what happened.[11] He was utterly uncompromising. He denied all liability for what had happened. He said that the government must reject the foreign efforts to interfere in the private affairs of Italy. There was no sign of any sort of apology. On the contrary, what had happened was all the fault of members of the clerical party.[12] They had planned it secretly and their intention was political. It had been a 'secret machination', desired by some of the clerical party. It was a conspiracy. What happened was illegal. Processions are never allowed in the streets. They are never allowed at night because darkness invites disorder. No one asked leave for a procession. If permission had been asked, it would certainly have been refused. The permission of the prefect was asked only for a bier followed by two or three carriages, in a private manner. The only hint of an apology was the dismissal of the chief of police.

More than one of the Italian ambassadors protested at the failure of foresight and duty on the part of the police in Rome. Launay in Berlin made himself resented by his masters in Rome because of the strength of language which he used.

The British ambassador at first accepted this theory that it was the fault of the clericals—almost:

It almost looks, indeed, as if it had been a pre-arranged plan, for making a little political capital, both in Italy and abroad, by so contriving things as to make it possible to propagate the idea, that there is no security from insults for the Pope, dead or alive, under the present order of things in Italy; and that the Guarantees Law is utterly worthless as a protection for the Vatican; and in short, that the truth of the often repeated phrase, of the Holy Father being a prisoner in His Palace, is now proved to demonstration by the facts which have occurred.

But on reflection Paget could not quite accept this version of events:

On the other hand, while every well-thinking person and the Press stigmatizes, as it deserves, the unseemly conduct of those who insulted the funeral procession, and, considering the vast concourse of people assembled, these do not appear to have been very numerous, the general opinion seems to be that the Government was lacking in foresight, and prudence.

---

[11] Letter of 13 July 1881, printed in *DDI*, ser. 2, vol. xiv, no. 102. This was actually circulated 27 July (evidently he took time for thought) and was not acquired by the press until the end of August.
[12] Mancini's circular, 27 July 1881, ibid., no. 16.

It may be quite true, as stated by M. Depretis in the Senate, and in the official circular . . . that the Government was authoritatively informed that the proceedings were to be conducted in an unostentatious manner, but if the Government were really not aware that something very different was intended, it must be acknowledged that they were extremely ill-informed, and were ignorant of what was known to almost everyone else in Rome.

It is hardly possible to credit that they were in this position, and under these circumstances their duty evidently was to follow the course suggested in the observations of Count Cambray Digny—viz. to insist with the ecclesiastical authorities upon one of the two alternatives,—either that the ceremony should be conducted in open day, with the assistance of the civil and military authorities, and with all the pomp, circumstance, and protection, which was due to the character of the Defunct, and which the Temporal Power was bound by the Guarantees Law to afford,—or else, if it was determined to effect the removal of the Body at night, that this should be done without any display or ostentation, so as not to attract the attention of the public, amongst whom on such an occasion, there were quite certain to be found a certain number of riotous and disorderly people.

I have ventured to enter thus fully into the subject, as it is one which appears not unlikely to create some sensation abroad.[13]

Paget had thus begun to realize what the consequences were likely to be in international politics.

Two days later Paget took the opportunity of talking to one of the Canons of St Peter's who had helped to arrange the funeral. On 20 July he sent a dispatch to Lord Granville reporting what the canon said:

The Pope Leo XIII gave orders, on the 1st of this month, to the Chapter of St Peter's, to make the necessary preparations, which were to be of the most modest and unassuming kind, for effecting the removal on the night of the 12th instant—

The Chapter met, and drew up a programme for the procession. It proposed that it should consist of the Funeral Car, drawn by four horses, on acount of its weight, and of carriages for the three Cardinal Heirs, and the members of the Chapter,—in all, about 10 carriages, without torches or any other Paraphernalia. This programme was submitted to Leo XIII, who considered the number of carriages too great, and as likely to attract attention, that a fewer number of followers might suffice, and gave orders to the Chapter to select four amongst themselves to follow, in one carriage, the remains to St Lorenzo, and that there should be one other carriage for the officiating Clergy.

There was a precedent for this extreme privacy, my informant observed, at the beginning of the century (1802), when the remains of Clement XIV were removed in the same manner, from St Peter to the Church of the SS. Apostoli. The arrangements were consequently made in conformity with Leo XIII's orders, and the person who gives me this information himself wrote out the programme.

But a few days before the 12th, the heads of some of the Catholic associations (Circoli Catholici) came to the Vatican, and insisted (the expression used was 's'attacarono come aquile'), first with the Cardinal Heirs [i.e. the executors], then with the Cardinal Secretary

---

[13] Paget to Granville, 14 July, PRO, FO 45/430, no. 298.

of State,[14] and ultimately with the Pope himself, upon the desire and intention of the Catholic Bodies to follow the coffin from Saint Peter's to Saint Lorenzo.

The Pope, and all connected with the Vatican, according to my informant, highly disapproved the proposed proceeding,—His Holiness foreseeing the consequences which probably would, and actually did result from it. His Holiness never sanctioned it—but was silent ('stava zitto').

The Circulars sent round to the Faithful to attend, and the bringing together of the vast concourse of people with torches and Bengal lights, was, my informant said, entirely the work of the Circoli Catholici—There must have been at least between three and four thousand persons with torches.

The effect of the Circoli was to make a political demonstration, which they knew beforehand would be a provocation of the national feeling, and would probably give rise to scenes which would enable them to proclaim that there was no security for religion, or for the Church in Rome. It was, he added, entirely the design and operation of the 'Zelanti', so well described by Padre Curci;[15] and they had only too well succeeded in their purpose.

My informant then gave me a description of what took place in the streets during the Procession, in which he was a participant, and certainly nothing could have been more scandalous and disgraceful.

All Rome, he said, appeared to have assembled in the streets, and the bearing of the general multitude was respectful and all that could be desired—taking off their hats as the Car passed etc etc.

The disturbance had been created by a certain number of individuals who, as soon as they were driven off at one place, repaired to another.

He then went on to speak of the negligence and want of foresight on the part of the Minister of the Interior—but in this he only repeated what is in everybody else's mouth, viz. that the Government should have insisted upon one of two things, either upon the Vatican consenting to the funeral being conducted with the honours due to a Sovereign, which, by the by, my informant assured me, would never have been accepted by the Vatican—or upon its being carried out in the strictest privacy—which would have been according to the Pope's desire.

The Minister of the Interior shielded himself, my informant observed, behind the communication made by Signor Vespignani, on the part of the Cardinal Heirs; but it was impossible the Minister could have been ignorant of what was publicly known throughout Rome for several days before.

The Cardinal Heirs were in good faith—but what occurred was beyond their control.

I observed to my informant that I was afraid that these events must have made a very painful impression upon His Holiness,—to which he replied that it had done so in more ways than one; for, irrespective of anything he might have felt about what took place during the procession, the success of the Catholic bodies in carrying out proceedings

---

[14] The papal secretary of state was then Ludovico Jacobini, cardinal from 1879. He had been an under-secretary at the Vatican Council, but his name was made while he was nuncio in Vienna. There he worked to diminish the force of the *Kulturkampf* in Germany, it was with this special aim that he was chosen as secretary of state, and he did not disappoint his backers.

[15] Carlo Maria Curci was a Neapolitan Jesuit who, after the Revolution of 1848, founded the famous and still flourishing Jesuit journal *La Civiltà Cattolica*. After the seizure of Rome by the Italians in 1870, he at once decided that a restoration of the temporal power was impossible. He began to publish this opinion openly at a time when the Curia regarded it as heresy. In 1874 the Jesuits turned him out.

directly contrary to His wishes must have brought home to His Holiness in very vivid colours, His own want of power and authority.

I remarked that I had seen it publicly stated that if the proceedings of the 12th had gone off peaceably, the Pope might possibly have taken an early opportunity of showing Himself on some public occasion outside the Vatican. My informant said that this was purely imaginary. That whatever Leo XIII's feelings and inclinations might be, it was the Jesuit Circle by which His Holiness was surrounded which is Master of the Situation in such a matter.

This led me to speak of Padre Curci's recent book.

Paget told his informant the canon of St Peter's that

I had been under the impression that it represented to a certain extent Leo XIII's own views. My informant replied, 'His Holiness' personal views possibly—His ideas as Pope can only be intransigenti.' He went on to say, that he feared Leo XIII's health would not much longer support the confinement of His present residence. That He had always been accustomed to change of air and sea bathing in the summer, and that the want of these was telling upon his constitution.

He informed me that there was a sad falling off in the amount of Peter's Pence, and that it barely sufficed now to defray the ordinary expenses of the Papacy. This he attributed in some degree to the non-combative policy of the present Pope, and he thought there might possibly be again an increase under a new Pope bent on a policy of action.

I think it my duty to add that it is fortunate for M. Depretis that Parliament is not now sitting, or he would certainly be called to a severe account for his recent shortcomings, for everyone feels the harm which has been done to the fair name of the country by allowing such scandals to occur within the capital, and that the finest opportunity has been lost for showing to the world the discomfiture of the enemies of the Italian kingdom both at home and abroad, that the Papal Guarantees Law is held sacred by the Italian Government and that the Papacy and Religion are surrounded by every security within the walls of Rome.

It seems probable however that the matter will not be allowed to drop,—for already a notice of interrogation upon the question has been addressed to the President of the Chamber, to be brought forward upon the reopening of Parliament in November.[16]

The pope's secretary of state Cardinal Jacobini issued a circular to all the nuncios. It stated that Leo XIII regarded the insults as insults to his own person, and that what had happened was a shameful outrage on religion and civilization, and proved without possibility of contradiction that the pope was a prisoner. As there was no nuncio in London, the British Foreign Office had to read this in the newspapers.

Towards the end of July there were meetings organized in the streets of Rome to demand the repeal of the Law of Guarantees and the occupation of the pope's palace by Italian troops. This was reflected in the next dispatch to Granville,

[16] Paget to Granville, 20 July, PRO, FO 45/430, no. 307.

dated 4 August.[17] But the dispatch was not written by Sir Augustus Paget, who fell ill at the end of July and was unable to cope with business. It was, therefore, written by his assistant Hugh Macdonell. Born in Florence, and with one of his sisters lady-in-waiting to Louis Napoleon's empress Eugenie, already a man of wide diplomatic experience and effectiveness, Macdonell was in Rome as secretary of the embassy for the four years 1878–82, later becoming the ambassador in Brazil and Denmark and Portugal. The Italian Foreign Office did not easily get his name; they tried Mac Donell or Mac-Donell. The different hand is very evident in the tone of the dispatch:

Under the title of 'The Law of Guarantees', the Italian papers have lately published a 'communiqué' from the Minister of the Interior stating that the Government have decided to stop all manifestations against the Holy See for the abolition of the said law. 'Those however', adds the notice, 'who seek its abolition are at liberty to petition Parliament, and with that object may form Societies and Clubs and hold meetings to further their purpose'.

The same papers now announce that 'anti-clerical' clubs have been regularly organised in different parts of Rome and throughout the Kingdom and that a general meeting will take place on Sunday next to determine the course to be pursued.

Thus the Government in order to extricate itself from an embarrassing position, created by their own want of judgment and moral courage, now show their weakness in treating with that restless faction which loves the Constitutional Monarchy perhaps less than the Priesthood.

The fact of the Government countenancing, if not directing the anti-clerical movement, is looked upon by Italians, who are not fanatics, as a tacit acknowledgment of complicity with the wrong doers. The stone thus set going cannot be stopped at the will of those who gave it the impulse—and the natural consequence is that scenes are daily witnessed in the streets, of insults to Priests,—the images of the Saints or of the Virgin, which figure at every street corner, are bespattered with mud or otherwise ill-used—and such like.

So far from 'the Italians beginning to tire and be ashamed of the events of the 13th', as the English papers seem to suppose, it is to be feared that the promoters of those disorders may seek encouragement in the anti-clerical attitude assumed by the Government—and that those events, far from 'frightening both sides into a composition' may yet add to the deadly controversy between the Vatican and the Quirinal.

Under these circumstances and in presence of the movement now set on foot, the Cardinal Secretary of State may well ask what would happen if on account of his ill-health the Pope were obliged to leave the Vatican. Such an event *was not impossible,*—for His Holiness, I am confidentially informed, is at this moment seriously indisposed—He has lately suffered from an attack of fever which has left him in a low and depressed condition:—weakened by sickness he fears that his health and strength are failing him. His Holiness suffers morally now, perhaps more than physically.

Those who can judge of his condition think that under the impression that his end is not far distant he deplores the state in which he may leave the Church. He sees that

---

[17] PRO, FO. 45/430, no. 321.

though animated by the best of intentions, the Policy of the Vatican, since his election, has led to little else but disappointment and failure—due as much to his friends as to his foes.

Last, though not least, the indignities offered to the remains of his predecessor, and the utter hopelessness of finding a *modus vivendi* between the Church and the State, have deeply grieved him. Beset by pecuniary embarrassments, he now also sees the discontinuance of 'Peter's Pence'. In short, disappointment and discouragement are daily working upon an already shattered constitution.

Given the truth of these reports it would have been perhaps more polite if the Italian Government admitted that it had suffered a surprize and acted with that energy which the interests of the Monarchy and the Church require.

Macdonell was evidently more of a pessimist than Paget. The predictions of diplomats are often as wrong as the predictions of anyone else who tries to say what history will do next. Here was a portrait of a pope likely to die any moment. Leo XIII lived for another twenty-two years.

Three days later began a series of fierce and sometimes riotous anticlerical meetings in the big cities of Italy. On 7 August, a Sunday, some 4,000 met at the Politeana theatre in Rome under the chairmanship of Signor Petroni,[18] who had long been in a prison of the pope and won fame because he refused to come out unless other papal prisoners were released. The object of the meeting was to denounce the law of guarantees and repeal it. A telegram of support was read from General Garibaldi: 'I support the abolition of guarantees and of the office guaranteed.' Oddly, this telegram was received by the audience with coolness. The veteran French socialist and revolutionary Louis Blanc, who was not far from his own death, provided a telegram of support from the novelist Victor Hugo and promised the support of 'French democracy'. Alberto Mario, who had fought at Garibaldi's side and was the husband of the revolutionary English girl Jessie White, won vast applause: 'to suppress the Papacy would be a humanitarian act . . . It is an institution of the past which it is the mission of Italy to abolish.' Before he could put the formal motion, a police inspector stopped the meeeting.

On Sunday, 14 August, there was another such meeting in Genoa, where Garibaldi's son-in-law (Stefano Canzio, who fought in Sicily with Garibaldi and married his young daughter Teresita) read a letter and was stopped when he spoke disrespectfully of king and pope. It was the eve of the feast of the Assumption and that night Rome was ringed with troops in expectation of tumults which did not happen.

Macdonell did not report to Granville on what was happening until 17 August. Then, surprisingly late, the dispatch took up the rumour that the pope

---

[18] See R. Ugolini and Vincenzo Pirro (eds.), *Giuseppe Petroni dallo stato pontificio all Italia unita* (Naples, 1990).

might decide to flee from Rome; a rumour which really mattered to the British government, because Britain (more probably a British possession like Malta) was mentioned by rumour as a destination. Fulda?—there was a *Kulturkampf* in Germany. Avignon?—there was militant anticlericalism in France. The Balearic Islands?—there was a fierce clerical-versus-liberal fight in Spain. Austria?— perhaps, but risky in the then state of opinion. Malta was an island with a Catholic population under a government which did not wish to alienate its subjects and was near enough to Italy to be close to events. It might attract a refugee Pope:

I regret to inform Your Lordship that, whether with or without the connivance of the authorities, the quarrel between Papists and anti-Papists is daily assuming more important dimensions, and, if allowed to continue, may lead to consequences far more serious than the Italian Government appear to have the necessary sense to foresee.

The deplorable scenes enacted in Rome on 7th have since been repeated at Siena and at Genoa. At the latter place the meeting was only dispersed by the Police when the President read a letter from Sigr Canzio (General Garibaldi's son-in-law) in which he openly declared that he would not assist at the meeting, as he had determined to withdraw from public life until the more serious and more important of guarantees—viz. the Monarchy—was abolished; and it is only after a delay of four days that the Government, pressed by the outcry of the more serious portion of the community, has decided on sending a functionary to Genoa to inquire into the 'incidents' which marked that gathering.

On the other hand the papers continue to announce and publish the programmes of other meetings to be held this week at Milan, Leghorn, Pisa, Girgenti and other places.

Not satisfied with these noisy demonstrations, the agitators seize every opportunity not only to disturb the Peace and show their hatred of the Vatican either by vociferating before every house and palace, or otherwise insulting those clericals who, perhaps imprudently, follow the custom of illuminating their dwellings on the festival of the Assumption and similar occasions, to display their devotion to the Holy See;—ending with an attempt to continue their manifestations before the Palace of the Vatican, when a squad of Bersaglieri put a timely end to the contemptible scene.

This state of things, I take the liberty to observe, is created by a limited number of individuals who call themselves Royalists, but are in reality Republicans, and who, with a following of vagabonds and ruffians, appear to have sufficient power to intimidate the Government and oblige them—if not to countenance the idea of the abolition of the Law of Guarantees—to revive a discord fraught with danger and discredit to both Parties.

The information which I have been able to gather from a conversation which I have had with Mgr Masotti, the Secretary of Propaganda, as to the state of feeling at the Vatican may be summed up as follows:

As Your Lordship is aware [nothing in the dispatches from Rome, so far, had made the Foreign Secretary aware of this, and Macdonell assumed as true what was not likely] His Holiness was opposed to the removal of the remains of Pius IX, and in vain endeavoured to persuade the Cardinals charged with the execution of the will of the late Pontiff to postpone the ceremony, thinking that his policy might perhaps eventually lead,—if not to friendly relations,—to a tacit understanding which might offer a safer opportunity for trying the experiment of an external ceremony conducted by the Vatican.

The Ultramontane Party, headed by the Cardinals in question, were however determined to carry out this programme; with the result which had already been brought to Your Lordship's notice.

The circumstances, brought about by the unpardonable want of foresight and subsequent attitude of the Government on the one side, and the intolerance of the Ultramontanes on the other, left no course open to His Holiness—due consideration being had for his moral and physical condition—than to espouse the cause of his adherents, and to do so thoroughly, in order to leave no doubt in the minds of his adversaries as to the full bitterness of the strife which they had thus voluntarily revived.

Considering the unfriendly disposition of the Government and the dangers to which the Vatican and the Pope might be exposed at the hands of an uncontrolled mob, the idea was then suggested that it would be well to prepare for such an eventuality.

The Pope, I am assured, never entertained the idea of his proposed departure from Rome; but his Ultramontane advisers gladly availed themselves of the fact that it had been discussed by his advisers to menace the Italian Government and thus give colour to a plan which had never been formed.

The Italian Government on their side, realizing the difficulties to which their senseless Policy might eventually expose them, seized the opportunity to allow publicity to be given to a rumour which they thought would do more towards crushing the anti-clerical movement than the arrest of the rioters, and thus help them to get out of an embarrassing position.

At the present moment however it is evident that neither Italy nor the Pope can see the advantage to be derived by Rome ceasing to be the centre of the Roman Catholic faith;— it is more than probable therefore that the present situation will gradually subside, but it is to be regretted that a question in which so many interests are involved should remain as unsolvable a dilemma as it was at its origin.

I must however add that in answer to my enquiries M. Masotti said that in the present alarm reigning at the Vatican it would be difficult to say what might occur if any overt act of violence were attempted or further insults offered to the Holy See. The question of the Pope's departure having now been stirred it will be looked upon as a possibility in case of dire necessity and His Holiness would then probably withdraw to Austria.[19]

The moderate Italian press, even when anticlerical, was totally opposed to these demonstrations. Anyone with a clear head could see that the alternative to the law of guarantees was not no guarantees but an international guarantee of the pope's independence, which would limit Italy's freedom of action and be resented by all the left wing and some of the extreme right.

A week after this, on 24 August, Mancini sent to Menabrea in London and to other envoys a statement of the position of the Italian government.[20] It was at last strong. In summary it said this: the relations between Italy and the pope are fixed by the law of guarantees. We cannot allow any foreign government to interfere in that relationship. We have been obliged to recognize the right to assemble for meetings and to petition. We cannot and ought not to stop people getting together to discuss whether laws ought to be changed, except when the meeting

---

[19] PRO, FO 45/430, no. 333.　　　[20] *DDI*, 2nd ser., vol. xiv, no. 168.

threatens to overturn public order and violate international obligations. Since the meeting in Rome on 7 August did not fulfil this condition, we quelled it, but that did not stop similar meetings in other cities and such meetings have done damage. The adversaries of the pope help those who regret the end of the pope's temporal power. The law of guarantees, protecting the pope, is essentially a liberal law and assures the pope of full spiritual independence. Government will do everything to protect the pope; to see that the law of guarantees is observed; to repress offences against him as it seeks to repress people who seek to divide Italy once again. This was strong language and a sufficient assurance to the powers.

Macdonell's prediction that the trouble would subside for the reasons given was slowly fulfilled, and as the funeral night receded into the past other crises—like Tunis and Egypt and Assab—started to be the main matters for the British envoys in Rome. The whole affair had a subtle effect in the extraordinary volte-face of the Italian government as it began to contemplate what was to be known as the Triple Alliance. Traditionally its ally was France, which had made Italian unity. The old enemy was Austria, against whose power Italian unity was forced through. From 1796 to 1881 France was the friend of Italian Liberals and Austria the foe. France's move towards a protectorate in Tunis, which the Italians thought their sphere of interest, was the chief cause of the swing in foreign policy. But the troubles after the previous pope's funeral had unwittingly shown that the Italian monarchy was at risk from the republicans, and the monarchy was believed to be essential to the fragile unity of Italy. In France a republican party, fiercely against kings, was dominant. It was not only Tunis but the predicament of the Italian government in face of the pope which pushed Italy towards that *bouleversement* of policy which made them the allies of Austria and Germany until 1914–15.

The international emotions had no effect on British policy until there were worries about the consequences of the Triple Alliance. Britain had backed Italian unity since the 1840s and was a natural though mostly quiescent ally. It could not often be an active ally, because in those years activity could only be antipapal; and, however Protestant its ministers, they had a priority which must make them hold aloof from campaigns against the pope: their concern over the lowering discontent and violence in Ireland. They did not like either of the popes—though they preferred Pope Leo XIII to Pope Pius IX—but they knew they might need papal authority in pressing peaceable courses on Irish nationalists who identified their nationalism with their Catholicism.

19

Eastern Horizons: Anglicans and the Oriental Orthodox Churches

Geoffrey Rowell

The English Reformation was essentially an event within the history of Western Christianity. The theological and political debates in England as on the continent of Europe were debates conditioned by the history of Latin Christendom, the development of the papacy, the struggle between pope and emperor, and the failure of a quest for reform in the Conciliar Movement. Eastern Christianity was far away and for the most part under the Muslim domination of the Ottoman Empire. Yet the appeal of developing Anglican apologetic to the undivided Church of the early centuries and to the writings of the Fathers as interpreters of scripture, ensured that Greek patristic theology became one of the well-springs of the theology of the Caroline divines, and found remarkable expression in the sermons and devotions of Lancelot Andrewes.[1]

A Church which appealed as part of its apologetic to the undivided Church of East and West against Western medieval practices and scholastic elaborations of doctrine would in principle find the non-papal yet episcopal ecclesiological stance of the Eastern Churches attractive, even if aspects of Orthodox worship, in particular the veneration of ikons, might be the source of reservations. In the nineteenth century it was to be a Tractarian claim that the existence of the Orthodox Churches provided an important plank against the arguments of Ultramontane papalism. Pusey once said that the Roman arguments would be overwhelming had not the Orthodox run out like a jetty to break up the incoming Roman tide. Anglicans of all colours could, therefore, value Orthodoxy as part of Anglican anti-Roman polemic. A bishop like Lancelot Andrewes was not alone in praying for the Eastern Churches as part of Christ's holy, catholic Church. The Nonjurors, anxious to affirm their primitive Christian identity, and looking for a larger body with which to link, turned towards the Orthodox as a way of affirming the legitimacy of their own self-understanding. Part of the later

---

[1] See Nicholas Lossky, *Lancelot Andrewes the Preacher (1555–1626): The Origins of the Mystical Theology of the Church of England* (Oxford, 1991).

motivation of John Mason Neale and other Tractarians and post-Tractarians, was to secure a clear acceptance by an ancient, patristically grounded, episcopal church, of their understanding of the Catholic character and continuity of the Church of England. One of the main concerns of the Tractarian and post-Tractarian opposition to the Anglo-Prussian Jerusalem bishopric scheme of the early 1840s that so exercised Newman was that it seemed to undermine the Tractarian 'branch theory' of the Church, which recognized the Orthodox patriarch of Jerusalem as the true bishop of that city. Anglicans had no business being there, and certainly not yoked together with Protestant Lutherans. It has in fact been one of the recurrent features of Anglican–Orthodox ecumenical endeavour (though perhaps it is in truth a feature of all ecumenical endeavour) that the pioneers and enthusiasts from the Anglican side were almost universally from the High Church tradition. When Orthodox bishops and theologians discovered that Anglican Evangelicals or Broad Church liberals existed, they had to reassess their understanding of Anglicanism, which had been vividly coloured by the enthusiasms of such men as Neale, H. P. Liddon, and W. J. Birkbeck.

Communications were another major barrier, both physical communications and the barriers of language. Anglicans could be sympathetic to the existence of the Eastern Churches in theory, and draw on the Greek Fathers theologically, but, until the nineteenth century, the difficulties of travel meant that contact with the Orthodox was limited to a handful of travellers to Russia, a few Greek and Russian visitors to England, and merchants and others who travelled in the sometimes difficult circumstances of the Ottoman Empire. Orthodox Christians, living under Muslim domination, attracted a natural sympathy from fellow Christians, and the nineteenth-century campaigns against the Bulgarian and Armenian massacres are coloured by a European Christian history reaching back to the Crusades. When travel became more possible in the nineteenth century, with the peace following the Revolutionary and Napoleonic wars, and the building of railways, coupled with Britain's economic and imperial expansion, Anglican contact with the Orthodox world inevitably increased. Just as communications made it possible for a cult of Pio Nono to grow in a way that contributed to the 1870 definition of papal infallibility, so travellers could penetrate remote regions of Turkey and find embattled and primitive Christian communities there. As evangelicals looked to the establishment of the Jerusalem bishopric as part of a millenarian programme concerned with the return of the Jews to the Holy Land, so the European and American encounter with the 'Nestorian' communities in the Kurdish mountains could lead to claims that the Lost Tribes of Israel had been discovered. There was undoubtedly a streak of romanticism in some of these claims in the journeys of George Percy Badger and

Athelstan Riley to the mountains of Kurdistan, and the archaeologist Austen Henry Layard struck a vein with his Victorian readership when he not only included in his account of his excavations at Nineveh the unearthing of the mighty Assyrian empire, with all its biblical resonances, but also described his visits to the strange, heterodox Islamic sect of the Yezidis, or 'devil-worshippers', and the various communities of Syrian Christians.

Anglicans who went to work among these communities could not look to them for theological legitimation in the same way that they did to the Chalcedonian Churches of Greece and Rome, for these Churches were the lineal descendants of those condemned as heretical by the early councils of Ephesus (431) and Chalcedon (451). But such apparently oppressed minorities welcoming English Christians who came offering the prospect of political protection also offered those same English Christians a welcome and a recognition from an ancient Church. Alongside the desire of English Christians to assist such Christian communities with printing of liturgical and theological texts, education, and renewal of their life went a concern to demonstrate the Christological orthodoxy of such Churches. This concern is an early example of the now commonly accepted ecumenical principle of endeavouring to reach behind the rigidities of opposed doctrinal formulae to a common understanding of faith. Such were some of the issues reflected in some of the salient encounters between Anglicans and Orthodox, and particularly the Oriental Orthodox, described and discussed in this chapter.

The patriarch Cyril Loukaris (1572–1638), who was much influenced by Calvinist theology, sent a protégé, Metrophanes Critopulus, to Oxford, corresponded with Archbishop Abbot, and presented the Codex Alexandrinus to Charles I. Towards the end of the seventeenth century there were proposals for the establishment of a Greek college in Oxford and the exiled metropolitan of Samos, Joseph Georgirenes, founded a Greek Church in Soho in 1677. The metropolitan Neophytus of Philippopolis visited England in 1701 and was awarded an honorary DD by Oxford, and honorary MAs were bestowed on his entourage: ''twas a mighty show, and the solemnity was very decent.' 'His Grace made us a very excellent speech, all in plain proper hellenistick Greek, commending the English nation for hospitality' and the Church of England 'in very round periods'.[2] John Covel (1638–1722), who had been Embassy chaplain

---

[2] Letter of E. Thwaite to Dr Charlett, in G. Williams, *The Orthodox Church of the East in the Eighteenth Century, Being the Correspondence between the Eastern Patriarchs and the Nonjuring Bishops with an Introduction on Various Projects of Reunion between the Eastern Church and the Anglican Communion* (London, 1868), p. xxii. The metropolitan was in fact Romanian (Letter of Archbishop Tenison to Dr Covel, 6 Sept. 1701, p. lix).

at Constantinople, became master of Christ's College, Cambridge, and vice-chancellor of the University, published a major work on the Greek Church just before his death, *Some Account of the Present Greek Church, with Reflections on their Present Doctrine and Discipline, particularly on the Eucharist and the Rest of their Seven Pretended Sacraments,* the first major Anglican work on the Greek Church. In 1716 a group of Nonjuring bishops entered into correspondence with the Orthodox patriarchs in search of a concordat of unity. The Church of Jerusalem was to be accorded primacy as the mother Church of Christendom, the churches of Antioch, Alexandria, and Constantinople had all their 'ancient canonical rights, privileges, and pre-eminences' recognized, and the patriarch of Constantinople was to be accorded an equality of honour with the bishop of Rome. The concordat proposed 'that the Catholick remnant of the British Churches . . . be reciprocally acknowledg'd as part of the Catholick Church in communion with the Apostles, with the holy Fathers of those Councils, and with their Successors'. The Nonjurors were to strive to revive 'the ancient godly discipline of the Church . . . and as near a conformity in Worship'. Homilies of St John Chrysostom and other Fathers were to be translated and read publicly.[3] The *Filioque* was to be interpreted in Cappadocian terms 'that the Father is properly the fountain and original whence the Holy Ghost proceedeth'. There were reservations about giving honour to Mary in any way which seemed to give the glory of God to a creature; about the invocation of saints; and about eucharistic devotion which seemed to imply the worship of 'the sacred Symbols of His presence'.[4]

In 1725, following further exchanges between the Orthodox patriarchs and the Nonjurors, Archbishop Wake wrote to the patriarch of Jerusalem making it clear that the correspondence the Orthodox had received did not come officially from the Church of England, but from 'certain schismatic Priests' who had written 'under the fictitious titles of Archbishops and Bishops of the Anglican Church, and have sought your Communion with them'. They had 'enticed many of the people to their party' and had 'established congregations apart from the Church', at length reaching 'such a pitch of madness as, on the demise of the first promoters of the schism, to consecrate to themselves new Bishops to succeed them'. Having given this warning to the patriarch, Wake went on to declare that 'we, the true Bishops and Clergy of the Church of England . . . profess the same Faith with you', and therefore, 'at least in spirit and effect' would not cease 'to hold communion' with the patriarch and pray for his peace and happiness. Wake concluded by earnestly entreating the patriarch to remember him in his 'prayer and sacrifices at the Holy Altar of God'.[5]

---

[3] Williams, *The Orthodox Church,* 5, 6.   [4] Ibid. 9–10.   [5] Ibid., pp. lvii–lviii.

For more than a century after these exchanges there was little official contact between Anglicans and Orthodox. Only in 1841, with the establishment of the joint Anglo-Prussian bishopric in Jerusalem, did Anglicans begin to become aware of and build bridges towards the Orthodox world. George Williams, later a fellow of King's College, Cambridge, and editor of the Nonjurors' correspondence with the Orthodox, was appointed by Archbishop Howley as chaplain to Michael Solomon Alexander, the first bishop. Howley instructed Williams 'to pay special regard to the Oriental Churches' and spoke to him of the Christians of the East 'with feelings of the most tender and compassionate sympathy and affection; claiming for them the utmost consideration and loving forbearance, on account of their long subjection to a degrading bondage'. The archbishop, moved almost to tears, cited a couplet of Homer about the soul-destroying effect of the experience of servitude.[6]

The 1840s saw the beginning of a major scholarly work by an Anglican on the Orthodox Church, John Mason Neale's *History of the Holy Eastern Church*, of which the first volume was on the *Patriarchate of Alexandria* (1847). The *General Introduction*, published three years later, celebrated the faithfulness of Eastern saints and martyrs in the glory of Byzantium and in the oppression of the Ottoman Empire. Neale conjured up a vision of a Church which extended

from the Sea of Okhotsk to the palaces of Venice, from the ice-fields that grind against the Solevetsky monastery to the burning jungles of Malabar, embracing a thousand languages, and nations, and tongues, but binding them together in the golden link of the same Faith, offering the Tremendous Sacrifice in a hundred Liturgies, but offering it to the same GOD, and with the same rites.[7]

Although Neale himself had only one first-hand experience of the East in his 1860 visit to Dalmatia, his translations of Orthodox hymnody were one of his most significant contributions to Anglican awareness of Eastern theology and devotion.[8]

For all Neale's scholarship there was a coloration in his work of the Orientalism which was a characterstic of much Western European culture in the nineteenth century. Neale was, after all, the author of three 'Oriental' novels.[9] Travellers like Alexander Kinglake (*Eothen, or Traces of Travel Brought Home from the East* (1844)), and W. M. Thackeray (*Notes of a Journey from Cornhill to*

---

[6] Ibid., p. xliii.

[7] J. M. Neale, *A History of the Holy Eastern Church: General Introduction* (1850), 1–2, 9; Leon Litvack, *J. M. Neale and the Quest for Sobornost* (Oxford, 1994), 77.

[8] See ibid., pt. II, 'Hymnologist of the Eastern Church', 89–176. On Neale more generally as a hymn writer, see M. Chandler: *The Life and Work of John Mason Neale, 1818–1866* (Leominster, 1995), 171–201.

[9] *Theodora Phranza* (London, 1853); *The Lily of Tiflis* (London, 1859); and *The Lazar-House of Leros* (London, 1859).

Grand Cairo (1844)), played on the differences between the familiar (and superior) West and the 'exotic' East. Litvack notes how Thackeray resorts to words such as 'strange', 'outlandish', 'incomprehensible', and 'unfamiliar' in his description of Orthodox worship in the Church of the Holy Sepulchre, while Kinglake in his account of Greek worship in Smyrna has more than a *frisson* of Protestant prejudice at what he clearly regards as ritual mummery. When you see a Greek, he wrote, 'with a shaven skull and savage tail depending from his crown, kissing a thing of wood and glass, and cringing with base prostrations and apparent terror before a miserable picture, you see superstition in a shape which, outwardly at least, is sadly abject and repulsive'.[10]

If the world of Byzantine Orthodoxy was strange and distant to Anglicans, it was even more the case with the Christian communities that are today usually known as the Oriental Orthodox Churches, or the non-Chalcedonian Churches—the Copts, the Syrian Orthodox, the Armenians, the Ethiopians, and the Syro-Malabar Church of south-west India. Not only were they remoter and smaller than the Orthodox Churches of Greece, Russia, and the Balkans; they were also labelled as heretical by the decisions of the Council of Chalcedon in 451 concerning the two natures of Christ, or, in the case of the 'Nestorians' or Assyrians, or the Church of the East, by the Christological decisions of the Council of Ephesus in 431.

In the mountainous east of Turkey, where a weak Ottoman Empire abutted on an even weaker Persian Empire, and where Russian imperial designs looked south towards the Persian Gulf, Christian minorities survived, minorities which were all too ready to look to Western Christian powers for protection from their Muslim rulers. The Armenians were numerous in the high plateau lands around Lake Van and the headwaters of the Tigris and Euphrates, spreading north-east towards the Caucasus and their holy city of Etchmiadzin. In the ancient monastic hill country of the Tur 'Abdin, there were centres of Syrian Orthodox Christianity. Further east in the Kurdish mountains and stretching down towards Lake Urmia were the Nestorians or Assyrians. From the early decades of the nineteenth century these ancient Christian communities became the focus of the rival attentions of Catholic and Protestant missionaries, adventurer explorers and political agents. There was an intertwining of religious and political motivation.

In the mid-1830s American Protestant missionaries arrived in Urmia. Asahel Grant, a medical doctor, thought the Nestorian communities to be the Lost Tribes of Israel and published an account of his travels and researches so describing them.[11] A fellow American missionary, the Revd Justin Perkins, set up a

---

[10] *Eothen*, quoted in Litvack, *Neale*, 69; on Orientalism, see Litvack, *Neale*, 63–74.
[11] Asahel Grant, *The Nestorians; or the Lost Tribes* (London, 1841).

printing press and began the task of translating the Bible into modern Syriac, the New Testament being completed in a parallel ancient and modern Syriac version in 1846. Bunyan's *Pilgrim's Progress* and Baxter's *Saints' Everlasting Rest* were also translated.[12] Anglicans first became involved with these ancient Christian communities through a Chaldean Christian, Isa (Christian) Rassam, who had acted as Arabic interpreter for William Ainsworth, a member of the Euphrates expedition of 1835–7 who had journeyed through Kurdistan following the end of the Euphrates survey. Returning with Ainsworth to England, Rassam, armed with an introduction from Colonel Chesney, the leader of the Euphrates expedition, made his way to Oxford, where he made the acquaintance of William Palmer of Magdalen College, staying with him for two weeks. Rassam, whose previous acquaintance with the Church of England had been through CMS clergy (Rassam had in fact married an English woman, Matilda Badger, sister of George Percy Badger, a CMS employee), found Palmer's enthusiastic Tractarianism attractive. The picture of a non-papal catholicism painted by Palmer was enthusiastically endorsed by Rassam, who encouraged Palmer to think that the Chaldeans (the Uniate branch of the Church of the East) would be willing to renounce their allegiance to the pope and enter into communion with the Church of England. The Chaldean patriarch should be sent to Oxford; the University Press should print the Chaldean service books; and young Chaldeans should be sent to Oxford to be educated in order to be ordained as bishops in their Church. Rassam discussed his proposals with President Routh of Magdalen, who seems to have been less sanguine than Rassam that the Chaldean bishops would so readily abandon their allegiance to Rome.[13]

As a result of these conversations, and further contacts with the archbishop of Canterbury, William Howley, the Royal Geographical Society, and the SPCK, a new expedition was proposed with the particular object, in addition to geographical exploration, of investigating the condition of the Nestorian Christians in the Hakkari mountains, searching for manuscripts, and opening 'a communication between the Church of England and the Nestorian Christians'. The SPCK, having made a substantial grant, made clear to Rassam the society's attitude to the Eastern Christian communities:

The Society does not seek to interfere in any way with the affairs of the Chaldean Christians, or of any of the branches of the Church of Christ existing in the countries of the East: but is very anxious to afford them such assistance as it may be able to do, consistently with its own principles, in order that they themselves may be able to improve their own condition, and become one more flourishing branches of the Heavenly Vine.[14]

---

[12] J. Richter, *A History of Protestant Missions in the Near East* (Edinburgh, 1910), 295, 297.

[13] J. F. Coakley, *The Church of the East and the Church of England: A History of the Archbishop of Canterbury's Assyrian Mission* (Oxford, 1992), 20–3.

[14] Ibid. 24, 27.

Following the visit of Rassam and Ainsworth, a new and more official mission was dispatched in the person of the Revd George Percy Badger, in 1842. Badger had moved from the CMS and Methodism to being ordained in the Church of England and to sympathizing with Tractarianism. He visited William Palmer of Magdalen at Oxford, the American missionary, Perkins, commenting tartly that 'in England he fell under the influence of Puseyism, and at Oxford embraced it with all the ardour of his impulsive temperament'.[15] Badger went with the commission of both the SPCK and SPG. He was to have a particular concern for the work of Christian education, and for the establishment of schools; to investigate the needs of the Syrian Christian communities for the scriptures, 'and to distribute copies of the Bible and of the Arabic version of the English Liturgy wherever they may be useful'; to procure manuscripts of the scriptures and Chaldean liturgies; and to explain to the Churches 'the doctrine and discipline of the Church of England, and to assure them that she claims no jurisdiction or authority over them, or over any of the Churches of the East'.[16] Badger carried letters from Archbishop Howley addressed generally to 'the Patriarchs and Prelates of the Holy Eastern Church' expressing respect and affection, and the archbishop's 'zeal and fervent desire for the welfare and peace' of the Eastern Churches. Badger, he wrote, 'will tell you all things that you may wish to know concerning our apostolical Church, and its feeling of love and kindness towards the ancient and apostolical churches of CHRIST in the East'.[17] A further letter was sent by Bishop Blomfield of London to the patriarch of the Church of the East, Mar Shimoon, addressed as 'Patriarch of the Church in Coordistan'. Blomfield wrote that Badger would inform the patriarch of the present state of the Church of England, and its desire to act in a spirit of 'Christian friendship and goodwill'. 'We have directed him to report to us concerning your welfare, and the present condition of the ancient Church in Coordistan.'[18]

Although Badger journeyed to the Hakkari mountains and spent time with the patriarch, Mar Shimoon, no permanent Anglican mission was established at this time. Outbreaks of fighting caused severe difficulties, and the SPCK and SPG were not willing to provide the funds to support the missionary enterprise Badger hoped to set up. Badger himself also transformed the idea of the mission to one which encouraged defections from the Uniates and also to a mission in opposition to the activity of the American Protestant missionaries.[19] English denominational perceptions were projected on to the Eastern Christian communities, not only by Badger, but also by Austen Henry Layard, the excavator of the

---

[15] Ibid. 36.
[16] G. P. Badger, *The Nestorians and their Rituals with the Narrative of a Mission to Mesopotamia and Coordistan in 1842–1844* (London, 1852), i, p. xv.
[17] Ibid. p. xvi.   [18] Ibid. p. xvii.   [19] Ibid. 43.

ruins of Nineveh and other Assyrian sites. In his work *Nineveh and its Remains*, published in 1849, Layard contrasted the 'Protestant' simplicity of the Nestorian Churches with the proselytized Chaldeans. He visited a Chaldean church at Bebozi.

In the church I saw a few miserable prints, dressed up in all the horrors of red, yellow, and blue, miracles of saints and of the blessed Virgin, and a hideous infant in swaddling clothes, under which was written 'L'Iddio, bambino.' They had recently been stuck up against the bare walls. 'Can you understand these pictures,' I asked. 'No,' was the reply, 'we did not place them here; when our priest (a Nestorian) died a short time ago, Mutran Yusuf, the Catholic bishop came to us. He put up these pictures and told us that we were to adore them.'[20]

By contrast, in the Nestorian church at Birjai, Layard noted that 'the ceremonies were short and simple'. 'Two priests officiated in white surplices . . . a portion of Scripture was read, and then interpreted', the prayers were chanted, with the congregation participating. 'There were no idle forms or salutations; the people used the sign of the cross when entering, and bowed when the name of Christ occurred in the prayers. The Sacrament was administered to all present,' and 'when the service was ended, the congregation embraced one another as a symbol of brotherly love and concord'. 'I could not but contrast these simple and primitive rites', Layard observed, 'with the senseless mummery, and degrading forms, adopted by the converted Chaldaeans of the plains—the unadorned and imageless walls, with the hideous pictures, and monstrous deformities which encumber the churches of Mosul.'[21] 'Our sympathies', Layard wrote, 'cannot but be excited in favour of a long-persecuted people, who have merited the title "the Protestants of Asia".'[22]

Three years later Badger published his account of his encounters with the Nestorians, including comments also on 'the Syrian Jacobites, Papal Syrians, and Chaldeans', as well as 'an enquiry into the religious tenets of the Yezidis'. Badger having been appointed an East India Company chaplain in Bombay, his work was edited and seen through the press by John Mason Neale. Neale contributed a prefatory notice in which he welcomed Badger's full account (including English translations of important liturgical texts) of the theology and worship of the Church of the East, but questioned Badger's enthusiastic endorsement of a Christian community which in Neale's view was, although venerable and of great interest, none the less christologically heretical. Badger, he thought, had displayed 'amazing ingenuity' in discovering 'points of resemblance between the Nestorian and English Communions'.[23] Badger concluded, full of enthusiasm,

---

[20] A. H. Layard, *Nineveh and its Remains: With an account of a Visit to the Chaldaean Christians of Kurdistan* . . . (London, 1849), i. 154–5.

[21] Ibid. 201.   [22] Ibid. 268.   [23] Badger, *Nestorians*, i, p. x.

by proposing a scheme for union between Anglicans and Nestorians drawn up by his friend, William Palmer of Magdalen College. Such a union, leading to Anglican support of the Nestorian community, would have an effect among the totality of the Eastern Churches. 'Like a city set upon a hill which cannot be hid, the light of Evangelical truth and apostolical order proceeding forth from this reformed body would in due course scatter the darkness which partly pervades the other Churches in this district.' The Chaldeans would throw off the 'yoke of servitude' to the papacy, rightly laying claim 'to all the titles and privileges of a true and living branch of the one, holy, catholic, and apostolic Church'. 'What heretical or heterodox sect', Badger asked, 'could stand against this phalanx of reformed Christians?'

One after another the Jacobite and Papal Syrian communities would abandon their errors and enlist themselves under the same banner of Gospel truth and primitive discipline. And when these Churches shall have become one in faith and charity, then . . . may we hope that from them will go forth a fervent zeal and love . . . which through the power of GOD shall reduce the followers of the false prophet to the sway of the Crucified One, and gather the heathen Yezeedees into the fold of the Shepherd of Israel.[24]

Badger had hoped that his book *The Nestorians and their Rituals* (1852) would be a spur to the Church of England coming to the assistance of the ancient Church of the East, but there was no immediate response. It was not until Edward White Benson became archbishop of Canterbury in 1883 that there was an active Anglican engagement with the Syrian Christians in a major way with the refoundation of the Archbishop's Mission to the Assyrian Christians in 1884. The letter of appeal for support which Benson issued referred to the work undertaken by the Revd Rudolf Wahl, an American Episcopalian priest, of Jewish and German origin and Lutheran background, whom Archbishop Tait had (somewhat misguidedly given Wahl's peripatetic and somewhat unstable background) commissioned to work among the Christians of the Church of the East.[25] Benson wrote: 'The object in view has not been to bring over these so-called Nestorian Christians to the Communion of the English Church, but rather to strengthen and encourage them in developing the work of their own Church.' The archbishop went on:

There appears to be no trace among these people of the ancient Nestorian heresy. They are a simple, much-oppressed, earnest race, possessed by a strong desire for instruction, and intense regard and affection for England and the English Church. . . . They are much afraid of connecting themselves with any ecclesiastical organization which would absorb them into itself.[26]

---

[24] Ibid. ii. 359.   [25] Coakley, *Church of the East*, 76–7.   [26] Ibid. 89.

Benson was much attracted by the Eastern Churches, and Athelstan Riley, who was to be his emissary on a journey to Armenia and Kurdistan in 1884, believed the secret of this attraction lay both in the antiquity and non-Roman stance of the Eastern Churches, and in his own interest in 'what may be called in a special sense *ecclesiastical* subjects—Church history, and architecture, liturgies, [and] ritual'.[27] Writing in 1888 to the metropolitan of Kiev to send greetings on the nine-hundredth anniversary of the conversion of Russia, Benson pointed out that 'the Russian and the Anglican Church have common foes'. 'Alike we have to guard our independence against the Papal aggressiveness which claims to subordinate all the Church of Christ to the See of Rome.' And there was need of a common vigilance against 'new and strange doctrines adverse to that Holy Faith which was handed down to us by the Holy Apostles and Ancient Fathers of the Catholic Church'.[28] Writing further to the metropolitan in response to the metropolitan's initial reflections on the conditions Benson foresaw to be necessary for a union of the Anglican and Orthodox Churches, Benson urged that the two primary conditions for union were 'the drawing together of the hearts of the individuals composing the two Churches' and 'a more or less formal acceptance of each other's position with toleration for any points of difference'. The question of 'the Historic verity and reality of each other's Holy Orders'—interestingly the word 'validity' is not used—ought to be addressed, and the *Filioque* clause in the Creed was also perceived to be a problem. On the first, Benson sent the metropolitan works by Stubbs, Courayer, Haddan, and Bailey.[29] On the second, he did not doubt that a formula of agreement was possible drawn from the mutually acknowledged works of the Fathers. But Benson believed the quest for unity should begin by mutual admission to communion, which would in God's time 'work out for us both spiritual and intellectual approaches'.[30]

In forwarding relations with the Syrian Christians Archbishop Benson was glad to make use of the services of Athelstan Riley, a young man of definite High Church conviction who had been introduced to him by Bishop Magee of Peterborough shortly before Riley had left England to visit the monasteries of Mount Athos. Riley had been at Eton with William John Birkbeck, who was to forge notable links with the Russian Church, and it was originally through Riley's influence that Birkbeck had himself been won to High Anglican doctrine and devotion.[31] His grandson recalled him in later life as 'small in stature,

[27] A. C. Benson, *The Life of Edward White Benson sometime Archbishop of Canterbury* (2 vols.; London 1899), ii. 155.

[28] Ibid. 157.

[29] The books were: *Episcopal Succession in England* (Stubbs); *Validity of English Orders* (Courayer); *Apostolic Succession* (Haddan); *Ordinationum Ecclesiae Anglicanae Defensio* (Bailey).

[30] Benson, *Life*, ii. 161.   [31] *Life and Letters of W. J. Birkbeck*, by his wife (1992), 4.

piercing blue eyes, well groomed hair and beard, always well dressed, be it in formal London suiting, country tweeds or ankle length travelling coat with fur collar and lining'.[32] In summer 1884 Benson asked Riley if he would be prepared to go as an official emissary to visit the Syrian Christian communities in the mountains of Kurdistan, and also to make contact with the Armenians. Riley left on 20 August, with an Eton contemporary, H. P. Cholmeley, travelling via Warsaw and Kiev to Rostov and Vladikavkaz, and then across the Caucasus to Tblisi, where, Riley noted, 'I attended in academical dress the celebration of the Liturgy in the Chapel of the Exarchate.'[33] By 8 September they were in Etchmiadzin, the seat of the Armenian catholicos, where they had a meeting with Archbishop Megerditch. Just over two weeks later they arrived in Urmia in Persia. Having already found themselves involved at Tabriz in controversy over the actions of Rudolf Wahl, who had been expelled from Urmia because of conflicts with the American missionaries. Riley was not impressed by the 'abominably fidgetty' Wahl's slack observance of the rubrics, and later received complaints from the Syrians that Wahl knew little Syriac and was rude, incompetent, and cowardly.[34] At Gavilan Riley was told that, whereas the French looked after the 200 Chaldean Uniates, and the American missionaries offered protection to the handful of Protestant Syrians, there was no protection afforded to the 300 old Assyrian families.[35] It was a comment symptomatic of the problems posed by the ancient Christian minorities in the Ottoman and Persian domains, minorities who looked to the Western Christian imperial powers for protection at the same time as Russian influence was extending into Azerbaijan. Well-intentioned efforts at protection by different missionary groups and consular representatives, frequently without any real political muscle to back them, all too often left the Christian communities ground between an upper and nether millstone and with a sense of abandonment and betrayal, when promises of aid and protection failed to materialize.[36]

Suspicion of proselytism was well founded from the experience of the Eastern Christian minorities with American Protestant missionaries, Roman Catholic endeavours to convert Eastern Christians to Uniate status, and Russian Orthodox expansionism. When Riley set out for a second visit to the Syrian communities, following Benson's founding of a formally constituted Assyrian mission, he went with the two priests appointed to head the mission, A. J. Maclean and W. H. Browne, to call on the Armenian catholicos at Etchmiadzin. The

[32] Quoted in J. Park, *Athelstan Riley, Patron of St Petroc Minor, Little Petherick* (Truro, 1982), 58.
[33] A. Riley, *Narrative of a Visit to the Assyrian Christians in Kurdistan* (London, 1884), 9.
[34] Coakley, *Church of the East*, 93–4.
[35] Riley, *Narrative*, 6.
[36] For discussion of these issues, see J. Joseph, *The Nestorians and their Muslim Neighbours* (Princeton, 1961), 93–119.

catholicos asked whether there were 'no poor and ignorant English that the Archbishop of Canterbury must send priests to the East? Give my salutation to His Grace and tell him that I do not want his aid.' Riley protested that the mission was an English not an American one. 'Your assurances of non-proselytism are vain,' was the reply; 'only a form, presently you will throw off the pretence.' The line the catholicos took, Riley was told, was a result of pressure from the Russian government anxious to exclude Western influence in missionary guise.[37]

If the Armenian catholicos was cautious, even though Benson's mission was concerned with the Assyrians rather than the Armenians, Maclean and Browne were able to begin educational work among the Assyrians, the detailed account of which has been well written up by Dr Coakley in his study *The Church of the East and the Church of England.* Riley reported on the conditions with which Maclean and Browne were confronted.

They are taxed up to starvation point; their houses are hardly fit for human habitation; men, women and children go about scarcely covered from the winter's cold by a few rags; and yet apostasy from Christianity, which would bring them instantaneous relief from their sufferings, is almost unknown.

I know no more touching sight than the interior of one of their poor Churches; the old priest clothed in a vestment of the meanest material, speaking hesitatingly the prayers that have come down from the cradle of Christianity, the poor villagers pressing forward to kiss a little common wooden cross . . . The monotonous chanting of the congregation conducted in low murmurs as if they were afraid of being heard outside.[38]

The mission, with Riley's enthusiasm behind it, and with two mission priests from the Anglo-Catholic tradition—Mclean, a Scottish Episcopalian, and Browne, a former curate to Arthur Tooth and then on the staff of St Columba's, Haggerston—was conducted on Oxford Movement lines. Riley did little to disabuse the American Presbyterian missionaries that he considered them schismatics or heretics. J. H. Shedd, reporting to the American Mission Board, complained that 'the High Church party (among the Syrians) simply ignore the Presbyterians, since they emphasize Prelacy and church discipline and ritual. I cannot see how this differs from the lapsed and corrupt Christianity of the Old Churches. It is a direct contrast with true Bible religion.'[39] Browne committed himself whole-heartedly to the harsh and poverty-stricken life of the Assyrian Christians of the Hakkari mountains. When Riley returned on a further visit in 1888 he was taken by surprise at Browne's changed appearance.

---

[37] Quoted in Coakley, *Church of the East*, 105.
[38] A. Riley, *Report on the Foundation of the Archbishop's Mission to the Assyrian Church* (London, 1886), 11, quoted in Benson, *Life*, ii. 181.
[39] Coakley, *Church of the East*, 116.

A thin, spare figure stood before me, clad in an English double-breasted cassock, which once was black, but now discoloured by travel and weather, and turned a rusty green. A high conical hat of black felt, round the bottom of which was twisted a black turban, covered his head; the face beneath the turban was rather pinched; and his hair descended to his shoulders. On his feet were sandals, or shoes of rope, used by the mountaineers in scaling the rocks of their native valleys, and in his hand a staff with a crooked head, as borne by monks and hermits . . .[40]

Considering that the Assyrian Christians of the Church of the East represented the descendants of adherents of the Nestorianism condemned at the Council of Ephesus in 431, there was some ambiguity in what was, for the most part, a whole-hearted Anglican endorsement of their Catholic identity. Maclean, who became a considerable Syriac scholar, wrote persuasively about the Christology he found the Church of the East professing. He believed there to be much reason 'for hoping that the so-called Nestorians of the East . . . are not really Nestorians at all. They use unorthodox language and regard Nestorius as a saint; but I believe their faith is right.' The issue seemed to be but one of words.[41] If it were only words that were at issue, then, providing that the Assyrians were prepared to subscribe to the 'forms of sound words' which enshrined the Catholic faith (presumably in this context the Chalcedonian Definition), then they might be 'restored once more to communion with the Holy Catholic and Apostolic Church'. Benson eirenically and ecumenically modified this to refer to 'communion with *the other branches of* the Holy Catholic and Apostolic Church'. Riley was not persuaded, telling Benson that such a change of wording would cut at the root of the Christian faith, and involved setting oneself above the decision of an ecumenical council. 'Before accepting such a theological position I hope I should allow myself to be burnt, and by God's grace I think I would.' Benson interpreted the branch theory differently. 'A branch may be dead, or withered, or dying or sapless or leafless, or without fruit—and the restoration of Communion would be the restoration to vitality of such a languishing branch of the Church.'[42]

Bishop John Wordsworth of Salisbury, who was largely responsible for the drafting of the response to the 1896 papal condemnation of Anglican Orders, and was also deeply committed to the furtherance of understanding and fuller communion with the Churches of the East, was an early pioneer in the work of seeking agreed theological statements to make plain the shared faith of Anglicans and Orthodox, both Chalcedonian and non-Chalcedonian. According to Alexis Larpent, who shared in much of his ecumenical work, Wordsworth stoutly maintained that it was no longer sufficient simply to resort to historical texts and

---

[40] A. Riley, *Progress and Prospects of the Assyrian Mission and the Assyrian Christians* (1889), 15–16, quoted in Coakley, *Church of the East*, 128.
[41] Quoted in ibid. 136.   [42] Quoted in ibid. 138.

conciliar decrees. Wordsworth questioned, for instance, whether it was right to accuse the Copts of heresy, or to suggest that they were in fact monophysite in their Christology, as was commonly supposed. He questioned, likewise, whether the Armenians could really be held to reject Christian orthodoxy, or whether the Assyrians were still to be considered Nestorians. Rather than attributing to the various Oriental Orthodox Churches heterodox opinions, it was necessary to ask those Churches themselves for their own account of their faith.[43] His ecumenical concerns were undergirded by personal acquaintance with the Eastern Churches, particularly in the two visits he undertook to the Middle East in 1898. His theological approach to the Oriental churches anticipates the dialogue of Roman Catholics, Anglicans, and Orthodox with those Churches with the longest history of separate identity from the mainstream of Christendom, and it was the personal contacts of those like Riley and Badger and Browne which made such an approach possible once Christians of those ancient communities had ceased to be viewed through the spectacles of either the Protestant Reformation or Roman Catholicism.

The endeavours of the Church of England to build bridges to the Oriental Orthodox Churches (as they are now generally known) were exemplified again in Bishop Westcott's prefatory note to the account written by Oswald Hutton Parry of his six months' sojourn in the monastery of Deir al-Za'afaran, the then residence of the Syrian Orthodox patriarch of Antioch just outside Mardin, where the hills begin at the northern edge of the Jezireh plain. Parry was to serve the Assyrian mission in Urmia for ten years from 1897 to 1907, and ended his ministry as bishop of Guyana.[44] Westcott traced Anglican interest in the Oriental Churches to the visit of Dr Claudius Buchanan to the Syrian Churches of the Malabar coast in 1806. In his *Christian Researches in the East*, Buchanan, who had come to Calcutta in 1797 after Charles Simeon had obtained an East India Company chaplaincy for him, had written of the Syrian Christians he had encountered at Travancore, and had brought to England a complete manuscript copy of the Peshitta (Syriac Bible). He urged the Church Missionary Society to send 'a few learned, prudent and zealous clergymen' to the Malabar coast to work with the Malabar Church with a view to reviving and confirming the faith in that Church, a work which 'might lead ultimately to union between our Churches'. The missionaries, when sent out, were instructed by the CMS Committee 'not to pull down the ancient Church and build another but to remove the rubbish and repair the decaying places'. 'The Syrians should be brought back to their own ancient worship and discipline, rather than be induced to adopt the liturgy and

---

[43] E. W. Watson, *Life of Bishop John Wordsworth* (London, 1915), 347.

[44] For Parry's work with the Mission, see Coakley, *Church of the East*, 234–50. Parry had been curate of St Ignatius, Sunderland, in the diocese of Durham—hence, presumably, Westcott's preface to his book.

discipline of the English Church'—indeed they should be positively dissuaded from so doing.[45] From that beginning, Westcott went on, Anglican interest in the Oriental Churches had increased, of which Benson's Assyrian mission was a notable sign.

Westcott believed that there were particular reasons for these Churches having a particular attraction and fascination for Anglicans. They were independent. They were eager for education in both the scriptures and their own ancient formularies. They were 'not committed to any modern errors'. Surviving centuries of persecution, they were 'characteristically national churches'. 'They guard with the most jealous care their apostolic heritage, and are still able to express through it the power of their own life.'[46] Roman and American missions both offended the traditions of such Churches.

The aggressive imperialism of Rome, in spite of the dignity of its services, the strength and devotion of its missionaries, the political influence of France, repels a nation proud of their own possessions handed down from their fathers. The American Missionaries necessarily offend the same feeling of religious patriotism from another side. They have no instinctive regard for historic continuity, and look with little reverence on customs venerable by ancient use.[47]

Anglicans, by contrast, were able to approach the Syrian Christians with a strong apostolic order and catholic sympathy, and with no desire to disparage their native traditions, and could welcome the task of building up, purifying, and strengthening a Church which had received so much persecution. 'It is under no temptation to seek either submission or uniformity from those whom it serves. It acknowledges the power of the Faith to harmonise large differences of intellectual and ritual expression . . . within the limits of the historic Creed.' Westcott urged a need for a greater understanding, particularly by Anglicans making it clear that they were not 'non-episcopalian missionaries', any more than Syrians were to be viewed as merely nominal Christians. There were even things, Westcott suggested, which Anglicans might learn from Syrians, in particular a revival of the order of deacons and the service of ordination for the wives of the parochial clergy.

The regulation of the order of Deacons—perhaps the most characteristic order of the Eastern Churches—deserves careful study, as likely to provide a solution of some of the problems suggested by the conditions of home work. Scarcely less interesting and important is the service of ordination for the wives of the parochial clergy, by which they are made a kind of deaconesses. Some such solemn dedication might be a help to many

[45] E. Stock, *The History of the Church Missionary Society* (3 vols.; London 1899), i. 97, 232–3.
[46] O. H. Parry, *Six Months in a Syrian Monastery, Being the Record of a Visit to the Head Quarters of the Syrian Church in Mesopotamia, with some Account of the Yazidis or Devil Worshippers of Mosul and El Jilwah, their Sacred Book* (London, 1895), pp. vii–viii.
[47] Ibid., p. viii.

women among ourselves who, placed by marriage in positions of heavy responsibility, are distracted by the trivial calls of modern society.[48]

The English nation, Westcott concluded, was called to be the missionary nation of the world. 'It is not more surely marked out by its history to bring the Christian truth to the peoples of India, than it is marked out by the endowments of the National Church to bring new life to the Churches which represent the old Patriarchates of Antioch, and Alexandria, and Jerusalem.'[49] That Westcott could write with such firm conviction; that John Wordsworth could take such a prescient approach to the theological stance of churches condemned by the early councils, and that Archbishop Benson should give such clear support to a non-proselytizing mission to the Assyrian Christians, are a measure both of the evolving character of Anglicanism, and of the impact of ecumenical encounter.

[48] Ibid., p. x.   [49] Ibid., p. xi.

Epilogue: The Changing Role of the Ecclesiastical Historian

Edward Norman

Until quite recently the leading scholars of ecclesiastical history saw their endeavours as a dimension of Christian ministry. In the English tradition they were often clergy serving in universities, colleges, and seminaries, who combined their teaching with the maintenance of a religious vocation: the study of the Church and of Christianity in their formation and historical context. This was not a peripheral ministry. Christianity is a historical religion; its founder, that is to say, did not commit his truths to a philosophical school, or to a priestly caste, or even to a written record, but to a living and continuing body of believers. He founded a Church. The revelation made by Christ, which confirmed the religious intimations of preceeding human experience and the divine education of the Jewish people—and added to it the gifts of forgiveness and salvation—was entrusted to historical process, to the understanding and witness of a new people. Complete in itself, it nevertheless required to be more or less perpetually restated in the images and earthly structures inseparable from a dialectical engagement with the world. Even in sequences of time, and in the history of particular nations and cultures, when events appeared static, there were actually subtle changes. The Christian Church has rarely been stable, set as it is upon the unsteady waters of human development, and impressions of timelessness, which frequently attach to it, may be authentic representations of its essential message but are no indications of its inherent propensity to accommodate to the world around it. How could it be otherwise? The world and the Church are not of a different kind: they are natural religion and revealed religion in a complementary relationship whose apparent incompatibilities are the consequence of a frail human purchase upon reality rather than a divinely intended mismatch.

Committed, then, to the diversity of historical process, and enriched by the cultures through which it passes, the Church has always had a considerable dependence on the provision of its own scholars, both theologians and historians, who would use the expertise of the available scholarly *apparat* to interpret its message and context. Since these scholars recognized their function as a distinct ministry, the history of the Church has included a history of learned men and women, both lay and clerical, dedicating their lives to explaining the nature of the Church to itself. John McManners lives in this tradition, and his scholarly and priestly work has been a notable example of a vital dimension of ministry.

The vocation of ecclesiastical history at its best impels its practitioners to uncover whatever the data will bear, in the conviction that truth is to be sought for its own sake and in all its variety, not disguised or knowingly subordinated to confessional apologetics. Thus it is a strenuous vocation posited on the integrity and professionalism of the historian. Of course, all representations of truth are unconscious projections of minds that are not neutral intellectual instruments; even where polemical purpose is avoided, cultural preconceptions are inescapable. Amidst the flux of all these difficulties, ecclesiastical historians down the ages have attempted to help the Church and the world to understand how they interact, and to consider how believers down the centuries have responded to revelation. Sometimes Church historians of a particular tradition have employed their insights and learning to justify the distinctive beliefs of their own branch of Christian understanding, often under direct Church patronage. Sometimes, and more frequently in modern times, Church historians have seen themselves as institutionally independent, yet as men and women who are dedicated to an enrichment of the faith through an exploration of its place in human experience during earlier epochs. Sometimes they have been lone voices, speaking up for the Christian vocation of learning in a world which has not always appreciated it. An admiring visitor who praised Baronius for his *Annals of Ecclesiastical History*, the last volume of which appeared in 1594, enquired how many secretaries and assistants he had employed to produce so massive a work. Baronius, who never employed anyone, answered in the words of scripture: 'I have trodden the winepress alone.' Whether Church history is a solitary or a collective enterprise depends upon the chance of individual temperament, available resources, or educational need.

The long succession of those who have considered the study of ecclesiastical history as an aspect of Christian ministry is, however, now becoming increasingly difficult to maintain. It is an important dimension to the current crisis of Anglican learning. Among those coming forward for ordination there are fewer whose gifts or capacities allow standards of intellectual training that are comparable to those in other professions. It should be truly worrying for Christians that, in an increasingly educated society, the ministry of the Church—of all the Churches—includes far fewer who are able to address it at the appropriate level. Many chairs in ecclesiastical history, originally endowed for specifically Christian purposes, have been secularized; seminaries have been first amalgamated and then closed altogether because the numbers needed to keep them in existence have not been coming forward; a leadership that has had to take progressively hard decisions about the proper use of diminishing resources has not, in general, felt able to accord as high a priority (or any priority at all) to the study of Church history as it once did, in, for example, the annexation of one of the Christ Church canonries to the Regius Professorship of Ecclesiastical History at Oxford in 1840. The corollary of the decreasing importance attached to doctrine in the Church of England is the reduced institutional interest in its formation and maintenance. Admittedly, commentators have identified and lamented this 'crisis' from at least the turn of the century, but the evidence points to an acceleration of the process.

In this country the Church of England still retains a voice in education—in the sense that it is concerned with the conveyance of precise religious doctrine—but its presence in education is much less substantial than appearance suggests. The Church schools and colleges are often hardly distinguishable from their secular counterparts, and it certainly cannot be said that the attempt to foster a 'Christian ethos' in them—despite the many heroic efforts of individual Christian schoolteachers and college lecturers—encourages vocations to the ministry or to a view of scholarship which is characteristically confessional. Moreover, the decreasing availability of intellectual talent has allowed the governing bodies of educational institutions which maintain a chaplaincy to appoint people who will be effective welfare officers rather than productive scholars. The Church, in short, with pastoral 'usefulness' exalted above clerical learning (a sort of ecclesiastical Benthamism that has been gaining the upper hand since the era of Church reform began in the 1830s), is not creating either a Christian intelligentsia or a corps of believers who can make a distinct contribution to the secular culture which surrounds them. Such omissions are perhaps more apparent in the modern Established Church than in any of its sisters who are less ashamed of denominational historicism, or dubious about its scholarly significance. One needs only look, for instance, at the group founded by Alan Sell, himself a prolific author and Congregationalist. Professor Sell is a layman and it could be that the laïcization of the study of Church history, which has to some extent taken place simultaneously, will prove a partial compensation. But there seems little awareness—in Anglican circles at least—that the Church is an institution whose message will always need, if it is to be authentically a Church, a body of scholars who will interpret its relationship to the world within a confessional tradition. Perhaps the crisis of historical learning in the Church is experienced most acutely in Anglicanism. There seems to be no counterpart in the modern Roman Catholic Church in Britain. There has been a splendid flowering of Catholic history in the last fifteen years produced by scholars like Dominic Bellenger,

John Bossy, Sheridan Gilley, Richard Rex, and Jack Scarisbrick; a recent conference in Oxford devoted to the 'Catholic view of history' highlighted this trend. However, it has not come from the clergy (with some exceptions like Bellenger, Geoffrey Holt, and Geoffrey Scott), and is neither narrow nor overtly 'denominational'.

It is plain that most ecclesiastical history will in the future be the work of lay people, and, though it will be seen by many as an authentic form of Christian ministry, it will not necessarily be integrated with the institutional Church and recognized, through priestly involvement, as an important means of identifying the Church's mission in the world. This prompts consideration of an even more serious dimension of the decline of ecclesiastical history as an acceptable ministerial vocation in the Church of England: the loss of interest in distinctive denominational history, pronounced by comparison with writers in the Free Church tradition such as Alan Sell (above), John Walsh, W. R. Ward, and the late Gordon Rupp in the Methodist Church, and Clyde Binfield on Baptists and Congregationalists. Denominational studies embody the truth that a universal organization like the Christian Church, and a religion which appeals to the different aspects of individual consciousness and cultural awareness, can only be understood by first examining the general in the particular. Yet the sense of such authors as the above that ecclesiastical history must borrow from the rapidly evolving though secular intellectual disciplines is sound. The danger is that the ensuing professionalizing of the subject might make it too dependent on intellectual modes and cultural attitudes alien to a world-view in which religion is understood to have unique insights and exclusive claims. Some modern secular historians, for example, sometimes treat religious beliefs, as materialists do, as merely a phenomenon. Because religion occupies so little space in their own perception of reality, they find it difficult to imagine how people in the past can really have been motivated by religious belief. Then the search is on for the 'real', non-religious reasons that underpin confessional allegiance. While the Marxists had systematic philosophical reasons for supposing that the persistence of religion was a symptom of an irrationally ordered society, liberal materialist historians have latterly told their readers that religious belief is no more than an aspect of cultural relativism; those susceptible enough to believe this to be true are conditioned by social class, or economic necessity, or cultural expectations. Alternatively, they are the victims of social authority. These methods and assumptions have admittedly had their uses for a much wider circle of historians than liberal materialists, including ecclesiastical specialists, for even secular Church historians are invariably sympathetic to Christian tradition, if detached. Of course, to see the human reasons for which people adopt religious ideas is unquestionably important, since the divine creation comprises real matter and engages a real humanity. But to the believer it is an understanding which simultaneously fleshes out a universal reality which discloses, if opaquely, the divine mind, and is an adjunct of revelation and not its replacement.

The problem is not the professionalizing of the subject, or the new insights of the secular intelligence. It is that the study of the Church is now being defined by methods which were devised for secular and not for religious purposes. The pursuit of learning is not neutral, and the outcome of enquiry is, of course, dependent on the kinds of questions asked at the outset and the sort of evidence that is deemed admissible. Just as it is unhelpful to separate the sacred and the secular when it comes to attempts at categorizing reality, so it is equally unhelpful if only the secular side of the equation is in practice accorded legitimacy when it comes to the intellectual methods and the modes of thought by which the enquiry is set on foot. Ecclesiastical historians should never undervalue the importance of sympathy for the traditions they examine, and be watchful that employment of the methodologies of secular enquiry is not at the price of absorbing their underlying secularity. Most do indeed recognize the risk, and are more than professionally capable of withstanding it. Fortunately for the discipline, there remain (even within the Anglican tradition) many practitioners like Jonathan Clark and Richard Sharp who are alert to the strategies deployed by those whose interest in religion is sometimes ideologically hostile to the unique claims of a tradition of understanding derived from revealed knowledge.

There is, it need hardly be said, nothing intellectually necessary about the association of modern methods and techniques in historical enquiry with secularization. That is, however, in the circumstances of Western culture, what often happens. The writing of ecclesiastical history in Islamic countries at the present indicates that there is nothing about a religious view of the world which is necessarily incompatible either with a developed material culture or with current intellectual disciplines. It is in the West, in societies like ours, that prevailing attitudes have a tendency to relativize the religious dimensions of the culture. Those who attribute this to an inherent conflict of scientific method and traditional thought are mistaken—though the common perception that such is the case itself produces a difficult climate for the acceptance of distinctively religious insights into the nature of human life. Relativizing religious experience derives not from scientific method and discovery but from historical and anthropological research: from comparative analyses of different religious traditions in which their claims to unique understanding are seemingly undermined by the discovery of their common rootedness in social or cultural need. Thus the education of the Jewish people into a knowledge of God, described in the Old Testament, becomes simply another folk wandering of the ancient world, in which an enslaved people find compensation for their lowly status, and eventually sacralize their conquest of territory and their absorption of the native divinities they find there. Christ can be seen as yet another prophetic figure, thrown up in the disorientation of life under a subsequent period of loss of national freedom.

But there is nothing about such historical understanding—true in itself— which actually lessens the religious interpretation of the same body of data, originally made by, and still conveyed in, the tradition of Christian believers. They see a real material creation, which necessarily determines the reception of information about the world by human enquirers. Religious truth is committed to the historical process, and to study history, in this case Church history, is to show how men and women, inseparable from that material creation, are nevertheless made specifically to transcend it. To observe the secularizing effects of modern intellectual culture in the West should not be to lament the intellectual methods involved, or to doubt their utility. But it is necessary to notice that they are *only* methods. They do not determine the ultimate significance of the outcome of enquiry, which derives from judgements of a different sort depending on a revealed body of information, and taken as part of a religious tradition.

Some of the most fruitful advances in understanding that have been made in the last century have come from the sociology of religion. This is a science specifically concerned with showing the non-religious reasons for which people adhere to religious ideas or styles of living. Who today could write about denominationalism, for example, without reference to Ernst Troeltsch's seminal ideas about the relationship between social and religious differentiation? This is a discipline which shows the nuts and bolts of religious institutions and the reasons for the social need of them. That is *all* it shows, however. Universal truths require particular worldly expression or embodiments to be known about by mortals at all. In Christianity, that is to say, God becomes a man; the treasure is in earthen vessels. It must be expected, therefore, that the human accidents attaching to divine mysteries will be very human. Tearing them apart in order to demonstrate their humanity may be intellectually amusing as an exercise in secular inconoclasm, but it does not, in the end, relate very much about the religious reality of which the worldly representation is an icon. Ecclesiastical historians today will fail in professionalism if they do not keep abreast with general intellectual advances, but they should never lose ultimate confidence in the separateness of the truths whose partial structures are illuminated by current methods of intellectual enquiry. Faith and reason are interdependent. The danger is that revealed truth will be devalued because natural truth shows the means by which it is relayed to our understanding.

At the present time a great deal of distinguished writing in ecclesiastical history is being produced—of which the present volume is witness—and the sense among both lay and clerical historians, that producing it is still a distinctly ministerial vocation, persists: the declining official interest of the Churches in reconstructing their past has been creatively offset by the talents of lay men and women who have moved into this field of study. Yet it is impossible to escape the impression that the initiative remains at risk of passing to an intellectual culture whose terms of reference increasingly preclude the idea that revealed religious traditions are authentic sources of unique knowledge. Religion has been departmentalized instead; dispatched to the realm of the emotions. In the imprecise afterglow of the Romantic movement and the Evangelical experience, religion is now commonly seen as an aspect of therapy, as something which helps the individual to find personal significance, as an adjunct to aesthetic sensation, a private choice rather than a public policy. Throughout the history of the USSR religion was identified as a social phenomenon because the masters of education recognized that relativizing religious claims to unique knowledge was the most effective means of diminishing its credibility, thus laying the foundations of an acceptable basis to official atheism. When the USSR collapsed, it turned out that the effort had been in vain. Religious belief had survived on a large scale. This was perhaps due to the close association between Orthodoxy and Russian and Ukrainian nationalism, and between Islam and Islamic family structures in the Muslim states of the Union; or perhaps to the relatively undeveloped state of public consumerism and the consequent retardation of secular leisure. These, it will be noticed, are explanations which employ the appropriate styles of modern analysis: they are themselves examples of ecclesiastical history using the modes of the prevalent intellectual culture. It no longer seems realistic to attribute the survival of religion in the USSR to direct divine forces, or to some mysterious operation of providence. As Professor McManners has accurately noted elsewhere, historians no longer concern themselves worrying over such matters. But for all that, they are explanations which, in the greater perspective, are easily compatible with a providential view of the world as an expression of a creative will, whose detailed operations are conveyed through material means which may be analysed and, at least in part, understood. Whatever the impulsion of events in the former USSR, however, it is clear that in the West the causes of the secularization of history are radically different. With us the ingredients do not add up to a coherent ideology. Here the relativizing of religious history derives from the dominance in modern cultural life of those who rarely exhibit overt hostility to religion; for these opinion formers (and therefore for the public at large) religious explanations for events are implausible when there are so many more obvious ones on offer. Hence the risk for ecclesiastical historians that, in bringing the full range of contemporary intellectual strategies to their work, they unwittingly adopt attitudes ultimately inimical to religion. One must hope, however, that the professional rigour most habitually exhibit will ensure that explanatory modishness for its own sake remains the exception rather than the rule, and one need look no further than the work of John McManners to see that interpretative discrimination so sensitively in operation.

McManners has been among those leading the way in deciding to write about aspects of religious history that are more than internal histories of the various Churches, and this has conferred a vitality on the subject that should not be easily overlooked. Scholars with very divergent perspectives and loyalties have cooperated together to revive and broaden the scope of Church history, not writing to a common formula, for, as McManners pointed out in the Introduction to the *Oxford Illustrated History of Christianity*, such a history 'raises problems which outrun by far the scope of the professional techniques available to us'.[1] Such cooperation has forged the unlikely but fruitful partnership of the Oxford historian, John Walsh (who has himself contributed so much to the present good health of the discipline), with the History Workshop at Ruskin College. At work here is a reaction to the élitism once inherent in Church history, a preoccupation with the leaders and their ideas rather than the lives of ordinary believers. There is also a recognition of the seriousness with which the Western world has come to take the non-Christians' understandings of religious truths. These are valuable changes, but one needs to be alert to the possibility of the further secularization of the subject. If all religions are treated with equal weight, there can be no arrangement of things—in making an appointment to a university lectureship in theology, let us say—which does not further dislodge Christianity from its traditional position in Western culture. At school level, the major world religions are taught in a very uncritical light by teachers understandably anxious not to cause offence to the ethnic minorities who are, in this country, the available embodiments of the traditions concerned. Christianity, on the other hand, is often presented as a mass of doubtful propositions and controverted teachings so that pupils can 'make up their own minds'. The result is probably confusion; but it is secularizing because it tends emphatically to relativize all religious experience and to regard religious belief, once again, as a 'mere phenomenon'.

The Church history of our time, exemplified at its best in the writings of John McManners, may therefore be seen in some senses as modifying a distinctive tradition, but it has used the latest techniques of modern historical scholarship to produce some fine and enduring work. There are encouraging signs of creative

[1] John McManners, *The Oxford Illustrated History of Christianity* (Oxford, 1990), 5.

synthesis, an approach to religious history appealing to fine scholars like Patrick Collinson (Professor McManners's successor in Sydney), that can account for both the 'vertical dimension' favoured by traditional ecclesiastical history and the 'horizontal dimension' characteristic of a modern religion-and-society approach, while embracing the best insights of insiders and outsiders to the religious tradition in question. Such developments are perhaps in keeping with the characteristic emphasis of our time on the relationship of the Church to the world; to the ways in which social and political structures have moulded Christian institutions and thought and have been in turn changed by them; to the Christian contribution in educational and welfare work, and to the conditions which have restricted religious influence in some Western societies and have marginalized public consciousness of Christian teachings. Newman's observation that all life is change, and that to be perfect is to have changed often, must surely have great appeal for those whose study of the Churches records so many changes. It is a peculiarity of the Christian mind: to inhabit a worldly residence where time means nothing and yet changes all things, and to be guardians of a timeless message which can be known about only when each successive generation changes the images in which it is represented.

BIBLIOGRAPHY OF JOHN McMANNERS'S WORKS

1953

'France', in A. Goodwin (ed.), *The European Nobility in the Eighteenth Century* (1953), 22–42.

'Les "Psalteurs" de la Cathédrale d'Angers', *L'Anjou historique*, 51/239 (1953), 35–7.

1955

English Historical Review (hereafter *EHR*), 70 (1955), 676–7, review of Enid Stoye, *Vincent Bernard de Tscharner, 1728–1778* (Fribourg, 1954).

1956

EHR 71 (1956), 672–3, review of Elinor G. Barber, *The Bourgeoisie in Eighteenth-Century France* (London, 1955).

1957

'The Revolution and its Antecedents (1774–1794)', in J. M. Wallace-Hadrill and J. McManners (eds.), *France: Government and Society* (London, 1957), 161–88.

1958

'An Eccentric Curé of Eighteenth Century France', *Tasmania Historical Research Association: Papers and Proceedings*, 7 (June 1958), 6–12.

1960

French Ecclesiastical Society under the Ancien Régime: A Study of Angers in the Eighteenth Century (Manchester, 1960).

Journal of Religious History, 1 (1960), 121–3, review of Burdette C. Poland, *French Protestantism and the French Revolution: A Study in Church and State, Thought and Religion, 1685–1815* (Princeton, 1957).

EHR 75 (1960), 129–32, review of Georges Livret, *L'Intendance d'Alsace sous Louis XIV (1648–1715)* (Paris, 1956).

Ibid. 132–5, review of Maurice Bordes, *D'Étigny et l'administration de l'intendance d'Auch, 1751–1767* (2 vols., Auch, 1957).

1961

'Church and State in Catholic Europe in the Eighteenth Century', *Tasmania Historical Research Association: Papers and Proceedings*, 9 (Aug. 1961), 75–92.

1962

'Paul Hazard and the "Crisis of the European Conscience"', in *Arts: The Proceedings of the Sydney University Arts Association*, 2 (1962), 73–86 (inaugural lecture at the University of Sydney, delivered 22 June 1961).

EHR 77 (1962), 334–7, review of René Taveneaux, *Le Jansénisme en Lorraine* (Paris, 1960).

Ibid. 373, review of *Registres des déliberations du bureau de la Ville de Paris* (Commission des Travaux Historiques, vol. 19), ed. Suzanne Clémencet (Paris, 1958).

Ibid. 380–1, review of Jacques Saint-Germain, *Samuel Bernard, le banquier des rois* (Paris, 1960).

1963

Journal of Religious History, 2 (1963), 342–6, review article, 'Religious History of Modern France', based on a book of that title by Adrien Dansette (Freiburg, 1961).

EHR 78 (1963), 789–90, review of Alice Wemyss, *Les Protestants du Mas-d'Azil: Histoire d'une résistance, 1680–1830* (Toulouse, 1961).

1965

With R. M. Crawford, 'The Future of the Humanities in the Australian Universities', in *The Future of the Humanities in the Australian Universities* (Australian Humanities Research Council, Occasional Paper 8; Melbourne, 1965), 1–11.

'The Historiography of the French Revolution', in *New Cambridge Modern History*, viii. *The American and French Revolutions*, ed. A. Goodwin (Cambridge, 1965), 618–52.

1966

Lectures on European History 1789–1914: Men, Machines, and Freedom (Oxford, 1966).

1967

EHR 82 (1967), 222, review of *Liber Memorialis Sir Maurice Powicke. Studies Presented to the International Commission for the History of Representative and Parliamentary Institutions: Dublin, 1963* (Louvain, 1965).

Ibid. 393, review of René Taveneaux, *Jansénisme et politique* (Paris, 1965).

Ibid. 396–7, review of Lionel Rothkrug, *Opposition to Louis XIV: The Political and Social Origins of the French Enlightenment* (Princeton, 1965).

1968

Journal of Ecclesiastical History (hereafter *JEH*), 19 (1968), 261–2, review of François Gaquère, *Le Dialogue irénique Bossuet–Leibniz: La réunion des églises en échec (1691–1702)* (Paris, 1966); Bernard Larney, *Entretiens sur les sciences dans lesquels on apprend comment l'on doit étudier les sciences, et s'en servir pour se faire l'esprit juste, & le coeur droit*, ed. François Gerbal et Pierre Clair (Paris, 1966); R. R. Palmer, *Catholics and Unbelievers in Eighteenth Century France* (Princeton, 1966).

The Social Contract and Rousseau's Revolt against Society: An Inaugural Lecture Delivered in the University of Leicester, 6 November 1967 (Leicester, 1968), repr. in Maurice Cranston and Richard S. Peters (eds.), *Hobbes and Rousseau: A Collection of Critical Essays* (New York, 1972).

Journal of Theological Studies (hereafter *JTS*), 19 (1968), 683–5, review of Robert T. Holtby, *Daniel Waterland 1683–1740: A Study in Eighteenth Century Orthodoxy* (Carlisle, 1966).

EHR 83 (1968), 196–7, review of Charles Ledré, *L'Abbé de Salamon: Correspondant et agent du Saint-Siège pendant la Révolution* (Paris, 1965).

Ibid. 850–1, review of Norman Ravitch, *Sword and Mitre: Government and Episcopate in France and England in the Age of Aristocracy* (The Hague, 1966).
Ibid. 851–2, review of C. B. A. Behrens, *The Ancien Régime* (London, 1967).

1969

The French Revolution and the Church (London, 1969).
History, 54 (1969), 277–8, review of J. H. Shennan, *The Parlement of Paris* (London, 1968).
EHR 84 (1969), 856–7, review of René Caisso, *La Vente des biens nationaux de première origine dans le district de Tours. 1790–1822* (Coll. des documents inédits sur l'histoire économique de la Révolution française; Paris, 1967).

1970

JTS 21 (1970), 251–2, review of Friedrick Heyer, *The Catholic Church from 1648 to 1870*, trans. D. W. Shaw (London, 1969).
'Religion and the Relations of Church and State', *New Cambridge Modern History*, vi. *The Rise of Great Britain and Russia*, ed. J. S. Bromley (Cambridge, 1970), 119–53.
EHR 85 (1970), 172, review of Dom Yves Chaussy, *Les Bénédictins anglais réfugiés en France au XVIIe siècle (1611–1669)* (Paris, 1967).
Ibid. 367–9, review of Arthur Hertzberg, *The French Enlightenment and the Jews* (New York, 1968).
Ibid. 852–3, review of Louis J. Lekai, *The Rise of the Cistercian Strict Observance in Seventeenth Century France* (Washington, DC, 1968).

1971

JTS 22 (1971), 292–3, review of John W. Padberg, *Colleges in Controversy: The Jesuit Schools in France from Revival to Suppression, 1815–1880* (Cambridge, Mass., 1969).
History, 65 (1971), 112–13, review of L. S. Greenbaum, *Talleyrand. Statesman Priest: The Agent General of the Clergy and the Church of France at the End of the Old Regime* (Washington, 1970).
EHR 86 (1971), 179–80, review of A. Sarramon (ed.), *Les Paroisses du diocèse de Comminges en 1786* (Paris, 1968).
Ibid. 180, review of J. Plongeron, *Conscience religieuse en Révolution: Regards sur l'historiographie religieuse de la Révolution française* (Paris, 1969).
Ibid. 406, review of B. Jennings and C. Giblin (eds.), *Louvain Papers, 1606–1827* (Dublin, 1968).
Ibid. 416, review of Bruno Neveu (ed.), *Sébastien Joseph Du Cambout de Pontchâteau (1634–1690) et ses missions à Rome* (Paris, 1969).
Ibid. 421, review of R. J. White, *The Anti-Philosophers: A Study of the Philosophes in Eighteenth-Century France* (London, 1970).

1972

Church and State in France, 1870–1914 (London, 1972).
EHR 87 (1972), 194–5, review of Jean Sareil, *Les Tencin: Histoire d'une famille au dix-huitième siècle d'après de nombreux documents inédits* (Geneva, 1969).
Ibid. 422, review of Jacques Roland-Gosselin, *Le Carmel de Beaune, 1619–1660* (Rabat, 1969).

1974

Ibid. 25 (1974), 215, review of Roland Mousnier, *The Assassination of Henry IV: The Tyrannicide Problem and the Consolidation of the French Absolute Monarchy of the Early Seventeenth Century*, trans. Joan Spencer (London, 1973).

JEH 25 (1974), 330–1, review of Jean Guerber, SJ, *Le Ralliement du clergé français à la morale liguorienne: L'Abbé Gousset et ses précurseurs (1785–1832)* (Rome, 1973).

EHR 89 (1974), 394–7, review of Colin Lucas, *The Structure of the Terror: The Example of Javogues and the Loire* (Oxford, 1973).

Ibid. 894, review of *Douai College Documents, 1639–1794*, ed. P. R. Harris (Catholic Record Society, 63; 1972).

1975

Reflections at the Deathbed of Voltaire: The Art of Dying in Eighteenth-Century France (inaugural lecture as Regius Professor of Ecclesiastical History, 1974; Oxford, 1975).

'Jansenism and Politics in the Eighteenth Century', in Derek Baker (ed.), *Church, Society, and Politics* (Studies in Church History, 12; Oxford, 1975), 253–74.

History, 60 (1975), 480, review of Maurice Larkin, *Church and State after the Dreyfus Affair: The Separation Issue in France* (London, 1974).

JEH 26 (1975), 420–1, review of P. Brooks (ed.), *Christian Spirituality: Essays in Honour of Gordon Rupp* (London, 1975).

Ibid. 441–2, review of P. Jansen (ed.), *Arnauld d'Andilly défenseur du Port-Royal (1654–1659): Sa correspondance inédite avec la Cour conservée dans les Archives du Ministère des Affaires etrangères* (Paris, 1973).

JTS 26 (1975), 222–3, review of William Wilson Mauross, *S.P.G. Papers in the Lambeth Palace Library* (Oxford, 1974).

EHR 90 (1975), 198, review of François Jacques, *Le Diocèse de Tournai (1690–1728) et ses divisions archidiaconales et décanales de 1331 à 1789: Cartes de géographie historique* (Brussels, 1973).

Ibid. 202–3, review of Bernard Plongeron, *Théologie et politique au siècle des lumières (1770–1820)* (Geneva, 1973).

Ibid. 900–1, review of *Correspondance du Nonce en France: Angelo Ranuzzi (1683–1689)*, ed. Bruno Neveu (Acta Nuntiaturae Gallicae, 10) (Rome, 1973).

Ibid. 905–6, review of Hugh Fenning, *The Undoing of the Friars of Ireland: A Study of the Novitiate Question in the Eighteenth Century* (Louvain, 1972).

1976

JEH 27 (1976), 253–4, review of John W. Carver, *Napoleon and the Lazarists* (The Hague, 1974).

Ibid. 320–1, review of Edward Dixon Junkin, *Religion versus Revolution: The Interpretation of the French Revolution by German Protestant Churchmen, 1789–1799* (2 vols.; Austin, Tex., 1974).

Ibid. 507–8, review of Marcel Courdurié, *La Dette des collectivités publiques de Marseille au XVIIIᵉ siècle: Le Débat sur le prêt à intérêt au financement par l'emprunt* (n.d., n.p.).

EHR 91 (1976), 861–4, review of Henri Grange, *Les Idées de Necker* (Paris, 1974); Jean Egret, *Necker* (Paris, 1975).

1977

'Living and Loving: Changing Attitudes to Sexual Relationships in 18th century France', *British Society for Eighteenth Century Studies Newsletter*, 12 (June 1977), 1–19.

'The World, the Flesh and the Devil', sermon preached in Christ Church Cathedral, *Friends of Christ Church Cathedral Oxford Newsletter* (1977–8), 15–20.

1978

JEH 29 (1978), 236–8, review of Claude Langlois, *Un diocèse breton au début du XIXᵉ siècle* (Paris, 1974).

History, 63 (1978), 130–1, review of Cissie C. Fairchilds, *Poverty and Charity in Aix-en-Provence, 1640–1789* (London, 1976).

Ibid. 161–2, review of Bernard Reardon, *Liberalism and Tradition: Aspects of Catholic Thought in Nineteenth Century France* (Cambridge, 1975).

'Aristocratic Vocations: the bishops of France in the eighteenth Century', in Derek Baker (ed.), *Religious Motivation: Biographical and Sociological Problems for the Church Historian* (Studies in Church History 15, Oxford, 1978), 305–26.

EHR. 93 (1978), 204–5, review of Willem Frijhoff and Dominique Julia, *École et société dans la France d'ancien régime: Quatre exemples, Auch, Avallon, Condom et Gisors* (Cahiers des Annales, 35; Paris, 1975).

Ibid. 451, review of *Lettres de Turgot à la duchesse d'Enville (1764–74 et 1777–80)*, ed. Joseph Ruwet (Louvain, 1976).

Ibid. 669–70, review of Harry C. Payne, *The Philosophes and the People* (New Haven, 1976).

1979

JEH 30 (1979), 499–500, review of Arlette Playoust-Chaussis, *La Vie religieuse dans le diocèse de Boulogne au XVIIIᵉ siècle (1725–1790)* (Arras, 1976).

Ibid. 500–2, review of Robert Kreiser, *Miracles. Convulsions and Ecclesiastical Politics in Early Eighteenth-Century Paris* (Princeton, 1978).

Times Literary Supplement (hereafter *TLS*), 14 Dec., 'The History of Death'.

EHR 94 (1979), 201–2, review of Thomas Bentley, *Journal of a Visit to Paris, 1776*, ed. Peter France (Brighton, 1976).

1980

EHR 95 (1980), 427–8, review of Michel C. Peronnet, *Les Evêques de l'Ancienne France* (2 vols.; Lille, 1977).

JEH 31 (1980), 119–20, review of Y.-M. Hilaire, *Une chrétienté au XIXᵉ siècle? La Vie religieuse des populations du diocèse d'Arras (1840–1914)* (2 vols.; Villeneuve d'Ascq, 1977).

Ibid. 399, review of Jean Schlick (ed.), *Églises et état en Alsace et en Moselle: Changement ou fixité* (Strasbourg, 1979).

'Believers and Worshippers', in Alan Bullock (ed.), *Faces of Europe* (Oxford, 1980), 173–99.

1981

Death and the Enlightenment (Oxford, 1981).

'Death and the French Historians', in Joachim Whaley (ed.), *Mirrors of Mortality: Studies in the Social History of Death* (London, 1981), 106–30.

'The Individual in the Church of England', in *Believing in the Church: A Report by the Doctrine Commission of the Church of England* (London, 1981).

History, 66 (1981), 524–5, review of Eva Jacobs, W. H. Barber, Jean H. Bloch, F. W. Leaky, and Eileen Le Breton (eds.), *Women and Society in Eighteenth Century France: Essays in Honour of John Stephenson Spink* (London, 1979).

Ibid. 525, review of Robert Darnton, *The Business of Enlightenment: A Publishing History of the Encyclopédie, 1775–1800* (London, 1979).

JEH 32 (1981), 122, review of William J. Callahan and David Higgs (eds.), *Church and Society in Catholic Europe of the Eighteenth Century* (Cambridge, 1979).

Ibid. 360–1, review of Robert Sauzet, *Contre-Réforme et réforme catholique en Bas-Languedoc: Le Diocèse de Nîmes au XVIIe siècle* (Louvain, 1979).

TLS, 11 Dec. 1981, p. 1445, review of Maarten Ultee, *The Abbey of St Germain des Prés in the Seventeenth Century*.

1982

Popular Religion in 17th and 18th century France: A New Theme in French Historiography (John Coffin Memorial Lecture 1982; London, 1982).

JEH 33 (1982), 451–2, review of F. Lebrun (ed.), *Le Diocèse d'Angers* (Paris, 1981).

Ibid., review of F. Lebrun (ed.), *Histoire des Catholiques en France du XVe siècle à nos jours* (Toulouse, 1980).

Ibid. 148–9, review of M.-H. Froeschlé-Chopard, *La Religion populaire en Provence orientale au XVIIIe siècle* (Bibliothèque Beauchesne, Religions Société Politique, 7; Paris, 1980).

1983

TLS, 25 Mar. 1983, review of Colin Jones, *Charity and* bienfaisance: *The Treatment of the Poor in the Montpellier Region 1740–1815* (Cambridge, 1982).

JEH 34 (1983), 306–7, review of James O'Higgins, *Yves de Vallone: The Making of an esprit-fort* (International Archives of the History of Ideas, 97; The Hague, 1982).

1984

EHR 99 (1984), 187–8, review of René Moulinas, *Les Juifs du pape en France: Les communautés d'Avignon et du Comtat Venaissin au 17e et 18e siècles* (Paris, 1981).

Ibid. 618–19, review of Louis Châtellier, *Tradition chrétienne et renouveau catholique dans le cadre de l'ancienne diocèse de Strasbourg (1650–1770)* (Paris, 1981).

JEH 35 (1984), 171, review of Richard M. Golden (ed.), *State and Society under the Bourbon Kings of France* (Lawrence, Kan., 1982).

1985

'Tithe in Eighteenth-Century France: A Focus for Rural Anticlericalism', in Derek Beales and Geoffrey Best (eds.), *History, Society and the Churches: Essays in Honour of Owen Chadwick* (Cambridge, 1985), 147–68.

TLS, 26 July 1985, p. 829, review of Catherine-Laurence Maire (ed.), *Les Convulsionnaires de Saint-Médard: Miracles, convulsions et prophéties à Paris au XVIIIe siècle* (Paris, 1985).

'The Use of History', *Royal Artillery Historical Society. Proceedings* 5 (1985), 16–32.
'Voltaire and the Monks', in W. J. Sheils, *Monks, Hermits, and the Ascetic Tradition* (Studies in Church History, 22; Oxford, 1985), 319–42.

1986

Abbés and Actresses: The Church and the Theatrical Profession in Eighteenth-Century France (Zaharoff Lecture 1986; Oxford, 1986).
JEH 37 (1986), 506, review of *Repertoire des visites pastorales de la France, Première série: Anciens diocèses (jusque'en 1790)*, iii. *Mâcon-Riez*, ed. Dominique Julia (Paris, 1983).
TLS, 3 Jan. 1986, p. 8, review of James Bentley, *Restless Bones: The story of Relics* (London, 1985), and David Sox, *Relics and Shrines* (London, 1985).
EHR 101 (1986), 242–3, review of E. Le Roy Ladurie, *La Sorcière de jasmin* (Paris, 1983).
Ibid. 510–11, review of Geoffrey Bremner, *Order and Chance: The Pattern of Diderot's Thought* (Cambridge, 1983).

1987

Introduction (with John Roberts) to J. S. Bromley, *Corsairs and Navies 1660–1760* (London, 1987).
TLS, 30 Jan. 1987, p. 117, review of Austin Gough, *Paris and Rome: The Gallican Church and the Ultramontane Campaign 1848–1853* (Oxford, 1986).
Ibid., 31 July 1987, p. 829, review of John Kent, *The Unacceptable Face: The Modern Church in the Eyes of the Historian* (London, 1987).
JEH 38 (1987), 501–2, review of *Repertoire des visites pastorales de la France. Première série: Anciens diocèses (jusqu'en 1790)*, iv. *La Rochelle–Ypres. Bâle* (Paris, 1985).
Ibid. 502, review of Marie-Louis Gondal, *L'Acte mystique: Témoignage spirituel de Madame Guyon (1648–1717)*, doctoral thesis (Lyons, 1985; published by the author, 1985).
EHR 102 (1987), 717–18, review of Charles Hoffman, *Church and Community in the Diocese of Lyon, 1500–1789* (New Haven, 1984).
Ibid. 728–9, review of Yves-Marie Hilaire (ed.), *Benoît Labre, Errance et sainteté: Histoire d'un culte, 1783–1793* (Paris, 1984).
History, 72 (1987), 531, review of Myriam Yardeni, *Le Refuge Protéstant* (Paris, 1985).

1988

'The Religious Observances of Versailles under Louis XV', in G. Barber and C. P. Courtney (eds.), *Enlightenment Essays in Memory of Robert Shackleton* (Oxford, 1988), 175–88.
'Authority in Church and State: Reflections on the Coronation of Louis XVI', in G. R. Evans (ed.), *Christian Authority: Essays in Honour of Henry Chadwick* (Oxford, 1988), 278–95.
JEH 39 (1988), 476–8, review of Lucien Ceyssens and Joseph A. G. Tans, *Autour de l'Unigenitus: Recherches sur la genèse de la constitution* (Louvain, 1987).
EHR 103 (1988), 688–92, review of Timothy Tackett, *Religion, Revolution, and Regional Culture in Eighteenth-Century France: The Ecclesiastical Oath of 1791* (Princeton, 1986).
Ibid. 1069–70, review of Claude Langlois, *Le Catholicisme au féminin: Les Congrégations françaises à supérieure générale au XIXᵉ siècle* (Paris, 1984).

TLS, 7–13 Oct. 1988, p. 1131, review of Georges Minois, *Le Confesseur du roi: Les Directeurs de conscience sous la monarchie française* (Paris, 1988).

1989

JEH 40 (1989), 625–6, review of Pierre Jurieu, *Lettres pastorales adressées aux fidèles de France qui gémissent sous la captivité de Babylon*, introduction by Robin Howells (Hildesheim, 1988).

Ibid. 463–4, review of E. J. M. Van Eijl (ed.), *L'Image de C. Jansenius jusqu'a la fin du XVIIIe siècle* (Actes du Colloque, Louvain, 7–9 Nov. 1985).

1990

The Oxford Illustrated History of Christianity (ed.) (Oxford, 1990).

JEH 41 (1990), 695–6, review of Pierre Blet, *Le Clergé de France, Louis XIV et le Saint Siège de 1695 à 1715* (Vatican City, 1989).

TLS, 2–8 Nov. 1990, p. 1185, review of Alan Charles Kors, *Atheism in France 1650–1729*, i. *The Orthodox Sources of Disbelief* (Princeton, 1990).

1991

TLS, 1 Nov. 1991, p. 27, review of John Bowker, *The Meanings of Death* (Cambridge, 1991).

JEH 42 (1991), 327–8, review of Colin Jones, *The Charitable Imperative: Hospitals and Nursing in Ancien Regime and Revolutionary France* (London, 1989).

EHR 106 (1991), 502, review of J. N. Tuck, *French Catholic Missionaries and the Politics of Imperialism in Vietnam, 1857–1914* (Liverpool, 1987).

1992

EHR 107 (1992), 494–5, review of Louis Pérouas and Paul Hollander, *La Révolution française: Une rupture dans le Christianisme? Le cas du Limousin, 1775–1822* (Treignac, 1988).

JEH 43 (1992), 487–8, review of Norman Ravitch, *The Catholic Church and the French Nation 1589–1789* (London, 1990).

1993

'Military Appreciations for Royal Visits', *Command* (Summer 1993), 19–20.

1994

TLS, 8 Apr. 1994, p. 25, review of Jean Meyer, *Bossuet* (Paris, 1993).

EHR 109 (1994), 191–2, review of Alain Cabantous, *Le Ciel dans la Mer: Christianisme et civilisation maritime XVIe–XIXe siècles* (Paris, 1990).

Ibid. 751–2, review of Suzanne Desan, *Reclaiming the Sacred: Lay Religion and Popular Politics in Revolutionary France* (Ithaca, NY, 1990).

1995

TLS, 19 May 1995, p. 27, review of John Rogister, *Louis XV and the Parlement of Paris, 1737–1755* (Cambridge, 1995).

INDEX

synagogues 301
  see also Great Synagogue
Synod, see Dort; Merse and Teviotdale; Rome
Syriac languages 387, 394
Syrian, Christians 383, 386, 388, 395, 396
  Sects 316, 389, 390, 392
Syro-Malabar Church 386

Tabriz 392
Tacitus 262
taille 32, 34
Tait, Archibald Campbell, archbishop of
  Canterbury 351 n., 359, 390
Talleyrand, madame de 86
Tamburini, cardinal Fortunato 109, 110 & n.,
  111, 121 n., 123, 124, 125, 126
Tandeau, abbé 139
Tasmania, University of 6–9
taxes 31, 36, 142
  see also lotteries; France: tax collectors; *taille*
Tblisi 392
  Chapel of the Exarchate 392
Temple, Frederick, archbishop of Canterbury
  (formerly bishop of London) 354, 355,
  356, 358, 359, 361, 362, 363
Temple, William 363
Temple of Solomon 235
Tencin, archbishop de 96
Ten Commandments 24
Terray, abbé 138–9
Tertullian 341
Test and Corporation Acts 191–2, 222–3,
  299
Teviotdale, *see* Merse, synod of
Thackeray, Wm.:
  *Notes of a Journey from Cornhill to Grand
    Cairo* 385–6
Théodicée chrétienne, la 335
Thermidor 241
Thessalonians, Epistle to the 294
The Times 193
Third estate 144
  see also Estates-General
Third Republic, *see* France
Thirty-nine Articles, *see* Church of England
Thirty Years War 42, 55, 58
Thomism 110
Thompson, Prof. J. M. 10
Thorowgood, Thomas 57 n.
Tiber, river 326, 369
Tigris, river 386
Timaios 261
Timothy, the apostle 62
tithe 193
Tobruk, siege of 3, 4
Tocqueville, Alexis de 5, 6, 10, 14
Toledo, archbishop of, *see* Moreno y Maisonave,
  cardinal

toleration 47
  in Britain 188–9
  in France 104, 155; *see also* French
    Revolution
  in Scotland 216
Toleration Act (1689) 188
Tolet, cardinal 34
Tooth, Revd Arthur 393
Tories 189, 193, 216, 229
  doctrines 225–6
Torrigiani, Cardinal 130
Tortona, bishop of, *see* Cavalchini-Guidobono,
  cardinal Carlo-Alberto
Totila, king of the Goths 155
Toulon, bishop of, *see* Lascaris, abbé de
Toulouse, archbishop of 330
  see also de Brienne
  Faculty of Catholic theology 328
Tournelle, madame de la 86
Tours, archbishop of 113
Tractarians 347, 381, 382, 387
  theory of the Church 382
Trafalgar 268
transcendental realities 320
Travancore 395
Trent, Council of 64, 66, 77, 78, 82, 100, 129,
  135, 165, 166, 238
Treuvé 27
tribunate, *see* Consulate
Tridentine Catholicism 150, 278, 279, 287
  see also Trent
Trinitarian 189, 210
  see also Orthodoxy
Trinity College, Dublin 197 n.
Triple Alliance 380
Troeltsch, Ernst 404
Troger, Paul 160
Troyes, bishops of, *see*, Cicé, J.-B.-M. Champion
  de; Coeur, abbé
Tübingen 294
Tuileries, palace 85, 248
Tunis 380
Tur 'Abdin 386
Turgot 267
Turin 108, 120
  court of 125
Turkey 382
Turks 176, 179, 180, 204
Tuscany 371 n.
  dukes of, *see* Emperor, Holy Roman (Leopold
    II)
Twelfth Night 261
tyrannicide 26
Tyrol 156
Tyndale, William 13

Ukranian nationalism 405
Ulster 228